Saskatchewan Politics: Into the Twenty-First Century

Saskatchewan Politics: Into the Twenty-First Century

edited by
Howard A. Leeson

Canadian Plains Research Center
University of Regina
2001

Canadian Plains Research Center
University of Regina
Regina, Saskatchewan S4S 0A2
Canada
Tel: (306) 585-4758
Fax: (306) 585-4699
e-mail: canadian.plains@uregina.ca
http://www.cprc.ca

National Library of Canada Cataloguing in Publication Data

Main entry under title:

Saskatchewan politics

(University of Regina publications, ISSN 1480-0004 ; 7)
Includes bibliographic references and index.
ISBN 0-88977-131-6

1. Saskatchewan—Politics and government. I. Leeson, Howard A., 1942-
II. University of Regina. Canadian Plains Research Center.
III. Series.
FC3528.2.S27 2001 320.97124 C2001-911631-4
F1072.S27 2001

Cover Design: Donna Achtzehner, Canadian Plains Research Center
Photo courtesy of Saskatchewan Property Management Corporation

Printed and bound in Canada by Houghton Boston, Saskatoon, Saskatchewan
Printed on acid-free paper

— Dedication —

This book is dedicated to Duane Adams, author of one of the chapters in this volume. Duane was a long-time civil servant with the government of Saskatchewan and a major architect of health reform in this province. He finished his chapter just prior to his untimely death. We hope that his chapter will serve to explain what Duane and his colleagues attempted to do for the people of Saskatchewan.

— Contents —

— Acknowledgments —

Any book is a partnership of many people. This book is the result of many more people than usual.

First I would like to thank all of the authors and their support staff who have contributed to this reader. All of them have donated their time and effort. No one has been paid for their work, and any author's royalties that come from this book will be put back into student scholarships or other worthy causes.

I would also like to thank the University of Regina, and in particular the Saskatchewan Institute of Public Policy, for providing me the space and time to complete the work.

Special acknowledgement should go to the following people: Aydon Charleton for doing his usual fine proofreading and commentary on the content; Brian Mlazgar for picking up mistakes and proofreading the final copy; Donna Achtzehner for the fine book cover; and Ede Leeson for reading the final copy and suggesting useful changes.

Howard A. Leeson

— Introduction —

This book was originally intended to be a reader for students in Political Science. As such, it is divided into sections dealing with institutions, political parties, and current issues. It was prompted by the fact that no comprehensive reader had been done on Saskatchewan politics in over twenty years. I did not expect that it would be of great interest outside the classroom. However, books have a way of going their own direction, especially when several authors are involved. Once the articles were finished it became apparent to me that one powerful theme permeated the work. That theme was change. In two short decades many of the foundations of Saskatchewan politics have either vanished or have been changed beyond recognition. Such a finding is obviously of interest to all of us who study or practice politics in the province, whether or not it is in the classroom.

For almost a century the roots of Saskatchewan have been anchored firmly in agriculture, cooperatives, socialism, and a distinctive, vibrant, rural community. To speak the name of the province was to conjure up images associated with the institutions and programs associated with these realities, the Wheat Pool, orderly marketing, Medicare, the family farm, and small towns with wooden elevators. Much has changed however.

In his article on agriculture Bob Stirling chronicles what has happened to agriculture and rural Saskatchewan, outlining how profoundly the industry has been transformed. He laments the fact that agriculture now "mirrors the needs of agribusiness," and is "boxed in by patents and trade agreements." But he does not believe that the directions of the past twenty years are irreversible. Rather he believes that ordinary people can still control their destiny and "take charge of that social project." Readers will have to judge for themselves if he is being realistic about the future.

Profound change has not been limited to rural Saskatchewan. In his article Brett Fairbairn reviews the role of government in the whole economy. He is blunt in his conclusion that "it seems that governments cannot plan economies." As we know from the *Regina Manifesto*, the assumption that government should be heavily involved in the economy has been an article of faith for many in Saskatchewan since the Great Depression. However, while rejecting the notion that government cannot plan the economy, Fairbairn does not adopt the simplistic approach of many who advocate removing government from the economy entirely. Rather he advocates a new, more modest approach that emphasizes community and education. He concludes that there is no guarantee of success with his approach. Instead he simply asks us to keep our "minds open," and our "heads up."

Nowhere is change more apparent than in the area of social services delivered by government. Duane Adams, before his untimely death this year, took time out of his busy life to explain why an enormous reorganization of the Medicare system had been undertaken in the 1990s. As deputy minister of Health when these profound changes took place, Duane was in a unique position. As he explains, he had to balance the white horse and the black horse, improvement of services with fiscal necessity. Some may find his observations too laudatory of those engaged in the process itself. We can excuse him some enthusiasm since it is apparent that he not only believed in Medicare, but he also believed that it must change if we were to sustain it. What he brings to the reader's attention then, is the view of those who were in the system at the time, what they thought they were doing, and where they thought they had succeeded. What is most profound about his article is his analysis of how financial and service concerns actually worked together to facilitate massive change; change that could not have happened had both factors not been present at the same time.

Looking at the present fiscal situation of Saskatchewan, there is little to suggest that for ten years debt and deficit were the main concern of the people of the province. In his article Michael Rushton examines the major elements of what many have described as the most profound fiscal crisis in Saskatchewan since the Great Depression. He begins with the assumption that budget deficits in the 1980s brought the provincial debt to "dangerous and unsustainable levels." Not all agree with this conclusion. But in the final analysis it does not matter. The issue of debt and deficit in Saskatchewan, as in the rest of Canada, drove the political agenda for most of the previous decade. Rushton concludes that the conventional wisdom about government debt has been changed forever in the province, and that no one will want to tamper with the new consensus that has emerged.

Change has also been profound in the political parties of the province. Taken together, the articles by Lynda Haverstock on the Liberal Party, Kevin Wishlow on the Saskatchewan Party, and Jocelyne Praud and Sarah McQuarrie on the NDP, paint a picture of a party system which has undergone enormous change in the last two decades. Most obvious is that one major party, the Progressive Conservative Party, has disappeared entirely, "put to sleep" by its members. It has been replaced by the Saskatchewan Party, which did not exist until after the 1995 election. The Liberal Party, with a long history in the province, has been relegated to virtual obscurity during much of the last two decades. Plagued by internal difficulties and the self-inflicted wounds outlined in detail by Haverstock, it faces an uncertain future. The CCF/NDP, which has governed Saskatchewan for 41 of the 57 years since 1944, has also changed decisively. Praud and McQuarrie detail these changes for us, concluding that the NDP has followed the path that many other social democratic parties in power have followed by pursuing policies which are often at odds with the social democratic origins of the party. Lastly, in his article on the Saskatchewan Party, Wishlow presents us with an interesting analysis about the rapid growth and position of this party. He challenges directly the assumption that the creation of the Saskatchewan Party is nothing more than the latest installment of the continuing Left-Right divide in the politics of the province. To understate the obvious, the party system in this province has undergone a transformation, one which seems not yet to have run its course.

Nowhere is change more obvious however, than in the fundamental mix of peoples in the province. In particular, several articles make us aware of the growing role and importance of Aboriginal peoples in Saskatchewan. From the emphasis on their role in the justice system as outlined by Whyte and Matthews, to the role of Aboriginal people in the last election detailed in the Voyageur and Green article, to Pitsula's direct look at the participation of First Nations in the electoral system, we become aware of the how the new face of politics in the province is developing. It will not be the face of the immigrant settler; it will be the face of the young Aboriginal person. Each of these articles has something to say about the role of Aboriginal people in the future. All of them conclude that Aboriginal people will play an increasingly important role. But the road to that new role will not be easy. The authors all argue that it will require some important changes to our conceptions about the role of First Nations and other Aboriginal people in the province. Abandoning the old concepts will not come easy. The adoption of new ones will likely be even harder.

If unsettling change is the main theme of the book, perhaps we can take comfort in the fact that some articles demonstrate the amount of continuity that remains in many areas of political life. In his article on the role of the lieutenant governor, Michael Jackson points out how stable the role of the monarchy remains in the province. In an unabashed way he proposes that it not only serves a useful purpose, but will continue to do so in the future. In talking about the "resurgence" of the office he concludes that it "has increasingly served to express the goals and self awareness of the provincial community." Whether he is right, and whether or not the office will continue to be relevant in the future, will remain questions in the minds of many.

Just as the institution of the monarchy remains, so too does the legislature. Here however, Merrilee Rasmussen points out that it has not remained unchanged. While it is still the focus of much of the political debate in the province, she laments the fact that the legislature has been increasingly marginalized. Indeed she says "the conflict between executive government and the legislature in Saskatchewan during the 1980s and 1990s has resulted in a permanent erosion of this democratic component of the institution of Parliament in this province." She concludes that the increasing control of the legislature by the executive branch, and the premier's office in particular, has added to an already growing cynicism about politics and politicians. Real democracy cannot exist where legislatures are simply the tools of powerful premiers. Change has occurred in the function of the legislature in Saskatchewan, but not change that she welcomes or thinks healthy for our democracy.

How MLAs are elected is the subject of Dan deVlieger's essay. As a former member of the last commission on electoral boundaries he outlines the work of that commission, the legislation that governed it, and the resulting boundaries. More importantly he outlines the mood of public mistrust about politicians, the legal situation that preceded the legislation, and the attempt by the Romanow government to draft legislation which would give the province a smaller legislature, but one that adhered more closely to the principle of one person, one vote. He concludes that the present legislation, for all practical purposes, eliminates the possibility of a gerrymander by any future governing party.

If premiers and cabinets are increasingly important, how are they chosen, by whom, and under what circumstances? In his article former premier Allan Blakeney tells us what goes into the choosing of a cabinet, and how they function when in place. What better person to do so than someone who has actually done this? What strikes the reader first is how little flexibility remains for a premier once all of the "structural variables" involved in appointing cabinet have been applied. What strikes the reader second, however, is how much power a premier has. The humourous story about a cabinet vote in which the premier is on one side and the rest of the cabinet on the other being described as a "tie vote" is highly instructive. It is clear from his article that cabinet remains the real focus of political power in Saskatchewan.

For some the real face of government in the province is found in the civil service. In particular the civil service in Saskatchewan continues to have a national reputation for excellence, both as "an incubator of ideas and a breeding ground for talent."

Many national figures in the public service have come from this province. Indeed, over the years there have been so many in Ottawa that they have been called the "Saskatchewan Mafia." In his article Ken Rasmussen explores the role of the bureaucracy in the political life of the province. He too concludes that change has come to this institution. He says that there is "a new balance in which its former leadership role has been curtailed." Overall, he believes that the public service here has become much more like that in other provinces.

Throughout the period under examination in this book federal-provincial relations affected every aspect of policy in the province. From the momentous events that surrounded the patriation of the Constitution in 1982, through Meech Lake and Charlottetown, to the unilateral cutbacks in transfer payments by the Chrétien government after 1993, the federal government and its policies have impacted heavily on politics in Saskatchewan. In their article on the negotiation and adoption of the Social Union Framework Agreement, Greg Marchildon and Brent Cotter outline attempts to try and bring stability to this area. Once again, Saskatchewan played a unique role in key federal-provincial negotiations. More importantly, these two participants detail how Saskatchewan's view of the Canadian federation, a view often at odds with other provinces, has influenced the shape of Canada. There is a surprising continuity in this area, obviously affected by the fact that two of the leaders, Allan Blakeney and Roy Romanow, were key participants in most of the major discussions over twenty years. But, it is more than that. The systemic forces that are described in this article obviously shape the province's approach to its place in Confederation, forces which circumscribe all leaders whatever their partisan background.

Finally, the book concludes with an article by Sperling and Wishlow about the role of the media in Saskatchewan. It is hard hitting. We all know the importance of the media in the political life of the province. Without the modern media we would not have access to vital information about important political choices. Indeed, the article begins with a quote from former premier Grant Devine about "marketing the message." How independent is the media? How biased a report do we get? Do powerful interests control the media in this province? These two authors answer these questions and more as they test the hypotheses of several important critics of the media. Some will be angry at their conclusions. Most, I think, will be moved to question more closely the role of this vital link in the political life of the province.

Change and continuity. In my own essay I try to outline the broad changes in the Saskatchewan polity during the past twenty-five years. I conclude that the old Saskatchewan is gone forever, lost in the welter of changing industries, ideologies, and peoples. A new Saskatchewan continues to be born, with new players and perhaps new goals. But what has not changed is the uniqueness of Saskatchewan. We will approach the new future still adhering to most of the basic attitudes and principles that have served us well in the past. Maybe, just maybe, we will get the best of both change and continuity.

Howard A. Leeson
Regina, Saskatchewan
December 2001

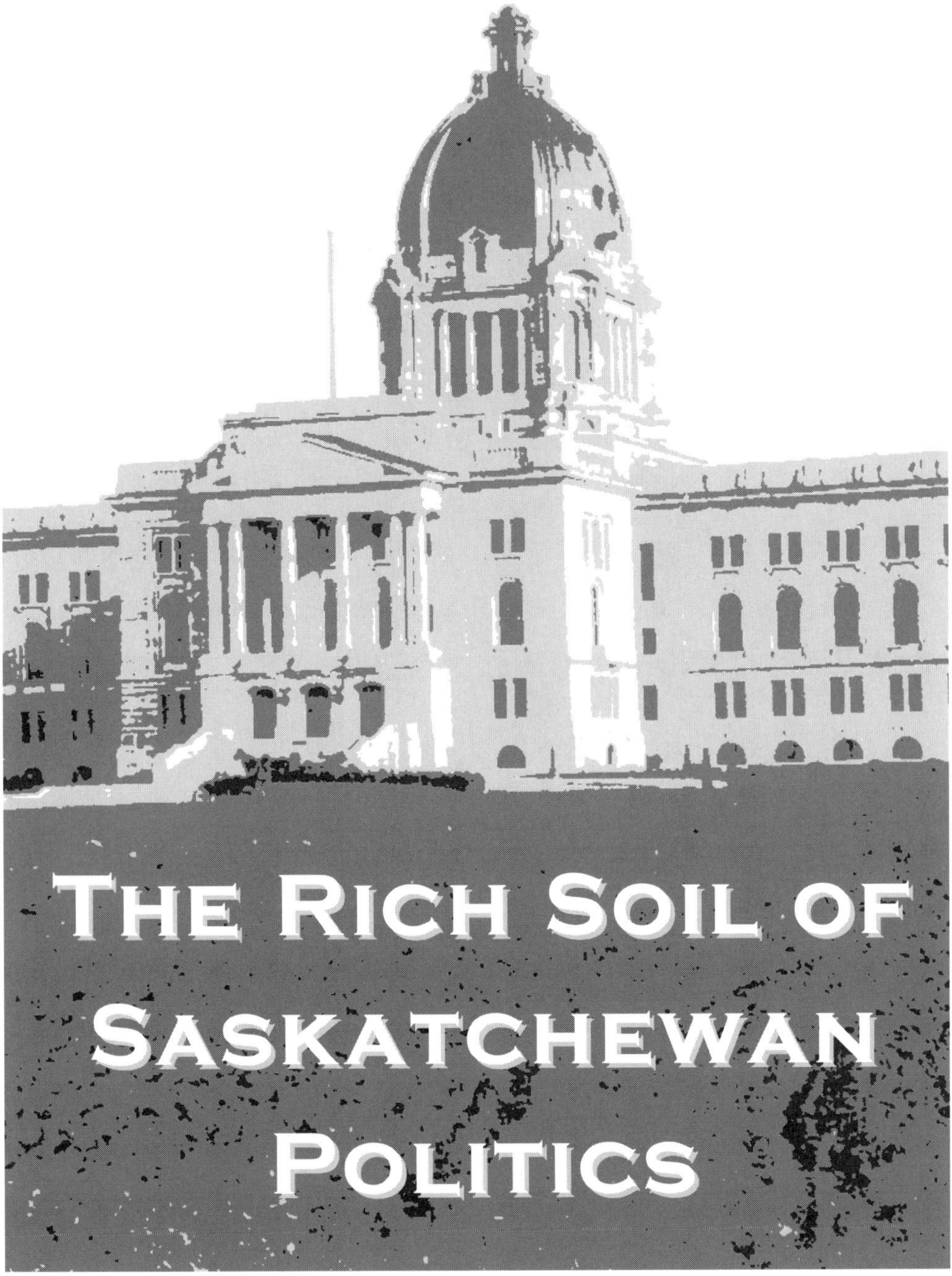
THE RICH SOIL OF
SASKATCHEWAN
POLITICS

The Rich Soil of Saskatchewan Politics

Howard A. Leeson

> *The wind turns in silent frenzy upon itself, whirling into a smoking funnel, breathing up topsoil and tumbleweed skeletons to carry on its spinning way over the prairie, out and out to the far line of the sky... where spindling poplars lift their dusty leaves and wild sunflowers stare, the gravestones stand among the prairie grasses. Over them a rapt and endless silence lies. This soil is rich.*
>
> W.O. Mitchell, *Who Has Seen the Wind*[1]

"This soil is rich." W.O. Mitchell's words are a metaphor for many things in Saskatchewan. His juxtaposition of the rich soil with an image of silence and gravestones reminds us of how tenuous the existence of human enterprise has been in this region. For thousands of years the land provided riches for First Nations people. They lived harmoniously with the seasons of its existence. But in the nineteenth century the medley of life on the prairies changed profoundly as Europeans flooded in. The sedate and fixed roles of grass, animal, and human, were altered forever as these settlers strove to mine the gold of wheat and other grains. By 1947, however, it appeared that the tenure of these new settlers might be brief indeed. The emptying of rural Saskatchewan had already begun. The production of food, it seemed, would continue, but without the descendants of many of the settlers who had given their lives to build the grain enterprise.

Rich soil might also be taken as a metaphor for politics in Saskatchewan. The fertile social soil of this province has provided us with a hundred years of unique and innovative political life. At the same time that W.O. Mitchell was writing his poignant tale of a young boy on the prairie, Seymour Lipset was writing about an extraordinary political transformation in Saskatchewan. He was intrigued by the fact that socialism seemed to have taken deep root in the province and that the people of Saskatchewan did not conform to the usual pattern of agrarian radicalism:

> The frontier character alone [of Saskatchewan] would not have created or maintained the conditions for rapid social change [to socialism]. Most North American frontier areas that were once centers of agrarian radicalism became strongholds political and economic conservatism within a few decades after their original settlement...[2]

In Saskatchewan, though, he concluded that socialism might endure: "Ostensibly ... Saskatchewan seems to have remained near the radical peak that it reached in

1. W.O. Mitchell, *Who Has Seen The Wind* (Toronto: Macmillan of Canada, 1947), 300.
2. Seymour Lipset, *Agrarian Socialism* (Los Angeles: University of California Press, 1959), 26.

1944."[3] Despite this view, he was not sanguine about the long-term prospects for the CCF as a vehicle for permanent social change.[4]

FOR OR AGAINST SOCIALISM

Was the CCF a socialist party? Did it usher in an era of socialist government in Saskatchewan after 1944? The answer, is yes, no, and maybe. Walter Young, whose book is considered by most to be the best study of the CCF, was ambivalent. He acknowledged that the CCF had socialist elements and originally was a "value laden movement." He also acknowledged, however, that as a movement becomes institutionalized into an electoral party, the goal of attracting a broader base of support acts to put pressure on the "purity" of the goals of the movement. Since compromise in a party of principle is often thought of as the enemy of truth, many become disillusioned when the party or movement is in government. This is what Young believed had happened to the CCF.[5]

In many ways the answer to this question is irrelevant. For most of those who eagerly awaited the New Jerusalem the appearance and rhetoric of socialism was sufficient. The *Regina Manifesto* was clear on the need to substitute socialism for capitalism, and if this meant the occasional bend in the road, or required compromise, it was understandable. For those who opposed socialism, this same appearance and rhetoric were sufficient to condemn all that the CCF stood for. For them, the CCF had to be opposed for what it said, and not necessarily for what it did.

Thus, after 1944, politics in Saskatchewan became organized around those who were for or against socialism. Elections were decided largely on the basis of support for the CCF/NDP, or the alternative free enterprise party.

SLOW CHANGE

During the period 1944–80 the objective social and economic reality of the province changed. Urbanization, mechanization, and the growth of large-scale farming destroyed many of the smaller rural communities and permanently altered the way farming was "done." Some argued that these changes were having an impact on the values of the communities and the people. However, others thought that the fundamentals of the social structure of the province changed little after World War II. Although farms had grown larger and mechanization had changed the manner of farming, they concluded that these were changes of quantity rather than quality. Politics, and the social structures that underpinned it in the province, seemed to some not to have changed at all. Writing in 1980, historian John Archer could say that "the sense of community was still strong [and] the traditions of self-help and cooperation are still live traditions."[6] In the same year political scientist Evelyn Eager concluded that "political motivation is basically the same, too."[7] For the outside world the image of Saskatchewan remained intact. It was the home of social democracy and Medicare, of the enduring contest between capitalism and socialism.

But change was "in the wind" after 1980, and Saskatchewan was to be blown about by it along with the rest of the world.

3. Ibid., 278.
4. Ibid., 286.
5. Walter Young, *Anatomy of a Party* (Toronto: University of Toronto Press, 1971), 11.
6. John H. Archer, *Saskatchewan: A History* (Saskatoon: Western Producer Prairie Books, 1980), 352.
7. Evelyn Eager, *Saskatchewan Government* (Saskatoon: Western Producer Prairie Books, 1980), 12.

FUNDAMENTAL CHANGE

The decade of the 1980s brought a profound ideological change to all liberal democracies, a change that has transformed many of our ideas about politics. It continues to reverberate in the world. The immediate roots of this change can be found in the economic crisis over oil pricing which began after 1973. Sharp rises in the price of oil, brought about by the oil cartel called OPEC, made it clear that the industrialized world could no longer count on cheap imports of energy and other natural resources. Huge transfers of wealth went from North America, Europe and Japan to oil-producing countries like Iran and Saudi Arabia, forcing governments and individuals to borrow heavily to finance current account expenditures. This in turn drove inflation and interest rates to unbearable levels and led directly to the economic crash of 1982. Traditional Keynesian prescriptions seemed not to work in this new confluence of debt and inflation. This led to the emergence of those who prescribed "market place solutions" to solve the problem. This approach is described by some as neo-conservatism but is perhaps more precisely known as neo-liberalism:

> The core ideological thrust of neo-liberalism is *laissez-faire* economic doctrine. In the hands of conservative politicians this is often combined with the values of social traditionalism [neo-conservatism]. However, the addition of such values does not seem to be a necessary element in neo-liberalism *per se* and different social values may serve as a point of differentiation between politicians or political parties that share an attachment to market economic doctrines.
>
> The rediscovery of classical liberalism resulted from developments in modern economic theory and its application to political questions. Monetarism, supply side economics, and public choice theory were particularly important in the revival movement and supply both policy advice and ideological sustenance.[8]

The leading proponents of the neo-liberal approach in the 1980s were Margaret Thatcher, Prime Minister of Great Britain, and Ronald Reagan, President of the United States. They quite literally burst upon the decade, overwhelming all before them. The forces of capital, held in check for decades by memories of the Great Depression and the long economic expansion after World War II, began again to dominate politics in liberal democracies. This new ascendancy was accelerated and expanded by the disintegration of communist governments throughout the world. Conceptions of politics, the role of governments, indeed, the very directions of social change, were drastically altered.

SASKATCHEWAN IN THE 1980S

The decade of the 1970s had been kind to Saskatchewan. Heavy demand for its agricultural products, together with huge increases in the price of its natural resources, meant that money flowed into the province in unparalleled amounts. This in turn fueled a construction boom, hastened the mechanization of grain production, and drove up the price of land in the province. It was a prosperous period in the province's history. Thus, when the NDP government of Premier Allan Blakeney, which had been in power since 1971, called an election for April of 1982, it expected to be re-elected.

8. Stephen McBride and John Shields, *Dismantling a Nation* (Halifax: Fernwood Publishing, 1997), 23.

But the worldwide crash of prices for oil and grain and the rapid rise in interest rates were about to precipitate an economic collapse in Saskatchewan. It would be devastating. The electorate, already inclined to make a change, reacted in 1982 to the uncertainty of the looming economic crisis by creating a political collapse for the NDP. The Progressive Conservative Party, led by Grant Devine, swept the NDP into opposition. Not since before1944 had the private enterprise forces had such a sweeping victory.

Few realized at the time that the political system of the province would not return to the traditional and familiar divisions of the past. Some thought that the election of the Conservatives was an electoral freak, that the electorate would "regain their senses" in the future, and that "balance" would return to political life in Saskatchewan. This was not to be the case. The government of Grant Devine would be in power for two terms and embark on a wide-ranging program of fundamental change.

Some, like Don Baron and Paul Jackson, described this change approvingly:

> In those early days as Premier, he [Grant Devine] did, in fact, bring an awesome package of reforms. In his first seven years, his government had virtually restructured the provincial economy.[9]

Others, like Jim Pitsula and Ken Rasmussen, concluded that the Conservatives had simply "adapted" the new right philosophy to the realities of political life in Saskatchewan:

> Although it is an international movement with a common ideological core, neo-conservatism [neo-liberalism in the sense that McBride and Shields use it] does not express itself in precisely the same way in every country or province... Local conditions and circumstances invariably modify the way neo-conservative [neo-liberal] principles are applied in a particular country... It is not surprising, therefore, to find that Saskatchewan has developed its own distinctive brand of neo-conservatism. The two main factors influencing the new right in Saskatchewan are the province's strong well-entrenched social democratic tradition, and the hinterland nature of the economy.[10]

According to Pitsula and Rasmussen, the new right in Saskatchewan was only partially successful in its program of change for two reasons. First, there was still strong support for the social democratic notion that government should play a major role in the economy. That is, the majority of the voting public in the 1980s still accepted the premise that a strong provincial government was necessary if the province was to marshall and deploy its resources with maximum efficiency. In short, the province could not afford capitalism, and voters knew this. Second, there was strong social support for the political tradition of using the state to offset the disadvantages of being a hinterland economy. Both of these, they argued, prevented the Conservative Party from being fully successful in implementing the neo-liberal agenda in the province. However, this lack of complete ideological success did not prevent the Progressive Conservatives from establishing themselves as a formidable electoral force in rural Saskatchewan and damaging their main adversary — the NDP — in the rural areas of the province.

---

9. Don Baron and Paul Jackson, *Battleground* (Toronto: Bedford House Publishing,1991), 22

10. James M. Pitsula and Ken Rasmussen, *Privatizing a Province: The New Right in Saskatchewan* (Vancouver: New Star Books, 1990), 3.

POPULISM AND THE PROGRESSIVE CONSERVATIVES

In order to understand why the Conservatives were so successful in the rural areas, one needs to understand the role of populism and the NDP in the province. There have been at least four types of populism on the prairies, and many more definitions.[11] In Saskatchewan populism has been chiefly of the social democratic type. As David Laycock explains:

> Its most obvious features were rejection of the two major parties as instruments of eastern business, support for state ownership of major industries, advocacy of a farmer-labour alliance against organized business, and support for a full extension of democratic rights and practices within the parliamentary system.[12]

The social democratic variety of populism is dependent in part on the maintenance of a large number of small rural landholders. Larger farmers tend to develop more orthodox economic views. The type of hinterland economy, or more precisely, the makeup of the agricultural hinterland economy, is therefore important in understanding the impact of population changes in rural areas on the political culture of the province. Thus, rural depopulation and farm consolidation over the period after World War II weakened social democratic political populism in rural areas, and concomitantly, the political party associated with it. The necessary implication of this decline was an increasing rejection of the role of government in a hinterland economy. Thus, by the 1980s the Conservatives were able to play to an increasingly receptive rural audience in Saskatchewan, not because neo-liberalism *per se* was attractive, but because of the decline of social democratic populism.

Rural depopulation began to accomplish what had been predicted earlier by Lipset and others. As farms consolidated the old CCF generation moved into the towns, and was replaced by younger farmers who had not farmed during the Great Depression. The institutions of the previous generation, the Wheat Pool, the Canadian Wheat Board, and the cooperatives, meant less to these newer farmers. They were more willing to accept private sector measurements and methods, to view the role of government less positively. Already socially conservative, they became more economically conservative, identifying less and less with urban economic interests. Old alliances with groups like urban labour were viewed as unproductive. Indeed, more and more farmers agreed that organized labour was an impediment to, if not the enemy of, their well-being. With these changes the de-radicalization of rural Saskatchewan arrived, albeit several decades later than predicted.

The Progressive Conservatives recognized and exploited this new reality. They successfully tailored their political rhetoric and policies to reinforce the identification of rural voters with the Conservative Party. As a consequence, NDP support did not recover from the 1982 election in some rural regions. Areas of the northeast, which had been called "Red Square" for decades because of their unwavering support for the CCF/NDP, elected Conservatives for the first time in 1982, and continued to withhold their support from the NDP in the 1986 general election. Although the NDP received more votes overall than the Conservatives did in the province, they failed to form a government in 1986 because the rural seats remained firmly Conservative. This change in the political culture of rural Saskatchewan became a major factor in succeeding elections and political debates.

11. For a good discussion of prairie populism see David Laycock, *Populism and Democratic Thought in the Canadian Prairies, 1910–1945* (Toronto: University of Toronto Press, 1990).

12. Ibid., 20.

A CHANGE IN THE NDP

In 1987 Roy Romanow became the leader of the NDP. The decade of the 1980s had been a frustrating one for New Democrats. Feeling cheated out of victory in 1986 by what they perceived as a rigged electoral system, they could only sit by helplessly and watch as the Conservatives attempted to dismantle much of what the CCF/NDP had put in place over the previous four decades. But with the election of Romanow as leader, optimism began to return in the party. Most thought that with the return to power of the NDP, the "damage" done by the Tories could be repaired. They expected that social programs and privatized Crown corporations would be reinstated and that the new government would continue the process of social democracy as it had been defined under Tommy Douglas and Allan Blakeney. Thus, there were high expectations when the NDP was elected in a landslide victory in 1991. For some members these expectations remained unfulfilled, as the new government seemed to turn away from many of the traditional goals of the CCF/NDP.

Three things account for the course that the NDP pursued after 1991 — the fiscal situation, party leadership, and the changing social structure of the province. The most significant was probably the fiscal situation that the government inherited from the Conservatives. Years of deficits had brought the combined debt of the province to almost $15 billion, some $12 billion more than in 1982. It left little room for flexibility at a time when governments were being pressed by bondholders to reduce debt. The government decided to make "putting the fiscal house in order" its top priority. This clashed with the high expectations of many inside the NDP. It appeared to them that the government was pursuing an agenda that was out of tune with the historical goals of the party. Few disputed that the deficit and debt needed to be addressed, but many questioned the speed with which the leadership moved on the issue. They argued that permanent damage would be done to the social infrastructure of the province. The government remained firm, and it convinced the party in convention to support its direction.

The leadership of Roy Romanow is the second reason for the decisive change in the NDP. Romanow had been a cabinet member in the governments of Allan Blakeney, holding the posts of deputy premier, attorney general, and minister of Intergovernmental Affairs. An articulate, intelligent and telegenic politician, he was considered by most in the NDP as the "heir apparent" throughout the Blakeney years. After some serious soul-searching caused by his personal defeat in 1982, he returned to the legislature in 1986, and in the next year he succeeded to the leadership unopposed.

Despite his many years in the party and public eye, little was known at the time about Roy Romanow's basic approach to politics. The fact that he had been acclaimed leader meant that there was no opportunity for the membership to find out more about his views in a leadership contest. However, most New Democrats were unconcerned with this in the last years of the Conservative government. They wanted a leader who could defeat Devine, and Romanow appeared to be the person who could accomplish that goal. Thus, many were surprised when the government seemed so fiscally focussed in the first years of office.

They ought not to have been. The new premier's conception of politics owed little to classical ideas about socialism and class conflict. For him prairie politics had been about cooperation and community, about coming together behind strong leaders to accomplish what outsiders would not do for the province. In order to do so he thought one had to get the support of the whole community to pull together, government and the people, business and labour, young and old, urban and rural. In his view internal division only weakened the community. The test of leadership for Roy Romanow was how well the goals of the whole community could be accommodated. Thus, "community leaders" played a large role in his government in the early days because they were entrusted by others in society with legitimate, constructive roles. They were builders. They could help in cleaning up the mess. By contrast, "special interest groups," with their special needs and pleadings, were perceived as deserving, but part of the problem. They seemed to constantly demand more from government than it could provide, especially given the tight fiscal situation.

The mixture of these two impulses produced in Roy Romanow a profoundly organic and conservative approach to politics, tempered by a genuine concern for social needs. Far from being a neo-conservative or neo-liberal as some have charged, he is closer to what Horowitz defined it in the 1960s as a "red tory."[13] The impact of his views on government and the NDP in the decade of the nineties was important and likely long-lasting.

Finally, important as current issues and style of leadership are for political parties, long-term structural change is even more important. The earlier conclusion by Lipset that socialism seemed able to survive and prosper in Saskatchewan, that it was immune to the conservatizing forces found in other rural areas of North America, now seems to have been premature. The NDP changed because the political and social milieu of Saskatchewan changed. Any political party is a mixture of electoral and policy purposes. Getting elected is as important as making change in a liberal democratic system. Power without purpose is superficial and eventually self-destructive. Purpose without power is ornamental and bitterly frustrating. The balance of the two, especially in a party espousing radical change in society, will eventually move toward the electoral side. Lipset himself forecast this four decades ago:

> Gradually, however, every large scale social organization falls victim to the virus of bureaucratic conservatism, and to the fear that further change to the status quo will injure its power and status; or the organization may become ... an indispensable part of the social order.[14]

As with some of the people of the province, the NDP of the 1990s became more conservative and more electorally oriented. There was less to distinguish it from its political competitors. This in itself has tended to further change the political culture, both within the NDP and the society at large.

These three forces — fiscal constrictions, party leadership, and gradual change in the NDP — all acted in the period up to 2001 to move political debate inside the NDP away from the "norm" of the previous decades, and to produce a political system less sharply defined by ideological differences.

13. "Another aberration which may be worthy of investigation is the Canadian phenomenon of the red tory. At a higher level, he is a conscious ideological conservative with some odd socialist notions ... or a conscious ideological socialist with some odd tory notions. It is because socialists have a conception of society as more than an agglomeration of competing individuals — a conception close to the tory view of society as an organic community — that they find the liberal idea of equality (equality of opportunity) inadequate." Horowitz wrote this in 1966. He was trying to explain why Canadians seemed not to be so fully committed to liberal conceptions of society, and why western Canadians in particular seemed to be such a curious mixture of economic radicalism and social conservatism. Gad Horowitz, "Conservatism, Liberalism, and Socialism in Canada: An Interpretation," *Canadian Journal of Economics and Political Science* 32, no. 2 (May 1996): 144–71.

14. See note 4.

THE POST-ROMANOW PERIOD

When the election of 1999 produced a legislature in which the NDP and the opposition parties had an equal number of seats, Premier Romanow responded by striking a coalition with the Liberals, another sign that ideological differences had become less important in the electoral system. In the fall of 2000 Roy Romanow announced his plans to step down as leader of the NDP and as premier of the province. In January of 2001, in a wide open leadership contest, Lorne Calvert, a former minister of Health from Moose Jaw, was elected leader. His early actions as premier indicate that he may steer the party back toward some of its more traditional stands on some issues, but there is little to indicate that he will move the party radically toward the sharper divisions of earlier years.

OTHER PARTIES

The decade of the 1990s also had a profound impact on the other parties in the provincial party system. It began with a two-party system firmly in place. The Progressive Conservatives were in power, and the NDP was the Official Opposition. The Liberal Party was represented by only a single MLA. By the end of the decade the Conservative Party had been "put to sleep" by its own members, while the Liberals had gone from a single member to the Official Opposition and back to third party in coalition with the NDP. As well a new party, the Saskatchewan Party, had come into existence, become the Official Opposition, and then won more votes but fewer seats than the NDP in the election of 1999. Once again, as in the election of 1986, the electoral system rewarded the government with sufficient seats to hold on to power, this time in coalition with the Liberal Party. Such change in the political actors of the province had not been seen since the 1970s.

The details of these changes are delineated in several chapters in this volume. Two important results should be noted. The first was the lack of a continuous and sustained opposition to the NDP government prior to 1999. At a time when the government was extremely vulnerable because of stringent fiscal policies, the opposition parties remained divided and racked with internal dissension, unable to provide voters with an effective or believable alternative. The government, at least until 1999, won by default on major issues and debate. The second was the hardening of the urban/rural divide in the province. The process begun by the Conservative Party in 1982 seems to have been completed by the Saskatchewan Party. That is, almost all of rural Saskatchewan is now represented by the Saskatchewan Party, while almost all of urban Saskatchewan is represented by the NDP. This divide will remain one of the most critical cleavages in Saskatchewan politics for the foreseeable future.

POLITICAL CHANGE IN THE NEW MILLENNIUM

If the decade of the 1990s brought important changes to the party and political system of Saskatchewan, what can we expect in the new millennium? The twentieth century will probably be remembered as the century of ideology, a century in which political behaviour was organized and acted out in the context of conflicting ideologies, with the eventual triumph of a new form of liberal individualism. Some, like John Ralston Saul, call it corporatism, and are deeply troubled by it:

> The idea of individualism dominant today represents a narrow and superficial deformation of the western idea. A hijacking of the term and — since it is a central term — a hijacking of western civilization. ... The end

> result will be a society addicted to ideologies — a civilization tightly held at this moment in the embrace of a dominant ideology; corporatism. The acceptance of corporatism causes us to deny and undermine the legitimacy of the individual as a citizen in a democracy. The result of such a denial is a growing imbalance which leads to our adoration of self-interest and our denial of the public good.[15]

Others lament the passing of sharp divisions between left and right, the inability or unwillingness of many to focus on the enemy, or to recognize government as a force for positive change. Still others welcome the "end of ideology," with the comment that it was destructive to the individual and his or her freedom. Whatever the reaction, the new century starts with a profound alienation and cynicism about government and politicians.

Saskatchewan, which for many decades had been a province of vigorous faith in political debate and participation, seems now to be succumbing to this trend. Turnout in elections is down, membership in political parties has declined, and the general attitude toward political involvement is negative. The phrase, "oh, they're all the same," is now heard in the province with regularity. Ironically, as noted above, there is increasing evidence that they are indeed all the same.

SOCIAL CHANGE

But, if the last century will be noted here and elsewhere as one in which broad ideologies dominated, the most significant change in the twenty-first century will likely be found elsewhere. After centuries of social rigidity the industrial revolution and other forces have profoundly changed one of the most basic social relationships, the relationship between men and women. Increasing conservatism has frustrated and slowed the change of social attitudes about the equality of men and women, but it has not stopped it. It will become a full reality in the twenty-first century. Saskatchewan will be no exception. This change has altered many of the basic political relationships and issues in the province, and it will do so with greater force in the future.

The slow re-emergence of Aboriginal peoples from a century of oppression and assimilation will also have a profound impact on politics in Saskatchewan. Anyone who has looked at the demographic changes predicted cannot help but conclude that the comfortable image of twentieth century Saskatchewan will soon disappear forever. We can expect the emergence of a credible Aboriginal political party sometime early in this millennium, and with it will come changes to the political institutions of the province. Enduring as it has been, the British parliamentary structure will likely not seem suited to emerging political realities. The relationship between Aboriginal peoples and other citizens of Saskatchewan will eventually come to dominate most aspects of social and political life.

THE FUTURE

The reality of a global economy and civilization with its dominant ideology of corporatism, the decline of traditional rural communities, increasing cynicism about politics and politicians, the changed role of women, and the possibility of an emerging Aboriginal majority in the province will all serve to create a new and different

15. John Ralston Saul, *The Unconscious Civilization* (Concord, ON: House of Anansi Press, 1995), 2.

Saskatchewan. The politics of the past will no longer seem familiar. Indeed it will look jarringly antiquated.

But this will not mean that politics in the province will be any less interesting. The political soil of the province remains rich. The wind will still blow.

THE LEGISLATURE

THE ROLE OF THE LEGISLATURE

Merrilee Rasmussen

INTRODUCTION

Legislatures and executives have been engaged in conflict for hundreds of years and, out of their struggles, the shape of parliamentary governments was determined. Three hundred years ago, the Glorious Revolution in England established the essential principles that underlie the concept of parliamentary government. In particular, it established the idea that executive governments are accountable to legislatures, both through the legal requirement that the executive must obtain prior legislative consent to its expenditures and through the abolition of the monarch's ability to suspend the laws enacted by Parliament.

Although developed long before the extension of the franchise to all adults, this accountability is premised on democratic principles. Of the three arms of government, legislatures are more democratic than executives and the judiciary for two reasons. First, they are elected, not appointed, and, second, they make their decisions in public, not in private. Because we assume, as C.B. Macpherson put it, that democracy is "a good thing,"[1] the executive government and the judiciary must defer to the legislature in order to maintain this connection to the democratic foundation on which the parliamentary system is based. When they do not, parliamentary democracy — and parliamentary legitimacy — is weakened.

The conflict between the executive government and the legislature in Saskatchewan during the 1980s and 1990s has resulted in a permanent erosion of this democratic component of the institution of Parliament in this province. The story of that conflict is the story of how the sovereignty that Parliament had won for itself through that confrontation with an English king more than three hundred years ago has been largely surrendered to the monarch of the modern era — the premier or the prime minister and cabinet. It has also reinforced a deep public cynicism about politicians and political institutions, including the legislature. If all politicians are alike, it hardly matters which ones are actually elected. This is a phenomenon that

1. C.B. Macpherson, *The Real World of Democracy* (Toronto: CBC Enterprises, 1965), 1:

> Democracy used to be a bad word. Everybody who was anybody knew that democracy, in its original sense of rule by the people or government in accordance with the will of the bulk of the people, would be a bad thing — fatal to individual freedom and to all the graces of civilized living. That was the position taken by pretty nearly all men of intelligence from the earliest historical times down to about a hundred years ago. Then, within fifty years, democracy became a good thing.

has occurred everywhere, but it is especially significant in Saskatchewan, which was built on a conscious and deliberate democratic foundation.

A telling indicator of this transfer of power from the legislative back to the executive is the *de facto* substitution of cabinet (executive) assent for legislative consent to government expenditure through the mechanism of the special warrant. A special warrant is a statutory mechanism created by the legislature for use in exceptional circumstances. However, its recent uses have permitted cabinet to circumvent the legal requirement, originating in the ancient Bill of Rights, to obtain the prior approval of the legislature to the executive's proposed expenditures. In order to assess the role of the legislature in Saskatchewan it is important to look back to the origins of parliamentary institutions.

THE ANCIENT BILL OF RIGHTS

Although not well known in our time, this Bill of Rights was enacted in 1688–89,[2] almost 300 years before its more modern Canadian progeny, and its significance for Canadians lies in the fact that it forms a major part of the conceptual foundation of modern, Westminster-style parliamentary systems of government. It embodies the concept of parliamentary sovereignty in the form of the rule of law — no person, not even the monarch, is above the duly enacted laws of the land — and in the requirement that money needed by the Crown can only be secured with the prior consent of the people's representatives in Parliament.

The significance of the Glorious Revolution — as the fleeing of James II, the adoption of the Bill of Rights, and the accession of William and Mary to the throne of England is historically referred to — is summarized succinctly by Philip Norton:

> James II, like his Catholic predecessors, asserted the divine right of kings: that is, that the powers and position of the monarch are given by God and that the privileges of Parliament derive from the grace of the monarch. Parliament resisted both the claim and the use to which it was put in furthering the cause of Roman Catholicism. Despite the presence of a large number of royal supporters, *the House of Commons in 1685 refused to grant the king money to maintain a permanent army and refused also to repeal the Test Acts*, which restricted public office to those who had taken the sacrament of the Church of England. *James promptly prorogued Parliament and it never met again during his reign.*[3]

James II continued to rule by royal prerogative, that is as Dicey has described it, by arbitrary authority,[4] and suspended various laws, including the *Test Acts* that had figured in his dispute with Parliament. Suspension of the law involved merely the King's declaration that the law was no longer in force, even though the law had not been repealed by Parliament. As a result of these actions by the King, leading figures of the day invited William of Orange to invade England, which he did. Shortly

2. The problem with the date of the enactment of the Bill of Rights is not a result of there being some vagueness about the precise time of its adoption. Rather, it is caused by the fact that after its enactment the beginning of the year was moved from March 1 to January 1. The Bill of Rights was adopted on February 2 and so, by the old manner of reckoning time, it was adopted in 1688 and by the new method it was adopted in 1689. Throughout this chapter, it will be referred to as the ancient Bill of Rights to obviate this problem and to distinguish it from its more modern and usual referents.

3. Philip Norton, "The Glorious Revolution of 1688 and 1689: Its Continuing Relevance," *Parliamentary Affairs* 42, no. 2 (April 1989): 136 (emphasis added).

4. As quoted in Peter Hogg, *Constitutional Law in Canada* (Toronto: Carswell, 1992), 13.

after William landed, James II fled the country. A convention was summoned, since there was no king to summon Parliament, at which it was determined that James II had abdicated and the vacant throne was offered to William and Mary, jointly. But a condition of the offer was their acceptance of the Declaration of Right, later enacted as law in the form of the ancient Bill of Rights.

Despite, or perhaps paradoxically because of, its significance, the ancient Bill of Rights is not widely known. It is overshadowed, for example, by Magna Carta, even though Magna Carta had been largely repealed since its promulgation was extracted by the barons at Runneymede in 1215.[5] And yet, the ancient Bill of Rights retains significance in our time both constitutionally and legally.

Philip Norton finds two reasons for this. First, he surmises that the "ignominious fleeing of a king"[6] is not sufficiently exciting for generations of schoolchildren to study and, second, he suggests that the Glorious Revolution has "produced a state of affairs that became taken for granted and one that consequently was not deemed worthy of extended study."[7] No doubt Norton is being somewhat facetious in his reference to the lack of excitement for children in studying the flight of James II (this hardly seems to be a criterion on which school curricula are generally based), but he makes a valid point when he suggests that the principles of law that were established in the ancient Bill of Rights can be taken for granted precisely because they have become axiomatic in a parliamentary system of government.

In addition, the development of cabinet government in the nineteenth century and "prime ministerial" government in the twentieth century, together with the domination of individual members of Parliament by party affiliation, has served to blur the distinction between the legislative and executive arms of government. And, as Norton maintains, the tensions that are now surfacing between executive and legislative are at least partly a consequence of society's general ignorance of this historical legacy. Professor S.M. Waddams agrees, pointing out that the practical manner in which government operates obscures the difference between its legislative and executive arms:

> In the modern parliamentary system where the government often controls the majority of the Legislature, we are sometimes apt to confuse the government with Parliament itself. But it still remains an essential principle of our constitution that the government cannot itself *make* law, and has only those powers given to it *by* law.[8]

This is not to confuse the origins of Parliament with democracy. The movement towards democratizing parliamentary institutions did not begin until the *Reform Acts* of the nineteenth century in the United Kingdom (passed initially amid the elitism of the "golden age" of Parliament and a view of democracy as "a bad thing"[9]), culminating in universal adult male suffrage by 1868.[10] Even at this legalistic and superficial level, democratization through the extension of the franchise was not complete in Canada until well into the twentieth century with the granting of

5. Part I of the Schedule to the *Statute Law (Repeals) Act 1969* (U.K.) repeals the whole of 25 Edward I (1297), confirming Magna Carta, except for articles 1, 9, 29 and 37.
6. Norton, "The Glorious Revolution," note 5.
7. Ibid.
8. S.M. Waddams, *Introduction to the Study of Law* (Toronto: Carswell, 1987), 8 (emphasis added).
9. See Macpherson, *The Real World of Democracy*, chapter 1, note 2.
10. *Reform Act 1867*.

the vote to women[11] and, finally, to status Indians.[12] But, while Parliament is an institutional Topsy and therefore comprises a myriad of facets that may even be contradictory, it retains a democratic thread, apart from the franchise, that reaches back to 1688 and the wresting of power (by a privileged and noble class, to be sure) from an absolute monarch. The essence of Parliament lies in its principled acknowledgement that sovereignty resides in the people through their representatives and does not flow from God into the person of the king. As Ivor Jennings, a leading writer on the English constitution, described it:

> [T]he Reform Act [1832] altered the fundamental assumptions of the Constitution. ... The British Constitution is democratic. The power of government rests in the last resort on the consent of the electorate.[13]

This modern democratic base is itself grounded on or linked to another key facet of the ancient Bill of Rights, the abolition of the suspension power. The suspension power is the power claimed by absolute monarchs to make and unmake laws by royal decree rather than by virtue of a legislative process. This power was specifically denied in section 1 of the ancient Bill of Rights, which declared: "That the pretended Power of Suspending the Laws or the Execution of Laws by Regall Authority without Consent of Parlyament is illegall."

Parliament, in asserting its supremacy, had established the proposition that the law is what Parliament, or more accurately stated, the Queen-in-Parliament says that it is. (In the provincial context, the legislature is the combination of the Legislative Assembly and the lieutenant governor acting together.) Its pronouncements are issued in the form of statutes enacted in accordance with a legally and constitutionally mandated procedure. Thus, even the Crown, or in modern terms, the prime minister or premier and cabinet, are required to obey the law until it is properly changed.

After the dramatic events of the seventeenth century that led up to the enactment of the ancient Bill of Rights — with James II fleeing England to be replaced on the throne by William and Mary in accordance with the principles contained in the Declaration of Right — it is surprising to find that any serious attempt to revive the suspension power could take place more than three centuries after these fundamental issues had been so dramatically settled. Nevertheless, in our time it has been the attempted revival of the suspension power by executive government that has prompted judicial review and confirmation of the continued legal applicability of the ancient Bill of Rights. In Saskatchewan, its revival has, as well, been coupled with unusual uses of special warrants, so that the two most significant aspects of the ancient Bill of Rights as a foundation for modern parliamentary government have been under assault at the same time.

The issue of the suspension power was considered by the Supreme Court of Canada in 1976 in the case of *Re Anti-Inflation Act*.[14] The federal government had enacted legislation to give it authority to impose wage and price controls under the

11. Women received the right to vote in federal elections by S.C. 1918, c. 20.
12. The *Canada Elections Act*, S.C. 1960, c. 39, repealed clause 14(2)(e) of the former Act, being R.S.C. 1952, c. 23, which disqualified Indians from voting. A corresponding amendment to the *Indian Act* respecting waivers of tax exempt status which permitted enfranchisement was effected by S.C. 1960, c. 8.
13. As quoted in Forsey, *The Royal Power of Dissolution of Parliament in the British Commonwealth* (1943; Toronto: Oxford University Press, 1968), chapter 1, note 13, p. 72.
14. [1976] 2 S.C.R. 373.

authority of the "peace, order and good government clause" found in section 91 of the *Constitution Act, 1867*. While the focal point of the reference was the constitutional validity of the federal legislation, a subsidiary issue in the case related to a provision of the *Anti-Inflation Act* (Canada) which authorized the federal minister of Finance to enter into an agreement with a province for the application of the federal Act within that province. The difficulty lay, not with the power of the federal government to enter into such an agreement, but with the power of the Ontario government to do so. The Chief Justice, Bora Laskin, described it in this way:

> [W]hat is at issue is the right of the Crown, although duly protected by an order in council, to bind its subjects in the Province to laws not enacted by the Legislature nor made applicable to such subjects by adoption under authorizing legislation. *There is no principle in this country, as there is not in Great Britain, that the Crown may legislate by proclamation or order in council to bind citizens where it so acts without the support of a statute of the Legislature.*[15]

In the same year, on the other side of the world, in another parliamentary state based on the Westminster inheritance, the New Zealand Supreme Court came to a similar, although perhaps more eloquent, conclusion in the case of *Fitzgerald v. Muldoon and Others*.[16] The *New Zealand Superannuation Act 1974* had established a compulsory superannuation plan which required employees to contribute to a pension plan at a prescribed rate that was matched by employers. The plan was opposed by the National Party which promised to abolish it if elected. After winning the 1975 election, the new prime minister issued a press release announcing the cessation of contributions as of December 15, 1975. But he didn't move to bring legislation into the New Zealand Parliament to effect the change in law. On March 22, 1976 an action was brought in court claiming a declaration that the prime minister's statement was illegal and asking for various forms of injunctive relief. The New Zealand Supreme Court did not hesitate to grant the declaration sought:

> [I]t is not disputed that the Bill of Rights is part of our law. The fact that no modern instance of its application was cited in argument may be due to the fact that it is rarely that a litigant takes up such a cause as the present, or it may be because governments usually follow established procedures. But it is not a reason for declining to apply the Bill of Rights when it is invoked and a litigant makes out his case.[17]

In this country, the enforceability of the ancient Bill of Rights was more or less taken for granted by the Supreme Court of Canada in its brief allusion to that fact when it considered the constitutional reference cases brought before it in the early 1980s on the questions surrounding the proposal to patriate the Canadian Constitution with a charter of rights and an amending formula.[18]

Surprise at the apparent exercise of the suspension power in modern times arises because it has its conceptual origin as a corollary to the notion of rule by divine right. How can it be seriously contended in an era that embraces the rhetoric of democracy that it is in any sense appropriate that the executive government should

15. Ibid., p. 433 (emphasis added).

16. [1976] 2 N.Z.L.R. 617.

17. C.J. Wild, from his judgement in *Figzgerald* v. *Muldoon and Others*, as quoted in W.A. McKean, "The Suspending Power Exhumed," *Public Law* (Spring 1978): 7–15.

18. *Reference re Amendment of the Constitution of Canada (Nos. 1, 2 and 3)* (1982), 125 D.L.R. (3d) 1, at p. 30.

be permitted to enact law by announcement? In this manner, the ancient Bill of Rights underpins the modern concept of the rule of law. And it is because of the judicial pronouncements delivered when these excesses have been called into question that the continued significance of the ancient Bill of Rights has been affirmed. This is the parliamentary model that Saskatchewan has inherited and built on.

THE SASKATCHEWAN CONTEXT

The evolution of parliamentary government in Canada and Saskatchewan is more overtly linked with conscious notions of "rep by pop" than was the development of Parliament in Britain. It is somewhat less Topsy-like than its English ancestor because the legal creation of the country (by virtue of the enactment of British statutes) and of the province (by virtue of the enactment of federal statutes) required the making of specific choices to be enshrined as law. The creation of the province occurred, in the words of Saskatchewan political scientist David Smith, "de novo, within invisible, geometrically determined boundaries" in which "state preceded society."[19]

As legislative histories go, Saskatchewan's is a brief one. The movement from rule by executive council to legislating assembly and from territory to province in 1905 occurred at a point in time during the maturation of the British and Canadian parliamentary models that is unequivocally founded on notions of representative democracy. The Saskatchewan legislature has had to evolve since that time as a liberal institution transformed by the need to provide itself with a democratic base.[20] While these concepts may appear to be contradictory, they have been synthesized to create the modern Canadian version of a functioning Parliament.

Under the Liberal governments that dominated Saskatchewan politics in the first half of the province's life, "the Legislature's job," according to Smith, "was to ratify government's decisions and by its assent to lay the foundation on which an electoral majority might be sustained."[21] This description encapsulates the relationship between the government and the important interest group of the time — the Saskatchewan Grain Growers' Association (SGGA). Overlapping membership in government and the SGGA, the importance of agricultural issues in Saskatchewan, and the pre-eminence of the SGGA as the voice of the Saskatchewan farmer resulted in the development of a symbiotic relationship between the SGGA and government:

> The period of Liberal rule was characterized by the close attention paid to the expressed wishes of the Saskatchewan Grain Growers' Association, an attention which strongly enhanced the party's position with the agrarian electorate.
>
> From the beginning, an interlocking of personnel between the provincial Liberal administration and the leadership of the Grain Growers' ensured continuous and sympathetic consideration of agrarian demands. W.R. Motherwell, Saskatchewan Minister of Agriculture from 1905 to 1918, was one of the founders of the Grain Growers' Association, and he became its first president. George Langley, who was taken into the cabinet in 1912, and C.A. Dunning who followed in 1916 and became premier in

19. David E. Smith, "Saskatchewan: Approximating the Ideal," in Gary Levy and Graham White (eds.), *Provincial and Territorial Legislatures in Canada* (Toronto: University of Toronto Press, 1989), 49.
20. See Macpherson, *The Real World of Democracy*, chapter 1, 4–11, note 2.
21. Smith, "Saskatchewan: Approximating the Ideal," 50, note 2.

> 1922, were both active and influential in the agricultural association. In 1921, in a direct bid for Grain Growers' support in a period of agrarian upheaval, Premier Martin brought J.A. Maharg, president of the Association, into the cabinet for a short-lived term as Minister of Agriculture. The relationship between the Association and the government was sufficiently close for the Conservative opposition occasionally to challenge the presumably non-partisan nature of the farmers' movement. During the 1917 legislative session so many cabinet ministers deserted the legislative chamber for the Grain Growers' Convention in Moose Jaw that proceedings at the center of government ground to a halt. Efforts were made in later years to avoid such conflict by having the legislative sittings completed before the holding of the Grain Growers' Convention.
>
> This close connection of Liberals and Grain Growers' Association was more than coincidental, and it was carefully guarded and cultivated by the government.[22]

By 1944, with the resignation from government of a number of Liberal members of the SGGA, the disappearance of the SGGA as the sole voice of the farmer and the emergence of other farm organizations, and after the devastating effects of drought and depression, this kind of relationship between government and non-government organizations ceased to exist.[23] Furthermore, the CCF government elected in that year did not have these kinds of connections to affect its relationship with the legislature. The CCF as a political party developed programs that were relevant to both its urban and its rural supporters. It also placed value and emphasis on accountability to its members. The party established a Legislative Advisory Committee empowered to meet with the government caucus and report to the Party's Council and to the Party in Convention.[24] According to Evelyn Eager, a Saskatchewan historian,

> [t]he CCF during the Douglas regime in Saskatchewan achieved a unique juxtaposition of two opposing principles: the operation of party democracy while in power and adherence to the traditions of parliamentary government.[25]

And the CCF's view of the role of government was fundamentally different. Douglas offered voters in 1944 a choice between "conditions as they were before the war: a period of free enterprise and all the poverty it caused, or a change to a commonwealth of social justice."[26] All of these factors had an effect on the relationship of government to the Legislature. Evelyn Eager described the political sentiments of the times in these terms:

> The Liberals said responsible government had ended after 1944 and a regime of rule by experts had taken its place. That was inflammatory language, but it signalled the changes in legislative atmosphere and activity that became evident in the post-1944 period.[27]

---

22. Evelyn Eager, *Saskatchewan Government: Politics and Pragmatism* (Saskatoon: Western Producer Prairie Books, 1980), 47.

23. Ibid., 51–55.

24. Doris French Shackleton, *Tommy Douglas* (Toronto: McClelland and Stewart, 1975), 141–43.

25. Evelyn Eager, "The Paradox of Power in the Saskatchewan CCF, 1944–1961," in J.H. Aitchison (ed.), *The Political Process in Canada* (Toronto: University of Toronto Press, 1963), as quoted in Shackleton, *Tommy Douglas*, 143.

26. Shackleton, *Tommy Douglas*, 124, note 7.

27. Smith, "Saskatchewan: Approximating the Ideal," 51, note 2.

Although the CCF government that won the 1944 election was new to the Saskatchewan legislature, it had an established understanding of the nature of Parliament and parliamentary tradition. Premier Douglas, for example, had served as a federal member of Parliament since 1935. The long period of control of government by the CCF/NDP (from 1944 to 1982, with a seven-year hiatus under the Thatcher Liberals) provided an opportunity for the development and establishment of a Saskatchewan parliamentary tradition based on this beginning. And the tradition thus established was one that afforded respect to the democratic aspects of Parliament and sought to use parliamentary institutions as a means for enhancing the accountability of government to people through the legislature. Two specific examples come to mind: one involving Crown corporations and the other review of regulations.

When the Douglas administration brought the first *Crown Corporations Act* before the Saskatchewan legislature in 1945,[28] it also proposed the creation of a Standing Committee of the Legislature on Crown Corporations. The purpose for creating this committee was to provide a forum in which the various Crown corporations could be called to account before the legislature. Without the existence of such a committee, the arm's length nature and structure of the Crown corporation would mitigate against accountability. In fact, Premier Douglas went further and insisted that a cabinet minister chair the board of directors of each Crown corporation to ensure a two-way line of communication between government and the corporation and therefore accountability by the minister to the legislature.

Similarly, in 1963, when legislation to provide for the central filing and publication of regulations was first enacted[29] under the government of Premier Woodrow Lloyd, a special committee of the Saskatchewan legislature was established to conduct a review of all regulations filed.[30] The committee still functions as it was originally established. It is asked to analyze regulations from a number of perspectives. In particular, the committee is mandated to examine regulations on the broad grounds of appropriateness by inquiring as to whether, even if legal, a regulation relies on an unexpected — and therefore, perhaps, improper — use of the legal power. The committee has an opposition member as its chair and is authorized to report to the legislature and may recommend that regulations be repealed or amended. The committee thus provides an all-party mechanism by which the use of delegated law-making power can be supervised and controlled by the legislature.

Both these committees were innovative solutions devised in Saskatchewan to deal with the problem of managing government control over increasingly complex matters of government while at the same time retaining legislative accountability.

28. *The Crown Corporations Act, 1945*, S.S. 1945, c. 17.

29. *The Regulations Act, 1963*, S.S. 1963, c. 79.

30. The only reason that the Regulations Committee was established as a "special" rather than as a "standing" committee was because of the sitting practices of the Saskatchewan legislature and its rules concerning committee meetings. A standing committee is not permitted to meet when the legislature is not sitting. Prior to the Devine government's taking office in 1982, the legislature would always prorogue in the spring when the budget was approved. Thus, if the regulations committee had been established as a standing committee in 1963, its work would have to have been completed during the time when the legislature was sitting. Because it was constituted as a special committee it was able to meet at any time.

Since 1982, it has become the practice to prorogue only when the government is ready to commence a new session. In this context, the distinction between standing and special committees becomes irrelevant. As a special committee, the regulations committee must be reconstituted after each election and provided with a mandate. A resolution to this effect is adopted as a matter of course when required.

The seven-year term of Liberal government under Premier Ross Thatcher from 1964–71 saw little change in the legislature and its relationship with executive government. The committees established by Douglas and Lloyd continued to function in the same manner; special warrants were used, but only as they always had been. The Douglas/Lloyd governments in Saskatchewan established a standard of respect for the legislature that was carried forward through the Thatcher era and on under the Blakeney administration. Perhaps Blakeney's roots in the Saskatchewan civil service, serving as secretary of the Government finance office when Douglas established the Crown corporations committee, provides part of an explanation for that phenomenon.

This respect for the legislature makes sense in its historical context. The essential features of Parliament remain essential, even if they have come to be taken for granted. In fact, the continued rejection of the suspension power and the requirement of legislative approval to executive expenditure remain the essence of the parliamentary system, even as they were in Britain in 1688. However, during the decade of the 1980s this respectful relationship changed.

On April 26, 1982, the Progressive Conservative party under the leadership of Grant Devine suddenly came to power in Saskatchewan with an impressive majority of the seats in the Saskatchewan legislature.[31] The Conservatives elected in 1982 were largely unknown as well as inexperienced in Saskatchewan provincial politics. Although Premier J.T.M. Anderson, who held office between 1929 and 1934, was himself a Conservative, he led a coalition government composed of Conservatives, Progressives, and Independents. From 1934–75 the Conservatives actually held only two seats in the Saskatchewan legislature. One seat was only secured in a by-election in 1953, and neither incumbent was subsequently re-elected.[32] This first Progressive Conservative government in Saskatchewan was elected on the strength of an anti-government vote and two appealing promises: mortgage interest subsidies — at a time when mortgage interest rates were climbing into the 20 percent range — and the removal of the provincial tax on gasoline.[33]

The new government implemented its major campaign promises almost immediately after the election: the gas tax was removed as promised by the enactment of a cabinet order on May 9, 1982 (the day on which the Devine administration was sworn into office) and the necessary legislation to put in place the promised mortgage interest subsidy program received royal assent on July 9, 1982, and was made effective retroactively to July 1 of that year.[34]

However, the manner in which the new government removed the gas tax on the day it took office perhaps foreshadowed more significant events to come. Removal of the provincial tax on gasoline had been a key promise in the election campaign. Party leader Grant Devine had announced that a Conservative government would remove the gas tax on the day that a Progressive Conservative administration was sworn into office, whether it was necessary to pass a statute or a regulation, or even

---

31. In 1982, the Conservatives received 54% of the popular vote and took 55 of the 64 seats in the Saskatchewan legislature; the NDP received 37% of the popular vote and 9 seats; the Liberals placed a distant third with 4.5% of the popular vote and no seats in the Legislature. By 1991, the Conservatives had sunk to 23% and 10 seats; the NDP had risen to 51% and 55 seats; the Liberals had risen to 21% and had been able to secure a single seat.

32. *Provincial Elections in Saskatchewan 1905–1983* (Regina: Chief Electoral Office, 1983).

33. James M. Pitsula and Ken Rasmussen, *Privatizing a Province: The New Right in Saskatchewan* (Vancouver: New Star Books, 1990), chapter 1, note 11.

34. *The Mortgage Interest Reduction Act*, S.S. 1982-83, c. M-21.1.

recall the legislature. That claim itself bespoke a level of ignorance about the nature of statutes and regulations, how they come into being, and about the functions of the legislature, implying as it did that a statute could be passed without recalling the legislature.

The practical difficulty that the Conservatives faced was that the gas tax was imposed by *The Fuel Petroleum Products Act*,[35] a statute enacted by the Saskatchewan legislature. The gas tax could not, therefore, be removed unless the legislature repealed the Act that imposed it. To do otherwise would be an invocation of the suspension power which had been declared illegal by the ancient Bill of Rights. Furthermore, it would be impossible to pass a law on May 9, 1982, the day that the Conservatives took office, as they had promised, because the legislature would not even exist until May 19, 1982 — 23 days after voting day when the official return to the writ was made by the chief electoral officer.[36] What was at stake, however, was the new government's credibility and an embarrassing exposure of the depth of its ignorance about government in general and the legislative process in particular.

The government found a solution, of sorts, by removing the gas tax through a tax remission order passed by cabinet pursuant to the authority granted by subsection 78(1) of *The Department of Finance Act* (now *The Financial Administration Act, 1993*). That provision permits cabinet to forgive a tax when it is in the public interest and public inconvenience, hardship or injustice would occur. It has been frequently used to remit tax, for example, paid by persons whose only income is from social assistance benefits or who are members of a religious order and have taken vows of poverty so that they do not actually receive the income they earn. Remission orders were thus usually enacted for the benefit of named individuals or small groups of people described by limiting criteria. *The Fuel Petroleum Products Tax Exemption Regulations*,[37] enacted on May 9, 1982, exempted almost all possible taxpayers from the liability to pay tax under *The Fuel Petroleum Products Act*, arguably nullifying the Act. There was, therefore, a strong possibility that this particular remission order was *ultra vires* because it is an established principle of law that delegated legislation cannot be exercised by the delegatee in such a manner as to nullify the statute passed by the legislature pursuant to which the delegation of power is made.[38]

The tenuous legality of these regulations was recognized by the government itself. When the legislature was subsequently called into session for the first time after the election, *The Fuel Petroleum Products Act* was repealed and replaced by *The Fuel Tax Act*. This new Act established a new taxation regime, imposing tax only on aviation fuel and locomotive fuel, and was enacted on July 9, 1982 but made retroactive in effect to May 9, 1982 — the day on which the remission regulations had been originally promulgated. The questionable legality of the remission regulations was thus legitimized by a retroactive change to the statute imposing the tax, a change that was made as quickly as possible after the new government took office, although not the very same day.

The Conservatives' first term of office saw the elimination of major sources of

35. R.S.S.1978, c.F-23.

36. The life of a legislature is counted from the day on which the official return to the writ is made. See section 4(1) of the *Canadian Charter of Rights and Freedoms*. Saskatchewan's *Election Act* fixes this day as the twenty-third day after polling day. Up until the twenty-third day after polling day, the legislature remains in a state of dissolution and does not exist.

37. Saskatchewan Regulations 72/82, Gazetted May 21, 1982.

38. See Denys C. Holland and John P. McGowan, *Delegated Legislation in Canada* (Toronto: Carswell, 1989), 181–89.

government revenue through initiatives like the removal of the gas tax and revised resource royalty schemes, and a dramatic increase in expenditures on programs like the mortgage subsidy plan and the home improvement loan program. The government was reelected to its second term of office on October 20, 1986, but its standing in the Legislative Assembly declined from 57 to 38 seats.

Once the election was over, the minister of Finance announced that the province's annual deficit was $830 million more than he had projected it to be in the 1986–87 budget estimates that the legislature had approved only three months earlier on July 3, 1986. A session of the Legislature was quickly convened on December 3, 1986 — a mere six weeks after the general election — and several pieces of legislation were enacted. These included *The Government Organization Act*[39] which permitted the rearrangement of the executive government without going to the legislature, a revamped mortgage interest subsidy program under *The Mortgage Protection Act*,[40] amendments to *The Farm Land Security Act*,[41] *The Farmers' Counselling and Assistance Act*[42] and *The Saskatchewan Pension Plan Act*.[43]

It is not clear why the government felt it necessary to reconvene the legislature so quickly after the 1986 general election. Regular fall sittings had only begun in Saskatchewan in 1973, and there was already a precedent for doing without a fall sitting because of the election calendar. In 1978, when the Blakeney government was returned for a third time, in a fall election, the legislature was not recalled until the following spring. Furthermore, the original purpose of the fall sitting when it was established during the Blakeney administration in 1973 was to provide a means for introducing major legislative initiatives which could then be analyzed by those affected during the period of adjournment that followed. In Saskatchewan's early legislative history, the short session, beginning in late February and proroguing by early May, had been sufficient for governments to accomplish what was necessary. The growth of the demands on modern governments had increased the legislative load and made it difficult to deal adequately with all the measures before the legislature, particularly in the case of major new legislative initiatives. This was especially problematic since the then prevailing view of parliamentary privilege precluded public consultation on the text of legislation prior to its introduction in the House. Thus, what motivated the initiation of the practice of sitting in the fall was the idea of sitting to introduce major as well as controversial legislation in order to permit broad public discussion during the period of adjournment before the "main" part of the session. But the fall sitting held in 1986 was not held for this purpose. In fact, all but one of the bills that were introduced in the 1986 fall sitting were passed prior to that sitting's adjournment.[44]

39. S.S. 1986-87-88, c. G-5.1.
40. Ibid., c. M-21.11.
41. Ibid., c. 1.
42. Ibid., c. 2.
43. Ibid., c. 8.
44. In addition to the acts mentioned in notes 10–14 (above), three other bills were introduced in the fall of 1986. Only *The Tabling of Documents (Postponement) Act* (Bill 8), which was introduced on December 23, 1986, the day on which the fall 1986 session was adjourned, was not passed. A postponement Act has been introduced any time the fall portion of the legislative sitting extends past 15 sitting days. The reason for this is that *The Tabling of Documents Act* requires documents to be tabled within 15 days of the commencement of the session. Since no one expects that the fifteenth sitting day will occur before spring, the documents are not prepared prior to that time and are therefore not ready to be tabled. A postponement Act postpones the tabling requirement so that it will occur when it had been expected. In 1986, December 23 was the fifteenth sitting day. Bill 8 was given Royal assent on July 22, 1987.

The most obvious explanation for the haste in convening the session in 1986 was that it was necessary to do so in order to enact important legislation as soon as possible. But it is difficult to see what was so critical about the legislation that was enacted that fall, other than the fact that *The Government Organization Act* made it possible for executive government to be restructured and rearranged conveniently by cabinet order without debate in the House.

Government reorganization had, in the past, resulted from budget initiatives. The passage of this enabling legislation, together with the use of special warrants, made it possible for the executive government to bypass the legislature totally, at least for a time. "Bill 5," as it was known, attracted criticism from both the opposition and the media. According to James Pitsula and Ken Rasmussen, who conducted a study of the Devine administration, "Most observers saw the bill as being legally, morally and constitutionally wrong."[45] Some interpreted its passage as an attempt by the government to neutralize the effectiveness of the opposition, which had grown from eight members in 1982 to 25 after the 1986 general election, by limiting the public scrutiny to which the government would be subject.[46] And, in fact, eight departments were affected by regulations passed by cabinet under this new legislation before the legislature was finally forced to reconvene on June 17, 1987.[47] All of these reorganizations were funded by special warrants.

This twenty-first legislature was also marked by unique events in Saskatchewan legislative history which revolved around the government's attempt to impose a fast-paced agenda of privatization on an unwilling opposition and an apparently unwilling population. Eventually, even Premier Devine himself, when the 1991 election loomed on the horizon, admitted that he had "gotten too far ahead of public opinion."[48] The resulting polarization of the populace erupted in the Legislature in two significant and unprecedented events. The first was a lengthy bell-ringing crisis, when the opposition New Democratic Party walked out of the legislature for seventeen days over proposals to privatize the Saskatchewan Energy Corporation. The second occurred during debate on legislation to permit the privatization of the Potash Corporation of Saskatchewan, when the government used time allocation and closure for the first time in Saskatchewan's legislative history.

The bell-ringing incident in 1989 may have marked a turning point, both for the government and for the opposition. SaskEnergy was the natural gas division of SaskPower, itself first organized as a Crown corporation by the CCF government of Premier Douglas in 1949 by an order-in-council passed pursuant to the authority of the then newly enacted *Crown Corporations Act, 1945*.[49] The corporation had previously existed as an agency of government and had been widely regarded as an essential public utility, building the necessary infrastructure that private capital had failed to secure for the development of the whole of the province. In fact, Premier

45. Pitsula and Rasmussen, *Privatizing a Province*, 253, note 16.

46. Ibid.

47. These included regulations establishing the mandates of the departments of Human Resources, Labour and Employment, Environment and Public Safety, Education, Consumer and Commercial Affairs, Finance, Tourism, Small Business and Co-operatives, Parks, Recreation and Culture, as well as regulations establishing the Saskatchewan Opportunities Program to provide summer employment for students.

48. Pitsula and Rasmussen, *Privatizing a Province*, 4, note 16.

49. S.S. 1945, c. 17.

Douglas pointed to rural electrification of Saskatchewan in the 1950s as his most important achievement as premier, more important than Medicare.[50]

The government's division of SaskPower into two parts had taken place before the introduction of the privatization legislation that sparked the bell-ringing crisis in the legislature in 1989.[51] SaskPower retained control over electricity and SaskEnergy controlled natural gas. Historically, the more lucrative natural gas side of the corporation had subsidized the electrical side, ensuring reasonable rates for power in the whole of the province. When the government had implemented this division of SaskPower in 1988, the division had provoked concern that privatization was imminent. However, the minister responsible for SaskPower at that time repeatedly gave his assurances in the legislature that the creation of SaskEnergy was not a prelude to privatization of the natural gas side of SaskPower. By 1989, however, all had changed. Now the government proposed privatization and the opposition walked out of the legislature, leaving the bells ringing, in an effort to stop the government from succeeding in that proposal. And it did. The government finally agreed to establish a three-person commission, chaired by Dr. Lloyd Barber, then president of the University of Regina, to investigate and report on the proposal to privatize SaskEnergy. In the meantime, the government promised not to move further with its privatization legislation. The legislation died on the order paper before the report was completed and was never reintroduced.

The opposition was heavily criticized for that walk-out. It was described as an obstructionist tactic. According to the critics, the appropriate action for an opposition was to stay in the House and debate the issues. Thus, when the legislation to privatize the Potash Corporation of Saskatchewan (PCS) was introduced into the legislature later in the 1989 session, the opposition stayed in the House to debate the issue. However, it seemed that the government was not interested in debate. Up until nearly the end of July, that is just days before a time allocation motion was introduced on August 4, only two government MLAs had spoken to the potash bill: the Minister responsible for the Potash Corporation who moved the motion for second reading of the legislation, and the deputy premier. Their comments cover a total of less than four pages in *Hansard*.[52] The government then invoked closure.

Closure is a procedural mechanism by which a government can force the conclusion of debate on an issue by preventing the debate from being adjourned. Time allocation is a means by which special time limits on the various stages of a bill are imposed so that, no matter how many MLAs wish to speak on a measure, the total time to be spent on it will be limited to a pre-determined number of sitting days or hours. There had been no limitations on debates of government motions in the Saskatchewan legislature as a normal rule, other than the limitations on the debate

50. Thomas H. McLeod and Ian McLeod, *Tommy Douglas: The Road to Jerusalem* (Edmonton: Hurtig Publishers Ltd., 1987), 173 and note 15.

51. See *The Saskatchewan Energy Corporation Act*, Bill 22, 1989–90 session, which was introduced into the Saskatchewan Legislature on May 8, 1989 but which died on the order paper when that session was finally prorogued without its having been enacted.

52. *Hansard*, April 18, 1989, pp. 895–97 and ibid., July 20, 1989, pp. 2836–37. The legislature was adjourned during the potash debate for lack of a quorum, on May 8, 1989. The quorum required is only 15 MLAs present of a total of 66. Later, the minister responsible tried to close debate on July 12, 1989 (*Hansard*, pp. 2603–07), but, according to the comments of Opposition MLAs, the Government had not indicated that it would be dealing with the potash bill on that day. Normally, the order of business for the day is provided by the government to the opposition in advance. Consequently, the minister was not permitted to close debate.

on the Speech from the Throne and on the budget.[53] Thus, while the use of time allocation and closure may have become quite common in other Houses, particularly in the House of Commons, it had never before been used in Saskatchewan. Closure was invoked for the first time in Saskatchewan's legislative history on Saskatchewan Day, August 7, 1989,[54] on a time allocation motion that limited all stages of the bill to privatize PCS to three days.

Parliamentary debate serves to expose a government's position to critical analysis and review and to permit time for public support to be mobilized, either for or against it. Closure stops the debate from occurring so that the details of the government's proposals are not exposed to public review and scrutiny, and the support cannot be mobilized. Eugene Forsey explained the opposition's obligation to be obstructionist in his analysis of the use of closure in the "pipeline debate" of 1956:

> On a great issue of public policy, a Government defeated in Parliament is entitled to appeal from Parliament to the people, because it believes the existing Parliament has lost the confidence of the people. Equally, on a great issue of public policy, an Opposition, facing a certain defeat in Parliament, is entitled first to try to rouse public opinion and so force the Government to back down; and secondly, if that fails, to try to force an appeal from Parliament to the people, and for precisely the same reason which entitles a defeated Government to appeal: that it believes the existing Parliament has lost the confidence of the people.
>
> A Government makes its appeal by dissolution. An Opposition makes its appeal by trying to force dissolution, by obstruction... Used as it should be, and almost always has been in Canada, only for the gravest reasons, it is a legitimate and indeed essential part of the parliamentary system; in the last resort, with the government's power of dissolution, the only way of keeping Parliament responsible to the people.[55]

Thus, closure is a device used not to prevent obstruction, but to conclude it "when it has performed its function."[56]

Not surprisingly, once closure had been used for the first time in Saskatchewan, it became easier for the government to use it on subsequent occasions. In 1991, the government again invoked closure to force the enactment of an interim supply bill.[57] Interim supply is the process by which funds are approved for government expenditure during each month while the main budget and the detailed estimates are under review in the legislature. Usually, interim supply bills are passed in a matter of a few hours, most often in a single day. In this case, debate had continued for four sitting days. The dynamics of the session were focussed on the general election that was imminent (the legislature would cease to exist on November 12, 1991 when its five-year life would constitutionally expire). The opposition pressed every

53. Rule 13(1) of *The Rules and Procedures of the Legislative Assembly of Saskatchewan* limits the address in reply to the speech of the lieutenant governor to six sitting days. Rule 14(2) limits the budget debate to five days.

54. Saskatchewan Day is a statutory holiday that falls on the first Monday in August. In an unusual sitting, the Saskatchewan Legislature convened on Saskatchewan Day in 1989 to deal with the closure motion targeted at completing the government's legislative initiative to privatize PCS. As the sell-out crowd cheered on the home town football team in Taylor Field, Saskatchewan MLAs sat in another theatre a little further south, making legislative history.

55. Eugene Forsey, "Constitutional Aspects of the Canadian Pipe Line Debate," in *Public Law* (London: Stevens & Sons Limited, 1957).

56. Ibid., 26.

57. "Votes and Proceedings of the Legislative Assembly of Saskatchewan," May 8, 1991.

opportunity available to it to criticize the government. It complained that the government was not providing any answers to the detailed financial questions it had raised in the context of the government's request for interim supply. While that may have been true, it was also true that the opposition would have had several other opportunities to ask these questions in the course of the continuing consideration of the whole of the government's budget and, to some extent, in some of the legislature's committees. Given all these factors, it was perhaps not unreasonable for the government to resort to closure to enact this bill.

But later in the spring of 1991, as the Government was facing the expiration of its term of office, it used closure again to pass its controversial amendments to *The Education and Health Tax Act*. The amendments were designed to effect harmonization of the provincial sales tax with the new federal Goods and Services Tax (GST). There was substantial opposition to the removal of at least some of the exemptions to provincial sales tax that were necessary to achieve harmonization, especially the exemptions for books and restaurant meals. Petitions signed by more than 50,000 persons opposed to this bill had been tabled in the legislature. There would be no other opportunities in this legislature for the opposition to attack the government's position on the issue. Nevertheless, the government persisted in its use of closure to ensure the speedy passage of this bill as well. Closure has been used several more times since Saskatchewan Day in 1989, and it appears now to have become a commonplace in Saskatchewan as well as in other jurisdictions.

As a result of the difficulties that the government had faced in the legislature over privatization in 1989, it decided to proceed with the privatization of the general insurance business[58] of Saskatchewan Government Insurance (SGI) in a different manner. SGI Canada Insurance Services Ltd., an ordinary private business corporation, was incorporated pursuant to the enabling provisions of *The Business Corporations Act*[59] on July 18, 1990, and SGI was the sole shareholder.[60] On the same day, employees at SGI were advised that a decision had been made to expand SGI's general insurance business "including the necessary step of selling shares in SGI Canada."[61] The Saskatchewan Insurance Office and Professional Employees Union Local 397, representing SGI employees, and several individuals representative of employees, the union, and policyholders, initiated a legal action on the basis that the decision to sell SGI's entire general insurance business was one that must be made by the legislature.[62]

The argument the plaintiffs advanced was not all that radical. All corporations

58. SGI was originally created in 1946 for the purpose of providing general insurance because of the extremely high premiums demanded by private insurers for ordinary coverage. Premiums established by the newly created SGI were one-tenth of the private insurers' levels. With the introduction of compulsory automobile insurance in Saskatchewan in 1946, it was also the insurer for the compulsory portion of automobile accident insurance required by virtue of *The Automobile Accident Insurance Act*, R.S.S. 1978, c. A-35.

59. R.S.S. 1978, c. B-10.

60. These facts are set out in the judgment of J. MacLeod in *Bury et al. v. Saskatchewan Government Insurance and SGI Canada Insurance Services Ltd.*, [1991] 1 W.W.R. 47.

61. Ibid.

62. Although the complete list of plaintiffs is not contained in the reported judgements of this case, I disclose that I was one of the plaintiffs in this action. I was requested to lend my name to the lawsuit as a policyholder and because of my previous employment with the Saskatchewan legislature as legislative counsel and law clerk. My actual participation in the case or in the framing of the arguments was minimal. Counsel for the plaintiffs was Bob Mitchell, an NDP MLA at that time and later the minister of Justice in the Romanow Government.

are creatures of statute. Ordinary, private business corporations are incorporated pursuant to the authority given by *The Business Corporations Act* and are limited in their activities by the provisions of that Act.[63] Crown corporations are conceptually structured in the same manner as private corporations except that they have only one shareholder — the Crown. In Saskatchewan, Crown corporations can be created by cabinet order or by special statute. In either event, they are limited in their functioning to doing only those things that they are authorized to do by the order-in-council or the Act creating them.[64] The plaintiffs' argument in the SGI case was based on the fact that there was no specific authority to be found in the legislation establishing SGI that would permit the corporation to make the decision to sell off a major component of its business. Mr. Justice MacLeod, in the Saskatchewan Court of Queen's Bench, agreed. He found that neither the board of directors of SGI, nor the cabinet, had the power necessary to effect the sale that was announced; that power belonged to the Saskatchewan legislature.

The timing of SGI's privatization announcements also bears examination. The legislature had been in session almost until the end of June in 1990. Two weeks after it was adjourned, SGI Canada Ltd. was incorporated and the staff were advised of the impending sale, expected to commence by late fall. Although the responsible minister, Grant Schmidt, had frequently said that the privatization of SGI's general insurance business did not require legislative approval, the opposition was of the view that the government wished to keep the issue out of the legislature because it could then avoid a coalescing of public opinion against the initiative as had occurred in the previous year over SaskEnergy. The government also realized that the opposition would not let the necessary legislation pass without a fight. The Regina *Leader-Post* reported:

> Mr. Schmidt conceded ... that the government kept the matter out of the legislature because of the NDP's walkout over SaskEnergy. "The NDP has no respect for democracy," Mr. Schmidt said. "They have obstructed the legislature in the past to the extent that it's difficult to function in an ordinary democratic way."[65]

As a Regina newspaper columnist pointed out a few days after the Queen's Bench decision came down,

> Traditionally, a democratically elected government presents its agenda to the parliament before the duly elected representatives of the people and has that agenda passed in the form of laws. Schmidt — who made it known the government planned to privatize SGI general business well before the last session ended — didn't bother.[66]

---

63. Prior to the enactment in Saskatchewan of *The Business Corporations Act* in 1977, corporations were even more limited in their ability to act than they are now. A significant change post-1977 is that corporations are now given "all the powers of natural persons" (see subsection 15(1) of the Act). Previously, it had been necessary for a company to have "objects" clauses and the company was limited in its powers to doing only those things that were specifically listed in its objects. The idea that corporations should be so specifically limited in their ability to carry on business is thus not surprising.

64. The order-in-council Crowns are created or continued by virtue of the authority of *The Crown Corporations Act*, 1993, S.S. 1993, c. C-50.101. That Act establishes a corporate regime for any specific corporation that might be established, i.e., granting generic powers and imposing generic duties. If it is necessary or desirable either to remove or add to the powers and duties that are established as a default position, a specific statute is necessary. The major utility Crowns — SGI, SPC, SaskEnergy, SaskTel — all are established pursuant to their own specific statutory authority.

65. Murray Mandryk, *Leader-Post*, August 31, 1990.

66. Ibid.

The government immediately appealed the decision of the Court of Queen's Bench to the Court of Appeal. On December 3, 1990, the Court of Appeal affirmed the judgment of the lower court in a four-to-one decision, saying that SGI had engaged in an "openly stated attempt ... to do indirectly what it had no statutory authority to do directly."[67] As such, the actions of SGI were *ultra vires* the corporation — beyond its legal authority to effect.

Another recurring issue throughout the Conservatives' term of office was their mortgage subsidy plan. It was a key feature of their bid for election in 1982. Interest rates were approaching 20 percent in 1982 and homeowners who had to renew their mortgages at those rates were facing payments far beyond their ability to pay. The first session of the twentieth legislature began with a Speech from the Throne on June 17, 1982, only 29 days after the official return to the writ of election following the April 26 vote. *The Mortgage Interest Reduction Act*[68] was the first bill introduced in the session and, when finally enacted, it was made applicable retroactively to the period beginning on July 1, 1982 and ending on June 30, 1985.[69]

The purpose of the mortgage subsidy plan was to subsidize the mortgage payments of homeowners who, as they were faced with mortgage renewals at the newer and higher rates, would otherwise have lost their homes. Lending institutions announced that they would take the amount of the mortgage subsidy into account when determining whether or not a mortgage applicant would qualify for a mortgage or a mortgage renewal.

In their second bid for election in 1986, the Conservatives revived the mortgage protection scheme. Interest rates had dropped substantially from the highs of the early 1980s, so the new legislation (now called *The Mortgage Protection Act*[70]), enacted on December 24, 1986 and applicable to the period September 1, 1986 to August 31, 1996, provided subsidies to homeowners to result in their paying an effective interest rate of 9.75 percent. The government's stated position was that it was important to introduce stability into the Saskatchewan housing market by ensuring mortgage rates at a specified level for a ten-year period.

In 1990, *The Mortgage Protection Act* was amended to raise the subsidized interest rate to 10.75%. This was accomplished by the enactment in the legislature of *The Mortgage Protection Amendment Act, 1990*.[71] The next year, in what some critics came to call his "press release budget," the minister of Finance, Lorne Hepworth, announced on February 20, 1991, that the subsidy rate for the mortgage protection plan would be raised again, this time to 13.25%.[72] This was the same subsidy rate at which the mortgage protection scheme had first been introduced almost 10 years earlier, although prevailing mortgage interest rates in 1991 were half what they had been in 1982. The minister's "Financial Initiatives Briefing Package" outlined the effect of the change to the program: 40,000 homeowners (out of a total of 65,000) would no longer receive benefits and average monthly benefits to the remainder would be reduced from $56 to $22 per month. It also provided the government's rationale for changes to the program:

---

67. *Saskatchewan Government Insurance and SGI Canada Insurance Services Ltd. v. Bury et al.*, [1991] 4 W.W.R. 1, p. 26, per J.A. Sherstobitoff.
68. S.S. 1982-83, c. M-21.1.
69. Ibid., section 13.
70. S.S. 1986-87-88, c. M-21.11.
71. S.S. 1990-91, c. 5.
72. Mark Wyatt, "Consumers Hit Hard," *Leader-Post*, February 21, 1991.

> Fiscal constraints have evolved to where government must alter its priorities. Consequently, the subsidy rate is being returned to the 13¼% level introduced in 1982. The increase in subsidy rate balances government's commitment to fiscal responsibility and protects homeowners against excessively high interest rates.[73]

Although the legislature was not then sitting and no law had yet been passed, on March 1, 1991 the mortgage protection plan benefits of approximately 65,000 Saskatchewan homeowners were reduced as if the amendment to change the subsidized interest rates had already been enacted. About six weeks later, on April 11, 1991, the fourth session of the twenty-first legislature was reconvened and, shortly thereafter, Bill 67 was introduced to raise the subsidized interest rate under the mortgage protection plan in line with the minister's February announcement. The bill received second reading on June 12, 1991, and could have been expected to be passed in due course. However, before it could proceed through all the necessary legislative steps in order to become law, the Saskatchewan legislature was suddenly prorogued.

Prorogation terminates a legislative session. Everything before a legislature at the time of prorogation and not completed dies on the order paper.[74] It cannot thereafter become law unless in a subsequent session of the legislature the legislation is again introduced and proceeds through the necessary three readings, committee review, and royal assent. Bills die on the order paper almost every time a session of the Saskatchewan legislature is prorogued. Usually, the bills that are left standing on the order paper at this time are opposition bills that were never expected to be enacted anyway.[75] However, this time the deputy minister of Finance announced that *The Mortgage Protection Amendment Act, 1990*, among others,[76] would be treated as if it had been passed. Since prorogation only occurs when the government requests it, it is certainly unprecedented for a government to prorogue without passing its own budget and the legislation necessary as a result of that budget. But, in spite of all that, the minister of Finance's position was simple:

> Our Government remains committed to reducing the deficit and increasing spending in the areas of health, education and agriculture. Therefore, although the legislation to increase the subsidy rate to 13¼% has not been passed, we will be taking steps to ensure the proper legal authority exists. When the legislation is passed it will be retroactive to March 1,

73. The Honourable Lorne Hepworth, minister of Finance (Saskatchewan), "Financial Initiatives Briefing Package," February 20, 1991.

74. Sir David Lidderdale (ed.), *Erskine May Parliamentary Practice* (London: Butterworths, 1976), 62–63.

75. From time to time, governments will table a bill as a white paper, intending that it should not be passed until there can be a thorough public discussion of it. Once that discussion has taken place, the bill can be rewritten as necessary and reintroduced in a subsequent session. The reason for tabling such legislative proposals as a bill is out of respect for the legislature and on the basis of the concept that the legislature ought to be the first to know about proposed legislation.

76. There were three other bills of the seventeen that died that were budget-related. *The Urban Parks Financial Arrangements Act, 1991* (Bill 60), would have established the provincial government's contribution to the Wascana Centre Authority, the Meewasin Valley Authority and the Wakamow Valley Authority at a lower amount than would be necessary without the legislation; The Municipal Revenue Sharing Amendment Act, 1991 (Bill 75) would have reduced the amount that the provincial government is required to contribute to the municipal revenue sharing pool; and *The Liquor Consumption Tax Amendment Act, 1991* (Bill 63) would have lowered the provincial sales tax on liquor from 10 percent to 7 percent to effect "harmonization" with the GST.

> 1991. In the meantime, Mortgage Protection Plan benefits will continue to be based on the subsidy rate of 13 1/4%.[77]

Such a statement by a government that commands a majority in the legislature is usually acted upon, precisely because it retains the legislature's confidence and will be able to ensure enactment of the laws it proposes. However, it was not clear, given the circumstances of the unusual prorogation and the necessity, fast approaching, for the government to call a general election within the next four months, that this was in fact the case this time.

The government's position was challenged in the Saskatchewan Court of Queen's Bench and, on August 18, 1991, Mr. Justice Barclay agreed that the Government's actions were improper, although he suspended the implementation of his judgment for six months in deference to the legislature.[78] The government launched an appeal, but the issue was rendered moot by the passage of legislation to amend *The Mortgage Protection Act* before the six months expired.[79]

The end of the Progressive Conservatives' decade in power began when Government House Leader Grant Hodgins announced in the legislature, on June 17, 1991, that he was no longer able to support the policies of the government and therefore found it necessary to resign from the cabinet and to sit as an independent MLA. Mr. Hodgins' resignation precipitated another constitutional crisis in Saskatchewan. As a result, the government prorogued the legislature without passing its budget — apparently because this was the only way for the government to get out of the legislature without holding another vote of any kind. And, once the premier prorogued the legislature, he proceeded for another four months (until the general election was finally held) to again finance government expenditures through the improper (and probably illegal and unconstitutional) use of special warrants.

Thus, as the Progressive Conservative government approached the five-year limitation on the life of the legislature in the fall of 1991, it was an administration that

---

77. Letter dated July 8, 1991, from the minister of Finance to Raymond and Alexandra Sentes in response to their demand for benefits to be paid to them on the basis of the 10.75 percent subsidy rate specified in the statute.

78. This issue was not raised in argument before the court by either side. J. Barclay chose of his own initiative to invoke the so-called "*de facto* doctrine" which was used by the Supreme Court of Canada in *Re Manitoba Language Rights*, [1985] 1 S.C.R. 721, to deal with the practical problems created by its declaration that all the laws of Manitoba were invalid because they had not been enacted in both French and English. The doctrine permitted the Supreme Court to also provide for the temporary validity of the English-only laws for the minimum period necessary for those laws to be translated, re-enacted, printed, and published. (This time was subsequently fixed in *Re Manitoba Language Rights Order No. 1*, [1985] 2 S.C.R. 347 as to expire on December 31, 1988.) Thus, the effect of the court's decision was suspended so as to enable the government of Manitoba to remedy the problem created by the decision and so as to avoid the chaos that would follow if there were no valid law in that province. Peter Hogg, in his authoritative work, *Constitutional Law of Canada* (Toronto: Carswell, 1992), 1257, describes the court's exercise of power as "radical." The court itself justified its creation of the doctrine on the rule of law and the fundamental assumption of the constitution that Canada is a country ruled by law.

Clearly, a decision finding the mortgage protection plan to be *ultra vires* would not have had that kind of impact in Saskatchewan; it would not have created chaos, it would simply have required the government to pay higher benefits to eligible recipients under the program. If the government's appeal of Barclay's decision had gone ahead, this argument would have been advanced on behalf of the Senteses (see note 77) in the Court of Appeal. In any event, a provincial election was held in October and the appropriate legislation to amend the terms of the plan was passed by the new NDP government at the session held immediately after the election and before the time when Barclay's decision would have become operative. The government abandoned its appeal as a result.

79. *The Mortgage Protection Amendment Act, 1991*, S.S. 1991-92, c.7.

had flouted parliamentary tradition and constitutional convention, that had probably lost the confidence of the Saskatchewan legislature, and that had certainly lost the confidence of the majority of the Saskatchewan people.

There is, however, a broader concern that emerges out of the situation that developed in Saskatchewan over this period: a concern for the extent to which the Progressive Conservative government has permanently undermined the democratic nature of government institutions in Saskatchewan and, in particular, the democratic aspects of the Saskatchewan legislature itself. Parliaments can be justly criticized for providing a mechanism by which an elite's decisions, most of which have already been taken in other places outside the legislature, are legitimated. But though parliaments may no longer be places where proposals are put forward and debated in a process of actual decision making (if they ever were such places), they must still command the respect of the people who will be called upon to obey the laws enacted as a result of those decisions. That is to say, parliaments cannot perform an effective legitimating function unless there is some perception in the mind of the electorate that the discussion and debate that takes place in the legislative chamber counts for something. In Samuel H. Beer's terms, parliaments must be able to "mobilize consent."[80]

Thus, legislative debate is a process by which government puts forward its proposals to an opposition that points out flaws. While government does not wish to alter its proposals in any respect and cannot legally be compelled to do so when it holds a majority of the seats in a legislature, if government cannot adequately explain and defend its proposals in a manner that makes them sensible to both the formal opposition inside the legislature and the informal opposition (media and pressure groups) outside the legislature, it can be forced to do something it had not originally intended.

It is this public, democratic, pressure that will ultimately hold government to account and which is channelled through a legislative process that requires openness and debate. In this sense, Parliament is both relevant and significant, even if less than perfect. The extent to which government can make its decisions privately — outside the legislature and in the absence of discussion and criticism — is the extent to which the democratic component of Parliament is weakened and lost.

The early manifestations of tension between the legislature and the executive government during the 1980s might have been ascribed to a new administration's inexperience with government. But the continued and heightened nature of that tension over an extended period of time and the spilling over of that tension into the government's relationships with the judiciary in litigation over judicial appointments, privatization of SGI, environmental issues, electoral boundaries, the timely release of public accounts, special warrants, the provincial sales tax, and the mortgage protection plan alterations, prompts a different explanation: that the significant hallmark of the Progressive Conservative government lay in its belief that simply because it held a majority of the seats in the Legislative Assembly it could do whatever it wanted. The government demonstrated this attitude in its cavalier approach to the legislature and to formal demands for executive accountability. This attitude, coupled with the idea that if the rules are not written down and codified

80. Samuel H. Beer, "The British Legislature and the Problem of Mobilizing Consent," in Philip Norton (ed.), *Legislatures* (Oxford: Oxford University Press, 1990).

as laws they need not be followed, had allowed that administration to court constitutional crisis with impunity while ignoring parliamentary tradition. In these respects, by October 1991, when the general election was held in which the government was defeated, the Saskatchewan legislature appeared to have been poised on the threshold of the seventeenth century, not the twenty-first.

The government of Roy Romanow was elected in October 1991 with as great a landslide as had been the Devine government almost a decade earlier, and it was elected in an atmosphere of both great cynicism and great hope. The cynicism was the product of an almost complete disenchantment with the Devine administration; the hope rested on the assumption that Romanow, as an NDP premier with direct ties to the legacy of the Douglas government and as attorney general and deputy premier in the Blakeney administration, would right all the wrongs for which Devine had been criticized.

Romanow's first major task was to put the province's financial house in order, and this proved to be an even larger task than had been expected. The first session of the new legislature was called very quickly after the new government was sworn into office on November 1, 1991, opening on December 2, 1991. Two key pieces of legislation were enacted in that hastily convened session, an amendment to *The Mortgage Protection Act*[81] and *The Appropriation Act, 1991 (No. 2)*.[82] These two Acts have important symbolic significance for the legislature, because they represent the two key principles enshrined in the ancient Bill of Rights. Amendments to *The Mortgage Protection Act* to raise the subsidy level on mortgage interest acknowledge the requirement that laws be amended by the legislature and not just announced by the executive government. *The Appropriation Act* acknowledged the requirement that the Legislature approve executive expenditure, even in the absence of a budget and estimates.

However, even though a different government was now in power, the events of 1992 were apparently similar to those of 1987 in Saskatchewan. The legislature was not called into session until April 27, 1992 and the budget was not presented until May 7, 1992. Special warrants were used to finance government expenditures for the whole of April and May. The reason given by the Romanow government for using special warrants in this manner was that the devastating financial mess left behind by the former government made it impossible to bring in a budget in advance of the fiscal year. Arguably, that was irrelevant. A legislature did exist and was available and, although it would certainly have been inconvenient, the legislature could have been summoned to provide interim supply as it had, quite properly, in the previous December.

However, special warrants were not resorted to in order to avoid the legislature, but to permit the government to function pending its recall. Special warrants certainly provided an attractive administrative convenience as an alternative either to rushing the government's budget preparations or convening the legislature solely for the purpose of obtaining interim supply, and the government had demonstrated its sensitivity to the need for legislative approval by bringing in an appropriation Act the previous fall. Furthermore, there have been no other improper or questionable uses of special warrants by this government in the years that have followed that

81. S.S. 1991–1992, c. 7.

82. S.S. 1991, c. 14. Note that this Act says that it operates "notwithstanding section 30 of *The Financial Administration Act*" which requires estimates to be prepared and presented to the legislature.

incident. Nevertheless, the fact that a government that had criticized the Devine administration from opposition in 1987 felt comfortable in using special warrants in this manner suggests that the practices established during the Conservative regime of the 1980s have produced a lasting legacy.

This theory is supported by the fact that *The Government Organization Act* remains in force long after the defeat of the Conservative government that saw to its enactment and despite the vociferous criticism that was levelled at it by the then NDP opposition. However, since the election of the NDP in the fall of 1991, the Act has only been used for minor re-alignment of departmental mandates, the most significant of which was contained in a series of regulations made under the Act effective March 17, 1993.[83] Although the list of regulations is lengthy, the actual alterations to mandates were not extensive. More importantly, no special warrants were issued to fund new operations in these departments. In fact, no special warrants were issued with respect to the 1992–93 fiscal year for any reason after these regulations were enacted. This was because the legislature was in session and these new departmental arrangements were the basis on which the budget and estimates were presented to the legislature on March 18, 1993, the day after these regulations were enacted by cabinet. No special warrants have been issued in any year since then, other than those necessary to top-up spent appropriations at the end of a fiscal year and, in the fall of 1998, to provide additional funds for the purpose of fighting forest fires.

Thus, while the NDP government has continued to use *The Government Organization Act* as the mechanism by which it effects executive government reorganization, it has done so in connection with its budget and estimates which have been submitted for legislative approval. In doing so, it has demonstrated its deference to the legislature, while at the same time retaining the executive flexibility that the Act permits. On the other hand, the Romanow government, in other circumstances, demonstrated its lack of concern for the legislature as an institution. A notable illustration occurred in 1998 when the legislature's Crown Corporations Committee conducted an investigation into the sale of Channel Lake Petroleum Inc. by a Saskatchewan Crown corporation. The matter came before this committee rather than the legislature's Public Accounts Committee because of the opposition's refusal to meet the Public Accounts Committee unless a public inquiry was held. Ultimately, what happened was a witch hunt, in which each political party tried to pin the blame for the criticism of SaskPower's disposal of the assets of Channel Lake on its own favourite scapegoat. It did not show the legislature at its most glorious, but at the time it made for good television.[84]

83. *The Department of Agriculture and Food Regulations, 1993*, R.R.S., c. G-5.1 Reg 52, *The Department of Economic Development Regulations, 1993*, R.R.S. c. G-5.1 Reg 59, *The Department of Education, Training and Employment Regulations*, R.R.S. c. G-5.1 Reg 56, *The Department of Environment and Resource Management Regulations*, R.R.S. c. G-5.1 Reg 55, *The Department of Highways and Transportation Regulations*, R.R.S. c. G-5.1 Reg 54, *The Department of Justice Regulations, 1993*, R.R.S. c. G-5.1 Reg 60, *The Department of Labour Regulations, 1993*, R.R.S. c. G-5.1 Reg 58, *The Department of Municipal Government Regulations*, R.R.S. c. G-5.1 Reg 53, *The Department of Provincial Secretary Regulations, 1993*, R.R.S. c. G-5.1 Reg 62, *The Department of Social Services Regulations*, R.R.S. c. G-5.1 Reg 61, *The Indian and Métis Affairs Secretariat Regulations, 1993*, R.R.S. c. G-5.2 Reg 57.

84. I should declare from the outset my involvement in this inquiry as one of the counsel for Direct Energy Marketing Limited, which acquired Channel Lake, and Lawrence Portigal, who became one of the central figures in the affair.

Channel Lake was a wholly owned subsidiary of Saskatchewan's electrical power utility, a Crown corporation called SaskPower or SPC. Channel Lake was an Alberta incorporated corporation. It was created from a moribund corporate shell owned by SPC, formerly called Many Islands Pipelines. In 1994, natural gas holdings of Dynex, a corporation in financial difficulty, were acquired by SPC for Channel Lake from the Bank of Montreal. In the fall of 1996, Channel Lake had incurred some significant trading losses in its buying and selling of gas contracts that resulted from the unexpected and significant rise in the price of natural gas and the consequent bankruptcies of two of the companies involved in its buy-and-sell contracts. This was an industry-wide problem and affected other players besides Channel Lake. However, Channel Lake, being a wholly owned subsidiary of a Saskatchewan Crown corporation, was subject to a different kind of scrutiny than that given to a privately held corporation.

In 1994, Channel Lake received a management letter from its auditors in relation to its trading activities. In 1995, Channel Lake did not file financial statements with the Crown Investments Corporation (CIC — the government's "holding corporation" for the Crowns), even though requested. And in December 1997, the provincial auditor's report criticized Channel Lake's operation and sale. All of this led to calls from the opposition for a judicial inquiry, which the government resisted.

The government's position was that the Public Accounts Committee, to which all reports of the provincial auditor are referred as a matter of course, could and would appropriately deal with the matter in due course. The opposition was insistent that a judicial inquiry be held and thwarted the government's attempt to have the matter dealt with by the Public Accounts Committee.

They accomplished this through two tactics: first, the Public Accounts Committee of the legislature is chaired by an opposition MLA, who refused to convene a meeting; second, the opposition gave notice of introduction of a series of several hundred bills called "Channel Lake Indemnification Act" followed by the name of a municipality in the province (similar to the filibuster on the metro Toronto legislation with the amendments by street name). When each of these bills was called for first reading it was voted down by the government majority, but the opposition called for a recorded vote each time, thus effectively stalling the proceedings of the House completely.

Finally, the government activated the Crown Corporations Committee, which is chaired by a government MLA, to review the matter and convened its meeting. The opposition finally backed down and participated in the Crown Corporations Committee inquiry.

The usual function of the Committee is to review the operations of the Crowns. Ordinarily, officials from the CIC, and the specific Crown corporation under review are called as witnesses to the committee. The committee was first set up in the late 1940s by the CCF government of Tommy Douglas as a mechanism to provide accountability by the Crown corporations to the legislature. Each Crown corporation board was chaired by a cabinet minister[85] who was held politically accountable, and the Crowns were perceived as instruments of public policy. This was also at a time before the evolution of the Question Period as we know it today, so the creation of

85. It is interesting to note, too, that although the Devine administration conducted a review of the Crown corporations under the chairmanship of Wolfgang Wolf that recommended the removal of

the committee was a bold and progressive initiative to allow a forum in which the operations of the Crowns could be reviewed, even though they were not government departments with budgets that had to be voted. (As an interesting aside, the refinement of the functioning of the committee occurred during the time that former Premier Allan Blakeney was, prior to his election, head of the Government Finance Office, now CIC.)

The Channel Lake inquiry was a rare activity for the committee and, indeed, for the Saskatchewan legislature. A similar type of inquiry was held in the 1950s into the activities of a former CCF minister, C.M. Fines, which also involved the activities of private persons outside the legislature. In the 1970s, the chair of the Regina General Hospital Board was called to the Bar of the House to testify about allegations that the hospital was "filthy." These occasions happen so infrequently that there are no general rules to deal with them and no corporate memory in the form of persons with experience with the previous instances.

The committee conducted its inquiry on obviously partisan lines. Each caucus had its own theory about what happened, and they attempted to make the facts fit the theory. However, throughout it was the opposition members on the committee who acted particularly outrageously. On various occasions they called for police involvement (as did the local media) and for various law societies to be notified of various people's actions. Legal counsel to the committee, Ted Priel, QC, repeatedly admonished committee members to refrain from leaping to judgments before they had heard all the facts. These problems were exacerbated by the fact that the committee's proceedings were carried live on cable TV and the transcripts of their proceedings were posted on the Internet. In addition, the local media carried all of the sensational bits, without any real regard to balance[87] in their reporting. The media's theory was the usual one: all politicians are alike. In all of this what was lost was that people outside politics were implicated and affected by what was going on.

There are rights to which individuals who are not members or officers of Parliament are entitled when they are called upon to participate in parliamentary proceedings. This point was recognized by the chair at the committee's opening session when she said:

> So for me it is going to be extremely important that we treat all our witnesses with courtesy, with dignity, and with respect. The principle of administrative fairness has to guide our deliberations and we have to

---

ministers as chairs of the boards of directors of the Crowns, Devine did not implement the recommendation. Ministers as chairs of Crown boards were removed by the Romanow government after a review by CIC, including the TASC (Talking About Saskatchewan Crowns) hearings, in a report entitled "Saskatchewan's Crown Corporations: A New Era," June 1997, thus also removing what was designed to be the accountability link between executive government and the legislature, for the stated reasons of providing "a more autonomous operational structure" and removing "political interference" (see page 6 of the report).

86. Jack Messer had been an NDP cabinet minister in the Blakeney government. He was appointed to head SPC in 1991 after the NDP were re-elected in Saskatchewan. The rumour had been that the SPC board and the former minister responsible, Doug Anguish, had wanted to get rid of Messer for a long time, but the premier stepped in and said no. Anguish had resigned to take a job in the NWT a couple of years previously, but many thought that he hadn't jumped, he was pushed.

87. I refer here to "balance" in the sense that no particular effort was made in the reporting of this matter to offer an analysis of the evidence that might be relied upon as objective. The media's view of balance in reporting seems too frequently to mean only that each side is equally criticized, regardless of the extent to which criticism may be deserved.

> make sure we get all the relevant facts tabled before this committee so that we can make a report and a decision to the House.[88]

It is interesting that she referred to the "principle of administrative fairness." The decisions of the Supreme Court of Canada since *Nicholson v. Haldimand-Norfolk Police Board of Commissioners*[89] have established a duty of fairness that is contingent on the consequences of a decision made by a tribunal or other decision maker, not by the characterization of the decision as judicial or quasi-judicial. There is another line of Supreme Court cases represented by *Wiswell v. Winnipeg*[90] and *Old St. Boniface Residents Assn. v. Winnipeg (City)*,[91] that establish that this duty of fairness does not arise in a legislative context. However, in the Channel Lake inquiry, the legislative committee was not acting in a legislating capacity; it was, according to its mandate, acting as a fact finder and, in excess of its mandate, members of the committee threw out many wild accusations of criminal and civil liability.

Of course, the ancient Bill of Rights, and article 9 in particular, apparently precludes the courts from looking at what Parliament does. However, the historical context that gave rise to the Bill of Rights was one in which parliamentary actors were singled out by the monarch for retribution. Courts are not reluctant to look at what legislatures do when it comes to issues such as constitutionalized manner and form requirements, as in the *Manitoba Language Rights* case.[92] As well, all of the old privilege cases involved disputes over Parliament's ability to control publication of its proceedings. That has not been an issue for over a century. The privilege developed in an age when members would be arrested and brought to the king's justice over their legitimate activities in the House and there was a real concern to keep Parliament's activities unknown to the king — hence the role of the speaker as liaison between the monarch and the House and the convention that members are not referred to by name.

There are limits to which the legislature and its committees may go and still be protected by parliamentary privilege. Lord Denning, in his memorandum of his dissent in the Strauss case, points out that the scope of article 9 is to be determined by the courts, since the Bill of Rights is a statute.[93] This point is emphasized by *Erskine May*.[94] This leads logically to the conclusion that the actions of a legislative committee are reviewable by a court.

There are no rules to guide the committee in its carrying on of an inquiry such as this. Witnesses are sworn and are advised that they have the protection of parliamentary privilege and section 13 of the Canadian Charter of Rights and Freedoms. However, the committee members themselves ask the questions and ultimately decide. They act both as prosecutors and as judges. They have been quick to call for the police and other authorities to be brought into the picture, which suggests strongly that they are biased in their views. Those appearing before the committee are witnesses only; they have not been charged with an offence or even with any accusation. But as witnesses, they have no right to cross-examine any other witnesses or to present their own case in response. And, although witnesses are entitled to

88. Committee Verbatim Transcript, March 31, 1998.

89. [1979] 1 S.C.R. 311.

90. [1965] S.C.R. 512.

91. [1990] 3 S.C.R. 1170.

92. [1985] 1 S.C.R. 721.

93. G.F. Lock, "Parliamentary Privilege and the Courts: The Avoidance of Conflict," in *Public Law*, 83–84.

have legal counsel present to advise them, legal counsel is not entitled to speak, except in respect of procedural issues and then only grudgingly.[95]

The questioning by the committee also gave a reasonable apprehension that it would make findings of fault, which, on the authority of the *Starr*, *Krever*, and *Somalia* cases, would have resulted in the committee's exceeding its mandate and its jurisdiction.[96]

The committee's report was ultimately tabled amid further problems. A draft report prepared by the NDP caucus, not including the chair of the committee, who was also an NDP member, was released on August 18, 1998 without the knowledge or consent of the committee.[97] Reports were actually prepared by each of the opposition caucuses and the committee's ultimate report is an attempt to blend all of them.

Defamation actions were then commenced by Channel Lake and DEML, in both Saskatchewan and Alberta, against Liberal MLA Jack Hillson in respect of his line of questioning in the committee, in which he attempted to establish a connection between Channel Lake and the Russian Mafia. Owen Mitchell, a trustee for the company that owned DEML, was also on the board of directors of YBM Magnex International, a U.S.-based company that was the subject of a cease-trading order on the Toronto Stock Exchange. Suggestions were made in the media that one of YBM's major shareholders was a Russian mob boss. Other members of the YBM board included, for example, David Peterson, the former Liberal premier of Ontario. Hillson tried to draw a connection to DEML. The connection Hillson tried to draw was described as a "flight of fancy" by the media. Mark Wyatt wrote in a Regina *Leader-Post* editorial on July 10, 1998: "Tough questions are one thing. But ludicrous, unfounded, defamatory allegations cloaked in the form of a question are something entirely different."

Hillson also carried his flight of fancy outside the committee rooms, where he spoke to reporters in a scrum in the hallway. Channel Lake and DEML base one aspect of their defamation suits on the argument that Hillson lost the benefit of his privilege as an MLA to say anything without fear of litigation when he repeated the substance of his allegations in this manner. Legal action was commenced in both Saskatchewan and Alberta, where Channel Lake was originally incorporated and where its purchaser, DEML, is located. The Alberta Court of Queen's Bench has held that the action may proceed in Alberta, although Hillson attempted to have it struck on the basis that the action should proceed in Saskatchewan. One of the factors that the court took into account in coming to its conclusion was the existence or not of

94. Lidderdale, *Erskine May Parliamentary Practice*, 201.

95. In one infamous committee meeting, the committee chair referred to Mr. Wilson, legal counsel to Portigal and DEML, in a highly offensive manner. She did not realize the microphones were still on after an adjournment was called. She did, of course, immediately apologize, but the remark provides something of the tenor of the proceedings. The remark was not picked up in the written *Hansard*, but was quite clear and on camera in the video *Hansard*.

96. These cases all deal with situations in which other proceedings can affect the ability of the state to provide a fair trial to persons charged with a criminal offence. The state's interest in preserving public order through the criminal law, and the protection afforded to individuals via the Charter through the right to be presumed innocent and other legal rights, takes precedence over such civil proceedings as inquiries. If charges are to be laid and prosecuted they must proceed first.

97. It was subsequently reported by an NDP MLA to his constituency executive that the report was prepared in the premier's office and presented to the NDP members of the committee for their endorsement, in the expectation that such endorsement would be provided without question. In fact, it was. Bryan Topp, the premier's chief of staff, attended on many days of the committee's hearings.

Hillson's privilege as an MLA against actions taken against him in defamation for what he said in legislative proceedings. The court said that the privilege exists in Saskatchewan as a result of a Saskatchewan statute, and suggested that it does not protect an MLA outside the province.[98] In Saskatchewan, Hillson was unsuccessful in his attempt to have the claim struck on the basis that it discloses no reasonable cause of action. However, these actions have now been settled by the parties and this important question of privilege remains open.

The courts did intervene in the legislature's purview in two cases involving the outcome of the 1999 general election, held on September 16. It was widely anticipated that the election would have occurred in the previous spring, but a province-wide strike by members of the Saskatchewan Union of Nurses, in defiance of legislation ordering them back to work, led to the election's delay. When the election was finally held, the results were almost a catastrophe for the Romanow government. The government ended up with only 29 seats, the Saskatchewan Party won 25, and the Liberals, ultimately with four seats, held the balance of power. The situation was complicated by the fact that a speaker had to be chosen, and neither the NDP nor the Saskatchewan Party could afford to sacrifice a member for this purpose. Ultimately, the NDP and the Liberals formed a coalition government, which included the Liberal leader, Jim Melenchuk, as minister of Education, Liberal MLA Jack Hillson as minister of Intergovernmental and Aboriginal Affairs, and Liberal MLA Ron Osika as speaker.

However, the results in two seats were very close. In one the race was between the Liberal incumbent (who was originally elected as an NDP member and crossed the floor to the Liberal party prior to the 1999 general election) and a Saskatchewan Party newcomer. In the other, the race was between the NDP chair of the Crown Corporations Committee in the Channel Lake inquiry and a Liberal newcomer. The courts became involved when an application was made for a judicial recount.

Under Saskatchewan's election legislation, a candidate is entitled to a judicial recount whenever the margin between the two candidates with the highest number of votes is less than the total of unopened ballot envelopes, rejected ballots and ballots objected to.[99] In the Wood River constituency, there was a tie: D.F. (Yogi)

98. *Direct Energy Marketing Limited v. Jack Hillson*, [1999] A.J. No. 695 at paragraphs 7, 59 and 64. There are no judicial decisions involving questions of privilege in a context that goes beyond the boundaries of the province by which the privilege is conferred. The privilege developed, of course, at Westminster, in a unitary state. In a federal state, jurisdiction is apportioned by subject matter between the federal and provincial governments, and between provinces on the basis of geography. The question is a complex one because it involves the interpretation of the statute by which the privilege is claimed, although the statute results from the necessity of the existence of certain immunities in order to preserve freedom of speech for the representatives of the people in pursuing the public business. Joseph Maingot, QC, in his seminal work, *Parliamentary Privilege in Canada*, at p. 32 quotes from the work of A. Todd, *Parliamentary Government in the British Colonies*, as a basis for concluding that provincial legislatures have inherent jurisdiction as legislating bodies to confer on themselves necessary powers, as well as jurisdiction under s. 92 of the *Constitution Act, 1867*. The question is whether that power may extend beyond the geographical boundaries of the province, or to state it in another way, whether the courts of another provincial jurisdiction are required to recognize the privileges granted by another in the interests of democracy. It may be prudent, in the interests of comity, for each jurisdiction to extend the privilege to members in other Canadian jurisdictions, especially in a technological age where information can be disseminated instantly across the country and can be the subject of legitimate public comment.

99. Subsection 155(1) of *The Election Act*, 1996, S.S. 1996, c. E-6.01. "Unopened ballot envelopes" contain ballots cast by absentee voters. The ballot envelope contains a voter declaration, and if objection is made to the eligibility of an absentee voter to vote, the objection is noted on the unopened envelope.

Huyghebaert, of the Saskatchewan Party, and Glen McPherson, the Liberal candidate, each received 3,162 votes. The tie-breaking vote was cast by the returning officer as required by *The Election Act*. When the recount was finally completed, McPherson ended up with a one-vote margin, and the vote of the returning officer was not required. In Saskatoon Southeast, Pat Lorje, the NDP candidate and incumbent (chair of the Crown Corporations Committee during the Channel Lake inquiry) received 36 more votes than the Liberal candidate, Grant Karwacki. On the recount, that margin increased to 38 votes. However, in both these cases mishandling by the judges conducting the recount affected the legislature's authority to determine its own membership: one by the delay the other by a failure to appreciate the difference between the role of the legislature and the role of the judiciary.

The preliminary count of the votes commences in each constituency immediately after the close of the polls and is conducted by the deputy returning officer. The DRO is required to personally deliver the ballot box to the returning officer within two days after polling day.[100] The time and place for the final count of the ballots by the returning officer is set out in the election proclamation. The ballots from absentee voters are added in by the returning officer at the final count and the candidate with the highest numbers of votes is declared elected for each constituency. The final count must be conducted, as much as possible, continuously.[101] Any request for a judicial recount must take place within four days after the final count is completed.[102] Once such a request is made, court officials are required to immediately notify the chief justice, who in turn is required to immediately designate a judge of the court to conduct the recount. The judge is also directed by the Act to proceed continuously in the conduct of the recount. Only five days are permitted to lodge an appeal from the judge's result on the recount,[103] and, once those-five days have elapsed with no appeal, the result is certified and forwarded to the returning officer. There is no doubt that speed the overarching objective to be achieved by these provisions of *The Election Act*. While it is important to ensure that the election process was conducted properly, mere technicalities will not be allowed to frustrate the will of the electorate. And although procedures must be in place to ensure that only valid ballots are counted and that they are counted accurately, these procedures must be completed without delay.

In the Saskatoon Southeast constituency, the judge at first instance thought his task was to assess the validity of the election. It was not. On an application for a recount, the judge's job is to count the ballots cast and any issues questioning the propriety of procedures employed by the returning officer during the count should properly be resolved by petition under *The Controverted Elections Act*. However, this judge pronounced that he had "inherent" power to "fill in the holes" that he thought were left in *The Election Act*'s provisions. The Court of Appeal contradicted him, holding that it is the legislatures of the provinces that have exclusive, inherent jurisdiction to deal with election issues: "The jurisdiction of the courts is limited to that conferred upon them by legislative enactments."[104]

100. Subsection 143(1) of *The Election Act*.

101. Ibid., subsection 147(1).

102. See sections 155 to 170 of *The Election Act*, which provisions govern the process to be followed on a recount, and from where these details are extracted.

103. As opposed to the more usual 30 days permitted to launch an appeal from a decision of a judge in the Court of Queen's Bench to the Court of Appeal.

104. *Lorje v. Karwacki*, [1999] S.J. No. 903, at paragraph 24.

According to J.A. Tallis:

> [A] judge presiding over a recount is not exercising the court's ordinary civil or criminal jurisdiction. Parliament or the legislature, as the case may be, is the guardian of its own prerogatives and privileges and the courts have nothing to do with questions affecting membership except insofar as they have been specifically designated by law to act in such matters.[105]

Unfortunately for the constituents of Saskatoon Southeast, however, this matter was only resolved after a petition to the Court of Appeal. The general election was held on September 16, 1999 and the decision in the Court of Queen's Bench was given on November 10.[106] The appeal was heard on December 21 and a decision rendered on December 23 by the Court of Appeal. While the Court of Appeal must certainly be commended for recognizing the importance of settling as quickly as possible who had been elected in the constituency, there is no doubt that this conclusion could have been arrived at much more quickly if the judge below had recognized the limits on his power in the context of a mere recount of the votes.

The recount in Wood River was conducted on October 22–23, 1999. Irregularities were noted and relevant documents marked as exhibits for identification and later argument. The court reconvened on November 9, 1999, for argument respecting the irregularities and to receive testimony respecting circumstances surrounding the voting procedures involved in the Absentee Voters Poll. By the time this judgement was given, however, the decision in Saskatoon Southeast had been made and appealed. The certification of the result on the recount in Wood River did not occur until January 27, 2000.[107]

CONCLUSION

Eugene Forsey was right — the danger of royal absolutism is indeed past, and there is no doubt that the danger of cabinet absolutism is growing. Regardless of the party in power, the premier's office endeavours as much as possible to control the legislature. The danger is that this desire for control fuels public cynicism and, perhaps worse, cynicism among party members. This in turn contributes to the perception that all politicians are alike, and, if they are, why should anyone bother to vote or get involved in electoral politics? The differences, such as they are, between parties thus becomes of significance only to party insiders who may personally gain from one party or another being in power.

The erosion of the legislature continues, albeit perhaps somewhat more slowly than at times in the past. The Devine Conservatives believed that they had a majority of the seats in the legislature so they could do whatever they wanted. The Romanow NDP was constrained by their awareness that mere numbers are not the whole story; there are rules that are not so black and white. But the erosion that

105. Ibid., at paragraph 26.

106. *Karwacki v. Lorje*, [1999] S.J. No. 774.

107. It would not, however, be fair to leave the impression that this delay was somehow intended as a deliberate interference with the legislature's prerogative of determining its own membership. The judge in question was a reasonably new appointment to the Bench and appeared to have developed difficulty in rendering judgments in a number of cases of various types, which had become the topic of private conversation within the legal community in Regina. It may be that the public criticism for the delay that arose in relation to the judicial recount assisted in bringing to light a problem of a more general nature.

continues is the continuing delegitimization of the legislature in the minds of those who are not of the "political" class. While there are distinctions that remain between Saskatchewan and legislatures in other jurisdictions, there is a growing sense that these are distinctions without difference.

THE MONARCHY

Political Paradox: The Lieutenant Governor in Saskatchewan

D. Michael Jackson

INTRODUCTION

Political paradox: an apt description of the Office of Lieutenant Governor in a Canadian province. According to a literal reading of the constitution, the incumbent of the office wields enormous executive power — yet is widely regarded as a decorative rubber stamp. The lieutenant governor is expected to be politically neutral, but is a federal patronage appointment and usually drawn from the ranks of the supporters of the party in power in Ottawa. This vice-regal appointee represents the Crown and the Queen for purposes of the province, yet is technically a federal officer. Like the Queen and the governor general, the lieutenant governor by constitutional convention exercises executive power on the "advice" of the First Minister and government of the day, but on the other hand has a minimal, vaguely defined discretionary right to act independently.

Saskatchewan takes this paradox a couple of steps further. An institution which represents monarchy and thus evokes ceremony and traditional social patterns not only cohabits with, but appears to thrive in, an egalitarian rural society, the foyer of social democracy in North America and the longest-running dynasty of CCF and New Democratic Party governments in Canada. Another seeming contradiction: Canada's first multicultural province, where people of British and French ancestry combined comprise less than half of the population, embraces an institution representing a monarch domiciled in the United Kingdom. Throw into the mix the historically close relationship of the Crown with the Aboriginal peoples. The Office of Lieutenant Governor defies attempts to simplify, dismiss, underrate or even eliminate it.

Modern studies of the provincial vice-regal office are striking by their absence: one book published in 1957, minimally updated up to 1985; and chapters in two books on the Crown in the 1970s.[1] As for the lieutenant governor of Saskatchewan, an indication of the low political profile of the office is the paucity of references to

1. John T. Saywell, *The Office of Lieutenant Governor* (1957; Toronto: Copp Clark Pitman, 1986); "A Team of Governors" in Frank MacKinnon, *The Crown in Canada* (Calgary: Glenbow Alberta Institute/McClelland and Stewart West, 1976), 90–106; "The Lieutenant Governors" in Jacques Monet, *The Canadian Crown* (Toronto/Vancouver: Clarke, Irwin & Company, 1979), 39–45. See also a booklet by George F.G. Stanley, *The Role of the Lieutenant Governor* (Fredericton: Legislative Assembly of New Brunswick, 1992).

it in John Archer's history of the province published in 1980: of the fifteen lieutenant governors to hold office to that date, only four are even mentioned.[2] Evelyn Eager devotes a useful chapter to the office in her *Saskatchewan Government* (1980), noting its ambiguity and limitations.[3] By far the most interesting study of the Saskatchewan lieutenant governors is found in the centennial history of Government House, Regina.[4]

Theory of the Crown

David E. Smith's definitive 1995 study of the Canadian Crown is appropriately entitled *The Invisible Crown: The First Principle of Canadian Government*.[5] Indeed, the vice-regal office may at first sight appear so faint on the political screen as to be almost irrelevant, if not invisible; yet it incorporates the essence, historically and constitutionally, of Canada's separate political identity in North America and that of the Canadian provinces. The lieutenant governor is the nominal chief executive officer of the province, an integral part of the legislature, a formal link through the Crown with the federal government, and the provincial representative of the Sovereign. In short, the lieutenant governor is at the apex of the entire constitutional structure of the province.

In constitutional monarchy, and more specifically in its Canadian variant — whose uniqueness is often not fully recognized — "the Crown" is the symbol, concept and institution of supreme executive power of the state outside the governmental structure and beyond political parties. The Crown, as it were, lends this power, which it legitimizes and ultimately safeguards, to the transitory executive administrations produced by the political electoral process. The Crown's representative exercises executive power in name only, almost always doing so "on advice" of the ministers who are nominally his or her "councillors." The cabinet is rarely mentioned as such in constitutional documents; its formal name in the provinces is the "executive council" (in the federal government, it is technically a committee of the Queen's Privy Council for Canada). Canadians enveloped with American paradigms of the separation of powers often need to be reminded that the historic "Crown in Parliament" of the British or Westminster model presupposes a cabinet drawn from, and forming an integral part of, the legislative branch, responsible to it and requiring its confidence, yet deriving executive power directly from the Crown. This Crown in Parliament is in contrast with the republican model, at least in the United States, where power is theoretically derived from the sovereign people and mediated through representation.[6] It is arguable which is more "democratic" and certainly which is more effective, but, as we shall see, the locus of power in the Crown is a definitive characteristic of the Canadian system.

The monarchy, which personifies the Crown, provides the head of state in the

2. John H. Archer, *Saskatchewan: A History* (Saskatoon: Western Producer Prairie Books, 1980).
3. Evelyn Eager, "The Lieutenant Governor," in *Saskatchewan Government: Politics and Pragmatism* (Saskatoon: Western Producer Prairie Books, 1980), 116–29.
4. Margaret Hryniuk, edited by Garth Pugh, *"A Tower of Attraction": An Illustrated History of Government House, Regina* (Regina: Government House Historical Society/Canadian Plains Research Center, 1991).
5. David E. Smith, *The Invisible Crown: The First Principle of Canadian Government* (Toronto-Buffalo-London: University of Toronto Press, 1995).
6. For a thorough discussion of the contrast between monarchical and republican theory and practice, see David E. Smith, *The Republican Option in Canada, Past and Present* (Toronto-Buffalo-London: University of Toronto Press, 1999), especially chapter 2.

Canadian federation. "Sovereignty is vested in one particular individual, the reigning monarch, acting in Parliament for some purposes and in the provincial Legislatures for others."[7] There are in fact eleven Crowns in Canada: that for the country as a whole and those for each of the ten provinces. While the Sovereign is one person, the Crown has separate personalities, and legislative, executive and prerogative powers are divided among them. The Canadian Crown demonstrates this by operating as a triumvirate: the Queen is Canadian head of state; the governor general carries out most of her functions for federal jurisdiction; and the lieutenant governors do the same for provincial jurisdiction. It is useful to reiterate the obvious: Canada, unlike unitary states with one sovereign government, comprises *two concurrent jurisdictions* which have both exclusive and shared powers and *together* govern the Canadian state. The provinces have constitutionally sanctioned, co-sovereign powers in the Canadian federation. The provincial Crown reflects, defines and asserts this constitutional reality.

THE PROVINCIAL CROWN[8]

This provincial Crown was not at all the same in 1867, the year of Confederation. The centralizing view of Sir John A. Macdonald, the first prime minister of Canada, is apparent in the *British North America Act* (now the *Constitution Act, 1867*), which treated the provinces as local units subordinate to the dominant central, or "federal," government. The status of the provincial Crown echoed the same viewpoint. The lieutenant governors succeeded the governors of the former individual colonies as chief executive officers of the new provinces, with many similar powers. But they were clearly intended as officers or agents of Ottawa, appointed, paid, and liable to dismissal, by the central government. Whereas the governor general was formally appointed by the Queen, the lieutenant governors were appointed by the governor general in council (i.e. the federal cabinet) and thus did not represent the Sovereign directly. Furthermore, the lieutenant governors possessed (and still nominally possess) major constitutional powers to subordinate the provinces to the will of Ottawa.

However, the typically Canadian process of evolution began almost immediately, as pragmatism and practical experience reshaped the political system. The provinces realized, clarified, exercised and defended their co-sovereign status as Canada gradually evolved into a more authentic federal state. Concurrently the status of the provincial Crown was re-assessed. As John Saywell put it, "what was in practice an exercise of legislative or administrative authority was in theory an exercise of prerogative powers by the Crown or its representatives."[9] In other words, and somewhat paradoxically, the practical working-out of federalism led to its theoretical definition in the provincial Crown. The status of the lieutenant governors and the Crown they represented soon evolved accordingly. Already under the *Constitution Act, 1867*, lieutenant governors possessed a Great Seal and summoned their legislatures directly in the Queen's name. While the Queen was technically part of Parliament only and not of the provincial legislatures, and the lieutenant governors were supposed to give royal assent to legislation in the name of the governor general, they

7. I owe this succinct and significant phrase to constitutional lawyer Ken Tyler.

8. For further discussion see my paper, "The Provincial Crown in Canada," presented at the International Conference on Monarchy in Toronto in October 1997, and summarized in my article "How the Crown Unites Us," *The Ottawa Citizen*, February 7, 1998.

9. Saywell, *The Office of the Lieutenant Governor*, 9.

never did so: a convention promptly arose of giving royal assent in the Queen's name.

Some major court decisions clarified and confirmed the autonomous status of the provincial Crown. The best known of these is the judgement by the Judicial Committee of the Privy Council in 1892 in the *Maritime Bank* case, where it was specifically stated that "the Lieutenant Governor [...] is as much a representative of Her Majesty, for all purposes of Provincial Government as the Governor General himself is, for all purposes of Dominion Government." The provinces did indeed possess supreme powers within their spheres, the Queen formed part of the provincial governments, and the lieutenant governor was the Sovereign's direct representative in the province.[10]

POWERS OF THE CROWN

The constitutional powers of the Sovereign and her representatives fall into two main categories: *statutory* and *prerogative*, both exercised "on advice" of the cabinet. Statutory powers are those conferred by acts of Parliament or the legislatures. Prerogative powers are the authority vested in the Crown through custom, tradition and precedent. This "royal prerogative" has been described as "the residue of discretionary or arbitrary authority which at any time is legally left in the hands of the Crown."[11] It includes a wide range of powers, administrative acts and appointments normally exercised by ministers of the Crown and especially the First Minister. The instruments of the prerogative are primarily orders-in-council, but also commissions, proclamations, writs, letters patent and warrants. The only use of the royal prerogative in which some discretion still exists for the Crown's representative is the exercise of the "reserve powers" — the right to summon and dissolve the legislature and to name the First Minister. Theoretically, the Crown's representative may override advice of the First Minister and refuse dissolution of Parliament or legislature (or dissolve them despite advice to the contrary) or may dismiss a ministry. These reserve powers are evidently for very exceptional use in constitutional emergencies.[12]

Certain other reserve or emergency powers of the Canadian Crown are statutory in nature. Under sections 55–57 and 90 of the *Constitution Act, 1867*, the lieutenant governor may withhold royal assent to legislation (as may the governor general in Parliament); or may reserve it for the pleasure of the governor general, i.e. the federal government, the latter power being an instrument of federal control over provincial legislatures. (The separate federal power of disallowance of provincial legislation is not a vice-regal one, although in the early years of Confederation federal governments consulted with lieutenant governors on its use and the latter were

10. Other relevant court decisions were *Hodge* v. *The Queen* (1883), which affirmed the basic principle that the provincial legislatures were not delegates of Parliament; the Ontario Queen's Counsel case of 1898, which upheld the right of provinces to confer the Q.C. title; and Bonanza Creek (1916), which stated that the division of executive and prerogative powers mirrored the division of legislative powers between the central and provincial governments.

11. A.V. Dicey, *Introduction to the Study of the Law of the Constitution*, cited in David Smith, *The Invisible Crown*, 32 and 90.

12. As Frank MacKinnon has put it, in a colourful image, "The Offices of Governor General and Lieutenant-Governor are constitutional fire extinguishers with a potent mixture of powers for use in great emergencies. Like real extinguishers, they appear in bright colours and are strategically located. But everyone hopes their emergency powers will never be used; the fact that they are not used does not render them useless; and it is generally understood that there are severe penalties for tampering with them." (*The Crown in Canada*, 122).

charged with communicating the bad news to their legislatures.) A statutory power granted to the lieutenant governor by provincial legislation is that of approving and signing special warrants, "an instrument signed by the representative of the Crown at the request of cabinet to approve expenditure from the Consolidated Revenue Fund"[13] in specifically defined circumstances outside the normal parliamentary appropriation process.

In an assessment of the role and importance of the Crown in Canada, and more specifically the lieutenant governor, two points should be made. First, the almost (though not quite) exclusive exercise of the royal prerogative by the government strengthens and accentuates the power of the executive branch of government *vis-à-vis* the legislative. This is the prime message of David Smith's *Invisible Crown*: "The lever of executive control is the Crown."[14] The exercise of the lieutenant governor's theoretical powers by the government is far more significant than the reserve powers remaining at the discretion of the vice-regal incumbent.

The second point is also one made forcefully by Smith: through its prestige and constitutional pre-eminence but especially through its reinforcement of the executive power, the Crown has contributed enormously to the strength and autonomy of provincial jurisdiction in Canada. Smith refers to "the coupling of monarchy to federalism,"[15] and the evolution towards "a constitutional amalgam in Canada [...] called compound monarchy."[16] The Crown, he argues, is key to understanding the theory and practice of federalism in Canada. Elsewhere he points out that in 1867 "the [original] provinces inherited cohesive societies that pre-dated Confederation and monarchical forms of government to give these societies institutional expression."[17] "The Crown," he emphasizes, "endowed the provinces with unlimited potential for action."[18] Without trumpeting the fact, and perhaps not always fully aware of its implications, the provincial governments have made full use of the powers of the provincial Crown as these powers became more defined. Smith notes how Saskatchewan under the CCF government starting in the 1940s and Quebec in the Quiet Revolution were able to experiment in social and economic policy, thanks to the powers conferred on them by the provincial Crown.[19] Once again, governmental exercise of royal powers far outweighs the personal authority of the lieutenant governor.

What, then, are we to make of the role of the lieutenant governor? Is he or she merely a figurehead paraded on ceremonial occasions to read the speech from the throne at the opening of the legislature, an automaton who gives royal assent to legislation and signs orders-in-council and other documents as dictated by the cabinet? Is the office of any practical use? In trying to answer these questions in the Saskatchewan context, we need to review the evolution of the powers and status of the lieutenant governors in Canada.

---

13. Smith, *The Invisible Crown*, 83.
14. Ibid., 90.
15. Ibid., 8.
16. Ibid., 11.
17. David E. Smith, "Empire, Crown and Canadian Federalism," in *Canadian Journal of Political Science/Revue canadienne de science politique* 24, no. 3 (September 1991): 471.
18. Ibid., 461.
19. Ibid., 463–64.

THE LIEUTENANT GOVERNOR: AN OFFICE IN EVOLUTION

Constitutional Powers

The constitutional powers of the lieutenant governors were, in the earlier years of Confederation at least, not the rubber stamp which they are, rightly or wrongly, considered to be today. As Saywell points out,[20] no British monarch has dismissed a government since 1834; no Canadian governor general has ever done so since Confederation. But lieutenant governors used the "prerogative of dismissal" five times between 1867 and 1903 to dismiss their provincial ministries: twice in Quebec and three times in British Columbia.[21]

Another reserve prerogative, that of refusing dissolution of the legislature, has been even more rarely used: in Quebec in 1879, New Brunswick in 1883, and Prince Edward Island in 1891. On several other occasions, however, lieutenant governors considered their options when dissolution was requested by their premier in what they considered questionable or controversial circumstances, and on occasion threatened not to comply.[22] The discretionary use of the prerogative of dissolution, linked to that of the appointment of the First Minister, is still conceivable in a minority government situation. In the Saskatchewan election of 1929, no party was returned with a majority of seats. The Liberal government of James Gardiner opted to meet the House, as was its right, despite the opposition Conservative protests that they had won more seats. The government resigned upon its speedy defeat in the legislature, whereupon Lieutenant Governor Henry Newlands proceeded to call on the leader of the opposition, Dr. J.T.M. Anderson, to form an administration from a coalition of Conservatives, Progressives and Independents[23] — the only Saskatchewan coalition government until 1999. A similar situation arose after an election in Ontario in 1985. When a Conservative minority government chose to meet the House and was defeated, the lieutenant governor called on the Liberal leader to be premier, given that his party had concluded an agreement with the New Democrats for their support on the legislature. In both the above cases, the lieutenant governor did not have to override ministerial advice and his course of action was reasonably clear and non-controversial. In a somewhat analagous but convoluted case in Newfoundland in 1972, however, the lieutenant governor chose to accept controversial ministerial advice to dissolve the assembly: following an inconclusive election the Conservative premier did not want to meet the assembly where

---

20. Saywell, *The Office of Lieutenant Governor*, chapter 5, "The Prerogative of Dismissal."

21. Only in Australia, in 1975, has this reserve power been used in modern times, when the governor general dismissed the Commonwealth (federal) government following a parliamentary deadlock where the Senate refused to vote supply; this caused a constitutional crisis which still reverberates in Australian politics.

22. See Saywell, *The Office of Lieutenant Governor*, chapter 6, "The Prerogative of Dissolution." Federally, the power was used once, in the famous "King-Byng affair"of 1926 where the governor general, Lord Byng, refused dissolution of Parliament to Prime Minister Mackenzie King. The consensus is that Byng was on sound constitutional ground. In a recent election King had failed to get the majority he was seeking, had fewer seats than the opposition Conservatives, and governed only with the support of the Progressives. Unwilling to face a vote of censure in the House of Commons, King requested dissolution. Byng instead called on the leader of the opposition, Arthur Meighen, to form an administration. But by happenstance Meighen's government was soon defeated in the House and King made such political hay of the imbroligio that governors general ever since have recoiled from the prospect of confronting their First Minister on dissolution. For details of the "King-Byng Affair," see Frank MacKinnon, *The Crown in Canada*, 129–32.

23. See Eager, *Saskatchewan Government*, 125, and Saywell, *The Office of Lieutenant Governor*, 152.

he faced defeat. Arguably, the lieutenant governor could have refused dissolution and asked the Liberal leader to try to form a government.[24]

Genuine discretion in exercising the powers of dismissal and dissolution, however, now appears to be a thing of the past. As Smith puts it, "When those powers are used [...], the controversy over the rightness of the action is so great as to imperil the use of the discretionary power. In other words, the reserve powers appear, correctly or not, to be a wasting resource."[25]

The normally routine prerogative power of royal assent to legislation provides further illustrations of provincial vice-regal intervention — and of its disappearance. Royal assent has not been refused by a British monarch since 1707 and has never been refused by a Canadian governor general since Confederation. However, lieutenant governors cast their vice-regal veto no less than 38 times between 1870 and 1945 — but on the advice or with the concurrence of their cabinets as a handy tool to avoid awkward legislation! There was one exception, when the lieutenant governor of Prince Edward Island withheld assent from a bill on his own initiative in 1945. This was the last time the power has been used.[26]

The *reservation* of royal assent by the lieutenant governor for the "Signification of the Governor-General's pleasure," i.e. the federal government, is another matter altogether. Like the federal power of disallowance with which it is sometimes confused, reservation was a clear centralizing device to permit the federal government to override provincial legislation. And it was by no means an idle threat. Saywell records that 69 provincial bills were reserved (and 112 acts were disallowed) between 1867 and 1937, the *ultra vires* legislation of William Aberhart's Social Credit government in Alberta being the last target. The policy clearly established by Sir John A. Macdonald in 1882 was that lieutenant governors should only reserve assent on direct instructions from Ottawa, and from the beginning he discouraged use of the power. However, lieutenant governors reserved assent on their own initiative more frequently than on instructions from Ottawa, either because they deemed legislation to be *ultra vires* or inappropriate, or because they simply disagreed with it: in those instances the power became another form of vice-regal veto, often to the embarrassment of Ottawa. But the power of reservation never really caught on as a normative constitutional practice and its use declined steadily after 1914. After 1937 it was considered obsolete, another example of the waning discretionary powers of the lieutenant governors as well as a sign of the trend away from centralization in the federal system.[27]

There was one brief revival of the power of reservation — and it occurred in Saskatchewan in 1961, the only example in the province's history. Lieutenant Governor Frank Bastedo, a prominent Conservative lawyer who had been counsel for the oil industry, and was an appointee of the Diefenbaker government, reserved royal assent on Bill 56, *The Alteration of Certain Mineral Contracts*, because he had doubts about its validity and whether it was in the public interest. The bill was intended by the CCF government of Premier T.C. Douglas as a last resort to rectify

24. See Saywell, *The Office of Lieutenant Governor*, 273–74.

25. Smith, *The Invisible Crown*, 31–32.

26. See Saywell, *The Office of Lieutenant Governor*, 221–23.

27. For a detailed discussion of the power of reservation, see Saywell, *The Office of Lieutenant Governor*, Chapter 8, "Provincial Legislation."

one-sided contracts between an oil company and farmers. Even the Liberal opposition conceded that the bill had some merit and some of its MLAs voted in favour. Bastedo's reserving of royal assent, recalled Allan Blakeney, a CCF minister at the time, came totally unexpectedly, catching both sides of the House by surprise. Liberal member Mary Batten exclaimed to Blakeney, "he can't do that!"[28]

In view of Macdonald's 1882 stricture that lieutenant governors should only reserve legislation on instructions from Ottawa, and of the understanding since 1937 that the power was obsolete, Batten was right. Bastedo had not consulted the federal government, much less received instructions from Ottawa, as Prime Minister John Diefenbaker was quick to point out. But in the sense that early lieutenant governors had often used reservation as a kind of personal veto in place of denying royal assent, Bastedo was following a precedent, albeit an anachronistic one. In view of his connections with the oil industry his motives were suspect, to say the least. In the event, sensitive to charges by the Saskatchewan CCF that the federal Conservatives were interfering in provincial jurisdiction, the Diefenbaker government hastened to conclude that the bill was *intra vires* and to pass an order-in-council giving it royal assent.[29]

The Bastedo incident had two consequences. Constitutionally, it confirmed that the power of reservation in Canada was indeed obsolete and would not be used again. The remedy for constitutional challenges to legislation was the courts or the political process, not the personal intervention of the lieutenant governor. In terms of the perception of the vice-regal office in Saskatchewan, the incident cast a chill on relations between the lieutenant governor and the CCF/NDP which lasted two decades. Many social democrats were already sceptical about the Office of Lieutenant Governor, considering it an elitist social institution, political anachronism, and symbol of federal power and patronage. The Douglas, Lloyd and early Blakeney administrations saw their worst fears realized in the Bastedo affair. According to Allan Blakeney, in 1961 the CCF cabinet was apprehensive that Bastedo, given his exaggerated opinion of his vice-regal powers, might go so far as to dismiss their administration.[30]

Federal Agent?

As has been mentioned earlier, the framers of Confederation and of the *Constitution Act, 1867* expressly identified the lieutenant governor as a federal officer, a role in their view more significant than that of provincial representative of the Crown. It was true that the governor general also had the dual role of representing the imperial government in London while representing the Queen for purposes of the federal government, but the imperial function was to disappear with the Balfour Report of 1926 and the *Statute of Westminster* in 1931. Whereas the Australian state governors represented the Sovereign directly from the time of confederation in 1901, their Canadian counterparts have never gained the same status in theory. Indeed, the only part of their constitutions that the provinces cannot amend is the Office of Lieutenant Governor (section 92.1 of the *Constitution Act, 1867*).

In the early years of Confederation the lieutenant governors could, and frequently did, act as the eyes and ears and agents of the federal government. This

28. Author's interview with the Honourable Allan Blakeney, July 1999.

29. See Eager, *Saskatchewan Government*, 127–29, and Saywell, *The Office of Lieutenant Governor*, 267.

30. Blakeney interview.

went beyond the constitutional prerogatives of reservation of royal assent and notification of disallowance. It involved information-gathering and intelligence for the prime minister and his cabinet, communication of and support for federal policies, and acting as buffer in the frequent event of federal-provincial disagreements. This activist role on Ottawa's behalf declined and all but disappeared early in the twentieth century. Prime ministers were able to use their national parties and their own ministers, senators and members of parliament, as well as the media, to communicate their policies. Eventually intergovernmental conferences and bureaucracies provided formal channels for federal-provincial relations. The role of the lieutenant governor as federal agent was eclipsed even more quickly than that of purveyor of discretionary constitutional powers (and never really came into play in Saskatchewan). By the mid-twentieth century, the lieutenant governor had caught up in fact and perception to the legal definition in the 1892 court decision: the provincial representative of the Sovereign.

What did not disappear, however, was the federal government's *appointment* of the lieutenant governor (again, contrary to the Australian system, where the state premiers formally recommend the appointment of the governors to the Queen[31]). It has always been a jealously guarded prerogative of the prime minister, who has usually named supporters of his own party as a reward for past services or loyalty. In the early years of Confederation, when the Office of Lieutenant Governor was relatively powerful, it was also more prestigious, sought after, and characterized by high-profile appointees. A century later, when the Office had declined in both power and prestige, it was no longer seen as a desirable position by anyone with political ambition. The prime minister's office generally selected incumbents by canvassing opinions among the local establishment of the party in the province, usually mediated through the minister responsible for patronage. Former politicians — senators, members of Parliament, provincial members of the legislature — predominated among the nominees at least until the 1970s.[32]

INFLUENCE OF THE LIEUTENANT GOVERNOR

The partisan nature of the appointment has limited the political effectiveness of the provincial vice-regal post — something that did not impair the Office of Governor General until the custom began in the late 1970s of naming former politicians to the position[33] and almost never impairs constitutional monarchs, as has been evident in the United Kingdom, The Netherlands, Belgium, the

31. The Sovereign actually appointed the Australian state governors on the advice of the British government, although presumably with input from the premiers, until as late as 1986, when the national and state governments passed the *Australia Acts*. Since then, the premiers recommend the appointment of governors directly to the Queen. See Smith, *The Invisible Crown*, 42–43.

32. It should be noted that, under section 59 of the *Constitution Act, 1867*, lieutenant governors are not appointed for a fixed "term." They hold office "during the Pleasure of the Governor General" i.e. the federal cabinet, but for five years after their appointment they can only be removed "for Cause assigned" and communicated to both Houses of Parliament. Only two lieutenant governors have ever been removed from office by this process (although some have resigned): that of Quebec in 1880 by the Macdonald government and that of British Columbia in 1900 by the Laurier administration. Federal governments tend to replace lieutenant governors within about a year after their fifth anniversary, but this is not a hard-and-fast rule. In Saskatchewan, for example, Henry Newlands was reappointed in 1926 after five years, the only such case in the province's history, and served a further four years in the position. William Patterson served for nearly seven years (1951–1958), as did Robert Hanbidge (1963–1970). Archibald McNab was lieutenant governor for nine years (1936–1945).

33. See footnote 68 regarding the politicization of the Office of Governor General.

Scandinavian countries and Spain, for example. Understandably, premiers and their cabinets did not view lieutenant governors of a different political stripe as impartial confidants, especially if they had held seats on the opposing side of the House in their own legislatures. It did not help when some lieutenant governors continued to indulge in partisan activity. As Saywell has put it,

> The decline in the influence of the Lieutenant-Governor [...] need not have been so rapid and so complete if one elementary maxim had been learned and scrupulously followed: the monarch may be politically biased but must be politically neutral. [...] To confide in the Lieutenant-Governor was too often like giving secrets to the enemy. [...] he was never beyond suspicion. [...] while normal constitutional development reduced the Lieutenant-Governor's power political partiality destroyed his influence.[34]

Not surprisingly, relations between lieutenant governors and premiers have ranged from the cordial and correct to the distant, formal and sometimes downright hostile. Few premiers have instituted regular meetings with their lieutenant governor, unlike the practice in the United Kingdom, where the Sovereign normally receives the British prime minister weekly, or even in Ottawa, where the prime minister calls on the governor general at Rideau Hall fairly frequently.

Most premiers were realistic enough to accept the constitutional right of Ottawa to appoint lieutenant governors. What rankled with them was the lack of consultation with the provinces on the selection of their royal representative. The federal government *might* observe the courtesy of informal consultation with a premier of the same political stripe, but it has always denied any requirement or even convention to do so. Provincial governments of a different party are simply informed of the appointment — if they are lucky, before the formal announcement is made. CCF and NDP governments, given that their party has yet to hold power in Ottawa, have never had the luxury of such informal consultation as might be conceded to their Liberal and Conservative counterparts. The first CCF administration of Premier T.C. Douglas in Saskatchewan learned this to its chagrin in 1944 when it requested consultation on the next appointment from the federal Liberal government — and was soundly rebuffed by Prime Minister Mackenzie King.[35]

SASKATCHEWAN: THE FIRST SIXTY-FIVE YEARS (1905 TO 1970) – PRESTIGE AND DECLINE[36]

Saskatchewan's vice-regal history began in controversy. The last lieutenant governor of the Northwest Territories, Amédée Forget, was appointed first lieutenant governor of Saskatchewan when the province was formed on September 1, 1905. It was his formal task to select the first premier, and the last territorial premier, Frederick Haultain, seemed a logical choice. But although leader of a non-partisan administration, he had shown definite Conservative leanings and opposed the agreements on the new provincial status. At the instigation of the federal Liberal government of Sir Wilfrid Laurier, Forget appointed Liberal Walter Scott instead.[37]

34. Saywell, *The Office of Lieutenant Governor*, 260–61.

35. See ibid., 25.

36. More detailed accounts of these years are found in Eager, *Saskatchewan Government*, and Hryniuk/Pugh, *"A Tower of Attraction."*

37. The story of Walter Scott and the history of his administration is found in Gordon L. Barnhart, *"Peace, Progress and Prosperity": A Biography of Saskatchewan's First Premier, T. Walter Scott* (Regina: Canadian Plains Research Center, 2000).

Scott's government swept the province in the first election in December 1905, and the Liberals remained in power until 1929. Forget was criticized for his selection of Scott, especially by the Conservatives, but the choice was not really his; furthermore, it was an understandable decision in the circumstances, and, not for the last time, illustrated the partisan reality affecting the Office of Lieutenant Governor.[38]

Forget was criticized, again by the opposition Conservatives, when Scott called a snap election in 1908 after only three years in office; but it was manifestly unfair to blame the lieutenant governor for the premier's undoubted right to request dissolution. The next controversial occasion, in 1916, also involved Walter Scott; only this time the tables were turned: a Conservative federal government had appointed one of its own, former MP Richard Lake, as lieutenant governor in 1915. That year in Manitoba the lieutenant governor, a Liberal appointee, responding to charges of corruption by the Liberal opposition, by threat of using the prerogative of dismissal effectively forced the Conservative government to launch an investigation which proved the charges and led to the demise of their administration. In 1916, the opposition Conservatives in Saskatchewan tried the same tactic in retaliation for the fate of their Manitoba counterparts: they levelled charges of impropriety against the government and, through Lieutenant Governor Lake, tried to force the government to either establish a royal commission or face dismissal. However, Scott held private discussions with Lake, and, although there was some friction and disagreement between the two, the matter was resolved without the lieutenant governor intervening. In light of the potential for misunderstanding revealed by this episode, Scott's successor, William Martin, undertook to keep the lieutenant governor better informed through letters and meetings, a practice which, however, did not become a regular feature until the 1990s.[39]

After World War I, Saskatchewan experienced few constitutional or political incidents between its lieutenant governor and government. We have already referred to two: the minority government situation in 1929, when the lieutenant governor acted appropriately; and the reservation of royal assent in 1961, when he did not. Otherwise Saskatchewan lieutenant governors functioned in a relatively low-key fashion, carrying out their routine constitutional duties and social obligations. The latter were considered particularly important for the first forty years of the province's existence. Government House in Regina, the imposing vice-regal residence constructed in 1891 for the governors of the Northwest Territories, continued as the pre-eminent venue for official entertainment by Saskatchewan lieutenant governors and invitations to functions were prized.[40] Lieutenant governors who were perceived as not doing their part to maintain standards of hospitality incurred grumbling and criticism. Even during the Depression years of 1929 to 1939, the lieutenant governors carried out a surprisingly active social calendar. But the Depression and World War II ultimately decreased the importance of vice-regal entertainment, as did the increasing egalitarianism of the post-war era. It was yet another factor in reducing the profile of the lieutenant governors in Saskatchewan.

38. For the details of the controversy over the Scott appointment, see Saywell, *The Office of Lieutenant Governor*, 104–07; Eager, *Saskatchewan Government*, 125–26; Hryniuk/Pugh, *"A Tower of Attraction,"* 60–61; and Barnhart, *"Peace, Progress and Prosperity,"* 44–45.

39. For a detailed study of the Scott-Lake episode, see Saywell, *The Office of Lieutenant Governor*, 54–56; Eager, *Saskatchewan Government*, 126–27, 208–11; and Barnhart, *"Peace, Progress and Prosperity,"* 136–38.

40. The history of Government House is admirably presented in Hryniuk/Pugh, *"A Tower of Attraction,"* and summarized in Robert H. Hubbard, *Ample Mansions: The Vice-Regal Residences of the Canadian Provinces* (Ottawa, London, Paris: University of Ottawa Press, 1989), 172–89.

This is not to discount the value of the vice-regal office in terms of representing the Crown and the Sovereign, which continued to enjoy considerable prestige throughout this period; or of promoting worthy causes across the province. Saskatchewan lieutenant governors have always put their personal stamp on the Office and chosen themes or activities of particular interest to them. For example, George Brown, the second lieutenant governor (1910–1915), demonstrated support for agriculture and his wife showed her interest in the suffragette movement led by Nellie McLung. Richard Lake was knighted in 1918 for his contribution to the war effort and particularly the Red Cross. Henry Newlands (1921–1930) promoted the army reserve and the Save the Children Fund. Archibald ("Archie") McNab (1936–1945) and his wife were deeply involved in World War II charities. McNab was renowned and appreciated for his breezy informality. Receiving King George VI and Queen Elizabeth at Government House in 1939 during their famous cross-Canada tour, he is reputed to have told the royal couple to come again — and next time, bring the kids!

Most of the lieutenant governors during Saskatchewan's first six decades as a province shared similar backgrounds: they had been politically active, were ethnically Anglo-Saxon and Protestant, and were usually professional people. There were exceptions. Forget, the first lieutenant governor, was a public servant when appointed governor of the North-West Territories and was French Canadian and Roman Catholic. Henry Newlands was a lawyer and judge, not known for any political affiliation. John Uhrich (1948–1951) was of Alsatian origin and the first Roman Catholic since Forget. However, Brown, a lawyer, had been a Liberal member of the Territorial Assembly. Lake was a federal Conservative MP from 1904 to 1911, although he served on the provincial Public Service Commission under a Liberal government from then until his 1915 appointment. Hugh Munroe (1931–1936), appointed by Conservative Prime Minister R.B. Bennett, was a Saskatoon surgeon who had been president of the provincial Conservative Party. Businessman Archie McNab had served as a Liberal MLA and cabinet minister.

Thomas Miller, who holds the unfortunate record of being the shortest-serving incumbent (15 weeks before his death in 1945), was a journalist, publisher, and president of the provincial Liberal Party; his was the appointment that CCF Premier T.C. Douglas had tried to influence. His successor, Reginald Parker (1945–1948), who also died in office, had been a Liberal MLA and cabinet minister. And *his* successor, John Uhrich, a medical doctor, was another Liberal MLA and cabinet minister; he too died in office. To cap it all, the next lieutenant governor was William Patterson (1951–1958), the former Liberal premier defeated by the CCF in 1944.[41] Starting with McNab, then, the CCF governments faced an almost unbroken series of former Liberal politicians in the vice-regal office until the appointment of Frank Bastedo, the Conservative lawyer (1958–1963) — and he dealt them the blow of the infamous reservation of royal assent in 1961. Bastedo's successor during Woodrow Lloyd's 1961–1964 NDP government was another lawyer, the friendly, likeable Robert ("Dinny") Hanbidge (1963–1970); but he was a former Conservative MLA and MP, who resigned from the House of Commons to take his vice-regal appointment. It was hardly a record to endear the Office of Lieutenant Governor to the CCF/NDP.

41. Allan Blakeney termed the CCF's relationship with Patterson one of "cool correctness" (Blakeney interview).

In September 1944, early in the mandate of the first social democratic government in North America, Premier T.C. Douglas announced the closure of Government House. He also recommended to the federal government that the position of lieutenant governor be eliminated and the duties carried out by the chief justice. While the position of lieutenant governor was beyond the control of the province, protected by the *Constitution Act, 1867*, Government House was not. The premier said "the upkeep of Government House is a frill which we cannot afford particularly when this province is struggling to provide social services. It is a relic of a bygone age."[42]

Douglas closed Government House in 1945 by repealing *The Government House Act*, without opposition in the legislature, although over the protests of some community organizations. Most of the furnishings were sold at a public auction for a fraction of their value. Eventually all but seven acres of the 53-acre grounds would be disposed of. The lieutenant governor's office moved to the Hotel Saskatchewan, where it was to remain for nearly forty years. Government House was leased to the federal government as a veterans' rehabilitation centre, which opened its doors in 1946. Ironically, Princess Elizabeth toured Government House in 1951 to meet convalescent veterans in the building where her parents had been entertained by Lieutenant Governor Archie McNab in 1939.

While the social democratic beliefs of the CCF certainly played a part in the closure of Government House and the proposal to eliminate the vice-regal position, the Douglas government was not alone in its antipathy to the Office of Lieutenant Governor. In 1934, at the height of the Depression, a motion was moved in the Saskatchewan Legislative Assembly to suspend the Office (it was defeated). During the 1920s, 1930s and 1940s Progressive, Social Credit and CCF elected members in western Canada periodically urged its abolition as an undemocratic institution and an inappropriate expense. They were sometimes joined by politicians in Ontario and Quebec. Liberal Premier Mitch Hepburn of Ontario, elected in 1934, resented the lieutenant governor as a functionary of Ottawa, threatened to starve out the incumbent, and closed Government House in Toronto in 1937. Alberta's Government House in Edmonton was closed in 1938 by the Social Credit administration of Aberhart, in retaliation for Ottawa's use of the powers of disallowance and reservation.[43]

From 1945 the Saskatchewan lieutenant governors operated in subdued fashion out of their modest suite in the Hotel Saskatchewan. Their staff was reduced from the complement of gardeners and domestic personnel in the halcyon days of Government House to a single secretary assisted by volunteer aides-de-camp. The lieutenant governors co-existed in a reasonably amicable, if distant, manner with their CCF ministers. The pomp and circumstance of the early years when Government House was open had given way to a more prosaic approach. But Frank Bastedo (1958–1963) went against the current in this respect just as he did in constitutional matters, placing great emphasis on the dignity of the Office. He and his wife entertained at, and attended, elegant social functions. The historic horse-

---

42. From the *Regina Leader-Post*, quoted in Hryniuk/Pugh, *"A Tower of Attraction,"* 106. See 106–07 for an account of the closure of Government House and the sale of its furnishings.

43. In 1997, the Parti Québécois government of Lucien Bouchard closed the official residence of the lieutenant governor of Québec; this was a barb aimed at Ottawa in the style of Mitch Hepburn sixty years earlier.

drawn landau, dating from the time of the Northwest Territories, was brought back into use, after years of neglect, for the opening of the legislature in 1960.

The "reservation" crisis of 1961, however, overshadowed Bastedo's brief revival of the vice-regal office. The indifference or grudging acceptance or even cordiality of many CCF politicians turned to anger and hostility which would take years to overcome. Allan Blakeney when premier refused to appear at the same functions as the lieutenant governor unless absolutely required (this resulted in the erroneous "rule," which persisted into the 1980s, that premier and lieutenant governor could not share the same platform). Although most of "Dinny" Hanbidge's service (1963–1970) was during the Liberal administration of Ross Thatcher (1964–1971), the Saskatchewan vice-regal office did not recover its lustre. Hanbidge's own informality reflected that of the times. He rejected the wearing of the governor's "civil uniform" for ceremonial occasions and, given that his wife was an invalid, stopped the use of the landau (which went into storage at the RCMP). He discontinued the traditional New Year's Day levee at the Hotel Saskatchewan. He was unpretentious, gregarious, showed his love of sports and was popular at the grassroots. The contrast with the Bastedo era was obvious, inevitable, and understandable. The lieutenant governor was no longer taken seriously as a factor in political life. The prestige of the vice-regal office was at its nadir, a fate it shared with that in most Canadian provinces at the time.

AN OFFICE IN TRANSITION, 1970–1980

Three Lieutenant Governors

The appointment of Stephen Worobetz as lieutenant governor by the Trudeau Liberal government in 1970 marked the beginning of a transition in Saskatchewan's vice-regal office. A Saskatoon surgeon, Dr. Worobetz was a supporter of the Liberal party, something he attributed, like many others, to the Liberals' policy on immigration which enabled his parents to emigrate from Ukraine to Canada early in the century.[44] But, in a distinct break with the usual practice of the last six decades, he was not active politically and had not held political office, either elected or within the party. In another break with previous practice, he was first approached by Premier Ross Thatcher to see if he would accept the post, before Prime Minister Pierre Trudeau called to offer it.

Indeed, Thatcher made it clear to the federal Liberals that it was high time a person of Ukrainian origin was appointed to the vice-regal office in a province where this ethnic group played a key economic and social role, and that Stephen Worobetz was the ideal candidate. The appointment was well received partly for this reason; but it was partly, too, because Worobetz himself was widely admired. He had been decorated with the Military Cross for courage under fire as a medical doctor with the Canadian Army in the Italian campaign in World War II. His quiet, modest and unassuming character won him general respect. He was the right kind of person to deal with the sometimes belligerent and abrasive Thatcher, and, for most of his time in office, with Allan Blakeney, leader of an NDP still smarting from the Bastedo period. Worobetz and Blakeney enjoyed a warm relationship. It was Blakeney who arranged for the provincial government to contribute to the rent for the suite which Worobetz had to take as a second home in the capital city.

44. Author's interview with the Honourable Dr. Stephen Worobetz, July 1999.

While personal relationships were cordial between lieutenant governor and premier, official contacts continued at the minimal level of before. Worobetz was not one to rock the boat and, feeling that he had little to offer in political terms, did not mind the lack of consultation. He recalled being approached on one occasion by some business people about legislation on gas and oil royalties which displeased them; he consulted with Chief Justice E.M. Culliton who explained to him the dormant power of reservation.[45] Fortunately for Worobetz — and the provincial vice-regal office — the matter went no further. Appreciated as a promoter of the volunteer sector, Stephen Worobetz remained as a low-profile but highly respected lieutenant governor until he returned to his medical practice in 1976.

The Trudeau government's next appointee was George Porteous, a 72-year-old former YMCA staff person decorated for his courage as a Japanese prisoner of war after the fall of Hong Kong in 1941. A proponent of physical fitness and seniors, and not one to stand on ceremony, Porteous adopted a modest approach to the vice-regal post — too modest in the view of Premier Blakeney, who tried to persuade the lieutenant governor to accept some help with his travel. Blakeney eventually convinced him to take a driver instead of driving himself or taking the bus, but he refused the use of the executive air service. One decision by the Blakeney government during the tenure of George Porteous was to have definite repercussions on the vice-regal function: the establishment of a protocol office in 1976. Intended to coordinate the government's hitherto fragmented approach to official visits, functions and ceremonies, the Protocol Office was a sign of the times. Diplomats posted to Ottawa were fanning out across the country to monitor the increasingly assertive provincial governments. Popular, and therefore official, indifference to ceremonial and tradition seemed to be running its course. Given their common interests, the Protocol Office was, if not an ally, at the very least a sympathizer with the Office of Lieutenant Governor, which until then had little if any support in the provincial bureaucracy.

George Porteous died in office early in 1978, two years after his appointment; the fledgling Protocol Office organized his lying-in state at the Legislative Building. His death created a minor crisis, because the government found to its surprise that it could not pass orders-in-council or special warrants or recall the legislature. While an "administrator," usually the chief justice, can fill in for the lieutenant governor in the event of absence or illness, this is not the case if a lieutenant governor dies in office.[46] Under pressure from the province, the Trudeau government speedily made its third vice-regal appointment for Saskatchewan: Cameron Irwin McIntosh, publisher of a North Battleford newspaper.

While McIntosh was an active Liberal (his father had been a Liberal MP for North Battleford for fifteen years), like his immediate predecessors he had not held elected or party office. With the benefit of hindsight, his tenure (1978–1983) was to mark a turning point in the fortunes of the Saskatchewan vice-regal office. But

---

45. Ibid.

46. Philippe Doré, Clerk of the Executive Council at the time, gave an account of this incident (typescript, Saskatchewan Legislative Assembly, 1978), where Chief Justice E.M. Culliton informed the government he could no longer function as administrator. The Letters Patent of King George VI of 1947 provide for the Chief Justice of Canada to act in the event of the death of the governor general, but no such provision applies to the lieutenant governor. Allan Blakeney suggested that the *Constitution Act, 1867* be amended to allow the administrator to function for 90 days following the death of a lieutenant governor, but no action was ever taken by the federal government.

it got off to a rocky start when McIntosh, still thinking and acting like a newspaperman, expressed a public opinion in favour of capital punishment. Premier Blakeney made clear his view that it was not appropriate for the lieutenant governor to take a public stand on controversial issues. At first it appeared that the cool, correct relationship between lieutenant governor and a New Democratic premier would continue. Consultations between the government and the lieutenant governor were virtually non-existent. The Saskatchewan lieutenant governor enjoyed the dubious distinction of having the smallest, poorest vice-regal operation in the country, based on the little suite in the Hotel Saskatchewan where McIntosh sometimes camped out and used the bathtub to store files.[47] His lack of experience, coupled with the absence of briefings for new lieutenant governors, was obvious when Blakeney came to see him to request signing the writ for the general election of 1978 (incidentally, a change from previous practice when the government simply sent over the document for signature). McIntosh asked what the lieutenant governor did if the incumbent government lost the election; Blakeney gave his nominal superior a quick lesson on the vice-regal prerogative of appointment.[48] McIntosh did not have to apply the lesson in 1978, but it proved useful in 1982 when Blakeney was defeated.

McIntosh did not repeat the mistake of the capital punishment affair. He not only made up for it, but won the respect and appreciation of the Blakeney government for his initiatives in two areas. First, he strongly supported the national unity campaign in which Blakeney was a prominent leader, following the election of René Lévesque's Parti Québécois government in Québec in 1977. Indeed, national unity was to be a prime theme of McIntosh's tenure; it was a theme his successors would assume as one of the ongoing roles of the lieutenant governor. Second, McIntosh threw himself with vigour and conviction into the program for the province's 75th anniversary in 1980, dubbed "Celebrate Saskatchewan." He criss-crossed the province tirelessly, speaking, lending his presence and sharing his enthusiasm. He was the first lieutenant governor to make use of the government's executive aircraft.

Good-humoured, jovial yet modest, energetic, Irwin McIntosh turned out to be the right person at the right time to persuade the NDP of the value of the vice-regal office. His firm support of the government's initiatives and his hard work went a long way towards excising the stigma which had afflicted the office. McIntosh publicly responded in defence of his government when the media, justifiably, criticized the paltry accommodation for the vice-regal office. On September 28, 1981, Premier Blakeney participated in a ceremony inaugurating the province's first lieutenant governor's flag. Until then, Saskatchewan had been the only province not to have a vice-regal emblem; but it became one of the first to adopt a new national pattern, displaying the provincial shield of arms surrounded by ten gold maple leaves, surmounted by a crown, on a royal blue background. Blakeney took advantage of the occasion to state his firm belief in the importance of the Office of Lieutenant Governor and the Crown for all Canadians. The same day, the Supreme Court of Canada handed down its judgement on the constitutional question posed by the Trudeau government and the negotiations were soon under way which led to the

---

47. It was a treatment which McIntosh's family remembered with chagrin after his untimely death in 1988 at the age of 62 and for them overshadowed the many real accomplishments of his time in office.

48. Author's interview with Dr. Howard Leeson, January 2000. Leeson accompanied Blakeney on this vice-regal call.

"patriation" exercise of 1982. The resulting *Constitution Act, 1982* entrenched the monarchy even more firmly in the Canadian political system.[49]

GOVERNMENT HOUSE REBORN

The NDP government of Allan Blakeney undertook another project of great significance for the Crown in Saskatchewan: the restoration of Government House. After its closure in 1945, the prestige of the mansion on Dewdney Avenue in Regina dwindled like that of the vice-regal incumbents who were now excluded from it. The lease to the federal government for a veterans' rehabilitation centre concluded in 1957. In 1958 the provincial government resumed operation of the facility under the name "Saskatchewan House" as a centre for continuous learning. The grand old edifice, stripped of its elegant furnishings, the victim of *ad hoc* renovations adapted to the requirements of its various tenants, was deteriorating inside and out. The CCF government had momentarily considered its demolition in 1958. The threat was more serious under Ross Thatcher's Liberal administration after 1964. This galvanized a dedicated group of citizens into action in 1969, under the name Saskatchewan House Committee (called eventually, after the restoration, the Government House Historical Society). In the vanguard of the heritage movement, this coalition vigorously lobbied the provincial government to preserve the House as an historic property. It presented a brief to the Thatcher government in 1970 and was successful in having Government House declared an historic site in 1971.

In 1974 the NDP government decided in principle to restore Government House as an historic property; the multi-million dollar restoration was undertaken between 1978 and 1980 as a 75th anniversary project. The facility was in Blakeney's constituency and he took a personal interest and considerable pride in the project. The Saskatchewan economy was booming, government revenues were escalating, and no expense was spared to restore the property to its original grandeur. The irony did not escape observers that the direct successor of the CCF administration which had closed the House was now scouring the province for the antiques and artifacts which its predecessor had sold for a song in the 1945 auction. But times had changed. On September 4, 1980, the 75th anniversary of the inauguration of the province of Saskatchewan in 1905, Lieutenant Governor McIntosh and Premier Blakeney presided at the official opening of the resplendent Government House Historic Property.

Government House was to be a museum, depicting the turn-of-the-century residence of Lieutenant Governor and Madame Forget; opened in 1981, the museum became a magnet for school groups from across the province. The House was also to be a venue for concerts, plays (especially the summer production of *The Trial of Louis Riel*) and functions of non-profit organizations, and an entertainment facility for the government, including the lieutenant governor. But, by a cabinet decision in 1977, it was not to accommodate the vice-regal offices.[50] Twenty years later, Allan Blakeney did not recall any conscious opposition to the idea and thought that it

49. Section 41 requires the unanimous consent of the Senate, the House of Commons and the legislatures of all ten provinces for any changes to the offices of the Queen, the governor general and the lieutenant governor.

50. Cabinet Minute #6485 records that Cabinet approved in principle that "the Lieutenant Governor be extended the opportunity to use portions of the building as is related to his duties [*sic*], but not for the establishment of a permanent office." (Cabinet Meeting, December 6, 1977.)

would have happened in due course.[51] Others attribute the decision to the lingering hostility to the Office of the Lieutenant Governor in the ranks of NDP politicians and officials. A trial balloon floated in 1981 to install the lieutenant governor's office (but not residence) in Government House was quickly shot down at the officials level, although Blakeney himself expressed mild interest.[52]

It was evident that Blakeney's personal support for the Office of Lieutenant Governor was well ahead of his party's. With his understanding of constitutional subtleties, Blakeney appreciated the strengths and nuances of the Crown for Canadian governance. He was also conscious that the ceremonial associated with the Crown lent a desirable dignity to the political process and its institutions. During the vice-regal tenure of Irwin McIntosh, Allan Blakeney had emerged from the negative era of the partisan lieutenant governors and the Bastedo episode; by and large his party had not.

THE RESTORATION (1980–2001)

The People

It is a truism to say that the personality of a lieutenant governor (as of anyone holding high office) has a major effect on the role and its public perception. In the case of the Saskatchewan lieutenant governors from the 1980s, the individuals involved shaped the office in a progressively positive manner, helped by the circumstances and their respective First Ministers. Lieutenant governors, despite their method of appointment and source of their salary, were by now considered by themselves and virtually everyone else to have no obligations to the federal government; the days of the "federal agent" were long gone.[53] The non-partisan role was also taken for granted, again despite the method of appointment and the background of the appointee. From the 1970s the Saskatchewan lieutenant governors were such as to inspire confidence among politicians and the general public alike.

Frederick Johnson, appointed in 1983 by the Trudeau government to succeed Irwin McIntosh, had once been an active Liberal, running (unsuccessfully) for elected federal and provincial office. However, he was a war veteran, had long been a superior court judge and a distinguished chief justice of the Court of Queen's Bench (when he had led a major reform of the courts), and was a respected personality in the province. Johnson brought a new dignity to the office, taking seriously the symbolic, decorative functions of the Crown, supported by his wife Joyce. What might have been construed as excessive formality in the Bastedo period was welcomed in the 1980s as a timely development. Saskatchewan had come of age and gained a new self-confidence and sense of identity. The people and communities of the province, bolstered by the success of "Celebrate Saskatchewan," by increased international exchanges, by a prominent place on the national scene despite their small population, and even by their enjoyment of royal visits, concluded that tradition and ceremonial were compatible with informality and egalitarian rural values. The Crown and the Office of Lieutenant Governor were beneficiaries as well as contributors.

---

51. Blakeney interview.
52. Author's personal conversations in 1981.
53. Jack Wiebe, lieutenant governor from 1994 to 2000, said that there was no contact between him and the federal government, in either direction, after his appointment (interview with the author, July 1999).

Sylvia Fedoruk had no evident political affiliation. Her appointment in 1988 by Brian Mulroney's Progressive Conservative government (over a number of Conservative contenders) was due primarily to her personal prestige as a distinguished cancer researcher at the University of Saskatchewan, of which she had become chancellor, and to the influence of the Saskatoon member of the federal cabinet, Ramon Hnatyshyn (later to become governor general). As the first female appointee, the second of Ukrainian origin, and a renowned curler and all-round athlete in a very sports-conscious province, Sylvia Fedoruk was taken to heart by the people. Her down-to-earth, frank approach and her rapport with children cemented the bond. She was a political neophyte; but her intellect and prairie common sense more than compensated for this, together with the fact that new lieutenant governors were at long last benefiting from orientations, briefings and ongoing support from government officials. Fedoruk made only one misstep while she was in office: a Regina *Leader-Post* reporter discovered that she had made a donation of $100 to the federal Progressive Conservatives. Fedoruk admitted it was a mistake, but an honest one — she often responded to fund-raising solicitations such as this without paying much attention to them, and had donated to other political parties too.[54] Thanks to Fedoruk's personal stature, and to the unwillingness of NDP opposition leader Roy Romanow to make an issue of it, the controversy soon dissipated. It was a clear reminder that the vice-regal post was now expected to be totally non-partisan.

When the affable John E.N. (Jack) Wiebe was appointed by Jean Chrétien's Liberal government to succeed Fedoruk in 1994, he was the first practising farmer to hold the vice-regal office — surprising in Canada's premier agricultural province. From the Swift Current area, Wiebe was a well-known Liberal, having served as a member of the Legislative Assembly in the 1970s and as fundraiser and provincial campaign organizer for the federal Liberals. But he had been an MLA popular on both sides of the House and his knowledge of the political process turned out to be an asset. He expressed his personal enthusiasm for his new non-partisan role[55] and he was as good as his word. His rural background, too, stood him in good stead. Gifted with a facility for relating to people and a naturally good-humoured disposition, Wiebe and his wife Ann were ubiquitous at Saskatchewan events and places and enjoyed widespread popularity.

Saskatchewan's second female lieutenant governor, Lynda Haverstock, was named by the Chrétien government late in 1999 and assumed office early in 2000. She differed from the pattern of the last thirty years in that she had been very recently involved in elected politics. Leader of the provincial Liberals from 1989 to 1995, she was the first woman to head a Saskatchewan political party. Haverstock was elected to the legislature in 1991 and brought the party from one MLA to eleven in the 1995 election, but resigned as leader during a caucus revolt later that year and served her remaining time in the legislature as an independent member, choosing not to run in the 1999 election. Articulate and incisive, Haverstock had been one of the opposition members listened to with respect by those on the government side of the House. This, and her distancing from the provincial Liberals, gave substance to her personal resolve, like that of Jack Wiebe, to emphasize the

54. Author's interview with the Honourable Sylvia Fedoruk, July 1999.

55. Author's conversations with J.E.N. Wiebe in 1994. Wiebe returned to politics when Prime Minister Jean Chrétien appointed him to the Senate in April 2000, barely two months after his leaving the vice-regal office.

non-partisan vice-regal role.[56] She held a doctorate in clinical psychology and was an acknowledged expert in farm stress. Haverstock was seen as a role model by many Saskatchewan women and her appointment was applauded across the province. She was thus a clearly justifiable exception to the now general public expectation that recent politicians should not be appointed to vice-regal office. With her husband Harley Olsen, a federal public servant, Lynda Haverstock was destined to carry the Saskatchewan Office of Lieutenant Governor into the provincial centennial year of 2005.

Traditions – New and Old

The very day Frederick Johnson took office in 1983 provided evidence of a new approach to the Office of Lieutenant Governor. For decades new lieutenant governors had been sworn in with a minimum of formality and publicity at a brief event in the legislative library. But for Johnson's installation Conservative Premier Grant Devine's government changed the format to a major, televised ceremony in the legislative chamber attended by over 500 invited guests and followed by military honours. The experiment was judged a success, reflecting the new interest in state ceremonial and sense that public occasions should indeed be as "public" as possible. Devine's government used the same formula at the installation of Sylvia Fedoruk in 1988 and added a farewell ceremony for outgoing lieutenant governor Johnson. Roy Romanow's NDP government used a similar format for the farewell for Fedoruk and the installation of Jack Wiebe in 1994; his NDP-Liberal coalition staged another major ceremony for swearing in Lynda Haverstock in 2000.

Already in 1980, "Celebrate Saskatchewan" year, there had been a revival of tradition. For the first time in many years, a military guard of honour greeted the lieutenant governor on his arrival at the legislative building for the speech from the throne, and Irwin McIntosh and his wife Barbara Lee arrived in the historic provincial landau, retrieved from the RCMP museum where it had been in storage since the days of "Dinny" Hanbidge. While McIntosh was grateful for the new attention to ceremonial, during his last few months in office he expressed the hope that accommodation would be found to enable the lieutenant governor to represent Saskatchewan with the dignity appropriate for official visitors. It was Frederick Johnson who fulfilled Irwin McIntosh's dream: in 1983 Grant Devine and his government made the decision to return the lieutenant governor's office to Government House, barely two years after the museum had opened. On Canada Day, July 1, 1984, a proud Lieutenant Governor Johnson welcomed his First Minister and guests at a formal dinner to inaugurate the new vice-regal offices. Prominent among the guests was an evidently pleased Allan Blakeney, now leader of the opposition.

Devine's government took another major step following the appointment of Johnson's successor, Sylvia Fedoruk: purchasing a modern townhouse in Regina as an official residence. (Renovating Government House to include an apartment, although momentarily considered, was neither practical nor economic.) Fedoruk's successors, Jack Wiebe and Lynda Haverstock, who, like her, came from outside Regina, were to appreciate this decision.

Government House and the new residence were not the only signs of vice-regal progress. Lieutenant governors had survived on a bare-bones budget and skeleton

56. Author's conversation with Dr. Lynda Haverstock, December 1999.

staff since the closure of Government House in 1945. While the federal government continued to pay the lieutenant governor's salary and some allowances, this was no longer enough. Lieutenant governors were travelling ever more, their presence in demand in all corners of the province from schools, service clubs, volunteer organizations, municipalities and Indian bands. Grant Devine again responded to Fred Johnson's call for help. A pro-active private secretary was appointed, was given the resources to hire support staff, and secured a modest entertainment allowance, together with increased travel funds, from the provincial budget.[57] Joyce Johnson became the first vice-regal spouse to benefit from a small but telling change in national protocol, which granted the title "His/Her Honour" to the spouse of the lieutenant governor as well as to the incumbent, just as the governor general's spouse automatically became "His/Her Excellency."[58]

The renewed vice-regal presence in Government House led to the expectation, amply fulfilled, that more functions would be held in the historic property. In 1985 Frederick Johnson reinstituted the New Year's Day levee, abandoned by Hanbidge in the 1960s. Hundreds of citizens flocked to Government House to exchange new year's greetings with the vice-regal couple and another popular tradition was renewed. The Johnsons held the first royal function at Government House since 1939 when they entertained the Queen and the Duke of Edinburgh during their visit in 1987. A unique feature of this tour was an educational program on the Crown, of which a highlight was an address by the Queen to an audience composed partly of school children in the legislative chamber, celebrating its 75th anniversary. The educational initiative continued with the publication by the Devine government of an illustrated educational booklet on the Crown on the occasion of the Duke and Duchess of York's visit in 1989, distributed to all schools and libraries in the province; a revised second edition was published in 1990 for the first visit of Governor General Ray Hnatyshyn.[59] In 1997, at the suggestion of Lieutenant Governor Wiebe, the Romanow government produced an educational video on the Crown, which among other things emphasized the status of the provincial Crown and the relationship of the Canadian Crown to the Aboriginal peoples.[60] The Crown, and the Office of Lieutenant Governor, had emerged from the era of official indifference.

PROVINCIAL HONOURS

An important element in the restoration of the vice-regal profile in Saskatchewan was the lieutenant governor's key role in the provincial honours system recognizing achievement and excellence. Canada had instituted a national honours system in 1967, centennial year, with the Order of Canada, and expanded it in 1972 with the

57. A study commissioned by the Monarchist League of Canada in 1999 found that the federal budget for the lieutenant governor of Saskatchewan (including salary) was $130,600 and the provincial budget $276,000 (both 1999–2000 Estimates). The entire annual cost of the monarchy in Canada, including the governor general, the lieutenant governors and royal visits, came to $22.4 million, or 74 cents per Canadian. *Canadian Monarchist News* 4, no. 3 (Autumn 1999): 14–18.

58. A title which, in the author's view, should replace the second-rate "Your Honour" for lieutenant governors, given their coordinate status with the governor general. The British government early in Confederation determined that lieutenant governors should not retain the title "Excellency" accorded to the colonial governors, and were entitled only to 15-gun artillery salutes instead of the 21-gun salutes granted to their colonial predecessors and the governor general — another symbolic anomaly.

59. D. Michael Jackson, *The Canadian Monarchy in Saskatchewan* (Regina: Government of Saskatchewan, 1990).

60. Saskatchewan Intergovernmental Affairs and Saskatchewan Communications Network, "From Palace to Prairie: the Crown and Responsible Government in Saskatchewan" (55-minute video, 1997).

Order of Military Merit and Bravery Decorations; other decorations and medals were added over the next three decades. As the provinces developed their own identity, it was not surprising that they gave some thought to honours within their own jurisdictions. This met with opposition from the authorities at Rideau Hall, responsible for administering the national honours on behalf of the governor general, on the grounds that only the Sovereign could authorize official honours of the Crown, that she had not authorized provincial honours, that the federal government would not advise her to do so, and that provincial honours were redundant anyway.[61]

Saskatchewan came to a different conclusion in 1980 when the question arose in the context of the "Celebrate Saskatchewan" festivities.[62] Roy Romanow, then intergovernmental affairs minister, authorized a study of the issue, which determined that a provincial honour was desirable, responding to popular demand, and in a politicized province like Saskatchewan must be clearly objective and non-partisan if was to have any chance of success. Reflecting the growing understanding of the viceregal role, there was no hesitation in determining that the lieutenant governor should present the honour in the name of the Crown. Grant Devine's Conservatives carried the project to fruition after their election in 1982 and announced the Saskatchewan Award of Merit in 1984 (the name was changed to Saskatchewan Order of Merit in 1988 when the honour was enshrined in legislation, *The Provincial Emblems and Honours Act*). It was only months after Quebec, starting the planning process later but finishing earlier, had established the first provincial order, *l'Ordre national du Québec*. Lieutenant Governor Johnson presided at the first of the annual investitures late in 1985; among the recipients was that Saskatchewan icon, the first CCF premier and first leader of the federal NDP, Tommy Douglas, making what was to be his final public appearance. The non-partisan credentials of the new honour were immediately established.[63]

Roy Romanow's New Democrats established a second honour, the Saskatchewan Volunteer Medal, in 1995 as a 90th anniversary project for the province. Early in 1996, at the first annual ceremony in the legislature, MLAs from both sides of the House escorted constituents to receive their medals from Lieutenant Governor Jack Wiebe. The lieutenant governor was visibly doing what he was supposed to do: non-partisan recognition on behalf of the people of the province.[64]

---

61. Ontario, despite Ottawa's objections, began a series of provincial medals in 1973, which incorporated the crown and were presented by the lieutenant governor. Alberta established an order in 1979 but, bowing to pressure from Rideau Hall, conceded that the insignia of the order would be a desk-top medallion and not a medal to be worn!

62. For a brief history of provincial honours, the process of beginning the Saskatchewan honours system, and a constitutional argument in favour of them, see D. Michael Jackson, "The Development of Saskatchewan Honours" (unpublished research paper for the Senior Management Development Program of the Saskatchewan Public Service Commission, 1990).

63. Other provinces followed suit with their own orders — Ontario in 1986 and British Columbia in 1989, the latter virtually copying Saskatchewan's legislation. Prince Edward Island adopted the Saskatchewan model in 1997, Manitoba in 1999 and New Brunswick, Nova Scotia and Newfoundland in 2001. Alberta converted its semi-order to a normal one in 1998. The lieutenant governor presents the order in all provinces with the single and prominent exception of Quebec.

64. The federal and Rideau Hall authorities eventually relaxed their attitude to provincial honours, thanks in large part to representations from Saskatchewan. After Sylvia Fedoruk, already a member of the Saskatchewan Order of Merit, was installed as lieutenant governor in 1988 and became chancellor of the order, she conspicuously wore her medal at Rideau Hall despite its "irregular" status. When Saskatchewan's Ray Hnatyshyn became governor general in 1990, Rideau Hall changed its tune and found a compromise to accommodate provincial orders by granting them a status in the national precedence of orders, decorations and medals in 1991, extending this to other provincial honours in 1998.

THE OTHER VICEROY: SASKATCHEWAN AND THE GOVERNOR GENERAL

The relationship between the federal and provincial viceroys was minimal, until Governor General Roland Mitchener began holding periodic conferences in the 1970s. On paper the lieutenant governor's subordinate status to the governor general remained unchanged, even as court decisions and evolving constitutional convention implied a coordinate partnership between the two royal representatives. However, in yet another paradox of the Canadian Crown, just when the federal government tried to popularize the notion of the governor general as head of state in lieu of the Queen, the prestige of the national vice-regal office steadily declined, due largely to the same government's dismissive attitude to it.

Ottawa clearly wanted to minimize the role of the monarchy and its symbols, as an element of its campaign to woo Quebec and of a so-called "Canadianization" program to create an indigenous national imagery. Jettisoning the word "dominion" and generally replacing the coat of arms by the maple leaf logo were among the outward and visible manifestations of this policy. The attempted makeover of the Office of Governor General was another. The appointment of Canadians to the national vice-regal office, starting in 1952 with Vincent Massey, had been long overdue; Massey and his immediate successors, Georges Vanier (1959–67) and Roland Mitchener (1967–74), ably maintained the Office's prestige. However, former diplomat Jules Léger (1974–79) failed to match the profile of his predecessors at the very time the Trudeau government made serious efforts to replace the Queen in all but name by the governor general. Its Bill C-60 met with opposition from those who saw it as thinly veiled republicanism, but also from provincial governments which objected to a federal appointee as Canadian head of state, questioned the putative status of the lieutenant governors under the proposed arrangement, and saw the bill as another centralizing device.[65]

Meeting in Regina at their annual conference chaired by Allan Blakeney in 1978, the premiers voiced their disagreement — and none was more vocal than René Lévesque, the Parti Québécois premier of Quebec. The federal government of the 1970s (and indeed its successors for the next twenty years), in David Smith's words, "misperceived the complexity of the Crown [and] failed [...] to recognize its federalist dimension. In this conceit they proved themselves true descendants of Sir John A. Macdonald."[66] It was no accident that the provinces "had incorporated the rites associated with parliamentary monarchy 'to affirm the status of the provincial government'."[67] The provinces generally showed themselves more monarchical than the federal government, for the reasons of history and tradition to which Ottawa often seemed oblivious, but also for their own constitutional integrity. Perhaps then it is no coincidence that the prestige of the lieutenant governors rose during the same period as that of the governors general declined, and not only in Saskatchewan. Starting in the 1970s, appointments to the provincial vice-regal

65. Bill C-60, among other things, described the Queen as "sovereign head" but the governor general as "First Canadian." For a discussion of the "Canadianization" of the Crown in general and this episode in particular, see Smith, *The Invisible Crown*, chapter 3, "Canadianizing the Crown."

66. Ibid, 55.

67. Ibid, 168.

offices became on the whole less overtly political just when those to the national one became much more so.[68]

In this context, visits to Saskatchewan of governors general ranged from influential to indifferent. Massey, Vanier and Mitchener could and did carry them off with aplomb. Léger and his successors had more difficulty in attracting public attention. Ed Schreyer, governor general from 1979–84, a former Manitoba NDP premier and of Ukrainian ancestry, was cordially received on his frequent but brief and low-key visits; yet when he joined in the province's 75th anniversary celebrations in 1980 he could not help but be upstaged by Prime Minister Pierre Trudeau. Jeanne Sauvé, a former Liberal cabinet minister and speaker of the House of Commons, and the first woman to be governor general (1984–90), attempted a grander style on her two visits. Born in the francophone village of Prud'homme, near Saskatoon, she had left the province at two years of age when her family moved to Quebec; but this was enough for Grant Devine's government to feature her as the guest of honour at a dinner in 1984 for Saskatchewan achievers from all over Canada. The style of this governor general was not such as to endear her to an informal rural population. An austere classical concert sponsored by Sauvé in Regina was unenthusiastically received. Lieutenant Governor Fred Johnson was nearly apoplectic when he caught one of Sauvé's staff changing his seating plan at a dinner at Government House. Local municipalities were offended when Rideau Hall staffers attempted to ban the singing of "God Save The Queen" and replace the toast to the Queen by a "toast to the Governor General." While this was in line with current thinking in Ottawa, it was a gross misreading of prairie sensitivities.

Sauvé's successor was Ray Hnatyshyn (1990–95), the former federal Conservative cabinet minister from Saskatoon and another person of Ukrainian ancestry, who was popular in Saskatchewan and restored positive feelings towards the national vice-regal office in his home province. Devine's Conservative government staged a major welcome for his first official visit in 1990. Thereafter, Hnatyshyn's trips to Saskatchewan, like Schreyer's, tended to be frequent, informal and low-key. He and his wife Gerda were warmly received as a hometown couple who had made good on the national scene, which compensated to a large extent for Hnatyshyn's recent partisan past.

His successor, Roméo LeBlanc (1995–99), a long-time federal Liberal politician and an Acadian from New Brunswick, had no such credentials. Romanow's NDP government dutifully arranged an official welcome and tour in 1995 to mark the province's 90th anniversary but LeBlanc, though pleasant and agreeable, struck no real chords in Saskatchewan apart from the tiny francophone minority; his only other visit, in 1998, passed almost unnoticed. The point had been reached where David Smith could write in 1999, "Notwithstanding the personal qualities of the appointees, which have often been extraordinary, the Canadian governor general has become a hermetic head of state — ignored by press, politicians and public."[69]

68. Although many of the British governors general before 1952 had political backgrounds in the United Kingdom, this had little relevance to the Canadian scene. Vincent Massey had Liberal antecedents and Roland Michener was a former Conservative MP and Speaker of the House of Commons; but both had been "laundered" by subsequent diplomatic posts and were perceived as non-partisan. Governors General Edward Schreyer, Jeanne Sauvé, Ramon Hnatyshyn and Roméo LeBlanc, whatever their individual merits and accomplishments, as former politicians were handicapped by their partisan past, especially when the opposing party won the election during their tenure (as happened to Sauvé and Hnatyshyn).

69. David Smith, "Republican Tendencies," *Policy Options-Options politiques* (May 1999): 11.

The welcome appointment late in 1999 of well-known journalist Adrienne Clarkson, the first non-politician since Léger to be governor general, with her husband, philosopher John Ralston Saul, augured well for a change in the fortunes of the national vice-regal office in the new millennium. Her first visit to Saskatchewan in 2000, like those to the other provinces, was characterized by a new energy and effort to raise the profile of the Office of Governor General. True, some things had not changed: the incomprehension of some Rideau Hall field staff with respect to provincial status and protocol; the push to label the governor general as head of state; and the apparently tacit understanding with official Ottawa to avoid mention of the Queen and the Crown.[70]

But Adrienne Clarkson herself turned her visit into a veritable *tour de force*, relating superbly to the public, young and old, rural and urban, and making her mark in the media in a way her predecessors had never been able to master. In a hushed Saskatchewan legislature packed with invited guests, she spoke eloquently, even poetically, of her impressions of the province, facing head-on the controversial issues of rural depopulation and out-migration of the young. It was a refreshing change from traditional vice-regal platitudes and reflected a new acceptance, indeed expectation, by the Canadian public that governors-general — and by extension lieutenant governors — should not fear to address the real issues of society.

POLITICS, PREMIERS AND MATTERS CONSTITUTIONAL

When Frederick Johnson took office as lieutenant governor in 1983 at the first major installation ceremony staged in the legislative chamber, he spoke glowingly of the advantages of constitutional monarchy. In the inaugural dinner which followed, with customary zeal he affirmed that, in the well-known dictum of the British constitutional expert Walter Bagehot, the Sovereign or her representative had three rights — "the right to be consulted, the right to encourage, the right to warn"[71] — and that he expected to exercise those rights. Johnson's expectations were not fulfilled. Constitutional matters were not the strong suit of Grant Devine and his Conservative administration, who had been elected in 1982 with a bare handful of experienced MLAs. The premier himself appreciated and respected the ceremonial, symbolic role of the lieutenant governor and at the personal level enjoyed cordial relations with the three incumbents who served during his nine years in office. Devine certainly took major steps to restore and enhance the prestige of the vice-regal office, including the return to Government House and the launching of the provincial honours system. However, he and his cabinet had no intention of allowing the lieutenant governor to play more than an honorific role. Devine, like his predecessors as premier, did not meet regularly with his lieutenant governors. When Johnson asked to see cabinet documents as a matter of routine, he was turned down. But the key issue on which the political and constitutional limitations of the vice-regal office became apparent for both Fred Johnson and Sylvia Fedoruk was a vexed one: that of special warrants.

As we have already seen, one of the statutory powers granted to the lieutenant governor is that of approving and signing "special warrants" at the request of cabinet, to approve government expenditures outside the normal legislative appropriation

70. Among recent governors general, Ray Hnatyshyn did speak warmly in public of the Queen and the Crown, but only after he left office (for example, in the video "From Palace to Prairie").

71. Walter Bagehot, *The English Constitution* (London: Kegan Paul, Trench, Trubner & Co., 1909), 75.

process.[72] Merrilee Rasmussen gives the following explanation in her thesis on the subject:

> A special warrant is a statutory exception to the basic rule of law that requires parliamentary consent to government expenditures... It is an exception that permits the Lieutenant Governor, at the request of Cabinet, to approve government expenditures in the Legislature's place under certain limited conditions ... the power to authorize by special warrant is given to the Lieutenant Governor and not to the Cabinet directly. This suggests that the Legislature has purposely provided to the Lieutenant Governor the legal ability to exercise independent action, recognizing that the conventions of the constitution will constrain the Lieutenant Governor to exercising that legal power only in situations in which a "constitutional fire extinguisher" may be necessary.[73]

Theoretically, then, the lieutenant governor, while normally accepting advice from the government to sign special warrants, in an emergency might exercise a reserve power to refuse such a request.

As Rasmussen points out, special warrants are normally "used towards the end of a fiscal year, when the Legislature is not sitting, to provide for any shortfall between the estimated amounts that were appropriated for the use of departments and the amount that is actually spent."[74] They are then retroactively approved by the legislature in supplementary estimates.

However, beginning in the 1980s, special warrants were put to frequent and questionable use in Saskatchewan. In 1987, the Conservative government chose not to recall the legislature and present its budget in the normal period of February-March and or even after the beginning of the fiscal year on April 1. Instead, the government resorted to special warrants "to finance ordinary and predictable government expenditures"[75] — an infraction of the intent if not the letter of the legislation. Howard Leeson, the editor of this book, wrote to Lieutenant Governor Johnson urging him to recall the legislature and require the government to present a budget. Johnson declined to do so, citing the governing legislation as justification for him not to refuse "advice," although he might balk at signing warrants if they were repeated indefinitely. For Leeson, the lieutenant governor's refusal to act called into question the very rationale for the existence of the Crown. Lieutenant Governor Johnson was clearly unwilling to test his reserve powers unless forced to by a prolonged and serious political crisis; as a former chief justice he knew, and preferred to stand by, the letter of the law.[76]

His successor, Sylvia Fedoruk, faced a more serious challenge in 1991 as the Devine government neared the end of its constitutional five-year mandate. In June of that year, faced with the possibility of losing a vote of confidence, the government abruptly prorogued the legislature in June without allowing the vote. An

72. The current legislative provision in Saskatchewan is found in section 14 of *The Financial Administration Act, 1993*. Other provinces and the federal government have similar legislation.

73. Merrilee D. Rasmussen, "The Decline of Parliamentary Democracy in Saskatchewan" (Master's thesis, University of Regina, 1994), 76. The words in quotes are those already cited from Frank MacKinnon (see footnote 12).

74. Ibid, 86.

75. Ibid, 91.

76. Johnson made his view clear in a conversation with the author at the time. See also Saywell, *The Office of Lieutenant Governor*, 26–27. Under threat of legal action by the NDP opposition, the government did recall the legislature in June and passed the budget.

unhappy Sylvia Fedoruk, her face like a thundercloud, entered the legislative chamber to declare a prorogation which evidently went against her personal judgement. Since a budget had not been passed, the government again resorted to a series of special warrants to finance its expenditures. There was a political and public outcry and the lieutenant governor came under considerable pressure to refuse her signature to the warrants. Fedoruk was placed in a dilemma: either sanction a use of the special warrant which was certainly unconventional and possibly illegal, or resort to a perilous and unprecedented use of the reserve power. She consulted constitutional experts and made clear to the premier her disagreement with the government's actions. Beyond this she was not prepared to go; she concluded that it was up to the electorate, and not to the edict of an appointed official, to render final judgement.[77] In November 1991, that electorate swept the Conservatives from office.

Johnson and Fedoruk, by their unwillingness to act in the highly questionable use of special warrants, and, in Fedoruk's case, of prorogation, undoubtedly circumscribed even further the already minimal exercise of the lieutenant governor's reserve powers. Like Sir Richard Lake in 1916, and unlike Frank Bastedo in 1961, Johnson and Fedoruk took a very restrictive view of their constitutional role. It has been cogently argued that Fedoruk should have refused prorogation in June 1991 and that in not doing so she missed a unique opportunity to restore constitutional credibility to the vice-regal office. According to this view, she and her predecessor would have enjoyed wide public support had they refused to sign the dubious series of special warrants.[78] But exercising unprecedented reserve powers of a "prerogative of prorogation" and a "prerogative of special warrants" would have taken the vice-regal office into uncharted and dangerous waters. It is yet another of the many paradoxes of the Office of Lieutenant Governor that New Democrats, who had decried Bastedo's use of reservation and had questioned the value of the vice-regal function at all, urged the lieutenant governor to exercise reserve powers when they were in opposition.[79]

On balance, Johnson and Fedoruk were probably wise to act as they did. They realized that in the late twentieth century the public expected the media, the courts, public opinion and ultimately the voters to deal with erring governments, not a federal appointee. Acting in the circumstances of 1987 and 1991, however great the provocation at the time, might have appeared to be yielding to partisan pressure and compromised the hard-won impartiality of the Office of Lieutenant Governor.

This did not mean, however, that the lieutenant governor had no worthwhile role to play in governance. The right circumstances appeared when Roy Romanow's NDP administration won the 1991 election. Romanow made it clear that he personally respected the Office of Lieutenant Governor and its incumbents and expected his political colleagues and public service to do likewise. Ceremonial occasions were given a high profile. Swearings-in of new cabinet ministers henceforth took place at Government House, which became Romanow's preferred venue for government entertainment. Far from avoiding the lieutenant governor on official occasions as had been the practice of his CCF-NDP predecessors (although not Grant

77. Fedoruk interview.

78. This view has been expressed by, among others, Ned Shillington, former NDP MLA and cabinet minister, who was in opposition at the time (interview with the author, March 2000).

79. Merrilee Rasmussen was also critical of the New Democratic government of Roy Romanow for using special warrants inappropriately ("The Decline of Parliamentary Democracy in Saskatchewan," 132–33).

Devine), he actively encouraged vice-regal participation at as many events as possible. Sylvia Fedoruk and Jack Wiebe returned the favour. Wiebe in particular proved to be a consummate diplomat and developed into a fine art the traditional vice-regal duty of receiving foreign diplomats and delegations, interpreting and promoting with enthusiasm Saskatchewan's history, culture and economy to visitors.

The most significant evolution in the lieutenant governor's role, however, was not ceremonial or international, but political: the effective application by Premier Romanow of Bagehot's principle, affirmed by Fred Johnson in 1983, that the Sovereign's representative had the right to be consulted, to encourage and to warn. Early in his first mandate, Sylvia Fedoruk proposed to Romanow that they hold regular monthly meetings, a proposal readily accepted by the premier. Saskatchewan thus became the only province where the practice existed and Fedoruk considered it one of the most worthwhile innovations of her tenure.[80] Her successor, Jack Wiebe, found the experience mutually beneficial: Romanow kept him informed on issues while Wiebe could contribute advice and encouragement based on his personal reading of the provincial scene. As Wiebe noted, being premier is a lonely job; rare is the opportunity to consult with a neutral observer in confidence.[81] Romanow found Wiebe, as a former MLA, particularly helpful in this regard; the fact that he had been on the opposite side of the House counted far less than their shared experience of political life. It was yet another of the many paradoxes in the Office of Lieutenant Governor that a partisan past could sometimes contribute to the non-partisan vice-regal role.

Lynda Haverstock found herself in a similar situation from 2000. She considered that Roy Romanow's understanding of and implementing the Bagehot principle allowed the lieutenant governor to properly fulfil her constitutional role and thus make a genuine contribution to the political order. She also had no difficulty in adapting to her apolitical status, associating comfortably with politicians on both sides of the House.[82]

So it was that by the beginning of the new millennium, the Office of Lieutenant Governor in Saskatchewan had attained an unprecedented equilibrium of prestige and political acceptance, more so than in many other provinces. This was thanks in large measure to Roy Romanow's immediate predecessors as premier, but especially to him. Romanow, like Allan Blakeney, understood the constitutional subtleties of the Crown; after all, he had been Blakeney's point man in the negotiations leading to the *Constitution Act, 1982*. But like Grant Devine, he also appreciated the ceremonial and symbolic functions of the lieutenant governor; by temperament he was sensitive to the public need for protocol and ceremonial and to the human face of the monarchy. Unencumbered by the CCF-NDP baggage of the 1940s to 1970s, he not only accepted but reinforced and extended Devine's support for the vice-regal office. Howard Leeson has suggested in his Introduction that Roy Romanow was a genuine "red tory"[83] (or, to coin a phrase, a "blue social democrat"). This is a very Canadian paradox. So, of course, is the Crown.

80. Fedoruk interview.

81. Wiebe interview.

82. Author's interview with the Honourable Lynda Haverstock, February 2001.

83. Howard Leeson, "The Rich Soil of Saskatchewan Politics," in this volume.

CONCLUSION: RESOLVING A PARADOX

The republican movement in Canada, unlike Australia, has never been very strong. On the whole, Canadians have seemed content with the status quo.[84] Opinion polls usually find those expressing an opinion either to be evenly divided on whether to replace the monarchy with a republic, or to be slightly in favour of the monarchy, a pattern that has continued for decades despite repeated assertions that only the "older generation" wants to retain the monarchy. Despite, too, the wave of immigration which has produced a multicultural mosaic in the country.[85] On the surface, maintaining the monarch of the United Kingdom as Canadian head of state in the third millennium is paradoxical, to say the least. Beneath the surface, however, the Canadian reluctance to debate, let alone abolish, an institution as curious as the monarchy is readily comprehensible. In a country locked in the smothering economic and cultural embrace of the enormous republic to its south, the monarchy inherited from and shared with Britain provides a unique strand of national identity; its symbols, however archaic and arcane to some, like those of parliamentary democracy give some sense of continuity in a nation prone to revisionist rewrites of its history. It is the epitome of a separate and unique political culture on the North American continent.[86]

Yet the monarchy in Canada has obvious weaknesses. The very notion of a hereditary family at the head of the state lacks a certain logic in the twenty-first century. For Canadians, sharing in what is clearly a primarily British royal family is bound to raise questions of its relevance to an increasingly multicultural North American society, as it always has for francophones. A non-resident head of state, despite his or her constitutional status, despite the roles of the vice-regal representatives, cannot help but be distanced from the Canadian citizenry. However, criticism of the monarchy in Canada has almost entirely revolved around these symbolic dimensions; with the notable exception of David Smith, little attention has been paid to the political consequences of the immense power conferred on the executive branch by the Crown through the exercise of the royal prerogative. Those voicing concern about concentration of power in the prime minister's office have usually neglected to identify its theoretical source. It is in the United Kingdom that there has been a genuine critique of the constitutional implications of monarchy: "The Royal Prerogative has no place in a modern western democracy," says, bluntly, one observer.[87]

While ignoring its constitutional implications, some commentators, usually academic or journalistic, have dismissed the monarchy as anachronistic, colonial, even

84. For a thorough discussion, see David Smith, *The Republican Option in Canada, Past and Present* (Toronto: University of Toronto Press, 1999).

85. A Gallup poll in October 1999 showed 48% of Canadians in favour of retaining the monarchy and 43% opposed. The figures for the 9 provinces other than Quebec were 54% in favour, 38% opposed (Quebec figures were 30% for, 58% against, but the number "for" had more than doubled since the last poll in 1997). Figures for the prairies were 50% for, 41% against. See *Canadian Monarchist News* 5, no. 1 (Winter 2000): 1–2. Polling by the government of Canada in 2000 for symbols on new bank notes found that the Queen, at 59%, was not only well ahead of other contenders but the only one to score a majority. Further polls in 2001 showed that support for the monarchy across Canada had increased to 55%.

86. For an American sociologist's study of the differences between Canadian and American attitudes, see Seymour Martin Lipsett, *Continental Divide: The Values and Institutions of the United States and Canada* (New York, London: Routledge, 1990). Note especially chapters 1, "Revolution and Counter-Revolution," and 3, "The Canadian Identity."

87. Jack Straw, MP, "Abolish the Royal Prerogative," in Anthony Barnett (ed.), *Power and the Throne* (London: Vintage, Random House, 1994).

absurd. Their numbers and profile increased in the 1990s, due in part to the tattered reputation of some members of the royal family, although never of Queen Elizabeth personally. The federal government's renewed effort to promote the governor general as "head of state" was part of this trend.[88] Members of Jean Chrétien's Liberal government (though not the prime minister himself) floated several trial balloons about ending the monarchy. Those interested in the issue watched closely the Australian debate and 1999 referendum on becoming a republic. Yet the republican option failed in Australia despite its strong lobby and highly organized anti-monarchy campaign.[89] In Canada, it made little headway, for the same reasons as in the 1970s: the innate reluctance of Canadians to seriously contemplate a republic, and the resistance of the provinces to an apparently centralizing device.[90]

Canadians were weary and leery of constitutional initiatives after two decades of them, starting with the "patriation" debate in the early 1980s and continuing with the rejected Meech Lake and Charlottetown accords. Given the entrenched status of the Crown in the *Constitution Act, 1982*, few were anxious to open another constitutional can of worms, especially one bound to be as controversial and emotive as the monarchy. Even those who preferred the republican option admitted that it was a non-issue and the object of mass indifference — which was probably just as well, because a full-fledged debate would not only be divisive but raise fundamental and troubling questions about the nature of sovereignty, now vested theoretically in the monarch. Canada had far more important issues to face.[91] In any event, the enormously successful Canadian tour by the heir to the throne, the Prince of Wales, in the spring of 2001, including his first-ever visit to Saskatchewan, underscored the deep-rooted, instinctive appeal of the monarchy to grassroots sentiment, and notably to the First Nations.

Surprisingly, those who were pushing for elimination of the monarchy did not appear to consider the interests of the Aboriginal peoples, whose loyalty to the Queen was very well known — witness their lobbying in London in 1981 to oppose the patriation of the constitution. For the First Nations, the treaties are sacred agreements between themselves and the monarch (First Nations prominently fly the Union Jack). The Aboriginal peoples instinctively understand the powerful moral, social and political resonances of symbol; and while their treaties are with the federal Crown, their respect extends to its provincial counterpart. But the most telling aspect of the efforts to downplay or remove the monarchy, from Bill C-60 in the 1970s to the proponents of the governor general as head of state in the 1990s, was the utter failure to take into account the provincial Crown and the lieutenant governor who embodied it. This was not only a constitutional non-starter, it was

88. The federal government's tacit policy on the governor general was supported by the Toronto *Globe and Mail*, which during the 1990s carried on an editorial campaign to replace the monarch as head of state by the governor general at the end of the present Queen's reign and select the governor general by vote of the Companions of the Order of Canada.

89. For an analysis of the Australian referendum, see Michael Valpy, "The Significance of the Referendum for Canadian Monarchists," in *Canadian Monarchy News* 4, no. 1 (Winter 1999): 3-4.

90. For an argument in favour of the Crown in Canada, see my address to the Association of Canadian Clubs, 1992–1996, "The Crown — A Canadian Institution," reproduced in *Canadian Speeches: Issues of the Day* 9, no. 2 (May 1995): 40–47.

91. Reflections on the republican-monarchist state of play in Canada at the end of the twentieth century are found in the May 1999 issue of *Policy Options-Options politiques*, with contributions by David E. Smith, Reg Whitaker, Gerald Henderson, David J. Elkins and Michael Valpy. Valpy is the only one to express outright support for the monarchy.

also a misreading of the pragmatic but also emotional reality of the provincial vice-regal office, and of its surprising success. Which brings us back to the question posed early in this chapter: what are we to make of the role of lieutenant governor?

The classic view of vice-regal powers is summed up in a phrase by Jacques Monet: "The Queen, the Governor General and the Lieutenant Governor are the custodians of the constitution. Their responsibility is to see that the rules are followed, both the written and the unwritten."[92] Merrilee Rasmussen, in dealing with the issue of special warrants, considers this role to be potentially critical: "[T]he reserve powers of the Crown are the only institutional check available to be used against a government that flouts the conventions of parliamentary democracy."[93] Thus, in an ironic paradox of history, the Crown, whose powers originally had to be limited by the executive and legislative branches, and which is the source of executive power through the royal prerogative, is now seen as the ultimate constraint on the over-powerful executive, given the progressive weakening of the legislative branch.

If the vice-regal offices in Canada are to genuinely fulfil this role of constitutional last resort, the political neutrality of the incumbents must be beyond question, which means the method of their appointment will have to be changed. Prime ministerial patronage for both the national and provincial representatives of the Sovereign should no longer be acceptable. Jacques Monet has proposed that the governor general be nominated by the full Privy Council.[94] We would argue that, given the constitutional status of the provinces and thus their vice-regal offices, the lieutenant governors should not be federal appointees at all. But there is no point in substituting provincial patronage for federal, as is the case for the Australian state governors. Selection of the lieutenant governor could be made instead by a provincial equivalent of the Privy Council convened for the purpose.

As it stands, in strictly constitutional terms, the lieutenant governor retains almost no power on his or her own. With the reserve powers of royal assent and reservation long gone, with the prerogatives of dismissal and dissolution apparently obsolete, and with the vice-regal reluctance to exercise discretion in the granting of special warrants or prorogation, the lieutenant governor has essentially yielded to the courts, the media, public opinion and the electorate the task of safeguarding the constitution and acting as a check on the executive. But not entirely. The lieutenant governor still incarnates legality in the province. In the words of Norman Ward, "the mere existence of the power will, in fact, tend to prevent the need for its exercise arising."[95] Or, as a British Columbia viceroy once said, "the lieutenant governor exists to deny the government absolute power."[96]

92. Jacques Monet, *The Canadian Crown*, 61.

93. Rasmussen, "The Decline of Parliamentary Democracy in Saskatchewan," 140. Rasmussen recommends specific, statutory vice-regal discretion in the granting of special warrants as a safeguard against their abuse (141–43).

94. Conversations with the author. The Privy Council is a formal body of which the federal cabinet is nominally a committee. It includes all present and former federal cabinet ministers as well as some honorary appointees and meets only rarely on ceremonial occasions.

95. Norman Ward, *Dawson's the Government of Canada* (Toronto: University of Toronto Press, 1987), 191.

96. The Honourable David Lam, in the video "On Behalf of Her Majesty: The Story of British Columbia's Government House and the Lieutenant-Governor" (Victoria, British Columbia Government House Foundation, 1991).

Still, the primary role of the lieutenant governor is now moral and symbolic. This is not to say it is not practical. The lieutenant governor, by carrying out so many of the decorative, ceremonial and social duties which are necessary in any society, frees the premier to get on with the business of governing. A lieutenant governor who can be consulted, encourage and warn provides an invaluable service to first minister and cabinet. Yet the function of symbol is crucial.[97] In this sense, the royal and vice-regal positions should both reflect and help define the values of the community, and their incumbents provide a personal, caring, non-partisan approach to issues of the day.[98] It may well be that the inability of the Office of Governor General to do this, especially since the 1970s, deprived Canada of a much-needed rallying point which could incorporate at the same time the continuous tradition of monarchy and the contemporary aspirations of Canadians of both official languages, of the Aboriginal peoples and of multiple cultures.[99]

In Saskatchewan, the resurgent Office of Lieutenant Governor helped fill the void. Since the 1980s, the lieutenant governor has increasingly served to express the goals and self-awareness of the provincial community. The Office is a prime vehicle for the recognition by society of deserving individuals and causes, notably through the bestowing of honours, but also through the simple yet effective non-partisan vice-regal presence in schools, hospitals, seniors' homes, cultural and sports events and First Nations ceremonies. (A good example is the annual vice-regal tour of schools in northern Saskatchewan initiated by Sylvia Fedoruk.)

The entire political process, in its widest sense, benefits from a strong vice-regal office. Our age is characterized by public scepticism, even cynicism, about politicians. The criticism heaped on them by the media is tantamount to undermining the system. Allan Blakeney, for one, believes that democratic government needs champions and that the role of the Queen and the vice-regal representatives is to embody, without too much clarity or precision, the few values we hold in common.[100] David Smith has said that one of the prime functions of the Crown is "to represent kingly virtues in the system."[101] The Queen herself demonstrated this function in her remarks at the Saskatchewan legislature in 1987:

> The Crown represents the basic political ideals which all Canadians share. It stands for the idea that individual people matter more than theories; that we are all subject to the rule of law. These ideals are guaranteed by a common loyalty, through the Sovereign, to community and country.[102]

At the dawn of the new millennium, there was an emotional farewell for Jack Wiebe. Premier Roy Romanow thanked him for his wise counsel and friendship; the lieutenant governor expressed in return his gratitude for the premier's strong support of and respect for the vice-regal office. Chief Perry Bellegarde of the Federation of Saskatchewan Indian Nations commended Wiebe on maintaining the integrity of the Crown. Jack Wiebe had not made a false move. He had had the good fortune

97. For an American study of social and political symbolism, see Robert Bellah, Richard Madsen, William M. Sullivan, Ann Swidler and Steven M. Tipton, *Habits of the Heart* (Berkeley: University of California Press, 1985).

98. Cf. Jacques Monet, "A Symbol of Community," in *The Canadian Crown*, 75–82.

99. I owe this observation to Ned Shillington (interview). David Smith says that the governor general in Australia is far more successful in this symbolic role, and that the state governors have much more prestige and visibility than their Canadian counterparts (conversation with the author, April 2000).

100. Blakeney interview.

101. In "From Palace to Prairie."

102. Cited in Jackson, *The Canadian Monarchy in Saskatchewan*, 53.

not to face a constitutional dilemma like his two immediate predecessors. It had been a felicitous, harmonious tenure at Government House.

Lynda Haverstock's installation early in 2000 brought out the best in Saskatchewan's now accepted tradition of state ceremonial. Despite her very recent political activity, there was a remarkable convergence among politicians lauding her appointment — not only Premier Romanow, but also Elwin Hermanson, who headed the recently formed Saskatchewan Party and was now leader of the official opposition, and Liberal Ron Osika, speaker of the Legislative Assembly. It was a sign that the Office of Lieutenant Governor was appreciated and more importantly, that it was *understood*. Haverstock illustrated another dimension of the Office and provided evidence of her personal poise when she earned the applause of a group of farmers protesting at the legislative building hours before her installation. In her inaugural address, she announced her intention to focus on Saskatchewan's youth and encourage them to "live life with a purpose." As a *Leader-Post* editorialist wrote in a piece entitled "A Good Beginning," this was a particularly relevant message, given the province's changing demographics. The writer continued: "If Lynda Haverstock's first day on the job is any indication, she is about to embark on a very successful term as Saskatchewan's lieutenant governor."[103]

Like her national counterpart, Governor General Adrienne Clarkson, Lynda Haverstock soon demonstrated a readiness to speak publicly, and substantively, about key issues affecting society, while carefully refraining from commenting on public policy. Her own view was that the lieutenant governor had a unique opportunity, through an intensive and non-partisan visit program across the province, to sense and express the interests, concerns and aspirations of the people, and to encourage pride and boost morale.[104] Haverstock consciously articulated Allan Blakeney's belief that the vice-regal office should champion democratic institutions: she set out to educate her audiences on the merits of parliamentary democracy and the responsibilities of individual citizens towards it. She also gave spirited addresses explaining and promoting Canada's constitutional monarchy, echoing a theme sounded by her three immediate predecessors.[105]

The crucial balance between the Queen's representative and the First Minister is always a fragile one, relying on responsible leadership and compatible personalities. After Roy Romanow's retirement from political life early in 2001, Premier Lorne Calvert continued the practice of regular meetings with the lieutenant governor and, if his enthusiasm for the Prince of Wales' visit was any indication, shared Romanow's positive view of the monarchy in Canada. If successive lieutenant governors and premiers followed their example, Saskatchewan would appear to have resolved, at the beginning of the twenty-first century, the historic paradox of the Office of Lieutenant Governor.

103. *Regina Leader-Post*, February 23, 2000.

104. Haverstock interview. Haverstock, as a former politician, was struck by the popularity of the vice-regal office — she had to turn down over 200 invitations in her first three months in office — and the increasing demand for substantive speeches by an apolitical person who had nothing to gain or lose.

105. Haverstock described herself as an "unabashed monarchist," a view reinforced by her audience with the Queen in London 2000 when she attended the 100th birthday celebrations for the Queen Mother (Haverstock interview). The practice began in the reign of the present Queen of granting Canadian lieutenant governors an audience with Her Majesty once during their mandate — another sign of the growing acceptance of the co-ordinate status of the provincial viceroys, which before then had mystified if not perplexed Buckingham Palace (see Smith, *The Invisible Crown*, 55).

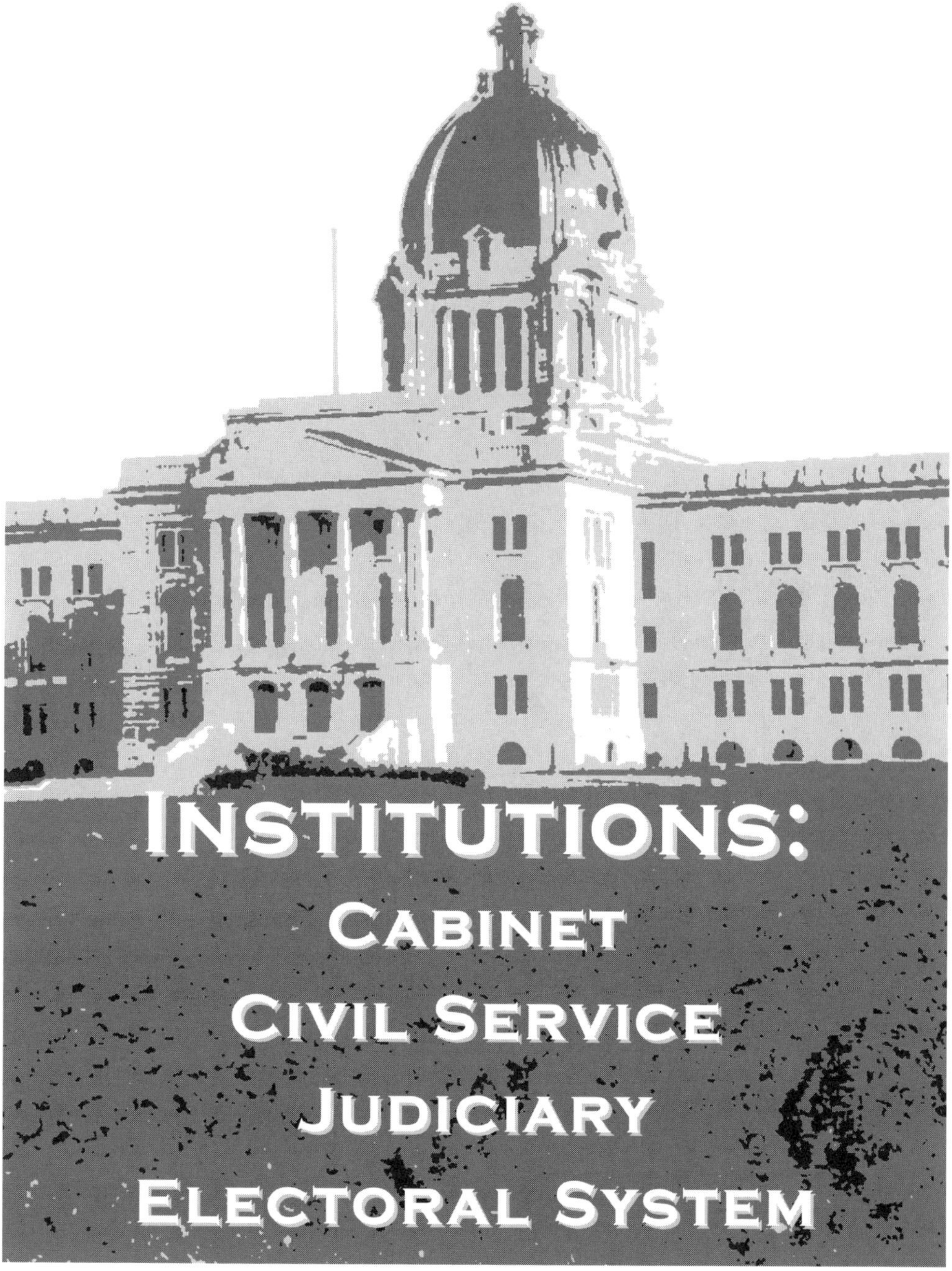
INSTITUTIONS:
CABINET
CIVIL SERVICE
JUDICIARY
ELECTORAL SYSTEM

Premiers and Cabinets in Saskatchewan: One Premier's View

The Honourable Allan E. Blakeney, PC, OC, QC

INTRODUCTION

In our parliamentary system of government as it operates in Canada, the Executive Council plays a key role. In the province of Saskatchewan members of the Executive Council are members of the cabinet. They constitute the group that directs the operations of the government. In formal terms, the representative of the monarch, the lieutenant governor, chooses members of the Executive Council who act in the name of the monarch. The legislature passes a budget by "granting to Her Majesty ... certain sums..." Similarly the legislature passes legislation. These acts are assigned to members of the Executive Council for administration.

The Executive Council appoints public servants, some by direct order of the Executive Council and some according to rules set out by the legislature in acts administered by the Executive Council.

It will be seen that the Executive Council — the cabinet — plays a key role in proposing how money should be raised and spent, what laws should be passed and how they should be administered, and who should be appointed as employees of the government.

Following an election the lieutenant governor calls upon a member of the legislature — normally the leader of the majority party in the legislature — to form a government by choosing a cabinet which can get the support of a majority in the legislature.

CHOOSING A CABINET

The leader of the government becomes the premier. How does a premier go about choosing a cabinet in Saskatchewan? A premier seeks to achieve several objectives when he chooses a cabinet. I will refer to the premier as "he," since all Saskatchewan premiers have been male (this may well change in the relatively near future). He seeks to unite his support group. If his cabinet requires the support of two or more parties to assure itself a majority in the legislature, then it may be necessary to have in the cabinet representatives of two or more parties. Even if this is not the case it may be necessary or desirable to have different groups within the governing party appropriately represented in the cabinet.

It is sometimes supposed that a premier looks at the caucus of his party and decides which members are "best qualified" to be cabinet ministers. The assumption is that a premier reviews the qualifications of the individual members — can they speak in public, can they give clear explanations in the legislature, can they handle paper and detail, do they meet the public well and project an air of confidence and reasonableness, and so on — and chooses ministers accordingly. All this is an accurate but a very partial picture.

A cabinet is a team. It is not simply a collection of competent people. Depending upon the criteria applied, a cabinet could consist entirely of white male lawyers and teachers from Saskatoon and Regina, but it would not be a good cabinet. It is not true that voters want simply administrative competence in their cabinet. They want to feel comfortable with the cabinet, that the cabinet or some members of it are aware of their concerns, and in some sense represent them.

The interests and concerns which need to be recognized when forming a cabinet vary over the years. Geography has always been a factor. A premier seeks to have the major cities and regions of the province represented, as membership in his caucus permits. Until recently it was acceptable to have an all-male cabinet, but now some gender balance is preferable. Once religious affiliation was perhaps more important than it now is. Ethnic representation is, I would judge, still a factor to be considered. The need to have some diversity of occupation — farmer, business person, teacher, professional person — is still a consideration. It is also desirable to have some seasoned veterans and some young blood so that over the years there can be some continuity in cabinet, but also some renewal. The voters sometimes make the process easier when elections come around by defeating some candidates who are cabinet ministers, but this is not the sort of help in achieving cabinet renewal that a premier ordinarily welcomes.

In certain circumstances, it is possible for a premier to select someone as a cabinet minister who is not a member of the legislature, provided that a by-election or general election is called soon after the appointment. There was an occasion when a Saskatchewan cabinet minister was not a member of the legislature. The Honourable Herb Pinder was selected as a cabinet minister by Premier Ross Thatcher in 1964. He had been a candidate in the 1964 provincial election and was involved in a very close contest. There was a recount which gave Mr. Pinder's opponent, Mr. Robert Walker, a small majority of two. Mr. Walker reached the conclusion that the election could probably be overturned by the proceedings under *The Controverted Elections Act*, and accordingly he resigned. A by-election was called in which Mr. Walker was elected. Mr. Pinder served as a cabinet minister for six months during the period of the recounts and the by-election. After his defeat he resigned as a cabinet minister, never having been a member of the legislature.

CABINET CHANGES

With a basic consideration of personal competence and attention to as many of the representation considerations as can be accommodated, a premier attempts to shape a team which will inspire confidence in the public and in the legislature.

A premier usually feels it necessary to have new faces in his cabinet from time to time. The reasons for this are both internal and external. For reasons internal to the cabinet and caucus, some changes in those who serve as cabinet ministers is desirable. Cabinets, like other organizational bodies, fall into patterns of decision making which often serve to discourage new approaches to old issues. A new face with a new perspective can often serve to encourage a new look at continuing issues — and most issues of government are continuing ones, but undergo subtle changes over time.

Similarly, some departments of government become fixed in their ways and fall into set positions in dealing with key interest groups — such as the Department of Education in its dealings with the teaching profession. There are several ways to deal with this matter, including a change of minister. This can often be made easier by a cabinet shuffle which involves new faces in cabinet.

In Napoleon's army each soldier was said to carry a field marshal's baton in his knapsack. Similarly, most caucus members, in their own mind, carry a cabinet minister's seal of office in their briefcase. If there can be changes in cabinet with new appointments from the caucus from time to time, this contributes to a happier caucus and, incidentally, a more disciplined one.

This process of rotation and change is not an easy one. In my time as premier, even when the intention to rotate cabinet ministers was well known and well understood, cabinet ministers who were replaced were never happy, and sometimes caucus members were also unhappy when other caucus colleagues were appointed to fill vacancies and they were not.

But with all its difficulties, some change of cabinet ministers is beneficial for internal reasons. It is also beneficial for external reasons. I do not like to think of government as part of the entertainment industry, but when most people gain their knowledge of public affairs from television, it is inevitable that some parallels will be drawn in the public mind. The television networks are well aware of this and regularly introduce "new" shows with new faces. The fact that the content of the "new" shows is remarkably similar to the "old" shows seems not to matter too much, as long as some new faces are introduced. Unfortunately, some of the same thinking seems to reflect itself in the media coverage of public affairs. Governments are frequently described as old and tired and devoid of new ideas. Most public issues do not require new ideas, but this does not dampen the pursuit by the media of novelty, seemingly for the sake of novelty alone. So premiers respond with cabinet shuffles to present old faces in new roles and by bringing new faces into cabinet. I followed the practice of having ministers make many of the important announcements on behalf of the government so that there would be many faces of the government in the media. I also hoped that if ministers announced good news, they would be accepted as appropriate spokespersons for the government when there was bad news. The premier was not, therefore, ever-present in the media.

Cabinet changes are not solely or even primarily a method of coping with the increasingly mindless, visually driven media. They are also a way to give the general public — and interest groups in particular — a new entry point into the government. Above, I used the Department of Education and the teaching profession as an example of the interplay of government and special interest groups. There are many parallel cases. An interest group will lobby as hard as possible with a particular minister. Sometimes the minister, backed by his or her cabinet colleagues, reaches a point where no further movement is possible. The appointment of a new minister to the portfolio gives the interest group another point at which to apply pressure and, occasionally, some further accommodation can be found when the personalities involved in the government-interest group interactions are changed. It is understood that there are cases where a government can never reach an accommodation with certain interest groups that are diametrically opposed to its philosophical and political agenda. Nevertheless, a government does not want interest groups — other than those which are implacably opposed to it — to conclude that the group's objectives can only be achieved by a change of government. A change of cabinet minister in a particular portfolio can sometimes prevent this conclusion from being reached.

As I have suggested, if a government has decided to change its policy with respect to a given issue, sometimes the most graceful and effective way to do this is by first changing the minister, either by a cabinet shuffle or by appointing a new minister from caucus.

Another factor to be considered is the age of cabinet ministers, and this was an issue which concerned me in the 1970s. The 1960s had glorified youth and this feeling was still strong in the 1970s. I had an extraordinary first Cabinet in 1971 and I knew it was not going to be easy or wise to replace many of them. After two elections, and facing our third, we would all be eight years older. Accordingly, as the small first Cabinet was added to, I gave some attention to the age of the new entrants. I tried, successfully, to keep the average age of the Cabinet well under 50.

A premier therefore attempts, in his appointments to cabinet and changes in these appointments, to create and renew his team so that it may perform its role in lawmaking, government administration, relating to particular and general publics, and generally setting a tone and direction for the government.

HOW CABINETS OPERATE

I turn now to the question of how the cabinet team organizes itself to carry out its functions. Different cabinets operate in different ways. Some federal cabinets have been large, have existed largely to perform their representative function (e.g. every province and some other interest groups having a cabinet minister), and to be a sounding board for the prime minister for a few major policy and political matters — in the words of Professor Donald Savoie, they are "focus groups." In this structure most of the policy issues are determined by cabinet committees or by the prime minister's staff. In the federal cabinet of Prime Minster Brian Mulroney, the Priority and Planning Committee had nineteen members — and was on many issues the effective decision-making body.

Provincial cabinets operate differently in different provinces. Some have a small inner cabinet (called by several names) that makes most of the decisions, while the full cabinet operates to deal with a few issues and to carry the decisions received from cabinet committees to the departments and agencies of government.

The Saskatchewan cabinet in the 1970s functioned primarily as a decision-making body. The key decision to be made when considering how a provincial cabinet will operate is the extent to which issues will be examined by cabinet committees before proceeding to cabinet for formal decision. I favoured a system with a small number of committees where most key issues came to the full cabinet for decision.

Committees are, of course, both necessary and desirable. In the 1970s we had a finance committee called the Treasury Board, a Cabinet Planning Committee, a committee on Crown corporations called the Crown Investments Corporation, a committee which reviewed legislation, regulations and orders-in-council, an *ad hoc* committee to deal with issues of collective bargaining, an informal political committee of cabinet, as well as some other, shorter-lived, *ad hoc* committees.

In order to arrive at the broad approaches which we wished the government to take, our cabinet had an annual planning conference, two or three days in length, which was usually held in the early fall. The structure of these conferences was not uniform. They were attended by all cabinet ministers, while frequently there were some members of the Legislative Assembly (MLAs) present and some senior public servants. On occasion we had conferences with a minimum of paper when the cabinet ministers and MLAs talked about the direction in which they wished the government to go in (say) the next ten years. This was a blend of what we would like to see the province look like in ten years' time, what we thought the public would accept or could be persuaded to accept, what our party workers wanted of us, and what was possible within the financial and administrative constraints under which we worked. In short, we engaged in elaborating visions, modified by the art of the possible. On other occasions, we drew more heavily on proposals by public servants based upon what they would wish their departments and agencies to achieve over the next (say) ten years.

This "gazing into the future" was modified by economic and financial projections which attempted to predict the trends in the provincial economy and to estimate what resources the government would have at its disposal. We considered social projections which attempted to outline the problems which were likely to arise and which would need to be dealt with by the people of Saskatchewan and their government.

Out of this process we attempted to arrive at a rough outline for government for ten years and a somewhat more detailed plan for governing over the next five years. We would assess priorities, identifying top priorities, which was usually easy, and identifying items of low priority, which was usually difficult. It was in this framework that we asked departments and agencies to prepare for legislative changes needed to achieve our objectives and to present proposals for spending in the next financial year (commencing in April). And we asked the committee of (usually five) cabinet ministers called the Treasury Board, referred to above, to review the spending proposals in the light of the broad plan arrived at.

The Treasury Board drew its staff from the Department of Finance. Its meetings to finalize the budget were usually attended by the Deputy minister of Finance and the Chief of the Planning Secretariat, who was the senior staff member to the Cabinet Planning Committee, referred to above. The Treasury Board met with departments and agencies over many weeks, considered their budget requests, and the resources that would be available, and presented a spending plan to Cabinet. The plan identified 15 or 20 key decisions. For example, it might identify a major highway expansion plan which would require an increase of half a point on the personal income tax. This plan was the subject of vigorous Cabinet debate, usually over a few days during which time two or three representatives of caucus sat in. Inevitably some important initiatives could not be proceeded with because the resources were not available. The finalized budget was reviewed with caucus and on occasion important modifications were made. This finalized budget became the basis of what was presented to the legislature and approved. Inevitably, changes had to be made during the course of the budget year. The proposals for change were presented to the Treasury Board, which attempted to deal with genuine changes in circumstances while still maintaining the budget plan arrived at by cabinet and caucus.

The many relatively smaller decisions made by the Treasury Board throughout the budgetary year were recorded in minutes which were circulated to cabinet in advance of cabinet meetings. Ministers could object to individual Treasury Board decisions and cabinet would then consider them, but any attempts to revisit battles fought during the budget finalization process were firmly discouraged.

The process of arriving at ten-year projections and five-year plans, and generally keeping government policies from becoming mere repetitions of what was done in previous years, requires a group of public servants who are charged with the responsibility of keeping the flow of policy proposals coming to cabinet and caucus. In our government this task fell to the Planning Secretariat. The Planning Secretariat would be aware of policy trends in the community, in the governing party as evidenced by resolutions at party conventions, and of the "blue sky" efforts of cabinet and caucus members when they engaged in broad policy discussions, particularly at planning conferences.

The planning group would also be aware of important background information such as likely economic trends over a period of years, demographic trends, educational attainment trends, and the like. Taking this material, they formulated proposals which were put before a committee of cabinet ministers — the Planning Committee. These were largely longer-range programs dealing with policy areas such as post-secondary education or housing. These proposals would be considered by the Cabinet Planning Committee and presented to cabinet. The usual result was that a priority decision was made which would find its way into the broad planning process and into the annual budget cycle.

Cabinet dealt with its law-making function by considering ideas for changes in law arising out of the broad planning process, from caucus, from departments and agencies and occasionally directly from a non-government group. Caucus was organized into committees, such as agriculture, health, justice and others. Proposals for changes in law were forwarded by individual MLAs to the caucus committees for consideration and recommendation to the fall caucus and cabinet. An outline proposal for a change in legislation was forwarded to Cabinet for consideration in principle. If it was approved in principle, it was referred to a department or agency to prepare a bill in legal form, with the assistance of the legislative drafting staff. Sometimes the change in the law did not require a change in legislation but rather a change in a regulation that could be made by the cabinet, pursuant to existing legislation. The process for a major change in a regulation was similar to that used for a legislative change in statute law.

When the bill (which is the name given to a proposed law in the legislative process) or a draft of the revised regulation had been drawn up in final form it was considered by the cabinet committee on legislation, regulations and orders-in-council. The job of this committee was to assure cabinet that the bills and regulations conformed to the principles already approved by cabinet and did not contain any unusual provisions or grant any extraordinary powers to the police or public servants in dealing with the public. This committee saved huge amounts of time for the full cabinet.

CROWN CORPORATIONS

The Crown corporations — SaskPower, SaskTel, SGI, SaskOil, Potash Corporation of Saskatchewan, and the rest — operated largely independently of government. They reported for some matters — particularly capital expenditures — to the Crown Investment Corporation (CIC), the board of which was made up of ministers responsible for Crown corporations. The CIC was, in effect, a cabinet committee on Crown corporations which attempted to give financial and broad policy direction to the corporations while leaving the direction and management to the individual corporations and their boards of directors and management.

A specific issue concerning the governance of Crown corporations was the approval of changes in rates charged by the utilities for the electric power, natural gas, telephone services and insurance rates under the compulsory auto insurance plan. Since these affected large numbers of the public and sometimes were politically sensitive, major rate changes were considered by the CIC and sometimes by cabinet.

The Progressive Conservative government of the 1980s set up a Public Utilities Review Commission, but abandoned the experiment after a few years. Saskatchewan has now reestablished a review board, but it is a real question whether in the Saskatchewan context a rate review board is worth the extra expense. As a number of rates became subject to competition from private competitors this matter became less of an issue.

INDUSTRIAL RELATIONS

One of the issues which concerns any cabinet is the wage settlements made between the government and its many employee groups in the government proper, provincial Crown corporations, and agencies and groups like teachers and health care workers whose salaries, wages, and benefits are paid largely from provincial government revenues. The government faces dilemmas in dealing with the remuneration of public servants, broadly defined. During the course of bargaining, the trade unions in many bargaining units regularly put forward arguments based upon amounts paid to employees doing similar work in other government bargaining units. Governments therefore try to maintain a measure of uniformity, or at least comparability, of remuneration among these groups of public servants. This promptly produces charges that the government has set guidelines, that the employer representatives at the bargaining table are mere talking heads mouthing the instructions they have received, and that there is no bargaining in good faith. There is clearly no answer to this conundrum and perhaps neither side wants an answer. Lack of precision is often the only way to reach an agreement in situations where there is no basis for agreement on the underlying principles governing bargaining, but only a need to reach a settlement. An *ad hoc* cabinet committee on collective bargaining tried to oversee this aspect of government on behalf of cabinet. It reported irregularly for information purposes and sometimes because cabinet decisions were required.

OTHER COMMITTEES

Cabinet also heard from an informal political committee which reported regularly on the current state of public acceptance of the government and its policies and on particular issues of political concern. I will later touch on the dynamics of the discussions arising ftom the reports of the political committee.

On occasion the cabinet had to deal with ongoing issues which were of major importance and which cut across several departments or agencies. These we dealt with by special committees which we sometimes staffed by creating secretariats.

An example of this is the proposal in the 1970s to acquire a major ownership position in the potash industry of the province. To manage this issue we set up an *ad hoc* cabinet committee — the Potash Committee — with a staff — the Potash Secretariat — to pull together all the threads and outline a coherent policy, design the appropriate legislation, consider the position of various groups in the community who would be affected and propose concrete action plans and contingency plans. These committees and their secretariats were dismantled when the major task was completed and ongoing follow-up work was assigned to an existing department or agency.

CABINET AT WORK

Supported by these structures, how did cabinet operate? We had a full cabinet meeting usually weekly. There was a formal agenda with almost all items supported by briefing material. During sessions of the legislature, this schedule had to be varied to provide for short, half-hour daily meetings at lunch immediately prior to a caucus meeting, which itself was immediately prior to the afternoon sitting of the legislature. We usually attempted to have a longer, half-day meeting each week to supplement the short daily cabinet meetings which tended to be focused on legislative business and legislative strategy.

Our practice was to structure the cabinet meetings to start with routine matters such as making appointments which were urgent but not a matter of great controversy, and reports of cabinet committees. The chief reports here were from the Treasury Board which made many decisions of a financial nature within the framework of the budget already approved. As noted above, these decisions were reported to cabinet in written form in detail, and cabinet ministers would have the opportunity to question the decision if they had strong grounds for doing so. The Treasury Board minutes were circulated to cabinet ministers in advance of the cabinet meeting and ministers were expected to indicate to the cabinet secretary if they proposed to raise objection to a Treasury Board decision. This process gave rise to surprisingly few problems, while keeping ministers informed of financial decisions and giving all of them some feeling that they could raise objections if the concerns were firmly and soundly held.

The committee on legislation, regulations and orders-in-council reported on its review of proposals for change. The committee soon came to understand how cabinet wished to deal with these matters and we were able to dispose of a large volume of material expeditiously. Very few booby traps went undetected.

Ordinarily we then proceeded to consider a report from the political committee of cabinet. This was a good deal less formal and was considered within the context of a general discussion on the state of our political standing with our electorate, which we called "state of the nation." I felt it was important to give all cabinet ministers an opportunity to comment on how our policies were being received by the electorate. If a government policy is being pursued in the face of some significant public opposition, it is often true that the minister or the department under fire becomes identified with the policy and tends to resent the criticism from his cabinet colleagues of how his/her department is handling the issue. A forum must be created where frank comments can be made which engender a minimum of resentment from other cabinet colleagues. A freewheeling discussion in the course of considering a report from the political committee of cabinet or a discussion on the general "state of the nation" seemed to provide this forum and keep the cabinet operating as a functioning team, collectively responsible for all major policies of the government.

It is not necessary that cabinets operate with this degree of collective knowledge and responsibility, but I considered it desirable in a small province like Saskatchewan, where there is a high level of public expectation that cabinet ministers be familiar with most areas of government policy and be able to explain the reasons why a particular policy is being pursued. The same reasoning led us to give fairly detailed explanations of government policies to caucus members so that the issues could be debated effectively in caucus and so that the decisions ultimately arrived at could be explained and defended by caucus members.

We then proceeded to reports, if any, from *ad hoc* committees such as the committee on collective bargaining or any special committee like the Potash Committee, and we then moved on to agenda items. These often included proposals for legislation, seeking Cabinet's approval in principle, or proposals for major new policies where approval was sought to put the idea into the budgeting process. If the idea was certain to cost a great deal of money, such as a childrens' dentistry program, there was no point in the Department of Health doing the very considerable groundwork necessary to include the proposal in its annual budget presentation unless cabinet and caucus considered that it was near the top of the priority list and had some chance of being included in the budget in the next year or two.

There were a large number of other items that found their way to the cabinet agenda, notwithstanding our efforts to keep the agenda manageable. The premier called the items in the order he chose. Some ministers were prone to leave the meeting for "urgent business" after items in which they had a special interest were dealt with. It was sometimes necessary to clear off many minor items and leave some important issues until later in order to ensure a good attendance for all items.

Discussion was sometimes longer than necessary in order to reach a decision. On any major issues I wanted all ministers to know why we reached our decision from among the reasonable alternatives so that they could explain and defend the decision to the public. I operated on the principle that for major issues it was often better to discuss and not decide than to decide and not discuss.

CABINET SECRETARY

A very important player in making this rather elaborate apparatus work effectively is the cabinet secretary. It is he or she who prepares the agenda, advises ministers and deputies about the type of material needed to support an agenda item, and sends back material which is insufficient. Much of the material is prepared by deputy ministers for the minister's signature and the deputies need to have someone to advise them on what they can do to assist their ministers. The secretary advises on whether a matter should go directly to cabinet or go first to one of the committees, what form the material should take, and what response the proposal receives from cabinet. The latter matter is a delicate one. The secretary will not disclose the discussion which occurred in cabinet. He or she will report the decision and may be able to offer advice to the deputy on whether the matter was clearly rejected or whether a revised proposal might have some chance of approval.

Sometimes if the secretary feels that a minister is determined to get a matter considered, the secretary will raise the matter with the premier who might have to speak to the minister. Another technique is to allow the matter to go forward and have other ministers shoot it down.

The cabinet secretary works with the staff at the Department of Finance and the Planning Secretariat to provide staff for cabinet committees and to detect and head off any emerging turf wars among the staffs at these central agencies.

In my government, the cabinet secretary had the more nebulous but crucially important task of finding out when there was unhappiness with cabinet or administrative procedures among ministers or deputies, or when there was some friction between a minister and his deputy. The secretary was often able to defuse some of these matters and on occasion consulted with the premier if they appeared serious and prolonged. The secretary's assessments of instances of personal friction became part of the mix of considerations governing shuffles of ministers and deputies.

REFLECTIONS ON HOW CABINET OPERATED

As I think back on the operation of our cabinet over eleven years, some patterns can be discerned. The 1971 cabinet was a group which had led our party to a decisive victory that year. All had been members of the legislature before 1971 except one, and he had been party president and had played a key role in the campaign. In this situation the premier is *primus inter pares*. Proper deference was paid to the premier but no more. Cabinet members had no hesitation in questioning my views or the advice I might be getting from public servants or non-elected political advisors. As time went on and others became cabinet ministers — people who were not part of the pre-1971 team and who had not been party officials — the position of some of the original cabinet ministers and particularly the premier became subtly more dominant. I was fortunate for our eleven years in office in having a core of cabinet ministers who did not feel inhibited in challenging me, or the deputy premier, Mr. Romanow, or any other minister. But a premier has to guard against the danger of an increasingly dominant role. A premier of another province with a 19-person cabinet (including himself) used to say that there were 37 votes around the table — each of the 18 ministers had one and he had 19. And in a sense it is accurate that a premier can usually see that his views prevail, but he is unwise to rely on any such power if his powers of persuasion should prove inadequate. I can recall cabinet considering a small issue on which my views would be well known. I tried to dispose of the issue quickly by having a vote. We did not do this often but rather aimed for consensus on any issue of substance. In this instance every vote was against the position I favoured. As we completed our polling around the table one minister, who frequently kidded me, followed my summing-up comment of "Well" with the comment "Oh, oh, another tie." It was not a tie. The majority won. But it did recall, if only in jest, the particular role of the premier.

CHANGES IN PROCEDURE

Over our eleven years in government there were changes. The role of government expanded. In response we developed more formal procedures, many of which I have described above. The government which we succeeded — Premier Thatcher's government — operated with a minimum of structure and, as it seemed to me, a minimum of cabinet involvement in many key decisions. We tried to have a collegial cabinet. This meant that minor decisions had to be kept off the cabinet agenda in order to leave time for the debate-and-decide model. The committee structures were developed to accomplish this.

In the early years we had fewer major policy debates since we were acting upon our 1971 election program. As this program became less topical and timely, we developed planning and budgeting procedures to allow us to do effective forward planning in ways which involved the caucus, the party and sometimes groups in the public.

In Professor Leeson's introduction to this volume he quotes Professor S.M. Lipset as suggesting that structures like cabinets make left-wing parties more conservative. Structures suggest due process, and due process inhibits rapid change. I believe it is not only structures but also the very fact of being in government that makes left-of-centre parties more conservative. The public generally resists rapid change. If a government feels it necessary to carry a substantial part of the public with it in effecting a change in policy, then change must proceed at a measured pace. The need to be somewhat cautious is increased by the fact that the public usually resists the process of change even when it can be persuaded to embrace the results.

During the 1971–82 period, our cabinet and caucus experienced the usual change in government-party relations when the CCF or NDP assumes office. The party in opposition develops policies and plans to carry out the party's vision for the province over the next 10 or 20 years. When there is an NDP government, the focus of the party is too often on what road should be paved or what nursing home should be built, on immediate and pedestrian projects, and less time is spent on the broader vision.

Between 1971–82 we attempted to keep a close liaison with the party. I attended almost all of the meetings of the party's provincial council and executive. One cabinet minister attended almost all monthly executive meetings and several attended quarterly provincial council meetings to keep abreast of sentiment in the party. In this we were honouring a longstanding tradition in the party.

Politics is the art of the possible, not only in what policies are pursued by a government but also in how they are presented to the public. In the 1970s the NDP government pursued a vigorous policy of expanding the social ownership of resource industries and utilities. Crown corporations were developed to operate in the areas of potash, oil, uranium and housing, and there were expansions in the areas of electrical power, natural gas and telephones. For the most part, however, these were presented not as part of a broad policy of greater public ownership of the means of production, distribution, and exchange — as referred to in the party's *Regina Manifesto* of 1933 — but rather as ways by which Saskatchewan people could control their own resources and utilities, in contrast to having them owned outside the province, or as a way to prevent the federal government from taking an undue share of Saskatchewan resource revenue to deal with burgeoning federal budget deficits.

The ideological framework later identified with Ronald Reagan and Margaret Thatcher, which was becoming widely accepted in the late 1970s allowed arguments based upon good business, or regional benefits, but was hostile to arguments based on left of centre ideology. This broad issue gave rise to some lively debates in cabinet. I can recall on one occasion a group of ministers argued that we should pay out a "dividend" of (say) $25 per person to all permanent residents of Saskatchewan as a Christmas bonus from the ample profits of the Potash Corporation of Saskatchewan in order to reinforce the business based arguments for public ownership. Others opposed this position, arguing that the profits should be used to reinvest in public enterprise and to strengthen social programs, to reinforce our key policy argument in favour of public enterprise. The second view prevailed. Whatever its merits in terms of ideology, it was probably a bad decision in political terms.

CABINET MINISTERS

I have spoken of cabinet as a body, as a group which develops policies for the government and acts as a board of directors overseeing not only policy formation but also financial management, lawmaking and general administration. I have emphasized the role of cabinet as a body and the collective responsibility of each minister for the decisions of the group.

Ministers have another role. Almost all ministers are assigned responsibility for directing the operations of one or more departments or agencies of government. The minister is not the general manager of his department. That is the role of the deputy minister (using Canadian nomenclature). Rather, the minister carries the proposals and concerns of the department to the cabinet table and carries back to the department the decisions made by cabinet. That is his/her internal role. The more important external role is to carry the policies and proposals of his/her department and of the government as a whole to the public. It is in order the better to accomplish this goal that it is desirable that ministers understand what decisions cabinet has made and, more particularly, why there were made. The minister's role is also to carry back to cabinet and caucus his/her assessment of the public reaction to the policies the government is pursuing and the way the government is being managed. This is a crucial duty of cabinet ministers. To do this job a cabinet minister must avoid enmeshing him/herself too deeply in the administration of the department for which he/she is responsible. Becoming heavily involved in the department will take too much of his/her time and will make him/her less objective in assessing the public's level of acceptance of the policies and administration of his/her department.

THE FUTURE

I have spoken of the operations of the cabinet in the 1970s and 1980s. In the twenty-first century many things will remain the same. But there will also be differences. The unrelenting increase in importance of the electronic media puts more and more pressure on the premier and cabinet ministers to spend more time on public communication and less on government administration. Ministers will probably spend more time consulting with citizen groups before decisions are made. There will be less time for full cabinet meetings. More matters will have to be left for decision by cabinet committees. Fewer issues will be decided by a full cabinet. This can conserve ministerial time. It raises the matter of competition among staffs to cabinet committees, but this problem can be managed. A further problem with increased reliance on cabinet committees is the best use of key cabinet ministers. They can be present if the important decisions are made in cabinet. It is more difficult to use these ministers most effectively if the important decisions are made in three or four cabinet committees. The tendency will be for only a few public servants to bridge the centres of decision making. This adds to the focus which concentrates powers around the offices of the premier and the minister of finance. This tendency should be resisted. It makes poorer use of ministerial talent and puts too much pressure on the premier and his office. This may be yet another reflection of the belief that government consists largely of "leadership" and only secondarily of management. Governments work best when each role is accorded its appropriate place.

Saskatchewan's Public Service: Converging to the Norm?

Ken Rasmussen

It is no exaggeration to suggest that over the past fifty-five years the public service in Saskatchewan has been a key institution in the province's quest to become a much more capable and competent policy actor. It has served both as an incubator of ideas and a breeding ground for talent. The Saskatchewan public service has been described as a public policy innovator gaining a strong national reputation based on its development or early adoption of many key public policies in the 1960s and 1970s.[1] The public service was also the source of talent for many of the commercial Crown corporations which defined Saskatchewan's aggressive, self-assured stance in the 1970s.[2] The reputation of the public service was further enhanced by the national influence of the so-called "Saskatchewan Mafia," the group of talented public servants lead by Al Johnson and Tommy Shoyama who left Saskatchewan for Ottawa in the 1960s and brought with them their progressive ideas and planning skills which were used in the development some of Canada's most innovative social policies.[3]

Many explanations have been offered as to why the Saskatchewan public service has had such an impact within the province and influenced national debates and policies. Prominent among these explanations is the history of self-sufficiency that characterized the earlier pioneer culture, which required successive governments to come up with made-in-Saskatchewan solutions to pressing problems.[4] Also high on the list was the galvanizing experience of the Depression, which created strong opposition to the supremacy of markets and a recognition of the social value of good, efficient and dedicated public service. Equally valid in explaining the prominence of the public service was the reality of a sparse, rural population which

1. Dale Poel, "The Diffusion of Legislation Among Canadian Provinces: A Statistical Analysis," *Canadian Journal of Political Science* 9, no. 4 (December 1976): 605–26; Eleanor D. Glor (ed.), *Policy Innovation in the Saskatchewan Public Sector, 1971–82* (Toronto: Captus Press, 1997); Albert Wesley Johnson, "Biography of a Government: Policy Formation in Saskatchewan, 1944–61" (PhD dissertation, Harvard University, 1963).
2. John Richards and Larry Pratt, *Prairie Capitalism: Power and Influence in the New West* (Toronto: McClelland and Stewart, 1979), 139–42.
3. Rodney Haddow, *Poverty Reform in Canada, 1958–1978: State and Class Influences on Policy Making* (Montreal/Kingston: McGill-Queen's University Press 1993); P.E. Bryden, *Planners and Politicians: Liberal Politics and Social Policy, 1957–1968* (Montreal/Kingston: McGill-Queen's University Press, 1997).
4. John Archer, *Saskatchewan: A History* (Saskatoon: Western Producer Prairie Books, 1980).

required state-led action to ensure that basic infrastructure was available including roads, telephones, rural electricity and rural natural gas. Other explanations have focused on the managerial or technocratic brand of social democracy endorsed by the CCF and later NDP governments in Saskatchewan which have dominated electoral politics in the post-war era. This tradition of "Fabian" technocracy was combined with a history of one-party dominance and resulted in long periods of stable relations between the government and the bureaucracy when competence could replace partisan responsiveness as the key to success. Finally, there was a strong bureaucratic commitment to accountable and rational decision making associated with governments that tended to hold office for extended periods of time.[5]

Whatever the reasons that lay beneath this legacy there recently appears to be a decline in the reputation of the public service, which has seen its image tarnished alongside growing public dissatisfaction with political institutions and political elites. The reasons for such a decline in the influence and prominence of the public service in Saskatchewan would include general environmental factors such as mounting debts and deficits, budget cuts, staff reductions and reduced opportunities for innovation, declining levels of service to citizens, strikes in the unionized parts of the public service, tensions between senior civil servants and ministers, better opportunities and salaries in the private sector, increasing politicization of the senior public service, and an aging cohort of middle managers with little opportunity for promotion. All of these factors have impaired the functioning of the public service, reduced its influence, limited its effectiveness and reduced its prestige as an institution in Saskatchewan political life.

The start of this slow decline in the influence and stature of the public service can be traced back to the political decision in the 1980s to diminish the role of the public service in policy formation and try and transform it into a managerial organization based upon the changed perception of the role of government associated with new-right ideology.[6] The ideas that influenced the changes in structure and orientation of the public service during the 1980s were drawn from the administrative reform efforts of other Anglo-American democracies and the federal government, all of whom were equally enthralled with "neo-conservatism."[7] There was a strong belief that the public sector could and should be managed in a more "business-like" fashion in the hope that managerial values would replace what were perceived by the new government in 1982 as those of a stolid, entrenched and typically underperforming career public service. To achieve this end there was an emphasis on a number of reforms associated with what has come to be called the New Public Management, including explicit standards and measures of performance, greater competition in the public sector, an emphasis on output controls, and, of course, contracting-out and privatization.[8] This was a reversal of traditional administrative reform assumptions in Saskatchewan which were based on the belief that the

5. Allan Blakeney and Sandford Borins, *Political Management in Canada* (Toronto: McGraw-Hill Ryerson, 1992), 146–59; Robert I. McLaren, "Serving Saskatchewan: A Study of the Saskatchewan Public Service" (unpublished manuscript, 1991).

6. James Pitsula and Ken Rasmussen, *Privatizing a Province: The New Right in Saskatchewan* (Vancouver: New Star Books, 1991)

7. Donald. J. Savoie, *Thatcher, Reagan and Mulroney: In Search of a New Bureaucracy* (Toronto: University of Toronto Press, 1994); Patricia W. Ingraham and B. Guy Peters, "The Conundrum of Reform: A Comparative Analysis," *Review of Public Personnel Administration* 8 (Summer 1988): 3–16.

8. Christopher Hood, "A Public Management for All Seasons?," *Public Administration* 69 (Fall 1991): 4–5.

biggest inhibition in the path of good public administration was meddling by politicians. Whereas in the past reformers tried to curtail the ability of politicians to interfere with the ability of competent and professional public servants to carry out their duties in an efficient and impartial manner, during the 1980s this was turned on its head. More political control was seen as a solution to social and economic problems, not more neutral, professional public administration. Thus an attempt was made to reduce the policy influence of permanent officials while emphasizing a more managerial orientation. Cabinet steered and the public service rowed. Overall, the argument during the 1980s was that the provincial state in Saskatchewan was badly managed and its performance could only be improved through a firm hand from the political leadership while creating a more managerial public service.

With the defeat of the Devine Tories in 1991 and the coming to power of the NDP there was an expectation of something of a restoration to the old pattern. Indeed the NDP were clearly wary of the techniques and language associated with the New Public Management (NPM) movement, which was always framed in the language of the market, betraying its outright hostility to government solutions in any form. For the most part the NDP government has chosen to emphasize more traditional values of accountable government, constitutional bureaucracy and transparent processes while downplaying any initiatives aimed at modernizing the public service such as those that were taking place in both Manitoba and Alberta.[9] The NDP did not engage in the inflamed rhetoric of administrative reform, and avoided language which portrayed the bureaucracy as wasteful, incompetent, out of control and unresponsive to political control. But while avoiding a reform agenda the NDP government has not attempted to rely on the public service as a major institution of social and economic innovation as was the case in the past. As a result the public service in Saskatchewan has entered a period of stasis in which it has neither become a policy innovator working closely with a government with clearly articulated goals, nor has it become a leader in the development of new techniques and practices of public management.

Contributing to this sense of stagnation is the fact that the public service in Saskatchewan over the past two decades has endured the all-too-common difficulties of delayering, downsizing, and decentralization associated with deficit management and policy retrenchment. This has resulted in the Saskatchewan public service losing somewhere in the vicinity of 1,000 positions — most through attrition and early retirements — to the point that it currently employees approximately 11,000 individuals. These developments have unavoidably resulted in diminished career opportunities, insecurity, low morale, and a general alteration of the terms and conditions of employment, the so-called moral contract, between employer and employee similar to that of other jurisdictions. These concerns are felt most acutely in the out-of-scope, mid-manager categories, where senior managers have been given a good deal of discretion in determining which of their middle rank will stay and which will go. Thus the Saskatchewan public service may not be what it once was, nor has it become something new. Rather it remains a public service that co-operates with government in devising and implementing its agenda, but it has been

9. Christopher J. Bruce, Ronald D. Kneebone and Kenneth J. McKenzie (eds.), *A Government Reinvented: A Study of Alberta's Deficit Elimination Program* (Toronto: Oxford University Press, 1997); Ken Rasmussen, "The Manitoba Civil Service: A Quiet Tradition in Transition," in Evert Linquist (ed.), *The Career Public Service in Canada* (Toronto: IPAC Monograph, forthcoming).

working with a government preoccupied with deficit reduction, agricultural crisis, partisan realignment and not reform of the public service.

The story of the public service over the past two decades is one of neglect and ossification. Neither the Tories nor the NDP have been interested in modernizing the public service. Nor is their any evidence that the present government will devote the time and energy to the reform of the public service that this would require. In this regard the public service in Saskatchewan will suffer from the same sorts of benign neglect seen in many other provinces, making a restoration of the public service to its former position of influence in the province unlikely and even unwelcome by most political elites in the province. What this chapter will describe is a slow process by which the Saskatchewan public service has converged toward the pattern of other provincial public services. This is not an entirely unexpected or unwelcome phenomenon, as the early periods of development were based on a variety of unique circumstances which were not instiutionalized by various leaders within the public service. Equally it is unlikely that the public service in Saskatchewan will ever return to its previous place of leadership in policy debates, given the more open and entrenched environment that decision making operates in. Ironically, one of the reasons for this decline in the role of the public service is that its past successes in initiating and developing policies have meant that the government of Saskatchewan now finds itself struggling to maintain existing commitments and is unable to occupy any new policy space.[10]

1982–1991: THE RISE OF MANAGERIALISM AND THE DECLINE OF POLICY INFLUENCE

The movement towards a more managerial orientation of the Saskatchewan public service came initially from the common recognition across the country that governments could not continue to grow forever.[11] The impact of this realization began to be felt in the career public service by the mid-1980s, when employment levelled off and even declined in terms of the number of permanent employees. Beginning at this time, it was common for positions within the public service to go deliberately unfilled, or to be filled with non-permanent personnel. Public servants were coming to recognize the fact that they were not going to have a "career" in the sense of moving smoothly up the ranks in an ever-expanding department.

While these "natural pressures" limited the growth of the public service in Saskatchewan during the 1980s, the biggest push in the direction of managerialism and subsequent decline in the role of the public service came from the distrust of professional public service expressed by the Progressive Conservative government of Grant Devine, which defeated the NDP in 1982. This attitude had two sources, one partisan the other ideological. It began with suspicions, not altogether unfounded, that the public service had grown too close to the previous NDP government. There was a feeling within the Devine government that the public service of Saskatchewan drifted from the classical assumption that it was to be a neutral or impartial instrument willing to serve any political party that formed a government. Rather, the

10. Ken Rasmussen, "Saskatchewan: From Entrepreneurial State to Embedded State," in Michael Howlet and Keith Brownsey (eds.), *The Provincial State in Canada* (Toronto: Broadview, 2001), 241–76.

11. David K. Foot et al., "The Growth and Distribution of Federal, Provincial and Local Government Employment in Canada," in David K. Foot (ed.), *Public Employment and Compensation in Canada: Myths and Realities* (Montreal: Institute for Research on Public Policy, 1978).

Tories saw the Saskatchewan public service as nest of NDP partisans, central planners and assorted party hangers-on, all eager to subvert the Reagan/Thatcher style neo-conservative revolution that the PC party was planning to implement.

This partisan hostility was accompanied by a strong anti-statist stance clearly evident in the senior ranks of the PC party. It is easy to argue that, more than any other government in Canada, Grant Devine's Tory party was influenced by the neo-conservatism of Ronald Reagan and Margaret Thatcher and the negative impression of government and the public service that went along with it.[12] This ideological position contained an overt hostility towards such things as public sector unions and the idea of the positive state, and naturally progressed to a lack of regard for the formal institutions of parliamentary government, including the public service.[13]

The earliest manifestation of these two strands of thought came in one of the largest purges of the public service in Saskatchewan history, which disregarded the whole notion that the civil service is and should be a neutral institution.[14] While it may be common for a new government to feel that the public service has grown too cosy to a party that has governed for an extended period of time, the level of the purge was unprecedented in Saskatchewan political history, although it should be noted that there was clearly a close connection between the bureaucracy and the government as symbolized by the fact that Allan Blakeney and other cabinet ministers had themselves been public servants. Adding to the PC government's suspicions were an inordinate number of order-in-council appointments which reached a peak at the end of the Blakeney era of some 1,200; there are less than 200 today.[15] Nevertheless, upon coming to office the government undertook a heavy-handed purge of the public service "which went well beyond the normal trend in past Saskatchewan experience."[16] Even more damning in the eyes of critics was the fact that since "these firings began almost the moment the Conservatives were elected, it is clear that no effort was made to see if the employees affected were prepared and able to work in a professional, impartial manner, and therefore effectively serve the new government."[17]

Something similar happened in 1964, when 20 years of CCF government came to an end and Ross Thatcher's Liberal party engaged in a wholesale purge and general attack on the notion of public administration.[18] Even the CCF, who initially tried to work with the public service and regarded professional public administration as essential, eventually found it necessary to place key people in the bureaucracy to get the kind of policy advice they wanted.[19] This kind of patronage involved

12. Pitsula and Rasmussen, *Privatizing a Province*, 6–21.

13. Merilee Rasmussen, "The Decline of Parliamentary Democracy in Saskatchewan" (Master's thesis, University of Regina, 1994).

14. Hans Michelmann and Jeffrey S. Steeves, "The 1982 Transition in Power in Saskatchewan: The Progressive Conservatives and the Public Service," *Canadian Public Administration* 28 (Winter 1995): 3.

15. Ken Norman, "Saskatchewan," in William A.W. Neilson (ed.), *Getting the Pink Slip: Severance and Firing in the Senior Public Service* (n.p.: Institute of Public Administration Monograph, No. 12, n.d.).

16. Michelmann and Steeves, "The 1982 Transition," 16.

17. Michael Cassidy, "Political Rights for Public Servants: A Federal Perspective (1)," *Canadian Public Administration* 28 (Winter 1986): 659.

18. Robert McLaren, *The Saskatchewan Practice of Public Administration in Historical Perspective* (Lewiston: The Edwin Mellen Press, 1998); I. McLeod and T.H. McLeod, *Tommy Douglas: The Road to Jerusalem* (Edmonton: Hurtig Publishers, 1987), 174.

19. Seymour Martin Lipset, *Agrarian Socialism: The Cooperative Commonwealth Federation in Saskatchewan* (Garden City, NY: Doubleday and Company, 1968), chapter 12.

in filling key senior positions is generally accepted practice in most provincial public services, but until the arrival of the Tories, it was accepted that these partisan appointments and dismissals would be confined to the most senior levels of the public service.

Despite the negative views of the public sector and the initial purge of "reds" in the bureaucracy, there was not a serious decline in the number of public servants in the province. If anything, the Devine government increased their numbers by creating a whole new layer of special assistants, personal assistants, communications advisors and press secretaries, who were there to counter the power of the public service which the government felt it could not trust. The Tories also increased the size of the cabinet — making it the largest in Saskatchewan history with 25 members — and they increased the number of departments, which saw the emergence of a Department of Small Business and Tourism, a Department of Economic Development and Trade, and a Department of Advanced Education and Manpower. The government did favour a policy of decentralization which resulted in some agencies moving to Moose Jaw, Swift Current, Melville and Saskatoon, which the government touted as something that would bring services closer to customers and economic prosperity to rural Saskatchewan. This policy also had the result of increasing the suspicions and concerns of public servants, few of whom had any desire to relocate to rural Saskatchewan.

More fundamental changes to the structure of the public service came after the 1986 election which saw the PC government returned to office with a substantially reduced majority. Quickly the government introduced *The Government Organization Act* (Bill 5) giving the cabinet the power to create and terminate departments without the approval or scrutiny of the legislature. Previously it was the practise that all government reorganizations would emerge from budget initiatives presented in the legislature and not simply through a cabinet minister's press release. The concern in the career public service was that this could increase the power of the cabinet at the expense of the legislature, and in the hands of a government hostile to the public service this was regarded as more than a potential threat. It allowed the cabinet to determine the objectives and purposes of departments or to disestablish departments, all of which gave the cabinet law-making power that had traditionally been the prerogative of the legislature. The immediate result was a reorganization of departments, largely through amalgamation and the creation of "super departments." An example was the creation of the Department of Human Resources, Labour and Employment in 1988, which amalgamated a number of social service- and employment-related departments in an effort to implement the government's policy agenda of social service and welfare reform.

An even more direct hit occurred to the public service in the first budget after the 1986 election which saw, for the first time, the government eliminate positions from the public service — in this case 2,000 positions were to be cut.[20] Most of this took place through early retirement and the deletion of permanent positions which were not occupied. The government came up with no plans for dealing with the difficulties associated with these redundancies in the manner of Manitoba and Alberta, both of which developed elaborate processes for dealing with mass dislocations. This decision resulted in all the difficulties associated with a lack of growth,

20. Government of Saskatchewan, *Budget Address* (Department of Finance, June 1987), 4.

such as hiring freezes, insecurity and declining morale. While some downsizing had begun as early as 1984, it was not until 1987 that the public service distinctly levelled off. Paralleling this shedding of personnel were some major initiatives in the area of privatization and contracting out, which had a substantial impact on the size of a number of government departments.

Privatization and contracting out directly affected the size of the career public service through the transfer of departmental activities such as running provincial parks, highway maintenance, construction, laboratory services and crop insurance to the private sector. Under the influence of British privatization guru Madsen Pirie, the government also "hived off" a number of activities that were formerly part of the regular public service and placed them into a series of five new "departmental" Crown corporations. These included the Advanced Technology Training Centre, the New Careers Corporation, the Property Management Corporation, the Saskatchewan Water Corporation and the Souris Basin Development Authority. These organizations were free from the confines of the *Public Service Act*, and were expected to operate in a manner that was more managerial, businesslike, and efficient, although within the confines of a policy framework supplied by superior institutions.

Privatization, contracting-out and hiving-off are common practises associated with the rise of new public management which attempts to separate policy development from policy implementation as much as possible. Related to this desire for increased efficiency was an emphasis on staff development, which concentrated on management skills not policy analysis. In the late 1980s the seminars organized by the Public Service Commission for senior managers and deputy ministers had titles such as "Managing Transition: The Challenge of Change," "Empowering Employees — Energy on Tap," "Managerial Moxie," "A Challenge for Creative Management — Managing in Times of Constraint." On top of this, mission and vision statements began to proliferate, all with the aim of having public servants manage in a less rule-oriented manner and with more of a focus on results. Perhaps the most explicit example of the influence of managerialism was the establishment of a performance pay policy in the 1985–86 fiscal year, which the government felt would "strengthen and support the development of an open participative management style and provide the link between an individual's performance and merit based adjustments."[21] The notion of explicit standards and measure of performance which are used to establish rates of pay have long been associated with the new public management, but their actual effectiveness in improving managerial behaviour is in some doubt.[22]

This new attitude towards both the principles of parliamentary government and the values and role of public service had a major impact on the relationship between the government and the public sector unions. The two were early and eager combatants from the beginning of the government's tenure in office. Issues such as privatization and contracting out, and persistent rumours that the government was engaged in wholesale patronage fuelled this mistrust. The government also imposed stringent guidelines on public service pay, passed draconian back-to-work legislation,

21. Public Service Commission, *Annual Report, 1985–86*, 13.

22. Patricia W. Ingraham, "Of Pigs in Pokes and Policy Diffusion: Another Look at Pay-for-Performance," *Public Administration Review* 53 (July/August 1993): 348–56; Jone L. Pearce et al., "Managerial Compensation Based on Organizational Performance: A Time Series Analysis of the Effects of Merit Pay," *Academy of Management Jorunal* 28 (June 1985): 261–78.

was the first government in Canada to use the "notwithstanding clause" in the Charter of Rights and Freedoms to deny public servants recourse to the courts, and altered labour legislation to favour employers, including public sector employers.[23] Senior officials fared little better when the government arbitrarily froze wages in 1984 announcing "that the salary adjustment for 2,300 public service managers, effective April 1, 1984 was to be 0%."[24]

However, the final act that capped nearly a decade of bad relations between the public service and the government occurred just before the 1991 election — the government's release of a plan called "Fair Share Saskatchewan." The purpose of this was to transfer large numbers of public servants to communities in rural Saskatchewan, which the *Globe and Mail* described as "a sort of Maoist pork-barrel scheme forcing white-collar mandarins to work in the countryside." No department was unaffected, with 1,371 employees being targeted for relocation. This was a wildly unpopular policy amongst all public servants and had very little appeal in small-town Saskatchewan, which viewed it as a gross attempt at buying their votes. This policy, which was announced on the eve of the 1991 election, went down to defeat with the government in no small measure because of the strong mobilization of the Saskatchewan Government Employees Union (SGEU) against this policy, which appeared to have no apparent rationale other than political opportunism.

One of the difficulties with the public sector reforms initiated in the 1980s was that the government was attempting to create a new administrative culture in the public sector without recognizing the impact that other policies, such as downsizing, salary freezes, and relocation were having on the public service. Rather than producing more entrepreneurial, creative behaviour, downsizing created just the opposite: defensive, cautious, anxious and pro-inertia behaviour. The downsizing was coupled with a desire on the part of the political leadership to improve the managerial capacity of public servants, while at the same time attenuating their policy advisory roles.[25] Further, the government moved decisively away from concerns about accountability and responsibility towards a business management emphasis on productivity, performance and service to clients. Efficiency was valued over accountability, and responsiveness over due process.[26]

1991–2000: THE REVIVAL THAT NEVER CAME

There was no question that the vast majority of public servants greeted with relief the defeat of the Devine government and with it, "Fair Share Saskatchewan." Roy Romanow summed up the feelings of many public servants when, shortly after the election, he noted that the "previous administration often gave the impression that it looked upon the public service as the enemy, rather than a vital partner."[27]

23. Ian McCuaig, Bob Sass and Mark Stobbe, "Labour Pains: The Birth of a New Industrial Relations Order in Saskatchewan," in Lesley Biggs and Mark Stobbe (eds.), *Devine Rule in Saskatchewan* (Saskatoon: Fifth House Press, 1991), 169–76; Leo Panitch and Donald Swartz, *The Assault on Trade Union Freedoms: From Wage Controls to Social Contract* (Toronto: Garamond Press, 1993), 110.

24. Government of Saskatchewan, *Budget Address* (Department of Finance, March 1984), 11.

25. B. Guy Peters and Donald J. Savoie, "Civil Service Reform: Misdiagnosing the Patient," *Public Administration Review* 54 (September/October 1994): 418–25.

26. Andrew Gray and Bill Jenkins, "From Public Administration to Public Management: Reassessing a Revolution," *Public Administration* 73 (Spring 1995): 87.

27. Roy Romanow, "Address to the Institute of Public Administration of Canada" (February 24, 1992), 1.

Expectations were high that the NDP government would have a different attitude towards the public service, would restore some stability to the career public service, and would even return the province to its "normal pattern" of state-led development. While the partisan pressures on the public service eased, the reality of the budget crisis meant that downsizing, career plateauing, and layoffs would remain the order of the day and the expectations of public servants were not to be fulfilled. The impression of senior and mid-level bureaucrats in the first couple of years of the Romanow government was that the public service in Saskatchewan had indeed become more professional, and that policy and process advice was welcome.[28] Yet there has been little evidence that the Romanow government really wanted to bring about any major structural transformations to the public service or wanted to innovate in the area of public management like Tony Blair and other social democratic leaders.

One of the areas the new government was very sensitive to was the fear of patronage and a wholesale purge of the public service. The government went slowly in dealing with the public service, and indeed left many key officials in place, including the Deputy Minister of Finance, all of whom proved capable of meeting the expectations of the new government. The government, of course, did dismiss some high profile appointees of the previous government, and even passed special legislation to help them in this task. The *Crown Employment Contracts Act* was passed within days of the first NDP sitting in December 1991. The rationale offered at this time was that

> public concerns were greatly intensified several weeks ago when it became apparent that the previous administration had entered into a number of secret employment contracts with certain employees and that these contracts provided unusually generous provisions in the event of voluntary resignation or involuntary dismissal.[29]

This decisive action to rid the bureaucracy of obvious Tory supporters was part of the NDP's plan to take control of the public service. Yet by passing this legislation they managed to accomplish this task in such a way as to not arouse public sympathy for those displaced or cause undue fear in the career public service. The exact wording of this Act stated that it did not apply to Crown employment contracts in which the employees were covered by a collective agreement entered by a Crown employer and a certified trade union, nor did it apply to anyone who was entitled to an appeal procedure provided by section 37 of the *Public Service Act*, which included all permanent members of the classified public service. Thus the government made it clear that it was targeting a small number of individuals and wanted the classified and unionized parts of the public service not to be concerned. If anything, many NDP members were openly critical of the government for not going far enough in purging the previous patronage appointments which were said to extend deep into the bureaucracy. But the minister responsible for the PSC maintained that the government sincerely wanted "to remove politics from hiring and firing within the public service of the province."[30]

28. The fact that it was an NDP government does not really explain these developments, especially in comparison with developments in Ontario at this same time. See Evert A. Lindquist and Graham White, "Streams, Springs and Stones: Ontario Public Service Reform in the 1980s and 1990s," *Canadian Public Administration* 37 (Summer 1994): 278.

29. Saskatchewan, Legislative Assembly, *Debates*, December 13, 1991, p. 354.

30. Ibid., April 27, 1994, p. 1889.

None of this implies that the current NDP government has not engaged in the usual patronage in areas such as press secretaries, executive assistants, as well as the more senior positions in the Crown corporations and the public service. The government has done this, but none of its actions fall outside the norms for provincial governments in Canada, which all reserve a number of order-in-council appointments for trusted advisors. Patronage, in the form of placing key individuals within strategic positions in the bureaucracy is clearly a part of every government's plans to gain control of the bureaucracy. But one important reason that it did not go very far with the NDP is that it does not have the same fears of a hostile bureaucracy that the previous government did. The NDP came to power with numerous former cabinet ministers and a deep understanding of bureaucratic processes. Indeed, the bureaucracy has found that its status as a source of policy advice has been partially restored and the government is receptive to its expertise and its ability to ensure that public controversy and bad decisions are avoided. The problem from the point of creative policy outcomes is more related to a lack of strong goals and direction coming from Cabinet as opposed to a lack of capacity or talent in the public service.

Despite a recognition of the need for a talented, neutral bureaucracy, the NDP government was mostly preoccupied with the problem of restoring the public trust that had been lost over the previous decade. The NDP government sought to restore public trust in the governmental process by increasing the accountability of both elected officials and the public service. They began by restoring the transparency of government decision making, increased the oversight role of independent watchdogs like the Auditor General, increased the duties and powers of legislative committees, and opened the proceedings of some legislative committees to public scrutiny. Many of the features of this new legislation were designed to bring more power, not exclusively to cabinet, but to the institutions of responsible government. Amendments occurred to a host of documents such as the *Tabling of Documents Act*, which were seen as being

> imperative to restore public trust and confidence in the institutions of democratic government in Saskatchewan. If safeguards are in place and the rules well understood the worst abuses of the political process evident in recent years will be avoided.[31]

By 1993 the government had passed a number of new or revised statutes such as the *Member's Conflict of Interest Act*, the *Crown Corporations Act*, and a new *Financial Administration Act* to name some of the most prominent. Much of this legislation emerged directly from the recommendations of the Financial Management Review Commission, which the government established immediately after the 1991 election, and which reported in February 1992. This Commission listed a number of sound recommendations for the improvement of public administration, most of which the government quickly acted upon[32]: the provincial auditor's oversight of the powerful Crown corporations sector was increased; Crown agency revenues were directed to general government revenues; one easy-to-read financial statement for all government spending and revenues was established; management control over government operations was tightened; limits to the amount of funds that could be committed to any project without legislative approval were established; the Crown

31. Ibid., December 11, 1991, p. 238.
32. Saskatchewan, "Financial Management Review Commission: A Progress Report" (November 10, 1992).

Investments Corporation was established as a cabinet committee; improved tendering and awarding of contract policies were instituted, and so on. The cumulative effect of these numerous reforms has been to enhance public accountability. Yet the hoped-for increase in public esteem for politicians and, by proxy, the public service, has yet to materialize. The focus on accountability might also reflect a return to the bureaucratic red tape and the negative stereotypes of the past, but it is also possible to see it as a much needed addition to the rampant managerialism of the 1980s. These procedures must be in place and observed and represent an important feature of what is essentially a model of "political" managerialism.

In addition, the NDP tried to reform the democratic institutions of the province and restructured the legislature, reducing the number of seats from 66 to 58. Reductions also came in the perks of cabinet ministers, deputy ministers and the presidents of Crown corporations. Reforms to the pension plans of MLAs were addressed by an citizens' panel, ending some of the provisions which had outraged citizens in other provinces. The government saw the need to act in both symbolic and substantive ways to restore public faith in government. None of this implies that the government has done all it could and should. For instance, public servants are still required to make presentations to the NDP caucus, as well as writing ministers speeches and giving them notes for debate in committee of the whole. And as long as politicians remain untrustworthy in the eyes of many citizens, it is unlikely that they will regard the public service as being possessed of more virtue and honour.

More recently, the government's concern for accountability turned up in the platform of the NDP in the 1999 election. They have promised to push forward in the direction of further accountability measures. In particular they are going to require government departments to publish annual plans with performance objectives and monitor the results and publicly report on how well they did. This kind of performance management regime is increasing common in all provincial governments, and while Saskatchewan is one of the late adopters of these measures, there is some sense that public management in the province is coming of age, allowing for both new management techniques to complement the more tradition role of providing policy advice. This is somewhat at odds with developments in other provinces in which the public service is encouraged to be an efficient manager of programs, and all policy making is centralized in increasingly large units attached to the premiers office.

THE UNIONS AND COLLECTIVE BARGAINING IN THE 1990S

One aspect of the relationship between the public service and the government that has been absent in Saskatchewan over the past decade has been the relentless bureaucracy bashing that was popular in other provinces. Saskatchewan has so far avoided the worst confrontations between governments and their own employees witnessed in other provinces. It is fair to say that relations between the government and it own employees represented by the Saskatchewan Government Employees Union (SGEU), while not always cordial, have not deteriorated as far as they have in other jurisdictions. The reasons may have something to do with the fact that Saskatchewan is the only province in Canada to have no special collective bargaining legislation for its own employees, having allowed them to organise under the *Trade Union Act* since 1944. One result is that the government is required to negotiate agreements through the process of free collective bargaining, and has never considered any special "social contract" legislation to deal with union difficulties.

The government reached its budget targets with relatively modest layoffs. Nor did the government require any across-the-board wage decreases or *de facto* wage cuts in the form of compulsory days off without pay as seen in other provinces.

This is not to say that the relations between the government and its unionized employees have been entirely satisfactory over the past decade. There was a series of rotating strikes by the SGEU prior to the signing of a collective agreement in 1992, and there has been constant pressure for pay equity legislation and employment equity, both of which have been slow to develop in Saskatchewan and have resulted in angry public demonstrations from the province's social justice organizations as well as unions. Indeed, Saskatchewan remains the only Canadian province without a comprehensive pay equity legislation. Yet the government has attempted to develop a new, positive and progressive relationship with public service unions and to a great extent, according to both the government and union leadership, this has indeed been achieved. It seems reasonably safe to suggest that Saskatchewan has one of the best, most productive relationships with its public sector unions in the country. This stems directly from the fact that the SGEU is regarded by the government as a legitimate representative of its employees and is a stakeholder whose input and contribution are necessary for the development and efficient operations of the public service.

This attitude has resulted in Saskatchewan moving in a new direction with regards to employer/union relations. An example is the recent creation of union-management committees (UMCs) in each department. Members of the UMCs have received training, ensuring an "interest-based" approach to problem solving. The government sees this approach as allowing joint ownership of most workplace issues and as a tool which provides an alternative to the adversarial, confrontational approach to labour relations that has characterized previous encounters between the government and the SGEU. The approach of UMCs involves seeing initial proposals as one answer to a problem identified by one of the parties, clearly defining the underlying problem, joint searching for alternative solutions to the problem, and determining the solution that satisfies the greatest number of interests of both sides.

The Public Service Commission has also helped improve the relationship with the SGEU by restoring the transparency and union involvement in the hiring process. That is to say, there is a policy in which the Public Service Commission advertises all openings. This occurs once a week, and the results of the internal competitions are made public. It is the view of the government that "all competitions are open competitions for Public Service Commission appointments."[33] The government is also happy that the number of order-in-council appointments has come down to 200, from 360 under the previous government.[34] The NDP also put student hiring during the summer on a fair, competitive basis, using a lottery system to distribute these positions. All of this aids in creating a process that is seen as open and fair by all participants.

Active involvement of the union is also found in the hiring process for all in-scope positions. The union's role used to be limited to that of silent observer, and any problems that unions observed could only be resolved through the regular grievance process. Now the union is more directly involved in a collaborative hiring process. Staffing panels, which are chaired by a PSC employee, include a representative from

32. Saskatchewan, Legislative Assembly, *Debates*, April 27, 1994, p. 1889.
34. Ibid., February 12, 1994, p. 525.

unions and management, with the union representative usually coming from the department where the open position is located. This process is viewed positively by the government because it encourages input from the union and provides a benefit to the employer by helping ensure that the correct candidate is put in place. Some have seen an additional value in these participative management/union structures, given the increased vulnerability of both management and employee groups by the machinations of elected officials in executive and legislative bodies.[35]

The Saskatchewan *Civil Service Act* also extends courtesies to the SGEU not seen in other jurisdictions. For instance, while all civil service acts allow the commission to make regulations, only in Saskatchewan does the act note that:

> Before submitting regulations to the Lieutenant-Governor in Council the commission may extend to any trade union representing employee in the public service an opportunity to peruse and examine the proposed regulations for the purpose of making any recommendation for changing therein.

This type of consideration is valuable and an important part of the whole process, and very much in line with the most progressive thinking regarding the issue of employee/employer relations.

If any problem exists with this structure it is the fact that it is a highly centralized apparatus which concentrates an excessive amount of decision-making authority in Regina. Both the Public Service Commission and the SGEU deal frequently over very minor details, which could be much more sensibly handled at the departmental and branch level. This, however, is a problem that emerges from the fact that the Saskatchewan Public Service is still a unified public service and tends to encourage promotion and appointment across departments, which is better handled through a centralized structure.

CONCLUSION: THE END OF A TRADITION IN SASKATCHEWAN?

Like other jurisdictions, Saskatchewan is slowly coming to accept the notion that modernization of public management practices might not be incompatible with traditional values such as accountability and transparency. As such it is currently in the process of rewriting the *Public Service Act* with the hope of decentralizing more personnel decision making to departments. The government itself is committed to greater public consultation, community-based decisions, partnerships, and the devolution of government programs and services to subsidiary governments. In addition it is developing a strong commitment to performance management and accountability through a process of business planning which is currently being pilot-tested in seven departments. What characterizes these modest reform initiatives is an interest in invigorating some of the traditional values and processes of public management, as opposed to completely abandoning the old model and reinventing the entire career public service along a entirely new standard. Thus the kinds of radical developments that have occurred in New Zealand, Britain and other Anglo-American democracies are not to be found in Saskatchewan.[36] Instead

---

35. Richarad C. Kearney and Steven W. Hayes, "Labour-Management Relations and Participative Decision Making: Toward a New Paradigim," *Public Administration Review* 54 (January/February 1994): 49.

36. R.C. Mascarenhas, "Building an Enterprise Culture in the Public Sector: Reform of the Public Sector in Australia, Britain, and New Zealand," *Public Administration Review* 53 (July/August 1993): 319–28; Andrew Flynn, Andrew Grey and William I. Jenkins, "Taking the Next Steps: The Changing Management of Government," *Parliamentary Affairs* 43 (April 1990): 159–78.

there is a recognition that public servants, despite all the talk about empowering, entrepreneurship and so forth, work in an environment which is bound by rules established by statutes, subject to the control of ministers, legislative bodies and external watchdog agencies, and increasingly citizens and interest groups. In such an environment it is certainly helpful to view the public service as a part of the structure of governance which must be made accountable to legitimate authority.[37] While this involves a much more modest reform effort, it is an important one that may helped the public service in Saskatchewan reclaim at least part of its distinctive tradition and role in this province.

The results can be seen in the senior and middle levels of the public service where individuals are now much more comfortable in dealing with policy issues.[38] They feel secure in providing advice, independent from a heavy partisan influence. A practical example can be seen in the operations of the legislative review committee which most senior officials must face at some point. The feeling is that the committee is a very cordial, professional and collegial body, which is in sharp contrast to its previous incarnation under the chairmanship of PC cabinet minister Grant Schmidt, where the proceedings were described by numerous participants as being "vicious." Indeed, overall there is a sense that encounters with the political nexus of cabinet ministers and special assistants are very professional and that the political side recognizes that the bureaucracy has the knowledge and expertise which can be used to diffuse a political crisis or to get a policy through the process with the minimum of aggravation to other departments or resistance from interest groups.

This is not to say that public servants have not felt the sting of downsizing and reduced budgets with an attendant loss of perks and prestige. Nor has the government ended the bureaucratic infighting that occurs between departments and branches, or the associated frustrations and delays of dealing with any hierarchical organization. In addition, the government is committed to including public servants in the policy-making process, particularly the Treasury Board process. In the last years of the Devine government it was generally accepted that the bureaucratic process, particularly the Treasury Board process, had imploded and cabinet ministers were making decisions on their own, without telling other cabinet ministers, let alone public servants. In short, the job of the public servant has not been eroded to the extent it has in other jurisdictions, where much of the discretion has been removed through power grabs by politicians and demands by citizens and interest groups.

What the Saskatchewan experience demonstrates is that in order for a public service to move effectively in a new direction there must be some acknowledgement of the traditional values associated with constitutional bureaucracy. More than that, in order to allow public servants the necessary space to engage in positive behaviours, there needs to be a recognition of the importance of the structures of accountability, openness, transparency and trust. Only in such an environment will public servants have the confidence to change their behaviour. Because bureaucracies are inherently resistant to change, the correct environment is clearly a paramount concern. Indeed, the Saskatchewan case might even put to rest the old public administration nostrum which states that as a bureaucracy is subject to democratic control

37. Savoie, *Thatcher, Reagan, Mulroney*, 218.

38. See Ken Rasmussen, "Policy Capacity in Saskatchewan: Strengthening the Equilibrium," *Canadian Public Administration* 42, no. 3 (Fall 1999): 331–48.

it becomes more rigid and dysfunctional, and as it becomes free of democratic control it tends to exhibit greater efficiency and effectiveness. A functioning career public service needs democratic controls as much as it needs freedom from them, and, as ever, the art of successful public administration is finding the balance. While no one would suggest that the public service in Saskatchewan will reach the level or renown associated with both the Douglas and Blakeney governments, it will not become simply a machine to implement policies developed by ministers and executive assistants. Rather, it will work with politicians in finding solutions to Saskatchewan's intractable problems. The public service in Saskatchewan appears to have found a new balance in which its former leadership role has been curtailed, but its more traditional role as valued advisor has been reinstituted. Thus the movement of the civil service towards the norm may be a change for Saskatchewan, but it is a change that should be welcomed by civil servants, politicians and citizens.

The Judiciary

John D. Whyte and Colleen Matthews

INTRODUCTION

The special context of Saskatchewan — agrarian, ethnically diverse, remote from cultural and capital centres, and significantly reliant on federal policies with respect to Aboriginal peoples, agriculture, transportation, trade, energy and transfers, combined with little electoral clout in the shaping of them — has produced a spirit for radicalism, but seldom with respect to public institutions. Notwithstanding the Britishness of the structures through which both the legislative and the legal processes are conducted, Saskatchewan has not pushed against constitutional restraints by seeking fundamental reforms, nor has it always been quick to adopt the limited reforms that have occurred elsewhere in Canada with respect to the basic structures of the state.

Saskatchewan's early experiments in labour relations, human rights and medical care have been pursued within established models of governance. This British institutional hegemony has occurred in the absence of a British demographic hegemony, testament, perhaps, to the innate soundness of British statecraft — or, more likely, just a reflection of the durability of formal governmental arrangements once constitutionalized.

In any event, this history of slow adaptation is not bound to continue, and this is especially so with respect to the institutions through which the legal process is implemented.

Saskatchewan is now coming face to face with the consequence of using, without significant modification, a legal system, and a court system, which fails to serve the needs of Aboriginal communities for public safety and social order. That system is also being challenged to meet the needs of Aboriginal people for appropriate and timely indemnification for harms, in particular, the harms suffered by Aboriginal children while they were held at residential schools.

The response of Aboriginal communities has been to demand tribal courts or peacemaker courts, to push for increased adoption of Aboriginal processes of healing in response to offending, to claim jurisdiction over law-making, to establish First Nations police services and to seek to exercise Aboriginal administration over, first, sentencing to the community under probation or conditional sentences and, then, over correctional institutions. Although not all Aboriginal spokespersons and groups claim that a parallel, autonomous criminal justice system is an essential condition of establishing a legitimate and effective system for protecting social order, almost all Aboriginal political voices state that adapting the existing system of justice is necessary so that Aboriginal values and culture are strongly reflected in it and Aboriginal people are major participants in its operation.

The justice system was undoubtedly one of the state instruments by which colonialist policies were pursued and may have been irremediably tainted by that role. Currently, it is the justice system that is most visibly involved in regulating the social crisis that has resulted from decades of socially destructive policies directed against Canada's Aboriginal peoples. These hard truths mean that the current legal system is not well positioned to be seen in a positive light by those Aboriginal political leaders trying to construct healthy communities.

At this stage in the province's vital project of establishing the full inclusion of Aboriginal people in social and economic life, it is not possible to guess how the justice system, in general, and the judicial function, in particular, will be reshaped. In the general area of public administration, and in the specific area of courts, as in many other areas, the assumption that there is trust and confidence in, and satisfaction with, our established systems cannot be sustained. The changes that will need to be made to respond to the need to create institutions that reflect greater social inclusion will not necessarily fit well with foundational legalist principles of separation of the judicial power, independence of judges, professionalization of court participants and formal closure to legal disputes.

The Canadian Constitution, both in its 1867 and its 1982 provisions, expresses a strong commitment to preserving the integrity of distinct minority communities and to not licensing the suppression of minority identities. Indeed, this principle was specifically identified by the Supreme Court of Canada in its remarkable 1998 decision in the Quebec Secession Reference.[1] Although we know the historical force of that commitment with respect to some minority communities — language and religious minorities, for instance — we are just beginning to learn its meaning with respect to indigenous peoples. Recently, the Supreme Court has given the concept of protecting the integrity of these communities significant weight in the context of specific Aboriginal practices,[2] in the context of protecting vital community interests,[3] and in the context of land and territory.[4]

The weight of this commitment in the shaping of political authority has not yet emerged, but we can assume that if the pattern of not effectively sharing political power with Aboriginal communities continues, with the continuing result of social exclusion and deprivation, the constitutional precept in favour of preserving the integrity of historical communities will force courts to order changes in how government, justice, and possibly the courts, are conducted and structured.[5]

In addition to Aboriginal communities, Saskatchewan contains the minority language community of *fransaskois* and this community, too, enjoys a degree of constitutional recognition. Language claims in Saskatchewan have centred on the language of court proceedings and legislation.[6] Capacity within the province to offer French language proceedings has not significantly strengthened in recent decades

1. *Reference re Secession of Quebec*, [1998] 2 S.C.R. 217.
2. *R. v. Marshall*, [1999] 3 S.C.R. 456.
3. *Guerin v. The Queen*, [1984] 2 S.C.R. 335; *R. v. Sparrow*, [1990] 1 S.C.R. 1075.
4. *Delgamuukw v. British Columbia*, [1997] 3 S.C.R. 1010.
5. *R. v. Williams*, [1998] 1 S.C.R. 1128; R. v. Gladue, [1999] 1 S.C.R. 688.
6. *R. v. Mercure*, [1988] 1 S.C.R. 234.

and the failure to be able to extend equal court services to members of both of Canada's official language groups continues the long-standing challenge of meeting basic constitutional commitments.

Another of the Constitution's foundational commitments that was identified by the Supreme Court in the Quebec Secession Reference is the rule of law. This principle simply means that public authority must be exercised according to law — through the use of formal legal rules and through administration of those rules in a way that complies with fundamental legal principles. The rule of law implicit in the *Constitution Act, 1867* and the establishment of the "Judicature" in Part VII of that *Constitution Act* was made more explicit in the Preamble to the Canadian Charter of Rights and Freedoms, a key element of the *Constitution Act, 1982*. It states, in part, that "Canada is founded upon ... the rule of law."

The 1867 Constitution, in recognizing the "Judicature," spelled out that the rule of law, or legalism, requires for its realization a specific agency of law whose chief role — the determination of law's content — as well as its traditional jurisdiction and its independence from interference from the other branches of government, are all constitutionally guaranteed. Hence, the judiciary in Saskatchewan enjoys explicit constitutional recognition and protection and its vital role of preserving the conditions for legitimate government is secured.

It is clear in Canadian constitutional jurisprudence that the central role of law, and of courts, in preserving the rule of law is obtained through ensuring that all the elements of judicial independence are beyond the reach of legislatures and the executive.[7] It is also obtained through preserving against encroachment the historic jurisdiction of courts[8] including, most significantly, the inherent jurisdiction of superior courts to review the actions of legislatures[9] and to supervise the conduct of the executive branch to ensure that it acts within its jurisdiction as established in formal legislation[10] and that its administrative acts accord with fundamental legal rules of procedural fairness.[11]

It seems unlikely that it will be easy to establish reconciliation between the two core constitutional commitments that have been identified — preserving the integrity of minority communities, especially the communities of Aboriginal peoples, and preserving the integrity of the agency through which government according to law is guaranteed. It cannot be expected that the current court structure, with its comprehensive jurisdiction, and with its current appointment rules, will not be affected by the imperatives of inter-societal accommodation.

In this task, the people of Saskatchewan face a fundamental choice. Either they can promote adaptation of the court system to reflect wider Aboriginal participation and to incorporate Aboriginal understandings of the appropriate responses to social conflict, or they can conclude that the alienating effect of the established

---

7. *Reference re Remuneration of Judges of the Provincial Court of Prince Edward Island; Reference re Independence and Impartiality of Judges of the Provincial Court of Prince Edward Island; R. v. Campbell; R. v. Ekmecic; R. v. Wickman; Manitoba Provincial Judges Assn. v. Manitoba (Minister of Justice)* (hereinafter Provincial Court Judges Reference), [1997] 3 S.C.R. 3.

8. *Labour Relations Board of Saskatchewan v. John East Iron Works Ltd.*, [1949] A.C. 134; [1948] 4 D.L.R. 673 (PC).

9. *Citizens Insurance Company v. Parsons* (1881), 7 AC 96 (PC) aff'g. (1880), 4 S.C.R. 215.

10. *Canadian Union of Public Employees v. New Brunswick Liquor Corporation*, [1979] 2 S.C.R. 227.

11. Section 7, Canadian Charter of Rights and Freedoms, Part I, *Constitution Act, 1982; Nicholson v. Haldimand — Norfolk Regional Board of Commissioners of Police*, [1979] 1 S.C.R. 311.

court system will not easily be expunged, even with court reforms, and accept the creation of an Aboriginal justice system or Aboriginal justice systems. In our view, the better inter-societal model for Saskatchewan is to establish, or change, public structures so that they genuinely reflect the province's pluralism, enable broad-based participation by members of minority communities and represent genuine power sharing.

Fortunately, although the court system, standing at the heart of the legal process, does not seem easily amenable to change, it is, in fact, a dynamic structure, capable of at least limited alteration to meet the needs of social contexts in which it operates.

While at this juncture it is not possible to predict the future shape of Saskatchewan's court system, it is possible to trace the course of its dynamism as Saskatchewan was settled by Europeans and evolved as a result of this settlement. This history does not likely prepare the province for the fullness of the challenge to change that it now faces. However, it does tell us that even fixed public institutions, like courts, can be altered to respond to deep social needs.

ENGLISH COURTS IN THE NORTH-WEST

In Britain, by the end of the 1600s, it had been established that Parliament had supremacy over the King in his Privy Council — over the original powers of government available to the king through the royal prerogative. However, royal prerogative powers were still used where Parliament did not legislate, and the King in Council was still the final executive authority in government. For a long time, the British Parliament had little involvement in the governmental affairs of the British colonies, leaving this largely to the King and his Privy Council.[12]

Just as the king, through the royal prerogative, had powers of government, he also had judicial power that was exercised through the king's prerogative courts. In 1640, an Act of the British Parliament abolished these prerogative courts and prevented the King and his Privy Council from exercising judicial power in matters that were within the jurisdiction of the English central court. However, this did not apply to the colonies. Orders-in-council were passed to provide for appeals from the colonies to the Privy Council rather than to the English courts.[13]

In 1833, the Judicial Committee of the Privy Council was created by statute. It became the final court of appeal for colonial courts, and had the ability to establish consistency in the common law throughout the British empire. (Generally speaking, the same judges were part of both the House of Lords, the final court of appeal for the United Kingdom, and the Privy Council, the final court of appeal for the colonies.)[14] In 1844, another statute authorized appeals to the Judicial Committee of the Privy Council from any colonial courts (not just the courts of appeal), even where colonial charters or local law restricted appeals. This was a continuation of the royal prerogative, formalized by statute. Although colonies could determine the types of cases that could be appealed as a matter of right, this did not prevent appeals by leave of the Judicial Committee.[15]

12. W.R. Lederman, *Continuing Canadian Constitutional Dilemmas: Essays on the Constitutional History, Public Law and Federal System of Canada* (Toronto: Butterworths, 1981), 64.
13. B.L. Strayer, *The Canadian Constitution and the Courts: The Function and Scope of Judicial Review* (Toronto: Butterworths, 1988), 10–11.
14. P.S. Hogg, *Constitutional Law of Canada: 1999 Student Edition* (Toronto: Thomson Canada, 1999), 31.
15. Strayer, *The Canadian Constitution and the Courts*, 11–12, 24–25.

English common law determined how laws were received in the British colonies.[16] When a colony was settled, British settlers were considered to have taken to the colony as much of English statute and common law as was suitable there. (The colonial courts could determine suitability.) This included the right to a representative assembly. The King in Council could provide for a governor, council, assembly and courts, but could not make new laws for the colony. Only the assembly and the British Parliament could do that. When a colony was acquired by conquest or cession, English public law applied to establish and operate colonial government institutions. Otherwise, the private law (such as contract law, property law, and tort law) and criminal law in force prior to the conquest or cession continued in effect until changed by the British Parliament or King in Council. In ceded colonies, there was no received right to a representative assembly; the King in Council and the British Parliament could make laws for the colony. However, once an assembly was granted, the position of the colony was the same as that of a colony acquired by settlement.[17]

It became important for a colony to establish a date for the reception of English law. After that date, English statutes were no longer automatically received in the colony. English statutes, as they existed on the date of reception, applied in the colony but subsequent repeal of those statutes, or enactment of new statutes, by the British Parliament did not apply in the colony. The date of reception could be established by judicial decision (the maritime provinces), by imperial power (in Quebec, by royal proclamation in 1763, although French civil law was restored by *The Quebec Act* in 1774), or by statute that adopted English laws as of a particular date (Ontario, the western provinces and the territories).[18] The date of reception for the former Rupert's Land and North-Western territory, which applies to Saskatchewan, is the date those British territories became part of Canada — July 15, 1870.[19]

The date of reception affected the application of statute law, but did not affect the application of English common law. Principles of English common law continued to apply, and the decisions of the highest courts in England continued to be precedents for the courts of the colonies until 1949, when appeal from the final courts in Canada to the Judicial Committee of the Privy Council in London was abolished.

At the time of Confederation, the courts and laws that existed in Canada (Ontario and Quebec), Nova Scotia, and New Brunswick were continued pursuant to section 129 of the *Constitution Act, 1867*. In section 101, the Act gave the Parliament of Canada jurisdiction to provide for the "Constitution, Maintenance, and Organization of a General Court of Appeal for Canada, and for the Establishment of any additional Courts for the better Administration of the Laws of Canada." It also provided, in section 92(14), that provinces had authority over the organization and maintenance of provincial courts.

At Confederation, Rupert's Land and the North-Western Territories (including

16. Aboriginal customary law continued to exist. An analysis of the practices and traditions of Aboriginal peoples is beyond the scope of this chapter.

17. Hogg, *Constitutional Law of Canada*, 27–33 and Lederman, *Continuing Canadian Constitutional Dilemmas*, 64–65.

18. Hogg, *Constitutional Law of Canada*, 29–30 and 34 and Lederman, *Continuing Canadian Constitutional Dilemmas*, 67–68.

19. Lederman, *Continuing Canadian Constitutional Dilemmas*, 78.

the area that is now Saskatchewan) were still British territory, owned or controlled by the Hudson's Bay Company. However, with the assistance of the British government, Canada was able to acquire these territories.[20] Pursuant to the *Constitution Act, 1867* and the British *Rupert's Land Act, 1868*,[21] Rupert's Land and the North-Western Territories were admitted to Confederation by imperial order-in-council effective July 15, 1870. Parliament received authority to legislate for the territories. Manitoba then joined Confederation as a province.[22]

In the 1870s, immigration and settlement of the west became a national policy. A series of treaties was negotiated with First Nations, and reserves were created. A land survey of the region had begun in 1869, and in 1872, the *Dominion Lands Act* provided for the acquisition of homesteads. In 1874, the first detachment of the North-West Mounted Police was established in the west.[23]

Finally, in 1875, the federal government, under Prime Minister Alexander Mackenzie, passed the *North-West Territories Act* (proclaimed in 1876). It provided for appointment, by the federal government, of a Lieutenant Governor and a Council to assist with the administration of the territories, and for the gradual introduction of representative government. Battleford was the capital of the North-West Territories until 1883, when the capital was transferred to Regina.[24]

The *North-West Territories Act* gave the Lieutenant Governor, on the advice and consent of the Council, power to make ordinances respecting a number of enumerated subjects. One of the subjects was the administration of justice, including the organization of courts of civil and criminal jurisdiction.

The Act provided for a Sheriff and up to three Stipendiary Magistrates to be appointed by the federal government, and for Justices of the Peace to be appointed by the Lieutenant Governor. The Stipendiary Magistrates were to hold office "during pleasure," to reside at such places ordered by the Governor in Council, and to preside over such courts as were assigned to them by the Lieutenant-Governor. Each Stipendiary Magistrate had jurisdiction throughout the North-West Territories and could exercise the functions of any Justice of the Peace or any two Justices of the Peace. Until 1886, Stipendiary Magistrates were also *ex officio* members of the Council appointed to assist in the administration of the North-West Territories.

A judge of the Manitoba Court of Queen's Bench "with any one of the Stipendiary Magistrates as an associate" had authority to try offences alleged to have been committed in the North-West Territories. For an offence punishable by death, a jury was required and a conviction could be appealed to the Manitoba Court of Queen's Bench. There was also authority for conveying the accused to Manitoba for trial by the Court of Queen's Bench if the offence was punishable by death or imprisonment in a penitentiary.

For the more serious offences (where the maximum punishment exceeded five years imprisonment) a jury was required unless the accused consented to proceeding without one. Less serious offences were to be tried in a summary way without a jury.

In civil matters, either a Stipendiary Magistrate or a judge of the Manitoba Court of Queen's Bench could, without a jury, hear claims that did not exceed a

20. Donald Creighton, *Canada's First Century* (Toronto: Macmillan of Canada, 1970), 17.
21. 31-32 Vict., c. 105 (U. K.).
22. Lederman, *Continuing Canadian Constitutional Dilemmas*, 77.
23. Creighton, *Canada's First Century*, 25–26.
24. J.H. Archer, *Saskatchewan: A History* (Saskatoon: Western Producer Prairie Books, 1980), 76.

specified amount. Larger claims required a jury if either party demanded one. Decisions respecting these larger claims could be appealed to the Court of Queen's Bench in Manitoba.

In 1875, the same year that the federal government passed the *North-West Territories Act*, it passed legislation establishing the Supreme Court of Canada. The Supreme Court was not the final court of appeal that it is today. Although there were no appeals as of right from the Supreme Court to the Judicial Committee of the Privy Council, appeals by leave (the prerogative appeals) were still available. And decisions of provincial appeal courts could be appealed directly to Britain, without going to the Supreme Court of Canada, until 1949 when appeals to Britain were abolished.[25]

Amendments to the *North-West Territories Act* in 1877 increased the jurisdiction of Stipendiary Magistrates. The least serious offences could be tried by a Magistrate in a summary way, without a jury. Where the maximum punishment for an offence did not exceed seven years' imprisonment, there could be a trial without a jury if the accused agreed. Where the maximum punishment for an offence exceeded seven years' imprisonment but the offence was not punishable by death, the charge was to be tried by a Stipendiary Magistrate and a Justice of the Peace with a jury of six. Finally, where the punishment was death, the charge was to be tried by one Stipendiary Magistrate and two Justices of the Peace with a jury of six.

By 1880, the types of offences that could be tried in a summary way, without a jury, were enumerated in legislation. All other criminal charges could be tried by a Stipendiary Magistrate and a Justice of the Peace with a jury of six. An offence punishable by death could be appealed to the Manitoba Court of Queen's Bench. (It was a jury of six that found Louis Riel guilty of treason in 1885, and a Stipendiary Magistrate who sentenced him to death. The case was appealed to the Manitoba Court of Appeal and the Judicial Committee of the Privy Council.)

Prior to 1880, the *North-West Territories Act* did not specify qualifications for Stipendiary Magistrates, other than to indicate that they must be "fit and proper" persons. In 1880, the provision was changed to provide for appointment, by the federal government, of "one or more fit and proper person or persons, barristers-at-law or advocates of five years' standing in any of the Provinces, not exceeding three" to act as Stipendiary Magistrates. Their salaries were specified in legislation.

In 1880, the population in the area that is now Saskatchewan was about 19,000. A census taken in 1881 indicated that approximately 1,000 were settlers and 15,000 were Indians. The remainder were said to be Métis and "English-speaking mixed bloods."[26]

Amendments to the *North-West Territories Act* in 1885 (three years after the introduction of the railway) increased the number of Stipendiary Magistrates to a maximum of four. They also provided that, in criminal cases requiring a jury, the accused could consent to be tried by a Stipendiary Magistrate without a jury. Further, the *Administration of Justice in North-West Territories Act* of 1885 provided that, whenever, under any Act in force in the North-West Territories, a power or authority was to be exercised by a judge of a court, in the Territories it would be exercised by a Stipendiary Magistrate. The court in the North-West Territories was becoming increasingly professional.

25. Strayer, *The Canadian Constitution and the Courts*, 29.

26. Archer, *Saskatchewan*, 67.

That same year the Territorial Council, by ordinance, created the "High Court of Justice" for the North-West Territories, to be staffed by Stipendiary Magistrates. However, the court was abolished the following year when the federal government created the Supreme Court of the North-West Territories.

In 1886, the *North-West Territories Act* was amended to establish "The Supreme Court of the North-West Territories." The court was to be a court of original and appellate jurisdiction and was to consist of five judges. (By the time Saskatchewan became a province, this had increased to not less than six judges, including the chief justice.) A person who had been a judge of a superior court of any province of Canada, a Stipendiary Magistrate of the territories, or a barrister or advocate of at least ten years' standing at the bar of any province or of the territories could be a judge of the court. Judges were to hold office during good behaviour, and were removable only by the Governor General on address of the Senate and House of Commons. Their annual salaries were set out in legislation.

The Act provided that the federal government could divide the North-West Territories into judicial districts. While judges of the Supreme Court had jurisdiction throughout the North-West Territories, each judge was expected to act in the district to which he was assigned. By order-in-council, the North-West Territories were divided into five judicial districts: Eastern Assiniboia, Western Assiniboia, Southern Alberta, Northern Alberta, and Saskatchewan.

In 1894, an amendment to the *North-West Territories Act* provided for the appointment of police magistrates in the Territories. These magistrates held all the powers then vested in two justices of the peace under any law in Canada, with jurisdiction in the territory defined by the order-in-council appointing them.

In 1898, the Yukon Territory was created out of the North-West Territories, and in 1905, Saskatchewan and Alberta became provinces.

COURTS IN SASKATCHEWAN

The Saskatchewan Act, a federal statute which came into force on September 1, 1905, created the province of Saskatchewan and thus has constitutional status. It provided that the Legislative Assembly was to be composed of 25 elected members and it continued the courts of civil and criminal jurisdiction. It provided that the Legislature could abolish the Supreme Court of the North-West Territories if it constituted a superior court of criminal jurisdiction.

In 1907, *The Judicature Act* was passed abolishing the Supreme Court of the North-West Territories as it affected Saskatchewan, and creating "The Supreme Court of Saskatchewan" as a superior court, with original and appellate jurisdiction. A separate appeal court had not yet been established. Judges of the Supreme Court sat *in banc* to hear appeals. A quorum for this purpose was three judges and no judge who took part in the trial or whose judgment was under appeal could sit on the appeal. Saskatchewan was not the only province that did not immediately establish a separate court of appeal. Although Ontario and Quebec had courts of appeal at Confederation, the other provinces did not establish separate appeal courts until some time after entering Confederation.[27]

In 1907, the Saskatchewan government also passed *The District Courts Act*. The legislation created eight judicial districts (Cannington, Moosomin, Yorkton, Regina,

27. Peter McCormick, *Canada's Courts* (Toronto: James Lorimer & Company, 1994), 29.

Moose Jaw, Saskatoon, Prince Albert and Battleford) and established a district court in each of those judicial districts. The jurisdiction of a district court was limited. A district court could not hear certain enumerated matters (including actions in which title to lands or validity of wills was in question), or claims that exceeded a specified amount. Each district court judge could also hear criminal matters and was constituted a criminal court for that purpose.

The Surrogate Courts Act of 1907 established, in each of the judicial districts set up under *The District Courts Act*, a surrogate court to handle estate matters. The judge of each district court was also the judge of the surrogate court for the same judicial district. (The surrogate court became part of the Court of Queen's Bench when the District Court merged with that court in 1980.)

Judges of the Supreme Court of Saskatchewan and the District Courts of the province were appointed and paid by the federal government, as provided for in sections 96 and 100 of the *Constitution Act, 1867*. However, the province determined where they were to reside. Supreme Court judges were to reside "at the seat of government in the province" and the district court judge of each judicial district was to reside at the place in the district to which he was appointed, as was determined by the Lieutenant Governor in Council.

The Magistrates Act of 1906 provided for the appointment of police magistrates and justices of the peace. Police Magistrates had the authority, within their territorial jurisdictions, of two justices of the peace. *The Magistrates Act* was replaced in 1907 by *The Police Magistrates' Act*. That Act authorized the Lieutenant Governor in Council to appoint a police magistrate for every city and town in the province. A police magistrate had the powers of two justices of the peace and could hear matters over which he had jurisdiction, in the judicial district in which he was situated. To be appointed a police magistrate, a person was required to be a member of the bar of the Supreme Court of Saskatchewan at the time of appointment. However, in 1913, the Act was amended to also provide for appointment of police officers as police magistrates.

In 1915, *The Court of Appeal Act* created a Court of Appeal for the province, consisting of four judges including the Chief Justice, and sitting at the city of Regina. The same year, *The King's Bench Act* was passed, abolishing the Supreme Court and creating "his Majesty's Court of King's Bench for Saskatchewan" — a six-member court, including the Chief Justice.

In 1958, *The Police Magistrates Act* was amended and renamed *The Provincial Magistrates Act*; police magistrates became "provincial magistrates." Provincial magistrates had jurisdiction throughout Saskatchewan and salaries were fixed by the province. The Attorney General had authority to assign a provincial magistrate to a city or town and to move the magistrate to another area. Finally, in 1963, *The Magistrates' Courts Act, 1963* established the Magistrates' Courts. To be appointed a judge of a Magistrate's Court, a person was required to be a member in good standing of the Bar of one of the provinces of Canada and to have been such a member or a provincial magistrate for at least five years. The salary was set out in the legislation. Judges of the Magistrates' Courts had jurisdiction throughout Saskatchewan but would sit in the place designated by the Attorney General.

Three court levels — superior, district and magistrates — modelled on their English counterparts, had also developed in the other provinces (except Quebec). The superior courts of the provinces, like English superior courts, tended to be small, with judges residing in one or two central locations and sometimes travelling on circuit. The judges heard a full range of civil matters and had exclusive jurisdiction over the most serious criminal offences.[28] Superior court judges also had appellate jurisdiction.

District or county courts (similar to English county courts) were decentralized, with judges residing in the communities they served. These judges had jurisdiction over civil matters involving lower sums of money and over the less serious criminal charges. They handled a larger number of criminal matters than did superior court judges.[29]

In addition to superior and district or county courts, cases were heard by magistrates and justices of the peace who were appointed by the provincial government. Magistrates courts were similar to English lay courts, although magistrates with legal training were common in Canada. Magistrates were closely associated with municipal authorities, often sharing responsibilities and facilities with them. Magistrates heard mainly criminal matters involving the less serious offences and the early stages of criminal proceedings, although their jurisdiction was expanded to include juvenile matters, some family matters and, in some provinces, small claims matters.[30]

During the 1960s and 1970s, two movements for reform in court structure developed in Canada. Prior to that, reforms had increased the jurisdiction of district court judges and magistrates but had not resulted in major structural change.[31] These reform movements — the transformation of magistrates courts into highly professionalized provincial courts and the merger of the district and superior courts — have engendered ongoing reform of Saskatchewan's trial courts.

As the jurisdiction of magistrates courts increased, there was an increasing awareness of the necessity of establishing professional standards of competence and neutrality with respect to the trial of any offence, regardless of seriousness. And with an increase in jurisdiction, and in qualification of judges, the cost of salaries and court administration would increase.[32] These factors prompted a movement for reform that resulted in the establishment of Provincial Courts.

New Brunswick created a Provincial Court in 1967, and Ontario created one in 1968. (Quebec had created a Provincial Court in 1965, but it was different from other Provincial Courts in that it heard largely civil matters. There was another court with jurisdiction over criminal matters, which later merged with the Provincial Court.[33]) The other provinces followed suit.

The Provincial Court of Saskatchewan was created by provincial statute in 1978. The current legislation is *The Provincial Court Act, 1998*. Provincial Court Judges have jurisdiction throughout Saskatchewan. Currently, there are 47 Provincial Court judicial positions in the province, including the Chief Judge and Associate Chief Judge. Judges sit in 13 permanent Provincial Court locations and hold court in 78 circuit points.

Judges of the Provincial Court are appointed by the provincial government,

---

28. Carl Baar, *One Trial Court: Possibilities and Limitations* (Ottawa: Canadian Judicial Council, 1991), 5 and 8.
29. Ibid..
30. Ibid., 5, 7, and 9. In Saskatchewan, *The Small Claims Enforcement Act, 1959*, provided for trial of small claims by provincial magistrates.
31. Ibid., 5.
32. Ibid., 10.
33. Ibid., 6–7.

although the provincial Judicial Council considers and makes recommendations to the minister of Justice respecting proposed appointments. Since 1998, the Act has required that appointments be made from the list of those whom the Judicial Council has approved for appointment. The 1998 enactment also increased the requirements for appointment to the Court. An appointee is now required to have been a member of the Bar for ten years, rather than five years, or to have other legal or judicial experience that is satisfactory to the Judicial Council. These two changes express the continuing professionalization of the Provincial Court.

Probably the greatest imperative behind rising standards has been the coming into force in 1982 of the Canadian Charter of Rights and Freedoms. Charter-based defences are available to all persons charged with offences and this has meant that Provincial Courts acquired responsibility for interpreting and applying constitutional principles. The point may be not so much that Provincial Courts apply the Constitution, but that Charter case law is marked by legal complexity.

In addition, the Provincial Court's jurisdiction over criminal matters has expanded. Amendments to the Criminal Code have reclassified criminal offences, giving the Provincial Court jurisdiction over many of the more serious offences. Jurisdiction has also been increased through the enactment of new offences. And all offences committed by youth under the age of 18 are tried in Youth Court, a division of the Provincial Court, unless they are transferred to adult court pursuant to the provisions of the *Young Offenders Act*.

The Provincial Court hears a number of offences created by provincial statute, like highway traffic, environmental, occupational health and safety, wildlife, and alcohol and gaming matters. Federal statutes have also created some regulatory offences which are heard in the Provincial Court. Traffic Courts operated by Justices of the Peace were established in Regina and Saskatoon, in 1977 and 1981 respectively, and are responsible for provincial highway traffic offences.

During the past several decades, federal criminal law reform has produced a significantly more complex law of criminal offending, as well as more complex sentencing law. It is now not possible to hold to the view that substantive criminal law, criminal procedure, or the law of sentencing that is administered in Provincial Courts, is less complex (or even less significant for most defendants) than is required in the criminal trial workload of the superior courts.

In civil matters, the Provincial Court does not play as large a role. The monetary limit for claims in Small Claims Court is $5,000, although that limit was moved from legislation to regulations in 1997, so that it can be increased more easily in the future. And, although the Provincial Court has jurisdiction in some family law matters, with the creation of Family Law Divisions in Regina, Saskatoon and Prince Albert, the Provincial Court's role in Family Law matters has decreased.

Appeals from decisions of the Provincial Court in the more serious (indictable) criminal matters are to the Saskatchewan Court of Appeal. The less serious (summary conviction) matters are appealed to the Saskatchewan Court of Queen's Bench (unless a summary conviction matter was tried with an indictable offence which is also being appealed, and leave to appeal to the Court of Appeal has been obtained). A decision of a Queen's Bench judge sitting on appeal on a summary conviction matter can be appealed to the Court of Appeal on a question of law alone, if leave is granted. Appeals of civil matters heard in Small Claims Court are to the Court of Queen's Bench.

The second reform movement of the 1960s and 1970s led to merger of the superior and district or county courts. The first merger occurred in Prince Edward Island in 1973. Mergers followed a few years later in Alberta, New Brunswick and Saskatchewan. In Saskatchewan, the merger occurred in 1980 — two years after the Provincial Court was established. Manitoba and Newfoundland courts were the next to merge, and in 1990, single superior trial courts were established in Ontario and British Columbia. Finally, in 1991, Nova Scotia announced that it would merge its courts.[34] The resulting superior courts are larger and more widely dispersed courts. In Saskatchewan, Alberta, Manitoba and New Brunswick, the superior trial court is referred to as a Court of Queen's Bench, following the English nomenclature.

"Her Majesty's Court of Queen's Bench for Saskatchewan" is established pursuant to *The Queen's Bench Act, 1998*. The court's judges are federally appointed, selected from the Saskatchewan Bar. The salaries, allowances and pensions of the judges are fixed and provided by Parliament. Judges hold office during good behaviour until the age of 75, and are removable only by the Governor General on address of the Senate and House of Commons.

There are 33 Queen's Bench judicial positions in the province, including that of the Chief Justice. The judges sit in 13 judicial centres. When a judge is appointed by the federal government, the province determines the judicial centre at which the judge is to reside. Each judge sits in more than one judicial centre, as determined by the chief justice of the court. Seven of the 33 Queen's Bench judges are assigned to the Family Law Division. All Queen's Bench judges have jurisdiction to hear any Queen's Bench matters, including family law matters.

In addition, there are currently eleven supernumerary judges. A supernumerary judge is one who no longer performs judicial duties full time, but remains available to perform such duties as may be assigned from time to time by the Chief Justice of the Queen's Bench. A judge is eligible to go supernumerary at the age of 65 years with 15 years of service or at the age of 70 with ten years of service. Supernumerary judges work approximately half time and draw full salary.

The constitutional entrenchment of the judicial function in Part VII (Judicature) of the *Constitution Act, 1867*, means that superior courts have an inherent jurisdiction. This means that, unlike the Provincial Court or statutory decision makers (administrative boards and tribunals), the superior courts have authority beyond that which is outlined in legislation. Provincial statutes set out the jurisdiction of the court, but do not limit the inherent jurisdiction.

The Court of Queen's Bench has jurisdiction over both criminal and civil law matters. A small group of the most serious, indictable offences, particularly murder, is within the exclusive jurisdiction of the Court of Queen's Bench. With other indictable offences, the accused can elect to be tried by a Queen's Bench Judge and Jury, Queen's Bench Judge alone, or Provincial Court Judge alone. All jury trials are in the Court of Queen's Bench.

Civil law matters, with the exception of cases handled in Small Claims Court, and most family law matters, are heard in the Court of Queen's Bench.

In the mid-1970s, there was an effort across the country to bring family law disputes into one court. The federal government agreed to jointly fund four pilot unified family courts, in St. John's, Fredericton, Hamilton, and Saskatoon. The Unified Family Court in Saskatoon was created in 1978.[35]

34. Ibid., 6.
35. Ibid., 7.

Due to the constitutional entrenchment of superior court jurisdiction, some family law matters can be heard only by federally appointed judges but others can be heard by provincially-appointed judges. Provinces with Unified Family Courts or Family Law Divisions have given the superior courts (federally appointed judges) responsibility for all family law matters. Creation of Unified Family Courts has therefore shifted family law matters formerly within the jurisdiction of the Provincial Court to the superior court (in Saskatchewan, to the Court of Queen's Bench). It has not created a new level of courts.

The Unified Family Court in Saskatoon is now part of the Family Law Division of the Court of Queen's Bench, which was created in 1994. Since 1994, in Regina and Saskatoon, and since 1996 in Prince Albert, all family law proceedings have been in the Court of Queen's Bench, Family Law Division. In other centres, the Queen's Bench and Provincial Courts can both hear child protection cases, child and spousal maintenance issues and maintenance enforcement default hearings. The Court of Queen's Bench has exclusive jurisdiction over divorce, matrimonial property, custody and access, and adoption.

Within the Family Law Division, Family Law Support Services has been created. It provides information to the public on family law issues through brochures, self-help kits, and parent education workshops; prepares custody and access reports for use by the court; and provides supervised access and exchange services.

Mediation Services is closely associated with Family Law Support Services in family law matters, but provides services to many other areas as well. Mediation Services was actually created in response to the farm debt crisis of the 1980s, but it was always meant to provide dispute resolution services in other areas as well. It began operation on July 1, 1988, with the proclamation of *The Saskatchewan Farm Security Act*, an Act that provides for mediation in actions on mortgages against farm land and in actions for possession of farm equipment. In the years that followed, family law fee-for-service mediation and court-ordered family mediation were developed, as were other mediation services like training and facilitation services. In addition, there are now other legislated mediation requirements. For example, *The Queen's Bench Act* requires that parties in contested civil matters, other than family law matters, attend a mediation session after the close of pleadings but before any further steps are taken in the action. Currently, this applies only in the judicial centres of Regina, Swift Current, Saskatoon, and Prince Albert.

Appeals from decisions of the Court of Queen's Bench are to the Saskatchewan Court of Appeal. Like the Court of Queen's Bench, the Saskatchewan Court of Appeal is a superior court, and hears both civil and criminal matters. Its judges are appointed and paid by the federal government.

There are currently eight judges, including the Chief Justice, on the Saskatchewan Court of Appeal. The court is located in Regina, although it holds sittings in Saskatoon four times a year. Appeals of decisions of the Saskatchewan Court of Appeal are to the Supreme Court of Canada.

As a result of Saskatchewan's (and Canada's) experiences with court reform, the court system has become significantly different from the English central trial court model and criminal adjudication has become less stratified than in the English system.[36] Hence, although the changes have been relatively modest, Canadian trial courts have become simpler and less hierarchical than they were at

36. Ibid., 9.

their origin. Perhaps Canadian court structure reflects Canada's easier relationship with tradition.

The evolution of Saskatchewan courts reveals the effect of changing conditions on court structure. We have already pointed out that the breakdown of the concept of simple crimes led to the professionalization of the Provincial Court so that its members have virtually the same formal qualifications as those in the superior court and, for most trials, the range of legal issues is as complex. It should, however, be noted that the concept of less serious crime has not become obsolete and, to some extent, the Provincial Court plays a large role, that the Court of Queen's Bench does not, in responding to wrongdoing that, while socially harmful, cries out less for denunciation and more for social assistance to aid offenders in meeting their developmental needs. In this way, members of the Provincial Court are caught in the tension between condemning wrongful conduct and recognizing that the better response would be to recognize the social and psychological context of the offenders and order remedies that might begin to meet the needs and dysfunctions that define that context. Provincial Court judges, in fashioning sentencing responses that meet this need for balance, and doing so in a very large volume of cases, are carrying a weighty share of the province's social need for wise and constructive judgment.

Given the twin factors of increased complexity of criminal law as it is administered in Provincial Court and the increased social burden of judging the hundreds of offences that reflect widespread social pathologies, it is questionable whether there continues to be a strong reason for breaking the trial court function in the administration of criminal justice into superior court jurisdiction and Provincial Court jurisdiction. Certainly, about a quarter of a century ago, the distinction between superior court jurisdiction and district court jurisdiction was felt to have become obsolete almost everywhere in Canada. The impetus for this merger of courts may also have been the unreality of the supposed distinction in the importance and complexity between the cases heard at these two levels of trial court.

The sense that there was no further need for the separation between superior and district court functions may also have come from changed patterns of mobility. The superior court was always a collegial court, which means that its members lived and sat in metropolitan centres. Their judicial work was conducted in proximity with each other so that the values and trends of judge-made law could be easily transmitted between them and, thus, the common law would be assured of even development and consistency. District courts were placed in regional centres. In part, it may have been felt that consistency of understanding in the members of that court was less significant because, first, of the lesser importance of the cases and, second, the corrective effect of appeals. However, the underlying reason for the existence of district courts was the difficulty and cost of being required to come to metropolitan centres for trials — worth the cost only when the case involved larger sums. This latter factor explains why, when court merger occurred, the newly merged superior courts were placed in some, but not all, of the regional centres.

Two types of mobility change lessened the case for both district and superior courts. More efficient information transfer has, even before the age of electronic information transfer, produced better conditions for achieving consistency in judge-made law, and a more mobile population has made the trip to major cities less disruptive and less costly. Both of these social factors were, in fact, in place decades before court merger, showing that court reform hardly occurs precipitously.

Another response to changing social conditions is the development of unified family courts. The steadily increasing demand on the civil justice system to regulate family dissolution produced the need for a simpler and more easily understood court structure and simpler court procedures, for family support services, and for more expertise in handling the difficult human issues that accompany separation and divorce — notably, the issue of parenting the children of the domestic partnership.

Family dissolution has also been one of the two sorts of civil disputes that have impelled the development of provincial mediation services. The other has been civil disputes between farmers and creditors arising from farm failures. Although segments of the legal profession initially expressed concerns about statutory mediation requirements, the experience has been positive. Most now view a mediation requirement as potentially positive, although some may simply treat it as a *pro forma* element of conducting a legal action.

The final social change that has been reflected in courts is the number of women serving as judges. Two of the eight Court of Appeal judges and 11 of the 33 judges of the Court of Queen's Bench are women. Ten of the 47 Provincial Court positions are held by women. No institution of society that displays high levels of imperfection in representing the diverse identities in society manages to sustain legitimacy. In light of the importance of the rule of law to maintaining the central principles of the liberal democratic society, the continued failure to include women in the province's courts could have been costly.

The challenges the province now faces are continuing the project of increasing gender representation in the courts and correcting other areas of significant under-representation. The most obvious categories of under-representation are Aboriginal people and members of visible minorities. A January 2001 judicial appointment has brought the number of Aboriginal judges on the Provincial Court to three. The responsibilities of the most recent appointee include the development of a northern Cree Court circuit.

The sense of pressure to improve the representation of all three categories — and possibly other sorts of disadvantage, such as disabled persons — can be expected to be felt by appointors to courts, and to be reflected in future appointments.

THE PROVINCIAL COURT AND JUDICIAL INDEPENDENCE

While the *Constitution Act, 1867*, sets out in some detail conditions for ensuring the integrity of the judicial branch and maintaining the independence of judges, those constitutional provisions (the "Judicature" provisions) do not relate to provincially appointed judges. During the 1980s and 1990s, provincial courts from many areas of Canada began to complain publicly about the loss of independence of provincial court judges arising from tough and often unilateral pay policies of provincial governments. These judges were able to point to section 11(d) of the Canadian Charter of Rights and Freedoms in the *Constitution Act, 1982* to show the constitutional obligation on governments to preserve their independence. That subsection says that any person charged with an offence has the right "to be presumed innocent until proven guilty according to law in a fair and public hearing by an independent and impartial tribunal." This subsection, as the foundation of judicial independence, is limited in that it pertains only to judicial adjudication in the context of persons charged with offences. However, such cases represent the lion's share of provincial court responsibility and subsection 11(d) serves as a significant constitutional guide with respect to that court.

Saskatchewan was one of those provinces whose unilateral judicial pay policies enraged members of the Provincial Court, and the Saskatchewan Provincial Court Judges' Association joined those of other provinces in a constitutionally based challenge to provincial practices with respect to judicial salaries and benefits.

Recent history of compensation for Saskatchewan Provincial Court judges commenced in June 1990 when *The Provincial Court Act* was amended to provide for the appointment, every three years, of three commissioners to inquire into and make recommendations respecting Provincial Court judges' salaries, remuneration, allowances and benefits. The recommendations of the Commission were not binding, but the minister of Justice was required to lay the Commission's report before the Legislative Assembly.

Prior to 1990, the government of Saskatchewan and Provincial Court judges had negotiated salaries and benefits for the latter. However, in 1989, after unsuccessful attempts to negotiate compensation issues, the province and the Provincial Court judges were at an impasse, and the judges threatened to commence a court action. The government agreed to establish a Commission to make non-binding recommendations respecting salary and compensation issues.

The Commission was appointed for a three-year period beginning October 1, 1990. It was chaired by Professor Douglas Schmeiser, and became known as the Schmeiser Commission. The Commission received written submissions and documents and held an oral hearing.

The Provincial Court Judges' Association based its submission on the principle of judicial independence. It argued for a salary of $135,500 (parity with federally appointed District Court judges) and a yearly cost of living increase for the next two years. The Attorney General did not recommend a specific salary. He supported the principle of judicial independence, but took the position that current compensation levels met this threshold requirement and that salary should be set in the Saskatchewan context and economic climate. The salary of Provincial Court judges was $90,000.

In its March 1991 decision, the Schmeiser Commission recommended a salary of $104,000 (approximating the 1991 provincial average) for the three-year period commencing October 1, 1990, with cost of living increases on October 1 in the next two years. It recommended increases in the additional salary for the Chief Judge (from $5,705 to $7,000) and for the Associate Chief Judge (from $3,000 to $3,500). In addition, the Commission made a number of recommendations on other matters, particularly with respect to pensions and benefits.

The recommendations of the Schmeiser Commission were not implemented. In October 1991, there was a change of government. Further meetings took place and, in February 1993, the Provincial Court Judges' Association and the Government of Saskatchewan entered into an agreement for the establishment of a binding process for determining salary and benefits. *The Provincial Court Act* was then amended in June 1993 to give effect to the agreement. It provided for the establishment a three-member Provincial Court Commission which was empowered to make binding recommendations on compensation issues, and non-binding recommendations respecting support staff, facilities, equipment, security of the court, certain benefits and any matters that could affect judicial independence.

The Commission was established in June 1993 and held hearings in August and September that year. It was chaired by Saskatoon lawyer Marty Irwin.

The Commission reported that there was unanimity among the submissions on the importance of the role of the Provincial Court judge and the need for judicial independence. The minister of Justice argued that the salary ($90,000) and benefits then in place met or exceeded those necessary to "reflect the station, dignity and responsibility of judicial office in Saskatchewan," that Provincial Court judges were among the highest income earners in the province, that there was a list of approved candidates for appointment to the court, and that further increases in salaries and benefits should be based on the economic health of the province.

The Commission, in its December 13, 1993 report, agreed with the submission of the minister of Justice that compensation must be "made in Saskatchewan," but also said that it would not want to award a salary range that excluded some of the legal profession's best candidates for the judiciary. The Commission declined to develop a formula that would base Provincial Court judges' salaries on other provincial salary scales. It also acknowledged that Provincial Court salaries must reflect provincial fiscal realities — and that the Saskatchewan economic climate could not support a dramatic salary increase.

The Irwin Commission recommended a salary of $108,000, effective April 1, 1993 with 2 percent increases on April 1 in 1994 and 1995, bringing the salary to $110,160 in 1994 and $112,360 in 1995. The Minister and the Provincial Court Judges' Association had made a joint submission for an increase in the Chief Judges' additional salary, to $7,000. The Commission therefore recommended this increase, as well as an increase in the Associate Chief Judge's salary to $3,500. There were other recommendations with respect to benefits.

The Irwin Commission's recommendations to increase the salaries of Provincial Court judges were not implemented. After release of the report, the Minister of Justice referred the issue back to the Commission for reconsideration, but the Commission declined to amend its report. The Government of Saskatchewan then enacted legislative amendments that set aside the compensation recommendations and revoked the Commission. The Act came into effect in May 1994 and, the same month, a lawsuit was commenced by Provincial Court judges, against the minister of Justice, the government of Saskatchewan and the minister in his personal capacity.

Issues related to compensation and judicial independence also arose in other provinces. By 1996, the issue reached the Supreme Court of Canada in appeals arising out of Alberta, Prince Edward Island and Manitoba. The Attorney General for Saskatchewan and the Saskatchewan Provincial Court Judges' Association intervened at the Supreme Court.

In June 1997, an out-of-court settlement was reached in the court action brought by Saskatchewan Provincial Court judges, and in September 1997 the Supreme Court of Canada rendered its decision in the Alberta, Prince Edward Island and Manitoba cases. The Supreme Court set out the constitutional requirements governing relationships between governments and provincial courts over matters of compensation.[37]

The Supreme Court of Canada held that judicial independence is an unwritten constitutional principle, the existence of which is recognized and affirmed by the preamble to the *Constitution Act, 1867*. The specific constitutional provisions usually cited as guarantees of judicial independence (the Judicature provisions of the

37. Provincial Court Judges Reference.

Constitution Act, 1867 and section 11(d) of the Charter) merely elaborate that principle. The court made it clear that judicial independence is a principle that now extends to all courts, not just the superior courts. Three core characteristics of judicial independence were identified as security of tenure, financial security and administrative independence.

The 1997 Provincial Court Judges Reference distinguished between the independence of an individual judge and an independence that "attaches to the court or tribunal as an institutional entity."[38] The institutional independence of the judiciary was said to reflect a commitment to the separation of powers among the legislative, executive, and judicial branches of government. This separation of powers requires that the relationship between the judicial branch and the other two branches be depoliticized. The legislature and executive cannot exert political pressure on the judiciary and the judiciary should "exercise reserve in speaking out publicly on issues of general public policy" that could end up before the courts, that are debated politically and that are not related to the proper administration of justice.[39]

The Supreme Court said that financial security for the courts as an institution has three components. First, although salaries can be reduced, increased or frozen, either as "part of an overall economic measure which affects the salaries of all or some persons who are remunerated from public funds, or as part of a measure which is directed at provincial court judges as a class," a special process must be used for any changes to remuneration, to avoid the possibility of, or appearance of, political interference.[40] To set or recommend a level of remuneration, an independent body — a judicial compensation commission — must be used. Although this process has now been held to be a constitutional requirement, the Supreme Court said that the recommendations of the commission would not be binding on a government. However, those recommendations are not to be taken lightly; if the government declines to follow them, it must justify its decision.

Second, the judiciary must not engage in negotiations with the government over remuneration. The Supreme Court indicated that salary negotiations are political, as remuneration is from public funds. Further, because the Crown is involved in criminal prosecutions before the courts, negotiations could undermine the appearance of judicial independence.

Third, any reductions to judicial remuneration cannot take the salaries below a basic minimum level required for the office of a judge. Public confidence in the independence of the judiciary would be undermined if judges were paid at such a low rate that they could be seen as "susceptible to political pressure through economic manipulation."[41]

Finally, the court indicated that the same principles apply to judges' benefits, including pensions.

With respect to compensation commissions, the court indicated that they must meet three criteria: they must be independent, objective, and effective. To meet the requirement of independence, commission members must have some kind of security of tenure. They should serve for a fixed term, which may vary in length. Appointments must not be controlled by one of the branches of government. The

38. Ibid., paragraph 118.
39. Ibid., paragraph 140.
40. Ibid., paragraph 133.
41. Ibid., paragraph 135.

commission should have members appointed by the judiciary and by the executive/legislature.

To meet the criteria of objectivity, commissions must refer to objective criteria, not political expediencies, when making recommendations on remuneration. The court said that the commission's objectivity can be promoted by ensuring it is fully informed (it could receive submissions from the judiciary, the executive and the legislature, although that is not a constitutional requirement). The court also recommended that the enabling legislation or regulations contain a list of relevant factors to guide the commission's deliberations.

Third, with respect to effectiveness of the commissions, the court said governments have a constitutional obligation not to change remuneration until they have received a copy of the report of the commission. They must also prevent government inaction from leading to a reduction in judges' real salaries due to inflation by having the commission convene within a fixed period after its last report, and the commissions' reports must have a meaningful effect on the determination of judicial salaries. Reports of the commissions need not be binding, as the allocation of public resources is generally the responsibility of the legislature, but the executive or legislature must formally respond to the contents of the commission's report within a specified time. Further, if one or more recommendations is not accepted, the government must be prepared to justify its decision in the courts if necessary. The standard of justification is said to be one of simple "rationality" under which the government must provide a legitimate reason for not accepting the commission's recommendation.

Following the Supreme Court of Canada decision, the Saskatchewan government passed *The Provincial Court Act*, 1998, which reflects the requirements set out in the decision, including the establishment of a commission.

The first Provincial Court Commission under the Act was established July 6, 1998, and is chaired by Robert G. Bundon. It held hearings on November 20, 1998 and issued its first report on December 16, 1998. The Commission's recommendations ratified the June 1997 agreement between the Saskatchewan government and the Provincial Court judges and set the salary for Provincial Court judges for the period from April 1, 1997 to March 31, 2000.

The Provincial Court Commission reconvened on July 1, 1999 to do an independent review of judicial remuneration and benefits for the period from April 1, 2000 to March 31, 2003. The Commission received submissions from interested parties and held public hearings on November 1–2, 1999.

The Saskatchewan Provincial Court Judges' Association asked the Commission to consider many of the same issues argued before previous Commissions: the unique role and responsibility of the Provincial Court judge, a comparison with national standards of remuneration for judges, judicial independence and the public interest in the administration of justice, the need to attract, motivate and retain the most highly qualified candidates, fiscal capacity of government, and increases in cost of living. With respect to the comparison with national standards of remuneration, the minister of Justice argued that the total remuneration package must be considered — that the salary is but one component of that.

The Commission issued its report on December 21, 1999. It acknowledged the principles of judicial independence set out in the Judges Reference and that compensation to judges must be sufficient to protect that independence. The

Commission also acknowledged that the Provincial Court is a busy court with extensive jurisdiction. The Commission referred to evidence that the national average of remuneration for provincial court judges was $138,776 and indicated it was imperative that the compensation be sufficient to "attract, motivate and retain" the most qualified candidates. With respect to the fiscal capacity of government, the Commission pointed to evidence that the province's budget would continue to remain balanced and that the general economic projection was one of growth. It believed the additional expenditure to secure the goal of judicial independence could be provided.

The Commission indicated that although it looked at factors unique to Saskatchewan, it strongly considered the national averages for judicial remuneration. Parity with federally appointed judges was a factor but not a dominant factor. The Commission was of the view that the comparison to the national average of provincial court judges was more appropriate.

The Commission recommended that the salary be $143,000 for the period from April 1, 2000 to March 31, 2003 and that the salaries for the Chief Judge and Associate Chief Judge be $153,000 and $148,000 respectively. It recommended that administrative judges receive additional remuneration of $3,000 for administrative duties assigned to them, and that the number of administrative judges be limited to four, as proposed by the Minister of Justice and agreed by the Chief Judge. The Commission recommended a $600 per diem rate for temporary judges, or $300 per half day. It also made recommendations with respect to allowances, annual leave and education leave, pensions and retirement, and it undertook to conduct a review of facilities and security provided for judges.

On January 13, 2000, the government of Saskatchewan announced that it would implement the Provincial Court Commission's recommendations regarding pay and benefits for Provincial Court Judges.

CONCLUSION

Any constitutionally recognized agency of the state lives under a number of imperatives. It must enjoy immunity from political interference that would prevent it from meeting its constitutional responsibilities. It must also continually assess whether it needs to change its structures and practices in order to meet those basic responsibilities in a constantly changing social environment. It must determine whether its character and role continue to fit the needs of the political community it serves.

Clearly, little has changed to alter the basic judicial goal of adjudicating conflict in accordance with law. This project, that has been established for centuries, is essential to public order, security of the person and government under law. Saskatchewan history shows that Saskatchewan courts have contributed immensely to the creation of an orderly and largely prosperous society. The establishment of law and order, and the rule of law, in a pioneer society has been the bedrock for today's mature political community.

Changing social conditions and changing political sensibilities have produced changes in court structure, particularly changes to the trial court function in the province. Threats to independence have been responded to, and attention to constructing a constitutionally appropriate relationship between courts and government has sustained a strong and independent judicial system — and has done so without lingering rancour or conflict.

Saskatchewan's political maturity is reflected in the place that its judicial system holds in Saskatchewan society.

Saskatchewan, however, faces an immense social challenge. Its Aboriginal population does not enjoy an equal place in its economy or its society. The courts are on the front line of this troubled relationship, daily dealing with the social dysfunctions that this historic inequity has produced. Needless to say, courts have not created our legacy or strained inter-societal relations. Yet they are implicated in its current manifestation. More to the point, it is within the courts' scope of responsibilities, and within their ways of meeting those responsibilities, that the task of constructing real social inclusion and social parity lies. The project of social order, including the operation of the court system, cannot be seen to be an aspect of oppressive inter-societal relations. Rather, it must be seen as one of the key engines for finding common purposes, for incorporating a common vision in Saskatchewan society and for constructing equal social participation.

Saskatchewan's judicial system, like Saskatchewan itself, is just now at the point of facing its greatest challenge.[42]

42. The authors wish to acknowledge the valuable assistance of Thomson Irvine, Crown Counsel, in the preparation of this chapter.

Top: Frederick W. Johnson, Lieutenant Governor from 1983 to 1988, seen here with his wife Joyce, brought a new dignity to the position and obtained long-overdue resources for the vice-regal office, including the return to Government House in 1984. He was the first chancellor of the Saskatchewan Order of Merit (photo: courtesy of D. Michael Jackson)

Bottom: Sylvia O. Fedoruk, chancellor of the University of Saskatchewan and the first woman to be Lieutenant Governor (1988-94), was also the first to have regular meetings with the Premier. She faced a constitutional crisis in 1991 over special warrants and prorogation of the Legislature (photo: Office of the Lieutenant Governor of Saskatchewan)

Top: John E.N. (Jack) Wiebe, Lieutenant Governor from 1994 to 2000, was the first farmer to occupy the vice-regal position; the province benefited from his political savvy and grassroots appeal. He presided over the first presentation of the Saskatchewan Volunteer Medal (photo: Office of the Lieutenant Governor of Saskatchewan)

Bottom: Lynda M. Haverstock, the second female Lieutenant Governor (from 2000). Her poise and non-partisan eloquence soon eclipsed her recent political role. Seen here with the Prince of Wales shortly after investing him as the first honorary member of the Saskatchewan Order of Merit in 2001, she is wearing the collar of office of Chancellor of the Order, donated by Sylvia Fedoruk, and the medal of the Order (the lieutenant governor became an ex officio member from 2001) (photo: Saskatchewan Protocol Office)

Top: Allan Blakeney, Premier of Saskatchewan 1971–1982 (photo courtesy Saskatchewan Archives Board)

Bottom: Grant Devine, Premier of Saskatchewan 1982–1991 (photo courtesy Saskatchewan Archives Board)

Top: Roy Romanow, Premier of Saskatchewan 1991–2001 (photo courtesy Oktober Revolution Photography)

Bottom: Lorne Calvert, Premier of Saskatchewan 2001–present (photo courtesy Executive Council Office)

Drawing Boundaries: The Work of Saskatchewan's Provincial Constituency Boundaries Commission, 1993

Dan de Vlieger

In 1993, within two years of being elected to office in October 1991, the New Democratic Party government of Saskatchewan brought into effect *The Constituency Boundaries Act*, S.S. 1993. Under the terms of this Act, a Constituency Boundaries Commission, consisting of three persons,[1] was established on July 28, 1993, charged with the responsibility of preparing an interim report and submitting a final report containing recommendations respecting constituency boundaries for 56 constituencies located in the "southern area" of the province. Northern constituencies are dealt with differently, as will be seen.

The Commission, assisted by two technical advisors,[2] commenced its work immediately, submitted an interim report on November 22, 1993, held a series of public hearings at six locations[3] around the province in January 1994 to receive reactions to the interim report, and presented its final report to the Honourable Herman Rolfes, Speaker of the Legislative Assembly, on February 15, 1994. At the six public meetings the Commission listened to 46 presentations from individuals and organizations. In addition the Commission received written briefs from another 25 individuals.[4]

This summary of the actual work of the Commission is obviously silent about the background that gave rise to the legislation establishing the Commission, and says nothing about the particular requirements the Commission was required to observe. Both these elements, need to be briefly mentioned in order to provide a meaningful context to the Commission's recommendations.

In relation to the legislative background, it is informative to look at the economic and political circumstances prevalent at that time in Canada generally and in Saskatchewan in particular.

In the early 1990s, with all parts of Canada in the throes of an economic recession and with the public clamouring for a reduction in the size of both public deficits and current government expenditures, governments and legislatures were

1. The Commission consisted of the Honourable Mr. Justice E.C. Malone (chairperson), Court of Queen's Bench, Dan de Vlieger (Deputy Chairperson), Dean of Arts, University of Regina, and Nancy Kent, Executive Director, Prince Albert Regional Economic Development Authority.
2. Mrs. Janice Baker and Mr. Donald C. McMahon.
3. The public hearings were held in Saskatoon (January 4), Prince Albert (January 5), North Battleford (January 6), Yorkton (January 11), Swift Current (January 13), and Regina (January 14).
4. Appendix D, *Final Report, Constituency Boundaries Commission, 1993.*

under considerable popular pressure to show that they had understood the public mood. In the case of several jurisdictions this meant being prepared to show a willingness to reduce (or at least not increase) the remuneration of elected legislators and in some instances, as in Saskatchewan, it also meant a preparedness to reduce the number of legislative seats to which people could be elected. Thus in Saskatchewan the newly elected government, in its 1993 *Constituency Boundaries Act,* mandated the establishment of boundaries for a total of 58 constituencies, a reduction of 8 seats (or 12 percent) from the number of constituencies returning members in the previous election.

In effect this meant a reduction of eight rural seats in the "southern area" of the province, since SS. 14(4) of the Act mandated that the two seats established in the "northern area" had to be maintained and also because the populations of Regina and Saskatoon and immediate surrounding areas had experienced a net increase in population relative to that of the rural population. It also meant that regardless of which way the boundaries of the 56 seats in the southern area of the province were drawn it was inevitable that some of the sitting members of the legislature, should they wish to contest the next provincial election, would be competing for the same seats with some of their current legislative colleagues. It was evident from comments made during the Commission's public hearings and from the submissions that it received that this reduction in the total number of constituencies was not met with universal acclaim.

While the public mood in the early 1990s was one of a mistrust of politicians in general, in Saskatchewan that mood was particularly acute in the wake of widespread suspicion that many elected legislators in the Grant Devine government had engaged in corrupt practices. This suspicion found a counterpart in the controversial legislation which had been introduced and passed by Premier Devine's Progressive Conservative government to govern the holding of the next provincial election. That legislation, *The Electoral Boundaries Commission Act, 1986–87–88* and *The Representation Act, 1989,* was seen by many people as a deliberate attempt to thwart the democratic process. The specific features found to be particularly odious in these two pieces of legislation were: 1) a designation that the seats in the southern part of the promise had to be either completely rural or completely urban, i.e, no seats could have both rural and urban voters[5]; and 2) an increase in the permissible variation of a constituency's population to 25 percent, either more or less, from the "constituency population quotient."[6]

Under the previous legislation governing provincial elections the permissible variation had been 15 percent, either more or less, from a constituency population quotient. This new provision allowed the variation to increase from a potential maximum of 30 percent between the largest and smallest constituencies to a potential maximum variation of 50 percent. Coupled with the deliberate designation of seats as either rural or urban this was certainly seen by many people, especially in urban

5. In fact the legislation went much further than dividing the southern area of the province between rural and urban seats. It also determined that for the urban seats, Saskatoon and Regina had to have eleven seats each, Moose Jaw and Prince Albert two each, and one each for Swift Current, Yorkton and the Battlefords.

6. In Saskatchewan the term "constituency population quotient" refers to a number arrived at by dividing the total population contained in the "southern area" by the number of seats allocated to that area. This view was in part based on the fact that in the last election won by the Progressive Conservative Party in 1986, the NDP as the leading opposition party had gained more votes on a province-wide basis than did the governing party under the leadership of Grant Devine.

areas, as a deliberate attempt by the government to try and ensure its re-election on the basis of gaining a majority of seats containing a minority of the population.[7] The clamour that accompanied the introduction of this legislation, both inside and outside of the legislature, was based in part on assertions that these legislative measures were unconstitutional. Acting under the threat of legal action by a coalition of individuals under the name of the Society for the Advancement of Voter Equality, the government of Grant Devine was prompted to refer the issue to the Saskatchewan Court of Appeal for a ruling under *The Constitutional Questions Act, 1978*.

The challenge that was launched before the Court of Appeal was based on the provisions of the Charter of Rights and Freedoms.[8] Since the introduction of the Charter in the early 1980s there had been an increase in the debate in Canada's legal and political circles about whether the terms of the Charter could be used to challenge the traditional practices of legislatures, both at the federal and provincial levels of government, in establishing electoral boundaries for constituencies. In Canada, although each citizen has the right to cast a vote, the political weight given to that vote could vary widely depending on where the voter lives.

At both provincial and federal levels of government in Canada the electoral systems in place are based on the practice of single-member seats with a plurality of votes determining the winner, sometimes quaintly named as a "first-past-the post" system. The arguments of the challengers to the Saskatchewan government's legislation may be characterized as being based on the notion that the slogan "one person, one vote" implies that under the equality provisions of the Charter of Rights and Freedoms, each vote should be equal to any other vote, or at least as equal as can be established in practice. The challengers to the legislation were encouraged in their position by the case of *Dixon v. the Attorney General of British Columbia, 1989*, in which then Chief Justice of British Columbia Madame Beverly McLachlin had found against the British Columbia government's attempts to determine electoral boundaries in such a way as to significantly vary the value or weight of a vote from one elector to the next. Some of the wording used by the Chief Justice in the Dixon case figured prominently in the arguments placed before the Court of Appeal in the late fall of 1990.[9]

The unanimous decision of the Saskatchewan Court of Appeal against the legislation delivered on March 6, 1991, was obviously a severe blow to the Saskatchewan government's electoral planning strategy[10] and it was not surprising that Saskatchewan launched an immediate request to the Supreme Court of Canada for an expedited hearing to appeal this case. This was granted. There was some urgency to this case being heard, but not only because of Saskatchewan's situation. There

7. The arguments against the government's legislation were presented by Roger Carter, QC, a former Dean of Law at the University of Saskatchewan and appointed by the Court, and two intervenors, Dr. John Conway, Professor of Sociology at the University of Regina, and Larry Kowalchuk, a lawyer from Saskatoon representing an anti-poverty group with the name of Equal Justice for All. The government's case was presented by Robert Richards and Thomas Irvine.

8. J.F. Conway, "The Saskatchewan Electoral Boundaries Case, 1990–91: A Final Note," paper presented to the Canadian Political Science Association, Ottawa, June 1993, pp. 14–20.

9. *Judgment*, Court of Appeal for Saskatchewan. In the Matter of the *Constitutional Questions Act*, R.S.S. 1978, Chapter C-29; In the Matter of a Reference Pursuant Thereto by the Lieutenant Governor in Council to the Court of Appeal for Hearing and Consideration of Certain Questions Relating to the Constitutional Validity of Provincial Electoral Boundaries, File No. 639, 6 March 1991.

10. The Saskatchewan legislature's constitutional mandate of five years was slated to end in October 1991.

were other cases on related issues winding their way through the courts in Alberta and the Northwest Territories, with another slated to be launched in Prince Edward Island.

In June 1991 a majority of the Supreme Court of Canada, in a 6-3 decision, overturned the decision of the Saskatchewan Court of Appeal. In the view of the Supreme Court, as delivered for the majority by the Honourable Madame Justice Beverly McLachlin, now a member of the Supreme Court, the governing principle was not that of equality of voting power but that of the right to "effective representation." This decision allowed the Saskatchewan government to call for an election in October 1991 on the basis of the legislation that had received such severe challenges. As it turned out, in the ensuing election the government led by Grant Devine was defeated by the New Democratic Party under the leadership of Roy Romanow.

It is against this background of economic, political, and constitutional elements that the new provincial government introduced legislation culminating in *The Constituency Boundaries Act, 1993*. The main provisions of the Act that were sharply different from the provisions of the legislation it replaced may be summarized as follows: 1) reduction of the number of seats in the legislature from 66 to 58; 2) no designation of seats as either urban or rural; 3) a permissible variation for the southern seats of 5 percent, either more or less, from the constitution population quotient.[11]

There were, however, some significant similarities between *The Constituency Boundaries Act, 1993*, and the legislation it replaced. The two most important were: 1) a series of provisions in Section 14(2) of the Act allowing the Commission to exercise its discretion (subject to the requirements of the 5 percent rule) to depart from a strict equality provision in consideration of geography, special community interests, or topography; 2) an order to the Commission in Section 14(4) to fix the boundaries of the constituencies north of the line dividing the province between a northern and a southern region (i.e. the constituencies of Athabasca and Cumberland) as prescribed in *The Representation Act, 1989*.

The work of the Commission was therefore one governed by conditions which on the one hand provided it with considerably more discretion than the Commission that had drawn up the boundaries for the constituencies on the basis of which the 1991 election was held, but on the other hand it also curtailed the exercise of this discretion by establishing the rule of permitting a deviation of only 5 percent from the constituency population quotient and prohibiting any change in the boundaries for the two northern constituencies. However, while it was noted by some that the restrictions imposed by the legislation were too onerous, these same restrictions highlighted geographical factors that made the work of the Commission unexpectedly challenging. The greatest challenge resulted from the major river systems that cut across the Saskatchewan landscape. The way in which this challenge presented itself

11. One other change, while not as significant as the three enumerated above, related to the composition of the Commission itself. Under the legislation of the government of Premier Grant Devine the Commission charged with the responsibility of drafting the constituency boundaries in place for the 1991 election had as one of its members appointed by the government the province's Chief Electoral Officer, an individual who at that time was appointed to that office by the government of the day, i.e., it was a patronage appointment. Under the new legislation the government reverted back to the practice of having, apart from the Commission's chairperson, the other two persons, nominated respectively by the government and the official opposition, appointed after consultation with the leaders of the opposition parties.

can be seen by comparing the prospective electoral map submitted in the Commission's *Interim Report* with recommendations contained in the Commission's *Final Report*.

Saskatchewan as a geographic entity is a rectangle and topographically it is relatively featureless. At first glance these aspects would appear to make the drawing of electoral boundaries relatively easy. In some ways that was the case, but given the fairly narrow permissible deviation of 5 percent, more or less, from the constituency population quotient (CPQ), a contemplated change from an initial prospective recommendation would bring unforeseen reverberations in its wake. This can be illustrated by looking more closely at how the Commission conducted its work.

The first task of the Commission was to establish the CPQ. The Act [SS 3 (1)] required that the results of the 1991 census be used to calculate this quotient. The 1991 census determined that Saskatchewan's population numbered 988,928. By subtracting the population (a total of 26,735) determined by that census as living in the northern area of the province, and contained in the Athabasca and Cumberland constituencies, the CPQ to be used for the 56 constituencies in the southern area was determined to be 17,182 (988, 928 less 26,735 divided by 56). The 5 percent permissible deviation from this number, up or down, was then determined as being 859. Consequently no constituency in the southern area could contain more than 18,041 or fewer than 16,323 persons.

Using the 1991 census data, broken into census enumeration areas (for Regina and Saskatoon it was possible to use population figures on a block-by-block basis), the Commission proceeded to examine how a potential division of the population into 56 constituencies of equal size might appear.

In approaching this task, two important considerations immediately came to the fore: 1) Saskatchewan, being a rectangle, it is imperative that one must start by drawing a map using the four corners of this rectangle; 2) Saskatchewan's population is, like everywhere else, not evenly spread across the province. The major cities of Saskatoon and Regina figure prominently, and so do the cities of Prince Albert, Moose Jaw, Yorkton, Swift Current and the Battlefords. Given these two major considerations, and regardless of how precisely boundaries of constituencies could be determined, the Commission had to start working from the premise that of the 56 constituencies whose boundaries had to be established, the location of 33 of them was roughly predetermined (i.e. one in each of the four corners, and 29 contained within or largely centred on the above-named cities).

Apart from these geographic and demographic factors there remained two other major aspects the Commission had to deal with. The first of these was the fact that Saskatchewan is dissected by the North and South Saskatchewan rivers and, although not quite as important, by the Qu'Appelle Valley. While these "cracks" in Saskatchewan's topography are not numerous, the accessibility of regions had to be kept in mind while drawing constituency boundaries. The second aspect, and one already mentioned, was the limitation resulting from the 5 percent variation.

Working within these parameters, the Commission was also confronted with the fact that the Act, by reducing the number of constituencies from 64 to 56 in the southern area of the province, made it impossible to give any real consideration to the previously existing boundaries between constituencies. In a sense this was a liberating factor for the Commission since it meant that whatever set of boundaries it considered, it could not begin to accommodate established political interests.

The Commission decided, for its interim report, to produce a set of recommendations for potential constituency boundaries that as closely as possible would match, for each constituency, the constituency population quotient of 17,182. It did so on the basis that after receiving reactions from the public, it would be able to make changes accommodating, where possible, a variety of concerns. This can be seen by looking at the description of proposed constituencies in Appendix A of the Commission's *Interim Report*. Of the 56 southern constituencies there were only four that would have a population base greater or smaller than 1 percent of the CPQ, and the average deviation for all 56 of these constituencies was only 0.47 percent (81 people).

In the Commission's *Final Report* the departures from the CPQ were somewhat greater. The reasons for this did not occur as the result of any large-scale revisions or any major change of views within the Commission, but rather from the parameters and limitations mentioned earlier. Given the fact that the Commission had to stay within the 5 percent tolerance, a change in the proposed boundaries for one constituency tended to have reverberations not only in the immediately adjacent constituency, but in constituencies bordering that one as well — in short, a domino effect.

The results of this domino effect can be seen in the Commission's recommendations for constituency boundaries in its *Final Report*. There were now 10 (as opposed to four) constituencies out of 56 that would contain a number of people greater or smaller than 1 percent of the CPQ, and the average deviation for all 56 constituencies was now 0.79 percent. The total number of constituencies that saw their proposed boundaries changed in the *Final Report* compared to what had been recommended in the *Interim Report* was 44 (or 79 percent).

If the magnitude of the changes between those originally suggested and those finally recommended, at least in terms of the percentage of constituencies affected, was surprisingly large, what is even more surprising to note is that each one of the 12 constituencies for which no change was recommended between the two reports was located in an urban area.

There are several conclusions that may be derived from the description of the work of the Commission. First, given the parameters within which the Commission had to conducts its work, the degree to which it would have been possible for the Commission, had it even contemplated doing so, to draw boundaries in such a way as to presumably provide an advantage to one party was virtually nil. Second, the large number of changes made between the two reports were minor in terms of the number of people per constituency affected. The fact that so many constituencies were affected resulted from the physical features of the landscape and the 5 percent permissible variation rule.

Finally, it should be noted that Saskatchewan has established the smallest permissible tolerance for drawing electoral boundaries of any provincial or federal jurisdictions, and while theoretically it is of course feasible to narrow such a degree of tolerance to a level smaller than Saskatchewan's, doing so would make the work of any electoral boundaries commission much more difficult, if not impossible, if such factors as accessibility and other physical features of a landscape have to be taken into account. Practically speaking, a level of tolerance of 5 percent eliminates any opportunity for gerrymandering on the part of an electoral boundaries commission.

APPENDIX A

LIST OF PROPOSED CONSTITUENCIES – SASKATCHEWAN 1993
INTERIM REPORT

Name of Constituency	Population	% Variation from Quotient
Northern Constituencies		
Athabasca	11,446	
Cumberland	15,289	
Southern Constituencies		
Arm River	17,210	+0.16
Battleford–Cut Knife	17,159	-0.13
Cannington	17,293	+0.65
Canora	17,236	+0.31
Carrot River Valley	17,096	-0.50
Cypress Hills	17,200	+0.10
Estevan	17,166	-0.09
Humboldt	17,155	-0.16
Indian Head	17,205	+0.13
Kelvington	17,282	+0.58
Kindersley	17,243	+0.35
Last Mountain–Touchwood	17,012	-0.99
Lloydminster	17,231	+0.29
Meadow Lake	17,171	-0.06
Melfort	17,162	-0.12
Melville	17,152	-0.17
Moose Jaw Palliser	17,291	+0.63
Moose Jaw Wakamow	17,353	+1.00
Moosomin	17,187	+0.03
North Battleford	17,152	-0.17
Prince Albert Carlton	17,331	+0.87
Prince Albert Northcote	17,405	+1.30
Redberry Lake	17,075	-0.62
Regina Centre	17,121	-0.36
Regina Coronation Park	17,156	-0.15
Regina Dewdney	17,251	+0.40
Regina Lakeview	17,215	+0.19
Regina Northeast	17,257	+0.44
Regina Qu'Appelle Valley	16,915	-1.55
Regina Rosemont	17,156	-0.15
Regina Sherwood	17,275	+0.54
Regina South	17,190	+0.05
Regina University	17,217	+0.20
Regina Wascana Plains	16,626	-3.24
Rosetown	17,251	+0.40
Rosthern	17,157	-0.15
Saltcoats	17,262	+0.47
Saskatchewan Rivers	17,264	+0.48
Saskatoon Eastview	17,287	+0.61
Saskatoon Fairview	17,182	+0.00
Saskatoon Greystone	17,208	+0.15
Saskatoon Idylwyld	17,273	+0.53
Saskatoon Mount Royal	17,201	+0.11
Saskatoon Northwest	17,106	-0.44
Saskatoon Nutana	17,221	+0.23
Saskatoon River Crossing	17,024	-0.92
Saskatoon Riversdale	17,256	+0.43
Saskatoon Sutherland	17,253	+0.41
Saskatoon Wildwood	16,890	-1.70
Shellbrook	17,133	-0.29
Swift Current	17,181	-0.01
Thunder Creek	17,232	+0.29
Watrous	17,224	+0.24
Weyburn–Big Muddy	17,111	-0.41
Wolf Willow	17,283	+0.59
Yorkton	17,048	-0.78

NOTE: The population of the proposed Saskatchewan constituencies is based on the Saskatchewan population of 988,928 from the 1991 Canada Census.

APPENDIX B

List of Proposed Constituencies – Saskatchewan 1993 Final Report

Name of Constituency	Population	% Variation from Quotient
Northern Constituencies		
Athabasca	11,446	
Cumberland	15,289	
Southern Constituencies		
Arm River	17,325	+0.83
Battleford–Cut Knife	17,587	+2.36
Cannington	17,014	-0.98
Canora–Pelly	16,755	-2.49
Carrot River Valley	17,070	-0.65
Cypress Hills	17,085	-0.56
Estevan	17,081	-0.59
Humboldt	17,155	-0.16
Indian Head–Milestone	17,455	+1.59
Kelvington–Wadena	17,104	-0.45
Kindersley	17,326	+0.84
Last Mountain–Touchwood	17,396	-1.25
Lloydminster	17,231	+0.29
Meadow Lake	16,492	-4.02
Melfort–Tisdale	17,205	+0.13
Melville	17,152	-0.17
Moose Jaw North	17,335	+0.89
Moose Jaw Wakamow	17,309	+0.74
Moosomin	17,228	+0.27
North Battleford	17,152	-0.17
Prince Albert Carlton	17,776	+3.46
Prince Albert Northcote	16,960	-1.29
Redberry Lake	17,066	-0.68
Regina Centre	17,090	-0.54
Regina Coronation Park	17,156	-0.15
Regina Dewdney	17,146	-0.21
Regina Elphinstone	17,323	+0.82
Regina Lakeview	17,226	+0.26
Regina Northeast	17,141	-0.24
Regina Qu'Appelle Valley	16,915	-1.55
Regina Sherwood	17,275	+0.54
Regina South	17,190	+0.05
Regina Victoria–University	17,206	+0.14
Regina Wascana Plains	16,711	-2.74
Rosetown–Biggar	17,193	+0.06
Rosthern	17,157	-0.15
Saltcoats	17,403	+1.29
Saskatchewan Rivers	17,260	+0.45
Saskatoon Eastview	17,287	+0.61
Saskatoon Fairview	17,182	+0.00
Saskatoon Greystone	17,208	+0.15
Saskatoon Idylwyld	17,311	+0.75
Saskatoon Meewasin	17,024	-0.92
Saskatoon Mount Royal	17,163	-0.11
Saskatoon Nutana	17,221	+0.23
Saskatoon Riversdale	17,256	+0.43
Saskatoon Southeast	16,890	-1.70
Saskatoon Sutherland	17,253	+0.41
Shellbrook–Spiritwood	17,351	+0.98
Swift Current	17,300	+0.69
Thunder Creek	17,315	+0.77
Watrous	17,243	+0.35
Weyburn–Big Muddy	17,279	+0.56
Wolf Willow	17,105	-0.45
Yorkton	17,048	-0.78

NOTE: The population of the proposed Saskatchewan constituencies is based on the Saskatchewan population of 988,928 from the 1991 Canada Census.

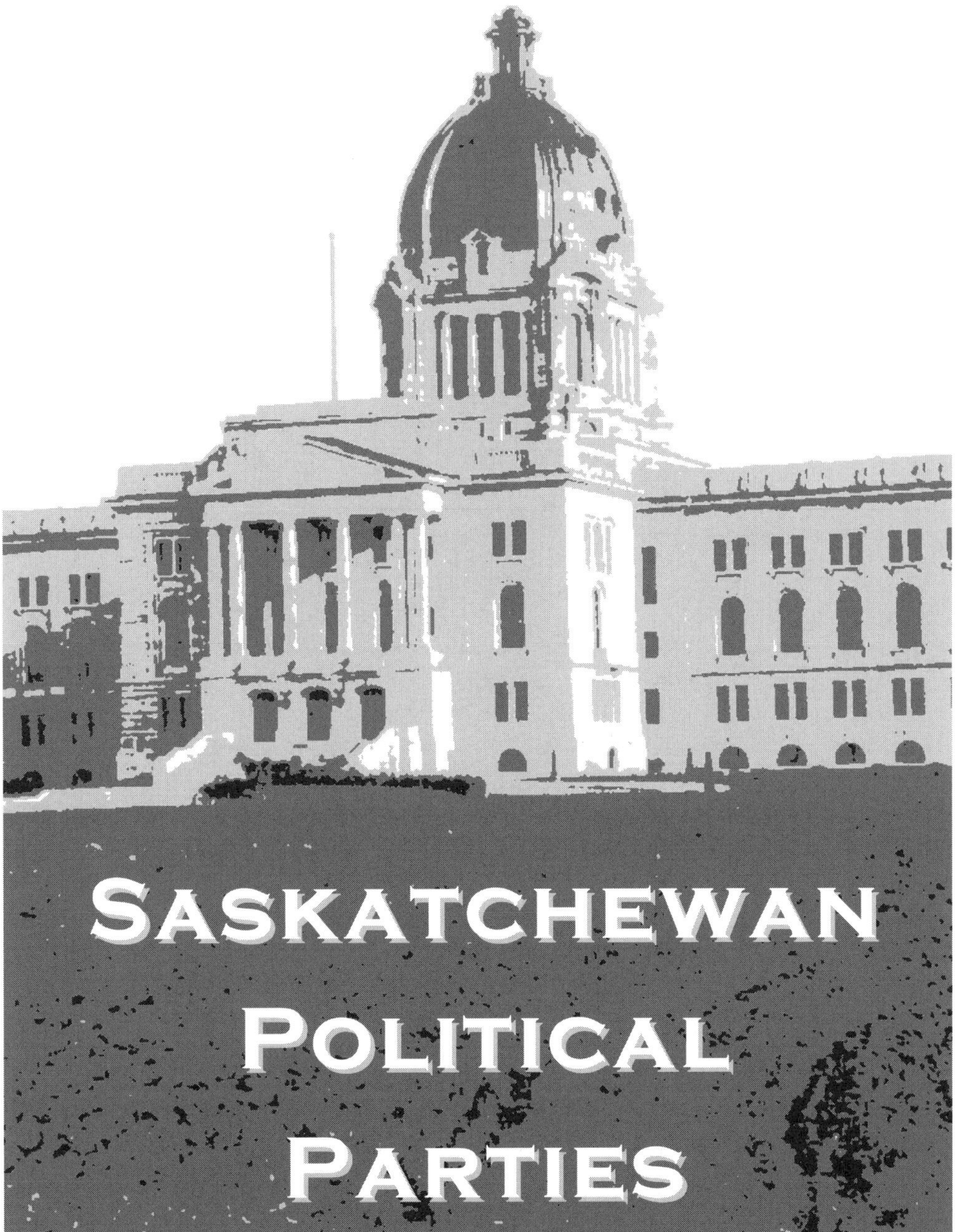

Saskatchewan Political Parties

The Saskatchewan CCF-NDP from the *Regina Manifesto* to the Romanow Years

Jocelyne Praud and Sarah McQuarrie

INTRODUCTION

For the last half century, the Saskatchewan CCF-NDP has defined the province of Saskatchewan and, in so doing, it has greatly contributed to the definition of Canada. Founded in Regina in 1933 by agrarian socialists and trade-unionists, the Saskatchewan Co-operative Commonwealth Federation (CCF) went on to form the first social democratic government in North America eleven years later under the leadership of Thomas C. Douglas. The CCF eventually became the "natural" governing party of the province. In their sixty-eight years of existence, the CCF and its successor, the New Democratic Party (NDP), have held power for more than forty years. Some of the most important accomplishments of the Saskatchewan CCF-NDP include the adoption in 1947 of Canada's first provincial bill of rights, the creation one year later of the Saskatchewan Arts Board, and the establishment in 1962 of Medicare, a system of publicly funded health-care services. The Saskatchewan Bill of Rights helped to pave the way for the two federal documents that protect the civil rights and liberties of Canadians, the 1960 Bill of Rights and the 1982 Charter of Rights and Freedoms. Nine years after the creation of the Saskatchewan Arts Board, the oldest arts support agency in North America, a similar agency was established at the federal level, the Canada Council for the Arts. Last but not least, Saskatchewan's Medicare was copied by the federal government and implemented on a national scale in the late 1960s. Clearly, the Saskatchewan CCF-NDP and, more specifically, its social democratic ideas, have had a tremendous impact not only on the province, but also on the country.

In consequence, no matter what their focus is, analyses of the Saskatchewan CCF-NDP have to refer to the concept of social democracy. But how do we define social democracy? As Kenneth McRoberts notes, this concept "does not lend itself to a precise definition, given the multitude of ways in which it has been used over the years."[1] Nevertheless, it is still possible to identify a set of ideas that have been constant in traditional social democratic thought.

One constant is that the state has an important role to play in strengthening democracy in the social, economic and political realms. With regard to the economy,

1. Kenneth McRoberts, *Quebec Social Change and Political Crisis* (Don Mills, ON: Oxford University Press, 1993), 254.

social democrats support state intervention and public ownership. In other words, they perceive the state as a full-fledged economic actor that intervenes in the mixed economy, regulates it and owns parts of it. For social democrats, the state also has to ensure wealth redistribution via progressive tax measures, publicly funded social programs such as health and education, and a social safety net to protect the most vulnerable members of society. Related to this and in part due to their ties to unions, social democrats are committed to strive for full employment and to enhance workers' rights. Lastly, with a view to strengthening political democracy, social democrats support "broadened participation in decision-making" through, for instance, "popular consultation by the state or worker control within private enterprises."[2] In sum, the democracy envisioned by social democrats is not simply political, it is also social and economic.

This chapter examines how the Saskatchewan CCF-NDP has developed since its inception in 1933 and, more specifically, how its approach to economic and social policy making has changed over the years. Two key periods can be distinguished in the development of the party: the first period involves the three decades of social democratic policy making beginning with the Douglas and Lloyd governments (1944–1964) and ending with the Blakeney government (1971–1982); the second and most recent period spanning from 1991 onwards concerns the Romanow government and its apparent move away from traditional social democratic policies. While the first section follows the CCF-NDP from its inception until the 1980s, the second section focuses on the Romanow years.

In the postwar period, the Douglas and Lloyd governments implemented a number of policies aimed at bringing social democracy to Saskatchewan. Crown corporations were created, and programs designed to improve the standard of living of non-affluent citizens — namely, rural electrification, hospital coverage, social aid and Medicare — were launched. The fact that these policies were not reversed by the Thatcher Liberals attests to their wide popular support. In 1971, the New Democrats were returned to power on a brand new platform, *New Deal for People*, which essentially pledged to strengthen social democracy in the province. This is what the Blakeney government did, especially with respect to the economy. In the early 1980s, as a right-wing wave was sweeping through Europe and North America, the Saskatchewan NDP was defeated by Grant Devine's Conservatives, who did not support social democratic ideals.

Shortly after regaining power in 1991, the New Democrats discovered that Saskatchewan's deficit and debt were much higher than expected. The Romanow government then designed a "balanced" plan to eliminate the deficit, combining tax increases and spending cuts. Through the 1990s, the government's deficit reduction strategy as well as its approach to economic and social policy making often appeared to be at odds with traditional social democratic ideas of state intervention, public ownership and consultation. While international and national factors account for this shift of direction, it is important to note that factors related to the party and, in particular, changes in its electoral support base, leadership and internal organization, also contributed to it. These factors should be of particular interest to present and future activists and intellectuals who are committed to working within the Saskatchewan NDP and bringing about a renewed social democratic vision.

---

2. Ibid., 254.

BRINGING SOCIAL DEMOCRACY TO SASKATCHEWAN

FROM THE *REGINA MANIFESTO* TO THE DOUGLAS GOVERNMENT

The Co-operative Commonwealth Federation (CCF) was founded with the *Regina Manifesto* in 1933, but within a few short years it had left behind many of the more radical propositions contained within that document. Over time, the party changed from a primarily rural socialist movement to an urban-dominated political party. This emphasis on electoral politics has played a defining role in the development of the party, forcing it to become more conciliatory to what it once would have considered hostile interests. Nevertheless, the history of the CCF-NDP in Saskatchewan has also proved to be one of social change. Through its legislation, CCF-NDP governments in Saskatchewan often enabled the province to become a leader in Canadian social and economic legislation.

The early 1930s are generally considered to be a period of radicalism in Saskatchewan politics. Seymour Martin Lipset writes that "[t]he period up to the elections of 1934 and 1935 was distinctly a radical, agitational stage."[3] The desperation experienced by Saskatchewan farmers in the face of the Great Depression rendered them increasingly receptive to the more unconventional political ideology of socialism.[4] In July 1933, the *Regina Manifesto* was adopted at the first national convention of the CCF. The *Manifesto* outlined fourteen points in the CCF program, including economic planning and social ownership, a plan for agriculture and co-operatives, socialised medicine, and a national labour code. The *Manifesto* also proposed guidelines for dealing with external trade and relations, the *British North America Act*, and issues of freedom and social justice.[5]

The *Regina Manifesto* is a product of the Great Depression. The second paragraph states, for example, that "our society oscillates between periods of feverish prosperity in which the main benefits go to speculators and profiteers, and of catastrophic depression."[6] Despite its scathing attack on capitalism, however, Alan Whitehorn argues that the *Regina Manifesto*'s primary focus was not on socialism. Unlike traditional socialist thought, which is international in nature, the *Regina Manifesto* made several references to "nation" and "nationalism."[7] This was perhaps designed to make the ideology of the *Manifesto* more palatable to Canadian and Saskatchewan electorates. The *Manifesto* closed by stating that "[n]o C.C.F. Government will rest content until it has eradicated capitalism and put into operation the full programme of socialized planning which will lead to the establishment in Canada of the Co-operative Commonwealth."[8]

These radical sentiments would soon find themselves under attack. The *Manifesto* also emphasised the CCF's intention on being elected to government, and the party would soon leave behind some of the ideals of its early days in order to fulfill that more immediate objective, albeit not entirely. During the 1934 general election in Saskatchewan, the CCF's campaign was distinctly socialist in nature,

3. S.M. Lipset, *Agrarian Socialism* (Berkeley: University of California Press, 1959), 128.
4. Ibid.
5. CCF, *Regina Manifesto (Programme of the Co-operative Commonwealth Federation, adopted at the First National Convention held at Regina, Sask., July, 1933)* (Regina: Service Printing Co., 1933), 2–8.
6. Ibid., 1.
7. Alan Whitehorn, *Canadian Socialism* (Toronto: Oxford University Press, 1992), 44.
8. CCF, *Regina Manifesto*, 8.

and the party advocated the nationalization of all resources, creating widespread fear in rural Saskatchewan that a CCF government would nationalize land.[9] In Lipset's words, many voters felt that socialism "had unfortunate connotations of atheism, confiscation of land, and dictatorship."[10] The CCF proved itself unprepared or unable to counter the anti-socialist propaganda spread by its political opponents.

After its defeats in the 1934 provincial election and the 1935 federal election, references to socialism were removed from party literature. Furthermore, having been badly beaten in Saskatchewan's urban areas, the CCF chose not to contest any urban seats in 1938. Following the 1938 election, the party began to expand from its agrarian roots, attempting to "break into" Saskatchewan's urban areas by making overtures to trade unions and small businesspeople. The CCF drew up a trade union program, which marked an important break from its focus on the socialization of industry. The party also drew up policies to protect small business from monopolies, again attempting to broaden its primarily rural support base.[11] In its attempts to attract support from a broader population, the CCF moved away from some of the more militant statements contained in its founding document.

It would take the CCF thirteen years to gain power in the province. During that time, Lipset notes several changes in the party's ideology. These included, for example:

> The virtual dropping of the explicitly socialist goal and its replacement by phrases such as "a new social order"... The elimination of any suggestion of land nationalization... The withdrawal of plans to socialise all, or even the majority, of private industry... An increased emphasis from 1936 through 1944 on social security... The inclusion of small businessmen as a group whose status would be preserved and strengthened under a C.C.F. government... The elimination of plans to change class biases in the educational system [and] ... [t]he development in the 1940's of a complete labour and trade union policy.[12]

In 1944, perhaps because of such shifts in ideology, the CCF won 53 percent of the popular vote in Saskatchewan, which translated into a majority of forty-seven seats. Upon achieving power, Premier T.C. Douglas had a formidable task ahead of him. Despite the modifications in the CCF platform, many politicians and businessmen feared that the party's success in Saskatchewan would lead to the spread of "socialism" elsewhere in Canada. This meant that Douglas had to devote much of his time in government fending off attacks from the federal government, at a time when the province was also in poor financial shape following the Depression.[13]

9. Peter R. Sinclair, "The Saskatchewan CCF: Ascent to Power and the Decline of Socialism," in Samuel D. Clark, Paul J. Grayson, and Linda M. Grayson (eds.), *Prophecy and Protest: Social Movements in Twentieth-Century Canada* (Toronto: Gage Educational Publishing, 1975), 189.

10. Lipset, *Agrarian Socialism*, 128.

11. Sinclair, "The Saskatchewan CCF," 189, 143–47.

12. Lipset, *Agrarian Socialism*, 151.

13. Ivan Avakumovic, *Socialism in Canada: A Study of the CCF-NDP in Federal and Provincial Politics* (Toronto: McClelland and Stewart, 1978), 170; M.J. Coldwell, *Left Turn, Canada* (New York: Duell, Sloan and Pearce, 1945), 154. When the party won the election in 1944, Saskatchewan's credit rating was very low on North American markets. Further, allegations by opponents of the new government that "the socalists would default on their debt" did not help the situation. See Thomas H. McLeod and Ian McLeod, *Tommy Douglas: The Road to Jerusalem* (Edmonton: Hurtig Publishers, 1987), 187.

In spite of these obstacles, the first two years of the CCF government were a time of innovation. The new provincial government began implementing policies congruent with its social democratic ideals by increasing state intervention in the provincial economy and by attempting to raise the standard of living of low-income groups. The new *Crown Corporations Act* (1945) allowed the government to involve itself directly in industry, establishing eleven new Crown corporations in its first year and a half in government. The new Crowns were specialized in three main areas: manufacturing, resource development, and provincial utilities. However, problems surfaced in several of the government-run industries, and the province's finances precluded other mass nationalization programs. Operating under the advice of the influential Economic Advisory and Planning Board, the provincial government decided to limit the industries in which it chose to become involved. The government also decided that, in order for the provincial economy to develop in step with those of Alberta and Manitoba, it would be necessary to allow, and even encourage, certain types of private investment. In 1947, the government announced that it would be encouraging the development of new mines in Saskatchewan through a reduction in royalty rates, and the 1948 budget announced assistance that would be given to both co-operatives and private enterprise through the Industrial Development Fund and the *Co-operative Guarantee Act*.[14]

Two of the Crown corporations that were launched by the Douglas government — the Saskatchewan Government Insurance Office (SGIO) and the Saskatchewan Power Corporation — deserve special mention in that they definitely helped to enhance the quality of life of Saskatchewan residents. Since its inception in 1945, the SGIO has provided affordable insurance rates to Saskatchewan residents. Further, as noted by Thomas McLeod and Ian McLeod, "over the years [the SGIO] proved to be a popular and profitable undertaking."[15] Until 1944, the Saskatchewan Power Commission was mainly responsible for regulating the numerous utilities owned by private companies and municipalities. On the government's instructions, the Commission started buying up the small power companies in the province, thereby resulting in the creation of a unionized, state-owned electric power network called the Saskatchewan Power Corporation (SPC). The SPC facilitated rural electrification and provided electric power to rural and urban residents at competitive rates.[16]

The CCF government also attempted to raise the standard of living of lower-income groups, through such programs as social aid and Medicare. Before 1944, Saskatchewan's relief programs were notoriously strict. Relief was administered by the province's municipalities, controlled by political interests, unreliable, and often insufficient to provide a decent standard of living to its recipients. Upon achieving power, the Douglas government acted immediately to improve relief, beginning by renaming the program "social aid." In 1944, the provincial government sent a voluntary social aid payments schedule to the provincial municipalities and expanded the role of social aid officers. Because of Saskatchewan's difficult financial situation,

14. Jean Larmour, "The Douglas Government's Changing Emphasis on Public, Private, and Co-operative Development in Saskatchewan, 1944–1964," in J. William Brennan (ed.), *"Building the Co-operative Commonwealth": Essays on the Democratic Socialist Tradition in Canada* (Regina: Canadian Plains Research Center, 1984), 164; Rand Dyck, *Provincial Politics in Canada* (Scarborough: Prentice-Hall Canada Inc., 1991), 445.

15. McLeod and McLeod, *Tommy Douglas*, 166.

16. Ibid., 59, 166, 172.

however, these measures had limited impact on the province's social aid programs. The payments schedule was voluntary, and social aid offices suffered from chronic under-staffing. It was not until the late 1950s, when the federal government agreed to provide financial assistance to the provinces for social aid, that the Douglas government was able to institute major social aid reforms.[17]

No discussion of the Douglas government would be complete without an analysis of Medicare. The *Regina Manifesto* articulated the CCF's commitment to socialised medicine, stating

> [a] properly organized system of public health services including medical and dental care, which would stress the prevention rather than the cure of illness, should be extended to all our people in both rural and urban areas.[18]

In the early days of Saskatchewan's CCF government, limited provincial finances precluded the introduction of a Medicare scheme.[19] Douglas, however, did not abandon the ideal of socialised medicine, and campaigned on a Medicare program during the Saskatchewan general election of 1960.[20]

The CCF was once again victorious at the polls in the 1960 election, which the government interpreted as an endorsement of its Medicare proposals. In 1961, Douglas decided to leave provincial politics to serve as the leader of the federal New Democratic Party (NDP), leaving the implementation of Medicare to his provincial successor, Woodrow Lloyd. Because of the opposition of Saskatchewan's doctors, the implementation of Medicare proved to be a controversial measure in Saskatchewan. The province's doctors were unwilling to co-operate with a scheme that they felt would result in reduced health standards, but they also objected to Medicare on ideological grounds, seeing themselves "as defending individual freedom and the doctor-patient relationship against the red tide of socialism."[21]

Opponents of the government's proposal formed "Keep Our Doctors" committees, and engaged in various forms of protest. The doctors themselves threatened the provincial government, and in July 1962, Saskatchewan's doctors went on strike for three weeks. The provincial Liberal Party supported the doctors in their protest, seeing Medicare as an issue that would reduce the popularity of the Saskatchewan CCF. The government program went ahead, however, and the government and doctors were able to reach an agreement. Through the "Saskatoon Agreement" of July 23, 1962, the government's program was amended to provide doctors with different practicing options.[22]

Despite its eventual victory with Medicare, the controversy exhausted the CCF government, while boosting the strength of its main opponent, the Saskatchewan Liberal Party. While part of this may be attributed to the less dynamic leadership of Woodrow Lloyd, the fact was that the Medicare controversy galvanized the Saskatchewan electorate:

---

17. Jim Pitsula, "The CCF Government in Saskatchewan and Social Aid, 1944–1964," in Brennan (ed.), *"Building the Co-operative Commonwealth,"* 205–10.

18. CCF, *Regina Manifesto*, 5.

19. It is worth noting that a medical insurance program was set up in 1946 in the regional health district of Swift Current. However, the doctors' union opposed the launching of similar programs in other regional health districts. For more details, see McLeod and McLeod, *Tommy Douglas*, 150.

20. Avakumovic, *Socialism in Canada*, 184–85.

21. Ibid., 185; Gerald Friesen, *The Canadian Prairies: A History* (Toronto: University of Toronto Press, 1987), 425.

22. Avakumovic, *Socialism in Canada*, 185–86; Friesen, *The Canadian Prairies*, 425.

> More clearly than ever before, CCF now meant "social reform" and government action whereas Liberal meant "freedom" and fewer government social initiatives... The "Medicare crisis," as it was known, sapped the strength of the government and provided ideal ground for a Liberal resurgence.[23]

After twenty years in government, the CCF lost to the Saskatchewan Liberal Party in 1964. The Medicare fight left the party's ministers physically and mentally worn out. Furthermore, the CCF's election manifesto did not contain any new proposals that could attract voters. The Liberal Party, on the other hand, presented the Saskatchewan people with a dynamic, exciting campaign, allowing them to capture 40.4 percent of the popular vote and thirty-three seats in the legislature while the CCF gained 40.3 percent of the popular vote and twenty-five seats.[24]

The fact that the Douglas government made a variety of important changes to Saskatchewan's political culture is undisputed. However, the degree to which these changes can be characterized as "socialist" remains debatable. Opponents of the CCF have often characterized the party as socialist in an attempt to frighten the electorate. However, although the *Regina Manifesto* states the need to replace capitalism with a system of social planning, the actions of the Douglas government tell a different story. In fact, the Douglas government can best be described as "social democratic," for while the government did become involved in the provincial economy, it also encouraged private development where it was felt that private industry could better develop the province. Furthermore, rather than challenging the class structure of Saskatchewan society, the government attempted to improve the lot of Saskatchewan's low-income citizens through a variety of redistributive initiatives. The government also adopted a gradual approach to the implementation of social democratic policies, accepting the importance of private industry to the development of Saskatchewan, and waiting until funding was available for its social aid programs. Most notably, the government waited seventeen years to implement its Medicare scheme. Nevertheless, as Lipset argues, the accomplishments of the Douglas government should not be minimized:

> The stronger a radical social movement becomes in a democracy, the less radical it appears in terms of the general cultural values. As it captures society, society captures it. The amount of change that the movement introduces into the culture as a result of assuming power appears relatively slight compared to its original goals... The winning of votes, particularly the decisive marginal votes of the middle class, calls for a policy of ideological opportunism and gradualism.[25]

The Saskatchewan Liberal Party would win both the 1964 and 1967 provincial elections. Shortly after the 1967 election, the Saskatchewan CCF would change its name to the New Democratic Party of Saskatchewan. This name change signified a formal linkage with organized labour and opened the party up to the criticism that it was abandoning its agrarian roots.[26]

---

23. Ibid., 185.
24. Ibid, 187.
25. Lipset, *Agrarian Socialism*, 157.
26. Evelyn Eager, *Saskatchewan Government: Politics and Pragmatism* (Saskatoon: Western Producer Prairie Books, 1980), 58.

The Waffle and the Blakeney Years

The Waffle emerged within the New Democratic Party in 1969. The Waffle is perhaps one of the more controversial aspects of CCF-NDP history, particularly in Saskatchewan where a disagreement over the Waffle may have contributed to the resignation of Woodrow Lloyd, the provincial leader. The Waffle was made up of party members who saw the movement as a return to the traditional values of the CCF-NDP. The movement also attracted several Marxists who hoped to shift the party's ideology toward socialism.[27] The *Waffle Manifesto* was characterized by Canadian nationalism and by a consequent anti-Americanism. Stating that "the essential fact of Canadian history in the past century is the reduction of Canada to a colony of the United States," the *Manifesto* called for the creation of an independent socialist Canada.[28] The *Waffle Manifesto* was debated at the annual convention of the federal New Democratic Party in October 1969, where it was defeated by 499 votes to 284.[29] Woodrow Lloyd was one of the 284 votes in favour of the *Manifesto*, which many members of the party elite saw as overly divisive.[30]

The impact of the Waffle is debatable. According to John Richards and Larry Pratt:

> The history of the Waffle was, from the perspective of the Canadian left, a tragic fiasco. The NDP leadership, in its refusal to make any accommodations to a potentially significant force for revitalization, alienated many and retarded by at least a decade the intellectual renovation the party desperately needed. By its dogmatism the Waffle also alienated many and, outside the NDP, proved quite incapable of any impact upon Canadian politics, degenerating finally into a series of fractious and irrelevant Marxist sects.[31]

While the Waffle may have had some influence on party policy, Waffle members were not able to attain positions on party executives or party nominations. This has been attributed to systematic lobbying on the part of the party's establishment, designed to prevent the election of Waffle members to positions of power within the party.[32] Internal party fighting subsided during the 1971 general election, however, and in December 1971, the Waffle unsuccessfully entered the race for provincial executive and council. The Saskatchewan Waffle voted to leave the NDP in October 1973.[33]

Woodrow Lloyd resigned as leader of the provincial party in early 1970 after an emergency meeting of the provincial caucus and executive, and in July of that year, Allan Blakeney was elected to replace Lloyd as leader of the Saskatchewan NDP. He had defeated Roy Romanow, who was considered to be to the right of the party, Don Mitchell, the Waffle's candidate, and George Taylor, who was considered to be the candidate of the labour-left wing of the party.[34]

---

27. John Richards and Larry Pratt, *Prairie Capitalism: Power and Influence in the New West* (Toronto: McClelland and Stewart, 1979), 253.
28. *Waffle Manifesto*, in Michael S. Cross (ed.), *The Decline and Fall of a Good Idea* (Toronto: New Hogtown Press, 1974), 44.
29. Dennis Gruending, *Promises to Keep* (Saskatoon: Western Producer Prairie Books, 1990), 56.
30. For an account of Lloyd's support of the Waffle and his subsequent resignation as Leader of the Saskatchewan NDP, see Gruending, *Promises to Keep*, 57–67.
31. Richards and Pratt, *Prairie Capitalism*, 255.
32. Ibid, 254.
33. Saskatchewan Waffle, "A Movement is Growing...Waffle Saskatchewan Section," pamphlet, 1969. For an account of the Waffle in Saskatchewan, see Gruending, *Promises to Keep*, 101.
34. Desmond Morton, *The New Democrats 1961–1986: The Politics of Change* (Toronto: Copp Clark Pitman Ltd, 1986), 108.

In 1971 Allan Blakeney led the NDP to victory in Saskatchewan, defeating the Ross Thatcher Liberals. Central to Blakeney's victory was the platform, *New Deal for People*, which contained seventeen different planks and ran the gamut of Saskatchewan public policy.[35] This social democratic platform called for government intervention in the provincial economy and various social programs designed to assist members of lower classes. It also evidenced the traditional social democratic concern for unions and working people, by proposing various changes to the province's labour laws.

One of the most controversial aspects of the platform was its strategy for government intervention in agriculture. Specifically, the platform called for the establishment of a Land Bank Commission, which was designed to increase the number of family farms in Saskatchewan by purchasing land and then leasing it to farmers with an option to buy. The *New Deal for People* also put forward several innovative measures in the areas of health care and workers' rights. More specifically, it proposed to abolish deterrent health care fees and establish a prescription drug program. As for unions, they were promised a new deal guaranteeing free collective bargaining, increases in the minimum wage as well as a reduction in the legal work week to forty hours. All in all, the popular platform contained over one hundred proposals and was delivered to every household in Saskatchewan. On June 23, 1971, the NDP was returned to power in Saskatchewan, with 55 percent of the popular vote and forty-five out of sixty legislative seats.[36]

Dennis Gruending, in his analysis of the Blakeney administration, writes that "Blakeney's caucus and executive in 1971 were right of centre; but party policy was more to the left than it had been at any time since 1944."[37] Social policy analyst Gordon Ternowetsky argues that the provincial government's public policy initiatives can be divided into two areas: 1971–1976, when issues of social justice figured prominently on the public agenda; and 1976–1982, when issues of economic development were more prominent. Like most social democratic governments, the Blakeney administration attempted to improve living conditions for working people and narrow income gaps between rich and poor by implementing a variety of "social justice" policies. These policies included income security programs, and government subsidization of services for individuals and families.[38] However, the success of these programs with regard to social democratic ideals is less clear than the success of Blakeney's economic policies.

In his examination of income inequality in Saskatchewan from 1971–1982, Ternowetsky argues that there was reason to expect a decline in income inequality during this period; GDP was increasing, and the province's social democratic government could be expected to prioritize equality among its citizens.[39] The Saskatchewan Assistance Plan (SAP) was the government's major policy initiative aimed at increasing the standard of living of Saskatchewan's poorest citizens.[40] Between 1971 and 1982, payments under SAP increased by 206 percent, well above

35. New Democratic Party of Saskatchewan, *New Deal for People* (Regina: Service Printing Co., 1971).

36. Gruending, *Promises to Keep*, 82.

37. Ibid., 85.

38. Eleanor D. Glor, *Policy Innovation in the Saskatchewan Public Sector, 1971–1982* (North York, ON: Captus Press Inc., 1997), 21.

39. Gordon Ternowetsky, "Income Inequality 1971–1982: The Saskatchewan Case," in Jim Harding (ed.), *Social Policy and Social Justice* (Waterloo: Wilfrid Laurier University Press, 1995), 153.

40. Ibid., 154.

Saskatchewan's Consumer Price Index (CPI). The majority of these increases occurred between 1971 and 1976. In fact, increases in 1977–1982 were below increases in the CPI.[41] The Family Income Plan witnessed a similar trend:

> [i]n its first year [1974] 23,513 families were aided by the program. By 1981 the family caseload fell to 7,204, even though unemployment and welfare caseloads were increasing.[42]

While Ternowetsky also documents a slight fall in income inequality between 1971 and 1982, he goes on to argue that the fall was insufficient, given the economic situation of the day and the professed ideals of the governing party.[43] Eleanor Glor takes a slightly different perspective on the Blakeney government's accomplishments in the field of social justice, arguing that prior to 1975, the government demonstrated a true commitment to the introduction of innovative social programs.[44]

The implementation of social democratic ideals under Premier Blakeney can best be seen in an examination of the government's economic policies. The government was actively involved in developing and stabilizing the provincial economy, most notably in natural resource sectors. This state intervention coincided with a resource boom of the 1970s when the government became actively involved in hard rock mining projects, and partnerships with industry were established in all northern mining projects.[45]

Especially controversial was the decision of the Blakeney government to take control of the province's potash industry. The government's decision grew out of a disagreement with potash mining corporations regarding the payment of resource royalties. On November 13, 1975, the lieutenant governor highlighted the potential problems with the proposed legislation, which Attorney General and Deputy Premier Roy Romanow had been heavily involved in drafting, stating in the throne speech:

> You will therefore be asked at this Session to approve legislation which will enable my government to acquire the assets of some or all of the producing mines in the province. ... Where the terms for an agreement for sale can be reached between my government and a selected potash company, it will not be necessary to invoke the legislation. Where such an agreement cannot be reached, however, the legislation will enable my government to expropriate the Saskatchewan assets of that company.[46]

Created without actually invoking expropriation, the Potash Corporation of Saskatchewan purchased its first mine, the Duval Mine near Saskatoon, for US $129 million. Within two years, the government had spent $520 million and bought 40 percent of the potash industry in Saskatchewan. Industry disaffection faded when American potash corporations saw the generous compensation awarded by the Saskatchewan government. The Blakeney government also intervened in the development of the province's oil and gas reserves under the *Oil and Gas Conservation, Stabilization and Development Act* (1973).[47]

---

41. Ibid.
42. Ibid.,155. Ternowetsky also documents decreasing expenditures and caseloads in the Senior Citizens Benefits Package.
43. Ibid., 158.
44. Glor, *Policy Innovation in the Saskatchewan Public Sector*, 23.
45. Ibid., 9.
46. Gruending, *Promises to Keep*, 144–45.
47. Ibid., 149; Dyck, *Provincial Politics in Canada*, 453.

The uranium industry also proved controversial for the Blakeney government. The 1970s saw a boom in the price of uranium, and Saskatchewan was estimated to have significant reserves of the mineral. According to Gruending, "Blakeney wanted a uranium mining and milling industry; it was consistent with his other industrial development policies. But by the 1970s, other people in the province had come to see uranium as a death-dealing substance."[48] A debate over the province's decision to develop uranium became an annual ritual at NDP conventions. While it is possible that this debate was beneficial to the party, it is equally possible that it served to discredit and delegitimize the party's environmentalists.[49]

THE 1980s

Despite its innovation in social and economic areas and a booming provincial economy, the Blakeney government was defeated by the Progressive Conservative Party in 1982. The possible reasons for this defeat are numerous. The superstitious may point to the fact that April elections were never good for the NDP; the 1964 election had been held in April.[50] Jim Pitsula and Ken Rasmussen point to discontent among the Saskatchewan electorate, arguing that the voters were ready for a change.[51] At a time of high interest rates, the Conservatives' promises to eliminate the gas tax and provide mortgage relief resonated well with voters who were tired with the Blakeney government's focus on constitutional matters. The NDP fought the campaign against the federal Liberal government's decision to scrap the Crow Rate, which provided federal subsidies for grain transportation. This proved to be a non-issue, however, as both the Progressive Conservative and Liberal Parties agreed that the Crow Rate should be kept. Furthermore, the chief electoral threat to the NDP was coming from the Conservative Party, making a campaign fought against the federal Liberal government almost irrelevant.[52] Without the Crow Rate as an issue, the NDP was left without a significant policy for rural Saskatchewan, and the government land bank had recently come under fire.[53] The government's decision to increase spending rather than cut taxes in the pre-election budget was criticized as a betrayal of the province's middle class, and the Blakeney government lost the support of trade unions, which had proved important election-time allies in the past, when it legislated striking hospital staff back to work.[54] As Gruending suggests, the election of a Conservative government in Saskatchewan was in step with trends toward conservative governments in other parts of the world, most notably Ronald Reagan's in the United States and Margaret Thatcher's in Great Britain.[55]

On election night, the Progressive Conservatives polled 54.1 percent of the popular vote, and won fifty-five out of sixty-four seats in the provincial legislature.[56] Led by Grant Devine, the new government would offer a radically different political

48. Ibid., 153.
49. Ibid., 168.
50. James M. Pitsula and Ken Rasmussen, *Privatizing a Province:: The New Right in Saskatchewan* (Vancouver: New Star Books, 1990), 26.
51. Ibid.
52. Pitsula and Rasmussen argue that the rise of the Conservative Party is attributable to the collapse of the Liberal Party in Western Canada during the 1970s, a perception of the NDP as "out of touch" with voters, as well as ideological changes. See Pitsula and Rasmussen, *Privatizing a Province*, 23–26
53. Ibid., 27–28; Gruending, *Promises to Keep*, 177.
54. Ibid., *Privatizing a Province*, 28–29.
55. Gruending, *Promises to Keep*, 214.
56. Pitsula and Rasmussen, *Privatizing a Province*, 33.

vision for the province of Saskatchewan. The Conservative government subscribed to what can be described as "neo-liberalism." This new political philosophy would alter the province's economic and social strategies, encouraging private investment at the expense of public intervention, and ignoring the interests of organized labour and the province's working people. However, in apparent contradiction to neo-liberalism, which is focused on removing government from the economy, the Devine government was active in the provincial economy, handing out massive subsidies to private industry.[57] This marked a dramatic departure from the social democratic NDP tradition, which had emphasized the importance of state intervention in the economy and the role of government in reducing income inequalities.

After the 1982 defeat, the NDP was keen to renew and revitalize its provincial policies. Party President Delaine Scotton stated that "as a political party, we suffered probably what all political parties suffer when they are in government. ... We became rather short-term in our policy development."[58] The NDP implemented five task forces, which were to gather information from across Saskatchewan, and formulate reports to present to a policy convention. The task forces were divided into five groups: rural life; equality, participation and human rights; social justice; people and the economy; and the environment. The policy conference was held on June 9–10, 1984, and would set party policy for the 1980s.[59]

By 1985, the NDP's situation was beginning to look more promising. The economic strategies of the Devine government had failed to bring in the expected windfall of private investment to the province. By 1986, the province had accumulated a $1.7 billion dollar debt, and the province's Crown corporations, which the Conservative government had prevented from expanding in the hope of encouraging private investment, had increased their debts dramatically.[60] According to Pitsula and Rasmussen, "[t]he key to the narrow PC victory was the timely intervention of the Mulroney government with a half-billion dollar farm deficiency payment."[61] In October 1986, the NDP won 3,500 more votes than the Conservatives. However, the NDP votes were concentrated in urban constituencies, and the Conservatives carried rural Saskatchewan, awarding Devine a second majority government.[62]

In 1987, Blakeney announced his intention to step down as provincial leader, and the party planned a leadership convention for November that year. At that convention, Roy Romanow was elected without opposition to succeed Blakeney as leader of the Saskatchewan NDP. Romanow had a reputation for being to the right of the party's political spectrum. Furthermore, as Pitsula and Rasmussen point out, years of Conservative government had changed the province's political culture, making a return to true social democracy unlikely.[63] Nevertheless, Romanow would

57. Ibid., 282–83.

58. Ron Piche, "75 Briefs Presented to NDP Task Force," *The Leader-Post*, April 2, 1982, A4.

59. NDP of Saskatchewan, *Task Force Reports*, 1984.

60. de Clercy notes that by 1987 Saskatchewan had the highest per capita gross debt among the provinces, reaching $10,172 as opposed to a provincial average of $5,658 (see Cristine de Clercy, "Leadership and Uncertainty in the Politics of Fiscal Restructuring: Ralph Klein and Roy Romanow," paper presented at the annual meetings of the Canadian Political Science Association, Brock University, June 2–4, 1996, 4–5). During their second term in government, the Conservatives began a privatization scheme in earnest. For an account of the privatization process, see Pitsula and Rasmussen, *Privatizing a Province*, 136–79.

61. Pitsula and Rasmussen, *Privatizing a Province*, 283.

62. Gruending, *Promises to Keep*, 230.

63. Pitsula and Rasmussen, *Privatizing a Province*, 285.

lead the provincial NDP and citizens of Saskatchewan in protests against the Devine government's plan to privatize the natural gas utility company SaskEnergy, and would eventually form a majority government.[64]

THE ROMANOW YEARS

DEFICIT REDUCTION

In 1982, Ed Tchorzewski, Allan Blakeney's Finance Minister, presented Saskatchewan's last balanced budget of the decade. It would take twelve more years before a finance minister could deliver another. Throughout the 1980s, the Conservative government of Grant Devine registered a series of deficits reaching a high point of $1.2 billion in 1987. Falling petroleum and wheat prices as well the government's various tax reduction measures contributed to depress public revenues and thus maintain these deficits. In the months following the 1991 election, the independent Financial Management Review Commission appointed by the newly elected Romanow government, pegged Saskatchewan's 1990–1991 deficit at $975.16 million (instead of $275 million as estimated by the outgoing Conservatives). It also estimated the province's total public debt amounted to $12.704 billion as of October 31, 1991. Following the release of these figures, three of the four major bond rating agencies downgraded the province's rating from "AA" to "BB."[65]

During the 1991 election campaign, the NDP did not present a comprehensive outline of the policies it would implement once in power. In its view, such an outline could be provided only once the extent of the Conservatives' financial mismanagement was fully revealed. The brief election platform which it released in the summer of 1991, *The Saskatchewan Way*, contained some general proposals concerning farmers, Aboriginals, health care and the environment.[66] It also promised that the NDP would order a ninety-day audit of the province's books, balance the budget within four years, and eliminate the debt in fifteen years. These were the issues that the NDP emphasized throughout the campaign. That October, an impressive 81 percent of Saskatchewan voters turned out at the polls.[67] The New Democrats won 51 percent of the vote and fifty-five seats while the Conservatives won 26 percent of the vote and ten seats, and the Liberals 23 percent and one seat, that of their leader, Lynda Haverstock.[68]

Shortly after the election, Roy Romanow's new government appointed Donald Gass to head the Financial Management Review Commission that was to investigate Saskatchewan's finances. Released in early 1992, the report of the Commission

---

64. By that time, the Devine government had already sold part, or all, of several of the province's Crown corporations including, for example, SaskOil, Saskatchewan Minerals and the Potash Corporation of Saskatchewan. See Gruending, *Promises to Keep*, 234.

65. All these figures are drawn from Neil R. Thomlinson, "Same Problems, Different Solutions: Balancing Budgets in Alberta and Saskatchewan," paper presented at the annual meetings of the Canadian Political Science Association, Brock University, June 2–4, 1996, 2, 4, 6. On the topic of deficit reduction in Saskatchewan, see de Clercy, "Leadership and Uncertainty," 2, 5–7.

66. See the specific proposals of the NDP 1991 platform in Lorne A. Brown, Joe K. Roberts and John W. Warnock, *Saskatchewan Politics from Left to Right '44 to '99* (Regina: Hinterland Publications, 1999), 53.

67. Thomlinson, "Same Problems, Different Solutions," 4.

68. Elections Saskatchewan, *Statement of Votes, Twenty-Fourth Provincial General Election, September 16, 1999*, Volume 1, 137.

first pointed out that a combination of factors, including weak markets, low international prices, economic uncertainty, and high government spending, accounted for the province's financial difficulties. Then, using the accounting principles established by the Public Sector Accounting and Auditing Committee of the Canadian Institute of Chartered Accountants, it revised Saskatchewan's 1991 deficit and debt upwards. Lastly, the report made a number of recommendations designed to improve public administration and increase public accountability.[69] The Gass Commission, with its alarming portrayal of the province's financial situation, gave weight to the government's argument that first and foremost it should apply its energies to deficit reduction and "balancing the books."[70] Over the next few years, the Premier and his ministers would often invoke T.C. Douglas and the CCF's commitment to balanced budgets and fiscal conservatism to justify the priority given to the deficit issue. The report of the Gass Commission set the foundation for the overall policy direction of the new Romanow government.

Following the release of the Commission's report, the NDP formulated its plan to eliminate the provincial deficit in four years. As the new Premier would often explain, the plan was balanced in that it was concerned with both revenues and expenditures and thus combined tax increases and spending cuts.[71] Central to the plan was the notion that the government still had an important role to play in the provision of services. In his comparative study of the deficit reduction approaches of Ralph Klein's Conservatives in Alberta and Roy Romanow's New Democrats, Neil Thomlinson points out that the former used the deficit reduction issue to drastically diminish the role and size of government. In Saskatchewan, however, tax increases and spending cuts were to be implemented while preserving a role for government activism.[72] So when describing her government's approach to deficit reduction, Janice MacKinnon (NDP finance minister, 1993–1997) highlighted its commitment "to preserve the social safety net so that the most needy in society would be protected" and "to protect health and education."[73]

The budgets of the next three years emphasized tax increases and spending cuts. Specifically, the 1992 budget announced a 10 percent deficit reduction surcharge on personal income tax, a 2 percent increase in the provincial sales tax over two years (bringing it to 9 percent), an additional three cents per liter in the diesel and fuel tax (bringing it to thirteen cents), and an increase in the tobacco tax of thirty-three cents per package. The 1992 budget also hiked corporate taxes including the general rate (from 16 percent to 17 percent), the capital surcharge on resource corporations (from 1 percent to 3 percent), and the capital tax on financial institutions (from 3 percent to 3.25 percent). On the spending side, cuts amounting to $344 million were announced. Transfers to hospitals, universities, schools and municipalities were to be reduced by 2 to 3 percent. As well, several changes concerning,

69. See Province of Saskatchewan, *Report of the Saskatchewan Financial Management Review Commission*, February 1992. For a summary of the report's recommendations, see Thomlinson, "Same Problems, Different Solutions," 5–6 as well as Ken Rasmussen, "Saskatchewan: From Entrepreneurial State to Embedded State," in Michael Howlett and Keith Brownsey (eds.), *The Provincial State* (Peterborough, ON: Broadview, forthcoming 2001), 27–28.

70. Rasmussen, "Saskatchewan," 29; Thomlinson, "Same Problems, Different Solutions," 5.

71. See Roy Romanow, "How to Balance a Budget," *The Globe and Mail*, February 17, 1995, A25.

72. Thomlinson, "Same Problems, Different Solutions," 7–8. A similar point is made by de Clercy, "Leadership and Uncertainty," 14.

73. Janice MacKinnon in Thomlinson, "Same Problems, Different Solutions," 13.

for example, the funding of optometric care, chiropractic services, the Saskatchewan prescription drug plan and senior citizens' heritage program were introduced. However, these cuts need to be put in the context of a number of spending increases in various social programs including childcare centers, home care and child hunger programs. Furthermore, before the budget was tabled, in an effort to "lead by example," the government had outlined a series of reductions in the expenditures relating to the operation of government such as the salary of cabinet ministers, the allowances of government members and Crown corporation executives, and the advertising and communications budgets of government departments.[74] The 1993 budget included more extensive tax increases and spending cuts and stated that the funding for health and education would decline in the following year.[75]

In 1995, the Romanow government's combination of tax increases and spending cuts as well as increased resource revenues produced a $119 million surplus.[76] Saskatchewan had eliminated its deficit in four years, according to plan and just in time for the election. Shortly before the election, the NDP government followed the examples of Manitoba and Alberta and passed a balanced budget law requiring that future provincial governments balance their books over the course of their mandates.[77]

While the Romanow government had delivered on its promise to "balance the books," some aspects of its balanced approach to deficit reduction appeared to be at odds with social democratic ideals of wealth redistribution and broad participation in decision making. To begin with, a heavy reliance was placed on consumption taxes such as the fuel, retail sales, and tobacco taxes. Consumption taxes are regressive as they fall on all the different segments of the population regardless of their ability to pay. Some critics also pointed out that increases in corporate taxes were relatively minor.[78] In the end, non-affluent citizens, social democracy's key constituency, may have carried a heavy burden of deficit reduction, not only through increases in consumption taxes and the personal income tax, but also through cuts to social services and programs, which are considered to be essential to this constituency. Furthermore, as Thomlinson's study indicates, the government's approach to deficit reduction was not elaborated after extensive consultation with Saskatchewan citizens.[79] Consultation did occur, but only after the government had decided on its course of action and with the main objective of explaining the latter to the population. Overall, the Romanow government appears to have been fairly inflexible with regard to the specifics and timetable of its deficit reduction strategy. The fact that the deficit was brought down as initially scheduled suggests that the government was also driven by electoral concerns when designing and implementing its plan. Lastly, one wonders why the NDP government felt compelled to follow the example of its Conservative counterparts in Manitoba and

74. See the Honourable Ed Tchorzewski, "Budget Address," *Saskatchewan Hansard*, May 7, 1992; Thomlinson, "Same Problems, Different Solutions," 9–10.

75. de Clercy, "Leadership and Uncertainty," 8. See the Honourable Janice MacKinnon, "Budget Address," *Saskatchewan Hansard*, March 1993; Thomlinson, "Same Problems, Different Solutions," 13–14.

76. de Clercy, "Leadership and Uncertainty," 8. See also page 4, de Clercy's figure of Saskatchewan's annual budgets between 1981 and 1996.

77. Ibid., 8, note 29; Thomlinson, "Same Problems, Different Solutions," 25–26. The law also provides that revenues from assets sales must go towards paying the debt.

78. Brown et al., *Saskatchewan Politics from Left to Right*, 58.

79. Thomlinson, "Same Problems, Different Solutions," 10, 18–19.

Alberta and pass a balanced budget law. While it is unlikely that this ordinary law will drastically constrain future provincial governments, the latter might use it to justify their inability to implement innovative redistributive policies and respond to input from the citizenry.

Economic and Social Policies[80]

Through the 1990s, the approach of the Romanow government to economic policy bore little resemblance to that of the Blakeney government two decades earlier. As revealed in the government's major economic policy statement, *Partnership for Renewal* (1992), the social democratic traditions of state intervention and public ownership, which had inspired economic policy making in the 1970s, were to be less relevant in the 1990s.[81] In this document, the government indicated that "it had lost faith in the ability of the state to successfully engage in economic development activity."[82] Five principles were outlined to guide the "new, limited role" of the state:

> working with economic development partners (business, labour, communities, aboriginal groups, co-operatives, and farmers); encouraging regional and community-led solutions to economic renewal; working in partnership with business on market-led projects; focusing support to maximize employment opportunities; and establishing a clear investment criteria to guide provincial economic development.[83]

According to these principles, the state's main role was not to directly initiate economic activity, but rather to facilitate and even broker partnerships between business and other groups considered likely to boost economic development. In *Partnership for Renewal*, the government also ruled out the use of Crown corporations to stimulate the economy. Consequently, it did not significantly expand the Crown corporation sector or reverse the Devine government's privatizations of Crown corporations. In fact, the Romanow government eventually sold its remaining shares in Sask Oil, the Potash Corporation of Saskatchewan, Cameco, and the Lloydminster Heavy Oil Upgrader.[84] The government appeared to perceive the state as an instrument to foster an attractive investment climate for business, not as a full-fledged economic actor and initiator, intervening in the economy and owning parts of it. This "mainstream" approach was not unlike that of the NDP's Conservative counterparts in Manitoba and Alberta.

On the other hand, the new government's proposed health care reform and statements concerning the need to protect health indicated that its approach to health policy would be more social democratic. During the 1991 election campaign, the NDP had announced its intention to proceed with the second phase of the health care system introduced by the Lloyd government in 1963. The first phase had consisted in eliminating financial barriers to treatment. As the government argued in its paper *A Saskatchewan Vision for Health* (1992), the time had come to proceed with the second phase and put in place a new community health care system based on the

80. Because of space constraints, the following analysis of social policy will concentrate on health and workers' rights.

81. See Province of Saskatchewan, *Partnership for Renewal: A Strategy for the Saskatchewan Economy* (Regina: n.p., 1992).

82. Rasmussen, "Saskatchewan," 31.

83. Ibid.

84. Brown et al., *Saskatchewan Politics from Left to Right*, 59–60.

"wellness model." Such a model emphasized a more preventive and holistic approach to health.[85] Moreover, as noted earlier, in their first mandate, elected officials went to great lengths to emphasize that protection of health and education were central to their deficit reduction plan.

While the Romanow government's approach to health care reform was more social democratic, the specific measures that were eventually carried out in the field of health ended up being fiscally driven. In a sense, the province's poor financial situation, which federal decisions to freeze and then cut provincial transfers further exacerbated, prevented the government's social democratic approach to health care reform from being fully implemented. First, cuts were made to a number of services and programs including hospitals, the drug plan, chiropractic services, the children's dental plan and optometric care. On the other hand, funding to home care, which was seen as a "wellness" initiative, was increased, and efforts were made to shield low-income groups from funding cuts. Second, fifty-one of the province's 132 acute-care hospitals were converted into less costly community "wellness centres," thereby reducing the number of acute beds from 5.1 to 3.3 per one thousand residents. Third, Saskatchewan's 426 health boards were replaced with thirty-two district health boards responsible for administering programs.[86] Moreover, as with deficit reduction, none of these initiatives stemmed from extensive consultation with citizens. In reference to the process of holding public meetings on health care reform between government officials and citizens, Thomlinson states that "it could hardly be characterized as a populist exercise in which the public directs government action" as "feelings of anxiety were skillfully manipulated in such a way as to promote acceptance of the government's policy initiatives."[87] In brief, health care measures were not inspired by the social democratic tradition of broad involvement in decision making. Not unexpectedly, huge protests followed the conversion of hospitals into wellness centers or rather, as the public perceived it, the closure of hospitals.

In McRoberts' view, social democratic governments usually endeavour to "arrange a 'better deal' for organized labour and lower income groups."[88] With regards to workers' rights, however, the record of the Romanow government appears weak. To begin with, the government waited for three and half years before introducing modest reforms to the *Trade Union Act* and the *Labour Standards Act*. Regrettably for the unions, progressive measures such as prohibition of replacement workers were not included in these reforms. Further, in its ten years in power, the Romanow government did not pass pay equity legislation or significantly increase minimum wage rates.[89] Even more disturbing for many was the passage of back-to-work legislation twice, first, in 1998 against SaskPower workers and, then, in 1999,

85. Thomlinson, "Same Problems, Different Solutions," 19–20.

86. Ibid., 9, 13–14, 19–20, 23. All the members of the health boards were initially appointed by the government. As for the Regina and Saskatoon district health boards, eight members are now elected and up to six members are appointed by the minister of Health. The remaining southern health boards, except that of Lloydminster, have eight elected members and up to four appointed members. Lastly, the members of the Lloydminster health board as well as those of the northern health boards are appointed (see Government of Saskatchewan, "Saskatchewan Health Districts" [http://www.health.gov.sk.ca/ph_district_governance.html]).

87. Ibid., 20.

88. McRoberts, *Quebec Social Change and Political Crisis*, 254.

89. Rasmussen, "Saskatchewan," 18; Lorne A. Brown, "The Saskatchewan CCF-NDP: Fifty Years of Evolution, 1944–1994," *Socialist Studies Bulletin* 40 (April/May/June 1995): 37. All these demands were put forward by unions. See Barb Byers, "What did we Win? Sask.—'Real People Again,'" *Canadian Dimension* 26, no. 1 (January/February 1992): 15, 17.

against striking nurses. All this highlights the minimal influence that labour and, more specifically, public sector unions have had on the NDP.

The elimination of the deficit in 1995 did not prompt the NDP to return to a more traditional social democratic vision for Saskatchewan. In fact, the 1995 and 1999 electoral platforms of the self-described "Romanow New Democrats," *The Saskatchewan Way — It's Working* and *Building A Bright Future Together — The Saskatchewan Way*, indicated that the NDP would not depart from its recently tried-and-tested "Saskatchewan" method of governing and that fiscal prudence would continue to play a determinant role in policy decisions. In its 1995 platform, the NDP emphasized its success in balancing the province's books and proposed to divide surpluses equally among debt repayment, tax relief, and spending on job creation and health care programs.[90] In the end, the New Democrats won forty-two seats (with 47 percent of the vote) while the Liberals and Conservatives won eleven and five seats respectively (with 35 percent and 18 percent of the vote).[91] The reduction in legislative seats from sixty-six to fifty-eight as well as the NDP's loss of some of the rural ridings affected by hospital closures help to account for its diminished majority. Again in 1999, the NDP electoral platform stressed the government's record of balanced budgets as well as its tripartite approach to spending surpluses and promised "Lower Taxes. Less debt. Better services."[92] To the surprise of many who expected a third majority NDP government, the party managed to capture only twenty-nine seats (with 39 percent of the popular vote), the Saskatchewan Party twenty-five (with nearly 40 percent of the vote), and the Liberal Party four (with 20 percent of the vote).[93] The Romanow government's inability to respond effectively to the farm crisis partly explains why the NDP lost almost all its rural seats to the Saskatchewan Party. Eluding the legislative majority by just one seat, the NDP ended up forming Saskatchewan's first coalition government in seventy years with the Liberal Party. In any event, the significant drop in voter turnout from 81 percent in 1991 to 63 percent in 1995 and 66 percent in 1999 appeared to highlight Saskatchewan citizens' growing disillusionment with the Romanow New Democrats' "Saskatchewan Way" as well as the other two parties' failure to provide clearly attractive alternatives.[94]

Explaining the Movement Away from Social Democracy

Overall, international and national factors as well as changes related to the party itself may largely explain the Saskatchewan NDP's movement away from social democracy during the Romanow years. First, the 1970s witnessed the rise of neo-liberalism (or neo-conservatism) which was to exercise a tremendous influence on the right- and left-wing parties and governments of industrialized countries.[95] Seeing the

90. See NDP of Saskatchewan, *The Saskatchewan Way — It's Working* (1995), 5–6.

91. Elections Saskatchewan, 137.

92. NDP of Saskatchewan, *Building A Bright Future Together — The Saskatchewan Way* (1999), 2.

93. At present, the NDP has twenty-nine seats, the Saskatchewan Party twenty-six, and the Liberal Party three.

94. Thomlinson, "Same Problems, Different Solutions," 22.

95. It is debatable whether neo-liberalism is a "new" ideology or rather a return to the pure economic liberalism of the nineteenth century. The key difference between neo-liberalism and neo-conservatism is that the latter also espouses very traditional social values. On the rise of neo-liberalism, see Stephen McBride and John Shields, *Dismantling a Nation. The Transition to Corporate Rule in Canada* (Halifax: Fernwood Publishing, 1997), chapter one, 17–34.

state and, more specifically, the Keynesian activist state as the main source of economic and social problems, neo-liberalism advocates a sharp reduction in its role in the economy and society as well as maximum economic and individual freedom. In part because of the perceived inability of Keynesianism to effectively address the economic stagnation and high inflation of the 1970s, neo-liberalism and its related policies became the new doctrine of the day. Throughout the industrialized world, governments began curtailing state involvement in the economic and social realms by deregulating financial markets and the economy, liberalizing trade, cutting spending on social programs, and reducing public revenues.[96] The prevalence of the neo-liberal doctrine as well as the growing financial and economic interconnectedness of industrialized countries have made it very difficult for social democratic parties to implement Keynesian policies. The Saskatchewan NDP is a case in point. Second, Canadian federalism has also influenced the latter's movement away from social democracy. As a rule, provincial governments are significantly constrained by the economic and financial policies of the federal government. Defenders of the Romanow NDP question whether the government of a have-not province such as Saskatchewan could have pursued social democratic policies while the federal government was focusing on deficit and debt reduction, cutting social transfers to the provinces, and liberalizing trade. Perhaps the NDP government did not have to eliminate the deficit as expeditiously as it did and in quite the manner that it did. Nevertheless, one could argue that the NDP had to do something dramatic about the close to $1 billion deficit (generated in part by very high debt servicing charges) left over by the Conservatives. Lastly, changes specific to the party itself, including changes in its electoral support base, leadership and internal organization, also contributed to the party's departure from its social democratic heritage. The following will focus on these specific changes as they are more likely to be altered by activists and intellectuals who are committed to working within the Saskatchewan NDP and renewing the party's social democratic vision.

Between 1944 and 1978, a progressive farm-labour alliance ensured the eight electoral victories of the CCF-NDP in Saskatchewan.[97] However, in the 1980s, as rural voters backed the Conservatives twice, it became clear that the NDP could no longer rely on their support and that the old farm-labour alliance no longer existed. The dramatic social and economic changes that have taken place in rural Saskatchewan for the past two decades explains why many rural voters have deserted the party. First and foremost, the size of farms has increased, farming has become more capital-intensive, and small family farmers have been replaced by corporate farmers who do not identify with social democratic ideals. Further, rural residents, including farmers, small business owners, primary sector workers, and seniors, have expressed their anxiety about the declining population, fewer job opportunities and deteriorating infrastructure of rural Saskatchewan by supporting right-wing populist parties such as the Saskatchewan Party and the Canadian Alliance, which emphasize low taxes, small government, and free trade as means to remedy these problems.[98] Indeed, through the 1990s, rural voters in Saskatchewan increasingly

96. On the displacement of Keynesianism by neo-liberalism, see Neil Bradford, "Governing the Canadian Economy: Ideas and Politics," in Michael Whittington and Glen Williams (eds.), *Canadian Politics in the 21st Century* (Scarborough, ON: Nelson Canada, 2000), 193–215.

97. On this farm-labour alliance, see Rasmussen, "Saskatchewan," 15–16 as well as Brown, "The Saskatchewan CCF-NDP," 28–29, 34–35.

98. See Rasmussen, "Saskatchewan," 15–16.

backed non-NDP parties in provincial and federal elections. More specifically, the Saskatchewan Party won almost all the rural ridings in the 1994 provincial election, and the Canadian Alliance captured ten of Saskatchewan's fourteen federal ridings in the last federal election in 2000.

Just as the electoral base of the NDP was shifting to include more urban voters, organized labour was becoming more marginalized within the party. While the CCF-NDP was never a classical labour party, organized labour did exercise some influence over party affairs at least up until the 1970s.[99] However, the weak record of the Romanow government with regard to workers' rights suggests that this is no longer the case. At present, although the electoral base of the party still includes trade-unionists and progressive farmers, it is mainly composed of middle-class professionals such as teachers, social workers, lawyers and public sector workers who reside in the cities.[100] According to Ken Rasmussen, these voters support quality public services, "particularly health care and education without sacrificing too much in terms of tax increases," as well as the values of "individual autonomy, protection of women's and minorities' rights, encouragement for self-expression and a diversity of lifestyles."[101] The more "materialist" concerns of organized labour for workers' rights, state intervention, and public ownership may not be among their priorities. The outlook of these middle-class professionals, who happen to occupy key positions in the party, could also account for the party's movement away from more traditional expressions of social democratic policies.[102] In sum, it appears that when progressive farmers and trade-unionists became less essential to the party's electoral success, the aggressive use of state power to redress social and economic inequalities advocated by these two groups fell out of favour within the New Democratic leadership.

This became clear when Roy Romanow took over as leader of the Saskatchewan NDP in 1987. A lawyer of Ukrainian descent, Romanow was first elected as an MLA in 1967 in the riding of Saskatoon-Riversdale and served as Saskatchewan's deputy premier and attorney general from 1971 until 1982. In this capacity, Romanow initiated justice reforms such as the provincial legal aid plan and the Saskatchewan Human Rights Commission.[103] As Allan Blakeney's minister of Inter-Governmental Affairs, he also played a key role in the negotiations leading up to constitutional reform in 1981. In July 1970, Romanow had lost the party leadership to Allan Blakeney when the supporters of Waffle candidate Don Mitchell decided to back the more leftist of the two leading candidates. Nevertheless, sixteen years later, Romanow was finally elected party leader.[104] It was under the leadership of Romanow, a man whose politics were not as progressive as those of his predecessors, that the party moved away from some of its social democratic heritage.

There is no doubt that Romanow's pragmatist/compassionate politics, which combine fiscal conservatism, moderate economic liberalism, and social progressivism, defined the NDP's approach to government in the 1990s. His predominant

99. Brown, "The Saskatchewan CCF-NDP," 28, 34

100. Rasmussen, "Saskatchewan," 17–18.

101. Ibid., 18.

102. Ibid., 17; Brown, "The Saskatchewan CCF-NDP," 34–35.

103. In 1993, under Romanow's premiership, Saskatchewan's human rights code was amended to make it illegal to discriminate against gays and lesbians.

104. For a short biography of Roy Romanow, see Dennis Gruending, "The Man who would be Premier," *Saskatchewan Business* 11, no. 8 (October 1990): 10–12.

concern for fiscal responsibility clearly came through in an interview that he gave in the spring of 1999. When asked which of his achievements he was proudest of, Romanow responded: "our record ... the balanced approach we restored to Saskatchewan government after nine years of irresponsible Tory government in the 1980s."[105] The rest of his answer, however, highlights that "balancing the books" was perhaps the accomplishment he was proudest of:

> I'm proudest that [we] were able to work with the people of Saskatchewan to reward the trust they placed in us to get the province back on its feet, to get the books back in order. I'm proud that their hard work and sacrifice enabled us to balance the books — we tabled our sixth consecutive balanced budget this year, with plans for three more — and to restore balanced, sensible government to Saskatchewan.[106]

While his fiscal views are not really at odds with those of former Saskatchewan NDP leaders beginning with T.C. Douglas, something he would stress on several occasions while premier of Saskatchewan, his economic views are. In contrast to his predecessors, Romanow assiduously courted the business community and favoured less direct state intervention in the economy. Dave Glaze writes that already before the 1991 campaign, Romanow was spending "considerable effort reassuring Chamber of Commerce types that the NDP had no intention of restructuring the economy," thereby signaling that a Romanow government would not be as directly involved in economic affairs as previous NDP governments had been.[107] More recently, reflecting on the future of the federal NDP, Romanow appeared to suggest that the party had to accept the economic realities of trade liberalization and globalization if it was to remain part of the Canadian political landscape:

> My advice [to the NDP] ... would be to debate the issues in terms of idealism and philosophy but laced also with pragmatism. If you run away from change, you're a conservative. We can pretend the WTO doesn't exist, that NAFTA isn't here, that e-commerce doesn't do a trillion dollars in trade a day. But if you pretend that [these] ... aren't relevant for today ... you don't speak to ordinary people. And there's nothing written in stone that says that the NDP is here to stay forever in Canada.[108]

Lastly, this fiscal and economic pragmatist also supports publicly funded social programs such as Medicare which reflect the compassionate and communitarian values of Canada.[109] In a sense, Romanow's views are similar to those of New Labour Tony Blair in Great Britain, the architect of the "Third Way," who defines his government's approach to the economy as "neither laissez-faire nor one of state interference," prides himself on being supported by "business leaders as well as trade unions," and claims to support the "centre-left values of solidarity, social justice, responsibility and opportunity."[110] Although Roy Romanow's views clearly influenced the policy direction of the NDP government in the 1990s, it is important to note that other factors related

105. Romanow in "Q&A with Roy Romanow," *Saskatchewan Business* 20, no. 3 (May/June 1999): 34.

106. Ibid.

107. Dave Glaze, "AECL if Necessary, but not Necessarily AECL," *NeWest Review* 17, no. 4 (April/May 1992): 7.

108. Romanow in David Roberts, "Canada Faces Potential Danger, Romanow Says," *The Globe and Mail*, January 24, 2001, A5.

109. Ibid.

110. Tony Blair, "What the Third Way Stands for: Tony Blair," *The Globe and Mail*, September 21, 1998, A23. In "Bidding Farewell to the Man Who Never Left Home," *The Globe and Mail*, January 26, 2001, A13, Jeffrey Simpson praises Romanow for having been a precursor of Tony Blair.

to the internal organization of the party may also have contributed to shifting the party away from some traditional social democratic policies.

While it would be simplistic to identify the present NDP as an elitist "cadre party" as opposed to a more democratic "mass party," several changes related to its internal organization signal that the party has been acquiring cadre characteristics. Generally speaking, a cadre party has the following features: a small and passive membership, an elite group of professional politicians and/or parliamentary representatives who have a tight grip over the party organization, a pragmatic platform designed to win elections, and corporate donations. In the 1990s, party members became demoralized by the fiscal policies of the Romanow government, and many left the party as a result.[111] More specifically, party membership decreased steadily: 42,000 in 1991–92, 30,000 in 1993, 21,000 in 1996–97, and 16,000 in 2000.[112] This decline has served to reinforce the influence of the party leadership, which is mainly composed of middle-class professional politicians.[113] In light of these developments, it is perhaps not surprising that the platforms the NDP put forward in the last two provincial elections mainly comprised pragmatic proposals directed largely at urban middle-class voters rather than a more traditionally social democratic program for Saskatchewan as a whole. To echo Rasmussen's observations, since the 1980s the party has become more focussed on developing winning electoral strategies than on elaborating innovative policies.[114] But perhaps most significant, one wonders what prompted this social democratic party to start accepting corporate donations in 1996, especially since the federal NDP does not do so.[115] In sum, these internal changes help to account for the party's movement away from some of the tenets of social democracy.

On the other hand, the decision of the party council to elect Romanow's successor via a direct system of one-member, one-vote rather than the traditional delegate system indicates that some party elites view such organizational changes as problematic and are trying to address them.[116] In the mid-1980s, a committee was struck to examine the constitution of the party. At that time, the committee strongly advocated using direct voting to elect the next party leader. However, its proposal was resisted by members of the party executive. In the end, the compromise that was reached provided that both the direct and the delegate methods of selection would be included in the NDP constitution and that the party council would decide which method to use. The party council chose the delegate method for the 1987 leadership convention and the direct method for the 2001 leadership convention.[117] Following

111. Lorne Brown, "NDP for you and me," *Canadian Dimension* 33, no. 1 (Fall 1999): 31–34; Mitch Diamantopoulos, "The Romanow Legacy," *Prairie Dog* 25 (January 2001): 4.

112. These figures were provided by the NDP of Saskatchewan. It should be noted that in 1995 party membership increased to over 26,000. Even at its lowest point, the NDP party membership was still larger than that of its provincial rivals.

113. Rasmussen, "Saskatchewan," 17, 24; Joe Roberts, "Saskatchewan Election 1999: What's Left? A Survey and Analysis of Left Opinions," *Briarpatch* 28, no. 3 (April 1999): 16–19.

114. Ibid., 24–25. Nevertheless, in Rasmussen's view, the Saskatchewan NDP "is still very much a mass-based political party" (Rasmussen, "Saskatchewan," 24).

115. Brown et al., *Saskatchewan Politics from Left to Right*, 77–78. Moreover, at the 1998 annual convention, delegates rejected a constitutional amendment proposing that corporate donations be banned. See Martin O'Hanlon, "Big Business Money OK for Sask NDP," *Canadian Press Newswire* (November 15, 1998): 1–2.

116. See "Saskatchewan NDP to Lay Groundwork for First Leadership Convention in 30 Years," *Canadian Press Newswire* (September 30, 2000): 1–2.

117. See Saskatchewan NDP, *Rules of 2000–2001 Saskatchewan NDP Leadership Contest* (2000).

the announcement that the new NDP leader would be directly elected by card-carrying members, 8,000 people joined the party, thereby boosting the party membership to 24,000.[118] Finally, at the leadership convention of January 26–27, 2001 in Saskatoon, Lorne Calvert, a United Church minister and former minister of Health and Social Services in the Romanow government, who promised to return the party to its social democratic traditions, was elected by the NDP membership on the fourth ballot.[119]

CONCLUSION

This chapter has assessed the impact which the Saskatchewan CCF-NDP, the dominant party of the province, has had on Saskatchewan. While the Douglas, Lloyd and Blakeney governments played a key role in introducing and strengthening social democracy in the province, the same cannot really be said of the more recent Romanow government. In keeping with the social democratic tradition of state intervention in society and the economy, the Douglas, Lloyd and Blakeney governments created Crown corporations, regulated the economy, and strove to reduce social and economic inequalities. By contrast, the Romanow government of the past decade pursued fiscal, economic and social policies that were often at odds with the party's social democratic traditions. While international and national political and economic factors can largely explain this shift, factors related to the party and, in particular, changes in its electoral support base, leadership and internal organization, have also contributed to it.

The story of the Saskatchewan NDP in the 1990s is not an unusual one. The last two decades of the twentieth century have witnessed social democratic parties and governments in Canada and elsewhere in the industrialized world moving away from traditional social democratic policies.[120] For instance, social democratic parties in Canada, New Zealand, Australia and Sweden have tackled deficit and debt issues by cutting the social programs that they helped to establish; at times, they have endorsed market solutions to social and economic problems; and they have been reluctant to protect the interests of working people and unions. However, their adoption of such policies has not left them unscathed. At present, many of them are going through an identity crisis. They are no longer clear on the basic principles and policies that they stand for.

At the dawn of the twenty-first century, social democratic parties are at a crossroads. Now that the deficit and debt issues have been brought under control, they have to decide what to do next. They are essentially faced with two options: either they can follow New Labour Tony Blair's "Third Way" strategy or they can attempt to elaborate a renewed social democratic vision. The first option would entail shifting further away from traditional social democratic ideals and perhaps even endorsing a form of "compassionate" neo-liberalism. The second option would involve a

118. These figures were provided by the NDP of Saskatchewan.

119. On the leadership race, see Paul Adams, "Race Tests Saskatchewan NDP," *The Globe and Mail*, January 26, 2001, A4; James Parker, "NDP Picks Calvert," *The Leader Post*, January 29, 2001, A1–A2; David Roberts, "Saskatchewan NDP Choose Calvert as New Leader," *The Globe and Mail*, January 29, 2001, A5.

120. For a critical assessment of the Ontario, British Columbia and Saskatchewan NDP governments, see the pieces included in "Forum: NDPs in Power," *Studies in Political Economy* 43 (Spring 1994): 137–67. For provincial and European examples, see James Laxer, *In Search of a New Left, Canadian Politics After the Neo-Conservative Assault* (Toronto: Penguin Books, 1997), 3–12.

much more demanding task. It would require social democratic parties to thoroughly re-examine the basic social democratic principles and policies that they want to espouse.

Could such an exercise take place in an old party like the Saskatchewan NDP or should a new left party be created? According to a small sample of NDP activists interviewed at the time of the 1999 provincial election, the solution does not lie in the formation of a new party, but rather in the rise of a new leadership intent on progressive policy changes.[121] However, such a view appears too elitist in that it assumes that only the leadership can renew the party's social democratic vision. It seems that a more open and democratic process including not only party elites, but also rank-and-file party activists as well as progressive activists and intellectuals from inside and outside the NDP would be more likely to bring about a renewed social democratic vision. For such a process to be successful, however, it is imperative that all participants be truly committed to discuss old and new social democratic ideas in an imaginative and non-dogmatic way. Though it is not clear whether the Saskatchewan NDP will launch such an exercise, the decision to use direct voting to select the new leader of the Saskatchewan NDP may end up being a first step towards such a form of policy and party renewal. If a renewed social democratic vision eventually emerges in the party, Saskatchewan and Canada will no doubt both be better for it.

POSTSCRIPT: THE 2001 NDP LEADERSHIP

The 2001 NDP leadership race proved unconventional for several reasons. First, the new leader of the NDP was also to become the Premier of Saskatchewan, replacing Romanow. Second, it was the first NDP leadership race that was to be determined by a direct membership vote, as opposed to the traditional delegate convention. Finally, an unprecedented number of candidates entered the race — four sitting cabinet ministers (Chris Axworthy, Buckley Belanger, Joanne Crofford, and Maynard Sonntag) and three party activists (Scott Banda, Lorne Calvert, and Nettie Wiebe) contested the party's leadership.

This new system of voting marked an important break from the history of the NDP. While social democratic parties have traditionally been concerned with issues of democracy, this was the first time that the party utilized direct democracy in selecting its leader. Every party member was given the option of voting by mail-in preferential ballot for leader or casting a vote at the leadership convention. Approximately 18,000 mail-in ballots were cast, in addition to 1,000 on the convention floor. The results of the mail-in ballots votes were tabulated, added to the results on the convention floor, and announced at the leadership convention. The preferential ballot allowed the party to continue its tradition of electing its leaders by holding multiple ballots until a candidate receives a majority of the popular vote, while allowing every interested party member to take part in the leadership process.

The direct membership vote enabled individuals not tied to traditional party structures to sell party memberships and launch viable campaigns. Perhaps most notable in this was the campaign of left-of-centre candidate Nettie Wiebe, whose platform focused on the need to resist neo-liberal globalization and shift government to the left. Throughout her campaign, Wiebe also articulated the need for the

121. Roberts, "Saskatchewan Election 1999," 16–19.

NDP to reconnect with its rural roots by presenting several strategies to prevent what she felt was the siphoning of wealth out of rural Saskatchewan. Wiebe finished third in the race, which could signify a willingness among some party members to see a major ideological shift in the party. Yet it is unclear whether the membership as a whole adhered to this view, since the majority still backed the two "establishment" candidates, Lorne Calvert and Chris Axworthy, both of whom favoured a less radical approach to change within the party and government. In the end, the majority of the membership elected Lorne Calvert, who was seen in the party as more ideologically in line with the traditional principles of social democracy than his predecessor and whose campaign, while more centrist than that of Wiebe, focused on social policy.

Although the race had been decided by the over 18,000 mail-in ballots which were sent before the convention began, the party was able to preserve the excitement of a leadership convention, in part because the results for each ballot were announced on the convention floor. On the fourth ballot, Lorne Calvert eventually emerged the winner with 58 percent of the popular vote. Justice Minister Chris Axworthy came in second, with the remaining 42 percent.

Overall, however, the effect of this convention on the NDP and its government remains to be seen, as the NDP leadership is now facing the challenge of retaining and expanding its membership base. The party must keep the political momentum created by this race to rebuild and renew the party and continue winning general elections. Furthermore, the NDP government is currently part of a precarious coalition with the province's Liberal Party. While Calvert may be willing to move his party to the left, such an ideological shift will likely prove to be a difficult task.[122]

122. We thank all those who helped us by reviewing this chapter, as well as the Faculty of Arts at the University of Regina for funding this research.

Rethinking the Polarization Thesis: The Formation and Growth of the Saskatchewan Party, 1997–2001

Kevin Wishlow

INTRODUCTION

August 1997 marked the birth of a new Saskatchewan political party. As if to affirm that brand loyalty no longer mattered in provincial politics, the founding membership named their new party the generic-sounding "Saskatchewan Party." But this was not to be a bland political offering, packaged for the non-discriminating consumer. Instead, the new party boldly promised to break with convention, putting together a fresh package full of creative solutions for a new breed of sophisticated customer, dissatisfied with "old-style politics." Liberals and Conservatives set aside their old partisan differences, promising to build a new alliance with the goal of defeating the NDP government.

Some observers would characterize the development as nothing more than the most recent incarnation of Saskatchewan's ongoing left-right divide. This chapter challenges that argument, proposing that something new is indeed happening to the Saskatchewan party system. With the decline of the post-war consensus and the rise of the neo-liberal regime, ideological differences have narrowed between Saskatchewan's major political parties. The Saskatchewan Party has gained its momentum, not by exacerbating a deep ideological divide that pervades the province's political culture, but by exploiting alienation in the rural hinterland. With its goal clearly set on achieving power and then keeping it, the party hopes to bridge the rural-urban divide by implementing a policy platform similar to the one orchestrated by Ralph Klein's Conservatives in Alberta.

The so-called Alberta model relies upon a mixture of libertarian logic and social conservative rhetoric to justify the diminishing role of the state in society. Paradoxically, the collection of a rich stream of resource revenue is used to maintain state support for scaled-down social programs and services that were once the hallmark of the welfare state. This approach to governance is reflective of citizens who increasingly view themselves solely as consumers, favoring policies that will both boost their spending power and cater to their immediate needs. The new scaled-down state is framed in the discourse of unending prosperity, in which equality of condition becomes secondary to equality of opportunity.

HISTORY

It sometimes becomes a convenient narrative device to develop plots in bipolar terms. Good is pitted against evil or the underdog rises up to overthrow the oppressor. In the end, it is good which triumphs and the oppressed who shed their chains. Former United States President Ronald Reagan's now infamous analogy depicting the former Soviet Union as the "evil empire" characterized global reality in simplistic bipolar terms. Reagan relied upon the narrative to justify the expansion of the United States military machine in the face of the perceived Soviet threat. But myth often betrays reality. In reality the Soviet Empire was beginning to implode. Such contradictions are just as endemic to Saskatchewan politics. Myth would have it that the upstart Saskatchewan Party was a political movement born solely at the grassroots — far removed from the seats of power in Regina. The reality, however, was somewhat different. The new party was spawned by a band of eight sitting MLAs who arguably saw the diminishing prospects of achieving power within their respective parties.

Table 1
The Original Eight Saskatchewan Party MLAs

MLA	CONSTITUENCY	PREVIOUS PARTY AFFILIATION
Bob Bjornerud	Saltcoats	Liberal
June Draude	Kelvington-Wadena	Liberal
Rod Gantefoer	Melfort-Tisdale	Liberal
Ken Krawetz	Canora-Pelly	Liberal
Bill Boyd	Kindersley	PC
Dan D'Autremont	Cannington	PC
Ben Heppner	Rosthern	PC
Don Toth	Moosomin	PC

In the summer of 1997, four Liberal and four Progressive Conservative MLAs — all from rural Saskatchewan — formed a new political coalition in the Saskatchewan Legislature (see Table 1). The strategic alliance put an end to media speculation about a merger between the two opposition parties. But the creation of the new legislative group did not coincide with the immediate death of either the Liberal or the Conservative parties. The Liberals would hang on in the Legislature with a scaled-down caucus of six MLAs under the leadership of Saskatoon doctor Jim Melenchuk, eventually going on to compete in the next provincial election. Humbolt MLA Arlene Jule would also leave the Liberals over differences of policy and leadership to sit as an independent. Jule would eventually join the Saskatchewan Party, assuming the position as its Indian and Metis Affairs critic. The exodus of Liberals was mirrored in the backrooms with the defection of one-time leadership contender Tom Hengen, who would play a key role as a strategist in the new party. By contrast to the Liberals, the Conservatives' legislative ranks were decimated, with most of the sitting members leaving to join the new coalition, with the exception of Jack Gooshen who would sit as an independent. Gooshen would not be accepted into the new fold, pending the outcome of charges of consorting with a 14-year-old prostitute.[1]

1. Mark Wyatt, "Charge puts Gooshen in limbo," *Leader-Post*, August 13, 1997, A3.

The mass of defections precipitated an array of Progressive Conservatives voices, expressing either their support for the new legislative coalition or their opposition. Former Conservative Premier Grant Devine publicly articulated his support for the new party, raising the possibility that he too "would become a member."[2] Others, like Martin Pederson, who led the Saskatchewan Progressive Conservatives in the 1960s, asserted that the Saskatchewan Party didn't "mean the death knell of either the Liberals or Conservatives."[3] The Conservatives may not have received the "death knell" but they would soon be placed in the cryogenic chamber. At a meeting in November 1997 the PC executive finally decided to put the party in hiatus, not ruling out the possibility that the Conservatives could one day be revived if the circumstances were expedient.[4] Nothing was clear-cut in this partisan realignment. The relationship between the Conservatives and the newly formed Saskatchewan Party remained ambiguous. It took Bill Boyd, who was leader of the Progressive Conservatives before defecting to the new party, more than a month to finally submit his resignation to the PC executive. Even then, Boyd would keep his party membership, claiming that he wanted have some input when the future of the Conservatives was decided.[5]

While an official merger never took place, it was beginning to look like the Saskatchewan Party was nothing more the Conservative Party with a new name, logo and a few new faces. Even in the backrooms old personnel didn't just stay around, they stayed in power. Tom Lukiwski exchanged his job as executive director for the PCs for the general manager of the Saskatchewan Party.[6] And while the PCs had faded away with barely a whimper, the Liberals were making a roar. With a leaner six-member caucus they weren't about to shut out the lights. Liberal loyalist Jack Hillson characterized his defecting colleagues as holding ideological beliefs fundamentally at odds with his own: "they saw government as an evil in society and I see the government as a positive good that can do things for people and with people."[7] With the removal of the defectors, Hillson was now convinced the Liberal caucus would be a more cohesive group, sharing a common political philosophy.[8] The North Battleford MLA seemed to suggest that the ongoing infighting in the Liberal Party was the product of a deep ideological divide and not personal differences. Internal squabbling had resulted in the ousting of former leader Lynda Haverstock two years before. Kicked out of the "club," Haverstock would retain her seat, sitting as an independent Liberal. She would never ponder joining the new coalition.[9]

In an attempt to differentiate themselves from the Saskatchewan Party, the remaining Liberals seemed to be trying to raise questions about the legitimacy of the new party as a true Liberal-Conservative coalition. It became convenient to

2. Vicki Hall, "Devine Supports New Party," *Leader-Post*, August 11, 1997, A1.
3. Mark Wyatt, "Former leader says PCs not dead yet," *Leader-Post*, August 16, 1997, A4.
4. Mark Wyatt, "PC Party Inactive," *Leader-Post*, November 10, 1997, A3.
5. Mark Wyatt, "Boyd resigns as leader of the PCs," *Leader-Post*, September 12, 1997, A4.
6. Mark Wyatt, "Constitution, policy platform ok'd," *Leader-Post*, November 17, 1997, A4. The article notes that even as late as November 1997 Tom Lukiwski held the dual role as a party organizer for the Saskatchewan Party and executive director for the Progressive Conservative Party of Saskatchewan.
7. Hillson quoted in Mark Wyatt, "Liberals to steer middle course," *Leader-Post*, August 18, 1997, A3.
8. Ibid.
9. Ibid.; Murray Mandryk, "Sask. Liberals in critical condition," *Leader-Post*, August 9, 1997, A4.

depict the Liberal defectors as a right-wing lunatic fringe who had found it increasingly difficult to accept the more moderate "middle course" advocated by most of the membership. In other words, the defectors weren't really Liberals anyway. But some of the so-called loyalists weren't exactly long-standing Liberals either. Melville Liberal MLA Ron Osika was a former Reformer, who continued to advocate a more coercive approach to law-and-order issues. Another remaining Liberal, Glen McPherson, had only recently crossed the floor to join the Liberals from the NDP. One could be excused for thinking that the ideological divide argument was a mere smokescreen used to mask internal divisions and leadership problems that persisted within the Liberal Party long after the Haverstock bloodletting. Still, it cannot be discounted that the renegade Liberal MLAs left the party for a new partisan organization espousing principles more closely aligned with their own. Just the same the defectors might also have come to realize the internal feuding within party was preventing the Liberals from establishing themselves as a credible alternative to the NDP — especially in light of the sagging fortunes of the Progressive Conservatives.[10]

The Conservatives had the most to benefit from a full political makeover. The Devine Conservatives had been indelibly demonized in the minds of Saskatchewan voters. Voters were not about to forget the ballooning debt the Tories had left the province with their defeat in 1991; nor were voters able to forget the corruption that now seemed endemic to the Devine caucus. At the time of the Saskatchewan Party's inception in August 1997, 11 former Progressive Conservative MLAs — all members of the Devine government — had either been convicted or pleaded guilty to charges of fraud.[11] With each conviction the Conservatives' fortunes seemed to slide further. Even the leadership of Bill Boyd, a former welder from Kindersely and a relative unknown in the Devine days, failed to rebuild the public's trust in the party. From 10 seats in 1991, the Conservatives under Boyd dropped to five members in 1995 — largely to the benefit of the Liberals. Given such gloomy fortunes, it becomes clear why Boyd enthusiastically greeted the prospect of some sort of fresh coalition with disenchanted Liberals.

Aside from the Conservatives and Liberals, another party had entered the fray — albeit largely looking from the outside in. The federal Reform Party — the forerunner of the Canadian Alliance — had registered a provincial wing in Saskatchewan on December 13, 1996.[12] There had been some media speculation that it would be Reform that would move in to fill the perceived right-wing void in Saskatchewan politics. A month after the formation of the Saskatchewan Party, there was still a push within Reform circles to actively establish a provincial party. In a survey of Saskatchewan Reform membership released by the party in early September, 53 percent of respondents voted to proceed with the plan. Another 34 percent of respondents believed that Reform should collaborate with the new Saskatchewan Party. One Reformer interpreted the results as "a very clear rejection" of the new upstart.[13] Like the Liberals, some Reformers had concerns about the legitimacy of the party. Unlike the Liberals, however, Reform voices were critical of what they perceived as the top-down structure of the Saskatchewan Party — with

10. Ibid.

11. See Barb Pacholik, "Petersen discharged," *Leader-Post*, August 26, 1997, A1.

12. Mandryk, "Sask. Liberals in critical condition."

13. Eric Schenstead quoted in Mark Wyatt, "Provincial Reform sentiment unclear," *Leader-Post*, September 4, 1997, A1.

14. Ibid.

the defecting MLAs switching partisan affiliation without the direct consent of their constituents.[14] In a strategy deliberately aimed at appeasing such criticism, the eight founding Saskatchewan Party MLAs offered to step down if the majority of their constituents demanded it.[15]

Questions about legitimacy did not stop prominent Saskatchewan Reform MPs Gary Breitkreuz and Allan Kerpan from throwing their support behind the new party. The pair gave the endorsement, only to receive a tongue-lashing by Reform's executive council. Christine Whitaker, a Reform executive councillor, went so far as to describe their involvement as "unforgivable."[16] Other Reformers like Elwin Hermanson, a former MP who lost his seat in the 1997 federal election, were urging some type of "constructive relationship" between the two organizations. Hermanson himself would serve on the steering committee of the new party before going on to be elected as its leader.[17]

The real issue was not ideology, or even legitimacy — a struggle for power was occurring in the province over which party could best challenge the NDP, and in the short term, which party could establish itself as the official opposition. Some in the Reform camp felt that if any party filled that void in Saskatchewan, it would have to be Reform itself — not an assortment of previously elected politicians. As Derrek Konrad, the Reform MP for Prince Albert, put it, if Reform did "anything provincially, it [would have to be] ... the Reform party." It could not simply be "just people fed up with the status quo" in their respective parties.[18] In the legislature, the Liberals were engaged in a struggle of their own to remain the official opposition even though they now held fewer seats than the Saskatchewan Party. The Liberals immediately turned to Speaker Glenn Hagel, citing precedents in Manitoba and Alberta as grounds for retaining their opposition status and the extra funding that came with it. In the Manitoba precedent, which occurred in 1920, the Conservatives retained official opposition status even though their party had fewer members than either the Labor or Farmer parties. A similar situation arose in Alberta in 1984 following the death of NDP leader Grant Notley. The NDP retained its position as official opposition even though the party now had only one sitting member, compared to two Social Credit MLAs.[19]

On August 21, 1997 Hagel, relying on Saskatchewan law and parliamentary precedent, came to a decision. The Saskatchewan Party was given the status of Official Opposition. The Liberals, who stood to loose two staff members and $60,000 in funding, accepted the ruling.[20] Despite the new coalition's heightened legislative status, it would be nearly a month before it would meet the requirements under Saskatchewan law to operate as a full-fledged political party. On September 17, 1997, it presented the province's chief electoral officer with a petition bearing the names of 3,000 supporters — enough to register as a political party in the province. The petition revealed that most of the party's support came from rural

15. Mark Wyatt, "MLAs offer to quit if constituency petitions them," *Leader-Post*, November 17, 1997, A4.

16. Christine Whitaker quoted in Murray Mandryk, "Reform MPs catch flak for backing new party," *Leader-Post*, August 12, 1997, A4. Also see Anonymous, "Reformers don't agree on new Party," *Leader-Post*, August 19, 1997, A1.

17. Anonymous, "Reformers don't agree on new Party."

18. Derrek Konrad quoted in ibid.

19. Bonny Braden, "Hagel to announce decision today," *Leader-Post*, August 21, 1997, A4.

20. Bonny Braden, "Opposition status shifts," *Leader-Post*, August 22, 1997, A1.

Saskatchewan. Only 16 percent (210) of the signatures on the petition came from the four largest urban centres of Saskatoon, Regina, Moose Jaw and Prince Albert. Yet these four cities held 26 of the province's 58 ridings.[21] The realization of political power would demand that the party move beyond its rural base.

A number of immediate challenges, however, needed to be addressed first. Foremost among these were the question of leadership and the development of a comprehensive policy platform. At their inaugural meeting members of the new Saskatchewan Party caucus chose former Liberal Ken Krawetz to act as their interim leader until a permanent leader could be chosen. Krawetz who had only recently taken a run at the leadership of the Liberal Party and lost, was now receiving the full endorsement of Conservatives like Grant Devine and former cabinet minister Grant Schmidt.[22] But the selection of Krawetz was only an interim solution to a more pressing challenge — finding a credible big-name candidate who could build on the party's rural base without having any of the baggage of the Devine era. Beechy farmer and former Reform MP Elwin Hermanson announced early on that he would consider running for the leadership under favourable circumstances. There were high hopes within the party, however, that a fellow Reformer — Blackstrap MP Allan Kerpan — would run for the leadership. In the end, Kerpan announced his intention to remain in federal politics, opening the door for Hermanson to announce his candidacy.

Three candidates would compete for the leadership of the Saskatchewan Party. MLA Rod Gantefoer (a former Liberal) and former Canadian Forces commander and Progressive Conservative candidate Yogi Huyghebaert joined Hermanson in the race. Hermanson was generally considered to be the first-ballot favourite in the mail-in vote that was scheduled to be completed by April 9, 1997, in time for the April 20 leadership convention. He counted among his supporters former Conservatives Bill Boyd, Jake Heppner and Don Toth, along with former Liberal MLA Bob Bjornerud. Fred Thompson, a former NDP cabinet minister and recent Saskatchewan Party convert would also side with Hermanson. A Conservative-Liberal split in caucus over the leadership was beginning to emerge, with interim leader Ken Krawetz and former Liberal MLA June Draude siding with Gantefoer. Huyghebaert failed to receive any high-profile endorsements.[23]

The differences in the platforms of three candidates were subtle. All three envisioned a diminishing role of the state in the economy, reflected in lower taxes and the privatization of some state-owned utilities. Hermanson took a more cautious approach, favoring referenda as mechanisms for testing public support for such hot-button issues as privatization and even abortion. Gantefoer and Huyghebaert were much more explicit, both stating their aversion to the state ownership of key utilities. In the end, Hermanson's seemingly more moderate populist approach, together with the backing of high-profile players, won out. Just as important, Hermanson, who once campaigned for Herb Swan (a minister in the Devine cabinet) was able to dispel any connection he might have had to the Devine Conservatives.[24] He was the fresh face the new party seemed to want and need.

21. Mark Wyatt, "Saskatchewan Party now official," *Leader-Post*, September 18, 1997, A4.

22. Mark Wyatt, "Sask. Party names its interim leader," *Leader-Post*, August 12, 1997, A1.

23. Mark Wyatt, "Sask. Party returns to the limelight," *Leader-Post*, April 4, 1998, A5.

24. See Bonny Braden, "Saskatchewan Party, the leadership candidates...," *Leader-Post*, April 4, 1998, D1, D3. Also see Annonymous, "Sask. Party leader gives his views," *Leader-Post*, April 21, 1998, A5.

In keeping with the Saskatchewan Party's grassroots "approach," it was not Hermanson's position to create policy. Rather, it was merely a matter of articulating it. Many of the core values in that policy had been agreed to at the Saskatchewan Party's inaugural convention nearly six months earlier. At a late November convention in Saskatoon, 150 party members gave their approval to the party's constitution and policy platform. That platform, adopted by a predominantly rural membership, advocated a mixture of libertarian and social conservative initiatives. Those initiatives would allow private surgical clinics, lower taxes, get tough with young offenders, and demand the mandatory employment of welfare recipients. In addition, the membership voiced their opposition to affirmative action hiring programs and pledged to support legislation that would make union membership optional in unionized workplaces.[25] If party organizers had hoped to give the impression that the Saskatchewan Party was indeed a grassroots movement, the convention seemed to fail in this respect. Conspicuously absent from the event were indicators that there was a groundswell of support for the new party. In fact, there were fewer people at the meeting than had attended the Conservative party's farewell convention the weekend earlier. *Leader-Post* columnist Murray Mandryk concluded that even though the former Liberal and PC MLAs didn't participate in the resolution debates, "their role in developing the party's seven founding principles, its constitution and the initial resolution package ... [meant that the] party ... [was] still somewhat top-down."[26]

Still, in politics what often matters more is how the public understands political events. The Saskatchewan Party's sweep of rural Saskatchewan in the 1999 General election demonstrated nothing short of a grassroots protest against the incumbent NDP government. The party took 26 rural seats — just three less than the NDP — and managed to capture 39.6 percent of the popular vote — surpassing the NDP by nearly a full percentage point. Saskatchewan's cities might hold the key to power, but it is a rural sense of alienation that the party has strategically sought to exploit. Saskatchewan Party General Manager Tom Lukiwski put it bluntly: "We made a strategic decision to go hard after areas of strength."[27] For the Saskatchewan Party, with its eight original MLAs from rural ridings, the "strength" was clearly in rural Saskatchewan. With Saskatchewan farmers reeling from one of the worst years since the Depression of the 1930s, the Saskatchewan Party waged an all-out assault against the NDP's handling of agricultural issues. It was a strategy that clearly worked. The debate during the 1999 election campaign did not focus on policy. Instead, debate focused on who could most effectively and legitimately fight for the interests of farmers.

ALIENATION AND THE ALBERTA MODEL

It has become convenient to characterize the Saskatchewan Party as the right-wing alternative to the NDP. Such rhetoric is especially in vogue in recent years given the developments in federal politics. Just as Canadian Alliance founder Preston Manning sought to "unite-the-right" federally to defeat the Liberal government, Saskatchewan Party supporters have characterized their new party as the political

25. Mark Wyatt, "Constitution, policy platform ok'd," *Leader-Post*, November 17, 1997, A4.
26. Murray Mandryk, "This Saskatchewan party wasn't great," *Leader-Post*, November 17, 1997, A2.
27. Tom Lukiwski, personal interview (August 25, 2000).
28. See Duane Booth, "Sask. Party's M.J. meeting draws 50," *Leader-Post*, August 23, 1997, A4.

vehicle that will defeat the left-wing NDP.[28] Others, like leadership contender Yogi Huyghebaert, have gone even further, depicting the Saskatchewan political reality as a microcosm of the bipolar politics of the Cold War. In an interview with *Leader-Post* reporter Mark Wyatt, Huyghebaert explained his entry into Saskatchewan politics as a mere continuation of a lifelong fight to stop the spread of communism.[29]

Huyghebaert's bipolar explanation of the Saskatchewan political system might be extreme, but it is far from revolutionary. The model has an established history of acceptance among political observers going back to the end of World War II. It has been acceptable to describe the province's party system as being polarized along clearly defined ideological lines — between socialism and unfettered capitalism. John C. Courtney and David E. Smith generally subscribe to this paradigm. However, the pair carefully describes the system as a division of "moderate democratic socialism versus a peculiar Prairie variety of liberalism."[30] Courtney and Smith are also careful to point out that there are no absolutes. Despite an overriding tendency toward ideological polarization within the political party system, the CCF/NDP and its right-wing competitor have generally been considered resistant to radicalism. Even within the broader framework of the polarization paradigm, there has been the acknowledgement by some analysts that brokerage politics has not eluded the Saskatchewan party system. In essence, the political competition has reflected the emergence of two major populist parties — one on the left, the other on the right. As Courtney and Smith write: "it is, of course, one thing to be progressive and leftist on the hustings; it is quite another matter to be so when elected to power."[31]

The CCF/NDP has consistently positioned itself as the party of the left, espousing and implementing social democratic policies. The party's strength has come from maintaining the loyalty of left-wing interests — namely the working class and less-prosperous farmers.[32] The right wing, until the creation of the Saskatchewan Party, has been represented alternately by the Progressive Conservatives and the Liberals. The core support for these parties has come from individuals of higher incomes and more-prosperous farmers. This view of Saskatchewan's party system is rooted in the work of American political scientist Seymour Lipset, who first advanced the concept of agrarian socialism to explain the existence of a social democratic party on the Canadian prairies. Lipset's notion of agrarian socialism has gained wide acceptance outside Saskatchewan as an explanation of the enduring popularity of the CCF/NDP and the features of the province's party system. Jane Jenson, for example, argues that "wheat farmers and workers came to define themselves in a similar relationship to the economy and provide continuing support to a left party." Essentially, partisan support is understood as being divided along class lines.[33] It follows then that the CCF/NDP has been defeated only when right-wing interests have united under the banner of one party. This occurred in the 1960s

29. Mark Wyatt, "Political pasts important," *Leader-Post*, April 6, 1998, A1.

30. John C. Courtney and David E. Smith, "Saskatchewan: Parties in a Politically Competitive Province," in Martin Robin (ed.), *Canadian Provincial Politics* (Scarborough: Prentice-Hall, 1972), 314.

31. Ibid., 316.

32. See Jane Jenson, "Party Systems," in David J. Bellamy, Jon H. Pamett and Donald C. Rowatt (eds.), *Provincial Political Systems: Comparative Essays* (Toronto: Methuen, 1976), 121–22; John C. Courtney and David E. Smith, "Saskatchewan: Parties in a Politically Competitive Province," 314.

33. Jenson, "Party Systems."

34. See R.K. Carty and David Stewart, "Parties and Party Systems," in Christopher Dunn (ed.), *Provinces: Canadian Provincial Politics* (Peterborough, ON: Broadview Press, 1996), 84–85.

with the Liberals, under the leadership of Ross Thatcher, and in the 1980s with the Progressive Conservatives under the leadership of Grant Devine.[34]

The polarization thesis would explain the existence of the Saskatchewan Party in the same context. Mired in scandal and corruption, the Progressive Conservatives could no longer maintain enough credibility with the public to carry the right-wing banner. The Liberals, plagued by infighting, were unable to organize themselves effectively to fill the void. Thus the emergence of a new right-wing alternative through the Saskatchewan Party, becoming successful enough in uniting right-wing interests in rural Saskatchewan to nearly defeat the NDP in 1999 election. Within this paradigm, it could be argued that the Saskatchewan Party failed to gain representation in the province's major cities because of the popularity of an alternative right-wing option — the Liberals. Lukiwski, for one, argues if right-wing voters in the cities had clearly understood the Saskatchewan Party was the best political vehicle to defeat the NDP, they might have cast their votes differently. Instead, the strength of the Liberals in the cities functioned to split the vote in favour of the New Democrats.[35] Such an explanation, however, assumes that Liberal voters perceived a clear ideological difference between the political parties — voting specifically for the Liberals because they viewed the party as more representative of their interests, in contrast to the NDP.

It is at this point that the polarization model begins to unravel. The model fails to explain the political developments that occurred following the election. The NDP, with 29 seats, entered into a coalition government with the Liberals. Cynically, it might be easy to dismiss the coalition as a simple marriage of convenience — the Liberals selling out ideologically and embracing socialism for power's sake, or the NDP willing to compromise its socialist principles to do the same. Using such a rationale, it might be argued that the Saskatchewan Party was the only political party to remain true to its ideological convictions. Such an evaluation of the position and role of the Saskatchewan Party in the province's party system is naïve. The decline of the Keynesian welfare state and the rise of the global neo-liberal regime have eroded the ability of governments of all ideological leanings to implement policy without regard for economic, social and political forces beyond their jurisdictions. In Saskatchewan, the NDP, while social democratic in origin, has begun to adopt some neo-liberal social and economic prescriptions — emphasizing austerity budgeting, regressive taxation policies and targeted social service benefits. Neo-liberalism, detached from partisan biases, espouses a *laissez-faire* economic doctrine, resurrecting the tenets of classic liberalism. In this context, neo-liberals believe that supply-side economic solutions are the best means to create wealth in society. That wealth, in turn, can be used by the state to fund scaled-down versions of social programs that were introduced at the height of the welfare state. An NDP/Liberal coalition works because in practice there is little ideological difference between the two parties.

In response, the Saskatchewan Party has been left to scrutinize the NDP, not on the basis of its ideologically flawed programs, but on its success in implementing a right-wing agenda. In its reaction to the spring 2000 budget, for example, the Saskatchewan Party directed its criticism of the new coalition government to gauging whether the tax cuts unveiled in the document were significant. The

35. Lukiwski interview.

NDP/Liberal coalition had announced changes to the province's income tax system that would move the province towards a flat tax regime. At the same time the government expanded the PST, also a flat tax. It became the strategy of the Saskatchewan Party to attack the government's integrity on tax policy, as opposed to making any overt ideological references. Saskatchewan Party leader Elwin Hermanson described the budget as a "broken promise made by the NDP in the 1999 election to decrease income taxes without raising sales taxes ... [while characterizing the government's claims of tax reduction as] another exercise in smoke and mirrors."[36]

The NDP/Liberal coalition had stolen some aspects of the Saskatchewan Party's policy agenda, leaving the opposition to criticize the government's integrity and management style. The onus was on the Hermanson team to demonstrate the government wasn't doing what it promised. Ideological distinctions between the competing parties were clearly diminishing. Given these developments the traditional bipolar explanation of the province's party system weakens, demanding the consideration of an alternative paradigm. Such a model most certainly demands a reexamination of the nature of Saskatchewan's political culture. With the blurring of ideological distinctions between Saskatchewan's political parties, it becomes more difficult to view class as the most significant determinant of partisan support. Throughout the Western industrialized world the rise of the neo-liberal regime has been marked by a transformation of the role of the individual to the state — citizenship has been replaced by consumership. As British political scientist Paul Hirst argues, "workers judge politics and political parties apolitically, in terms of the expected benefits to themselves and their families."[37] It is Hirst's suggestion that this shift itself is a product of the welfare state. Bolstered by a comfortable social safety net, workers have now begun to place more emphasis on private consumption and leisure. Likewise, they have come to realize that their lifestyle and buying power are directly related to the state's economic performance.[38] The argument explains why wage-labourers will favor *pro-business* policies — including regressive taxation, relaxed labour standards, and targeted, rather than universal social welfare benefits. Workers fear that if they don't support parties promoting *pro-business* policies and programs, they could pay the price with their jobs. It is also in this same context that workers begin to view taxation as an impediment to their buying power as consumers.[39]

There has been change in the working class with respect to its confidence in the state. As a resource-based economy dependent upon agricultural production, Saskatchewan farmers and workers have never been oblivious to the impact of global trade and events on the local economy. In the post-war years, however, workers looked to the state as a buffer to offset the shortcomings of the global market. And then, as is readily apparent now, there were social and economic differences within the farming community.[40] As Lipset concluded, radicalism was spawned as a solution to the uncertainty created by the "industrial business cycles

36. Elwin Hermanson quoted in *Hansard* (March 29, 2000), 323.
37. Paul Hirst, *After Thatcher* (London: Collins, 1989), 33.
38. Ibid.
39. Ibid. (emphasis added).
40. See Lipset, *Agrarian Socialism*, 29–30.
41. Ibid., 67.

and the shifting price of wheat."[41] Out of the economic and social despair of the Depression of the 1930s, "there were growing doubts whether political democracy founded on capitalism could, in fact, continue to result in progress."[42] At the turn of the millennium, farmers still remained tied to the shifts in the world market, but few in Saskatchewan's working class — as identified by Lipset and Jenson — openly expressed doubts about capitalism. What has emerged is a curious political discourse that blurs ideological categorization. Voters demand services from government, such as health care and road construction, all the while advocating a diminished role of the state in society. The apparent paradox still remains consistent with Hirst's argument. The citizen as consumer views "civil society primarily as a marketplace."[43] David Beetham characterizes the shift as one in which the new citizen demands "the expansion of consumer powers in the marketplace ... [whereby] the rights of consumer choice and consumer redress in respect of those services that remain in the public sector."[44] In other words, citizens might view accessible and affordable health care as important. But they are no longer convinced that the state should hold the monopoly on delivering those services. As long as citizens receive adequate redress for their taxes paid, they remain happy. Instead of looking to the state as the means to offset the vagaries of the market, the working class is now receptive to employing market solutions to meet social needs.

An electorate in which fundamental ideological divisions are absent cannot support a party system polarized between right and left. At the national level the brokerage theory has been one of the most popular models used to explain the Canadian party system. The theory argues that the major parties must disguise their "central ideological interests [of protecting the capitalist system] and merely promise to satisfy the most important interests felt by voters at any point in time."[45] To achieve this, the major parties have opted to emphasize "ethnic and regional concerns instead of class interests."[46] The brokerage model has taken on a new dimension, given the rise in voter support for region-based parties during the 1990s with the Bloc in Quebec and the Reform Party in the West. Michael Marzolini describes the emergence of these parties on to the federal scene as the "native son or daughter effect."[47] Voters might actually have greater confidence in the abilities of national party leaders, such as Jean Chretien of the Liberals, but vote instead for a region-based party leader. Survey data collected by Marzolini following the 1999 federal election revealed that the primary loyalty of voters was to their region even though "a plurality of people in every region still believe[d] that the Liberals ... [were] the best party to represent the national interest."[48] While "Reform voters tended to be more impressed with Jean Chretien than they were with Preston Manning[;] ... [he] was the native son, and like Gilles Duceppe and Lucien Bouchard in Quebec, could be counted on to protect his region's interest."[49] Protecting

42. Ibid.

43. David Beetham, "Political Theory and British Politics," in Patrick Dunleavy *et al.* (eds.), *Developments in British Politics* (New York: St. Martin's Press, 1993), 363.

44. Ibid.

45. Rand Dyck, *Canadian Politics: Critical Approaches* (Scarborough, ON: Nelson, 1996), 375.

46. Ibid., 376.

47. Michael Marzolini, "The Regionalization of Canadian Electoral Politics," in Alan Frizell and Jon H. Pammett (eds.), *The Canadian General Election of 1997* (Toronto: Dundurn Press, 1997), 195.

48. Ibid., 204.

49. Ibid., 199.

the regional interest has translated into issues of regional importance, resulting in further regional polarization. Marzolini, as an example, compares Atlantic and Western Canadians. Westerners are more focused on deficit cutting, while Atlantic Canadians are more concerned about jobs.[50] During the 1999 election campaign, Preston Manning successfully exploited these underlying sentiments to achieve substantial Western support. In this respect, Reform operated very much as a Western-based brokerage party, promising to fight for what voters in Western Canada believed to be the most important issue — the deficit as opposed to employment.

It is my argument that the Saskatchewan Party behaved in the 1999 provincial election much the same as Reform — as a region-based brokerage party. Rural voters, experiencing a complex barrage of setbacks to their local economies, had come to view the Saskatchewan Party and its leader, Elwin Hermanson — himself a farmer — as the most representative of their interests. The NDP, by contrast, had come to be viewed by rural voters as the party of the more prosperous cities, representing big government with close ties to the big labour and corporate interests of the heartland. Rural support for the Saskatchewan Party is not simply a voice of protest and discontent, it also reflects a belief among rural voters that a credible voice, "a native son or daughter," is needed to speak out for their interests. In the past twenty years, rural residents have experienced tremendous upheaval and despair. Plummeting grain prices, combined with rising production costs, are hastening the demise of the small family farm in favour of large-scale commercial operations. Add to this the closure of 51 hospitals in the province, the consolidation of schools, rail line abandonment, deteriorating roads and local grain elevator closures, and rural Saskatchewan appears to have taken a full economic and social assault. The Saskatchewan Party has successfully been able to exploit the discontent the assault has created. Yet as a powerful opposition, with a clear intention to govern, the Saskatchewan Party must also appeal to popular sentiments among urban voters if it is to secure power in the next election. Rural Saskatchewan might have given the party its momentum, but there is evidence that the party, both at the grassroots and at the leadership level, is positioning itself to attract urban voters, all the while avoiding any overt displays of ideology. Just as the Canadian Alliance's Stockwell Day went to great lengths to display himself as a moderate in hopes of winning the Ontario heartland, the Saskatchewan Party's Hermanson must also do the same to win the Saskatchewan heartland — the cities.

Winning the heartland might very will be realized in the implementation of the Alberta model of Ralph Klein's Conservative government. The model relies heavily upon supply-side, Thatcher-style economic theory offset by a rich stream of resource royalties as a means to building a prosperous economy. The Klein government achieved a balanced budget in the mid-1990s without raising taxes. There was a

50. Ibid., 195–96.

51. Reforms announced by the Alberta government in 1993 resulted in an average decrease of 20 percent in overall government spending between 1992 and 1996. In terms of health-care spending cuts, the Alberta government decreased its share of funding to health services by 17.6 percent during the first round of cuts. Cuts to universities and colleges amounted to 16 percent during the four-year period. In September 1993 the Klein government cut individual monthly welfare payments to $394 from $470, while also reducing the number of benefits including the payment of damage deposits to renters. Sources: Stockwell Day, "Lessons from Alberta on Fiscal Dividends and Taxation," *The Fraser Institute* [http://fraserinstitute.ca/publications/books/fiscal_surplus/chapter6.html], Mary Nemeth, Dale Eisler and Brian Bergman, "To tax or cut: Saskatchewan raised taxes, Alberta cut programs. Both

considerable price, however, in terms of significant cuts to welfare benefits, education and health care, coupled with a hike in health-care premiums.[51] The "Klein revolution" has been realized in more than just tight fiscal management. In choosing to ignore corporate pressure to introduce US-style right-to-work legislation, the Klein government has demonstrated little desire to tighten the province's relatively relaxed labour laws and standards. There are still no laws in Alberta that require workers to pay dues if they choose not to hold a membership in the union that represents them.[52] Critics have cited this as one reason why Alberta has the lowest unionization rates in Canada. It is a reality, that when combined with Canada's lowest hourly minimum wage rates ($5.90), has made the province a relatively attractive place to do business.[53]

Making Alberta attractive to corporate investment has also meant a conscious effort on the part of the province to expand the range of services offered by the private sector — from the privatization of state-owned liquor stores to the contracting-out of health-care services. The Klein government, looking for ways to reduce waiting lists for health-care services, has consistently sought solutions in the market. Alberta's controversial Bill 11 — the *Health Care Protection Act* — formalizes the market approach to health delivery. The legislation, given royal assent on May 30, 2000, sets out the rules for the operation of privately owned surgical clinics, providing services ranging from gall bladder to nose and throat surgeries — all paid for through the province's health-care insurance program.[54] The bill's passage not only opens new opportunities for investment, it also symbolizes a profound change in public thinking about the role of the state. State services such as health care, and even education, come to be viewed primarily as consumable goods — not as cornerstones of a just society.

The Klein government's zealous drive to retool public health care is eclipsed only by its unflinching resolve to cut taxes. Beyond any single issue, tax cuts remain the fulcrum of the Alberta model. Even as the Alberta government has moved on to record budgetary surpluses, largely owed to resource royalties, it has proportionally given greater favour to tax cuts and rebates over restoring funding to besieged

are about to balance budgets," *Maclean's* (February 13, 1995): 16–23; Brian Bergman and Donna Korchinski, "Ralph's Way: Alberta is alone in trying to slash the deficit without raising taxes, *Maclean's* (March 7, 1994): 18–23; Alvin Finkel, "The Klein Revolution," *Canadian Dimension* (October/November 1994): 19–22.

Health-care premiums in 1995 rose from $30 to $36 per month for a single person. Source: Mary Janigan, Kathryn Welbourn, Mark Cardwell and Mary Nemeth, "A prescription for medicare: ten ways to heal the health-care system," *Maclean's* (July 31, 1995): 10–16; Bergman and Korchinski, "Ralph's Way."

52. For a discussion on the Alberta debate on right-to-work legislation see Christopher Serres, "Bombshell for organized labour: Alberta's unions battle for survival against right-to-work legislation," *Alberta Report* (September 4, 1995): 14. Also see Alberta Federation of Labour, "What's Wrong with Alberta's Labour Law?" *AFL Submission to the Provincial Legislative Standing Policy Committee on Learning* [http://afl.org/presentations/labourlaw00.html].

53. Government of Alberta, "A Reminder ... Minimum Wage to Increase," Government of Alberta News Release (September 30, 1999) [http://www.gov.ab.ca/can/199909/8204.html].

54. Government of Alberta, "Alberta Health Care Protection Act (Bill 11) Passed," Government of Alberta News Release (May 31, 2000) [http://www2.gov.ab.ca/healthfacts/PrinterFriendly.cfm?ID=213]; Government of Alberta, "Minister approves first contracts under Health Care Protection Act; releases criteria assessments," Government of Alberta News Release (September 29, 2000) [http://www.gov.ab.ca/can/20009/9729.html]; Brian Bergman, "The Alberta Test: Ralph Klein wants private clinics to play a bigger role in health care. Will he back down?" *Maclean's* (April 3, 2000): 42.

services. Alberta's 1998 budget provides a good example of this. In spite of the province's distinction of having the lowest level of taxation in Canada, then-Treasurer Stockwell Day proceeded to announce $285 million in further tax reductions, while another $585 million was allocated for debt reduction. In sharp contrast, the Klein government opted, after successive years of slashing funding to health, education and social services, to propose only modest spending increases in those areas. For the year ahead, projected increases in each of those respective areas would be less than $200 million. Increases would be held to that level over the next two budgets.[55] Not surprisingly, these relatively modest increases in spending have done little to shorten diagnostic service waiting lists in the health-care system, reduce classroom sizes in the K-12 system, or temper escalating university tuition costs.[56] This has not, however, served to sidetrack the overriding agenda of the Klein Conservatives. The Alberta government remains firmly opposed to scrapping health-care insurance premiums, arguing that it is more prudent to keep "costs reasonable." Instead, rhetoric has focussed on the promise of yet more tax cuts, even though Albertans spend more than any other Canadians on *out-of-pocket* health-care expenses.[57] In fact, Alberta, as Canada's second wealthiest province, spends proportionately less per capita on public health-care funding than the relatively poorer jurisdictions of Manitoba and Nova Scotia.[58]

Even so, the province certainly does not rank at the bottom, surpassing neighbouring Saskatchewan.[59] Much of Alberta's capacity to provide the level of state services it does — while maintaining a low overall rate of taxation — is owed to the province's collection of lucrative resource royalties. In 1999 net revenues from the Alberta resource sector totaled nearly $5 billion.[60] For the same period, the Saskatchewan government by comparison collected $943 million.[61] With skyrocketing world energy prices in 2000, and a provincial election on the horizon, the Klein government acted to "free-up" some of some of the growing windfall of resource royalties, expected to be nearly double the revenue collected the previous year. Instead of setting aside the funds for a day that would see less robust oil prices, the province opted for what some Albertans likened to a tax refund. All residents, 16 and over, were given $300 to offset the cost of rising fuel bills. In addition, residential electricity customers received a $20-per-month credit on their power bills. The same week of the announcement also witnessed a pledge by the Klein government to spend $200 million on post-secondary infrastructure improvements. There were no commitments, however, for providing more funds to shore up operating

55. Government of Alberta, "Budget '98 Highlights," *Budget '98: Agenda for Opportunity* (February 12, 1998) [http://treas.gov.ab.ca/publications/budget/budget98/highli.html]; Government of Alberta, "1998–2001 Fiscal Plan," ibid.

56. Brian Bergman, "Taking Advantage: With its soaring economy, oil-rich Alberta is the envy of Canada," *Maclean's* (September 18, 2000): 22.

57. A 1997 Statistics Canada survey determined that Albertans spend $1,800 per household on "out-of-pocket" health-care expenses. Cited in Ashley Geddes, "Reducing health premiums not top priority, Treasurer Day says," *The Edmonton Journal*, September 1, 1999, A1 (emphasis added).

58. Canadian Institute for Health Information, *National Health Expenditure Trends: 1975–1999* (1999) [http://cihi.ca/medrls/execnhex.htm].

59. Ibid.

60. Government of Alberta, *Annual Report 1999–2000* (Edmonton: Alberta Ministry of Resource Development, 2000), 39.

61. Government of Saskatchewan, *Public Accounts 1999–2000* (Regina: Saskatchewan Department of Finance, 2000), 31.

62. Brian Bergman, "Taking Advantage...," *Maclean's* (September 18, 2000): 22 (emphasis added).

expenses.[62] What the Klein government has achieved is to entrench the conviction that unending prosperity is integrally linked to state's retreat from society. Premier Klein routinely characterizes Alberta's current prosperity as the product of a favourable tax regime, not skyrocketing energy prices: "the way you don't create prosperity is through taxes."[63] For Albertans who have an underlying fear that yet another "bust" in the oil patch could be just around the corner, there is understandably some comfort in the message.

Ralph Klein's brand of populism is analogous to a well choreographed, albeit sometimes improvised, ballet. Klein has moved to exploit socially conservative sentiments when it has proven politically expedient, while moving to resist those sentiments when they have proven too radical. The Conservative premier has demonstrated an intuitive ability to know the limits of both social conservativism and liberalism in the realm of the mainstream electorate. Klein, who once entertained the possibility of running as a Liberal candidate, rose to the leadership of the Alberta Conservative Party on a wave of rural, socially conservative support, much of it coming from the religious right. Klein, in his bid to become party leader, orchestrated a campaign much like that waged by the Saskatchewan Party during the 1999 election. As journalist Mark Lisac observed, "Klein carefully appealed to rural voters in ways the other contenders could not or would not," going so far as to promise costly rural oriented programs such as irrigation projects, while advocating cuts in expenditures to health and education."[64] Klein won the leadership in 1992, receiving most of the support from rural Alberta and Calgary. As premier, that support was reflected in the backing of most of the rural Conservative members of the legislature. Klein gave rural conservatives a greater say in government. But in so doing he also fashioned himself, and the *new* party he created, as the dragon slayer of the elites — speaking out for rural Albertans and speaking out for the little guy.[65] The Klein Conservatives, like Hermanson's Saskatchewan Party, owe their political momentum to the alienation of the hinterland.

In power, Klein's rural power-base has not been ignored. But more often than not, the socially conservative faction has been listened to when it has been more politically expedient to do so. As Brooke Jeffrey puts it, Klein has consistently resorted to socially conservative rhetoric and policies as a method of "scapegoating" — a way of diverting public attention away from the social consequences of the government's neo-liberal economic programs. In the Klein vernacular, the poor and the socially and economically marginalized have come to be characterized as "lazy," acting solely as "special interests." It is a diversionary tactic that the Klein government frequently used early in its regime to explain the province's growing poverty rate, in the face of an onslaught of spending cuts and subsequent service reductions. Between 1993 and 1995 Statistics Canada data showed the number of Albertans living below the poverty line had nearly doubled. To put this in perspective, the capital city of Edmonton now held the distinction of having the highest per capita poverty rate of any large Canadian city. It has become convenient to blame the victim.[66]

Socially conservative-inspired rhetoric also became an expedient way of masking major spending cutbacks to the Alberta Department of Justice. The loss of $40

---

63. Klein quoted in *Calgary Herald*, September 1, 1993, A1, Cited in Brooke Jeffrey, *Hard Right Turn* (Toronto: HarperCollins, 1999), 122.

64. Mark Lisac, *The Klein Revolution* (Edmonton: NeWest Press, 1995), 70.

65. Ibid., 71–72 (emphasis added).

66. Jeffrey, *Hard Right Turn*, 131, 145–46.

million from the department's budget in the early 1990s meant less funding for policing and cuts to the province's Law Reform Commission. As Jeffrey observed, the premier diverted attention away from the cuts by resorting to law-and-order rhetoric. He frequently demanded the reinstatement of the death penalty for those convicted of murder, going so far as to demand an extension of the penalty to offenders as young as eight. Such tough talk certainly satisfied the socially conservative wing of the party, but Klein's posturing was nothing more than mere rhetoric, given that criminal justice issues are a matter of federal jurisdiction.[67]

Through it all, however, Klein has demonstrated himself to be a liberal — keeping radical socially conservative elements within his party at bay. The most notable example is the Klein government's handling of the case of Delwin Vriend. The lab instructor at King's University College in Edmonton had been fired from his job because he was gay. Vriend would eventually respond by challenging Alberta's *Human Rights Act* as unconstitutional on the grounds that it did not specify sexual orientation. The Supreme Court would rule in April 1998 that gays and lesbians — while not specifically mentioned — should receive protection under the act. There had been tremendous pressure within the Conservative caucus, including from then-Deputy Premier Stockwell Day, to invoke the notwithstanding clause in the Canadian Constitution to override the Supreme Court's decision. In the end, the Alberta government backed down. Instead, it vowed to utilize the Notwithstanding Clause if there was any move by the Supreme Court to sanction gay marriages, while in the same instance proposing to develop a policy framework that would open the door for gay couples to assume the same benefits and obligations as heterosexuals.[68] It was a position that appeared to quiet some social conservatives, but it was also a position that conveyed the impression that the Alberta government was no longer prepared to stomp on individual and minority rights. In accepting the Supreme Court decision, Klein characterized himself as a liberal, proclaiming that "it's morally wrong to discriminate on the basis of sexual orientation."[69]

Premier Klein may very well be a liberal by conviction, but his decision speaks more of his instincts for political survival. The Klein Conservatives, and Klein in particular, had come to recognize that even though the invocation of the notwithstanding clause could win the adulation of social conservatives, the party faced the prospect of receiving the disdain of a broader base of liberal support — much it situated in the cities. The debate that surrounded the Vriend case might at first assessment give credence to the Alberta redneck stereotype. But the Alberta government's own polling was saying something else. The majority of respondents to a survey conducted in the fall of 1998 favoured extending equal financial benefits to same-sex couples. The same respondents also favoured allowing homosexual couples to adopt foster children in certain circumstances. One gay activist, in assessing the province's political culture, put it this way: "no one in Alberta votes in terms of gay rights; they vote on economics, not social issues."[70] In Klein's Alberta model, neoliberalism comes as part of the standard equipment, social conservativism is a disposable option. The Klein brand of populism may sometimes appease deep-rooted

67. Ibid., 132–33.

68. Brian Bergman, "Not with standing: Alberta sends mixed signals to homosexuals," *Maclean's* (March 29, 1999): 22.

69. Joe Woodard, "Ralph gets moral, and Alberta gets gay rights: how Klein snookered public opinion to satisfy homosexual … and the media," *Alberta Report* (April 20, 1998): 12–17.

70. Bergman, "Not with standing," 22.

socially conservative sentiments, but its more enduring quality is found in its ability to tap an even more pervasive sense of individualism among Albertans.

IDEOLOGIES AND ASPIRATIONS

The Saskatchewan Party might have its sites set on the province's larger urban centres, but its roots remain firmly planted in rural Saskatchewan soil. The party now boasts in excess of 10,000 members, with three-quarters of them residing outside the province's four largest urban centres. In terms of occupation and social class, there is substantial support from farmers, agricultural service sector employees, small business owners and professionals such as lawyers and accountants. Party organizers caution, however, that such statistics are somewhat misleading.[71] Tom Likiwski, for one, argues that the higher proportion of civil servants and government contractors in the cities has a chilling effect on membership. Lukiwski reasons that those individuals with close ties to government are more reluctant to buy a party membership for fear of losing either their jobs or a contract.[72] His point might have some validity. But in the voting booth, where biases are secret, the Saskatchewan Party failed in the 1999 general election to get enough votes to win seats in the province's cities. Party Leader Elwin Hermanson dismisses any suggestion that electoral support is polarized between rural and urban voters:

> While the Saskatchewan Party won almost every rural seat in the 1999 election, we also did very well in most urban constituencies. In fact, the Saskatchewan Party ran a strong second in almost every constituency that we did not win. The so-called rural-urban split is not based on fundamental differences in the priorities between rural and urban voters. The split is the direct results of a government that has demonstrated little concern for rural communities.[73]

Certainly the Saskatchewan Party did achieve second-place finishes in most urban ridings, and in two ridings — Saskatoon Southeast and Regina Wascana Plains — the party's candidates narrowly lost to the NDP incumbent. In Regina Wascana Plains, for example, the Saskatchewan Party's Dan Thibault, with 38.95 percent of the vote, nearly edged out the NDP's Doreen Hamilton, who received the support of 40.2 percent of all voters. Adam Neisner, Jr., the Liberal candidate, received just over 20 percent of the vote to finish third. Some party insiders, such as Lukiwski, reason that had Liberal voters known the best way to defeat the NDP was by voting for the Saskatchewan Party, they would have done so.[74] Using this rationale, it would seem quite plausible that the Saskatchewan Party's consistent second place finishing in the cities could have translated into a number of victories — had voters been convinced that the Saskatchewan Party, not the Liberals, had the best chance of forming the government. The rural-urban split was simply a consequence of the Saskatchewan right's failure to unite.

Of course, such a scenario remains firmly rooted in the polarization paradigm. A counter argument can also be made that traditional NDP supporters, disgruntled with the government's performance and foreseeing an NDP victory in the public opinion polls, voted strategically. They sought to voice their disapproval

71. Lukiwski interview.
72. Ibid.
73. Elwin Hermanson, personal interview (September 21, 2000).
74. Lukiwski interview.

without toppling the government, casting their votes instead for the Liberals. Opinion polls released by Saskatchewan's two daily newspapers during the 1999 election campaign had predicted an NDP majority government, with the approval of 48.9 percent of all voters.[75] A final poll released by UCAL Management Consultants just before election saw the NDP with as high as 50 percent of the vote, while the Saskatchewan Party lagged behind at 29 percent.[76] With what seemed an easy victory in store for the NDP, traditional supporters — nurses and other public sector professionals and workers — gambled that a vote for the Liberals would send a message of protest to the government. Relations between the NDP and registered nurses in the province had strained considerably after the government had ordered striking members of the Saskatchewan Union of Nurses back to work only two months earlier. The action also added further tension between the party and the organized labour movement as a whole — eroding the NDP's core base of support.

Still, the Saskatchewan Party's leadership is convinced that the party has and will continue to make inroads into traditional NDP territory, by appealing to popular sentiments. Declaring that his party is "not married to a specific ideology,"[77] Hermanson echoes the mantra of Ontario Premier Mike Harris' "common sense" revolution. Electoral success in the new century, he asserts, will demand a "smaller, more practical common sense" approach to government.[78] But while Hermanson tries to create the impression that his party is ideologically neutral, he readily acknowledges where its true ideological convictions rest. Just as significantly, he does not attempt to conceal the party's strategy for both assuming and maintaining power:

> The Saskatchewan Party is a "free enterprise" based populist political movement that attempts to stay in touch with the priorities of Saskatchewan people and then reflect those priorities in the development of public policy. As a result, the Saskatchewan Party is attracting supporters from all political backgrounds including those who have voted NDP and those with no previous affiliation.[79]

The Saskatchewan Party is clearly positioning itself to function as a brokerage party in a political culture that its leadership has identified as shifting to the right.

In the language of "common sense," overt references to ideology are exchanged for the dictum of "freedom of choice." Citizens as consumers are viewed to be free to choose the quality and type of services delivered by the state. If farmers don't like a state-run agency marketing their grain, they are believed to have the freedom to choose an alternative. If the sick are unhappy with the health-care treatment they receive from the state, they too are believed to possess the freedom to look for an alternative. The notion of universality is traded for accessibility. In other words, everyone — the aggregation of individuals in the market — is considered to have the right to access the quality and type of services they demand. The emphasis is on "equality of opportunity," not equality of condition.[80] The state is thus viewed by the

75. See Mark Wyatt, "Opinion Poll suggests another NDP majority, " *The Leader-Post*, August 31, 1999, A1, A2. Also see Mark Wyatt, "Poll puts NDP ahead," *The Star-Phoenix*, August 31, 1999, A1, A4.

76. Barrett Pashak, "High taxes and rural rage," *Alberta Report* (October 4, 1999): 8.

77. Hermanson interview.

78. Ibid.

79. Ibid.

80. Ibid.

81. Ibid.

Saskatchewan Party as the facilitator for establishing an "environment that encourages private sector, value-added economic growth and job creation."[81] In the party's view, the market is entrusted with generating wealth. There are to be, however, no corresponding obligations imposed on the market to redistribute equitably the wealth it generates.

The discourse of "common sense" ultimately resides within the broader framework of majoritarian democracy. This is reflected both internally in the party's decision-making processes, and externally through the party's policy platform. Internally, leadership selection and review is open to the direct vote of the entire membership. In terms of candidate selection, the constituency associations have the final veto — based upon the vote of the local membership. This also means that incumbent candidates, even if they are sitting members of the legislature, can be challenged. Externally, the "common sense" approach is realized through the promotion of policies advocating free votes in the legislature, voter recall and set election dates. The underlying conviction is that elected representatives must be directly held accountable to the will of the majority of voters who elect them. It is the Saskatchewan Party's contention that it is the will of the majority that should establish the priorities of "practical public policy."[82] The interests of economically and socially marginalized groups thus become secondary to the interests of the majority. This is a consequence of majoritarianism that the party readily accepts. Using the rationale that the Canadian Charter of Rights and Freedoms "has been used to advance the rights and interests of groups ahead of the rights and interests of the individual," the Saskatchewan Party endorses the use of Section 33 of *The Constitution Act, 1982*.[83] The clause expressly gives a provincial legislature the constitutional right to pass legislation that operates notwithstanding the Charter of Rights and Freedoms. In effect, elected provincial legislatures, not appointed judges, are given the final say in the application of laws they pass within their sphere of jurisdiction.

Majoritarianism, populism, and radical liberalism can sometimes present a curious mix — if not a paradox. Hermanson might be right — asserting that "parties who remain tied to narrow political ideologies will not survive."[84] Majoritarianism enshrines populism, causing parties that celebrate free enterprise to take contradictory policy positions. Not surprisingly, the Saskatchewan Party, carrying the momentum of rural electoral support, advocates state support for the farm industry. In December 1999, Hermanson, as opposition leader, was pressuring the new NDP/Liberal coalition government to force Ottawa "to immediately provide $1 billion to Saskatchewan farm families."[85] The emphasis on this occasion was not simply on offering general tax concessions to the agricultural industry, but also on providing a direct cash payment to farmers from the state. The position stands in sharp contrast to the party's policies regarding economic development. Membership at the party's founding meeting in 1997 agreed that "under a Saskatchewan Party government, there will be no direct investments, loans or grants given to businesses."[86] The contradiction deserves some explanation.

82. Ibid. See also Lukiwski interview.

83. Saskatchewan Party, *Resolutions* (October 31, 1998).

84. Hermanson interview.

85. Hermanson quoted in *Hansard* (December 8, 1999), 47.

86. Saskatchewan Party, *Resolutions* (November 14–16, 1997).

Hermanson makes no secret that the party's position on agriculture appeals to its rural power base. Yet, he readily concedes that the position also presents a dilemma for the party as it seeks to attract urban voters. In defence of the party's farm platform, Hermanson argues the unique circumstances the province's farmers face in respect to a global grain trade war in which other countries, subsidizing agricultural production to a greater degree than does Canada, demand state intervention.[87] In the end though, he concedes the party will need to focus more on broad-based issues such as tax cuts, education, and health care, if it is to win acceptance with urban voters:

> The farmer that has the concern of his property taxes being far too high and increasing too quickly has the identical concern of the property taxpayer in Regina. We have to talk about issues that are relevant to people that are involved. But it doesn't mean to put those people at odds with one another. Because people in the city, as long as you are talking about fairness in lowering taxes to agriculture, they are fine with that. But they are not happy with what they might see as unjustified handouts to people in agriculture.[88]

Fundamental to the party's majoritarian ethic is a crucial need to hit upon issues and policies that receive the greatest possible popular support. Whether the Saskatchewan Party can be successful in identifying broad-based popular sentiments while at the same time striking a balance between rural and urban issues, remains to be seen. Hermanson himself acknowledges that the rural-urban question remains a matter of considerable debate within caucus.[89] There is recognition by party strategists that Saskatchewan's rural and urban cultures are indeed diverse — each with its particular set of values, norms and expectations of government. Still, the party's success or failure in striking a popular chord could very well be indicative of a shift in the province's political culture.

In its bid to hit upon popular issues that bridge the rural-urban divide the Saskatchewan Party has advocated policies emanating from a mixture of neo-liberal and socially conservative values. This becomes the party's interpretation of middle ground in Saskatchewan politics. In this context, the Saskatchewan Party's social conservative impulse is more reflective of its populist tendencies than a clearly defined moral agenda. And just as the party has had to search for common values between the rural and urban communities, it has also sought to strike a balance between neo-liberal and socially conservative interests — a reflection perhaps that the party is indeed an amalgam of diverse partisan affiliations. The phrasing of the party's position on Section 33 becomes representative of a political party trying to reconcile its liberal/conservative divide, all the while remaining cognizant of popular sentiments. In providing its rationale for advocating the use of the Notwithstanding Clause of the Constitution, the Saskatchewan Party recognizes the sanctity of individual rights, while in the same instance dictating that a constitutional mechanism guaranteeing them should remain subject to legislative review — and ultimately public scrutiny. As noted above, a Saskatchewan Party resolution in 1998 proclaims:

87. Hermanson interview.
88. Ibid.
89. Ibid.
90. Saskatchewan Party, *Resolutions* (October 31, 1998).

> that while the Canadian Charter of Rights and Freedoms does at least somewhat protect the rights of individuals, it has also been used to advance the rights and interests of groups ahead of the rights and interest of the individual.[90]

What emerges is a seemingly contradictory policy statement that bridges — albeit awkwardly — differences between neo-liberal and social conservative factions within the party. Of greater significance, however, is the freedom the resolution gives the party leadership — if in government — to implement policies and programs that have popular support.

It might be argued that the Saskatchewan Party's efforts to appeal to popular opinion have influenced its socially conservative stance on issues such as crime — an issue Hermanson identifies as uniting rural and urban voters. There is an underlying conviction in Saskatchewan Party policy that coercion is the best way to deter crime. This is reflected in policies demanding harsher sentences for young offenders, hard work for the incarcerated, restitution from parents of convicted young offenders who have committed property crimes, and favouring the rights of victims "over those found guilty of committing crimes."[91] By contrast the governing NDP has taken a somewhat less aggressive stance. The party, presumably identifying the same socially conservative sentiments among voters, promised during the 1999 election campaign to get tough on crime. Included in the NDP crime-fighting package was a pledge to introduce tougher penalties for repeat young offenders and to provide specific funding to put more police officers on the street. In making the campaign announcement, NDP Leader Roy Romanow seemed to appeal directly to socially conservative values: "the simple fact of the matter is the officer on the beat is the most effective way to fight crime and make our communities safer."[92] The NDP's "get tough" stance on crime, when compared to Saskatchewan Party policy, suggests a competition between the two parties for an emerging middle ground among the electorate. That middle ground is comfortable with a reduced role of the state in society, yet paradoxically insists on the state's support for key services such as health care and highways. This same group interprets what it perceives as a "breakdown" in the current social order as a deterioration of widely accepted institutions and values — chief among them deference to authority. Young people, it is reasoned, break the law because there is a collapse in authority, whether it be the state or in popularly held notions of family.

Similarly, deteriorating community values — not socio-economic realities — are seen to have created welfare dependency. The economically marginalized, using the same rationale, have lost their incentive to work. The emerging discourse of the political centre thus comes to justify the rollback and targeting of social programs. Social conservatism supports the neo-liberal regime — providing the moral rationale for a system that promises equality of opportunity, but does not deliver equality of condition. Independence, self-reliance, employability and family become part of the new vernacular used to mobilize public support for changing social and economic realities. As further evidence of this shift in Saskatchewan politics, the NDP in government has openly appealed to these sentiments as it has moved away from the principle of universality and begun to target social service benefits. Not surprisingly, the cornerstone of the NDP government's social policy, unveiled in the spring of

91. Saskatchewan Party, *Resolutions* (November 14–16, 1997).
92. CTV News, Regina, August 25, 1999.

1998, was promoted as the Building Independence — Investing in Families strategy. The news release outlining the strategy sought to demonstrate the government's commitment to moving adults off the welfare rolls and targeting benefits to the morally innocent — children. At the same time the government characterized itself as a protector of the popularly held notion of the family as a fundamental building block of Saskatchewan society:

> ensure that families will be financially better off working than they would be on social assistance; assist families in making the leap from dependence to the workforce; help families remain in the workforce; help with the cost of raising children and improve child health in lower income families; and provide training and employment for individuals and parents.[93]

The NDP does not define family in its discourse, demonstrating perhaps the greater importance the party places on attracting socially conservative interests, than advancing a particular model of society. This may in part be explained by the party's need to maintain left-of-centre support, both in and outside the party.

In contrast to the NDP, the Saskatchewan Party is more specific in how it defines family. In attributing existing social problems on "a divergence away from the traditional family unit, [the party's membership define that unit as a] ... mother and a father raising their children in a responsible and loving manner."[94] It can easily be deduced that this model does not include single parents or homosexual couples. In a refined policy statement on social policy adopted at the party's annual convention in April 1998, the membership appeared to reiterate the objectives of the NDP government's social assistance strategy:

> The Saskatchewan Party favors replacing the current social welfare system of cash assistance with one that strives to move fully-employable men and women into the workforce immediately.[95]

Even though the resolution retains the language of NDP policy, it remains consistent with earlier Saskatchewan Party policy statements in its tone. In providing its rationale for the resolution, the membership not only endorses a welfare system that discourages "dependence ... [but advocates] a system based on mandatory employment."[96] The differences in tone between the two parties may very well speak to the deep-rooted ideological commitments present within the NDP and the Saskatchewan Party that persist despite the realities of brokerage politics.

Reflecting a core ideological bias the Saskatchewan Party has demonstrated a greater willingness than the NDP and the Liberals have shown to confront more sensitive moral issues, such as abortion. At its founding convention the party's membership pledged that if in government "the Saskatchewan Party will conduct a binding referendum on the issue of public funding for abortion in Saskatchewan."[97] Certainly it can be argued that the resolution is merely consistent with the party's majoritarian philosophy. After all, in rationalizing the resolution the membership cites the 1991 provincial plebiscite in which roughly two-thirds of the electorate

93. Government of Saskatchewan, Social Services Department, "Saskatchewan Launches Most Significant Program in 30 Years," News Release, March 26, 1998.

94. Saskatchewan Party, *Resolutions* (November 14–16, 1997).

95. Saskatchewan Party, *Resolutions* (October 31, 1998).

96. Ibid.

97. Saskatchewan Party, *Resolutions* (November 14–16, 1997).

favored the removal of public funding for abortion. Despite the plebiscite results, the abortion issue has proven historically to be both a highly divisive and visceral debate — not something a party with such broad-based populist ambitions would want to tackle. For this reason the policy position would seem to be more reflective of deep-rooted moral sentiments among the Saskatchewan Party's core membership than a clear-cut desire to implement direct democracy.

Just like the Canadian Alliance and its predecessor the Reform Party, there is evidence to suggest a link between the Saskatchewan Party and the Christian right. Both Hermanson and founding Saskatchewan Party MLA Don Toth attended Full Gospel Bible Institute in Eston, Saskatchewan. The Bible Institute has been a bastion for social conservatism, producing such notable voices on the Christian right as Roy Beyer. Beyer, an evangelical pastor, played a leading role in founding the Canada Family Action Coalition.[98] The coalition, which has gained influence in Alliance circles, encourages its members to become active politically as a means of imposing its unique interpretation of "Judeo-Christian moral principles" on Canadian society. That interpretation stands in uncompromising opposition to abortion, while also advancing a narrowly defined notion of "family" that excludes single parents, homosexual and common-law couples: "we believe that the family, based on the marriage of a husband and wife of the opposite sex, is central to the fabric of society."[99]

Such socially conservative values might match those held privately by Hermanson and others in the Saskatchewan Party. However, Hermanson, like the Alliance's Stockwell Day, insists that the party does "not promote any particular religious or political philosophy," preferring instead the populist label.[100] Aside from the party's position on abortion, the Saskatchewan Party has shown a tendency to shy away from radical socially conservative positions despite the underlying sentiments of some members. One such instance occurred at the party's 1998 leadership convention. Delegates voted overwhelmingly to defeat a policy resolution calling for the abolition of the Saskatchewan Human Rights Commission. Some dissenting members had charged that the Commission has been "primarily used by radical leftists and radical gay movements ... [as a means of] shoving a lot of things down our [the public's] throats."[101] In the end, however, the majority of members conceded that the concept of human rights was indeed valid. At the same time there was a general consensus that any move to trample on those rights would undermine attempts to present the party as a moderate alternative to the NDP.[102]

Presenting the party as a more moderate voice has also meant reverting to libertarian logic, rather than overtly attacking institutions perceived as protecting the rights of minority groups. The credo of "equality for all, special privileges for no one" supersedes any discussion of current social, economic and historical realties.[103] Using this same logic the Saskatchewan Party remains steadfastly opposed to affirmative action programs that seek to improve the employment opportunities for

98. John Geddes, "New Might on the Right: A classic product of the Bible Belt," *Maclean's* (September 11, 2000): 22.

99. "About CFAC," *Canadian Family Action Committee* [http://www.cfac.org].

100. Hermanson interview.

101. Reg Hoegl quoted in James Parker, "Sask. Party delegates defeat resolution to abolish SHRC," *Leader-Post*, April 6, 1998, A4.

102. Ibid.

103. Saskatchewan Party, *Resolutions* (October 31, 1998).

socially and economically marginalized groups. To put it another way, the party rejects "hiring practices designed to give groups or individuals an advantage based on race, culture, gender, sexual orientation or any other arbitrary" criteria. The membership reasons that people should be hired strictly on the basis of "competence and qualification ... [arguing that] reverse discrimination doesn't undo the past and only serves to create a new set of victims who are discriminated against because of their sex, race, gender or sexual orientation."[104] The argument appeals directly to Saskatchewan's libertarian subconscious. Socially conservative discourse might appeal at a very visceral level to the Saskatchewan public's sense of social order. The libertarian argument, in comparison, is equally as pragmatic, functioning to manipulate the public's sense of what is rational and ultimately reasonable — and in so doing, becoming the language of "common sense." In this respect, the Saskatchewan Party has exploited underlying libertarian values in Saskatchewan society in the same way as it has drawn upon socially conservative sentiments as a means of mobilizing broad-based public support.

What emerges is a potent synergy between the expectations of voters and the political parties that must compete for their support. It really becomes a question of who will lead — the parties or the electorate. Parties possess great power, and not simply through the prospect of forming a government. Through the mastery of language, political parties also possess the capacity to lead the public into uncharted territory. For this reason, an important question arises on how the Saskatchewan Party would behave if in government. Clearly, on policy alone the party seems unlikely to challenge the neo-liberal regime. But as the political party searches for the middle ground among the electorate, we are left to speculate on the extent such a government would temper or advance libertarian and socially conservative agendas. It also comes to be a matter of speculation about the extent to which the party will either resist or appease socially democratic values that have persisted despite the decline of the welfare state. This question becomes particularly relevant as the party sets out to win over the urban vote.

It is the Alberta model, and above all the Alberta notion of prosperity, that emerges repeatedly in Saskatchewan Party rhetoric, as the party constructs a vision of where it wants to take the province it one day hopes to govern. The vision feeds on a prevailing consumer consciousness among the electorate. At a visceral level the vision also preys upon the envy factor — the growing restlessness of Saskatchewan residents who watch the frenetic pace of economic activity next door, while friends and relatives leave for new jobs in a rapidly expanding economy. During the 1999 election campaign Elwin Hermanson frequently referred to the "exodus" of Saskatchewan residents heading to Alberta in search of lower taxes. Staged media events included testimonials of Saskatchewan expatriates who had moved to Alberta to save taxes. One such testimonial appeared in a *Leader-Post* article, outlining Hermanson's tax-cutting strategy.[105] A Lloydminster businessperson was cited who claimed to have saved between $1,000 to $5,000 in taxes by moving to the Alberta side of the border from Saskatchewan. Even after the election Hermanson, in demanding a 20 percent cut in provincial income tax, was still referring to the Alberta model, challenging the NDP government here to narrow the gap between

104. Saskatchewan Party, *Resolutions* (November 14–16, 1997).

105. Bonnie Braden, "Businessman moved to escape taxes," *Leader-Post*, August 24, 1999, A4.

106. Neil Scott, "Sask. Party leader calls for flat-tax system," *Leader-Post*, October 2, 1999, A4.

Saskatchewan and Alberta's tax levels.[106] Thus tax cuts and the Alberta model become synonymous. Lowering the rate of taxation, and ushering in a flat-tax system is not just viewed by party strategists as a way to bridge the gap between rural and urban voters; tax cuts are also central to the party's strategy for economic prosperity.

To narrow the Saskatchewan Party's strategy to tax reduction would be to ignore the party's broader neo-liberal agenda as it relates to the delivery of services and the treatment of the labour market. Consistent with the Alberta model, the party membership supports the expansion of private investment in the delivery of state-funded services. If the Saskatchewan Party were to form government, the equivalent of Alberta's Bill 11 could in all likelihood find itself in Saskatchewan legislation. At its inaugural meeting, the party adopted a resolution committing it to "explore partnerships in the health-care field with private sector providers to address the issue of waiting lists."[107] Using the same rationale as Ralph Klein, the membership maintained that "it is possible for private care to work under the public system."[108] Given the public opposition Bill 11 received in Alberta, however, it becomes difficult to predict the strategy the party would employ to begin contracting out health-care services.

In terms of an overall strategy for privatization, the Saskatchewan Party has already demonstrated a somewhat more cautious approach than the Klein Conservatives — reflecting perhaps the party's populist inclination. Hermanson claims the party would not contemplate selling any of the province's large state-owned utilities unless a prospective buyer "came along with an offer" to purchase one of them.[109] Such a sale, however, would hinge on whether the public accepted the deal in a referendum. When it comes to the future of the foreign investment arms of those Crown corporations, Hermanson is much more explicit. He indicates that his party would be prepared to act solely on its electoral mandate to sell those interests — whether or not those ventures were profitable.[110] Party policy itself argues that privatization must occur only if "the market is right for sale."[111] What seems to be guiding this more calculated approach to privatization is a history lesson. The membership, recalling the failed attempt in 1989 of the Devine Conservatives to privatize SaskEnergy amid a groundswell of public opposition, has come to recognize that the sell-off of public services using "strict ideological arguments" can backfire politically.[112] Hence, the "common-sense" approach.

A lot has changed in the past decade. With the entrenchment of the neo-liberal regime, and the consequent deregulation of the marketplace, Crown utilities such as SaskTel have had to compete out of necessity. SaskTel positioned itself not as a public utility, but as a local brand label offering an expanding array of pricing packages and consumer driven products. In a consumer culture it is not so important that SaskTel be recognized as being owned by "the people"; rather, it is more important that SaskTel be recognized as the local brand. The SaskTel label gives the same level of comfort and assurance of service that an American tourist might find upon

107. Saskatchewan Party, *Resolutions* (November 14–16, 1997).
108. Ibid.
109. Mark Wyatt, "No Crown privatization: Hermanson," *Leader-Post* (11 September 1999), p. A6.
110. Ibid.
111. Saskatchewan Party, *Resolutions* (November 14–16, 1997).
112. Ibid.

seeing a Starbucks sign in Bangkok. The tourist has no investment in Starbucks, but she finds comfort in its familiarity. Staying competitive, though, demands more than merely promoting the brand label — it requires ongoing streams of revenue and investment to research and develop new products and services, while keeping the price of existing products and services competitive. Lopping off the investment arms of such Crowns as SaskTel arguably hinders their capacity to remain competitive, strengthening arguments for their privatization. This aside, the growing consumer consciousness among voters might make privatization of some state enterprises more palatable than a decade ago. In other words, it doesn't matter who owns the local brand, only that there is indeed a local brand. The Saskatchewan Party would theoretically get to impose an ideologically driven agenda within the emerging norms and values of the neo-liberal regime — all of it laced in the language of "common sense."

In respect to labour policy, the Saskatchewan Party has been more explicit. Following the Alberta lead, the party argues in favour of the relaxation of labour laws and standards as part of its strategy to make the province more competitive. The membership officially supports the principles consistent with US-style "right-to-work" legislation, calling for a revamping of both the *Labour Standards* and *Trade Union Acts*:

> give workers the right not be a member of a union, and ... give union members the right to refuse to allow any portion of their union dues to be paid for any cause not related to the main function of the union.[113]

The same libertarian logic reemerged in a private members' bill, introduced by Saskatchewan Party Labour Critic Randy Weekes, that proposed a "freedom of speech" clause in the *Trade Union Act*. The proposed amendment effectively gives employers the right to speak to employees about their views in the event of the formation of a union. The bill also carefully points out that "freedom of speech," either by the employer or employee cannot be exercised through "intimidation, coercion, threats, or undue influence."[114] Such a clause could conceivably have far-reaching implications. First, it is difficult to fathom how the freedom of an employer to communicate with employees in the period leading up to a certification vote — with the exclusion of sentiments favouring the organization of a union — would not constitute a threat. Second, the same clause could potentially restrict the ability of a union to picket or boycott an employer that refused to abide with the spirit of provincial labour law. Even the union's education of potential members about the consequences of not forming a union could be considered a threat in itself.

Unions, in themselves, do not necessarily bring about higher labour costs. But unions do provide workers — through the collective bargaining process — with greater leverage to improve wages and working conditions. "Right-to-work" legislation threatens to weaken that leverage. Proponents of such laws seldom characterize them as a way to bring wages down. The issue is not explicitly raised in Saskatchewan Party policy documents. Instead, the language conveys the impression that the legislation will bring about some sort of democratization in the workplace. Like Alberta's Ralph Klein, Elwin Hermanson's plan is anything but democratic. The

---

113. Ibid.

114. Bill 234 1999–2000 in Legislative Assembly of Saskatchewan, *An Act to amend the Trade Union Act to provide for Freedom of Speech in the Workplace* (2000).

115. Saskatchewan Party, *Resolutions* (October 31, 1998) (emphasis added).

same party committed to replacing the current social welfare system with one based on mandatory employment, is also committed to keeping Saskatchewan's minimum wage low.[115] In 1998, Hermanson was on record as describing the NDP government's decision to raise the province's minimum wage by 40 cents an hour as poor public policy that could "potentially [have a] devastating impact on the economy, on jobs, on businesses and on people."[116] As an alternative, Hermanson suggested that the government should have moved to cut taxes instead, while keeping Saskatchewan's base wage competitive.[117] The Saskatchewan's Party's position would seem to hold little comfort for those workers earning a minimum wage. Using Statistics Canada's definition of poverty, a single adult with no dependents earning $6 per hour (the Saskatchewan minimum wage effective January 1, 1999) would fall well below the poverty line. A single parent with one child would fall even further below. To put this in perspective, Statistics Canada would calculate the poverty threshold for such a person at $18,890 in annual income. An individual earning minimum wage (working 40 hours per week) would earn $12, 480 annually before taxes.[118]

The plight of the working poor never directly enters Hermanson's discussion on competitiveness and economic growth. Instead, he talks about the need to create new jobs and Saskatchewan's "huge positive potential" to do that.[119] Hermanson believes that potential resides in the province's "aboriginal population who tend to be more on the unemployed side."[120] He is convinced that if these people can be moved off welfare and trained, they will "fill a need in the workforce that will give us [the people of Saskatchewan] a Saskatchewan advantage in supplying or fulfilling labour requirements down the road."[121]

What the Saskatchewan Party seems prepared to advance is a low-wage economic strategy, without Alberta's lucrative stream of resource royalties. Combined with a low tax regime, it is a strategy that would also seem to reduce the state's capacity to provide services — particularly those such as education, health care and income subsidy programs that would be helpful to the working poor. Hermanson claims tax reduction would be the first priority of a Saskatchewan Party government — with programs to reduce provincial income tax by 20 percent in four years and completely eliminate the provincial sales tax within a seven-year phase-out period. At the same time the party has pledged to maintain existing funding levels for education and health care, while increasing the province's highways budget by $50 million per year. During the 1999 election campaign Hermanson conceded this would in part be accomplished through job losses in the civil service. He has reasoned that the cost of the initiatives would be more than offset by the expanded tax base the resulting economic activity would create.[122] That economic activity would not happen overnight — not to mention the party's longstanding commitment to maintaining a balanced budget. Those are factors that Hermanson himself recognizes.

116. Mark Wyatt, "Minimum wage hike slammed by Saskatchewan Party," *Leader-Post*, December 2, 1998, A1.

117. Ibid.

118. For a further discussion on Statistics Canada's Low Income Measure and other systems of poverty measurement see David P. Ross, Katherine Scott and Peter Smith, *The Canadian Fact Book on Poverty 2000* (Ottawa: Canadian Council on Social Development, 2000), 13–42.

119. Hermanson interview.

120. Ibid.

121. Ibid.

122. Saskatchewan Party, "The Way Up," *Election Platform of the Saskatchewan Party* (1999), 4, 5, 20. Also see Mark Wyatt, "Sask. Party in favor of spending cuts," *Leader-Post*, April 21, 1998, A6.

Much of it would depend, according to Hermanson, on the particular circumstances in which a Saskatchewan Party government found itself upon gaining power. For this reason Hermanson does not rule out the possibility of government spending cuts in key areas such as education. After all, as the Saskatchewan Party leader characterizes it: "if we don't stimulate that positive attitude in Saskatchewan where people stay here, we are not going to have students for the university — and that is the greater concern."[123] In essence, short term pain for long term gain:

> We have to approach these issues ... on the basis of what is the best thing to do. We have principles — the principle of equality, fairness and what will grow the economy and what will provide the service infrastructure the people of this province need.[124]

For Saskatchewan residents who have already endured a decade of austerity budgeting and public service reductions under the NDP, the prospect of yet more cuts may not be enticing. There is a difference in the Saskatchewan Party approach. For the province's middle class, the party's platform provides for more than an accelerated neo-liberal program of reform, it offers immediate rewards in terms of substantial of tax reductions, set against the Alberta paradigm for prosperity. It is an idea built on the notion that citizens as consumers can enhance their spending power immediately. Moral comfort comes in the belief that all that spending might someday provide services to those members of society who "need it the most." Greed is not only good — it's a virtue.

The Alberta model has not passed unnoticed by the Saskatchewan Party — both in its economic rationale and in its strategy for cultivating public support. If anything the party has already learned from its mistakes—knowing when to unleash socially conservative rhetoric and when to temper it. The membership's overwhelming support — despite some heated internal debate — for the Saskatchewan Human Rights Commission is but one example. Its carefully worded strategy for privatization is another — suggesting that despite the rise of the neo-liberal regime, remnants of a distinctive political culture remain in Saskatchewan. Like Klein, Hermanson has demonstrated a primordial desire to achieve economic reform, over any other aspect of public policy. His language of "common-sense," like that of Klein, appeals not only to the underlying libertarian subconsciousness of voters, but to their rapidly developing consumer sensibilities.

CONCLUSION

It would have at one time made sense to characterize the Saskatchewan Party as a right-wing populist party operating in the left-right polarity of Saskatchewan politics. In the neo-liberal regime, however, in which its primary political competitor — the NDP — now espouses the need for tax cuts, targeted social programs and austerity budgeting, old arguments die quickly. I am not about to suggest that elements of Saskatchewan's social democratic tradition do not persist. But under critical evaluation the ideological differences between the NDP and the Saskatchewan Party begin to dissolve. The political competition between the parties increasingly has come to focus on the best approach to facilitate reforms to the market — the "sensible approach" of the NDP's Roy Romanow compared to the "accelerated approach" of the Saskatchewan Party's Elwin Hermanson. The polarization

123. Hermanson interview.
124. Ibid.

thesis fails to explain partisan divisions that increasingly emphasize regional cleavages over class.

The difference between Saskatchewan's two major parties, in the end, is less a matter of ideology than of who speaks for whom. The Saskatchewan Party as it exists now remains a regional party built on the momentum of rural discontent — created ironically by the same neo-liberal policies the party's leader now prescribes. Hermanson as the rural native son promises to challenge the elites in the urban heartland — not just in Regina, but in the corridors of power in Ottawa as well. But gaining that power ultimately demands developing a platform that transcends rural and urban differences — something of which the Saskatchewan Party's leadership is acutely aware. That platform and model can be found in Alberta. There, Conservative Premier Ralph Klein rose to power by appealing to rural discontent, and then went on to stay by appealing to Alberta's liberal middle ground.

With ideological differences narrowing among the province's political parties, the Saskatchewan Party will increasingly behave as a brokerage party, seeking to further broaden its appeal among voters, in a political culture that has moved to the right. In contrast to the NDP, the Saskatchewan Party has no social democratic tradition to reconcile its agenda, only the unbridled faith in the market. While the NDP is tethered to rationalizing its policies and programs in the language of communal values, its primary competitor can in good conscience employ the libertarian lexicon of "common sense." If the Saskatchewan Party gains ground in urban ridings, it will be because the party is effective in speaking to voters' consumer sensibilities. Those sensibilities emphasize not just the here and now, but the "me." In a radical consumer culture what matters most is individual spending power and service. Arguments favouring universality and communal values become of secondary importance. The Saskatchewan Party's past success may have been built on rural alienation, but the party is clearly positioning itself to appeal to the citizen of the neo-liberal regime.

The Saskatchewan Liberal Party

Lynda Haverstock

INTRODUCTION

Long before the technological revolution, the "Baby Boom," World War II, the Great Depression, World War I, and even Saskatchewan's birth as a province in 1905, there was a Liberal Party. For most of the twentieth century, the Saskatchewan Liberal Party was the dominant force in shaping the province's public policy as either the governing body or as the only viable alternative to the government of the day.

In the last 25 years, however, the Saskatchewan Liberal Party has been relegated to a mere shadow of its former self, at times with neither a leader nor any sitting members in the Legislative Assembly. Rife with internal controversy, it is now perceived as its own worst enemy. There has been an episodic, soap opera-like quality to it since its defeat as government in 1971 until the 1999 election, when three of the four elected Liberal members, including the leader, forfeited the balance of power to sit with the New Democratic government.

This chapter will attempt to examine how a political party with such a rich heritage finds itself in what some have termed "a perpetual state of self-annihilation." Glimpses into its strengths and weaknesses may give some insight into whether this party can ever capture the imagination and confidence of Saskatchewan voters again and take the reins of power. This will be discussed within the context of the party's historical roots and with a view to the formidable challenges facing all of us in the new millennium. Perhaps no political party in its present state is the solution.

WHAT IS LIBERALISM?

Liberalism was *the* radical doctrine of the nineteenth century. It grew from dissatisfaction with the high Tory emphasis on loyalty to church, the Crown, and the class system. The Liberal view rejected authoritarianism and advocated representative democracy. Its ideology was based upon civil liberties such as freedom of expression and religious tolerance, full participation in the political process, and less government interference. The fundamental tenet was that "every citizen ... ought to be as free as possible [from the aristocrats] ... so that society as a whole would achieve the optimum allocation of its resources and thereby maximize its general welfare."[1] Given the Liberals' disdain for the class system, they rejected government domination that would diminish the role of individuals in improving their own

1. Peter Brock, *Fighting Joe Martin: Founder of the Liberal Party in the West: A Blow-by-blow Account* (Toronto: The National Press, 1981), 43.

lives. The belief was that any individual who worked hard could and should be able to reap the rewards from his/her labour.

There has been some modification of Liberal ideology over the past one hundred years. Modern day Liberalism would support a much stronger role for government in regulating the private economy and providing public support for the economically and socially disadvantaged, while stopping well short of full socialism.[2] It is from this shift in philosophy that the term "free enterprise with a social conscience" was coined to describe Liberalism today.

Because Liberalism does not easily fit into a Left-Right spectrum based on social class and does not cater readily to special interest groups, it has been a complex concept to convey. With the recent trend of political parties abdicating their philosophies and taking a more centrist approach, it has proven even more difficult for Liberals to map out and defend their political territory. However, one clear distinction was evident in the early years and remains. Conrad Russell writes that Liberalism has always been about power — how power is controlled and how it is dispersed. It is about how to help the powerless and underprivileged help themselves.[3]

This is in stark contrast to those who believe in and support the welfare state, which is more about power for and of the government (in managing the masses) than it is about people participating in improving their circumstances. The Liberal concern about power is equally distinct from those who adhere to right-wing doctrine, which usually entrenches economic power in the hands of the already powerful. While most see the conservative and socialist ideologies as unlikely bedfellows, it is their willingness to use the power of government in these controlling ways that has seen them join forces in the past.[4] This will be discussed later in review of the recent 1999 provincial election results.

A guiding principle underpinning true Liberal policies is what is called "minimum oppression." The present writer's term for this concept is "individual empowerment." It places the individual at the centre, with the premise being that an empowered individual results in a stronger, healthier society (collective).

Minimum oppression requires one to recognize and be concerned about the power of the state (government). Furthermore, it requires an understanding of the role of the state in keeping in check the power of the mighty — such as multinationals and monopolies — because of their lack of interest in and commitment to individuals. While government may be "an engine of liberty," only a fool would dismiss its significance as a potential threat to that same liberty. Because of its respect for individual integrity and its suspicion of the overt power of big government and big business, Liberalism is the strongest proponent of personal responsibility, accountability, and initiative. When the Liberal Party is perceived as something it is not — as being too socialist leaning or being more conservative than the Conservatives — it loses elections. Three other realities have equally contributed to the demise of Liberal governments: perceived strong federal/provincial Liberal ties; three-party politics; and the party executive's abdication of its responsibility for grassroots organization.

2. Dr. Paul Johnson, *Glossary of Political Economy Terms: 1994–99* (http://www.auburn.edu/~johnspm/gloss/l.html).

3. Conrad Russell, "The woman Tony Blair most fears. Conrad Russell on the politician who is Gladstone's heiress," *The Times* (London), November 6, 1999.

4. David E. Smith, *Prairie Liberalism: The Liberal Party in Saskatchewan, 1905–1971* (Toronto: University of Toronto Press, 1975), 233.

1905–1944: ONE-PARTY DOMINANCE

The fortunes of the Saskatchewan Liberal Party can be divided into two main eras: prior to the election of the socialist Co-operative Commonwealth Federation (CCF) in 1944 and the time since. David E. Smith's book, *Prairie Liberalism: The Liberal Party in Saskatchewan 1905–1971*, provides the most detailed analysis available of the provincial party for the first 66 years of its existence. This short chapter cannot do justice to Smith's thorough work and his book is highly recommended to students of political science.

From 1905 to 1929, the Liberals had a virtual lock on Saskatchewan politics. Some of this was a natural corollary to being in the position of influence when the province joined Confederation. Huge numbers of immigrants flooded the province and the party became known for its superb organizational skills and innovative policies, and it was not beyond using patronage to its advantage. The Liberal government's philosophy made newcomers feel welcome and unthreatened. As will be noted later, in large part it was the Liberals' unwillingness to compromise their open position in immigration that ultimately brought the government to its knees.

The first three sessions of the first-ever Saskatchewan legislature resulted in Acts that established the executive, legislative, and judicial branches of government. Liberal legislation resulted in putting the entire education system in place, as well as providing the statutory basis for municipal government. Great emphasis was placed on public health and welfare, public utilities, establishing a favourable climate for business, as well as passing an unparalleled number of Acts promoting cooperatives for handling grains, dairy products, and hail insurance to protect farmers.[5]

With the exception of their legislation promoting racial and religious tolerance, most Liberal policies were popular and would be considered, by today's standards, quite innovative:

> This was particularly true in the area of health and welfare which saw legislation for a child welfare bureau, mother's allowances, treatment of mental diseases, the creation of a Department of Public Health to replace the old council created in 1909, the education of the deaf and blind, old age pension, new legislation for sanatoria and union hospitals, the introduction of vocational education, relief and debt adjustment legislation. Highly significant to the area of public or co-operative enterprise and similar to their earlier acts which created the Saskatchewan Co-operative Elevator Company and the Saskatchewan Co-operative Creameries was the Power Commission Act, the precursor to the Saskatchewan Power Corporation.[6]

Of particular note was the intent of J.M. Uhrich, Liberal minister of Health, to introduce "state medicine." In January 1935, Dr. Uhrich presented a comprehensive proposal that complemented his government's public health programs. Because of the desperate economic conditions of the Depression, followed by the war years, Uhrich had to settle for legislation that established "'mutual medical and hospital benefit associations and municipally-sponsored and operated medical and hospital services."[7] All bills requiring significant expenditures were put on hold and little more than emergency/housekeeping measures were passed. Ironically, as the economy

5. Ibid., 46.
6. Ibid., 150.
7. Ibid., 223–24.

improved after World War II, it would be the CCF that would take credit for the concept of medicare.

The power and influence of the Liberal Party was profound "as they acquired, through deliberate effort, a reputation for honest government" and "it was a measure of Liberal governments in Saskatchewan that a majority of the populace looked upon the Liberals as their protectors."[8]

The early years were a time of unprecedented growth for the province and an attempt was made to strike a balance between competing interests. Regina became the capital; Saskatoon received the university; Prince Albert was given the penitentiary; North Battleford and Weyburn got major mental hospitals; and many small centres received judicial land and registry offices.[9] From 1901–11, the population increased by 439 percent to 491,279. By 1916, that number had mushroomed to 647,835. Saskatchewan became the third most populated province in Canada and remained so until the CCF came to power. There were 836,000 inhabitants in the province by 1944. The most recent statistics have Saskatchewan's population at 1,015,800.[10]

The Liberal Party's continued success was not only the result of cunning strategy, exceptional organization, and a popular legislative record. It was also due to the fractured nature of the opposition. However, by the late 1920s, two distinct issues arose from which organized dissension grew: the farming crisis and racial and religious prejudice. Anger at federal agriculture and immigration policies was most evident in farm organizations. The provincial party underestimated the seriousness of the antagonism toward "foreigners" who were not of British descent and the influence of the Ku Klux Klan (KKK). The KKK had infiltrated the province, selling thousands of memberships and inciting many electors into opposing the Liberals.[11] The final result was the election of a minority coalition government in 1929 made up of the Conservatives, the Progressives, and the Independents, which they termed a "Co-operative Government." This occurred in spite of the Liberals receiving the largest percentage of popular vote and the greatest number of seats in the Assembly.[12]

For the first time in 24 years, the Liberals were the Opposition. Within a few short months, the coalition government was faced with the crash of the stock market on Wall Street, the subsequent fallout on the overall economy, and years of drought. Religious and racial hatred no longer preoccupied people's minds as financial despair took hold of their lives. It is not surprising that the "Co-operative Government" did not survive; circumstances beyond its control brought about its demise in 1934 and the Liberals became the governing party once again. It should be noted that during this time of economic turmoil, the coalition government Conservative Premier J.T.M. Anderson tried, without success, to lure Liberals from the Opposition to sit with the Government.[13] This did not meet with success, unlike Premier Roy Romanow's endeavour in 1999 to entice the Liberals to cross the floor and provide him with the numbers the NDP needed to form a majority government.

The most vocal and identifiable critics of the Liberal government — especially

8. Ibid., 49.

9. Ibid.

10. Statistics Canada, CANSIMII, table 051–0001.

11. Smith, *Prairie Liberalism*, 147.

12. Ibid., 193.

13. Ibid., 207.

during the 1920s and throughout their return to power from 1934 to 1944 — were farmers. The United Farmers of Canada — Saskatchewan Section (UFC-SS) took direct political action and formed the Saskatchewan Farmers' Political Association. This Association soon aligned itself with the Independent Labour Party of Saskatchewan, which was not surprising since old Progressives could be found in both organizations.[14] This began a process of cooperation between farmers and labour that resulted in the formation of the Farmer-Labour Party (FLP) in 1932. The Depression helped fuel increased participation of agrarians in politics. The capitalist system was condemned and social ownership promoted. Some of the more extreme views generated fear amongst the voters and contributed to the re-election of the Liberals in 1934. However, this did not deter the FLP from doing what none of the previous parties, except the Liberals, had done. It used the tremendous organization of the UFC-SS to spread the word about socialism and undertook to build an organizational structure that ultimately put the Liberals to shame.[15]

"The opportunity to act upon discontent" finally presented itself. Prior to 1938, no viable alternative to the Liberals was apparent.[16] Now, frustration with years of rule by one party and extraordinary grief from the Depression could be expressed by coalescing around a new party. To the surprise of some, support for the FLP (which later became the CCF) did not come from the "poorer, socially outcast groups."[17] Rather, former Conservative support was transferred to the FLP because of their joint disdain for the Liberals. Prosperous farmers who had previously been active in the Saskatchewan Grain Growers' Association and the UFC-SS joined as well. The "Dirty Thirties" created strange alliances with an important focus — to take power away from the governing Liberals and, through superb organization, to keep power.[18]

There was one albatross that the provincial Liberals had that the new party did not — their ties to the federal Liberal Party, which often was the government of Canada. At times, national policies were seen as detrimental to Saskatchewan and the West. Conflict between Liberals about whether the provincial and federal wings of the party should be considered one and the same had existed since 1905 and remains today. Some leaders have distanced themselves from their federal counterparts, while others have nurtured this relationship.

One thing is certain: a Liberal government in Ottawa posed and continues to pose problems for provincial Liberals everywhere. Barry Wilson's book, *The Politics of Defeat: The Decline of the Liberal Party of Saskatchewan*, describes the deleterious effects of federal policies on provincial party fortunes. This is an advantage to opposing political parties that will never face the same challenge. Neither the CCF/NDP nor the Saskatchewan Party have to fight the policies of their federal parties on the provincial stage — the former because the CCF/NDP will likely never be in power as a federal government and the latter because they have deliberately disassociated themselves from any formal ties with a federal party (until the recent involvement of some sitting Saskatchewan Party MLAs in the leadership election of Stockwell Day and the Canadian Alliance Party).

14. Ibid., 211.
15. Ibid., 215.
16. Ibid., 220.
17. Ibid., 219.
18. Ibid., 220.

Interestingly, this political strategy of holding the provincial Liberals responsible for unpopular federal policies has been employed successfully for decades, up to and including the present day. This method was especially effective in the late 1930s when the CCF was able to paint the Liberals as inept: both Ottawa and Regina had Liberals in power and conditions remained economically deplorable (which was consistent with world conditions). The people, however, were "depression weary" and the election results of 1938 showed that voters wanted to "recapture the radicalism that once had been part of Saskatchewan Liberalism."[19]

The CCF had finally taken hold as the official opposition and it became apparent that they were not going to disappear. "Partisan politics began for the first time to permeate all associations — farm, municipal, and professional."[20] Many Liberals viewed this shift of politics to an "all-day, every-day occupation" as dangerous. Even today, many see this tendency, which remains prominent in Saskatchewan, as detrimental to economic growth.

Delay of the next election because of World War II worked to the Opposition's advantage. Many of the more innovative Liberal policies could not be implemented because of monetary limitations. The CCF honed its organization while the once-powerful Liberal machine grew rusty. Former Liberal Premier Jimmy Gardiner's continuing influence from Ottawa had weakened the provincial structure. The party's campaign was less than impressive and at the end of the 1944 election, the Liberals' popular support had fallen by 10 percent. This translated, however, into a loss from 38 seats to five. The party was decimated and the CCF began its twenty-year reign in Saskatchewan.

The election heralded in something equally new. Traditionally, Liberal policies had always been consensus-based. Rarely would legislation be seen as favouring one group over another. However, "because of its commitment to socialist principles, the CCF found it could not be all things to all men"[21] and businesspeople became suspicious and concerned about the new government's policies. By default, the Liberals were sought out as protectors by this particular group and the term "free enterprise" crept into the Liberal vernacular. This move was in direct contrast to Liberal practices of the past. The party most certainly would never have been viewed as defending a *laissez-faire* economy because of its commitment to progressive, reform legislation. The fears of the business community brought about a specific change in many party members, who were pegged as "right-wing Liberals" if they vigorously supported business's concerns and "left-wing Liberals" if they promoted more progressive social reforms. It was this confusion over right/left views in this new context, its ultimate influence on the leader's effectiveness, as well as party disorganization and federal-provincial party struggles that kept the Liberals in the role of Opposition for more than twenty years.

1944–2001: "THE BAD," "THE GOOD," AND "THE UGLY"

"THE BAD": 1944–1959

Following the election that catapulted the CCF into power, the Liberals tried to regroup. Significant Liberal strength was retained in rural Saskatchewan but urban

19. Ibid., 241.
20. Ibid., 242.
21. Ibid., 252.

support had moved to the CCF. It remains a stronghold for the NDP today. With their broad electoral base in decline, the Liberals were no longer seen as the Party that represented the greatest number of interests. Consumed by problems and unable to regain seats in two by-elections, the party wanted a change in leadership. In 1946, William J. Patterson resigned as leader and was replaced by Walter Tucker.

Tucker was deemed a "left-wing Liberal," which signaled a shift to more "progressive" policies once again. Given that the province already had the Douglas government that was viewed as too left-leaning by many, the election of Tucker as leader was not received well by a significant number of party members. The electorate had an opportunity in 1948 to go to the polls and state their preference. Despite party disunity and their failure to run candidates in 11 constituencies,[22] the Liberals increased their seats from five to 19. They had come very close to defeating CCF candidates in six seats. Had the Liberals closed ranks, they likely could have denied Douglas his second majority government. A rather new and insidious tendency to undermine the party from within was born during this time in Opposition. Sadly, it became a pattern that has never quite been broken — even when the party regained power.

Increased popular support for the Liberals in the election of 1952 failed to translate into seats. In fact, the party lost seats and unhappiness was the order of the day. Continued calls to dissociate from the federal party prevailed but no action was taken, even though "one of the favourite pastimes of the CCF [was] imputing blame to provincial Liberals for federal government actions."[23] This desire to separate federal and provincial forces was to have an influence on the selection of the next leader. Following Tucker's resignation to run federally, several leadership hopefuls came forward at the 1954 convention.[24] The victor was Hammy McDonald, who had positioned himself as the one most distant from federal influence.

McDonald only had two years as leader to prepare for the 1956 election. His centrist approach to Liberal politics alienated many party members and sent them in droves to the Social Credit. The anti-CCF vote, which exceeded 50 percent, was split, thus re-electing Douglas once again. But Liberal fortunes were about to change — all because of a man named John Diefenbaker. As federal Liberals faltered and the federal Conservatives assumed power in 1957, the provincial Liberals hoped to capitalize on this unusual circumstance.

Finally, the Liberals could turn their attention to the CCF instead of their own infighting. However, with another provincial election on the horizon and with the announcement by the leader that the party was broke, it was apparent that Hammy McDonald was not going to be the solution to Liberal resurgence. He had defined his role as leader as one who must reconcile the differences between "left-wing" and "right-wing" Liberals, and stay removed from giving direction in policy matters. He had seriously overlooked "the obvious sharing of political sympathy between Tory and socialist" and their shared desire to defeat the Liberals.[25] As the CCF celebrated its fifteenth year in power, it was apparent that a new leader was needed to go toe-to-toe with Douglas. That individual was none other than W.R. (Ross) Thatcher — a political figure who restored the Saskatchewan Liberal Party to government.

22. Saskatchewan, Chief Electoral Office, *Provincial Elections in Saskatchewan, 1905–1986* (Regina: Chief Electoral Office, 1987), 12.

23. Smith, *Prairie Liberalism*, 262.

24. Ibid., 265.

25. Ibid., 267.

"The Good": 1959–1971

The defeat of the federal Liberals in 1957 brought Jimmy Gardiner's control of the provincial Liberal Party to an end. After 43 consecutive years in politics, this formidable former provincial premier and federal Agriculture minister found himself without influence.[26] Dissatisfaction with Hammy McDonald and frustration with the Tommy Douglas administration motivated several prominent Liberals to scan the horizon for an individual who could provide a clear option. Their eyes settled on Ross Thatcher, a former CCF member of Parliament for 10 years from Moose Jaw, who had then sat as an Independent and finally as a Liberal.

Thatcher's years with the CCF had fueled his contempt for socialism. He believed that socialism in Saskatchewan — "the only place in North America where it had been given a chance to prove itself — was financially irresponsible and administratively inept."[27] A strong proponent of "enlightened social reform," Thatcher attacked what he saw as "social welfare with socialism," which he deemed financially unsustainable. Furthermore, he argued that Saskatchewan Crown Corporations had proved to be a dismal failure under the CCF, unless they could remain monopolies as had been established under Liberal governments (for example, Saskatchewan Government Telephones and the Saskatchewan Power Corporation). According to Thatcher:

> Crown Corporations inspired by the CCF were not only unprofitable in themselves but they had discouraged private investment in the province, thus stultifying the economy and limiting social services which might be soundly financed by the Saskatchewan Government.[28]

He espoused these and other views articulately in the famous 1957 Mossbank Debate with Tommy Douglas. He was an obvious contender for the leadership, not only because of his attacks on socialism but as a result of his outspoken criticisms of Liberal lethargy and factionalism. By 1959, he had won the leadership race on the first ballot, and within months had reversed the party's fortunes, both financially and organizationally.

After years of little reflection on party principles and ideas, the Liberals went through a process of self-examination. The results led to progressive policies that were to be balanced with responsible administration. Social security became the party's primary policy, as well as improved services for the "mentally disturbed" and a province-wide plan of prepaid medical and surgical services. The plight of Indians and Métis had always been a major concern for Thatcher and their issues became a cornerstone of future Liberal government policy under his tenure. Unlike his immediate predecessor, Thatcher did not hesitate to impose his views on the party, which were inextricably linked to his belief that without economic prosperity for all there would be no significant social advancement.[29]

Thatcher's Liberal Party was far more pragmatic than either the CCF or the federal Liberals wanted to acknowledge.[30] Socialist sympathizers painted Thatcher as conservative and his Liberal counterparts in Ottawa tagged him as a "right-winger."

---

26. Barry Wilson, *Politics of Defeat: The Decline of the Liberal Party in Saskatchewan* (Saskatoon: Western Producer Prairie Books, 1980), 3.
27. Smith, *Prairie Liberalism*, 274.
28. Ibid., 275.
29. Ibid., 279.
30. Ibid., 284.

Neither could reconcile his ability to compromise his commitment to private enterprise and his rigid adherence to ethical monetary practices with his determination to defend valuable social programs, even if the CCF had implemented them.

The new leader's unrelenting efforts to increase grassroots organization through membership drives, fundraisers, and policy meetings paid off in the 1960 election. Although the CCF was once again victorious, the Liberals demonstrated that, with Thatcher at the helm for only a matter of months, the party had finally overcome years of inner turmoil and with it, greater electoral support. The final election results, however, pointed out yet again that the only way to force the socialists from power was by consolidating anti-CCF support. Thatcher made this his priority.

Fascinatingly, federal and provincial Liberal ties were again strained but not for the same reasons that had existed in the past. With the Conservatives running the nation, the federal Liberals considered provincial CCFers as potential federal Liberal voters.[31] Thatcher vehemently opposed any formal alliance of the kind and went so far as to ask for unanimous agreement from his members against such an arrangement. He used the situation to distance the provincial party from its federal counterpart while wooing provincial Conservatives and disenchanted socialists to the fold.[32] The public tension between Thatcher's provincial party and the federal Liberals would be seen by some as advantageous politically. In addition, Thatcher began to focus on getting young people involved in the political process; this, too, stood the party in good stead.

A pivotal issue preceded the 1964 election. The CCF's introduction of a health-care scheme called Medicare resulted in the Liberals significantly modifying their original support of the concept of state medicine that Liberal minister of Health, Dr. J.M. Uhrich, had first raised as early as 1935. In 1962, doctors were so opposed to the proposition that they approached the Liberals to "defend their cause." A withdrawal of all doctors' services lasted three weeks. The Liberals demanded a plebiscite on the proposed policy, shifted gears while the actual bill was before the Legislative Assembly, and finally supported it while advocating that the legislation should include the cost of drugs.[33]

It has long been known that Thatcher made statements that the public must come to understand that health care is never really free; without this awareness he believed that Medicare itself would be at risk 30 years hence. This view and his future government's health policy on deterrent fees would ultimately bring about his fall from power. However, his thesis would also hold considerably greater credence "30 years hence" as health-care costs soar and Medicare is viewed by many to be at risk.

Thatcher's desire for dynamic candidates was to have considerable influence on the types of individuals who ran for office in the election of 1964. Indeed, of the contingent of Liberal MLAs who finally took their seats on the Liberal government side of the House, most were well-educated, youthful professionals, proprietors, and managers. One-third were farmers. With this kind of caucus, the new premier was optimistic about governing in a truly businesslike manner, something he believed

31. *Leader-Post*, November 27, 1962, p. 1.
32. Smith, *Prairie Liberalism*, 295.
33. Ibid., 296.

the CCF was devoid of doing after having years of "some teacher or preacher or someone who knows nothing about business ... in charge of enterprise."[34]

Unlike his recent predecessors, Thatcher strongly imposed his policy opinions on the party and it was welcomed with relief by many. Members finally had clear statements of principles that they had helped forge, but the defining stands on issues were "pure Thatcher" and there was little opposition.[35] This deference to the leader only worked because of Thatcher's prompt gains in the 1960 election.

In the years leading up to the 1964 Liberal victory, grassroots work focussed on membership drives and the funds that accrued from them. Constituency organization kept everyone busy. History has shown that the CCF had always been able to bring the membership and the leader on side regarding party policy. In the long run, the fact that Liberal members forfeited direct involvement in this arena would render the membership impotent in policy development and the leader too powerful.

Thatcher became renown for one-man rule. His domineering personality style in organization, policy, and even the treatment of his colleagues simplified overall decision making and practice. It also created a political party run entirely from the top down, placing the responsibility for its success or failure fully in the lap of Ross Thatcher.

Finally out of the Opposition ranks, the Liberals embarked on an approach to investment that brought results to Saskatchewan.[36] The potash industry began to flourish and the Prince Albert Pulp Mill came to fruition. Frugality was the order of the day throughout the civil service and in ministerial travel and entertaining. Aboriginal training and employment became a focal point, both in the civil service and within companies who wished to do business with the government. Social programs were preserved and even the controversial Medicare, over which some claim the 1964 election was won, was kept.

Because of the upswing in the economy and the federal announcement that Saskatchewan would "soon pass from the status of 'have not' to 'have' with a cessation of equalization payments,"[37] Thatcher called an unexpected election in October of 1967. The premier was optimistic going to the polls but devastated by the results. Although the Liberals returned with a majority, their popular support had waned. Immediately, dissension grew within the party. The economic downturn of the late 1960s drove Thatcher to become obsessed with cutting back. His actions created deep dissatisfaction amongst his cabinet, the caucus, and local Liberals who said they had to endure the wrath of a disenchanted public. Thatcher was the lightning rod for their disdain.

One of the people closest to Thatcher was Dave Steuart, the "Minister of Everything." Steuart has stated that the government's general policy at the time was simple — "cut back costs, save money, and prepare for the worst."[38] Public fights ensued as the university was told its funding would be controlled; teachers were incensed with the imposition of a 6 percent salary limit. Steuart then had the unfortunate task as Finance minister to deliver the 1968 budget that pronounced

34. Ibid., 275.
35. Ibid., 279.
36. Wilson, *Politics of Defeat*, 14.
37. Ibid., 16.
38. Ibid., 17.

nothing but bad news. Taxes, including utilization fees of $2.50 per day on hospital use and $1.50 for a doctor's visit, were raised to avoid a deficit budget, borrowing, or cutbacks.

The day became the beginning of the end for the Liberals. The NDP opposition called it "Black Friday." Consumers, union members and civil servants throughout the province were outraged. As Thatcher had predicted, wheat prices dropped, potash markets weakened, jobs became scarce, and education and health care costs soared. All attempts to improve economic fortunes through such ventures as the Meadow Lake Pulp Mill fueled attacks by the NDP that the Liberals were selling out the province's resources. Internal conflict grew within party ranks as members and MLAs felt power slipping away. They held the leader fully responsible and were angered by his autocratic behaviour and disinterest in their views.

Indeed, according to Steuart, Thatcher was becoming increasingly more controlling. The premier also had serious health problems that required hospitalizations that he tried to keep under wraps. The NDP spread rumours that he was being treated for alcoholism even though they knew the seriousness of his diabetes and that he had even suffered a stroke. By the time Thatcher called the election in 1971, he was maintained on oxygen throughout the campaign.

On election night, the Liberals received just 7 percent less of the vote than in 1967. The results, however, were significant. Virtually all of the Progressive Conservative vote went to the NDP and Thatcher's Liberals were reduced to a mere fifteen seats. The man once described by former Liberal MLA Jack Wiebe as "the most incredibly honest politician one could know" and "a Premier who didn't make decisions for raw political gain"[39] was resoundingly defeated. Four weeks later, Thatcher was dead. He was 54 years old.

"THE BAD": 1971–1989

The defeat of the Thatcher Liberal government in 1971 carries with it compelling stories, many of which have been documented by Dale Eisler in his book, *Rumours of Glory: Saskatchewan and the Thatcher Years*. One is a poignant description of Thatcher's visit to congratulate Allan Blakeney on the NDP's electoral success:

> This was the first time that Ross Thatcher had walked back into a hall packed with socialists since his days two decades before as a member of the CCF. It was the final act of courage for a man who never sidestepped a difficult or challenging situation.
>
> As they walked into the packed hall and jubilant NDP celebrants caught sight of Thatcher, a few scattered boos slowly became a resounding chorus. On the stage at the front of the hall, Blakeney saw Thatcher, quickly grabbed the microphone, and called his supporters to order.
>
> "My friends," Thatcher said after reaching the microphone and with Blakeney next to him, "I came to your headquarters for one reason, to congratulate Allan Blakeney on a magnificent election. It was a great election, Allan, great, great. You must have done a far better job than we did. It will just take a couple of days to pack our files and leave."
>
> As Thatcher, looking drawn and spent stepped off the stage and began to leave the hall, the years of bitterness and hatred felt by many in the party

39. Interview with Jack Wiebe, 1999.

he deserted, suddenly vanished. The crowd spontaneously began to sing "For He's a Jolly Good Fellow."[40]

This was more than the Liberal leader, who had been pivotal in bringing the party from the wilderness to government, would receive from many of his own. Thoughtful analysis of the pre-election circumstances proved that the provincial Liberals, yet again, had paid a price for having the federal Liberals in office in Ottawa. Furthermore, it was apparent that all of the Progressive Conservative vote had gone against the Liberals and for the New Democrats despite the latter's clear message of greater government control over farmland and resources. With the voting age reduced to 18 years for the first time, it was also evident that it was the NDP who appealed most to the younger, left-leaning urbanites.

However, Thatcher accepted full blame for the result and indicated to both the caucus and the party executive his intention to step down as leader shortly after the election. Following his announcement, he was told that his statement was "not good enough, that he alone was the reason for the defeat and that [he] should resign now."[41] It was after this particular rebuke by former Liberal Speaker of the Legislative Assembly Jim Snedker that Dave Steuart, one of Saskatchewan's most determined and passionate politicians, got to his feet to defend Thatcher. The subsequent caustic dressing down of the accuser did all but remove the skin from Snedker's bones. Steuart, small of stature, big of heart, with incomparable wit, was to become the next leader of the Saskatchewan Liberal Party.

When the deflated, leaderless Liberal caucus of fourteen sat together in the legislature for the first time, Thatcher's faithful right-hand man, Dave Steuart, was the Acting House Leader. The group assumed the role of Opposition with as much enthusiasm as they could muster. Behind the scenes, the party was assessing its status. At the time, finances were reported to be more than sound with some $935,000 in bank accounts and investment certificates. Some of these monies were later used to purchase a building in Regina. There were 41,000 signed-up members and even though the number of Liberal seats had been reduced greatly, the party took solace in its solid 43 percent base of popular support. Given this reassuring information and that the Liberals were perceived as the only alternative to the NDP, the position of new leader was coveted.

Several former MLAs wanted the job but had been unwilling to let their ambitions be known until Thatcher's departure was a certainty. By the time the leadership convention took place in Saskatoon on December 11, 1971, the result was a *fait accompli*. Once Steuart had decided to seek the job, he put the wheels in motion that ensured his victorious outcome. His opponents, photogenic and conservative-minded Cy MacDonald and the surprise candidate, former MLA and Rosetown farmer George Leith, described as "a principled outsider," did not have a chance against Steuart's formidable determination and skill as a campaigner. Steuart said later that younger members in the party were longing for a John F. Kennedy type of leader and that, to them, Leith filled the bill.

As his tenure lengthened, Steuart surprised many by his willingness to open up the party to fresh ideas. A *Leader-Post* article (April 11, 1975) toward the end of his time as leader cites George Leith as stating that Steuart's leadership had brought

40. Dale Eisler, *Rumours of Glory: Saskatchewan and the Thatcher Years* (Edmonton: Hurtig, 1987), 267.
41. Ibid., 269.

welcome changes. This was confirmed when the body of disgruntled Leith supporters (formed after the 1971 leadership convention and calling itself the 171 Group) disbanded in 1975 because they no longer viewed the party as undemocratic.

According to columnists of the time, Steuart was faced with the major challenge of motivating a party distraught over its loss at the polls, and doing it quickly. To those who were familiar with his personal and political history, he was more than a colourful pragmatist; he was a person who led by example, had done every conceivable job throughout party ranks and understood what "loyalty to the leader" meant. Newspaper articles from 1972 to 1976 show how focussed Steuart was on holding the Blakeney government accountable. He was prolific, thoughtful, and unrelenting in his attacks. He was also adept at fundraising out-of-province, which allowed the party to leave the bulk of the finances raised in Thatcher's days untouched. But tensions were growing.

Unlike his predecessor, Steuart was committed to giving "rank and file" Liberals a greater voice. He also wanted to end the infighting between the federal and provincial wings of the party, which Thatcher had nurtured in order to distance the Saskatchewan Liberals from Ottawa's policies. Despite Steuart's determination to end the factionalism, suspicion and distrust prevailed. From those who desired a more open party came little of substance. From those who thought the inclusion process a waste of time came complaints. Although his leadership had shown great promise with three out of four by-election victories, increased resources and organization, as well as some enthusiasm over the decentralization of power, the party was faltering.

Steuart was "damned if he did and damned if he didn't." Now the concern was that the leader "did not step in" often enough. By 1974, fundraising was drying up, constituency workers were unmotivated, and internal bickering about how to handle federal and provincial Liberal needs, especially regarding finances and unpopular federal policies, prevailed. The one bright light according to then sitting Liberal MLA Jack Wiebe was the respect the caucus had for each other's ideas — something that had been lacking under Thatcher's reign. Wiebe stated that even though the Liberals took a beating at the hands of the New Democrats, a healthy relationship existed between all members of the legislature and it was a rewarding experience. In his view, this camaraderie began to change when the Progressive Conservatives elected several members in the next election.

By the time the writ was dropped for the 1975 campaign, the Progressive Conservatives (PC) had chosen a new leader. The PC Party had been rendered irrelevant for years in provincial politics except for the impact it had on Liberal fortunes when supporters voted for NDP candidates. The arrival of Dick Collver, an energetic, youthful, free enterpriser was basically greeted with shrugged shoulders — the Liberals viewing him as a non-starter. This dismissive attitude was to prove fatal.

According to Barry Wilson, everyone underestimated Collver's "energy, organizing ability, and ambition."[42] He was able to attract dedicated workers with his no-nonsense yet charming style and his message of anti-left-wing politics. Some of them came directly from the Liberals who were well primed for his autocratic approach. Although his public statements were "often vague and appeared ill

42. Wilson, *Politics of Defeat*, 83.

thought-out,"[43] the media loved covering "the new kid on the block." With his raised profile, strong conservative rhetoric, and unparalleled willingness to work hard, he appealed to many individuals with local credibility to take up the cause and become candidates. The Tories were on their way to resurgence and no one knew but them.

The 1975 election results could have been different if Steuart's orders had been carried out. When it became clear that the PCs were a greater threat than anyone had predicted and that the Liberal Party's organization at the grassroots was weak, the leader gave a directive that all "money, workers, and efforts"[44] must focus on winnable ridings. Unfortunately, the election committee ignored his demand, with disastrous consequences.

Besides poorly organized constituency campaigns, the provincial Liberals were being blamed for unpopular federal policies. As well, the NDP strategy to focus the campaign on the strength of their leader proved effective. By the time the polls closed, it was apparent that Blakeney's government would retain a majority, with 39 seats, and that the Conservatives had garnered a surprising 27.6 percent in popular support, with seven new members in the Legislative Assembly. The Liberals remained the Official Opposition with fifteen seats.

The writing was on the wall for Dave Steuart. Despite the election of some very bright and dynamic MLAs, he knew that his days as leader were numbered. His attempts to reconcile federal-provincial differences were viewed as a failure by many within the party and as detrimental to the primary goal of becoming the government. His determination to replace Thatcher's domineering style with greater collegiality was seen as weakness. This was particularly frustrating given the positive reactions toward Collver by former Liberal Party faithful because of what Wilson termed his "thinly-veiled streak of authoritarianism."[45] Perhaps the most significant factor in the 1975 election, however, had little to do with any of the above.

Realities in Saskatchewan had changed considerably for one reason — a strong economy. Finally, the province had hit "the good times." Grain prices were high, oil and gas prices were high, potash and uranium were desired and lending institutions got involved in agriculture as never before in order to capitalize on inflation. The latter resulted in encouraging farmers to make huge investments in purchasing land and livestock. No one feared "the socialists" anymore, except those who disapproved of the NDP's continuous expansion of the bureaucracy, as well as their tendency for government involvement in every aspect of Saskatchewan business. The general public, however, no longer shared these concerns.

Steuart indicated his intention to step down as leader. He believed that he had an obligation to support his caucus, especially the novices, and show them the ropes. According to sitting members, he did just that. Wiebe offered this point of view:

> The new Caucus was very strong, especially in quality ... but the legislature became a different place, primarily because of the presence of the Tories who took everything too personally. In the great potash debate, the Conservatives didn't even participate. Even though we initially continued to have good relationships with the NDP members, estrangement became more and more evident between all members by 1978.[46]

43. Ibid., 84.
44. Ibid., 92.
45. Ibid., 97.
46. Interview with J. Wiebe (1999).

In usual Saskatchewan fashion, the mid-1970s were to bring some controversial political issues to the forefront. While the NDP was in court defending the very system of controls it had condemned Thatcher for implementing to see the potash industry of the 1960s through bad times, some key NDP policy planners were drafting their intention to "acquire the assets of some or all of the producing potash mines in the province."[47]

Steuart and the Liberals rose to the occasion with fervour. They attacked the plan "on business rather than ideological grounds."[48] In the legislature, their point man in the attack was Ted Malone. Collver's Tories made the odd choice of essentially remaining mute. The potash issue served to unite the Liberal caucus and party members. Following 40 days of heated debate, however, the massive NDP majority easily passed the controversial legislation. In some circles, Blakeney's nationalization of the potash industry is still viewed as having negatively influenced investment in the province from that day forward.

Despite public unease with the policy, the media refused to discuss it further and the Liberals were unable to keep the issue in the forefront. Their short revival fizzled. The focus soon shifted to finding a replacement for Steuart.

Several candidates were rumoured to be interested. In the initial stages, sitting MLAs Gary Lane, Ted Malone and Tony Merchant went through the motions of garnering support. It was no secret that there was no love lost between Lane and Steuart and some found it curious when Lane, after months of organizing, dropped out of contention. At the time, there was no hint that he would be joining the Conservatives. Before going, however, he helped to undermine Steuart's leadership.[49]

Later, Steuart was to say that he thought the party would permit him to leave graciously but realized that this would not be the case. Barry Wilson clearly describes the pain Steuart experienced at the hands of some Executive members, as well as his frustration over Lane's meetings with several MLAs.[50] The "unsinkable" Liberal veteran was to claim that it was the worst time of his political career.

A leadership convention was set for December 11, 1976. Steuart was convinced to remain until his successor was chosen. The protracted race was to take its toll on a party unable to keep its internal strife from public view. Battles between the federal and provincial wings continued; personality conflicts deepened the divisions. In the end, only two contestants contested the leadership of the Saskatchewan Liberal Party. Both were Regina lawyers, both had legislative experience, and both had some devoted followers who called themselves Liberals but remain political rivals to this day. Generally, the membership expressed unenthusiastic support for their only choices.

Ted Malone was a 39-year-old who had grown up in affluence. His early responsibilities in the party included organizing federal ridings, which resulted in some Liberals viewing him suspiciously as a "fed." Despite his involvement as campaign manager for Regina Lakeview in two provincial elections and his work as both a constituency president and member of the provincial executive, Malone was labeled an "[Otto] Lang" federal Liberal.[51]

---

47. Throne Speech, 1975.
48. Wilson, *Politics of Defeat*, 107.
49. Ibid, 101.
50. Ibid., 101–2.
51. Ibid., 114.

Malone first joined the legislature after winning a by-election upon the death of incumbent Liberal MLA Don McPherson (Regina Lakeview) in 1973. Appearing thoughtful and measured, especially during the raucous "Potash Debates" in 1975, Malone was presented as the "safe" option. Some expressed concern about his formal manner, believing that he lacked the needed warmth and demeanor to relate to "average" folk.

In contrast, contender Tony Merchant was the 31-year-old son of former Liberal MLA Sally Merchant, who had graced Thatcher's benches in the 1960s. He and his sister, Adrian (then married to MP Otto Lang), had been raised in a one-parent household after the loss of their father in World War II. Merchant's political interests were generally viewed as federal. He evoked strong reactions from others — both positive and negative — but his reputation inside and outside the legislature was legendary. Many commented on his tireless work as an MLA and his commitment to a broad range of worthy issues; others saw him as overly ambitious.[52]

The final tally put Malone ahead by 107 votes. Merchant's unorthodox and highly criticized method of gathering youth delegates failed him when 400 young people simply did not turn up to cast their ballots. The chasm between the candidates' camps never healed. Indeed, the wounds reopened repeatedly to the detriment of both federal and provincial Liberal fortunes.[53]

Malone inherited a deflated party. His challenges were daunting. By 1977, two by-elections were imminent, neither easily winnable. The first, Prince Albert-Duck Lake, became vacant upon Dave Steuart's departure to the Senate. Election after election, Steuart had barely won his seat, labeling himself "Landslide Dave." The second, Saskatoon-Sutherland, was left unrepresented following the tragic death of Liberal Evelyn Edwards. The Liberals recognized that the personal popularity of these individuals had played a significant role in holding both seats.

Once the campaigns were in full swing, it was apparent that while the Liberals had been engaged in an exhausting eight-month leadership race, the Conservatives had devoted themselves to organization. The party found itself marginalized as the media focussed almost exclusively on the NDP and the Tories. To the astonishment of many, both seats were won by Collver's Conservatives.

These PC gains were an omen for both the Liberals and the New Democrats. They demonstrated dissatisfaction with Blakeney's government and the dismissal of the Liberals as a relevant voice. According to party executive member John Embury, a tactical error was made placing the new leader in the spotlight during the two futile battles. By doing so, the losses were unfairly set in Malone's lap.[54]

The Tories now had nine members to the Liberals thirteen. The need was for the latter to definitively assert themselves as Her Majesty's Loyal Opposition. Examination of *Hansard* shows that the Liberal caucus far outshone their opposition rivals at the time. Interestingly, however, the media remained starstruck by the rising Tories — with significant help from the government. The NDP's unrelenting focus on the Conservatives gave them attention, especially following accusations that Collver's group were bigots like Anderson's Ku Klux Klan-ridden coalition government of 1929. Author Barry Wilson believes that there is more than a modicum of truth to Malone's assertion that "the NDP created the Tory monster."[55]

52. Ibid., 115, and interview with D. Steuart.

53. Ibid., 117.

54. Ibid., 123.

55. Ibid., 125.

The last thing the provincial Liberals needed was another humiliating defeat, but the Pelly by-election in June of 1977 delivered just that. The race was for second place in the NDP stronghold. The Liberals came in third. Within months, Colin Thatcher left to join his former colleague Gary Lane on the Conservative benches. Upon hearing of the Liberal defectors, former leader Dave Steuart exclaimed to Dick Collver that he would live to regret welcoming the Liberal defectors. Before long, Collver would agree.[56]

The Lane and Thatcher desertions tied the number of sitting members at ten and resulted in the Liberals losing official Opposition status. There were rumours of other MLAs stepping down to seek federal seats or simply returning to their previous jobs. Continued wrangling over finances and accusations against MP Otto Lang by both Malone and the party president kept internal tensions in the public eye. This polarized members even more. Speculation became reality when Glen Penner (Saskatoon-Eastview) and Bill Stodalka (Maple Creek) abandoned the proverbial sinking ship. Others declared that they had no intention of seeking re-election. Finally, the inevitable happened. For the first time in its history, the Saskatchewan Liberal Party was reduced to third-party status in the legislature.

Regardless of laudable attempts by Malone to reignite the Liberals through "think tank" sessions, which produced some exciting and innovative policy suggestions, he was leading a party in organizational chaos and financial instability. The "kitty" was depleting and fundraising was becoming a challenge. Their legislative performance went virtually unnoticed as the PCs continued to receive the bulk of the media attention through their questionable antics.

The Saskatchewan Liberal Party's habit of placing the blame for its woes on its leader reappeared. Criticism reverberated throughout the organization —"Malone would not take advice"; "he did not stroke enough egos"; "he was a poor organizer"; "he "micro-managed." After his first year "in charge," Malone had been unable to reverse party fortunes and simplistically the fault was deemed his.

A federal election was expected in the spring or summer of 1978. Malone complied with requests from the federal wing to delay nominations and minimize fundraising activities. These decisions had serious consequences in the ensuing months. As well, it was during this sitting of the legislature that something sordid began to appear. Attacks became more personal and vindictive in nature and the move to discredit the increasingly popular Collver became the *modus operandi* of the governing New Democrats. It has even been suggested that the NDP were assisted in this undertaking by ambitious Tories who wanted to rid themselves of their strong leader and replace him with someone they could more easily manipulate.

The anticipated 1978 federal election never arrived. Instead, Blakeney dropped the writ and the ill-prepared Liberals scrambled to mount a campaign. The NDP's polling indicated that their attacks on Collver were working, and that an early provincial election would all but destroy the disorganized Liberals. The NDP were willing to take the risk.[57]

Despite what Barry Wilson described as "the most unusual policy to be offered by a Saskatchewan political party in years"[58] (i.e., public referenda on unions and

56. Steuart interview.
57. Ibid., 140.
58. Ibid., 141.

the right to strike; and adopting a more European approach to democratic reform), the Liberal campaign went nowhere. Even the "new and improved, more approachable" Malone had little impact. From the moment the writ was dropped, the media counted the Liberals out of contention. By 9:30 p.m. on October 18, 1978, the devastating results were known. For the first time since Saskatchewan had become a province, there would be no Liberal representation in the legislature. Shortly after his shutout at the polls, Malone announced his resignation; ironically, within a month the provincial executive unanimously endorsed his leadership.[59]

With less than 14 percent of the popular vote, the party would not qualify for the $75,000 government rebate. The Liberals faced a future mired in hundreds of thousands of dollars in debt and organizational chaos, with a federal election around the corner. Blakeney's strategy of capitalizing on anti-Ottawa sentiments and instilling fear about Collver in the electorate had worked as voters coalesced in camps either for or against the NDP. In seven short years, the Saskatchewan Liberal Party "had slipped from power to irrelevance."[60]

Events over the next year were to seal the Liberals' fate. Federal fortunes had been promising leading up to Prime Minister Trudeau's election call in 1979. The final tally, however, mirrored the provincial party's results. All sitting members of Parliament were wiped out, including veteran heavyweight Otto Lang and rookie Ralph Goodale. The majority of the candidates lost their deposits. With party coffers at an all-time low, the conflict between the federal and provincial wings grew more intense over who would control the spoils.

Most members agreed that both campaigns had been abysmal failures but a faint flicker of hope remained. With Joe Clark's minority Conservative government leading the country, perhaps the provincial Liberals could spend their time rebuilding to the benefit of Liberals as a whole.

The new decade, however, did not bring the desired resurgence. Clark's short-lived government was defeated on a budget vote, throwing the country into another election; Pierre Elliott Trudeau was returned with a large majority despite receiving virtually no support from the West. Regionalism had reared its ugly head and more than remnants linger twenty years later.

Malone had agreed to remain as leader until a convention could be planned to elect a replacement. He had been functioning on a part-time basis while trying to build a law practice. All aspects of the party were in disarray, although they were having surprising success at reducing the debt.[61] The time of being flush with monies, however, was over.

A leadership convention was finally convened for June 14, 1981 in Saskatoon. Ralph Goodale, a 31-year-old former Liberal member of Parliament, declared his candidacy, and he was acclaimed when no other contenders stepped forward. Raised on a farm in southern Saskatchewan, Goodale had earned a law degree and worked briefly as a broadcast journalist. He had also been an advisor to Otto Lang when Lang was the federal minister of Justice. At the youthful age of 24, he was elected as a member of Parliament for Assiniboia until his defeat in the devastating elections of 1979 and 1980. He attempted to gain a provincial seat in an Estevan by-election, which went to the NDP in the autumn of 1980.

59. Regina *Leader-Post*, November 1, 1978, p. A3.

60. Ibid., 150.

61. Wiebe interview.

Many members believed that Goodale's energy and experience would be the party's best chance at bringing a Liberal voice back to Saskatchewan politics. He was well spoken, "clean cut," and determined. With no elected MLAs or MPs, he essentially became the party in the public eye.

At the same time, turmoil was beginning to mount within the provincial Progressive Conservatives as moves were made to undermine Collver and oust him from his post. The Tory leader's lawsuit with the Saskatchewan Government Insurance Office and continuous — now negative — media coverage led his party to see him as a liability. Collver agreed to step down in order to protect what he had spent years building. Following a hotly contested leadership race, an agricultural economist from the University of Saskatchewan was chosen as his successor. Grant Devine had run unsuccessfully for the Tories in the previous election. Now, he was the Leader of the Opposition with no political experience whatsoever.

Former PC leader Dick Collver remained in the Legislative Assembly but sat as an Independent. An unusual strategy then began to unfold. Whenever the NDP stepped up its attacks on its only threat — the Conservatives — it was Collver who would jump to his feet to deflect attention away from the vulnerable Opposition. Dennis Ham (MLA for Swift Current) contends that Collver's decision to sit as an Independent was done to help the Tories. Collver viewed his former colleagues as less skilled than the experienced New Democrats, but he was convinced that they were poised to become government if they avoided embarrassing mistakes.[62]

Before much time had lapsed, Collver formed a new political entity — the Unionist Party, whose primary goal was western separation. Despite criticism from both supporters and family, Ham joined the cause, stating that extreme measures might bring much needed attention from Ottawa. Ham had been a popular MLA locally but this move spelled political suicide for him. However, he reported that since he was not seeking re-election, he was now free to dissociate himself from those in the Tory Opposition whom he viewed as disloyal, manipulative, and devoid of a conscience. As well, even though Ham had nominated someone other than Collver during the PC leadership race of 1973, he believed that the former leader deserved better treatment than Ham witnessed behind closed doors at PC caucus meetings.[63]

One would have surmised that the distractions taking place in the Conservative ranks might benefit the Liberals. However, Premier Blakeney called an election for April of 1982 and caught the disorganized party at an exceptionally weak time. Goodale had first raised the need for assembling a field of candidates and a precise policy platform the day he was acclaimed leader.[64] This was much easier said than done. Federal Liberal policies were deeply unpopular and provincial rebuilding was going to take more time than a mere nine months. The party went into high gear, determined to deliver candidates in all 64 seats. Shortly before nominations closed, 15 loyal members had to be parachuted into constituencies so that there would be a Liberal on every ballot. Amidst the rhetoric and debate, Goodale's Liberals were discounted as a viable option. His federal ties were seen as a hindrance and "on election night, the Liberals were crushed in the Tory landslide."[65]

62. Interview with D. Ham.

63. Ibid.

64. Saskatoon *Star Phoenix*, June 13, 1981, p. A1.

65. Regina *Leader-Post*, June 14, 1985, p. A4.

It was a demoralizing night for Liberals and New Democrats alike and an unprecedented victory for the Devine Conservatives. Despite receiving 37.64 percent of the popular vote, the NDP only elected nine members. Many cabinet ministers did not survive the onslaught. The Tories took all remaining 55 seats, capturing 54.07 percent of the vote. As in the last election, the Liberals failed to elect any members. However, this time their popular vote was the lowest in Saskatchewan history — a mere 4.51 percent.[66]

The fortunes of the Saskatchewan Liberal Party had never been so bleak. It was at this time that a joke took root about Liberals being able to hold their meetings in a phone booth. But unlike previous unsuccessful elections when the leader's head was demanded on a plate, the party remained largely united in its time of grief. Absent a willing successor and without having to fight off internal blame for the loss, Goodale retained his position. There is conflicting information about the state of the party's finances at the time. One report put the election bill at $175,000 and an accumulated debt of $170,000.[67] In an interview three years later, Goodale indicated that in the early 1980s, the party had been "$300,000 in the hole on federal campaigns and a corresponding amount in debt on the provincial side."[68] Regardless of the actual number, the days of having five separate bank accounts and owning its own building were distant memories.

In Premier Devine's first mandate, the lack of a presence in the legislature hurt the Liberals. Even though Goodale frequently advanced credible criticisms of the government, the media focussed almost exclusively on the NDP. World conditions were serious and Saskatchewan felt their effects. Drought was pervasive, farm debts were continuing to climb due to high interest rates, and the overall economy was in a slump.

Two notable events took place as life in the political wilderness unfolded. The first reinforced age-old alliances that pitted provincial Liberals against each other during the 1984 battle to win the leadership of the federal party. Clear delineations appeared as many associated with Liberal leader Ralph Goodale backed John Turner. Supporters for leadership hopeful Jean Chretien complained that Turner supporters were receiving preferential treatment from the provincial party office and that Goodale was biased. These divisions were to run deep and carry over years later when Turner supporters were seen to move en masse behind Paul Martin, who subsequently sought the position against Jean Chretien in the early 1990s.

The second significant event also occurred in 1984. Bill Sveinson had been elected as a Tory in the Devine landslide. "Considered by many as a maverick on the right-wing of the Tory caucus,"[69] Sveinson crossed the floor of the legislature to sit as a Liberal in spite of there being no sitting Liberals in any Legislative Assembly west of Ontario. Sveinson had been convinced to convert by some Regina Liberals generally viewed as anti-Goodale. Within eight months, the leader asked party president Red Williams to "take the necessary steps to lift Sveinson's party membership."[70] The MLA's constant use of parliamentary tactics to delay the passing of legislation were seen as theatrical and Goodale believed "counter-productive and damaging to

66. Saskatchewan, *Provincial Elections in Saskatchewan*, 141–48.
67. Saskatoon *Star Phoenix*, June 9, 1982, p. D9.
68. Ibid., November 19, 1985, p. A9.
69. Regina *Leader-Post*, April 7, 1984, p. A4.
70. Ibid., December 21, 1984, p. A1.

the better role Saskatchewan Liberals would want to play in this province's public life."[71] Sveinson, however, believed that it was his commitment to support John Roberts and not John Turner in the federal race that was the nail in his coffin. He had been kept at a distance from the moment he had arrived at the party gates and had received no guidance or sense of inclusion from the leader.[72] With his expulsion, a Liberal presence was absent once again in the Saskatchewan Legislature.

In the year preceding the 1986 election, the party established a platform based on fiscal responsibility and integrity in government. From the outset, the policies appealed to rural voters. While support was not sufficient to predict forming government, it appeared that the Liberals could make substantial inroads, thus redrawing the province's political map. Hopes were dashed, however, when Prime Minister Brian Mulroney announced a multi-million dollar farm aid package shortly before the writ was dropped.

The ensuing campaign, in which the Tories and the New Democrats tried to outbid one another, demonstrated that urban voters were as easily swayed as their rural counterparts by promises to buy them with their own money. Only the Liberals refused to get into the bidding war. Only the Liberals warned of the dangers of running deficits and accumulating debt. But the public simply did not respond to Goodale's message of fiscal restraint. A meagre 9.99 percent of the Saskatchewan electorate voted Liberal.

When the results were counted, the NDP had edged out the Tories in the popular vote — receiving 45.2 percent and 44.61 percent respectively. Because New Democrat support was concentrated in urban areas, the Conservatives realized a majority government of 38 seats. The NDP had increased their numbers to 25 members. Although the Liberals had run third in all but two constituencies, Goodale won his seat in Assiniboia-Gravelbourg. Local supporters were ecstatic that they had been able to deliver a party leader to the legislature for the first time since 1978.[73]

The disappointing showing meant that the party was not afforded official party status in the legislature. The Devine government voluntarily provided Goodale with almost $50,000 in annual funding to facilitate the hiring of staff but the media and public generally continued to view politics in Saskatchewan as a two-party affair. Both prior to and following the election, Goodale intimated that the party had met with considerable success in wiping out the debt he had inherited in 1981. At the same time, The Toronto *Globe and Mail* reported that the leader had not been paid in six months and that, in addition to outstanding bank loans, the party had $75,000 in bills due immediately.[74] Several versions were likely correct at different times. After being wiped out in the elections of 1978 and 1979, the Liberals ran campaigns in 1980, 1982, and 1986, as well as financing three by-elections. It is not surprising that the party coffers went from full to depleted to "less broke" throughout its protracted time in the political wilderness.

Things other than direct expenditures also influenced party fortunes. It was common knowledge that the governing Conservatives did their best to keep former Liberals happy with contracts and work. This interfered with efforts of the party

71. Ibid.

72. Ibid., December 22, 1984, p. A4

73. Saskatchewan, *Provincial Elections in Saskatchewan*, 151–57.

74. Toronto *Globe and Mail*, April 29, 1986.

faithful to launch a substantive and lasting comeback. It is a method used too frequently by those in power, regardless of political stripe, and contributes to the disdain the public has toward those who appear to get involved in politics for their own personal gain.

In spite of Goodale's proclamation that he was finished with federal politics,[75] the party suffered another major setback in the summer of 1988 when he resigned as leader and MLA to run federally in Regina-Wascana. His former constituents in Assiniboia-Gravelbourg were particularly devastated and questioned his decision to leave only two years after they had worked so hard to produce the much-needed victory.[76] Throughout the previous year, Goodale had begun what he called "a 40-month plan" to build the membership base, constituency organization, and to raise funds.[77] With improved Liberal fortunes in Manitoba, Ontario, and Alberta, and a resounding 97.2 percent vote of confidence in a leadership review,[78] his announcement came as a surprise. However, Goodale was faced with the harsh reality that the party had placed third in the two May by-elections in 1988, with vote totals actually down from the 1986 general election.

Another consideration came with the departure of Allan Blakeney and the election of Roy Romanow as leader of the New Democrats. Romanow "was determined to keep the NDP in the political mainstream"[79] and with Devine fully entrenched with rural voters, some questioned where the Liberals could position themselves. Furthermore, it had become apparent that the provincial Liberals had been unable to capitalize on their federal cousins' rare absence from power in Ottawa. For almost seven years, Ralph Goodale had worked to plant and nurture the Liberal message in the minds of the electorate but it had not taken hold.

With Goodale's departure, the Saskatchewan Liberal Party relinquished its only presence in the legislature. Even more serious, there was no one — federally or provincially — to give the party a voice and identity, since there were no sitting Liberal MLAs, and the Liberals were again shut out in the 1988 federal election. A leadership convention was set for late March of 1989 and the search for a new provincial leader began.

"The Ugly": 1989–2001

To add insult to injury, the Saskatchewan Liberal Party placed third in the by-election to replace former leader Ralph Goodale in the Assiniboia-Gravelbourg constituency. Understandably, throngs were not stepping forward to declare their intentions to seek his vacant post.

High profile Liberals tried to put the best face on the situation. Saskatoon businessman Neil McMillan admitted that even though he would like to be premier one day, the timing was inconvenient. Party president Bob Crowe, Regina lawyer Cam McCannell, and federal campaign coordinator Gord McKenzie ruled themselves out of the race, as well.[80] Upon being approached about his possible candidacy, University of Regina President Lloyd Barber expressed the negative sentiments many were feeling about politics in general at the time:

75. Prince Albert *Herald*, November 2, 1986, p. 3.
76. Regina *Leader-Post*, December 13, 1988, p. A8
77. Ibid., March 25, 1987, p. A16.
78. Ibid., November 23, 1987, p. A4.
79. Ibid., August 23, 1988, p. A4.
80. Saskatoon *Star Phoenix*, September 1, 1988, p. A6.

> I have no interest in politics and, in fact, I'm totally fed up with politics. Politicians are only interested in getting power and not in telling the electorate the truth about what's going on. I really feel politics has become a bleak landscape in Canada.[81]

As the months progressed, three individuals formally announced their intentions: Regina-based June Blau, a former president of the Saskatchewan Union of Nurses; Neil Currie, a retired senior federal bureaucrat residing in Turtleford; and Peter Kingsmill, a small-town newspaper editor. Several delegate selection meetings were held throughout the province before a latecomer appeared on the scene. That individual was Lynda Haverstock, the present writer. For the sake of consistency in this chapter, the author will be addressed in the third person.

Haverstock was first asked to consider seeking the leadership in September of 1988 but had not taken the suggestion seriously. Her only involvement with the Liberal Party had been as a regional director in Saskatoon. She had acquired a reputation at provincial conferences for stating strong views on policy matters, particularly in agriculture. Regular Liberal meetings were not the order of the day. Like many "workers" in the party, commitments to more demanding organizations and boards, as well as her employment as a practicing clinical psychologist, lecturer, and researcher took precedent over infrequent Liberal activities.

Although other approaches were made, Haverstock remained disinterested until the leadership hopefuls visited Saskatoon to vie for delegates. Having already discounted the New Democrats and Conservatives as the answer to Saskatchewan's woes, she was dismayed when none of the contenders spoke of the fundamental need for systemic change in politics or about the substantive issues that were causing her concern. After the meeting, Haverstock shared that perhaps there was no party, including the Liberals, to which she could fully commit. Within days, Neil McMillan met with her, made an impressive pitch, and others followed suit with offers of support if she were to seek the leadership.

There were several considerations. Besides job commitments, which included a caseload of therapeutic clients, Haverstock was booked to give dozens of farm stress workshops throughout ravaged rural Saskatchewan. Unwilling to cancel these engagements, she agreed to let her name stand if her campaign committee understood that she would be unable to attend any delegate selection meetings. This meant that the only opportunity to win the support of members would be on the convention floor.

With commitments in hand regarding organizational and monetary assistance, for both before and after the convention if she won, she consulted with family. During those discussions, she shared the five personal commandments that would guide her throughout the next six and a half years, never knowing how central they would become in the final days of her future position as the Saskatchewan Liberal Party's thirteenth leader.

It was during the convention held in Regina at the Hotel Saskatchewan that Haverstock got her first insight into longtime party infighting. There was a propensity for members to categorize each other into Saskatoon Liberals and Regina Liberals, federal Liberals and provincial Liberals, Malone/Goodale/Turner Liberals and Merchant/Chretien Liberals, Liberals who were willing to do anything for a vote

81. Regina *Leader-Post*, August 26, 1988, p. A1.

and Liberals who were not. It was also obvious that several individuals resented her interest in taking over "their" party. To her astonishment, the political neophyte realized that there really was no unified Saskatchewan Liberal Party with a shared vision and common objectives. There would be many more surprises awaiting her after her victory.

Prior to the convention, the number of leadership candidates was reduced to three when Peter Kingsmill dropped out of the race to back Haverstock. By the time the votes were counted, a decision was made by all campaign managers to withhold the actual totals of the first ballot win because of the skewed result. For the first time in the province's history, a political party had elected a woman as its leader.

At her first news conference, Haverstock chose to address sensitive personal issues immediately, anticipating media curiosity. Rather than wait for the inevitable, she indicated that she was a high school dropout, teen mother, and divorcee, who had suffered from debilitating health problems and financial hardship. The 40-year-old explained some of the challenges she had faced that she felt qualified her for the job. Although limited in political experience, it was the new leader's contention that her far-from-picture-perfect past helped her to relate to the realities of others in need.

Other statements in this first official meeting with the media set a certain tone. Haverstock said that [she] "would not compromise her convictions for any person, any thing, or any party" and she "would not support the use of patronage"[82] for the sake of maintaining party loyalty if elected premier. She claimed that the common political practice of providing jobs to friends and supporters too often resulted in mediocrity and unnecessary expense to the taxpayer. This statement was to cause considerable reaction from some party members, especially those who had been kept "happy" with contracts from the ruling Conservatives.

Haverstock echoed the mantra of leaders past by emphasizing the need to promote local constituency organization, find good candidates, raise funds, and have an inclusive policy development process, without knowing how truly lacking the party was in all of the aforementioned. She also commended people for "being willing to [be] risk-takers, idea-makers, and accept a new [kind] of politician."[83]

At the time, the number of comments and questions from reporters and members about her age and appearance did not seem important. Later in her tenure, however, it became an annoyance. Former leaders, some of whom had been considerably younger than she, had never been described physically in newspaper articles nor was it implied that they were "too young" for the job. Haverstock came to view frequent statements in reference to her age as paternalistic, as well as an indication of a level of discomfort with her gender.

A new provincial executive had been elected at the same convention. The successful candidate for president, Vic Karwacki, had run on a mandate which included his intention to fire the executive director — the only "corporate memory" in the Saskatchewan Liberal Association (SLA) Office. The president made good on his pledge. The action resulted in the creation of a hostile environment with the remaining skeletal staff, who associated the leader with the dismissal. It would be eighteen months before a permanent replacement was hired to fill the pivotal position of executive director.

82. Saskatoon *Star Phoenix*, April 3, 1989, p. A3.
83. Ibid.

In order to gain insights into the party, to understand all aspects of its organization, and to identify key individuals with whom she should meet, Haverstock sought former Leader Ralph Goodale's counsel. These attempts proved unsuccessful. It was also apparent that those who had talked her into seeking the leadership were now "missing in action," too busy to become involved in the building process. Even the assurances that her salary as leader would be commensurate with her previous income were false. Before long, Haverstock took out a second mortgage on her Saskatoon home in order to pay herself.

The party was in financial difficulty. Two lawsuits had been pending against the Saskatchewan Liberal Association for some time and money was scarce. Targeted meetings with groups like the Saskatchewan Federation of Labour (asking if they would participate in the party's business/labour policy development) were discouraging at best. Equally disappointing was the realization that most "Young Liberals" appeared more interested in political gamesmanship than contributing to reforming the seedy side of politics.

Choices had to be made and the leader decided that the only way for the party to grow was for ordinary people around the province to hear the Liberal message. In the process, it was hoped that visits with noteworthy locals would incite them to become interested in seeking nominations, thereby reducing reliance on party stalwarts to simply fill candidate slots.

By extension, it was hoped that grassroots organization would be strengthened as new people were drawn in and neighbours threw their support behind credible local contenders. Without field organizers and with little assistance available from the party office, Haverstock knew that provincial constituency executives would continue to struggle. They, too, required a rallying point.

Dave Steuart outlined to Haverstock how Thatcher had mobilized local Liberal organizations. She followed his advice and began calling constituency presidents on weekends to discuss their successes and needs. This practice was short-lived after she received a sharp dressing down from the party president for "invading his turf."

This solidified the new leader's decision to focus on a listening tour and defer to the executive's mandate to fulfil the responsibilities of financial accountability, fund raising, organization, and internal party communications. The first stop was Saskatchewan's north where Haverstock simply moved in with strangers who welcomed her initiative to better understand their day-to-day issues. Later, she drove herself from one rural town to the next, meeting in local coffee shops and businesses. At one point, the leader had managed to visit 22 communities in three days. The intensity of the travel usually precluded volunteers traveling with her. As time progressed, this practice drew criticism. Thus began the portrayal of Haverstock as "the lone Liberal," which was reinforced by the 1991 election results.

Less than five weeks after taking over the helm of the Saskatchewan Liberals, the media complained that Haverstock was no where to be found.[84] Initial criticisms focussed on her failing to capitalize on the "middle ground" between the "privatize anything, mega-project obsessed" Tories and the "excessively emotional, anti-privatization" New Democrats. Within ten weeks, the complaints deepened. Comparisons were drawn between Haverstock and her predecessor, Ralph Goodale,

84. Regina *Leader-Post*, May 6, 1989, p. A2.

the latter praised as a permanent "fixture around the legislature in the days before he had a seat."[85] Reporters appeared incensed when she stated:

> We have set our own agenda and I'm sorry if I wasn't functioning to yours. As [the legislative session] was a waste of time and money for the people of this province over the last three months [of bell ringing and counter-efforts to avoid bell ringing], it would have been a waste of my time here, too.[86]

It was explained that the Liberals were just starting to develop policies and concrete proposals, let alone a comprehensive platform. Haverstock stated that she was unwilling as party leader to unilaterally make up policy. An article acknowledged this position as "fair" but also reported that some Regina Liberals were already "anxious."[87] This was the first of what would become frequent references to internal party dissatisfaction. The leader had been in her position for a total of 76 days.

Life in politics did not get easier with the passage of time. Problems endemic to the party prevailed. Money and organization remained scarce but positive signs were emerging. News reports around the province indicated that "old Liberal workers [were] dusting off their credentials" and "returning to the fold."[88] Three areas were providing hope. Community meetings were bringing out a broad cross-section of people from whom good candidates might stem, and unlike the Regina and Saskatoon press, local coverage was encouraging. Second, the policy group headed by Ken Svenson implemented a process that set the party apart. Participants were optimistic that it would result in an innovative, thoughtful, and deliverable platform document. Lastly, the general public seemed to be getting the message as long as the leader could take it to their own backyards.

Although hundreds of visits took place, it was impossible to visit every city, town, hamlet, and farm. Virtually no follow-up occurred thereafter, thus diminishing the party's ability to capitalize fully. Because of financial constraints, substantial mailings were out of the question. Time was the most precious commodity as requests grew to address groups ranging from the Stockgrowers Association, Chambers of Commerce to school boards and advocacy organizations. The provincial Liberals only identifiable presence at any public events was their leader and help was sorely needed.

Perhaps the most visible sign that the Liberals were making progress was the lengths to which the governing Conservatives tried to discredit Haverstock. Attempts to replace the former psychologist in the area of farm stress were proving difficult and she continued to be inundated with requests for stress workshops. The leader was compelled to give presentations every week at some rural municipality in the province until someone could be hired by Saskatchewan Mental Health. It was obvious that the PCs felt threatened. In short order, they sent out a publication entitled "A Look at Lynda," in which they misrepresented her professional remarks to farm families, called into question her morality, and even questioned whether she had, indeed, spent time in a wheelchair. The mail-out signaled that the Tories were worried. Eventually, they even accused the Liberal leader of marrying just to improve her public persona.

85. Ibid., June 17, 1989, p. A4.
86. Ibid.
87. Ibid.
88. Ibid., February 5, 1989, p. A4.

After five long years, Premier Devine could no longer avoid calling the election. There had been debate about whether the Liberal leader should run in Rosetown-Biggar or Saskatoon Greystone — the largest urban constituency in the province. The latter was seen as the greatest risk since the cities were predicted to go entirely New Democrat; furthermore, the NDP's local candidate in Saskatoon Greystone was the popular and dedicated incumbent Peter Prebble. The final decision was based on Haverstock's years of involvement and profile in the city.

Most Liberals were under no illusions. All information pointed to an NDP avalanche. The goal was to replace the Conservatives as the alternative to the New Democrats. Haverstock indicated that the best outcome for Saskatchewan citizens would be a minority government with Liberals holding the balance of power. (This had worked effectively in 1972 at the federal level; Trudeau's minority government implemented several New Democrat policies, in exchange for support. In addition, Ontario Liberal Premier David Peterson had to rely on New Democrat Leader Bob Rae in the mid-1980s to remain in power. Rae's small caucus had considerable influence as a result and became government after Peterson called an early election.)

By the time the 1991 writ was dropped, Haverstock had personally knocked on every Saskatoon Greystone constituent's door, not once but twice. Fund raising for the provincial campaign had resulted in the formidable sum of $155,000 and that was the total the party ultimately spent. The full slate of 64 candidates included the broadest cross-section of individuals since the days of Ross Thatcher.[89] They worked with tremendous dedication despite their battles being portrayed as futile. Central to the party's campaign was its platform entitled "Facing Reality in Saskatchewan," a reasonable document in which candidates and members alike took pride.

Voter discontent with the Tories resulted in an NDP sweep of 55 seats and 51.05 percent of the popular vote. Although the Liberals received a comparable share of the vote *vis-à-vis* the Conservatives — 23.9 percent versus 25.54 percent — only the leader was elected. The once-dominant Tories took nine seats.[90]

It was good news and bad news for the Saskatchewan Liberals. The dramatic increase in popular support represented an upward trend. Equally significant was the fact that they had come in second in 29 constituencies. Their support was balanced across rural and urban areas. Some saw this as a weakness and labeled it "the inch deep/mile wide phenomenon." Others viewed it as the perfect foundation on which to build. Finally, there was a party with the potential to draw all parts of the divided province together.

The election of a single member to the Legislative Assembly denied the Liberals official party status and the funding that accompanies it. In response to Haverstock's request for resources, newly elected Premier Roy Romanow provided the Liberals with the same funding (indexed for inflation) that had been granted to Mr. Goodale in 1986. While helpful, the sum was paltry in comparison to what would have been available had even one other Liberal been elected.

The lack of official party status also meant less time in question period, which afforded the Conservatives the advantage of raising every pertinent issue first. In addition, the new Liberal MLA would have to rely on the goodwill of other members for any initiative requiring a seconder, such as introducing a private member's bill or an emergency debate. This type of cooperation proved rare.

89. 1991 Saskatchewan Liberal Handbook on Candidates.

90. Report of the Chief Electoral Officer (1991 Edition).

To his credit, Premier Romanow called a fall session of the legislature shortly after taking office. Standing committees were reactivated after years of Conservative neglect. Haverstock was placed on several committees, including the most demanding.[91] It was a huge learning curve and she received an education, in short order.

The Liberal leader chose to do the unprecedented and voted in favour of the government's throne speech. The decision was based on giving the new government a chance. Immediately, the response from both sides of the House was ridicule. As well, conflicting schedules were established for the Standing Committees of Public Accounts and Crown Corporations. When Haverstock attended one meeting, she had to be absent from the other. Soon, constant references about her lack of commitment permeated the Legislative Assembly.

One particular strategy was implemented shortly after Haverstock's arrival as an elected member and continued until she was no longer the leader of the Saskatchewan Liberal Party. It appeared that a decision had been taken to isolate her from the day-to-day niceties of general conversations. This occurred in both the House and halls of the legislative building. Few MLAs replied to simple greetings. As well, every time the member from Saskatoon Greystone had the floor, boisterous interruptions from the overflow New Democrat members seated beside her were so loud that she could not hear her own voice. These experiences were confusing but seemed to point to one reasonable explanation. In spite of outnumbering the Liberals 55 to 1, the government saw them as their only threat.[92]

The party continued to face the ongoing obstacles associated with inexperience after years in the political wilderness. Some new faces had arrived on the scene but few who had fought the lonely battles of the last 20 years welcomed the newcomers with open arms. The more dedicated the new volunteer, the less acceptance he or she received. As well, flickers of gender bias were becoming more evident. Following the election of a female president, some executive members expressed concern about the public perception of a party whose key positions of leader, president, and acting executive director were filled by women. It did not register with the complainants that the Saskatchewan Liberal Party had only men occupying these positions for the last century.

A disturbing trend was developing as the make-up of the party executive changed. In spite of obvious growth in Liberal popularity, fewer efforts were made to raise money while greater efforts were made to curb already limited spending. This primarily affected constituency organization and communication with members. More distressing, however, was that confidential information disseminated at executive meetings made its way within hours to newspaper columnists. This and other displays of disloyalty to the party negatively influenced hardworking volunteers. It also led many to suspect that some Liberals were either being rewarded for causing inner turmoil or that their motives were to slow the party's progress.

It was during this time that Haverstock received warnings from party members — many of them former 1991 candidates — who related overhearing high-profile

---

91. Haverstock sat on The Standing Committee on Public Accounts, The Standing Committee on Crown Corporations, The Constitution Committee, The Rules and Procedures Committee, and by 1994, The Board of Internal Economy.

92. The former Devine government had "punished" Haverstock's husband before leaving office. The Romanow government was to take this to new heights.

Liberals discussing their concerns about the leader's increasing popularity and what would have to be done. Two schools of thought had been expressed. First, those who had anticipated a "caretaker" leader were not anxious to have a person committed to "the new politics" become premier. Others were concerned that if party fortunes continued to grow, few would be willing to replace Haverstock and their preference for leader would be left in the cold. The information was troubling since those cited were central to all party activities.

The federal Liberals were in a state of transition throughout these early years of Haverstock's tenure. Kim Campbell had replaced Conservative Prime Minister Brian Mulroney and the race to become leader of the Liberal Party of Canada was heating up. Remembering the accusations surrounding her predecessor's involvement in the Turner/Chretien battle of the 1980s, Haverstock stayed at arm's length and made no public or private commitments to any candidate. This was to no avail. Supporters of the two frontrunners, Paul Martin and Jean Chretien, simply surmised that if Haverstock was not supporting their person, she must be secretly supporting their adversary.

Public displays of questionable behaviour arose during the federal Liberal nomination meeting in Regina Wascana, contributing to further divisions. Because of allegations of wrongdoing lodged by all candidates, the provincial leader had to ask the president to appoint an arbitrator to scrutinize potential membership irregularities. The bitterness between the Merchant/Goodale camps was palpable.[93] Former president Sylvia Kish tore up her membership in protest and media reports were rife with party conflict.

As the 1993 legislative session was winding down, Haverstock was broadsided. Two "party faithful" publicly renounced the Leader within weeks of each other. Angry over the termination of his friend Peter Sheridan, whom he had been instrumental in hiring as executive director of the party, the vice-president of finance, Rod Gantefoer, sent an internal report critical of the party leadership to a prominent political reporter.[94] Shortly thereafter, a former provincial candidate, Randy Roman (Moose Jaw) demanded the leader's resignation because "she rants and raves ... like a wild woman at these people who are researching for her."[95] What remained unpublished was the reason for Roman's outburst. Haverstock had refused to comply with what she saw as unethical demands from an employee, who happened to be a close friend of Roman's. This former legislative researcher wished to remain on the payroll while running as a federal Liberal candidate, even though he would no longer be legitimately employed. He stated that "as long as [he] periodically showed up in the cafeteria of the Legislative Building, no one would know the difference." Within hours of the leader's refusal, the researcher left and did not return to the office. Days later, Roman's remarks were printed in newspapers throughout the province.

These two episodes were disturbing to Haverstock. As a former professional in different fields, a former member of several boards and organizations, and particularly, a former psychologist who made her living working with people by establishing trustful relationships, the criticisms called into question her entire reputation. The

93. Regina *Leader-Post*, March 6, 1993, p. A1.
94. Saskatoon *Star Phoenix*, June 3, 1993, p. A3.
95. Moose Jaw *Times-Herald*, June 17, 1993, p. 1.

comments devastated her family and friends; former clients and former colleagues also voiced concern.

Haverstock realized for the first time that the media would report information regardless of its inaccuracy. No attempts were made to determine whether this was a pattern with the leader before entering public life. Any effort to do so would have shown otherwise. The result, however, left the leader vulnerable. All anyone had to do from that day forward was to threaten that they would go to the media and imply that she was difficult if she did not comply with their demands. It was not just ambitious Liberals who tried to use this to their advantage. The New Democrats and Conservatives saw it as the Liberals' Achille's heel.

Many party members denounced "the character assassination," stating that "some people don't like the new style politics. They want to sit in the back and overthrow leaders."[96] Dale Eisler, author of the 1987 book on Ross Thatcher, summarized his views of the attacks on Haverstock as follows:

> Not only was Haverstock seen as an outsider, but she talked about breaking away from "old-style politics" ... code language ... [for] an end to a party that existed primarily as a vehicle for individuals to access the spoils of power. In other words, she became a threat to some of her own people... The reason for the rumours of mutiny is clear. After years in the political wilderness, the Liberals have suddenly become a viable option...[97]

It had been four years since Haverstock had become leader of the Saskatchewan Liberals. Popular support had grown, the party had more visibility and appeared to be making steady progress. Behaviour in the legislature suggested that the Liberals were the Romanow government's greatest worry. Observations like the "Premier ... pops up like a jack-in-the-box every time Haverstock asks a question in the assembly"[98] were reported with regularity. Yet, prognostications on the Liberal leader's demise continued.[99]

Media reports focussed on the need for the Liberals to win the seat vacated by NDP MLA John Solomon. This would provide the party official status and funding for the first time in 15 years. Despite the constituency's strong New Democrat base, press statements said, "It's not really overstating the case to suggest the very survival of the Saskatchewan Liberal party — or Lynda Haverstock's leadership thereof — hinges on the results of the upcoming Regina Northwest byelection."[100]

Long before a by-election was in the offing, however, internal party discussions had been focussing on the need to demonstrate momentum. One suggestion was to consider accepting a disenchanted member from the government benches in order to gain official party status. Few knew that a New Democrat MLA had contacted Haverstock and indicated that he and several others in his caucus were interested in crossing the floor to sit as Liberals. Most were rural members who feared obliteration in the next general election. Others were concerned about the pending results of a Commission whose mandate was to reduce the number of provincial constituencies, creating the possibility that they could lose their redrawn seat to another New Democrat in a nomination showdown. After many

96. Saskatoon *Star Phoenix*, June 18, 1993, p. A1.
97. Ibid., June 10, 1993, p. A7.
98. Regina *Leader-Post*, May 7, 1993, p. A4.
99. Ibid.
100. Ibid.

months, the discussions took an interesting turn when Romanow suddenly appointed the contact person to cabinet.[101]

Haverstock's hesitation to finalize negotiations was based on the MLAs involved, as well as the concept of "crossing the floor." It was difficult to view persons willing to share confidential memoranda and disregard party loyalty as principled. Regardless, pressures mounted. No consideration was given to accepting more than one MLA because legitimate questions could be raised about how "liberal" the Liberal caucus would be if former New Democrats outnumbered the one sitting Liberal. Finally, it was decided that the best scenario would involve a government MLA from a constituency that had received substantial Liberal support in the 1991 election. After considerable resistance, Haverstock acquiesced. It was to become one of the most fateful decisions of her political career and a personal disappointment.

Shaunavon (subsequently Wood River) MLA Glen McPherson fit the criterion. He represented an area of the province that had once been fertile Liberal ground. Unpopular with his former colleagues, many New Democrats stated that they were not unhappy with his departure.

During the news conference to announce McPherson's defection, the "new Liberal" signed the required code of ethics. Shortly thereafter, he abrogated the agreement, furious with the leader for her refusal to name him party whip or house leader in order for him to receive added pay. Although it had been made clear throughout negotiations that no such assignments would transpire, the message was ignored. While the party warmly welcomed McPherson, determined not to repeat the problems experienced by Bill Sveinson in the Goodale years, the damaged relationship with the leader would only grow worse. Some of his actions led many Liberals to question if he were actually working in the interests of the NDP.[102]

National polling was done in preparation for the 1993 federal election and results showed the party well ahead. The Chretien Liberals were poised to make great gains. The poll also "found Haverstock to be the most popular politician in the province."[103] This was the impetus for including the provincial leader in the federal campaign and, to the surprise of many, she suddenly received praise from some of her harshest backroom critics.[104] Election night left the federal Tories with only two seats in the entire country. The Chretien wave sent five Saskatchewan Liberal members of Parliament to Ottawa. Haverstock was exhilarated but the new spirit of federal-provincial party cooperation was short-lived. In spite of the provincial leader's requests to the Saskatchewan minister's office for joint meetings between sitting Liberal MLAs and MPs, the first would only occur two years later — one week after Haverstock's resignation.

Enthusiasm over achieving official party status and the federal party's October

101. It should be noted that this was not the first time this had happened. Shortly after Haverstock's election as leader and before she had won a legislative seat, PC MLA Sherwin Peterson (Kelvington–Wadena) contacted her to indicate his interest in crossing the floor to the Liberals. Within days, Peterson was appointed to the Devine cabinet.

102. Regina *Leader-Post*, June 28, 1996, p. A4.

103. Ibid., September 3, 1993, p. A4.

104. During the 1993 election, a longtime Goodale supporter told Haverstock that many Regina Liberals resented her for "stealing" the former leader's job. It was the first time that the "new" leader was able to attach meaning to the hostility she continued to experience in Regina. These resentments emerged four years later when Goodale supporters set up phone banks and worked tirelessly to encourage a vote for a leadership review at the 1995 Liberal convention in Regina.

success spilled over to the 1994 by-election in Regina-Northwest. Following a three-way contested nomination, the leader joined the hardworking victor, Anita Bergman, at the doors. Bergman had been a federal candidate, placing a close second. The New Democrats mounted a strong campaign in the Regina seat and the Liberals pulled out the stops. Party supporters came from across the province and beyond to assist.

The virtual disintegration of the Conservative vote and the collective efforts of determined party workers resulted in the unexpected by-election win of Bergman in what should have been a *fait accompli* for the NDP. It sent a serious message to the Romanow government. Liberal MLAs now numbered three. Not only did this fuel optimism among the party faithful, it attracted the attention of those who had remained in the background until success appeared imminent.

The next session of the legislature was filled with acrimony. Contempt for Haverstock was standard fare amongst the New Democrats. One press report described the "NDPs loathing of the Liberal Leader [as] moving from political disagreement to personalized hatred."[105] At one point, the deputy premier threatened to fire Haverstock's husband, which eventually transpired.[106]

A review of the pressing issues of the day explains, in part, why the Liberals were forging ahead in the polls. The Conservatives were yet to elect a new leader and were bogged down by seemingly endless criminal charges against former Tory MLAs. Romanow's government was trying to keep the province's financial nose above water while implementing unpopular healthcare reforms, expanding gambling, retroactively changing its own legislation, unilaterally canceling farm assistance, and blaming the Devine years for every challenge facing Saskatchewan. The Liberal Party was well poised to differentiate itself from the other two but failed to fully capture the moment.

With the arrival of the ambitious McPherson and Bergman's hiring of the disgruntled former "researcher turned federal candidate" as her assistant, the leader found the caucus anything but unified. "Unidentified Liberal insiders" were cited frequently in news articles, some of which pointed to her colleagues. Furthermore, the two most capable and principled Liberal employees in the Legislative Building — Elaine Hughston and Vonda Croissant — were treated with disdain by the caucus. Hughston's ruffling of feathers extended beyond the legislature. Many Liberals complained that she was too demanding and considered her lack of diplomacy as damaging to the leader. Croissant's lengthy legislative experience was ignored by both MLAs, who chose instead to the follow advice of "private advisors." The refusal to adhere to a common strategy remained a pattern even after the arrival of a new chief of staff, Kevin Stringer.

Throughout this time, faces were changing at the Saskatchewan Liberal Association Office (SLA). The provincial executive hired Emmet Reidy as executive director. Finally, the party had someone with considerable experience, albeit from the Thatcher era. However, significant challenges arose as the "new politics" leader came face-to-face with one who had no interest in or commitment to doing politics differently.

In public, Reidy's comments were firm and supportive of Haverstock. He

105. Regina *Leader-Post*, May 4, 1994, p. A4.
106. Ibid.

brought individuals back to the party who had been active "in the good years." Behind closed doors tensions grew, as disagreements over issues such as acceptable fund-raising practices became commonplace. Differences between the leader's staff and the SLA were also intensifying. The executive director did not keep his disregard for Hughston hidden, which served to reinforce negative attitudes about her within Party ranks. Not even highly successful events could bring the divided together. During one of the worst winter storms of 1995, over 1,000 people attended a leader's dinner in Regina. Instead of rejoicing, the key organizers undermined one another.

The Conservatives had held a leadership convention and elected MLA Bill Boyd (Kindersley) to replace interim leader Rick Swenson. In the Legislative Assembly, the Opposition had enough veteran members to use their experience to their advantage. Boyd's feisty nature added periodic comic relief to an otherwise mean-spirited setting. Several "Tory" private nembers' bills were essentially lifted directly from the Liberal 1991 platform document. Generally, though, they were saddled with the legacy of the Devine years. No one predicted that unpopular federal Liberal policies would help breath life into the deflated Conservative Party, as well as enhance the fortunes of the New Democrats in rural Saskatchewan.

As 1995 rolled in, the PCs arranged a clandestine meeting with Haverstock at the Hotel Saskatchewan. A proposal was made to merge the Liberal and Progressive Conservative parties prior to the call of the general election. Such an alliance would create ready-made constituency organizations in parts of the province where Tory support remained strong. It would also allow the Parties to run one instead of two candidates against the New Democrats and pool financial as well as human resources. This, however, was never a viable option for the Liberals. Several Conservative MLAs and two employees from the former Devine government were under investigation for criminal offences. The last colour the Liberals wanted to be painted was Tory blue.

A provincial election call was anticipated within months. The NDP and PC strategy in the legislative session had been to try to force Haverstock to answer for federal policies like the death of the Crow Benefit, cuts in transfer payments, and gun control.[107] The primary goal for the caucus was to maintain a Liberal presence while not becoming apologists for the Chretien government.

The federal Liberals' proposed gun control legislation enflamed rural residents and reignited the Conservatives' base support. Initially, the provincial Liberals agreed with the federal proposal. But as information came forward about the costs of a gun registry relative to the overall justice budget, it was difficult to defend. In addition, it became clear that the policy would adversely affect rural and northern Canadians, without seriously limiting access to illegal guns in urban centres. The provincial party reversed its position and Haverstock became a lightning rod for discontent.

Several members of the Party accused the Leader of disloyalty to the "Liberal Family." Former Leader Dave Steuart warned Haverstock that her overt criticisms would come with a cost, stating that "the chances of her being appointed to anything in the future is zero because she dared to stand up to the 'feds'."[108]

---

107. Ibid., April 18, 1995, p. A8.
108. Interview with D. Steuart, 1999.

Despite the desire to have all parties in the Legislative Assembly "on board" to present a united front against Ottawa's gun control policy, the New Democrats and Conservatives leapt at the chance to capitalize on the Saskatchewan Liberal Party's reversed position. Headlines throughout the province focussed on the Haverstock "flip flop." The 1995 legislative session was less than pleasant for the leader, who was attacked on all fronts — from the NDP, the Conservative Opposition, rural candidates unhappy with the Chretien government, federal party faithful who accused her of disloyalty, new legislative employees with personal agendas, and a campaign committee with questionable motives. All the while, the MLA from Shaunavon was conspicuous by his absence.

Anyone familiar with Saskatchewan politics knew that the chances of the Liberals replacing the ruling New Democrats in the upcoming election were remote. Every provincial government in the previous 60 years had received a second term, even the infamous Devine Conservatives. As well, the odds of going from one seat in 1991 to dozens in 1995 were poor. Yet, provincial executive members and political scientists alike predicted grandiose numbers. (University of Saskatchewan Professor John Courtney indicated that less than 20–30 seats should be seen as a failure for the Liberals). Realistically, the Liberals needed to become Her Majesty's Loyal Opposition with enough elected members to build an experienced core to govern in 1999. In Haverstock's mind, a second Romanow mandate was inevitable. A third term was not.

Pre-election polling placed the governing New Democrats at 51 percent of decided voters. The Liberals trailed at 30 percent with the Tories at 25 percent; 25 percent of the electorate was undecided. The Liberal Party did minimal polling of its own and inexplicably spent its only polling resources on a pollster from Ontario who had little knowledge of Saskatchewan. What was determined, however, was that the leader was the party's most visible asset.

Every effort was made for Haverstock to accept speaking engagements, participate in debates organized by professional groups, as well as visit communities across the province prior to the writ being dropped. Nomination meetings were also a priority. Many had been delayed causing frustration at the local level; at some nominations, attendance ranged from 30 to 500 people. One surprising priority was to arise, which would require significant attention. There was no guarantee that the Liberal leader could actually win her own seat.

The redistribution of Saskatoon Greystone posed real problems for the leader and the constituency campaign team. The redrawn seat now excluded previous areas of support for Haverstock and included strong NDP neighbourhoods. Had the revised 1995 boundaries existed in 1991, "the New Democrats would have won the seat by 607 votes."[109] As is the case with most leaders, Haverstock had to rely on the devotion of campaign workers and constituency supporters to return her to the legislature.

By now, the provincial executive had been infiltrated by many who had their own ideas about who should become leader. Concerns were expressed that the leader's stand on patronage was inhibiting fund-raising efforts. Haverstock viewed this as an excuse. Meetings with people such as Arthur Child, owner of Burns

109. Saskatoon *Star Phoenix*, June 18, 1995, p. A1.

Foods, had convinced the leader that many individuals and companies were interested in "the new politics."[110]

As the impending election grew near, there was a consensus that the party would benefit from a high-profile campaign manager. Regina engineer Wayne Clifton was well known to Reidy and agreed to the position. As weeks moved into months, Clifton never allowed his name to be used publicly. He did, however, appoint his friend, Graham Parsons, to write the platform document. *De facto*, executive director Emmet Reidy became the campaign manager. Individuals who had been crucial to the 1991 election strategy group, leader's tour, platform development, and even the leaders' debate were essentially marginalized from involvement in the 1995 campaign.

The NDP attempted to time the election to the Liberals' disadvantage. Frequent polls showed increasingly that Haverstock had correctly read the sentiments of the province's electorate. Growing support for the party and sustained support for its leader were evidence that she and many of her team of candidates were gradually convincing voters to trust the new politics — to believe that Saskatchewan could have, "commerce with morality, science with humanity, and politics with principle." At the grassroots, people began to embrace this vision, her code of conduct for candidates and elected members, as well as the Liberal commitment to genuine, systemic change. Unfortunately, it would be the same backroom politics she had vowed to eliminate that would deny Haverstock the chance to deliver on the message that captured the imagination of so many Saskatchewan citizens.

Not only did the Liberal leader's stated intention to remove backroom politics fail to materialize, it was precisely this type of behaviour at the Regina headquarters that many believe affected the outcome of the election. Those close to the leader began to question the intent of decisions being made with respect to the campaign. The strategic planning for three key elements became most suspect: the leader's tour, the platform document, and the production of the provincial advertising campaign. Any questions directed at those in control were met with angry and defensive outbursts, aimed with venomous intensity at Haverstock. Just days before the writ was dropped, the leader was summoned to Regina for the filming of the much-awaited television commercials. Upon arrival, she was dismayed to discover that she was expected to "wing it" because no scripts had been prepared. In addition, provincial campaign strategists seemed eager to sever communication with the Haverstock's constituency campaign organization, managed by Hughston. This created confusion and frustration for those trying to organize the leader's time in Saskatoon Greystone.

As anticipated, Romanow called the election for June 21, 1995. By the time the writ was dropped the Liberals were in "catch up" mode. The Liberal platform document entitled "Restoring Health to Saskatchewan" became a flashpoint in the campaign. Candidates were placed at a disadvantage trying to explain its complex set of policies. (The first time the leader had an opportunity to review the completed platform was mere hours before she and Parsons were to present it at an all-candidate's meeting). This substantial 80-page manual was problematic in several ways. Not only was it too extensive for a short campaign, but within hours of its public release,

110. Following Haverstock's departure as leader, Child bequeathed $1 million to the Reform Party of Canada.

a typographical error was discovered. Although the printers offered to reprint all of the booklets, a decision was made to "white out" the digit in question. Further, a controversial table had been added that neither the leader nor the candidates had seen. These two incidences called into question the whole platform, whose overall contents were ignored. The other parties, as well as the media, mocked it.

Two factors affected the outcome in some winnable seats. First, it was well known to the SLA office which local constituency organizations were weak. Had the campaign manager not refused offers of assistance early on from experienced out-of-province organizers (some central to the successful Regina-Northwest by-election campaign), Tory seats like Cypress Hills would likely have gone Liberal. Second, no targeted polling had been done to identify tight races to ensure Haverstock frequented critical seats. Impressions were left with desperate candidates that the leader had final say on where she would go. It never struck anyone that such matters are not left up to any leader in the midst of a campaign. It was during these telephone conversations with campaign headquarters that constituency campaign managers and workers began receiving the message that Haverstock "had to go."

Once on tour, Haverstock frequently encountered situations that appeared to be designed to embarrass her or, at the very least, invite negative publicity. One such tour stop was in Arm River for a banquet, where she found herself face-to-face with disgraced former PC MLA Gerald Muirhead. In front of television cameras, he stated his commitment to the local Liberal candidate. Not only had Harvey McLane's campaign organizers invited Muirhead, but no attempt was made by the provincial campaign to avoid such an encounter even though they were fully aware it was to take place. The incident created a feeding frenzy for the media accompanying the tour and became front-page news.

Haverstock did not shine in the leaders' debate. Although disturbed by the meeting she witnessed between Romanow and Conservative leader Bill Boyd prior to the televised debate, the problem lay more with her own lack of preparation. Little time had been set aside for the leader to focus on the job at hand. Those assigned from the provincial campaign team to assist did as little as possible, with one exception. Essentially, Haverstock entered the fray with no defined strategies, which was significantly different from her 1991 experience. The NDP/PC approach throughout the program was to discredit the Liberal leader and they did so with some success. Interestingly, the greatest impact appeared to be on nominated Liberal candidates and campaign organizers rather than the public at large.

At the time, chief of staff Kevin Stringer, a former assistant to Alberta Liberal leader Laurence Decore, observed that the provincial campaign team underutilized everything that would have won seats and overemphasized the negative at every turn. At one point, Clifton informed the Leader that she should begin making a list of anyone loyal to her, implying that she would need it in short order. It was obvious that he knew something she merely suspected.

The Liberal campaign provided the NDP with a clear avenue of attack. Even though the provincial wing of the party opposed the federal gun control bill, the Tories were the beneficiaries of this issue and retained significant support in rural areas. Their simple message targeted to select seats proved effective.[111] When the

111. Regina *Leader-Post*, June 10, 1995, p. A 14.

results of the election were tallied, the New Democrats were re-elected to a second majority government with 47.21 percent of the popular vote and 42 seats. The Conservatives were reduced to 17.92 percent and five members. While the Liberals surged to 34.7 percent — the highest since 1971 — they managed to elect only 11 MLAs, unexpectedly at the expense of the NDP.[112] Only 64 percent of eligible voters had exercised their franchise.

For the first time in two decades, the Saskatchewan Liberal Party was the Official Opposition. It was the only party to increase its percentage of popular vote, but the remarkable rise from irrelevance to prominence went uncelebrated. John F. Kennedy once said, "victory has a thousand fathers; defeat is an orphan." As headlines proclaimed "Liberals the losers in this election,"[113] and news reports called the result "a crushing [Liberal] defeat"[114] and "a case of dashed hopes,"[115] disappointed candidates and party workers responded in kind. Within days, however, it would be the "successful" candidates who would be called to a private meeting by Wood River MLA McPherson and the groundwork to replace the leader was laid.

Less than a week after the election, articles appeared which stated "that lines are being drawn for a potential battle over Lynda Haverstock's leadership at the party's convention this fall."[116] Columnists reported that Haverstock had "exercised a great deal of control over the campaign ... [including] obsessive control over the platform."[117] Furthermore, "Haverstock is blaming the campaign committee for the Party's failure to elect more members rather than take responsibility herself."[118] While defeated Regina Liberal candidates headed by the unseated former Regina Northwest MLA Anita Bergman held a post-mortem, some members of the provincial executive and SLA office were making plans of their own. Regardless of how the election results were interpreted, many recognized it was the Liberal Party that was best poised to become Saskatchewan's next government.

The writing was on the wall. By the time the new eleven-member Liberal caucus met officially for the first time, several MLAs had their eyes on the leadership. Many were recent recruits to the party and not well known to the leader. They were the unknown commodities, unlike McPherson and Gantefoer. At the end of the meeting, Haverstock chose to address the issue head-on and stated that even though she was aware that some of them wanted her job, it was important for them to learn their own first. A caucus committee was struck through which all decisions and concerns would be addressed and subsequent times were established to begin planning for the legislative session. Haverstock would never take her seat across from the premier as Saskatchewan's Leader of the Opposition, due, in large part, to the ambitions of the newly elected caucus.

Much was written of Haverstock's "phantom enemies."[119] In fact, however, most party insiders knew who was vying for positions of power and who wanted the leader gone. Prior to the campaign, provincial executive member Hewitt Helmsing

112. Ibid., June 22, 1995, p. A1.
113. Ibid., p. A10.
114. Ibid., p. C2.
115. Saskatoon *Star Phoenix*, June 22, 1995, p. A1.
116. Regina *Leader-Post*, June 26, 1995, p. A1.
117. Ibid., June 27, 1995, p. A7.
118. Ibid., June 26, 1995, p. A1.
119. The Watson *Witness*, October 25, 1995, p. 4.

brought Harvey McLane forward as a candidate for the election. It was no secret that he wanted McLane to seek the leadership. Emmet Reidy's undermining comments to constituency managers during the provincial campaign were reported so frequently that there were no doubts about his lack of support for Haverstock. The party's annual convention was set for the November 11 weekend in Regina, which the leader viewed as inappropriate and disrespectful of veterans. Requests to move it were rejected.

Haverstock wanted to call for a full leadership convention, to flush out contenders and allow all party members to express their will. In her view, it could prove to be a healthy exercise for the party. Several prominent supporters disagreed with her contention, believing instead that they should simply try to win the leadership review question outright. Later, it was apparent that some of those who advised against a full convention had ulterior motives. Organizing against a review would require the same level of commitment as those who were determined to win it. Some defeated candidates had established phone banks and had been actively promoting the need to replace the leader for weeks.

Between the orchestrated leaks to the media, the inability to solidify the caucus behind common objectives, the backroom dealings of the "old guard," and the determination of many Regina Liberals to win a leadership review, Haverstock was weary. Parts of the convention appeared uneventful but behind the scenes the pressure to dump the leader was enormous.

Two incidents received the bulk of the media attention. The first involved a taped message from former leader Dave Steuart, who was unable to attend the convention in person. The retired Senator, now living in British Columbia, was asked by Haverstock supporters to give a short, uplifting "pep talk" to the delegates. The intent was for a phone to ring through a sound system from the infamous "Liberal phone booth" and for Steuart to congratulate the party on its showing. He agreed to take part in the levity.[120] Steuart kept in regular contact with many people in the province and was always well informed about the latest Liberal goings-on. It came as no surprise to Haverstock when he called her and made his sentiments about the dissidents well known. Haverstock even shared some of Steuart's comments with caucus staff because of his colourful witticisms and classic one-liners about those he saw as troublemakers. Days before the convention, Haverstock was told that Steuart's contribution was no longer part of the plan. The majority of her committee was also informed that no tape would be played. This, however, was not the case. Instead, a tape of Steuart was played following the leader's speech and prior to awards presented to lifelong Liberals.

The message was neither uplifting nor entertaining. Instead, it was critical of those who were publicly discrediting the party and made reference to specific individuals. One MLA appeared to be anticipating the tape as, before it was played, he instructed those at his table to "stay put" because a surprise was coming. The evening deflated, caucus members bolted, and Haverstock demanded that all members of her advisory committee meet to explain what happened. At the debriefing, two individuals admitted that they decided to play the tape after they had heard it. The leader was disgusted. Steuart had been used and by her own supporters.

120. Interview with Elaine Hughston.

This decision by supposed Haverstock loyalists proved to be one of two fatal wounds for the Liberal leader at the convention. Even her most devout supporters left the dinner questioning the leader's judgement. As if pouring gas on a fire, those in caucus who had been plotting a revolt used the next few hours and "the Steuart tape" to rally the troops for the coup.

As the leadership review votes were being counted on Sunday morning, the caucus summoned Haverstock. All MLAs were present except Buckley Belanger (Athabasca). Ken Kravetz (Canora-Pelly) and McPherson (Wood River) indicated that the caucus wanted certain concessions regardless of the outcome of the leadership review vote. When the leader indicated that it was the members who dictate what the party stands for, she was told that the caucus did not care about "her members," "her party," or the platform on which they had been elected. By now, the behaviour and attitudes of some of the MLAs did not surprise Haverstock. However, she was shocked by the lack of courage of others to speak up for their liberal ideology. Haverstock said she would not respond to them. Instead, she would report to "her members" and "her party" forthwith.

Saskatchewan's thirteenth Liberal leader met with her family and closest confidantes for mere moments and informed them of her decision. Remembering the personal commandments she had shared with her daughter in 1989, the choice was made easier. Shortly thereafter, she received the results of the vote. Only 52 percent of the members did not want a leadership review. The narrow victory served to reinforce what she had already decided.

Within minutes, Haverstock stood before a room of 600 delegates and stated that while the 52 percent vote was constitutionally adequate to avoid a leadership convention, the deep divisions in the party would persist unless she resigned. In a media scrum, the former leader indicated that constant undermining had begun prior to the June election and "now they're going to have to do something with all that destructive energy."[121] She observed that because of the naivete of the caucus, "they need a chance to learn ... when there is no excuse for division."[122] Haverstock then appealed to the party to hold a one-person, one-vote leadership convention so that all 15,000 Saskatchewan Liberals could participate.

Many Liberal members, especially those who had not attended the Convention, were bewildered and commented that the caucus had highjacked the party. In defense, McPherson informed political reporter Dale Eisler that the caucus actions were in response to the "duplicitous and mean-spirited nature of Haverstock's leadership" as demonstrated at a two-day caucus meeting held in Outlook ten days prior to the convention. This was to become the second incident to receive an inordinate amount of negative publicity.

The Wood River MLA stated that "this was when any semblance of caucus solidarity behind the leader evaporated" because he had been able to prove to the caucus that Haverstock had solicited the support of a former Liberal MLA from McPherson's constituency, Roy Nelson, to help oust the sitting member. As evidence, McPherson said that his campaign manager, Dick Lemieux, had received the information directly from Nelson. Lemieux had then shared his claim with Melfort MLA Rod Gantefoer and executive director Emmet Reidy. During the Outlook

121. Regina *Leader-Post*, November 13, 1995, p. A1.
122. Ibid., November 14, 1995, p. A3.

Caucus meeting, McPherson openly accused the leader of arranging to get rid of him. When Haverstock denied any such involvement, McPherson contacted Lemieux by phone and Lemieux repeated his statement to the caucus. McPherson indicated to Eisler that it was later that night that seven caucus members pledged to withdraw support from the leader regardless of the leadership review vote.[123]

No one questioned the near-impossibility of "deposing" a duly elected MLA. Nor did anyone contact Roy Nelson to get his version of events, and McPherson's allegations were printed verbatim. Nelson, upon reading the news article, contacted the newspaper and stated that the story was false. No retraction was printed, whereupon Nelson wrote a letter to the editor, in which he stated that McPherson's and Lemieux's comments were fabricated. His letter said that "Haverstock did not in any phone call to myself suggest I do what I could to get MLA Glen McPherson ousted from caucus."[124]

Following her resignation, Haverstock indicated her intention to remain as the MLA for Saskatoon Greystone. No decision had been made immediately following her resignation as to whether or not she would sit with the Liberal Opposition. However, the actions of the caucus assisted with that decision when the former leader received word from the legislature that a security guard had been forced to let her "colleagues" into her office. This prompted Haverstock to ask Romanow's chief of staff, Gary Aldridge, for space outside of the designated Opposition offices. She was told that the only way she would be granted an office would be if she declared herself an Independent. She stated that she would be an "Independent Liberal" and the move to the basement began.

Public humiliation was far from over. Haverstock's executive assistant, Vonda Croissant, helped the former leader transport her property from the office of the Leader of the Opposition. In the process, and without Haverstock's knowledge, Croissant removed certain items she felt might be tampered with and delivered all financial records to an outside accountant for an immediate audit. These actions, coupled with the removal of personal items belonging to both Haverstock and Croissant, resulted in public accusations of theft. By November 17, the firing of the longest serving legislative employee of the Liberals was on the front pages of Saskatchewan's newspapers.

Less than five months after being elected MLA for Melville, and only three years after seeking a nomination as a federal Reform candidate, Ron Osika became the interim leader of the Saskatchewan Liberal Opposition. With the next Legislative Session just months away, there still was time to develop a strategy, as well as convince apprehensive Liberal members that the caucus revolt would yield positive results. Boyd's Conservatives, however, were the ones to "come out of the chute racing."

The Tories' late November annual meeting was the antithesis of the Liberal convention — upbeat, celebratory, and united.[125] Their approach prior to and during the 1996 sitting of the legislature was the same. As early as January, news articles reported that "it's been the tiny, discredited Tory rump that has led the charge on SaskPower hikes, Workers' Compensation Board and occupational health and

123. Saskatoon *Star Phoenix*, November 14, 1995, A1, A2.
124. Regina *Leader-Post*, November 24, 1995, p. A11.
125. Saskatoon *Star Phoenix*, November 27, 1995, p. A3.

safety fee hikes, and ... the government's decision to make farmers payback GRIP overpayments."[126] They outshone Her Majesty's Loyal Opposition, in spite of having half the number of members in the legislature. All the while, the Tories faced a barrage of accusations and ridicule from the New Democrats because of the continuing criminal charges against Conservatives who had served under Grant Devine. The "Liberal Caucus [was] too consumed by their own [individual] leadership aspirations" to be watchdogs for the public purse.[127]

By February, party executive director Emmet Reidy announced the Liberal leadership convention would be held in Saskatoon on November 15–16, using a standard delegate-selection process; the date was subsequently moved to November 22–23. A province-wide membership vote was rejected because it "would require a change in the Liberal party constitution."[128] It was during this announcement that Reidy stated "the party is not considering revoking Haverstock's membership for declaring herself an 'independent Liberal'."[129]

Within days, however, SLA president Dennis Barnett announced that the party executive "will not be renewing Haverstock's membership" and "this decision is based solely on Ms. Haverstock's decision to sit as an independent member of the Saskatchewan Legislature."[130] Speculation, however, pointed to the intent of "torpedoeing any chance [the former leader] might have had to mount a bid for her old job."[131] Although "much finger-pointing ... [was] directed at Glen McPherson and Gerard Aldridge ... thought to be ringleaders in the caucus coup,"[132] neither was at the executive meeting despite publicly endorsing the decision.[133] It was the vice-president of finance, Jim Melenchuk, who made the motion to rescind the former leader's membership. Tom Hengen was the seconder. Both became contenders for the leadership at the fall convention.

Interest was mounting in the position to become the Saskatchewan Liberal Party's new leader. Several MLAs were testing the waters. Melfort-Tisdale MLA Rod Gantefoer had begun a series of meetings to garner support. Hewitt Helmsing's choice, Harvey McLane (Arm River) was doing the same. Ken Krawetz (Canora-Pelly), Gerard Aldridge (Thundercreek), Glen McPherson (Wood River), and interim Leader Ron Osika (Melville) were also trying to evaluate their chances for success. Four individuals from outside Caucus were touted as possible candidates: Jim Melenchuk, a Saskatoon family physician who had run unsuccessfully in the 1995 campaign; defeated 1995 candidate Barry Thienes, an optometrist from Shaunavon; Radville lawyer, Rod MacDonald; and educational consultant, Tom Hengen.

Before the 1996 legislative session ended, the Liberal Opposition's ineptitude had become common fodder in media reports. The lacklustre performance led many to question whether the Liberals represented a credible alternative to the NDP. The blame was placed on chief of staff Bill McDonald, who was dismissed. Caucus house

126. Regina *Leader-Post*, January 17, 1996, p. A4.

127. Ibid.

128. Ibid., February 8, 1996, p. A9.

129. Ibid.

130. Prince Albert *Herald*, February 20, 1996, p. 5.

131. Regina *Leader-Post*, February 23, 1996, p. A4.

132. Following the defeat of Regina Northwest Liberal MLA Anita Bergman, Aldridge hired her constituency assistant, the former disgruntled legislative researcher who was considered responsible for several negative media reports against Haverstock.

133. Ibid.

leader Glen McPherson justified McDonald's firing because of the employee's "attempts to call the shots on the day-to-day operations of the House."[134] Given that these are the usual responsibilities of chiefs of staff, McPherson's comments led to further speculation about the Wood River MLA's motives.

With the date of the leadership convention finalized, six candidate forums were announced, as well as a new system for voting. Results of the first ballot would be determined by a full membership vote established at delegate-selection meetings. Thereafter, only those present as delegates at the convention could caste votes and would not be bound by the results of the membership vote in the constituency they represented. Amidst the party's difficulties, five contenders announced their intentions — MLAs Ken Krawetz, Gerard Aldridge, and Arlene Jule and two members of the provincial executive — Jim Melenchuk and Tom Hengen. The race was on.

Halfway through the delegate-selection process, the two frontrunners were in a "dead heat." Melenchuk and Hengen were substantially ahead of Krawetz. By then, both Aldridge and Jule had dropped out of contention.[135] During the leadership campaign, the New Democrats called a by-election in North Battleford to fill the vacancy left by NDP minister Doug Anguish, who had retired to the private sector. The Romanow Government was confident that it would retain the seat. In 1995, Anguish had won handily by 1,200 votes over his closest challenger. Many were caught off-guard when popular local city councilor and legal aid lawyer, Jack Hillson, became the new Liberal MLA in a region that had voted CCF/NDP for most of the past four decades. The victory occurred just days before the November 22 convention and provided a boost to the occasion. It also served as a warning to the New Democrats.

At the end of the first ballot, Hengen was ahead by 18 votes, but Melenchuk's victory was sealed when Krawetz endorsed him after the third ballot. The final tally resulted in 60.2 percent support for Melenchuk and 39.8 percent for Hengen from a total of 921 votes cast. The new leader of the Saskatchewan Liberals described his own leadership style "as a blend of corporate management and military."[136] Without a seat in the legislature, Melenchuk rewarded Canora-Pelly MLA Ken Krawetz by giving him the position of acting leader of the Liberal Opposition, replacing Ron Osika. Columnists assessed the convention a success, stating that the party could now undergo much-needed healing and that, with time, unanimity might prevail.

This was not to be. After a less than auspicious performance by the Liberals in the 1997 legislative session, there was dissatisfaction amongst the MLAs. The devastating results of the federal election in June of that year served to deepen the MLAs' concerns. Every Saskatchewan Liberal member of Parliament had been defeated except the federal minister of Agriculture, Ralph Goodale, and he had lost all rural polls but one, essentially being elected by urban supporters. The successful performance of the Reform Party of Canada led provincial Liberals to fear the formation of a provincial wing of Reformers. Within short order, secret meetings were held between Melenchuk, a handful of his MLAs, and members of the Conservative Party about merging into a new party. According to Rod Gantefoer, previously a

134. Regina *Leader-Post*, June 28, 1996, p. A4.

135. Although Aldridge dropped out of the race, Krawetz complained that, because of awkward leadership rules, his deletion from the ballot would prejudice Krawetz's candidacy. Therefore, the first ballot included Aldridge.

136. Regina *Leader-Post*, September 6, 1996, p. A4.

staunch Melenchuk supporter, serious discussions transpired until the Liberal leader was informed that he would not automatically become leader of the proposed entity.

Although it was reported that the idea of a combined right-of-centre party was rejected by a majority of the Liberal caucus, rumours circulated that several MLAs were continuing to negotiate with Boyd's Tories, as well as some federal Reformers. Melenchuk directed Opposition whip Harvey McLane to contact all elected members and require them to sign a pledge of allegiance to the Liberal Party. Neither Gerard Aldridge (Thundercreek) nor McPherson (Wood River) had been invited to participate in the talks about amalgamating "because of being disruptive forces in the caucus."[137] When Aldridge got wind of the ongoing discussions, he went to the media. According to Rod Gantefoer (Melfort-Tisdale), the Thundercreek MLA's accusations served to coalesce the already unhappy Liberal MLAs. The new leader had been at the helm for eight months when four members of his caucus joined with the Conservatives to form what was to be named the Saskatchewan Party. The "deflated ... Melenchuk told a news conference" that "lots of carrots were dangled in their faces ... they saw an opportunity to jump to the front of the queue with this new party"[138] and they took it. Some speculated that the MLAs who abandoned the Liberals did so, in part, because they did not want to be saddled with keeping the Liberal Association afloat with their own loan guarantees of up to $10,000 each.

Besides the defections of MLAs Ken Krawetz, Bob Bjornerud, Rod Gantefoer, and June Draude, Humboldt MLA Arlene Jule announced that she would sit as an Independent. This resulted in a significant shift in numbers in the legisature. The Liberal Opposition was reduced to six sitting members from 11, the "new" party had eight, the total of Independent MLAs now equaled three,[139] and the governing New Democrats maintained their majority with 41 seats.

Prominent Liberals were present for the announcement of the merger between the Liberals and Conservatives. Former leadership hopeful Tom Hengen participated in the news conference, fully supporting the new alliance. The provincial Liberal Party executive and council tried to diminish the damage by showing solidarity. They immediately gave leader Jim Melenchuk "a ringing endorsement"; "jubilant" party president Anita Bergman exclaimed that the Liberals "were ready to go forward to the policy process and to government in 1999."[140] Ralph Goodale sent a letter to all Liberal Party members condemning the "backroom connivers" for their disloyalty and "suggesting that this is not the way that Liberals do things."[141] Five days later, speaker Glenn Hagel named the Saskatchewan Party as Her Majesty's Loyal Opposition. Once again, the Liberals were supplanted as the clear alternative to the governing New Democrats.

In short order, the former Tory Caucus and their backroom organizers convinced rank and file members to lay the provincial wing of the Saskatchewan Conservative Party to rest. Bill Boyd made it clear that he was willing to forfeit his position as

137. Ibid., August 9, 1997, pp. A1, A2.

138. Moose Jaw *Tribune*, August 8, 1997, p. 2.

139. The fifth Tory MLA — Cypress Hill's Jack Gooshen — had been charged with attempting to obtain sex from a minor and had removed himself from the Conservative caucus by this time. He was not invited to join the new party and was declared an Independent by the Speaker of the House. Gooshen was found guilty of the offence in 1999 and resigned his seat as an MLA.

140. Moose Jaw *Tribune*, August 18, 1997, p. 1.

141. *Western Producer*, August 21, 1997, p. 7.

leader in order to facilitate the emergence of a fresh face to head the new alliance. The Saskatchewan Party later chose former Reform MP Elwin Hermanson as its leader.

By now, the provincial Liberals had elected a new party president, Rod MacDonald. MacDonald informed former Leader Lynda Haverstock that the party wished to make "an unconditional and sincere apology for the removal of her membership."[142] He "admitted that the party [had] lost membership and financial support over the Haverstock controversy" and that his actions were in response to members' expressed wishes.[143] Haverstock accepted the apology "from the president on behalf of Liberal members" and stated that this would not affect her status as an Independent Liberal in the Legislative Assembly. Liberal leader Jim Melenchuk tried to put a different interpretation on the situation and stated that he "had been in fruitful discussions with Lynda over the last three or four months,"[144] implying that the member for Saskatoon Greystone was contemplating a return to caucus. This was never the case and the former leader reiterated her position to Melenchuk both verbally and in writing.

In spite of the many setbacks for the party, optimism grew in the spring of 1998 when Saskatoon MLA Bob Pringle resigned. This provided Melenchuk with the opportunity to obtain a much-needed seat, which would finally put him into the legislature with his remaining caucus. However, it was not to be. The NDP convincingly won the Saskatoon Eastview by-election, albeit at a reduced plurality from the 1995 campaign.[145] The fact that Liberal support was also down from the previous election did not bode well for the party. Only 50 percent of eligible voters cast their votes, indicating that many NDP faithful had stayed home. The Liberals were unable to capitalize on the dissatisfaction with the Romanow government and the Liberal leader remained on the outside looking in.

This loss was to be followed by another serious blow. Athabasca MLA Buckley Belanger announced his resignation from the Liberal caucus and the Liberal Party. Belanger had been a strong supporter of former leader Lynda Haverstock and felt isolated within the Liberal caucus. The reassignment of his duties as critic for Northern Affairs to another Liberal MLA was seen as a form of punishment and had caused Belanger embarrassment. The popular MLA raised the stakes when he stated that he would resign his seat, seek the NDP nomination, and if successful, run as a New Democrat in a subsequent by-election. These actions were a testament to Belanger's values but also provided a basis for comparison with those MLAs who simply crossed-the-floor or formed a new party without allowing their constituents an opportunity to voice their opinions. Belanger went on to win the New Democrat nomination in the contested race and became the MLA for Athabasca for the second time in three years by a landslide in the by-election. Re-elected again as a New Democrat member in the 1999 provincial election, he was named to Romanow's cabinet.

142. Prince Albert *Herald*, March 17, 1998, p. 7.

143. Ibid.

144. Ibid.

145. The Romanow government's victory was significant given that the Channel Lake Inquiry had caused it considerable embarrassment. Furthermore, hospital waiting lists had become a key issue. Often, the electorate view by-elections as a safe time to send a message to those holding power. In spite of this, former Saskatchewan Union of Nurses' president, Judy Junor, recaptured the Saskatoon Eastview seat for the New Democrats.

There appeared to be no end to the turmoil of the Saskatchewan Liberal Party. Six MLAs had been lost in the space of a year. The leader made a proclamation that "anybody who runs in the next election will sign a notarized statement of commitment that they will not run for any other party if they lose a Liberal nomination ... violators of that code will be subject to civil litigation."[146] Many in the party regarded the public statements as inappropriate, voicing concern that it was a negative message to be sending with a provincial election looming and that it had a note of desperation about it.

As 1998 drew to a close, former leader Lynda Haverstock informed her constituents that she would not be seeking re-election at the end of her term. This allowed time for interested individuals to launch serious bids for Saskatoon Greystone, especially Liberals who could draw on previous areas of strength in the constituency. The 1999 legislative session would be the last before a general election and all parties had something to prove. Romanow was determined to get a third mandate. The Saskatchewan Party MLAs had to receive democratic support for their actions and capitalize on the public's lack of enthusiasm for the government. The Liberals simply needed to survive. To many members, the defections and the decline of the party were far too reminiscent of the disastrous 1970s.

An opportunity was afforded the Liberal Party in late June of 1999. Three by-elections were called in Cypress Hills, Regina Dewdney, and Saskatoon Fairview — the former vacated by Tory MLA Jack Gooshen following a criminal conviction, the latter due to the resignations of two long-serving New Democrats Ed Tchorzewski and Bob Mitchell. Of the three seats, the rural constituency was winnable for the Liberals, having lost in 1995 by just 143 votes. While simply increasing Liberal support in the two NDP strongholds would be acceptable, it was crucial that the party be the undisputed alternative to the government and add to its shrinking caucus with a victory in the Cypress Hills seat. As the polls closed, however, it would be another huge disappointment for the beleaguered Liberals. The same candidate who had come within a hair of taking the seat four years earlier was within 33 votes of losing his deposit. More ground was lost in Saskatoon Fairview, as well. The only solace was the increase of support in Regina Dewdney, attributed in part to the Liberals' left-wing agenda in the legislative session. The Saskatchewan Party added to their number of MLAs by taking the rural seat the Liberals had desperately needed.

Before long a leaked "confidential letter" made its way into the newspapers calling for the Liberal leader's resignation. Former executive director Emmet Reidy stated that the party "should seriously consider replacing leader Jim Melenchuk before the next election if [it] wants to win any seats"[147] and "stop the party's downslide." In his letter to the provincial executive, Reidy criticized the leader's appointment of Wood River MLA Glen McPherson as the campaign manager for the upcoming election. McPherson had been in charge of the disastrous campaign in the Cypress Hills by-election. In addition, the letter questioned the caucus strategy that supported IBEW union workers and encouraged striking nurses to break the law. This, too, had occurred under the Wood River MLA's direction. Responses from political reporters attributed Reidy's comments to his having an "axe to grind" because Melenchuk had fired him.[148] Even though there were some who agreed with

146. Saskatoon *Star Phoenix*, September 2, 1998, p. A2.
147. Regina *Leader-Post*, July 16, 1999, p. A4.
148. Ibid., July 17, 1999, p. A5.

Reidy's analysis, few were prepared to have the party go into an election without a leader.

The Saskatchewan Liberals were preparing for the 1999 election campaign. Sitting MLAs included Ron Osika, Glen McPherson, Harvey McLane, Gerard Aldridge, and Jack Hillson. For a year, predictions had been made that the Saskatchewan Party was positioned to take 20 to 22 rural ridings, calling it "the greatest hazard that has confronted the NDP in its 54 years as the primary force in the province."[149] Meanwhile, headlines described the once formidable Liberals as having the ability to give "lessons in political suicide."[150] Like the Tories in 1995, many Liberals feared obliteration. Lifelong members were bewildered by the caucus's left-leaning stances even though it was no secret that Melenchuk relied solely on Glen McPherson for decisions made in the legislature, as well as for political advice.

Melenchuk's public commentary continued to try to put the best face on the situation. He claimed that the party "at this point in time [is] within reach of forming Official Opposition ... and considering the inept NDP handling of the nurses' strike, forming government is not out of the question in many people's minds."[151] For a number of grassroots members, the campaign would be deemed a success if the Liberals retained two elected members, thereby maintaining official party status. What no one expected was that the party would receive a most unlikely gift — the balance of power.

It is said that politics is about luck and timing. Since almost every Saskatchewan government has had a second term guaranteed, Opposition parties patiently wait for the moment when the government must seek a third mandate. By the time the election was announced for September 16, 1999, political pundits had predicted another Romanow victory. They also speculated that the Saskatchewan Party was best poised to remain the Official Opposition. Few anticipated that the results would be so close. The final count left the New Democrats with 29 seats, the Saskatchewan Party received 26, and the Liberals were reduced to three elected members. Elwin Hermanson's new party actually received the highest percentage of the popular vote — 39.6 percent compared to 38.7 percent for the NDP. The Liberal Party garnered 20.2 percent. It was to make for interesting times and strange bedfellows.

A seat in the Legislative Assembly no longer eluded the Liberal leader. In a tight, three-way race, Melenchuk won with 36 percent of the popular support, 145 votes ahead of the NDP incumbent. Former MLAs Ron Osika (Melville) and Jack Hillson (North Battleford) retained their seats. An unusually close race in Wood River left the Liberals with the possibility of gaining a fourth member. Glen McPherson and his closest rival were tied and a judicial recount was inevitable. Although the New Democrats won almost every urban seat, they went down to defeat in rural Saskatchewan, which was dominated by the Saskatchewan Party.

The electorate had handed the Liberals tremendous power. The party was now in a position to influence the direction of public policy on a case-by-case basis. Premier Romanow's initial response to his minority government situation was to

149. The *National Post*, December 7, 1999.

150. Prince Albert *Herald*, July 20, 1999, p. 4.

151. *Saskatchewan Business*, May/June, 1999, p. 36.

discount any alliance with the Liberals and he stated so unequivocally. Melenchuk made similar comments. Both had been harsh critics of how the Saskatchewan Party had been founded, calling it "an anti-democratic act that amounts to nothing less than a political coup d'etat."[152] Furthermore, the Liberal leader promised his 1999 candidates that there would be no deals with the NDP. Ninety-six hours later, the premier and Melenchuk had changed their positions and the province had its first "coalition" government in 70 years. Opposition leader Elwin Hermanson condemned the Liberals, stating that they "overturned the voters' verdict and gave the NDP back its majority."[153]

By the end of September, Saskatchewan had a most unusual political arrangement. All three Liberal MLAs were absorbed into positions within the government that for all intents and purposes made them New Democrat members. Melville MLA Ron Osika was appointed Speaker of the Legislative Assembly, in spite of his earlier claims that he had ruled out the possibility. This act on the part of the government struck at the heart of goodwill in the legislature. The practice of electing rather than appointing a Speaker had been adopted by an all-party Rules and Procedures Committee and sanctioned by the House in 1992. The decision to overturn this democratic reform was considered inappropriate and undermining of the gains that sitting members had sought for years. In addition, Leader Jim Melenchuk, whom Romanow had accused of being "unable to run a one-car parade," was placed in charge of the half-billion dollar Department of Education. North Battleford MLA Jack Hillson took over as minister of Intergovernmental and Aboriginal Affairs, minister of Municipal Affairs, and provincial secretary.

Liberal Party stalwarts were at a loss as to why Melenchuk chose to forfeit the opportunity to essentially guide the Romanow government's agenda. Comments made by Jack Hillson at the time he entered the Romanow cabinet gave one version of the situation. According to the North Battleford MLA, Melenchuk made his agreement with Romanow without consulting his Liberal colleagues or the party. Since the three MLAs had no clear, common vision to articulate and questioned whether they could work together effectively, no one wanted to try to be the voice of the Liberal Party on his own.[154] This led to an "every man for himself" approach rather than a unified decision that took the party and its membership into account.

Melenchuk supporters gave their own take on the events surrounding the alliance. They reported that Jack Hillson was going to move into cabinet on his own, thereby leaving Melenchuk to have to cope with third-party status alongside Ron Osika on the Opposition benches. They claimed that their leader "took the deal, too, in order to preserve the image of a united party."[155]

Letters to the editor expressed divergent views on the coalition. The Liberal MLAs were accused of being afraid to wield the power they were given. They were labeled "betrayers of voters' wishes" and "greedy for forfeiting their independence for higher salaries now and higher pensions later." Romanow and Melenchuk were blamed for fueling public cynicism by their reversed positions on an alliance. Many New Democrats expressed their support by writing that the NDP/Liberal arrangement would prevent another costly election and that the chance for good

152. Saskatoon *Star Phoenix*, October 1, 1999, p. A12.
153. Ibid., p. A1.
154. Discussion with Jack Hillson.
155. Saskatoon *Star Phoenix*, October 2, 1999, p. A2.

government was now at hand.[156] Meanwhile, three former Liberal Party presidents stated that they most feared a loss of the Liberal Party's identity and that the implications of this action would only be felt in future elections. President Rod MacDonald reported that the party had had no involvement in any of the discussions and that "these guys have completely sold out their constituents ... rural Saskatchewan ... and the Liberal Party."[157]

Shortly after the announcement, some members of the party executive and former candidates gathered in Regina to discuss the situation. Noticeable by their absences were the party president and a number of Saskatoon candidates, as well as several provincial executive members from outside Regina. The Liberal leader's decision to enter into the agreement with Premier Romanow received an endorsement from the majority of the 40 people present. A few questioned how the Liberals would exist in the legislature as a distinct Opposition caucus. Furthermore, they wondered how this would affect the Liberal MLAs' ability to overtly criticize the government or even receive recognition for their ideas and contributions made within cabinet. These views were in the minority, however, and supporters of the coalition carried the day.

As the contents of the seventeen-clause coalition agreement became known, criticism mounted. Columnist Doug Cuthand described it as:

> something like a cross between marriage vows and a treaty. The Liberals promise to love, honour, and obey and the NDP will not stay out late and come home smelling of hard liquor and cheap perfume.
>
> They both agree that their treaty will be in force as long as the rivers flow or until they have their first spat.[158]

He noted that the document was between two unequal parties and in the long term the Liberals would, like First Nations people, be the losers.

The annual Liberal convention was set for November 13, at which there would be an automatic question posed to members about whether they wanted a leadership review. Speculation mounted that Melenchuk's disregard for party input would leave him open to harsh criticism. But prior to the event, party members and the media reported that there would be no bloodbath and that "Grit knives [would] stay sheathed." There appeared to be a consensus that the Liberal Party could not survive another divisive leadership struggle, thereby securing Jim Melenchuk's position.

One surprise awaited the delegates. Former executive director Emmet Reidy, who had called for Melenchuk's resignation in the summer, found his way to the microphone and called for the members to reject the leadership review question. Some wondered if his newfound enthusiasm for the leader stemmed from the contract he had received from the governing New Democrats. Before the voting, veteran members expressed concern about the number of unfamiliar faces who had been bussed in for the occasion but their queries went unanswered. By the time the ballots were counted, a leadership review had been rejected by 52 percent of voting delegates (ironically, the identical margin that had resulted in Haverstock's resignation 24 months earlier). Fourteen people had tipped the outcome in the leader's favour, and Melenchuk accepted the result as sufficient support to continue.

156. Ibid., October 8, 1999, p. A13.

157. Prince Albert *Herald*, September 30, 1999, p. 1.

158. Saskatoon *Star Phoenix*, October 8, 1999, p. A13.

The spring 2000 legislative session provided both the party and the public with an opportunity to evaluate if the Liberals successfully differentiated themselves within the ranks of the Romanow New Democratic government. Melenchuk supporters and NDP faithful remained convinced that the Liberals were making a valuable contribution. Detractors continued to question why anyone would support the party in the future if a Liberal vote could conceivably become a vote for the NDP. The first time that the electorate was able to express its opinion, however, took place when Wood River MLA Glen McPherson decided to step down from politics rather than face a potential showdown with the rival Saskatchewan Party candidate. The results of the June by-election were a shocking disappointment for the Liberals. The party lost 75 percent of the support it had garnered in the 1999 general election. In spite of the warning signs, there was no evidence that the leader or the provincial executive heard the voters' message.

Amidst rumours of the premier's impending retirement, long serving cabinet minister and deputy premier Dwain Lingenfelter unexpectedly announced his departure to the private sector and vacated his seat of Regina Elphinstone. Many had seen Lingenfelter as a strong contender for leader of the New Democratic Party and the most likely to keep the Saskatchewan Party at bay. He appealed to voters who had qualms about the influence of "old" Devine Tories in the backrooms of Hermanson's new party. These same people had no desire to see the NDP return to its anti-business/pro-union days under a left-of-centre leader. On the heels of Lingenfelter's departure, Roy Romanow formally announced his intention to retire from the premier's chair. Soon the way was paved for two more by-elections that would allow the public to express its will.

As contenders lined up to vie for Roy Romanow's position, many wondered what this would mean for the alliance the premier had forged with the Liberal leader. Some questioned how long North Battleford MLA Jack Hillson would remain, given his statements that he would re-evaluate his status in light of Romanow's departure and the party's poor performance in the Wood River by-election. As the NDP leadership race drew to a close and the victor, Lorne Calvert, assumed the position of Saskatchewan's thirteenth premier, Hillson made the announcement that he was resigning his cabinet post and leaving the coalition to sit on the Opposition side of the House as a Liberal.

As he penned a new coalition agreement with Premier Calvert, Liberal leader Jim Melenchuk called the North Battleford MLA's loyalty and motives into question. A few short weeks later, two back-to-back events afforded Liberal members the opportunity to assess their party's standing with the public. By-elections in both Regina Elphinstone and Saskatoon Riversdale were called for February 26 and March 19, respectively. The results showed conclusively that support for the Liberals had virtually collapsed since the 1999 election. They captured a mere 5 percent of the popular vote in both constituencies. It was clear that the only perceived alternative to the governing New Democrats was the Saskatchewan Party, which received an impressive 35 percent in the two NDP strongholds. As Hillson acknowledged the final tallies as confirmation of the disastrous impact the alliance had had on Liberal Party fortunes, Melenchuk interpreted that the results showed "an endorsement of the coalition."[159]

159. Regina *Leader-Post*, February 28, 2001, p. A4.

In between these two by-elections, the Saskatchewan Liberal Party held its annual meeting in Prince Albert on March 3, 2001. Two motions had been submitted calling for a leadership convention if members voted for a leadership review following an amendment to the party's constitution. Both Melenchuk and Melville Liberal MLA Ron Osika addressed the delegates and called for support of the coalition. Osika "blamed the party's poor performance in the recent Regina-Elphinstone by-election on infighting, in effect attributing the humbling defeat to Hillson,"[160] while the leader stated that he would remain in the coalition "even if the party dumps him."[161] North Battleford MLA Jack Hillson, in turn, posed two questions to those in attendance. He asked if "we [are] committed to a party that offers Saskatchewan a vision of how we build this province on Liberal principles ... or will we reject having an independent voice in favour of propping up an unpopular and tired NDP government?"[162]

Besides the blunt discussion, the disquieting practice of "instant Liberals" reappeared at the convention. Reminiscent of the Ralph Goodale/Tony Merchant federal nomination meeting for Regina Wascana and the 1999 provincial annual convention, media outlets reported that Melenchuk supporters had arranged for busloads of newly recruited Aboriginal youth to defeat the proposed motions and secure his leadership. The accusations were confirmed to the embarrassment of most members and made worse when reporters determined that these young people had little knowledge of the party or their reasons for being there except to "put my paper in the box."[163] This time, Melenchuk's effort to avoid a leadership review proved unsuccessful. Rank-and-file Liberals voted overwhelmingly in favour of a leadership convention with a final count of 257 to 93.[164]

The spring 2001 by-elections put the number of NDP government members at 29. Premier Calvert requested that Liberal MLA Ron Osika (Melville) step down from the Speaker's chair and appointed him to cabinet as minister of Municipal Affairs. Long-time New Democrat MLA Myron Kowalsky replaced Osika as Speaker, thereby reducing the NDP government members to 28 compared to 26 for the Opposition Saskatchewan Party. Despite the results of the March 3 vote, and his subsequent replacement as leader, Melenchuk remained in the Education portfolio.

It is the consensus of all the political parties represented in the Saskatchewan Legislative Assembly that the voting public would be less than welcoming of an early election. Given the litany of travails of the Liberal Party since 1996, including six defections, eight by-elections losses, and winning only three seats in the 1999 election with 20 percent of the popular vote, it has the most to lose. In the same vein, the new premier needs time to establish his own identity and reshape a party that has been in power for ten years. Although many might see the Saskatchewan Party as the likely beneficiary in the next general election, a tired electorate might make them pay if voters feel that they have been sent to the polls too early. As of March 2001, Saskatchewan politics continued to be predictably unpredictable. The province's Liberal Party remains consistent only in its dysfunction, unable to live up to its once magnificent past.

160. Ibid., March 3, 2001, p. A2.
161. Ibid., p. A15.
162. Ibid., p. A2.
163. Ibid., March 5, 2001, p. A4.
164. Ibid., p. A1.

CONCLUSION

This chapter began with a definition of Liberalism, an examination of its roots, and a brief review of the role the Saskatchewan Liberal Party played in the development of the province. It also peripherally explored the party's internal strengths and weaknesses and followed its journey throughout the last century.

As a result of this information, one might surmise that the party has outlived its usefulness and, like a great nation that has fallen from her days of glory, is not likely to regain the stature or significance it previously held. In light of the challenges facing Saskatchewan, however, the present writer contends that the ideology of Liberalism is as relevant and needed today as it ever was. What is required is an appropriate vehicle through which this political philosophy can be expressed.

For many years, the provincial Liberal Party has been unable to articulate what sets it apart from the other political players. Nor has it been able to overcome the problems usually associated with parties that have remained in opposition too long — disorganization, inability to raise money, disloyalty, inexperience at running successful campaigns, and lack of cohesiveness. It remains unknown if the deep and destructive divisions found within the Saskatchewan Liberal Party can be healed with the right combination of people.

Presently, two significant forces are represented in the Legislative Assembly in almost identical numbers. On the one hand, the Saskatchewan Party takes the view that government should exercise less control in most areas such as business and resource management, and yet it accepts government control in some moral issues. Despite their attempts to occupy the middle ground, the New Democrats continue to over-manage enterprise and are even willing to compete directly with private sector small businesses, all the while rejecting government influence or interference in questions of morality. It is interesting to note that the extremes of both of these parties likely evoke fear in large segments of the population. The edges of Liberalism, namely socialism and conservatism, would be perceived as much less threatening. There appears, then, to be considerable room for a political party that better reflects the needs of the province economically, environmentally, and technologically, while instilling a sense of hope in people.

As political parties blur their messages and modify their ideologies in order to appeal to the broadest base of support, the question remains whether the Saskatchewan Liberal Party can distinguish itself as a necessary entity for the times. Fewer people are joining political parties and buying memberships. It appears that citizens are less inclined to participate in their democracy even by casting their votes. All of this leads to one conclusion. There is a need for a party of vision, a party of courage, and a party that will treat the people, the process, and itself with dignity. Time will tell if that will be the Saskatchewan Liberal Party.[165]

EDITOR'S POSTSCRIPT

The Liberal party has continued to suffer some internal difficulties since this chapter was written. In October of 2001, after a hard-fought leadership contest, Liberal delegates elected David Karwacki from Saskatoon as the leader of the party. He defeated Jack Hillson, the sitting MLA for the Battlefords. Soon after his election the new leader asked both Liberal MLA's serving in the coalition cabinet, Jim

165. This chapter was written before Prime Minister Jean Chrétien appointed Lynda Haverstock as Lieutenant Governor of Saskatchewan.

Melenchuk, the former leader, and Ron Osika, to withdraw from the coalition. They declined, and have chosen to sit as independents, while remaining in cabinet. This has reduced the Liberal caucus in the House to one person, Jack Hillson. It remains to be seen if the new leader will be able to revive the party before the next election.

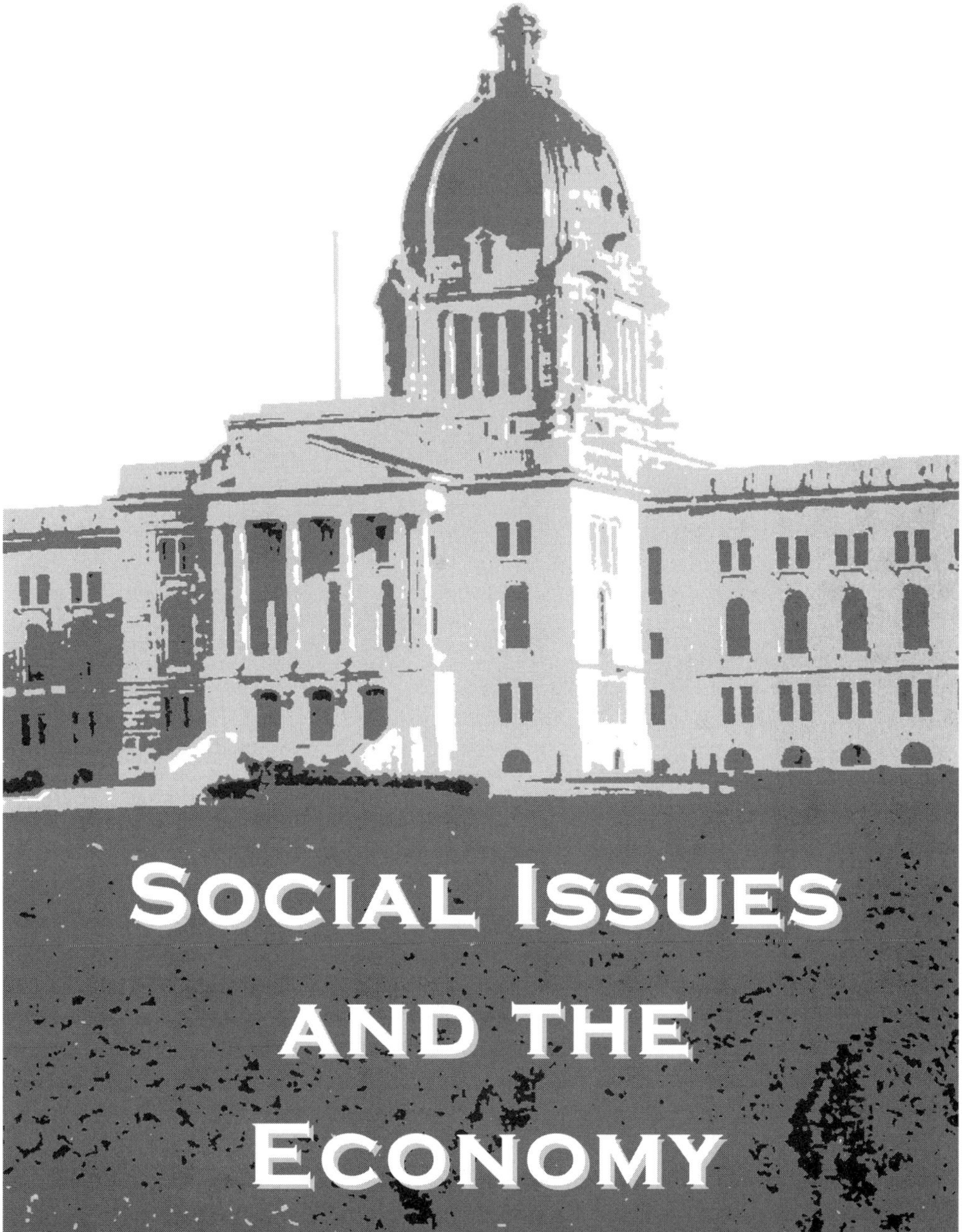

Social Issues and the Economy

Public Finance in Saskatchewan: 1980–2000

Michael Rushton

The key elements of the story of public finance in Saskatchewan over the past two decades are well known across Canada. Through the 1980s, budget deficits and the resulting provincial debt soared to dangerous and unsustainable levels, and through the 1990s the deficits were eventually turned into surplus budgets and the provincial debt, especially the debt/GDP ratio, began to fall. In this chapter we want to get behind that familiar story and examine some of the details.

In the first section we look at revenues of the provincial government, how they have evolved, what is the present state, and what does the future hold? The second section covers provincial government expenditures. The final section deals with the question of policy towards the provincial debt.

Figure 1 sets the stage, showing total revenues and expenditures for Saskatchewan as a percentage of provincial Gross Domestic Product (GDP). Here we see the path of the budget deficit from the early 1980s to the mid-1990s. In 1991 the deficit reached 4 percent of GDP, which was clearly unsustainable. Through the early 1990s a combination of expenditure reductions and tax increases led eventually to a balanced budget, and small surpluses thereafter.

But also interesting in the figure is that the provincial government's share of the economy is about the same now as it was twenty years ago, at about 20 percent. However, we will see below that the components of total revenue (TR) and total expenditure (TE) have changed over the decades.

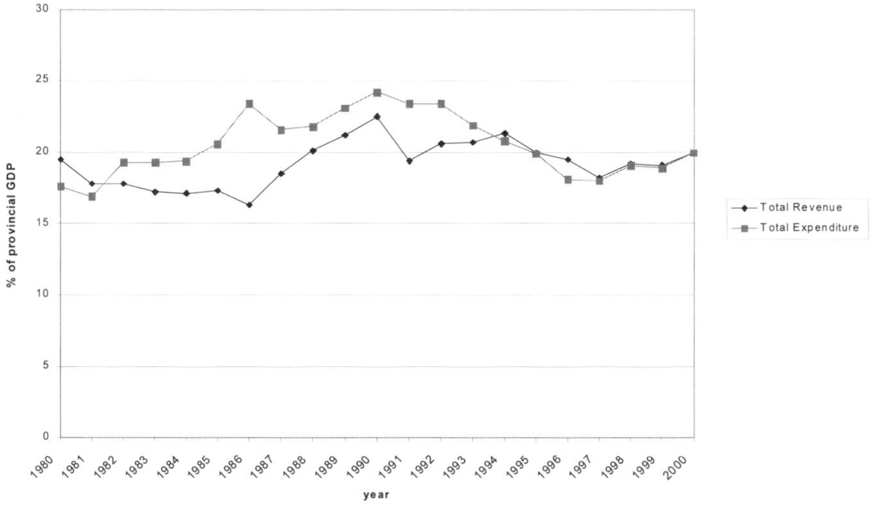

Figure 1. Government of Saskatchewan total revenues and expenditures, 1980–2000

SASKATCHEWAN GOVERNMENT REVENUES

Figure 2 shows the total and own-source revenues for the provincial government in the 1980s and 1990s. We see that at the end of the 1990s own-source and total revenues were about the same as in 1980: about 20 percent of GDP for total revenues and around 16 percent for own-source revenues, the latter number could be interpreted as a kind of "aggregate" tax rate by the province. The amounts transferred from the federal government to the provinces are always a point of some contention, with provinces claiming that they are not receiving enough to be able to deliver the services they are constitutionally obligated to provide, and the federal government claiming that it has a duty to maintain some controls on its total expenditure, including transfers to provinces. But as Figure 2 shows, for all the changes to the details that govern transfers that have occurred since 1980, there has not been a radical change in the proportion of provincial revenue that comes from federal transfers, at least in Saskatchewan, since the early 1980s.

Figure 3 shows the breakdown of revenue by source. The most important single tax for Saskatchewan is the personal income tax, followed by the sales tax. In the March 2000 budget, a plan was introduced to shift this balance in favour of the sales tax; in the past Saskatchewan has relied more heavily on the personal income tax than other provinces, and there is a concern that the disincentive effects of the income tax are harming provincial economic growth. It is especially a concern with neighbouring Alberta's plan to adopt an 11 percent flat tax levied on personal income in 2001. Saskatchewan will be phasing in a new income tax structure, with an 11 percent rate for low-income earners and with marginal rates of 13 percent and 15 percent at higher levels of income. The tax reform is discussed in more detail below.

In the budget for 2000–01, personal income taxes are expected to raise $1.247 billion (note that Saskatchewan's population is almost exactly one million, which has the useful feature of letting us easily translate most economic statistics into per person terms). Sales taxes will raise $815 million, and corporation taxes $589 million. Excise taxes on fuel, tobacco and other items will raise $538 million. Resource revenues are forecast to amount to $751 million in 2000–01, over half of which is accounted for by oil, followed by potash and natural gas in importance. It must be realized when reading Figure 3 that dividend revenues (transfers from Crown corporations), at $1.194 billion in 2000–01, were unusually high, due to a transfer of $695 million from the retained earnings of the Saskatchewan Liquor and Gaming Authority; in 1999–2000 dividends were only $153 million. Finally, transfers from the Government of Canada are estimated at $941 million for 2000–01, to bring total revenues for 2000–01 to an estimated $6.382 billion.

FEDERAL-PROVINCIAL TRANSFERS

We saw in the previous section that transfers to the provincial government from the government of Canada amounted to about 15 percent of provincial government revenue in 2000–01, with the average over the past two decades slightly higher than that. How are these transfer amounts determined?

EQUALIZATION

Equalization is a federal-provincial transfer program enshrined in the Constitution, for the purpose of ensuring that all Canadian provinces have the necessary revenues to provide comparable services to their residents while levying comparable tax rates, even though the province's tax base may be far below the

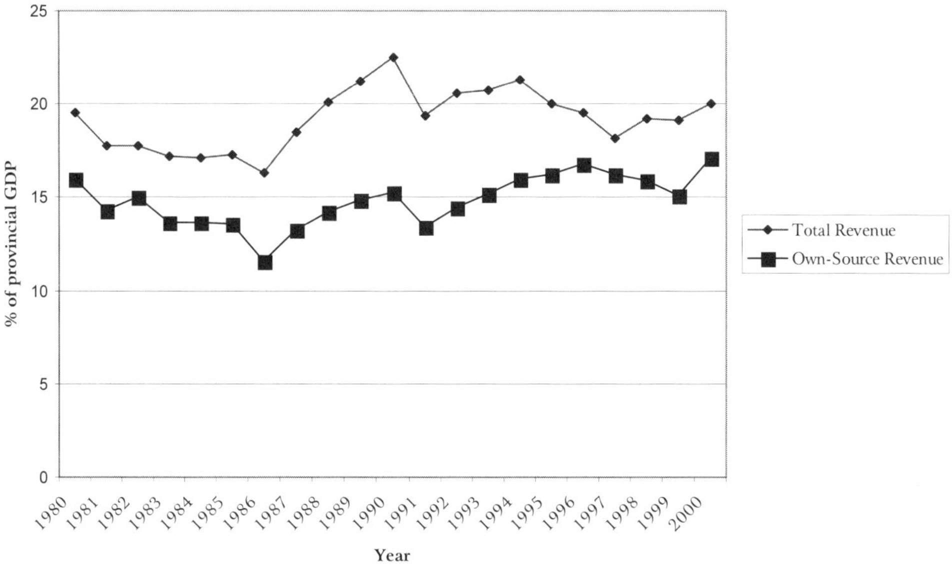

Figure 2. Government of Saskatchewan Total and Own-Source Revenues, 1980–2000.

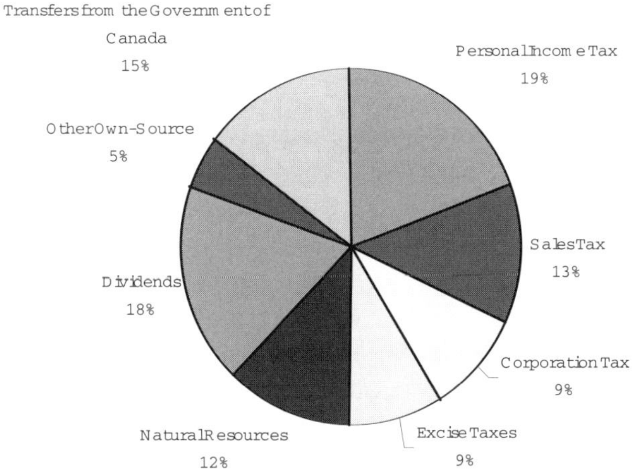

Figure 3. Government of Saskatchewan Sources of Revenue, 2000–01.

Canadian average. The design of the formula matches, roughly, the goal. For each potential source of provincial government revenue (personal income, sales, corporate profits, natural resources, etc.), calculate by how much the province's tax base per person exceeds or falls below the tax base per person in the five provinces of British Columbia, Saskatchewan, Manitoba, Ontario and Quebec.[1] The results are then added for all revenue sources, weighted by the national average tax rates. If this total reveals that the province in question has a lower overall tax base per person than the five-province standard, the province receives an equalization payment such that the sum of 1) the equalization payment, and 2) what the province could have raised on its own had it applied the national average tax rate, is equal to, per person, what the five-province group would have raised by applying the national average tax rates. If it turns out that the province in question has more tax base per person than the five-province standard, it neither receives equalization nor does it pay into the system. At present British Columbia, Alberta and Ontario are the non-recipient, or "have," provinces. Note that the system is not perfect equalization, for two reasons. First, equalization only applies where a province is a recipient, not when it would otherwise be a contributor. Second, it uses a five-province standard for the tax base, rather than all ten. The important province left out of the mix is Alberta; equalization will not bring poor provinces up to the wealth of that resource-rich province.

Saskatchewan has a higher-than-five-province-standard tax base in oil and gas revenues, sale of Crown leases, and, of course, potash. But these are dominated by the fact that Saskatchewan is below the five-province standard in personal income tax base, business tax bases, and property taxes. For the purposes of the 2000–01 budget, equalization is anticipated to be $336 million.

The student of Saskatchewan public finance will want to keep the following points about equalization in mind: 1) a boom in the provincial economy translates into fewer extra dollars in the provincial treasury than you might expect, for as the tax base rises own-source revenues will rise but equalization entitlement will fall; 2) equalization will not compensate a province that chooses to lower its tax rates — the entitlement is based on what the province *could* have earned had it applied national average tax rates, and is not based on what it actually did earn; 3) equalization will not help a province that has particularly high demands on spending, since the formula is entirely based on government revenues, not government expenditures; 4) equalization entitlement will rise as the rest of the country, or at least the other five provinces in the five-province standard, do well — Saskatchewan is equalized up to their level; and, 5) equalization entitlement will fall as other provinces cut their tax rates in areas where Saskatchewan is a "have-not" province, since the national average tax rate is used in the calculation of the entitlement. For example, large cuts in income tax rates in Ontario lead to a fall in Saskatchewan's equalization entitlement.

Canada Health and Social Transfer

The Canada Health and Social Transfer (CHST) is in principle meant to help provinces pay for health care, post-secondary education and welfare, although in practice it comes with virtually no strings attached.[2] It came into being in 1996 when

1. Those who want more detail on the system should consult Robin W. Boadway and Paul A.R. Hobson, *Intergovernmental Fiscal Relations in Canada* (Toronto: Canadian Tax Foundation, 1993), chapter 4.
2. For details and analysis of the CHST see Tracy R. Snoddon, "The Impact of the CHST on Interprovincial Redistribution in Canada," *Canadian Public Policy* 24, no. 1 (March 1998): 49–70.

two previous transfer programs were combined: Established Programs Financing, which was a lump sum ostensibly for health and post-secondary education, and the Canada Assistance Plan, which was a shared-cost arrangement on expenditures on welfare. The 2000–01 budget predicts CHST transfers of $495 million.

Why have lump sum transfers? There are two main reasons. First, in Canada there is an imbalance between the spending responsibilities of provincial governments and the degree to which provinces can effectively raise revenue through provincial taxes. Provinces will have difficulty raising enough revenue on their own because they are to some degree in "tax competition" with each other, especially so with taxes on capital income, because of its high mobility. It is generally thought to be more efficient to have the federal government raise more revenue than it needs for its own programs, and then give a portion of it back to the provinces. Note that since provinces vary widely in their per person contributions to federal revenues, but receive transfer funds back on a more equal per person basis, the CHST is in a sense "super-equalizing," to use Tom Courchene's term.[3]

Second, one could imagine that there are inter-provincial "externalities" — benefits that accrue to province A as a result of expenditure by province B — in the areas of health, post-secondary education, and welfare. When externalities are present, provinces will tend to spend amounts in those areas below the optimum, as they will not take account in their budget-making of the benefits to those residing in other provinces. One way to increase provincial spending in a particular field is to subsidize it. And so, in the 1960s federal provincial transfers in these fields were shared-cost, that is the federal government would pay provinces a portion of the amount provinces chose to spend in those fields. If there are inter-provincial externalities, shared-cost programs make sense; subsidies are a traditional economic solution to the externality problem.

However, a payment to provinces that does not depend on the amount of provincial spending (although there are some demands on provinces: that they abide by the terms of the *Canada Health Act*, that certain non-discriminatory policies apply to welfare, etc.) is not nearly as effective in getting provinces to spend more in these areas. In that sense this transfer program is really about health and social spending in name only.

THE ECONOMICS OF PERSONAL TAXES[4]

In the 1999 budget address the minister of Finance announced that a committee would be struck to examine the personal income tax in Saskatchewan, with an eye to making it more efficient, more equitable, and perhaps to move to a system which applies "made-in-Saskatchewan" tax rates and credits to taxable income, rather than relying on the federal income tax as a guide. The Personal Income Tax Review Committee submitted its *Final Report*[5] in November 1999, and the budget speech of March 2000 adopted the thrust of its recommendations. It is very important to realize that the Review Committee's recommendations reflected

3. Thomas J. Courchene, *Social Canada in the Millennium: Reform Imperatives and Restructuring Principles* (Toronto: C.D. Howe Institute, 1994), 115.

4. Some of this section is drawn from Michael Rushton, "Interprovincial Tax Competition and Tax Reform in Saskatchewan," *Canadian Tax Journal* (2000).

5. Saskatchewan Personal Income Tax Review Committee, *Final Report and Recommendations* (Regina: Department of Finance, 1999).

long-standing concerns in Saskatchewan, and that the March 2000 tax reforms were more than a decade in the making.

In 1985 the Saskatchewan government introduced the *flat tax* as part of the provincial personal income tax. It was levied at a flat rate on net income. This was an important step in Saskatchewan tax history because it represented a departure from the traditional way of levying provincial income taxes, which was to use as a tax base the amount of basic federal tax owing. Using basic federal tax as a tax base carries with it the use of the rate structure of the federal income tax as well as the federal system of deductions and credits.

To illustrate, the form one fills out to determine Saskatchewan income tax for 1999 begins by asking one to take 48 percent of federal tax (which is then followed by various surtaxes and tax credits). But federal tax is found by applying a rate of 17 percent to taxable income up to $29,590; 26 percent to the next amount of taxable income up to $59,180; and 29 percent on any income above that, less all the various federal tax credits. So all of these rates are implicitly adopted into the Saskatchewan income tax.

In the 1980s the federal government allowed Saskatchewan to introduce the flat tax as a temporary measure, but was in general against allowing provinces to completely depart from using the basic federal tax as the tax base.

The flat tax was introduced for two main reasons. First, it would be a revenue source for the province that was not subject to variation as the federal government changed its income tax provisions. When the basic federal tax is a province's tax base, any change in tax rates coming from a federal budget would immediately impact Saskatchewan's tax base, and in turn Saskatchewan's tax revenues.

The second reason for the flat tax was that it lowered the differential in total tax owing between families with one earner and families with two earners and an equivalent total household income. In Saskatchewan, reducing this differential has traditionally been claimed to be "supporting the family."

The obvious question to ask here is which families are being supported and who is bearing the financial burden of the support. It is a difficult issue. The principle that we would expect most Canadians to agree upon is that income taxes should be based on "ability to pay." We would want to tax one-earner and two-earner households with equivalent household income the same if we thought that the two-earner households had equivalent ability to pay and that that was the end of the story. However, the issue is complicated by the fact that the one-earner couple receives the benefit of the stay-at-home spouse's untaxed household labour. One could argue that this benefit *should* be taxed, and so the one-earner couple should pay more. Still, the tough question is "how much more?" A recent study by James Davies and Kenneth Boessenkool[6] uses the technique of "adult equivalence scales" — a way of measuring to what degree two can live as cheaply as one — and finds that horizontal equity in Canada would be enhanced by lowering the tax burden on single-earner couples. But this is still a point of some contention, and Neil Brooks' critique of the increased departure from using the "unadorned individual" as the unit of account in the personal income tax has some resonance in Saskatchewan.[7]

6. Kenneth J. Boessenkool and James B. Davies, "Giving Mom and Dad a Break: Returning Fairness to Families in Canada's Tax and Transfer System," *Commentary* (Toronto: C.D. Howe Institute, 1998).

7. Brooks' prediction that "in the year 2000 and beyond this issue, so far from being a pivotal one, will not be on the tax policy agenda" was evidently not fulfilled: Neil Brooks, "Comment," in Richard M. Bird and Jack M. Mintz (eds.), *Taxation to 2000 and Beyond* (Toronto: Canadian Tax Foundation, 1992), 200.

His influence was evident in the argument made by the Ontario Fair Tax Commission that having the individual as the basis of taxation is necessary to "recognizing and supporting the autonomy of women,"[8] and that the spousal credit, which lowers the tax burden on one-earner couples, "institutionalizes the presumptions of dependency of women on men and discriminates between women who work in the home and women who work in the paid labour market as well as in the home."[9]

In 1988 the Saskatchewan Department of Finance issued a discussion paper on tax reform[10] that is remarkably similar to the Review Committee *Report* of 1999. The 1988 *Dialogue* raises concerns about the problem of high marginal tax rates and their distortionary effects in the economy, the dependence of Saskatchewan government revenues on changes to the federal income tax, and the bias against one-earner couples — all of which inform the 1999 *Report*. The *Dialogue* proposes an income tax that would have the married (or equivalent) tax credit equal to the basic personal credit, which would greatly reduce the tax burden on one-earner couples. It also raises the idea of Saskatchewan setting up its own income tax rate structure that would be applied to taxable income rather than basic federal tax. Finally, it notes that a progressive income tax does not require steeply graduated marginal rate bands, as long as there is a substantial basic personal credit. It was a prescient Tom Courchene and Art Stewart who, in their discussion of the *Dialogue* in 1991, made the prediction that Saskatchewan was "on the inside track in the matter of how the tax collection agreements are likely to evolve ... [and] the tax collection agreements as we know them will soon be history."[11]

The impetus for the 1999 Tax Review Committee was the federal government's decision to allow provinces to apply tax rates to taxable income rather than basic federal tax, so long as the province continued to use a common definition of taxable income. When the federal government said that new systems could be in place on January 1, 2001, Alberta was quick to announce that it would be taking advantage of the opportunity. And in the 1999 budget speech, Saskatchewan formed the Tax Review Committee to examine this issue. In particular the Committee's mandate was to investigate whether moving the personal income tax to be applied to taxable income rather than basic federal tax would improve "fairness in the system, support for the family, simplicity for both the taxfiler and the Government, and competitiveness in attracting jobs and investment to Saskatchewan."

The last point was raised in the context of a fear that Alberta's low tax rates were attracting business investment away from Saskatchewan, as well as Saskatchewan's best and brightest.

The March 2000 Budget presented changes to the personal income tax that were very close to what was recommended by the Tax Review Committee. As recommended there is a move to a tax-on-income, rather than a tax-on-(federal)-tax system, with rate bands exactly as suggested: 11 percent on taxable income up to $35,000; 13 percent on taxable income between $35,000 and $100,000; and 15

8. Ontario Fair Tax Commission, *Fair Taxation in a Changing World: Highlights* (Toronto: University of Toronto Press, 1993), 29.

9. Ibid., 30.

10. Saskatchewan, *A Dialogue on Saskatchewan Income Tax Reform* (Regina: Department of Finance, 1988).

11. Thomas J. Courchene and Arthur E. Stewart, "Provincial Personal Income Taxation and the Future of the Tax Collection Agreements," in M. McMillan (ed.), *Provincial Public Finances Volume 2: Plaudits, Problems, and Prospects* (Toronto: Canadian Tax Foundation, 1991), 293.

percent on taxable income above $100,000. Also as suggested the 11 percent rate will apply to taxable capital gains on qualified farm property and small businesses, the same rate that applies in Alberta; this measure was meant to remove all incentives for those wishing to dispose of such assets to move to Medicine Hat. Finally, the system will be fully indexed to inflation. The tax credits are slightly less generous than the Tax Review Committee recommended: $8,000 for the basic personal credit and the spousal (or equivalent) credit, rather than $8,500; the child credit will be $2,500 rather than $3,000; and the seniors supplement to the age credit will be $1,000 instead of the recommended $1,500. But the important point is the equivalence of the basic credit and the spousal credit, this being the main manifestation of "support for the family" and following on the recommendations presented in the 1988 *Dialogue*.

An important aspect of the Review Committee's recommendations, which took it beyond the initial mandate given in the 1999 budget speech, was the question of the high reliance on personal income taxes relative to the sales tax, especially compared to other provinces (except Alberta, the only province without a provincial sales tax).

Under full implementation of the tax changes it is expected that combined income and sales taxes will fall by about $260 million per year. Over $400 million will be cut from income taxes, but this will be offset by increased sales tax revenues; even had the Review Committee's recommendation of a cut in the sales tax rate to 5 percent been followed, there would still have been an increase in sales tax revenues due to base broadening. There is no scientific guide to the optimal balance between income taxes and sales taxes. Income taxes have the advantage of being capable of being set at increasing marginal rates, and so are able to lend some progressivity to the system. But progressivity comes at a cost: the higher the marginal rates, the more the economy is distorted by the tax system, in terms of decisions regarding work, schooling, savings and investment. This leads to high "deadweight loss" in the tax system; it costs the economy more than a dollar for the government to raise an extra dollar in revenue. In Canada the deadweight loss from raising an extra dollar of income tax revenue has been estimated at over thirty cents; in other words the private economy loses at least $1.30 for every extra $1 the province collects in income tax. Sales taxes have a lower deadweight loss, in part because the rates are lower, and in part because sales taxes do not tax the returns to saving, and so do not have harmful effects on the economy's savings rate. The right balance between sales taxes and income taxes depends on the degree to which one is prepared to let total economic activity in the province fall in order to have some progressivity in tax rates, and on the degree to which one thinks that the personal income tax base is our best measure of "ability to pay." The Review Committee held the belief that Saskatchewan had an over-reliance on income taxes, in that high income tax rates were driving away talented people and business investment, and that a broader sales tax base would not have effects quite as harmful. This is not an issue that will ever be finally resolved; as the economy changes in the future, as other provinces change their tax structures, and as the people of Saskatchewan continue to think about the tax system, there will be further changes to the income tax/sales tax mix.

Changing the sales tax proved to be more controversial than changing the income tax. The Review Committee's recommendation was to greatly broaden the sales tax base and to reduce the rate from 6 percent to 5 percent. Instead, the budget broadened the base, but by much less than was recommended, and the rate remains at 6 percent. The base was expanded to include various services, and used goods over $300 (except autos, which will have sales tax applied to private sales of used autos, with a $3,000 exemption). The exemption for various goods used as inputs in production will continue. The sales tax was not extended to children's clothing, or to home heating and electricity, although it had been recommended. Two sales tax issues attracted the most attention. First, the tax was not extended to restaurant meals as the Committee had recommended, which led to widespread media comment that heavy public lobbying by the restaurant sector, between the time of the release of the Review Committee *Report* and the budget speech, had worked. Second, the sales tax is now to be applied to off-reserve purchases by Status Indians, as recommended by the Committee. This move was accompanied by a promise by the province to move to cease collecting excise taxes on gasoline and tobacco purchases on reserve. The expansion of the sales tax to off-reserve purchases is expected by many to generate a legal challenge.

What is striking to this economist is the salience of the sales tax base, relative to the major changes in the personal income tax, as a public issue. This is evident in the government's reluctance to follow through on all of the Committee's recommendations on expansion of the sales tax base, even at the cost of being left unable to decrease the rate. The changes to the personal income tax, which represent a much greater change to the tax system and to an ordinary individual's tax burden, received much less coverage in the media or in legislative debates. It cannot be denied that the visibility of a tax matters.

SASKATCHEWAN GOVERNMENT EXPENDITURES

Figure 4 shows how the components of operating expenditure (i.e. expenditures not including interest or debt repayment) have shifted since 1980. Adjusted for inflation we see that there has been a steady climb in per person expenditures on health care. We also see a decline in operating expenditures per person on combined non-health spending, the biggest components of which are education (at all levels) and social services. One can also see fairly clearly a "wave" pattern in non-health expenditure, which matches the electoral cycle; the one exception to the wave is 1995, when expenditure control in an effort to balance the budget dominated electoral concerns.

What explains the increases in health care expenditure? There are a number of factors in play.[12] One is simply public demand; health care is always a salient political issue, and shifting public expenditure in the direction of health could be seen partly as a result of satisfying public preferences. The very fact that there is more income per person in 2000 than in 1980 would lead us to expect more expenditure on health care per person, just as there would be more expenditure on all "normal" goods.

A second issue is the rate of inflation in the health sector; note that the deflator used in calculations for Figure 4 is the Consumer Price Index, and the rate of inflation in health has generally been higher than that. One reason is that drug prices have had a high rate of price increase. Also, payments to doctors and nurses are

12. A good summary of factors contributing to rising health care costs is in Joseph P. Newhouse, "Medical Care Costs: How Much Welfare Loss?," *Journal of Economic Perspectives* 6, no. 3 (Summer 1992): 3–21.

going to rise faster than the economy-wide rate of inflation. The reason often cited for this is what economists refer to as "cost disease."[13] Doctors and nurses deal interactively with patients, and there are few things that can be done, or that have been done, that can reduce the amount of time they must spend with their patients. This would be especially true in such areas as long-term care. In this *limited* sense we could say that productivity increases only very slowly in the profession; the stress is on "limited" because of course the *quality* of health care has improved greatly. But the time element has not changed much. Still, salaries for health care workers must keep pace with salaries in the rest of the economy if people are still going to remain willing to enter those professions, and salaries are going to increase with the general rate of productivity growth in the *entire* economy. And so health care is going to become relatively more expensive over time.

If this argument seems hard to follow, think of another example of cost disease where it is most obvious: the performing arts. It will take two workers — one on violin and one on piano — about twenty-two minutes to perform Beethoven's *Sonata No. 6 in A Major*. That is the same amount of time it took in 1802 when Beethoven composed the work. So in one sense there has been no increase in labour productivity in this area for 198 years. Of course, the *quality* of the performances may have increased greatly over that period, given improvements in how musicians are trained and so on. But the *quantity* of labour required remains the same. Still, we could not expect musicians' wages to remain the same as they were in 1802; if their wages do not keep pace with the rest of the economy, no one would want to be a professional musician in the year 2000. And so live performances of music face a cost disease; they become expensive relative to other goods in the economy over time.[14] Note that this is not a pessimistic result. The changes in relative prices are the result of something good happening in the economy; sectors like manufacturing and natural resources and agriculture becoming much more productive over time. But it is a result that asks people to note that relative prices will change in a particular way over time.

Another reason sometimes given for rising health care expenditures has to do with the question of the incentives facing physicians who are paid on a fee-for-service basis and are in the position to tell patients what services it is that they require. One could certainly see how such an incentive problem can lead to a high *level* of health care expenditure, but it is less clear how this situation would lead to a high *rate of increase* in expenditure.[15]

Figure 5 gives the breakdown of operating expenditures in the Saskatchewan budget for 2000–01. We see that over half of Saskatchewan's operating expenditure is not spent directly by the provincial government but is transferred to health districts, schools, universities and colleges, community-based organizations, RCMP services, and so on. Of a total operating expenditure of $5.291 billion in 2000–01, $3.018 billion is transferred to third-party organizations.

Individuals receive transfers of $846 million in the 2000–01 budget (and keep in mind how this translates into per person terms with Saskatchewan's population of one million). The main programs here are the Saskatchewan Assistance Plan (i.e. welfare), housing support, agricultural support, the prescription drug plan, student aid, family and youth services, community living, and treaty land entitlements.

The rest of the budget is composed of the operating costs of executive government — salaries, operating expenditures, and pensions and benefits — at $1.132 billion, and capital expenditures at $295 million.

SASKATCHEWAN GOVERNMENT DEBT

We will begin this section with some economic analysis of provincial government debt in general, and then turn to the position of the Saskatchewan government in the year 2000.

Governments borrow because they want to raise the revenue necessary to pay for their current expenditures over a period of time rather than completely during the present time period. There are three things to understand at the outset.

First, it is the ratio of government debt to the province's GDP (the total amount of output produced by the province in a year) that is relevant, not simply the level of debt itself. This is because GDP is the measure of the province's ability to finance the interest charges on its debt. Individual debt provides an analogy: we could not say whether an individual with a debt of $25,000 has a debt burden that is high or low unless we knew something about her income, for example whether she was employed at minimum wage or was earning over $100,000 per year.

Second, any expenditure by the government must be paid for through the raising of revenues. The revenues can be raised now or they can be raised later, but in government expenditure as in household expenditure there are no free lunches.[16] The government borrows by issuing bonds. When the bonds mature the government must repay the bond's owner the principal. The government cannot escape the burden of paying for its expenditures by simply issuing new bonds whenever old ones become due. This would lead to a perpetual government debt. But the interest that government would have to pay on that debt, even if it never paid off the principal, would, in present discounted value, equal the value of the debt itself.

Third, whether the debt that a province issues is held by its own residents or by non-residents does not matter. The notion that if a resident holds some of the government debt it is not really a burden on the province, since "we owe it to ourselves," neglects the fact that there is an opportunity cost to the funds the resident has put into provincial bonds: the funds could have been invested elsewhere. For example, suppose a Saskatchewanian named Howard is considering whether to buy a Saskatchewan government bond worth $100 or an Ontario Hydro bond also worth $100. If the Saskatchewan government could sell the $100 bond to Howard, that would mean $100 less that the Saskatchewan government would have to raise in the bond markets on Bay Street. If Howard opts for the Ontario Hydro bond, and so the Saskatchewan government sells its $100 bond to a Toronto trader instead of to Howard, then the province as a whole has just increased both its assets (Howard's ownership of the Ontario Hydro bond) and its liabilities (Toronto trader's ownership of the Saskatchewan government bond) by $100. So there is no change in the provincial economy's net worth. On the other hand, if Howard buys the Saskatchewan government bond, and so the province has no transactions with either Ontario Hydro or Bay Street traders, again there is no change in the provincial economy's net worth. So the proportion of Saskatchewan government debt held by residents is not a very interesting number.

When should a government borrow to finance its expenditures? There are considerations of efficiency and equity.

Regarding efficiency, recall the earlier discussion of the deadweight losses from taxes: it costs the economy more than $1 to raise government revenues of $1, because of the distortionary effects of taxation. Deadweight losses tend to rise exponentially with tax rates. That is the reason why economists generally argue that

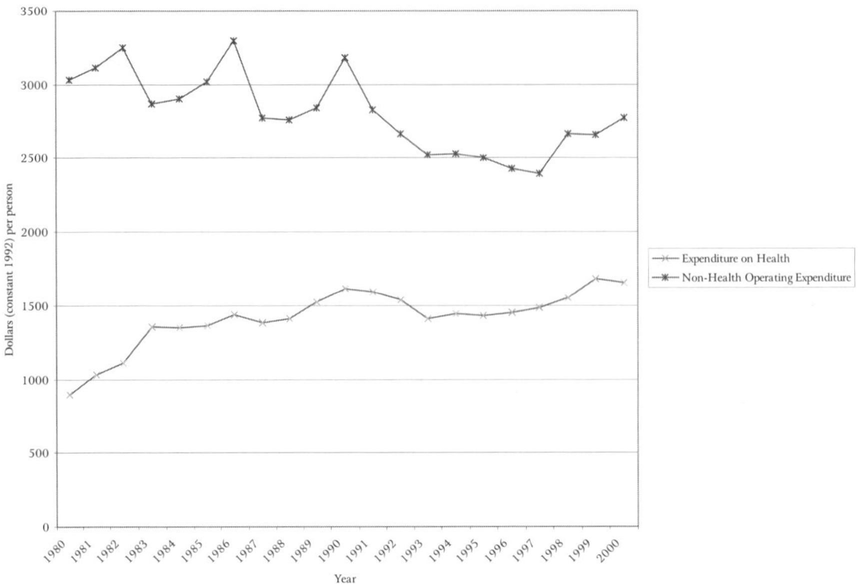

Figure 4. Government of Saskatchewan Operating Expenditure, 1980–2000.

taxes should be applied to a wide range of goods and services at a low tax rate rather than to a limited number of goods and services but at very high tax rates: the overall deadweight loss will be lower. What is true across goods and services is also true over time: there will be less deadweight loss from taxes if the government applies a constant income tax rate of 20 percent rather than 10 percent in some years and 30 percent in other years. When we apply this result to government debt policy, it would suggest that managing the government's borrowing so that tax rates will be relatively constant over time rather than variable is a good idea. In practice this would mean that allowing the government deficit to rise during economic downturns, and to fall into a budget surplus during economic good times, is good policy. It would also mean that if the government faces a one-time expenditure of great magnitude, borrowing — and so spreading the tax burden over a number of years — is a good idea. Note that this would be the case whether the one-time expenditure is for a capital project or for a current emergency.

Turning to equity considerations, the issue arises as to which generation, in fairness, should pay for current expenditures. One way to answer would be to first ask "who benefits?" If the expenditure is on capital, then future generations will benefit and so could be asked to bear some of the cost. If the expenditure is on current goods and services, then one might suggest that it is only fair that the current generation of taxpayers pay for it. There are a number of complications. First, exactly how will we define "generation"? Second, we would want to account for the fact that in all likelihood future generations will be richer than the current one, and so will have higher ability to pay, which may be a justification for passing some of the burden forward. Third, defining "capital" expenditure is not that easily done. Some component of health and education spending — on services, not just buildings and

13. See William J. Baumol, "Containing Medical Costs: Why Price Controls Won't Work," *The Public Interest* 93 (Fall 1988): 37–53.

14. The seminal work in the field of cost disease is William J. Baumol and William G. Bowen, *Performing Arts: The Economic Dilemma* (New York: Twentieth Century Fund, 1966).

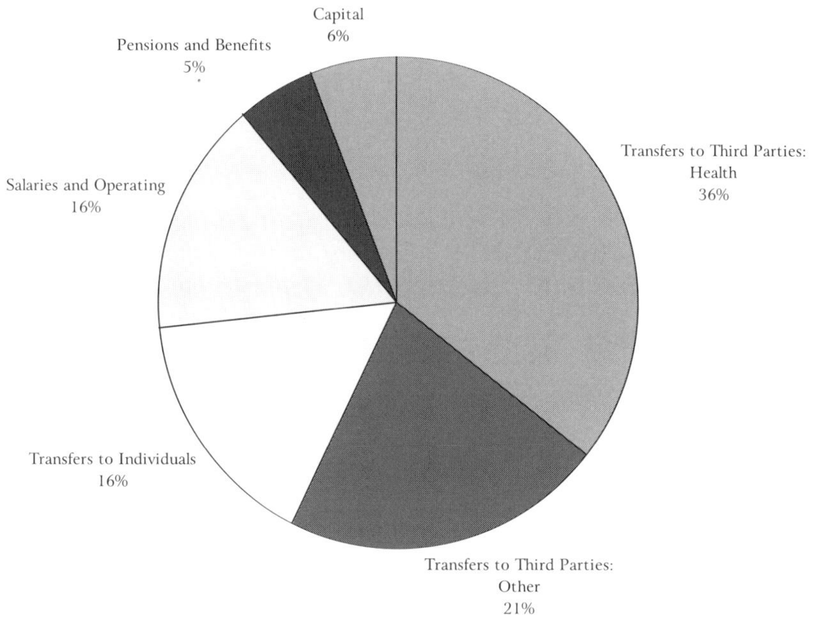

Figure 5: Government of Saskatchewan Operating Expenditures, 2000–01.

equipment — will benefit future generations, and so could be called "capital." But there is no agreed-upon method for determining the degree to which current expenditures benefit future generations.

Turning now to Saskatchewan, the total debt of the provincial government's General Revenue Fund, forecast for the year 2000, is $11.255 billion. Of this, $3.989 billion is Crown corporation debt and $7.911 billion is general government debt for a gross debt of $11.900 billion. There is guaranteed debt by Saskatchewan at $355 million, and the government has $999 million in sinking funds, which must be subtracted from the gross debt to obtain total debt. Total debt to GDP was estimated at 35.7 percent in 2000. Budget forecasts are that total debt will fall by $162 million by 2003–04, and with forecast economic growth that would leave a total debt to GDP ratio of 31.2 percent. The total debt to GDP ratio in Saskatchewan peaked in 1993 at just over 70 percent, and has steadily declined since.

Saskatchewan's debt to GDP ratio in the early 1990s was unsustainable in the sense that fears were arising about the government's ability to honour its debt. A vicious circle can develop where a lack of confidence in the provincial economy causes economic activity to decline, which further worsens the province's ability to meet its financial obligations.

But the province is now in a position where government debt is no longer in the headlines, and must ask itself where to go from here. The 2000 budget speech introduced a new approach to budget deficits and stabilization. Legislation was promised that would create a Fiscal Stabilization Fund. Previously, the provincial government had relied on the profits of the Liquor and Gaming Authority to stabilize its finances. In the future, all profits from the Liquor and Gaming Authority will be paid into the

15. We cannot do justice here to the complexities of the issue of supplier-induced demand. See Robert G. Evans, *Strained Mercy: The Economics of Canadian Health Care* (Toronto: Butterworths, 1984).

General Revenue Fund. The new Fiscal Stabilization Fund will be available to offset any temporary revenue declines or exceptional expenditure demands. The long-term target is that the balance of the Fiscal Stabilization Fund will be 5 percent of the prior year's revenues. It actually begins with a balance higher than that, with a starting balance of $405 million from the 2000–01 budget, which is about 7 percent of the forecast revenue for 1999–2000.

With the Fiscal Stabilization Fund as a cushion, the province is opting for a slow rate of debt repayment from 2000 to 2004, resulting from modest forecast budget surpluses, and the rate at which the debt to GDP ratio has been declining will level off.

Although the province's *Balanced Budget Act* requires balanced budgets over a four-year cycle, the political fact is that there is very little public support for even a modest budget deficit in a single year. The debt load that accumulated through the 1980s and early 1990s led to sharp expenditure reductions and tax increases that Saskatchewan people never want to see again. That the provincial debt must ultimately be paid for, and that high deficits do not bring prosperity, are now part of the conventional wisdom in the province. Saskatchewan has enjoyed budget stability since the mid-1990s, and we would not expect any government to want to tamper with that stability any time soon.

16. In many parts of Saskatchewan one would say instead that there are no free dinners.

The White and the Black Horse Race: Saskatchewan Health Reform in the 1990s

Duane Adams

> *"When we began Medicare, we pointed out that it would be in two phases. The first phase would be to remove the financial barrier between those giving the service and those receiving it. The second phase would be to reorganize and revamp the whole delivery system — and of course, that's the big item. That's the thing we haven't done yet."*
>
> Tommy Douglas from the 1982 film, *Folks Call Me Tommy*

And this is what the Saskatchewan Health Reform of the 1990s was all about.

The Saskatchewan health system reform, begun in December 1991 and remaining incomplete at the end of the decade, has been at times as challenging and traumatic as the introduction of Medicare in 1962. At its inception the minister of Health privately speculated that the vastness of the conceived undertaking was going to take more than a generation to complete. This foresight is turning out to be accurate. It is therefore premature to judge the ultimate value to Saskatchewan citizens of this seminal social reform. Nor for all its controversy is there evidence to justify setting aside the first decade of health reform as a social experiment gone astray. Indeed quite the opposite conclusion is warranted.

The Saskatchewan health reform, initially known as Wellness, was structured in two stages: a complete reorganization of the governance machinery and delivery capacities of the health system, to be followed by the reorganization and renewal of the primary care health services which would be offered through these new delivery structures. The governance restructuring has been completed within the decade. The structure now awaits the cues and support to begin the final stage of health reform — the renewal of the primary care health services. The majority of promised benefits to the people will come from this long-awaited service delivery renewal.

As often has been the case historically, while Saskatchewan may have been a little ahead of the times in articulating its health renewal vision, the vision was not capricious or inappropriate. All of Canada has since followed in the same direction, as is noted in the communiqué of the First Ministers' Meeting on Health in which they state that they all agree that "improvements to primary health care are crucial to the renewal of health services" and that the "First Ministers will continue to make primary health care reform a high priority."[1] While on the national scene this

1. Communiqué of the First Ministers' Meeting on Health, Ottawa, September 11, 2000.

declaration has caused not a ripple, back in Saskatchewan elements of the reform remain highly controversial and divisive.

Tracking the evolution of the health reform policies and initiatives of the 1990s, one can see moments of real public policy brilliance and political courage. But one can also witness some limits of political endurance under the pressure of prolonged public unrest. At this point in history, this author questions whether there was a widespread comprehension of the motives and potential public benefits of the Wellness reform by the provincial government. And by implication, one then questions whether the reform was adequately explained to constituents as a consequence. On the other hand, the reasons for and implications of governmental spending cuts and restraints in the early 1990s were well articulated, perhaps to the detriment of the system changes that the Wellness reform advanced for different reasons.

For the implementers of the Wellness reform, most days throughout the decade were a period where one had to have faith in the goals of the reform, hang on to one's hat, and live through the day with a bit of good humour. It was not a period in which to relax, be complacent, or to think one could fully understand what was going on everywhere in the health system. Only when the goals became blurred for lack of reinforcement midway through the decade, did the faith of some begin to waiver.

The purpose of this chapter is to chronicle the objectives of the Saskatchewan health system reform, the reasons and logic for it, to annotate the major reform policies and activities of the period, and to provide some appraisal of the value of the reform effort at the end of the decade. To date, there is no other written record of this period of health policy activity in Saskatchewan. Furthermore, the heavy reliance on electronic technology in developing policy options and implementing decisions has meant that there is only a very small written record of these activities available. As deputy minister of Health, the author of this chapter was closely involved in the health reform from its inception until mid-1997. He has drawn a great deal of material for this chapter from his personal knowledge and notes of the experience, confirmed with other key players of the period and archival records where they are available. Later researchers will need to draw heavily on oral history to obtain the facts. In the year 2001, the reasoning behind some of the earlier decisions is being sought. It is for this reason that more explanation is provided in this chapter than might normally be expected in a summary script.

THE CHANGING HEALTH SERVICE LANDSCAPE IN THE 1990S

By the beginning of the 1990s, pressures had become overwhelming to modernize the health system in Canada, its governance structures, and its medical and management performance. Also it had become imperative after a decade of the highest cost increases in history to bring the system's fiscal demands under control so that the system could be financially sustainable in the future. The only question that seemed outstanding was, what would trigger the reforms and where?

Many health Commissions,[2] advisory groups, independent researchers and

2. For example, see Alberta, *The Rainbow Report: Our Vision for Health* (Edmonton: Premier's Commission on Future Health Care for Albertans, 1989); British Columbia, *Closer to Home: The Report of the British Columbia Health Care Programs on Health Care and Costs* (Victoria: Crown Publications, 1991); Nova Scotia, *The Report of the Nova Scotia Royal Commission on Health Care: Towards a New Strategy* (Halifax: Royal Commission on Health Care, 1989); Ontario, *Deciding the Future of Our Health Care: An Overview for Areas for Public Discussion* (Toronto: Queen's Printer, 1989); Saskatchewan, *Future Directions for Health Care in Saskatchewan* (Regina: Saskatchewan Commission on Directions in Health Care, 1990). For a complete list see the final *Report of the National Forum on Health*.

government officials had begun to conclude that the present health system was inordinately expensive, and population health status was not improving as a result of investing more into existing programs. The federal government continued to reduce its fiscal contribution to the provincial health schemes (through the federal Established Program Financing (EPF) transfer formula) and it was feared that the insured health services might be lost if they were not placed on an affordable footing by governments. Private health expenditures for non-insured services were increasing proportional to public expenditures, and some expenditures were moving abruptly from the public to the private purse. Although concerns at the beginning of the decade were primarily financial, it was not long before issues of accessibility to health services and the quality of care arose.

As for the health system, it has always been a captive of the "medical" model of health care as opposed to its being a reflection of the "population health" model of health service. Emerging medical evidence indicated that the balance of emphasis in the health system had to be moved away from institutional services and more towards community-based service alternatives with enhanced attention on preventative health measures, coupled with expanded individual and community responsibility for personal health. Targeting new health investments to high-risk groups such as children, Aboriginal people, and seniors was advocated to supplement the "universal" health programs of the past. The concept of "evidenced based medicine" was gaining ground among practitioners and health decision makers, suggesting many medical procedures in the health system were of dubious value. Intense pressures were being placed on the health system to be more responsive, more publicly accountable, and more inclusive of consumers in health decision making.

While hospitals, long-term care programs and physician services remained the most expensive services in the health system, drug services and an extended range of community-based and preventive services such as home care were being added to the roster of services of a modern health program (as had occurred in Saskatchewan in the 1970s). Meanwhile, government health insurance support tightened up and restraints were placed on institutional capacity and costs.[3] Challenges to a single tiered health system increased in Canada and new ways of charging the public for some of the health care costs were advocated in certain provinces.

In Saskatchewan, the New Democratic Party came to power in October 1991 and immediately faced a crippling public debt and an unsustainable public expenditure pattern. Because health expenditures consumed one-third of the total provincial budget and generally rose faster than other public sector expenditures, the Saskatchewan Health budget contributed to at least one-third of the province's fiscal problem and potentially also to its solution. Concurrently, public expectations for more and better public services were high.

The Saskatchewan demographic trends presented daunting challenges for the provincial government. The trends were known in 1991 and were confirmed again

3. Cost constraints put serious administrative and fiscal pressures on institutions and service delivery. This led to an increase in challenges to a single-tiered health system. New forms of charging the public for some of the health care costs were being advocated. And, as government's insurance support tightened up, and restraints were put on institutional size and costs, more costs for health care were shifted to the private and personal sector. Over the past two decades costs paid through the private sector rose from 25 percent to 28 percent, prompting some observers to conclude that the system is slowly being privatized (*Striking a Balance Working Group Synthesis Report, 1997*: http://wwwnfh.hc-sc.gc.ca/publicat/finvol2/balance/three.htm7).

by the 1996 Canadian Census that Saskatchewan was fast becoming demographically dominated by an older white population on one hand, and a young Aboriginal population on the other. The young, newly educated population was emigrating to other provinces, contributing to a proportional shrinkage of the income- and tax-generating population.

The growth in numbers of the very young and the very old (the highest users of health services) puts an immense strain on the income and tax-generating population to pay for the required health, social and education services in a society. Unlike most other provinces, Saskatchewan could not expect to grow out of this predicament, as its overall population growth was essentially flat. The cost of servicing these two groups of people was growing at a faster rate than the available public revenues to the health system. This trend was expected to continue at an increasing rate. Further, the migration of population from rural to urban centres, a trend that accelerated throughout the decade, posed additional pressures on the health system. The large provincial investment in fixed capital health infrastructure in many rural areas of the province was now too large and also inappropriately located and programmed to meet the future needs of the potential user populations.

When assessing where the resources existed to address the new needs of the health system, few, if any, new financial resources were going to be available from the province in the foreseeable future. And of course the existing resources were largely tied up in the present health infrastructure and were not easily available for reallocation.

There were more than 400 separate, independent boards running fragments of the Saskatchewan health system. There was little co-ordination among them, but many jealousies and a lot of unhelpful competition. Each health institution and program was protecting itself, its own money and personnel, and its own community economic interests. No one was looking out for the interests of the whole person, family or community. And, from the point of view of the 400 institutions, there was no incentive or reward for taking a more integrative, co-operative, holistic approach to their business. It was virtually impossible to redirect resources from an existing institution into new community-based initiatives or social programs that would prevent the need for a treatment service in the first place. In essence, the system was hostage to the powerful health delivery stakeholders and local economic interests.

Three additional facts were relevant in setting the direction of Saskatchewan's health reform. First, for most population health needs, community-based services are generally more cost-effective, more appropriate, and usually more desirable than institutionalized services. Medical evidence shows that quality of life is better outside of institutions. Hospitals are inherently unhealthy locations. To limit the spread of disease and sustain a person's independence, hospitals should be used for specialized diagnostic, short-term intensive and acute purposes that cannot be met in other settings.

Second, community services are more flexible and generally more mobile and portable (unlike institutional services). Moreover, people's needs often cannot be met by one narrowly defined health service, but rather by a combination of services over a period of time as their needs change. There was, and still is, a need to blend existing resources and programs into a new recipe to deliver a more holistic, tailored and responsive service for individuals and families. This was virtually impossible to do in the pre-1990s health delivery system. It requires the use of additional types of health workers in a primary care environment and the remixing of resources to support the alternative services and personnel.

Third, providing non-acute services through a hospital setting is the most expensive way of doing so. For instance, the Health Services Utilization and Research Commission (HSURC) reported that in 1991–92, 48 percent to 65 percent of adult medical hospital days, and 26 percent to 48 percent of pediatric days in Saskatchewan hospitals, were used for non-acute care.[4] This type of practice places enormous utilization pressures on a hospital, which only can be met by investing more and more resources into the hospital settings. Solutions to the over-utilization and inappropriate utilization of hospitals, along with controls on rapidly rising hospital costs, are to be found in an array of alternate community and home-based programs, which coincidentally are often more beneficial for the patient or client.

In Saskatchewan in October1991, the incoming new minister of Health, Louise Simard, knew of these pressures. As Opposition health critic, she had travelled the province for two years to hear the public's views as a watchdog on the previous government's appointed "Saskatchewan Commission on New Directions for Health Care." Ms. Simard had been particularly impressed with the concepts of the "determinants of health" theory[5] of societal health, with the challenges of "evidence based medicine," with the performance of community health workers, with the call for more democracy in the direction of the system, and with the evidence of inefficiencies and dysfunctional rigidities in the traditional health services. This prior knowledge and these inclinations of the incoming minister conditioned rather quickly the direction and speed of change in Saskatchewan's policy.

On January 13, 1992, Simard and her deputy minister were asked to attend a meeting with Premier Romanow in Saskatoon that he had agreed to hold at the request of the Chairpersons of the three Saskatoon hospitals and the Saskatoon Health Authority (a body that possessed a mandate to rationalize hospital services in Saskatoon). The chairpersons had come to tell the premier that they did not feel much health reform progress could be made in that city if all the hospital boards remained in place with their existing mandates. Following the meeting the premier asked the minister if she agreed with the assessment, which she did. The decision was taken at that point to consolidate the governance responsibilities of the public hospitals (but not the privately owned St. Paul's Hospital) and the Saskatoon Health Authority into a single health service corporation in Saskatoon. This pattern of corporate consolidation was immediately established for the three hospitals and the Wascana Rehabilitation Centre in Regina as well. And so began the structural consolidation features of the Saskatchewan health reform.

Also in January 1992, to research and bring together the most contemporary thinking on health service governance and programming, the minister established the "Wellness Project" and selected a small number of people (eventually seven people of whom two had a social services background) to form a quiet study group. Reflecting the nonconformist nature of the unit, it was known as the "skunkworks"

4. Health Services Utilization and Research Commission, *Barriers to Community Care*, Summary Report, No. 3 (Saskatoon: HSURC, 1994), 1.

5. The "determinants of health" theory was first comprehensively articulated in the 1986 Health and Welfare Canada report, *Achieving Health for All: A Framework for Health Promotion*. This theory expands the definition of what factors influence health by including the relevant additional factors of housing, employment, education and the environment. The concept includes empowered health consumers and health professionals, and a new generation of health services.

and was located apart from the Health Department. The *Saskatchewan Vision for Health, 1992* document reports that "Meetings were held across the province to discuss health reform. During these discussions, the wellness approach was confirmed as the best overall framework within which to identify and address reforms to the health system."[6] The group was given slightly more than two months to submit ideas to the minister. With difficulty, this was achieved and the ideas formed the basis of the public vision document for the Wellness reform.

THE INAUGURAL INTENT OF THE HEALTH REFORM

From the outset, the Saskatchewan health reform was conceived to be about the quality of life of Saskatchewan people. Its conception was not initially or essentially about saving money as some critics later charged. The reform was baptized "Wellness" and its vision statement proclaimed, "Wellness refers to our physical, mental and spiritual well-being. It means getting healthy and staying healthy Wellness means improving our quality of life."[7] The approach chosen to reach the improved quality of life goal was through a major reform and reorganization of primary care health services, which itself required a major restructuring of the governance and delivery machinery of the health system before progress could be made.

Contemporary primary care health practice expects that a health system will reconcile itself with the "determinants of health" concepts and adopt a holistic approach to preventive services, diagnosis and service prescription. The well-being of an individual is dependent upon one's physical, mental, emotional and spiritual state, as well as one's home, community and work environment. Therefore, all these factors need to be the concern of primary health service providers. Since no one professional person can have all the necessary knowledge and skill to assess and address all these potential factors, a team of professionals is needed and is preferably located on a site together.

In a general sense, the primary care reform was to provide assistance, education and support to citizens to remain healthy individually, in their family and community lives, in their work settings, and in their society, thereby improving the quality of life for themselves and those around them. This Wellness vision was an attempt to move the context of health beyond the "treatment and care of the sick" to one of the "sustenance of a healthy society." This Wellness vision is the essence of the "determinants of health" theory of a healthy society which has been gaining ground world-wide.

In this model, health providers are challenged to empower individuals through education, consultation and enhanced co-ordination and integration of service with the capability to protect their own well-being. To achieve this, the primary health services delivery model encourages, if not insists on the view that community involvement in health services decision making is essential.

Within the health "care" programs, the reform also was designed to provide a co-ordinated system of interdisciplinary assessment, coupled with a professionally supervised and co-ordinated system of patient placement and movement throughout the health system. To facilitate this service integration for the patient, the structural changes to the governance and management system of all health programs would be reconstructed so that all services would fall under one authority

6. Saskatchewan Health, *A Saskatchewan Vision for Health: A Framework for Change* (August 1992), 10.
7. Ibid., 11.

and management regime. In such an integrated system, the whole spectrum of potential services from home, to community, to nursing home, to hospital could be considered and matched for the most appropriate service requirements for a patient and his/her family. The traditional health system could not do this.

Thus, the initial objectives of the health service reform were: 1) to reorganize the primary health care delivery system and introduce into it the concepts of the Wellness model of programming; and 2) to consolidate the diagnostic, treatment, rehabilitation and continuing care health services into an integrated, managed care system to provide a seamless array of unique, specialized and fully co-ordinated health and assisted-living services, accessed mainly through the primary care health system.

In addition, the pre-reform structure of the health care system was not financially sustainable, nor did it foster a health service delivery environment that could support the Wellness vision of service. Both to provide a foundation for the new service delivery goals and to create a financially sustainable structure for treatment services, the traditional health system had to be integrated throughout. This would allow for the resource and service flexibility that the Wellness model demanded and the health system as a whole would require on the basis of efficiency and effectiveness criteria.

In August 1992, the provincial cabinet established several key principles to guide the reform: increasing community involvement in the health system; emphasizing disease and accident prevention, healthy lifestyles and population health; improving the balance between institutional services and home- or community-based care programs, to provide the right service at the right time in the right place — as close to home as possible; co-ordinating and integrating health services for a more responsive, efficient and client-centred system; and ensuring a financially sustainable publicly funded health system.

At the point when the principles of health reform (the Wellness model) were announced by the government and enunciated by the minister of health, it was known to Saskatchewan Health and to the health sector that additional public money was going to be very difficult to find in order to sustain the existing health services or enhance the system with the addition of new primary care services. It was not known to the sector, however, that the province was verging on bankruptcy and that the troubled provincial finances were about to emerge as full-scale crises for the government. Therefore, while the health sector was not aware of the magnitude of the provincial financial exigency, it was not unenlightened of the fiscal trouble ahead either. Yet when health reform was inaugurated in August 1992, the health sector was not unduly pessimistic or cynical about the stated objectives of the Wellness reform. In fact, some health stakeholders were very excited about the opportunities the new health goals and objectives offered the system and its workers.

The principles of the health reform were not at all a mere rhetorical statement of momentary political value. There is an inherent logic and interdependence to the Saskatchewan health reform principles, which is as valid today as it was in 1992. To relieve the utilization and cost pressure on hospitals, more community service alternatives needed to be provided, but there was no new provincial money to start the work of creating service alternatives. Resources to instigate the new programs had to be found within the health system where the majority of public resources were lodged: the hospitals, nursing homes, the Medicare physician payment system, and the provincial drug plan.

Because of the lack of home-based health programs and an appropriate patient assessment system, the institutional system was congested with inappropriate utilization from bottom to top. That is, many nursing home and small hospital beds were occupied by people who should have been serviced by home care. Consequently, people who required nursing home care could not get into nursing homes and were held unnecessarily in acute hospital beds, straining the capacity of hospitals. The hospitals, with patients coming through the front doors, could only argue for more capacity and more resources to look after all the people in this hospital modality. The forecast of being able to handle the patient volumes in this way was impossible to justify or finance — then or in the future.

It was widely known that outdated provincial legislation, policy and funding practices made it virtually impossible for the health system, even voluntarily, to move towards integrated governance arrangements. (That was one major reason why the Saskatoon Hospital Board chairs told the premier not to expect much progress in health reform given the existing hospital corporate structure.) Furthermore, at the local level, existing budget and management structures, along with the territorial behaviour of the traditional health administrations and professional groups, were making it difficult to integrate health programs and services such as home-care, community health, rehabilitation programs, mental health, public health, hospital and nursing home services. This lack of service co-ordination meant that service delivery was fragmented. There were gaps in service existing alongside much duplication of service; and it was difficult to consider the needs of the whole person.

There was ample evidence to suggest that the delivery of health care needed to be improved or risk the inability to serve the public in the future. Building the community service options would allow decongestion of the system from top to bottom, meanwhile providing more appropriate care to people all along the continuum of service.

The integration of health services administration and delivery created new opportunities to develop a more appropriate range of health services for all people at a sustainable cost. Integration is a service delivery concept whereby the governance, planning, decision making and delivery of several types of public services are brought together under the same governance, administrative and delivery structure. Integration offers enormous opportunities to blend the roles of health service providers, mix the resource allocation to support these providers, treat the client as a whole person, break down the territorial barriers in health and social systems, and offer help to individuals and communities in an effective way. It also may eliminate the incentive for sub-sectors of the health system to sustain spending in low priority programs and perhaps conceal opportunities for redirecting public resources to address more important public needs.

In addition, it was also believed that cost efficiencies could more likely be found at a sub-provincial level in places that a central bureaucracy could not penetrate or affect. Finding and using these efficiencies could soften the impacts of the provincial cost constraint policies. (For example, by 1993 it was known that the hospital system had perhaps $100 million or more in accumulated reserves that could be tapped to soften the impact of health system changes in a transition, although the provincial health department had no access to these reserve accounts.)

Public participation in health system decision making was intended to provide a genuine foundation for "public ownership" of the health system, the services provided and the responsiveness of these services to individuals, families and communities. Public participation was not only wanted by Saskatchewan citizens but it was also essential to the success of the Wellness approach to health services. Moreover, it was also an attempt to counter the pressure of the medical model of health care. New forces and ideas were needed to encourage health boards to develop programs and community solutions that would affect population health. Initially an overreaction to this intent occurred to the near exclusion of physicians in the decision-making process by some district health boards. In the latter half of the decade, physicians seem to have re-established a better balance of their influence in the health system.

There was also a pressing need to sensitize the delivery of treatment services in order to become more helpful, responsive and acceptable to patients and families. The minister of Health hoped through the application of the principle of public participation that more women, Aboriginal people, more community-based workers and volunteers would contribute their knowledge and experience to the programs of the health system. No presumption was made that public participation would affect fiscal management of the health system a great deal, but rather that public participation would affect resource allocation decisions within the system. It was also expected that more public participation would bring a new sensitivity to health care administration and its relationships with health workers (a relationship that was historically fraught with tension).

Community-based health solutions need the contribution of a diverse, interdisciplinary mix of talents and skills. The pre-1990 health system was working in narrow silos, which were defined and regulated by health professional associations and by years of tradition and bureaucratic rules. Moreover, the public glamour and the resource hungriness of Medicare and hospitalization had placed the less highly profiled community-based services in a highly defensive position. As the last in line to receive new annual resource consideration (either provincially or locally), the community-based health options perpetually needed to muster all their influence simply to maintain a status quo position in the health service resourcing equation.

While initially the Saskatchewan Health Care Association suggested that the new integrated health system should be piggy-backed onto the larger hospitals in the province, this option was rejected by the minister of Health since it was considered very likely that these hospitals and their special interest supporters would have redirected resources away from the vital community services in order to prop up their acute hospital services in a tight money situation. Moreover, one objective of the Wellness model was to reduce the reliance on institutions in pursuit of improved responses to population health needs. Focusing the leadership for health reform on the hospital system (and its reliance on the municipal government system) would surely have defeated the objective of creating new community-based health service alternatives, in part to relieve the pressure on the hospitals themselves, and in part to offer services to people who needed health assistance but not hospitalization.

It was known that in some cases, the expansion of the community-based services (particularly home care services) threatened the survival of certain small hospital institutions because both the small hospitals and the home care programs were competing with each other to service the same patients in small communities and thereby keep their funding allocations up. Without knowing it, some citizens were being retained for unnecessary days in smaller hospitals to help justify the hospital's existence.

Fourteen hundred community health workers were direct employees of the provincial health department. These workers needed to be assimilated with other community workers at the local level. But the health department could not devolve these workers until a new sub-provincial health corporate structure was available to absorb the employees. Similarly for hospitals and nursing homes, the minister and some of her senior cabinet colleagues concluded that the level of self-interest and protectionism of these programs was such that little change could be expected from within their traditional governance and management model.

In order to offer even a possibility that all the health workers (community as well as institutional workers) could work in teams and also look for ways to expand their functions (or devolve some of them to other workers), the old management patterns and any unnecessary walls of professional protection had to be removed. One aspect of achieving this was to break up the traditional bureaucratic/supervisory power structures that governed the workers. Another aspect was to reconsider the regulated professional roles through the workers' professional associations.

All of this led to the conclusion that regions or districts were needed for programmatic and operational reasons, not ideological or political reasons. Regionalization had to be adopted not so much because it was considered an ideal governance structure, but because there was no other organizational vehicle that could integrate the full range of health (and hopefully, in time, social) services in order to provide a coherent response to the anticipated new Wellness Centres, eliminate internal protectionism in the old system, and thereby alter the power balance and program directions of the health system. In fact, choosing this option would create a new and sometimes tense political dynamic in provincial politics by devolving some of the provincial government's power to these new district boards and eventually to their elected members.

Nevertheless, the organizational vehicle chosen to implement the principles and objectives of the Saskatchewan health reform was a regionalized (district) system of health governance, a fully integrated health governance and service delivery model, governed by a new "public" health corporation in each district, with partially elected and partially appointed boards that were jointly responsible to their own electorates and also to the provincial minister of Health.

Discussion and decision making about this governance were largely completed by summer1992 when the Wellness health reform was announced, but it was not formulated in law until the *Health Districts Act* was passed in May 1993 by the legislature. Prior to passage of the legislation, four interim districts had been established: Saskatoon, Regina, Prince Albert, and Lloydminster.

STRUCTURAL REFORM ACTIVITIES

Reformulating the health system's corporate and governance structures was a huge and complex work. To achieve it necessitated some flexibility or compromise at the time, which later critics have alleged to have been unwise (such as the absolute number of districts in Saskatchewan). Nevertheless, a whole new health corporate infrastructure was created in approximately six months and for the most part has subsequently worked well after it developed some experience.

HEALTH SERVICES UTILILZATION AND RESEARCH COMMISSSION

It was known that the traditional "information" on which health decisions were made was often inadequate, speculative and emotive. Thus, a body independent from government called the Health Services Utilization and Research Commission (HSURC) was created to provide research findings to the government, the health professional associations, the health institutions and the public on the health system's performance and on ways to improve it. It was mandated to undertake scientifically based analysis of the appropriateness of health care services and facility utilization in Saskatchewan.[8]

Because of its competence and credibility, the Commission has become a major force in promoting positive change in the Saskatchewan health sector. It turns out that the public trusts and accepts hard evidence and scientific findings if the findings are communicated in understandable language by a credible professional person and not from a political source. Hard evidence bolstering difficult decisions was a powerful tool in dealing with the emotionally based arguments of interest groups.

THE PROVINCIAL HEALTH COUNCIL

The Provincial Health Council was created to advise government and the private sector on affordable "healthy" public policies that could improve population health through inter-sectoral policy and programming action. The utility for society of having an institution like the Provincial Health Council with a mandate to pursue intersectoral healthy public policies was in advance of its time and has not properly been appreciated. Many of the ultimate recommendations required new public and private investments to initiate the policies. Other recommendations required significant changes to the way government and its departments did business and set priorities. At the time when the Council reported, the government was struggling to bring its massive deficit under control and to reshape the size and commitments of the public sector. New public investments to advance the intersectoral public policies were not seen as feasible by the government. In addition, it became apparent at that time that neither the government nor the bureaucracy would redirect its attention and energy away from cost containment and cost reduction initiatives in order to meet the challenges advanced by the healthy public policy advocates.

Having completed its work of setting futuristic public policy goals, the Provincial Health Council was retired by the government at the end of its short mandate to leave the implementation of its work to others. The unconsidered consequence of ending the work of the Provincial Health Council was that Wellness advocacy efforts of 1,000 or more citizens which the Council had mobilized and who were dedicated to the advancement of Wellness ideals were lost.

HEALTH DISTRICTS

Initially four new interim health districts were created to advance the first ready districts. Then the *Health Districts Act* was passed by the legislature to appropriately empower these first districts and to enable the creation of all other health districts and health corporations throughout the province. The purpose of these amalgamations was to integrate and to co-ordinate all health service delivery functions at a sub-provincial level within a defined geographical territory. On the one hand,

8. The mandate and composition of the Commission, along with its publications is found on the internet at: www.hsurc.sk.ca

this permitted the decentralization of certain provincial health service delivery functions, and on the other hand it allowed the amalgamation and centralization to the districts of a variety of locally and municipally owned and governed hospitals and other health programs. However, the Act did not provide health districts with any taxation power.

Local initiative brought about the creation of 33 geographically unified health service districts for the delivery of virtually all health services in each territory. (The far northern Saskatchewan territory was given an additional two to three years to organize its three health districts to enable the northern communities to work through their special cultural and geographic problems of health service delivery.) When a corporate structure was in place to govern these districts, then approximately 400 existing health corporations were amalgamated into the 30 new health district corporations (three in the north were created later) along with all their separate administrative staff and program delivery structures and functions. Duplication in administrative staffing was removed at this time. The health department estimated that the overall cost saving of these amalgamations was about 25 percent of the top administrative costs of the health system. A curious side effect of these amalgamations was that when most district administrative officers were put in one physical location, although the amalgamations actually reduced the total number of this staff, the size of the district administration looked larger, causing worker, union, political and public criticism of "enlarged administration," a perception that could not be dispelled!

Small Hospital Conversions

The acute care component of 51 small hospitals (publicly thought to be 52) was closed out. These facilities were converted into health centres and began their reprogramming into the Wellness model of health. In half the cases, the small hospitals were also operating chronic care beds. This capacity was not touched.

Before health reform began, Saskatchewan had 132 hospitals and approximately 174 nursing homes for a population of one million people. Many of the hospitals were very small, staffed as hospitals but operating as nursing homes. At the outset of health reform, 51 of these small hospitals were converted to health centres and their programming redirected to community-sensitive health initiatives such as chronic care monitoring and evaluation, nutrition counselling, first responders services, itinerant physician services, mental health and addictions services, and public health awareness communication. Later three other large urban hospitals were amalgamated into other existing hospital facilities and closed, and several other small rural hospital facilities are currently being converted or reprogrammed by District Boards.

The decision about which small hospitals to convert was based solely on evidence provided by hospitals to the Department of Health. Small hospitals that claimed to serve on average eight or less acutely ill patients per day for the two previous years, and where the population in those communities had access to emergency service in approximately 50 minutes driving time, were selected for conversion. If the Department of Health had chosen the criteria of ten or less acutely ill patients per day on average, an additional 20 small hospitals would have been converted. Until the health service reconfiguration of the first conversions took effect, it was not possible to estimate the service impacts of more conversions. Therefore the smaller of the two targets was chosen.

The conversion of these small hospitals was a watershed in the health reform. The drama of the event was seen provincially and nationally as symbolic of the massive reform that Saskatchewan once again had initiated. Tackling this volatile issue was seen by the press and by the health professional associations as a reflection of the determination and political courage the provincial government was prepared to expend to address its fiscal problems. After this event was announced, there were no doubters hidden in the weeds waiting for health reform initiatives to blow over!

While the transition from a small community hospital to a health centre was highly contentious at the time, the scientific evaluation of health outcomes as a result of the action is encouraging. In its report, *Assessing the Impact of the 1993 Acute Care Funding Cuts to Rural Saskatchewan Hospitals*, the Health Services Utilization and Research Commission said: "Cutting the acute care funding to 52 rural Saskatchewan hospitals has not adversely affected the health status of residents in these communities."[9] In fact, the shift from acute care facilities to Wellness centres has already been shown to improve the health of the population. HSURC also found that

> Overall mortality rates declined, with the largest decreases in communities whose hospitals lost their acute funding. Death rates from heart attacks and motor vehicle accidents — life threatening events known to be sensitive to emergency service response times and capacity — declined after the 1993 acute care funding cuts to a greater extent in affected communities than in communities that retained their small hospitals.[10]

This evidence lends support to the message that the primary objective of health care reform is improved service, not cutting costs at the expense of people's health.

HEALTH CENTRES

The opportunity to begin the development of Wellness health centres was provided by the conversion of the small acute hospitals in 1993. The community clinic experience in Saskatchewan (beginning in the 1960s) offered some valuable insights into the programming possibilities for new health centres. Also Canadian experience had been gained in Quebec, Ontario and elsewhere in the world as to how the programming in these centres might contribute to population health and the care needs of rural communities.

While the rural health centres were not an ideal model of what was intended as a Wellness centre, they did provide one model of what was possible in smaller rural communities. The ideal principal role of the health centres was to draw together the complete range of public and non-profit health (and certain social services), integrate and focus these services for application to a particular person or community, and then assist citizens sensitively to use this service roster in an efficient and appropriate manner.

Health Centres were planned to be the principal point of contact with the health system. In this model, an advanced-trained nurse would be the point of entry to the health and social system. Doctors would be a part of the health centre team of professional workers, but they would be used for their unique medical knowledge and skill. Other professional workers would be available to offer non-medical and paramedical advice and assistance such as educational, social service, justice, housing,

9. Health Services Utilization and Research Commission, *Assessing the Impact of the 1993 Acute Care Funding Cuts to Rural Saskatchewan Hospitals*, Summary Report, Number 13 (Saskatchewan, 1999), 9.
10. Ibid.

etc. More program emphasis would be placed on the prevention of disease and the avoidance or amelioration of personal dysfunction, on education, on community and family support and assistance systems.

Hospital diagnostic, institutional treatment and care services would be continued as referred specialized services, accessed initially through the primary care health centres.

Payment systems for doctors and any other health workers paid on a fee-for-service system would be adjusted to provide incentives to assist citizens to remain healthy, as opposed to compensating physicians and others on the basis of specific treatment interventions. Changing the physician payment system for primary care physicians, while not resisted in principle by the Saskatchewan Medical Association, was not accomplished in this decade. Some pilot projects have been established to demonstrate the advantages and challenges of the payment and service delivery system.

These first health centres evolved to meet their own community needs with a core of emergency services, observation and assessment health services, palliative and convalescent care, laboratory, x-ray and community services.

The major reconfiguring and enhancement of primary care services throughout the province is the next and final stage of health reform.

Devolution of Saskatchewan Health Community-Based Staff

Saskatchewan Health then devolved its direct patient service delivery functions to the districts to achieve further integration of these services with other district-based community services. This devolution involved moving 1,400 health service workers from the provincial payroll and having them rehired in the district corporations where they were providing service. It principally included the program fields of mental health, public health, and addictions services.

Labour Force Reorganization

The collective bargaining arrangements were reorganized and rationalized so as to allow workers of similar professional training to be represented by the same union, and to rationalize the collective bargaining agreements within the same union and the same district so as to assist the workers and simplify collective bargaining both for management and labour.

Working through the difficulties for labour, both organized and unorganized, and the individual job adjustments that had to be made for some health workers was an especially complicated problem, one that was seriously underestimated at first. The previous structural arrangement of the health system had resulted in 25 collective agreements covering 81 health sector employers, approximately 30,000 employees represented by 382 local unions in 538 bargaining units. Representation by trade union was based on place of employment, not occupation. Furthermore, there was a significant number of unorganized health work units. All this led to diversity amongst contracts for the same type of workers. For instance, a nurse represented by one union could earn a different wage or benefits package than a nurse represented by another union. Transferring from one institution to another stirred stormy debate amongst employees and employers, such as how or if to recognize seniority that was gained in a similar position but in a different institution in the same district.

From the outset of reform, the provincial government attempted to work collaboratively with the health labour movement and not hastily strong-arm labour into new policy positions or relationships that the movement had not thoroughly considered. The government had encouraged the unions to work voluntarily with the department and the districts to maintain a positive and participatory labour relations environment. Collaboration was needed in order to conclude transfer/merger agreements within the districts to provide a framework for the movement and job assistance of staff impacted by the restructuring of health services. Inter- and intra-union transfer agreements were negotiated, but they were not universal in their application across district employers, affiliate employers and trade unions.

This particular work was initially left to the unions to sort out among themselves, but it proved too difficult to achieve without a neutral facilitator. Eventually the four major health unions requested the appointment of an independent commissioner to assess the problems and recommend solutions to the jurisdictional issues province-wide. Consequently the process took a long time to complete and caused more stress for workers, unions and management than was necessary.

In the end, the Saskatchewan Association of Health-Care Organizations (SAHO) maintained the right to bargain collectively on behalf of all health public sector employers in their organization. As a result of the amalgamation of bargaining units, the number of collective agreements was reduced from 25 to 9. Furthermore, each union was able to serve its members regardless of the site location within the same district because the district Health Corporation was the sole public employer in that district. Employees were reassured that if they transferred or were reassigned to a different health program within the same district, they did not forfeit their accumulated seniority, benefits or wage. This labour legislation and readjustment has contributed to the enhancement of mobility and flexibility of labour, and consequently to a more cost-effective and efficient delivery of health services.

While labour reform in the health industry was achieved under stressful circumstances, it was accomplished on the basis of collaboration and consultation. All parties to these agreements (health workers, the health district corporations and the health unions) have acknowledged periodically that they have benefited in the end because the labour reform has simplified collective bargaining, has protected the job security and seniority of workers in the same district, and has reduced the anxiety of labour force adjustment. If the number of districts is reduced in the future, a similar process with labour will have to be repeated. It is an activity that deserves very close attention by those who might engage in future health reform.

HEALTH FINANCING AND RESOURCE EQUITY

In retrospect, provincial health cost containment policies (in the context of the government's desperate financial situation) were a major incentive to advance certain health reform activities, particularly structural changes and measures that positively impacted the efficiency of the health system. The provincial fiscal crises also solidified the government's political stamina to see through controversial health system changes, determination it might not otherwise have had if the changes had not led to greater fiscal stability. In this sense, the fiscal pressure may be seen as helpful, although supremely unpleasant, in advancing the health reform agenda.

At the beginning of the health reform, the Department of Health and the government had concluded that the global amount of public funding made available for health services was adequate to provide the services needed in Saskatchewan.

The difficulty to be faced by the reform was that the resources were largely tied up in the wrong places. They were being consumed by the inappropriately utilized health infrastructure, in locations where the people had moved away or where the programs did not fit the needs of the people.

Of critical importance to the inter-district resource equity policy that the reform was attempting to drive into the health system was changing the method of funding the health system. The decision to globalize most health funding from the provincial government into a population-needs based formula was vital in order to offer the maximum possible financial flexibility to districts to reallocate resources to the priority health needs in their districts. The needs-based funding system supports a health outcomes approach to district program planning. It shifts attention away from the level of activity of health care providers, to the actual health of the population. This approach was intended to improve the equity among districts in their ability to address health needs. That is, health dollars were to be allocated where the needs were greatest. It encourages the provision of the appropriate services at the right time. It discourages the unnecessary institutionalization of citizens.

To complicate this financing transition on top of "flat" line or reduced district budgets, three additional financial movements needed to be made: money had to be moved to follow citizens for their services; money had to be reallocated from historically overfunded to underfunded districts; and money could move only from institutional cost centres to community-based cost centres.

First, one of the fundamental principles of Saskatchewan's health care system is the freedom to choose where and from whom to receive health services. Consequently funding to districts recognizes the choices made by consumers of health care services and allocates funding to those districts in which the service is actually provided, not where the citizen is resident. Therefore, while per capita funding initially flowed to the home district of a citizen, it eventually was moved to the district where the citizen received his/her services. This generally meant a flow or money from rural to urban centres.

Second, to achieve financial equity across the districts, the financial objective was to allocate from the health department to districts an equal per capita amount of money, having adjusted the per capita for certain measures of health need and demographics. Unavoidably, this caused some districts to face higher levels of financial stress because when the budgets of the 400 previous health corporations were merged to form the 30 new district budgets, about one-third of the districts initially possessed budgets higher than their fair share by up to 40 percent; one-third were lower than their fair share; and about one-third were on target. Although it was accepted that achieving real financial equity across the districts would take several years of inter-district financial adjustment, trying to embed some financial equity in the system was painful for all. But aside from the difficulty of reallocating resources away from districts, at the same time the reallocation could not be done quickly enough to meet the needs of the underfunded districts.

Third, the new funding arrangement created a one-way financial valve, which allowed funds to be moved from institutional programs to community-based programs, but not the reverse. This feature was designed to protect funding for community programs relative to the fiscally hungry acute care institutions.

An intriguing observation about this financial scenario is that the majority of the underfunded districts adopted health reform measures more quickly than other districts and were also the quickest to put in place new community-based programs to reach out to their populations in need. (Perhaps this had to do with the fact that the underfunded districts had a less-inflated physical infrastructure to sustain.) Of course, when some new money was reallocated to these underfunded districts within the equity provisions of the new funding formula, they were in a very good position to use it well. The Prince Albert District was a notable example of this phenomenon.

By 1996, the provincial government concluded the pace of change in the health system (especially health facility conversions) was too quick, and the level of uncertainty for the public to be too intense. The provincial government decided to infuse more money into the health system to give some relief to the local impacts. This action has proven to be more contentious than was anticipated. While there was a factual basis for reaching this "rate of change" conclusion, the result was that by relieving the financial pressure to change, those districts that were resistant to change remained so. Their unsustainable financial practices simply continued each year. Meanwhile other districts that had faced and dealt with the consequences of change earlier were offended that the resisters were continually bought out of their deficits — at a financial penalty to the entire health system, to the provincial government, and to other public programs.

In recent years the funding formula has been distorted to an unrecognizable state from its inception by adopting a line-by-line financing approach — mainly to fix certain problems that had become major political problems for the government. While this financing approach is used elsewhere in Canada, it is not helping to create a stable district financial ledger or a sustainable health system in Saskatchewan. Sometimes tight money is better than a small bit of loose change!

As the decade closed, health costs were once again rising to levels which are claimed to be unsustainable in the mid- and long term. While the federal government has infused $23.4 billion dollars over five years into the Canada-wide health system beginning in the 2000–01 fiscal year, the rate of the escalation of this money in its later years is below what is expected in wage rate settlements.[11] Given that wages and related personnel remuneration costs consume more than 70 percent of the health budget, this financial forecast is extremely worrisome. More financial struggling is predictable.

It is important to note that in spite of losing scores of millions of dollars in health and social transfer payments from the federal government in this decade, Saskatchewan did not reduce spending on health.[12] Rather it replaced the entire amount of the federal reductions while redirecting many millions of dollars into community-based programs. Health premiums and user fees have not been imposed to pay for health services. The provincial government held to this financial policy while at the same time holding total spending for health services approximately constant for five years. The importance of this fact is that government's fiscal policies

11. After allowing for certain money to be spent directly by Ottawa for health care, the remainder available for transfer payment increases to the provinces results in less than $4 billion annually. This amount alone was reduced by the federal government in 1996 with the introduction of its CHST transfer payment. Vastly more had been reduced in the expected federal cash transfer payment to provinces over the period 1982–94. The nature and amounts of these federal fiscal reductions for health and social purposes are examined in Duane Adams (ed.), *Federalism, Democracy and Health Policy in Canada* (Kingston: Institute of Intergovernmental Relations, Queen's University, 2001).

12. Canadian Institute for Health Information, *National Health Expenditure Database: National Health Expenditure Trends, 1975–1997, 1999.*

were, in gross terms, a restraint on cost escalation, not a reduction of the gross funding base of the health system. Where individual programs or districts experienced actual base funding reductions, those reductions reflected the effects of reallocating financial resources internally within the system. In other provinces, the base budgets of their health departments were slashed in absolute terms.

Public Accountability

Greater and more transparent public accountability for health service policy and delivery was instigated. A serious attempt was also made to rebalance the public accountability of the provincial minister of Health with the accountability of the District Health Boards whereby the minister of Health would be accountable for province-wide standards and the overall performance of the system, but each district would be accountable for its own operational and patient-specific activities, decisions and behaviours. Achieving this balance of accountability would have allowed a greater degree of health debate at the provincial level, and would have encouraged far less political interference from the provincial level in the affairs of districts. This dual accountability of the boards was written into the *Health Districts Act*.

Over the course of the decade, this rebalancing of accountability was not successfully achieved because the public and the media would not hold to this division of accountability. That is, if a complainant was not satisfied with a district's decision it would appeal to the minister of Health and expect an intervention. To reject this call would make the provincial minister appear insensitive (a politically unacceptable attitude), or intervening with the district was seen as "micro management" of a district's affairs (an inflammatory action in health system governance.)

The provincial auditor states that if the Department of Health would identify its system-wide standards and measurements for the health system and population health, then the provincial minister could be held accountable for these alone. It would then be much easier for the provincial minister to deflect local decisions and events back to the communities involved. This level of measurement and new balance of accountability has not yet been achieved in the reformed health system.

Evidence-based Decision Making

For the first time in health administration history, an attempt was made to de-politicize health decision making at the provincial level by using an "evidence-based" approach for the most important policy issues. This approach to decision making and to public explanation of policy was assisted by the work of the HSURC. While it was commonly known within the health system and to some extent throughout the provincial political sector that this de-politicization effort was being made, its adoption was highly dependent on the attitude of successive health ministers and the support that they could muster in the cabinet to sustain this approach. It worked well in the early years of the reform and seems to have been a very credible and effective tool to diffuse contentious situations with communities. That is, the public could accept facts when they would not accept opinions, especially political opinions. Nevertheless this important approach to decision making was lost in due course when the NDP government had to respond in kind to its political opposition.

Health Providers Human Resource Committee

In 1995, the Health Providers Human Resource Committee was established with the mandate to consider and advise on issues related to the education, regulation and utilization of health providers in Saskatchewan. The committee considered the implications for health providers of the reforms and the need to secure their support for the Wellness model. The committee sought the input of 166 groups and individuals representing health professions, educators, unions, employers and consumer groups. Based on this advice, the committee presented recommendations in the area of education, regulation and utilization of providers.

The chief purpose of this committee was to ensure the safe delegation of service functions down and among the hierarchical chain of the health professions to enhance each professional occupation in order to make better use of the time and skills of professionals throughout the chain. One intended effect of this was to release physicians' time for activities that required their particular training, and to replace the time with that of advanced trained nurses. (To some extent, this will offer some relief to the rural doctor shortage.) It has taken until spring 2001 before appropriate enabling legislation to provide a legal foundation for this advancement could be achieved.

THE SASKATCHEWAN HEALTH INFORMATION NETWORK

A major overhaul of the management and client-based information systems of the health sector was begun. It initiated the transfiguration of all health data systems into a patient-centred, relational database, that was a fully-integrated patient and management record system, using the most modern data processing and transmission technology available. The new system was intended for the use of patients, health workers, and the administration of the health system itself. It is now known as the SHIN system (the Saskatchewan Health Information Network system).

TELE-MEDICINE

The planning and development of the use of tele-medicine was begun in order to test its viability to improve health services in rural and remote Saskatchewan communities.

THE WHITE HORSE/BLACK HORSE PHENOMENON

One major ambiguity that has had to be faced throughout most of Saskatchewan's health reform is public confusion about the motive for the reform. Was the main purpose of the Wellness reform altruistic, based on virtuous and sound principles, and dedicated to a renewed health system and an improved quality of life for Saskatchewan people? Or, was the Wellness reform a cover story to distract public attention from the severity of impacts of drastic health cost-cutting and governmental spending restraints? For the people implementing the reform activities both inside and outside government, it was never entirely certain which motive was dominant deep inside the government. And for the press, public and reform critics, a similar schizophrenia existed. The ambiguity led to serious strategic communication difficulties with the public because the same action or policy by the government could be explained as contributing to the Wellness goals; or alternately, it could be explained as contributing to the government's cost restraint policy. Furthermore, while cost restraint was a necessary and legitimate goal for the government in the early and mid-1990s, that goal alone could not sustain public support indefinitely. From the outset, the "quality of life" (or Wellness) goals had set the Saskatchewan health reform apart from other provincial health reform ventures in

Canada that followed later in the decade. These reform policies in other Canadian provinces were focused almost exclusively on cost efficiency and cost cutting. Over time, these efficiency objectives alone could sustain little public support in the other provinces, just as was the experience in Saskatchewan.

Since the Saskatchewan Department of Health was charged with implementing the Wellness reforms as well as the government's health cost restraint policies, the department needed to be very clear for itself as well as for its clients which "horse" it was riding when a policy was explained and implemented. This led to the shorthand terminology to explain the two contrasting motives of health reform as the "white horse and black horse" phenomenon. The white horse represented Wellness and all the high hopes for that initiative; the black horse represented cost cutting and the negativity that this policy generated.

If one follows the history of the white horse and black horse, it can be seen that the two policies emerged quite distinctly in time and then from about 1995 onwards each had its own moment of dominance, while frequently scraping sides with the other. As was explained earlier in this text, the Wellness reform moved ahead quite positively through 1992 and the early months of 1993. During this period, the Department of Health and the health sector were aware of a very tight — but not catastrophic — money situation. With the report of the Gass commission on the provincial fiscal situation in 1992,[13] the crises in provincial public finances became clearer. The government began to explore its options for severe reduction in public spending. These decisions were announced in its spring budget of 1993. The most dramatic of its decisions affecting the health system was the conversion of 51 small, acute care hospitals to health centres. And this is also where the confusion over the motive for the health reform began. Conversion of these small hospitals served both the goals of the Wellness reform and also those of the fiscal restraint policy of government.

It was estimated by the health department that the decision to convert these small hospitals would save the province about $50 million after an equivalent amount was reinvested in these communities through the health centres to begin the Wellness programming. Given the provincial fiscal environment at that time, this potential saving could not be ignored. Moreover, health experts had advised for many years that a better, more positive health outcome could be expected in these small communities if the health investment were used for more community services and less for inpatient services. Simultaneously, the minister of Health argued that the new district boards should be established before any changes were forced on the health system. The minister did not win this debate with her colleagues.

The conversions proceeded before the new district boards were established, which placed the new boards in the position of great public controversy from the moment of their birth. Simultaneously these new district boards had also to amalgamate all the public health corporations in their territory, establish their own corporate structures, hire their management staff, deal with the placement of people from the converted small hospitals, address the labour unrest that was emerging, and deal more generally with a flat or reduced overall budget line from the province. In these circumstances, it is no surprise that the inaugural goals of the Wellness reform were submerged for a period of time

13. Saskatchewan Finance, *Report of the Saskatchewan Financial Management Review Commission*, Don Gass, Chairperson (February 1992), 189.

As the new health governance system settled in and as the districts were able to undertake their own community health needs assessments, much was generated in the way of new community programming. Yet these important achievements could never compete well for media attention with occasional sad stories of mishandled cases found somewhere in the health system. As the decade has run its course, the inability of districts to receive recognition for their many new initiatives has contributed to a distorted public knowledge of what the health system now can offer. This is most unfortunate. The good work of districts is largely unknown.

But the reality of the matter is that the principal promise and service goal of the reform — a restructured and renewed primary care system — was not addressed in any significant way during the decade. While the provincial government did approve on two occasions the direction to proceed with primary care reform and to offer physicians a new payment system to be a part of this renewed health system, after discussion with the Saskatchewan Medical Association, the Department of Health concluded that the provincial government did not have enough available resources to sustain the up-front transitional costs of this primary care reform. Modest demonstration projects were initiated successfully, but a critical mass of projects province-wide could not be undertaken. This awaits another day.

Meanwhile, throughout the later part of the 1990s, politicians themselves lost sight of the colour of the horse on which they were riding. Attempts were made by provincial politicians to put health reform to bed (to say it was over), to put distance between themselves and the concept of Wellness (by dropping the word from all their communications), and to pour more money into the health system. By the end of the decade, appeals to the provincial government were being heard from the Saskatchewan Association of Health Organizations, and others, to recommit to the Wellness goals for a renewed health system to provide the inspiration and direction for the next decade of change. To some extent this lost vision explains the appointment in the summer 2000 by the provincial government of the Fyke Commission on Medicare.[14] But curiously the public call for a reconfirmation of the vision for health renewal is what the First Ministers of Canada provided in their September 2000 accord.

OTHER OBSERVATIONS ON THE IMPLEMENTATION EXPERIENCE

LEADERSHIP CHALLENGES

The Saskatchewan health reform presented major challenges in finding and preparing people to take leadership roles in the movement. The adoption of the Wellness model, coupled with the structural integration, required totally new ideas and skills in the governance of the system, the administration of programs, the conceptualization and management of service programs, the use of technology information systems, communication with the public and media, and working intimately with communities, health workers, unions and health professional associations. No

14. The terms of reference for the Provincial Commission on Medicare, August 22, 2000, are found at http://www.medicare-commission.com/pcmtermsofref.htmhttp://www.medicare-commission.com/pcmtermsofref.htm. In summary the mandate of the Commission is to identify key challenges in reforming and improving Medicare; to recommend an action plan for delivering health services through a model which is sustainable and embodies the core values of Medicare; and to investigate and make recommendations to ensure the long-term stewardship of a publicly funded, publicly administered Medicare system.

longer could one rely on knowing one narrow part of the health system, managing behind closed doors, communicating policies without explanation or justification, relying on policy and procedural manuals which had been developed over 30 years.

To take community ownership of the health system, the government required leaders who could focus on the complex needs of individuals, families and communities, and work outside the strictures of the medical model and the emotionally captivating demands of health institutions. There were few established health leaders who possessed these qualifications. Several strategies were adopted to capture new leadership.

People who expressed an interest in playing a leading role in advancing health changes were given some, but not enough, training. People with training and experience working in communities, as opposed to people who worked in institutions and bureaucratic hierarchies, were sought out. During the process of community consultations and town hall meetings, community opinion leaders were identified. Then these initial leaders sought out others within their communities. A conscious effort was made to draw more women into the reform network, as they generally possess a more comprehensive understanding of family health needs and care. As well, some high-profile leadership from the health professions was acquired, particularly from the related nursing professions. A very large local planning and development network was created, involving hundreds of people, in a community health development process.

The formal educational system was of no value in providing or training new leadership for the health reform. With the exception of a few outstanding professionals in the educational system, it was not even a major influence in conditioning the directions for the Wellness Model. The formal educational system takes so long to change that it could not keep up to the rapid rate of change in the health system. Nor has it done so at the end of this decade of reform. This was a great disappointment because the educational system should be a natural ally for the promotion of change and a major contributor to the preparation for change. It simply could not adjust itself rapidly in order to adapt to the changes required by this major societal reform.

Health District Numbers and Boundaries

Voluntary local health planning committees were established initially. These planning committees, in consultation with consumers and providers of health services and community leaders, as well as with the Department of Health, were asked to identify and gain the support of the communities to be involved in their respective districts in order to propose boundaries for the health district, recommend the processes and strategies for the establishment of an Interim Board, identify issues that should be addressed by the health district board, and begin the process of a health needs assessment in their districts.

Realizing that some communities might not have the appropriate skills to conduct all of these formulating tasks, assistance in the form of advice and technical support was offered through the Department of Health in all of these stages. Each team was comprehensive in itself so that it could provide support and assistance to deal with most issues initially encountered by the local committees and planning groups.

Setting local boundaries had been problematic throughout Saskatchewan history. The minister therefore concluded that imposing boundaries for districts, established by the department, was probably going to produce locally insensitive service patterns and perhaps coercive intercommunity relationships. The potential consequences of such peremptory action were unwanted.

The minister asked communities to join together voluntarily to create health districts with a population of not less than 12,000 people in a land mass that was contiguous. While this population base was small, on the basis of previous experience with Saskatchewan Home Care districts it was known that this population base could support a small but good home care program. It could also support a small system of community health centres. Therefore it was concluded that the 12,000 person population base was the minimum viable small district.

The district boundaries established voluntarily reflect trading patterns of the communities and to some extent an intercommunity power-balancing choice. It would appear that individual communities chose to align themselves where they felt they could achieve the most favourable treatment within the new district — mostly from an economic perspective, rather than a health service perspective. The alliances most certainly reflect a rural worry about cities subsuming and overlooking their interests. On a map, the district boundaries do not look "neat," and they may not reflect efficient health delivery patterns, but they were effective in terms of community relationships as well as in commencing major social reform.

With regard to the number of districts created, the governmental consideration was always a trade-off between the geographic size of the district and the number of people who lived within the territory. The minister wanted the district to be small enough that the people in it could identify with their district and the decisions of the health board. At the same time the population count was important in order to assure that there was minimum service delivery viability in the territory. No one knew what minimum population count would assure service delivery viability because the integrated service delivery concept had never been tested in a rural setting (although primary care models had been developed on a small population base elsewhere in the world).

The Department of Health quietly hoped that less than 20 districts would be proposed to provide the balance between efficient administration and democratic participation. But the local negotiation of district boundaries appears to have been affected by the government's decisions concerning cost constraint, and the eventual decision to convert 51 small hospitals into health centres. This precipitated a rural wariness of urban districts' motives concerning future resource allocations. The result was the configuration of 33 health districts (three in the far north).

By the end of the decade, with the subsequent migration of population from rural to urban areas, a few districts have fallen below the population criterion of 12,000 people. Other districts have found it very difficult to adopt a developmental mode of operation because their resource base is so small that it limits the possibilities for internal resource redirection into new health ventures.

In the late 1990s, a debate has emerged about the size and number of districts. It is really a consideration of the districts' service efficiency versus their democratic effectiveness. While the outcome of this debate is not yet known, no scientific evaluation has been undertaken of the costs and benefits of the efficiency/democracy equation.[15] Since it is known that governance of the Canadian health system is not noticeably democratic, the objective evaluation of the Saskatchewan experience with elected/appointed health boards will undoubtedly be awaited nationally with a great deal of interest.

Ownership of Health Facilities

Ownership of health facilities, public or private, was not an issue in the Saskatchewan health reform. What was critical was whether privately owned facilities functioned within the public health system law, regulation, program and financing rules of the publicly controlled system. In Saskatchewan there were a large number of privately owned, not-for-profit nursing homes and at least thirteen privately owned hospitals. Most of the private owners were religious organzations.

Regarding hospitals, only Catholic religious organizations were involved. Where duplicated hospital services existed in the same city, the religious organizations adjusted their service mission to a large extent so as to serve the long-term ill people through nursing homes. All of the church-sponsored hospitals agreed to serve under service contracts with district boards, while retaining their own boards and CEOs. Their service contracts are renewable annually.

Regarding the private not-for-profit nursing homes, the same conditions applied. They operate under service contracts with the district boards, with the same terms and conditions for patients as in a public facility. The transitional problem for nursing homes was that some citizens had originally contributed to the construction of the nursing homes, with the understanding they would have preferential admission to these homes in later years of their lives. The health reform required that under a publicly financed nursing home scheme, preferential admission would not be allowed. Rather admission to all nursing homes, private or public, would be governed by the priority of need of a citizen determined through a professionally conducted medical and social assessment. Thereafter the placement officers would do whatever was possible to situate the citizen in a socially and culturally compatible home.

The debate in Canada about public and private health facilities is really about public versus "for-profit" privately owned facilities, and whether the rules of admission and payment for the citizen are the same in the two different types of ownership arrangement. In Saskatchewan this was not a significant issue because there were only two private "for profit" nursing home corporations running six "for profit" private nursing home facilities. These facilities functioned within the public rules and standards of the health system and received public financing in the same way as publicly owned nursing homes. In this situation, facilities had to make any profit from their ventures through "efficiencies" of operation.

Elected/Appointed Boards

The first district health boards were appointed by the minister of Health to quickly establish the new governing structure. The Department of Health advocated an elected district health board system to empower and substantiate the concept of "community ownership" of the district health system, its service directions, programs and practices. While this rationale may have affected some part of the collective political mind, the eventual decision to choose boards through a part-elected, part-appointed process was difficult and centred on three options: 1) an elected system where the board members were accountable to the public for their decisions, not to the provincial government, and they therefore could reject provincial political

15. Dr. Ken Rasmussen, University of Regina, has undertaken some research on Saskatchewan Health Districts and democracy. He thoughts are contained, for example, in "Institutional Change and Policy Outcomes: District Health Boards in Saskatchewan" (paper presented at the Annual Meeting of the Canadian Political Science Association, St. Catharine's, Ontario, June 2–4, 1996).

influence even when it is in the public interest; 2) an appointed system, which might be unfairly accused of partisanship but might indeed be more responsive to provincial government influence. It would shift more of the responsibility and accountability for the district board decisions back to the provincial minister of Health; or 3) a balance of elected and appointed board members which might slightly favour either elected or appointed membership, with accountability to both the minister of Health and the public.

Those wanting all elected boards were encouraging a more democratic governance approach to the health system. They felt appointed representatives would be seen as partisan political appointees. Those wanting appointed boards were concerned that newly elected boards should be assured of the range of experience needed to take charge of a rapidly changing health system. It was also suggested that many very experienced people who might be wanted for board service were too busy or unwilling to stand for election.

In addition there were no assurances that an election system would provide representation from very important population groups whose perspectives in health decisions are vital, like the Aboriginal communities and women. It is also desirable on each board to have certain types of expertise, such as law, financial management and so on. A way had to be found to make this expertise available to boards which did not gain it through the electoral process.

To work through these contentious positions the minister appointed a commissioner to consult with the appointed boards and the public to determine what system of representation was preferred. After four months of consultations, the advice to the minister was submitted in a document entitled *Report of the Saskatchewan Commission on District Health Board Elections* in September 1994. The majority of those consulted indicated a strong preference for elected boards. It was thought that elected boards would be more accountable and more responsive to the needs of the electorate.[16]

To minimize the disadvantages of an all-elected or all-appointed board membership process, the government chose the middle ground. The *Health Districts Act* stipulates that each board will be composed of a core of eight elected representatives with the option for the minster of Health to appoint four additional representatives. The two largest urban boards would be composed of a maximum of fourteen representatives, of whom six could be appointed. This permitted some cross-representation with surrounding rural areas that used the urban centres as health referral centres. Members would be elected on a ward system to make sure that different communities in the district and/or groups found representation on the board.

The intention of allowing for appointed members was to ensure that district boards had some element of gender balance, representation from minority groups, and a reasonable degree of expertise to plan and manage all aspects of their health system.

The intention of allowing for elected board members was to encourage more democratic governance of the health system. And to disarm any criticism of partisan appointments to the boards, the appointed representatives by law were named by the minister of Health on the recommendation of the elected boards.

16. Saskatchewan, *Report of the Saskatchewan Commission on District Health Board Elections* (Saskatchewan: Saskatchewan Health, 1994), 3.

In practice this mixed approach to board composition has worked well. The boards report that once they all meet, no distinctions are made as to whether a person is elected or appointed. In terms of board performance, there is no concrete evidence that an elected board governs better than an appointed board, or vice versa. To a large extent, the choice of method of obtaining board members has to do with the choice between democratic and administrative principles.

Health board election dates were set to avoid coinciding with municipal elections so as to avoid the impression that health boards were synonymous with municipal government. (Some powerful municipal interest groups had indicated that they preferred to subsume the new health boards into municipal governance control.) While initially separating health board elections from municipal elections might have been wise, in practice this has proven to be problematic. There is insufficient public profile for health board elections to encourage effective democratic processes in choosing representatives to the health boards. In the 1999 health board elections, two-thirds of the seats went uncontested and voter turnout averaged only 10 percent. It is not yet known what this poor electoral result means. Is it an electoral process failure — a reflection of public disinterest in health board participation — a lack of personal satisfaction from this type of community work — a failure by the health system to seek out candidates and encourage them to stand for election? Or is it a conscious decision by potential health board candidates to avoid the stresses inherent in health service governance?

Certainly improvements can be made to the electoral process for health board election and the use on the boards of these public representatives. The timing of health board elections can be changed to coincide with other municipal elections. Another concern is that uncontested re-election of members might lead to a staleness of ideas on the board. The role of board members has to be meaningful; their contribution to the health system needs to be publicly recognized and appreciated; the electoral process has to be better profiled and communicated; and the authority of these public representatives respected by the provincial government.

CONCLUSION

Given the fiscal crises faced by the provincial government in 1991, there were only three health system options from which the government could choose: radically change the system to make it better and financially sustainable in the long term; let it whither and shrink over several years by funding reductions at the margin; or permit a two-tiered health system to emerge. From an ideological perspective, it could not tolerate the third option. By ruling out this option, and also with pride in its historic contributions to the Canadian health system, it could not stand aside and let the Saskatchewan system flounder. It had no real choice except to proceed with major changes to the health system and accept the political consequences of doing so. In choosing this option, it decided to introduce the most modern concepts of a contemporary health system — which it called the Wellness model.

Saskatchewan drew on worldwide experience to plan its health reform initiatives but the dearth of practical information left Saskatchewan largely on its own in pursing this social reform. For several years now, as information about the Saskatchewan health reforms spreads around the world, a great many international visitors have made their way to Saskatchewan to examine and learn from this province's health reform experience. The fundamental principles of the reform, its governance structures, and the opportunities offered in the integrated delivery structure are all recognized and applauded. The great difficulties in implementing the reforms are also widely recognized, so that many other jurisdictions have yet to proceed with their own policy changes.

For the most part, the impacts and struggles over the health system changes in this decade have not been about health care, but rather about the community and individual *economic* impacts of the changes. The opposition to the new health policies has largely been an exercise in community and self-interest protection (personal, political and professional).

The overarching factors which motivated and sustained the Saskatchewan health reform in its most difficult moments were the initial vision of improved health and quality of life for the entire population; the determined and committed leadership of so many citizens to the vision of this future health system; and the extensive involvement of the public in transforming the traditional health system at the community and district levels. In a strange way, the financial crisis helped. This reform could not have achieved any degree of success without these factors dominating the event: a motivating vision, determined and committed leadership, extensive democratic participation throughout. Re-inspiring these forces in Saskatchewan will condition the eventual outcome of the 1990s health reform for the next generation.

Economic Development and the New Role of Government

Brett Fairbairn

Approximately 125 years ago, many people believed that governments had only a limited role to play in economic development. Governments set tariffs and monetary exchange rates, acting as gate-keepers between their national economies and the world economy, and they enforced systems of property rights, contract law, and so on that enabled some citizens to prosper. In essence, governments set up categories and compartments within which economies would develop according to private impulses. In Canada, most of this role was federal. Provinces were active mainly as cheering sections and lobbyists for their industries, though their laws and taxes also made some difference. But by approximately 50 years ago, many people were quite sure that governments had a large role to play in managing economies, in fact that economies required active government steering and planning. No longer limited to tariffs, money, and commercial law, governments now were thought to use fiscal policy (taxation and spending) to even out highs and lows in economic cycles (Keynesianism), to remove market imperfections through active intervention, and to undertake direct, targeted economic investment in key sectors. Provincial governments in the postwar era came to see themselves as key agents of economic development. This was true of both left- and right-wing governments, of oil-rich Alberta as well as more agrarian Saskatchewan.[1]

Since the 1970s, the twentieth century's infatuation with planning has unraveled due to a variety of disappointments. These included the high interest rates and recession around 1980, large deficits, and the questionable results of some megaprojects. Whatever the causes, there has been a loss of faith in government leadership in relation to the economy. There seem to be two truths to draw from these experiences. First, it seems that governments cannot plan economies. But second, it seems that the role of government remains indispensable — we have not returned to the situation of 125 years ago, when the role of the state was thought to be minimal. Today's truth seems to lie somewhere between the two extremes.

The current situation poses a dilemma, especially for politicians at the provincial level: for if a government's role is not to plan the economy, yet governments are still part of the picture, then what, precisely, do they do? To be blunt, how exactly can a cabinet minister or a member of the legislature affect the economy? The present moment is one in which politicians must pretend to voters that they have more influence than their civil servants tell them they actually possess. Fortunately the

1. The classic examination of this era is John Richards and Larry Pratt, *Prairie Capitalism: Power and Influence in the New West* (Toronto: McLelland and Stewart, 1970).

situation is not all bad. The state is an institution with vast resources of personnel, information, and regulatory and spending power; it should never be underestimated. These resources can be deployed in ways that influence a society's collective goals, values, and aspirations, promoting improvement and development in broad ways and broad areas; and, they can be deployed in ways that provide practical aid to citizens and communities who are themselves engaged in economic development. With respect to the economy, the role of politicians is less that of the planner or CEO, and more that of a coach, a priest, or a figurehead: someone around whom collective and individual action come together; a mediator for problems in search of solutions; a facilitator for accomplishments mainly by others.

The purpose of an economy is to sustain people. Within Canada — a country repeatedly ranked as having one of the highest qualities of life in the world — Saskatchewan has a somewhat less-than-average economy. Is this a cause for concern? People in most other parts of the world would be happy with Saskatchewan's economic performance and living standards; but, to judge by the weight given in public debate to the need for jobs and income, most Saskatchewan people are not. In fact, while the province's wealth and economy have continued to grow in absolute terms, personal income per capita relative to that in other parts of Canada has fallen from a high point in the mid-1970s when it exceeded the national average, to about 93 percent of the national average in recent years. The main reason for the relative decline is worsening terms of trade: the prices of Saskatchewan exports have fallen relative to the prices of the things Saskatchewan people buy.[2] The result for the province as a whole is a "cost-price squeeze" that would be familiar to any farmer: despite constant gains in production and productivity, income does not improve. It is like running on a treadmill. No matter how much faster we run, we don't get ahead. This apparent impasse has caused many people to question and rethink economic strategies and institutions. Such questioning and rethinking have not yet gone far enough.

For generations, an enduring aspect of the Saskatchewan mentality has been a feeling that the provincial economy is lacking in depth, is too dependent on raw commodities, does not generate sufficient growth, and is inadequate to provide for, especially, the young people of the province. The last point is a critical one: Saskatchewan people want to know that the economy can sustain their communities from generation to generation. In a sense, it is not production that concerns the public so much as reproduction. The fact that the province's population is roughly constant conceals the true extent of the problem, because the rapid population growth of a handful of urban centres statistically balances the decline of large rural regions. This does not mean that the cities experiencing the population growth necessarily feel better off: instability, inequality, and poverty are widespread, perhaps increasingly so. The economy appears to be failing to sustain most of the communities that people care about.

Before spending most of this chapter on problems and on questions of change and improvement, it is important to put matters in perspective by noting what people in Saskatchewan do well. Saskatchewan has an immensely productive economy

2. For an excellent review of provincial economic performance and a detailed review of economic-development strategies and initiatives, see Peter W.B. Phillips, "Whither Saskatchewan? A Look at Economic Policies, 1975–2000," *Canadian Business Economics* (November 1998): 36–49; on growth and terms of trade, pp. 36–37.

that generates large revenues in world trade. This economy is based on a rich and (for its population) vast natural environment. The province delivers high-quality products and services. The population is educated (lagging behind the rest of Canada in overall terms, but better than most parts of the world), skilled, and highly motivated. In some of the most important areas for the future — First Nations and Métis communities, education for young people — there is movement and promise. Having said this, Saskatchewan people remain acutely conscious of the challenges they face.

GLOBALIZATION AND GEOGRAPHY

Globalization, if by that we mean freeing up of trade, markets, capital, and institutions on an international scale, is nothing new. It is roughly a two-hundred-year-old process (at least) whose latest wave has captured the popular imagination in the last two decades. Earlier waves of globalization are in fact the reason that Saskatchewan's present economy exists: Saskatchewan was drawn into the European orbit and the world economy in order to trade commodities produced here for goods and services from the colonial heartlands.

Saskatchewan has already seen four economies in the last six or eight generations. In every case, geography and resources were key considerations. In every case, world markets dictated sweeping transformations. The first economy, that of the First Nations, was centred around hunting and gathering, as well as trade. The second economy, the fur-trading economy, was built to extract resources and transport them over long distances for European markets. The third economy, the grain-export economy, bought extensive European settlement and the establishment of additional modern institutions in western Canada such as policing, railroads, churches, towns, and a modern state.

The grain economy boomed in the early to mid-twentieth century, and has been in serious decline for over a generation. Grain prices have generally tended downward since a peak after World War I, but later and smaller peaks in the 1940s and 1970s interrupted the overall trend. Farm population has declined continuously since the 1930s, but faster in some periods and perhaps especially quickly in recent decades. On the surface, this looks like the painful but normal transformation of an agrarian economy to an industrialized one, much as it has occurred in every other industrialized society. This is certainly true in the sense that Saskatchewan's economy has developed as an integral part of an international, industrial economy. But industrial economies are always regionally differentiated. For a region to become part of an industrial economy does not mean factories spring up; it may mean just the opposite. As a matter of fact, neither the Saskatchewan economy nor Canada's as a whole became dominated by manufacturing in the postwar era. After the 1950s manufacturing actually declined as a proportion of national output.[3] What increased were new primary industries of mining, petroleum, and forestry. Already by 1960 forest and mineral products had grown to 58 percent of all Canadian exports, while old staples of grain, fish, and furs had fallen to 15 percent.[4] Some

3. On the broad postwar Canadian patterns see J.M. Bumsted, *The Peoples of Canada: A Post-Confederation History* (Toronto: Oxford University Press, 1992), 277.

4. Paul Phillips and Stephen Watson, "From Mobilization to Continentalism: The Canadian Economy in the Post-Depression Period," in Michael S. Cross and Gregory S. Kealey (eds.), *Modern Canada 1930–1980s* (Toronto: McClelland and Stewart, 1984), 41.

regions — notably in southern Ontario and other metropolitan areas — did develop as manufacturing centres, but for most of Canada the industrial economy meant renewed specialization in activities closely related to natural resources.

The new resource industries are, in effect, Saskatchewan's fourth economy, overlaid on top of the previous ones. Saskatchewan's boom in oil, potash, and uranium in the 1970s was a powerful boost to the province's economy for a number of years. More recently, the announcement of a vast set of new forest-products developments in 1999, involving according to official estimates half a billion dollars in private investment, has brought renewed attention to the forest sector. Forestry and mining jobs, head offices, and service industries contribute mightily to the economies of several Saskatchewan centres, and go a long way toward explaining why the larger cities can grow and prosper when the agricultural areas around them are suffering. Saskatchewan's cities are far less economically dependent on agriculture than most people realize. Even in Saskatchewan, agriculture has been reduced to just one industry in the provincial economy — an important industry to be sure, and one to which many people feel a personal and sympathetic attachment; but an increasingly separate industry all the same. The rural-urban split in the 1999 provincial election has its roots not only in differing rural and urban cultures, but also in divergent economies.

The other resources are no panaceas, however. Forest and mineral commodities have also shown signs of long-term price declines or instabilities that are not so different from the earlier resource economies. For a period in the 1980s-90s, prices of potash, oil, and uranium were all weak. This points to a basic problem of dealing with generic commodities on global markets: commodities that are interchangeable and freely traded are subject to price-reducing competition from around the world. Most of the time, there will be someone who can produce more cheaply than Saskatchewan can, even if this is only because of state subsidies or unpaid social and environmental costs. Trading in generic commodities is simply a poor economic strategy. This is why "adding value" and "preserving identity" have become mantras of economic development in Saskatchewan.

All four of Saskatchewan's economies have been based on the natural environment and its resources. The environment is and always has been the foundation of Saskatchewan's economy. This ought properly to be seen as a strength, since it has made possible the peopling of Saskatchewan and the creation of a high quality of life. In Saskatchewan, renewal and preservation of the environment should be a priority much as, in businesses, the renewal and preservation of capital stock is treated as a basic goal and necessity. That this has not always been the case — that furs and later soil were in some areas overexploited and abused — contributed to some of the crises in the province's development. It remains to be seen whether current forms of mineral and forest exploitation are environmentally sound and sustainable, but in Saskatchewan of all places people should be acutely conscious that environmental problems make economic problems worse.

One of the basic social-economic problems in Saskatchewan today is that the population is distributed to fit the economies of the past. Farming was an extensive resource industry that created a widely distributed population. Mining and particularly forestry may affect large land areas, but do not require that these areas be settled — the jobs, offices, and services are much more concentrated than in older farming or fishing economies. Similarly the First Nations and Métis populations in the North — populations that are growing relatively rapidly — are located there because of past economies that were based on animal and other resources. It is an open question whether the population of the North can be sustained by economic activities distributed within the North.

The relationship of economics, geography, and population is put into question all over again by contemporary waves of economic change. In an era of renewed globalization, the key issue is whether and how development can occur while being constrained within a region such as a province, a community, the North, or a rural area. In other words, can we ensure that jobs will exist where people are, or do people have to migrate North to South, rural to urban, interprovincially, or internationally in order to follow investment capital? Classical economics has argued that every region can find its niche in world trade — the theory of comparative advantage. Even if some region were better at all things, it would still pay for that region to specialize in what it does the best, and to leave the rest for others. This means we should not worry overly: there must be something that it pays to do in Saskatchewan. But comforting as this notion is in theory, in practice it is no more reassuring than other nineteenth-century liberal ideas, such as that specialization of labour will produce social harmony, or that nationalism will create world peace. Classical liberals have had vast confidence in progress through the free action of unregulated forces; this optimism has rarely been shared by regions that found themselves cast in the role of hinterland, as Saskatchewan has been to Ontario, rural areas to urban, northern areas to southern ones.

The development of a North American economic unit does not necessarily improve matters. The North American Free Trade Agreement (NAFTA) helped establish a common market in goods and to some extent in capital; the proposed federal Multilateral Agreement on Investment (MAI), which in recent years was desperately resisted by socially minded groups, would have advanced the process. Yet despite the changes, there is no real free market in labour between countries. In other words, goods, investment, and jobs are increasingly permitted to move freely — but people are not. Perhaps it makes sense for Saskatchewan people to move elsewhere, to Vancouver, or even south of the border, to follow jobs and economic activity. But if Saskatchewan people can't leave to go where jobs are, or if we don't want them to, then some kind of territorial economic strategies are essential.

It may be that a new economy is emerging that is less geographically constrained than economies of the past. This new economy is associated with information technology and information-based services. If any place in the world should be interested in — should be a leader in — new kinds of development, then it should be Saskatchewan, a province that has struggled for over a century with limits imposed by geography. But it is not enough to realize that a transformation may occur; not enough to desire to take advantage of it. The emergence of a new economy requires a basic rethinking of economic strategy and of the role of government.

INEFFECTIVENESS OF TRADITIONAL GOVERNMENT POLICIES

One sign of the ways in which economy and society have changed is the ineffectiveness of traditional tools of government. While macroeconomic fiscal policy, centrally planned investment, megaprojects, and programs of economic stimulation may still have some place, their effectiveness at solving the particular problems of today's economy is increasingly open to question. People generally don't believe that traditional kinds of government policy make much difference to the economy — and they have reason for that belief. An important recent study by Peter Phillips noted that in the last quarter-century Saskatchewan governments have tried four general kinds of economic policies: broad fiscal measures, mercantilist trade policies (such as export promotion and "Buy Saskatchewan" campaigns), microeconomic tax and subsidy policies, and policies to create a climate for entrepreneurship and innovation. The first three of these were failures. The jury is still out on the fourth.[5]

The magnitude of government failure to influence the economy is best expressed by looking at fiscal policy. Saskatchewan in the 1980s and 1990s provided a laboratory in which two successive governments carried out a monumental experiment in public spending and taxation. In the 1980s, the Devine government cut taxes (notably the fuel tax but also royalties from the petroleum industry) while generally maintaining spending, and even introducing new programs, for example, to subsidize home improvements and mortgages. The result was a budget deficit that grew to over one billion dollars per year. In essence, a billion dollars or about 5 percent of the province's gross domestic product was borrowed and pumped into household budgets, government services, economic-development megaprojects, and all the other areas of the economy touched by provincial taxation and spending. It might have been logical to expect that the result would be exceptional growth in the provincial economy, yet this did not happen! The 1980s remained difficult for Saskatchewan people. Then, in the 1990s, the Romanow government made the elimination of the deficit its top priority. The result was that a billion dollars a year was taken *out* of the provincial economy. Taxes were raised, services restricted, creditors paid off. The result this time could have been expected to be an economic contraction, a recession or depression. Yet again, the predictable did not occur. The Saskatchewan economy even continued to grow despite increased taxation and reduced government spending. What are we to make of all this?

First, it seems that the capacity of governments to affect overall economic performance by direct means, such as raising or lowering taxation or spending, is now far more restricted than many have believed. Governments may pretend to be managers of the economy; the record says they are not.

Second, the fact that Saskatchewan's economy can have a billion dollars put in or taken out with so little apparent overall effect should give pause for thought about the nature and integrity of our economy. Apparently, the Saskatchewan economy is so full of "leaks" that wealth quickly disperses and disappears, probably beyond the provincial borders. The same problem means that the megaprojects of the 1980s brought much less benefit to people of the province than their size suggested. Many of the benefits flowed to contractors, head offices, managers, or investors based elsewhere.[6] The hard reality that provincial governments, and perhaps electors, have been reluctant to face, is that billions of dollars spent by provincial governments on spending or tax cuts or megaprojects have next to no effect on the provincial economy as a whole.

All this should come as no surprise. Billions of dollars flow through the hands of Saskatchewan farmers, yet rural communities continue to decline: the wealth concentrates in the hands of, mostly, non-Saskatchewan-based implement and chemical companies, railroads, and agrifood corporations. Billions of dollars in northern

5. Phillips, "Whither Saskatchewan?"

6. Compare Eric C. Howe, "Government-Funded Mega-Projects Make Public Poorer," *Star-Phoenix*, September 16, 1993, and Peter Phillips's comments quoted by Bruce Johnstone, "Economist Says Diversification Didn't Protect Provincial Economy," *Star-Phoenix*, January 9, 1999.

lumber and minerals are extracted, yet the North remains poor. These are characteristics of leaky economies that allow profits, capital, and wealth to escape instead of recirculating within the rural or northern area, or within the province as a whole. Leakages of course are also linkages, and reflect the extent to which Saskatchewan's economy is integrated into the wider continental economy.

Given what are truly spectacular failures of traditional kinds of policy, Saskatchewan governments in the twenty-first century will have to continue to reconceptualize their role with respect to economic development. Direct measures to manage development through overall fiscal policy, or to generate wealth through megaprojects, have been proven ineffective. The alternative is to develop careful, nuanced, sector-specific strategies that recognize the limited tools available to government, and use those tools to reduce key bottlenecks for particular kinds of enterprises. This may sound simple, but entails a difficult shift in thinking away from planning and toward process facilitation, away from picking winners and toward helping others to experiment. The days are likely gone when governments could decide that thirty thousand jobs shall be created, that hog production shall triple, that potatoes shall grow beside Lake Diefenbaker, that information technology will be concentrated here or there, that the forest industry shall flourish in the northeast (to cite a series of in some cases ill-fated economic pronouncements from the period 1995–99). Voters may wish that governments could decide such things. The targets might even be met; but if so, it will be largely by good luck. Practically speaking, governments do not have the power to make such things happen.

To some extent, governments may have to become more humble. But equally, they need to recognize the tremendous resources they possess to facilitate and support development in less directive ways. The greatest challenge for governments is to move from trying to plan outcomes, to working to facilitate processes. They have perhaps begun to move in this direction, but the challenge is larger than it seems. Governments and their staffs must reconceptualize themselves as helpers, not experts; as facilitators, not target-setters; as knowledge-brokers rather than analysts, regulators, or deliverers of programs. In the early twenty-first century, successful governments must work in an open-ended way with private, public, and social enterprises, supporting a less-planned and more bottom-up kind of development.

SUCCESSES OF PRIVATE, PUBLIC, AND SOCIAL ENTERPRISE

Like all successful economies in the industrialized world, Saskatchewan's economy is a mixture of different forms of ownership, each of which has played a vital role in development. The rhetoric of the Cold War — free market or state planning — concealed the reality that all Western economies have in fact been mixed economies, not one-sided capitalist economies. What the dénouement of the Cold War showed was that open, diverse, somewhat balanced, and pluralistic societies and economic systems outperform those that are monolithically organized around a single form of ownership.[7] The question, post-1989, is not whether to have a market economy, but *what kind* of market economy to have. The appropriate balance of sectors and forms of ownership may well be different for particular regions

---

7. Henry Mintzberg, "Managing Government — Governing Management," *Harvard Business Review* (May-June 1996): 75–83. An abridged version with many of the references to nonprofits and alternative forms of ownership edited out was published as "The Myth of 'Society Inc.'" in *Report on Business Magazine* (October 1996): 113–17.

and circumstances. Promoting an appropriate balance has to be a keystone of any economic development policy. This means government needs a nuanced understanding of the respective strengths and weaknesses of different sectors, and of its own roles in supporting them.

The private sector — businesses oriented toward the profit interests of investors — has been a main engine of growth and expansion. Private businesses have pursued profitable resource extraction and contributed to the growth of service-delivery hubs around the province. They are often good at mobilizing capital, enhancing productivity (more production with less labour), and creating linkages to wider markets. If there are deficiencies, these lie, first, in a tendency towards boom-or-bust cycles. Since the earliest days of the province, a significant part of the Saskatchewan mentality has been the wild optimism of excessive boosterism — the dream of every pioneer hamlet that it would become a thriving metropolis — followed by the hard reality of a crash. The booms and the busts have contributed to a second tendency, a tendency towards concentration of successful private enterprises in the larger centres. These tendencies are expressions of the basic profit motive that makes private enterprise productive: investors seek high returns, are guided by perceptions, and gravitate as a result towards hubs. It is natural, predictable, and possibly even desirable that profit-oriented enterprises gravitate in this way to follow their economic interests; but it leaves geographically and socially marginal populations underserviced.

Of course, the concept of the private sector is an abstraction that conceals a wide diversity of enterprises. These range from farms (which are private, yet hard to characterize historically as behaving in an investor-oriented fashion), to small commercial enterprises, to huge multinational food and resource companies. There are important differences between those forms of private enterprise that are widely distributed and rooted in specific communities — agriculture and small local business — and those that are larger and more mobile in their investments and activities. Such differences have important ramifications for economic policy. Small businesses are best favoured by creating a generalized climate of favourable conditions, infrastructure, and human resources; it is not surprising that taxation levels and competitiveness issues are frequently raised by small-business representatives. The very large private enterprises are in a league of their own, likely best dealt with by government through carefully defined and specific partnerships. Large and small-medium enterprises also differ in the kinds of workforces they require: typically large enterprises want broadly educated employees from a good public system; they then conduct much of their specialized training themselves, or work directly with post-secondary institutions to develop specialized programs. Small-medium enterprises often want employees who come ready-made with all the necessary skills, which in the emerging economy is almost impossible to achieve.

To the extent Saskatchewan people have learned over the years to take their boosterism with a grain of salt, they have sought balance and stability by encouraging and accepting the development of public enterprises — those owned by the state — in specific fields. In general, such state enterprises or Crown corporations found a niche because they provided for long-term stability of planning and investment, less driven by boom-and-bust cycles than private enterprise; and because they provided province-wide benefits or standards of service. Implicitly, state enterprise existed in part to develop and cross-subsidize services to rural, remote, or marginal populations. The two great limitations of this approach are, first, that such cross-subsidization is sustainable only if the state enterprise has a monopoly position, which Crown corporations are generally now losing due to federal competition policies; and, second, that the provincial level of thinking leads to a relative centralization and a remoteness from people and communities.

In practice, state enterprise won acceptance from the population where it dealt with matters of basic, standardized service and infrastructure: electricity, natural gas, telephones, and (though not organized as a Crown corporation) highways. Even in these cases, however, public attitudes, especially in recent years, show a deep-seated suspicion of monopoly and of centralization that is expressed in criticism of service, resistance to rate increases, demands for an independent utilities-review commission, and hostility to what amounts to normal corporate behaviour. By contrast, in other areas such as natural resources (oil, potash, uranium, and so on, where Crown corporations were developed systematically in the 1970s), acceptance was even less: the Conservative governments of the 1980s were able to privatize these enterprises without effective public opposition. Arguably the strongest current sector of the provincial economy — the new resource industries of mining, petroleum, and forestry — is now almost entirely managed by private enterprise. The provincial review of Crown corporations in the mid-1990s generally confirmed the structure and management orientation of the remaining Crowns.[8] Media coverage since that time suggests that the wider issues of public trust, mandate, and acceptance have not been resolved.

Some Saskatchewan people have been content to rely on the market to meet all needs; others have relied on the state. Those who were content with neither alternative helped develop a third sector, which in some other industrialized countries is increasingly referred to as the social economy. The social economy consists of mutuals, nonprofits (including not only associations and charities but some large institutions such as universities and hospitals), and co-operatives. The largest, most formal, and most market-oriented of these social enterprises are the co-operatives. While co-operatives, and to a lesser extent other social enterprises, are well-developed in Saskatchewan — an expression of decades of dissatisfaction with what could be accomplished by private business and government — it is a mistake to think Saskatchewan is unique. Other parts of Canada and other industrialized countries — the United States, Germany, Japan, Italy, France, in fact all prosperous countries — also have large co-operative movements, particularly in rural and agricultural regions. The main unique feature in Saskatchewan is that few private companies keep head offices here, so that the co-operatives stand out on lists of provincially based enterprises. Rather than seeing co-operatives as a unique Saskatchewan invention, which they are not, it would be better to say that Saskatchewan people have pragmatically created a balanced economy by using every tool at their disposal, including co-operatives.

Co-operatives in Saskatchewan serve rural communities and small towns, though increasingly also inner-city neighbourhoods that see themselves as marginalized by urban development. The attractiveness of the co-operative form is that the business is rooted in the community through local ownership by a group of users.

8. See Crown Investments Corporation of Saskatchewan, *Saskatchewan Crown Corporations Review 1996*; also TASC (Talking About Saskatchewan Crowns), *A Report on the Public Review of the Future of Crown Corporations in Saskatchewan* (September 1996); and John Allan (ed.), *Public Enterprise in an Era of Change* (Regina: Canadian Plains Research Center, 1998).

As a result, the business cannot easily move away or transfer its capital elsewhere as an investor-oriented firm might do; capital is recirculated within the community of members. The business also is not as remote and centralized as a provincial corporation would be; members are involved, developed, and trained as leaders. Co-operatives typically have multi-tier structures, in which local or primary co-operatives maximize local involvement and benefit, while central co-operatives maximize efficiency and create vertical integration. While this approach has a proven worth for geographically and socially marginalized populations, and complements the strengths of private and state enterprises, it, too, has its limitations. The key problems for co-operatives are, first, that they are hard to form, requiring a great deal of consensus-building, persuasion, and education; and second, that once formed, they become institutionalized. Highly institutionalized co-operatives continue to recirculate capital, provide services where other forms of enterprise might not, and train and develop local leaders; but their dynamism and vision tends to decline, creating difficulties in reproducing the co-operative movement among new generations of members. Unless balanced by active development of new co-operatives, the result is that those interested in more visionary possibilities of development may overlook co-operatives as too stale or too conservative. A different problem arises where there is not a critical mass of co-operatives in a single sector. In this case, the individual co-operatives may be too isolated, lack access to central services, and lack mutual support. Linkages among such co-operatives need external support.

It goes without saying that Saskatchewan's economy will remain a balance of different forms of ownership, and that its success will depend in large measure on each sector doing what it does best and functioning in a fashion complementary to the others. This has interesting implications for government policy. First, it seems unlikely that the provincial economy has much to gain from a government pitting any one sector against the others. Policies of moderation and balance seem inescapable, if overall results are to be positive. In the 1990s, the Romanow government pursued this kind of balance at least on a symbolic and rhetorical level: there were sales-tax reductions for small business (following sales-tax increases to eliminate the deficit); partnerships with large private businesses, for example in meat packing and forestry; the review of Crown corporations that gave a green light to their development strategies; and the recognition of co-operatives through incorporating their name into the Ministry of Economic and Co-operative Development.

But while government policy must be balanced and convey a sense of balance, it is also true that each sector has different strengths and weaknesses, and therefore that policy ought to be different in each case. To optimize growth and development, government policy should support each sector to do what it does well. It should also assist each sector to overcome its distinctive weaknesses and barriers. And government must do this while resisting the temptation to plan and predetermine outcomes, which would only arouse opposition or denature the various forms of enterprise. What is increasingly needed is not planning authorities or boosterism, divisive politics or quick fixes, but well-conceived, long-term strategies put into practice through carefully thought-out and well-designed policies and programs. Neither Saskatchewan nor any other jurisdiction has ever found a perfect answer; this is to say, there is plenty of room for innovative policy development. At the same time, the task of fine-tuning economic strategy for a diverse economy is complicated and made more urgent by today's economic transformations.

THE NEW ECONOMY

The new economy, of course, is information-based.[9] It entails growth in service and knowledge industries. Beyond this, much is unclear, but some patterns can be identified. We can conceptualize the new economy as one that is different in important ways from the past "industrial" model of how an economy works. The industrial economy that dominated from about the 1930s to the 1970s was based on standardized manufacturing activities, segmented into specialized subunits, and controlled by rigid hierarchies that sought ever-greater efficiencies by increasing scale and cutting cost. In the last quarter-century every aspect of this system has come under pressure: standardization, specialization, hierarchy, concentration on cost-cutting rather than quality. The crisis of the industrial economy involves regional crises in many different industries. Within the North American economy the crisis of Western grain farming has been paralleled by the crises of Atlantic fishing, West Coast forest products, Mid-West United States and Central Canadian automobiles and steel, oil and gas, and (in different parts of the United States) also textile and defence industries — to name only a few. It is a mistake to think that economic problems are unique to Saskatchewan or are particular to agriculture or any single industry. In general, *all* traditional industries are suffering. How people perceive this situation depends on the particular industrial structure of the region they live in. In Saskatchewan we are familiar with a farm crisis, but — without denying there is a farm crisis — we also need to see this as a symptom of larger changes that affect the entire economy. The failure to see the breadth of changes in the economy is probably a reason for the failure of many government economic-development policies over the last twenty-five years.

We might legitimately object that Saskatchewan has always been internationally oriented, and that industries like agriculture have been based on small, flexible units — family farms — rather than on bureaucratic industrial corporations. To the extent these statements are true, they constitute relative strengths of Saskatchewan in dealing with the new economy. However, they are not as true as we would like to think. Our international orientation has been in the sale of fairly standardized, interchangeable raw commodities, marketed in centralized fashion through huge companies or parastatal entities like marketing boards: this is a variation of industrial-era thinking. Our farms do remain in the hands of families, but as economic units they are increasingly integrated into vast industrial systems within which farmers are cast as mass-production specialists. This is simply more mass-industrial thinking. Although we think of Saskatchewan as being somehow different from the wider economy, it is not. Even our most traditional industries are caught up in the larger models.

The new economy involves not just a new technological base but also new forms of organization and new ways of thinking. It should be seen not just as the creation of new firms, the internet, or software companies; it should be seen also as basic changes in existing enterprises as they learn to organize and manage their activities in knowledge-based ways.

More information-based enterprises require less in the way of plant, machinery, land, and physical resources than their industrial-era predecessors. By contrast,

9. A relatively early and still very interesting discussion of the information economy and its implications is Manuel Castells, *The Informational City: Information Technology, Economic Restructuring, and the Urban-Regional Process* (Oxford: Basil Blackwell, 1989).

human intelligence, skills, and creative teamwork count for more. Enterprises of the new economy are more typically small and flexible rather than large and monolithic; even when information-based businesses become large, these typically have a high degree of internal flexibility, for example in the form of entrepreneurial centres or shifting alignments of project teams. Human resources are also more fluid, changing and flowing between units or between companies. While organizations of the industrial era were characterized by hierarchy and strict internal functional specialization, the new organizations are best conceptualized as networks whose nodes temporarily bring together people of differing skills around common problems.

We can see this much by studying the successful firms of Silicon Valley, but Silicon Valley is an exceptional case. The more important point is that such changes in thinking and organizational design are occurring broadly throughout the international economy. It is not only that firms whose business is information are adopting new approaches. More and more firms are beginning to realize that their business has always been based, to a greater or lesser degree, on information.

As individuals, more and more people in communities across Saskatchewan are earning a living by participating in the information economy. The new economy can already be seen in Saskatchewan in the growth of knowledge-based industries such as information processing, biotechnology, scientific research (such as the Canadian Light Source synchrotron announced in 1999), industries that for the most part are based in the larger cities. However, even in small towns in Saskatchewan, there are people who earn a living by consulting to or contracting with firms and agencies in the cities, in other parts of Canada, or indeed around the world: designers, artists, writers, researchers, trainers, analysts, advisers — whether such people are employees in existing enterprises or are independent professionals, the new economy is represented to some degree in almost every region of the province. It is by no means clear, however, that these developments are enough to make Saskatchewan a leader in the new economy.

It is significant that new-economy enterprises form and operate in clusters. These may be geographic, but they may also be network of related organizations working across great distances. The reasons for this clustering are different from the reasons for the clustering of industrial-era firms, which had to do with factors like land and transportation costs. New-economy enterprises often cluster in relatively expensive places like Silicon Valley, Denver, Dallas, or Massachusetts; within Saskatchewan, some are based in Saskatoon when they could likely be located more cheaply in a small town a hundred kilometres away. Why do information-based businesses behave in this fashion? Why do businesses for whom distance is relatively unimportant not locate more frequently in remote places? There are likely two main reasons. The first is synergies that come from personal interactions and from association with a group or a place. This is really a question of the *culture* of the new information economy. People involved in it want to stick together; but also, they derive marketing opportunities and advantages from doing so. Perception, image, and reputation are clearly affected by who is networked in what way with whom. Being located in a centre that is known for computers, for biotechnology, or for innovative automobile production is presumably worth it to those who are there. The second reason is more concrete: information-based enterprises depend critically on human resources, which is to say on talented and educated people. They tend to locate in a setting that is attractive to the kinds of people they need.

These patterns are important in relation to the participation of places like

Saskatchewan in the new economy. A recent American study identified the less-populated, more agricultural states of the Mid-West, including all of those adjacent to the Canadian Prairies, as among the laggards in the development of new-economy jobs.[10] Clearly, for a place like Saskatchewan to participate in this kind of employment requires something other than a *laissez-faire* approach. Effective strategies will have to include encouraging some geographic clusters like Innovation Place in Saskatoon; and also encouraging nongeographic clusters using networking of firms and individuals around the province, with each other and with the outside world. Education for a talented and skilled knowledge work force is essential; but so too are services, amenities, environments, and images that make the province and places within it attractive to knowledge workers. The province and its people will have to think of themselves and market themselves in new ways, in order to foster perceptions and attitudes that are supportive of knowledge industries. This means developing and reinforcing information-oriented cultures, identities, and workforces. The new economy requires not only changes in how institutions organize themselves, but also changes in how people think.

The productivity gains in the production of "things" — whether steel or wheat — mean that jobs and occupations concerned directly with making things are declining; and the returns to companies from these activities are slim. Growth is in jobs that design and move and market and add value to things. In short, though it may seem odd to say it this way, growth is in office jobs. The postmodern economy is one in which process is critically important, and people manage processes from their desks. Substance still matters — people need food, clothing, and shelter — but increasingly creativity and productivity focus around *how* such physical things are designed, produced, distributed, and consumed; as well as around nonphysical determinants of health and well-being.

This transition is hard for many people to accept, because our natural way of thinking about the economy revolves around material production. When we think of a higher standard of living, we think of having homes and things to put in them. When we think about honest work, we think about work that involves getting our hands dirty to make something. We are right to see dignity in growing food from the soil, digging coal out of the rock face, or running machines on the assembly line. But due to increased productivity, the new economy requires many fewer of these kinds of jobs, but many more intellectual workers who deal in abstract products and services. Information-based work is still real: it can improve people's lives by delivering better material products, quicker, more tailored to people's needs and desires; not to mention by delivering intangibles like education, news, entertainment, or for that matter health care and social services. The idea that information-based work is somehow less real or less valuable, that providing services is not a real job, is a barrier in places like Saskatchewan to full participation in the emerging economy.

The trick is to see the emergence of the new economy as something that affects all occupations without eliminating any of them. Job numbers will decline in one area and increase in another, as in past economic transformations; but the changes will not be total. Just as the relatively new resource industries of forestry and mining co-exist in Saskatchewan with the grain economy (and even with furs and

---

10. Robert D. Atkinson, Randolph H. Court, and Joseph M. Ward, "The State New Economy Index: Benchmarking Economic Transformation in the States" (Progressive Policy Institute Technology & New Economy Project, July 1999); see especially the map and indices on p. 7.

hunting-gathering), the emerging new economy will be overlaid on top of all of these rather than wholly displacing any of them. People in Saskatchewan will continue to perform jobs they know, with some significant changes and new technology; but there will also be new jobs and new areas of growth. Judging by past transformations, the key question from the point of view of social-economic policy will be whether the growth in employment in some areas will match the decline in others — "match" not only in the sense of quantity but also geographic and demographic "fit." If not, there will be adjustment problems. Policy objectives should include promoting optimum development of the new economy, promoting wide geographic and demographic participation in it, and providing mechanisms to help people who are changing jobs — or whose jobs are changing.

The authors of the US study of the new economy criticized old approaches to economic development by governments that focused on physical infrastructure, gap financing for big industrial projects, incentives to attract industries, and cutting taxes and government services in hopes of making an area appear attractive to business. These ideas reflect the thinking of the industrial-era economy. Governments have to move from "hunting and gathering" (industrial recruitment) to "gardening" (promoting growth from within).[11] "Corporate tax subsidies, abatements, and assurances of low labor costs" are strategies that are "increasingly out of touch with the factors that constitute success in the New Economy: good public education, an R&D infrastructure, availability of job-specific skills training, quality of life, quality of government, and innovative economic development efforts. ... Low costs with a poor quality of life are not the tickets to success."

New approaches recommended by the U.S. researchers are as follows: 1) co-invest in the skills of the work force: high standards in public education, a degree of choice and specialization among schools, programs to encourage minority and disadvantaged students, increased scholarships, skills alliances with industry and unions for workforce training; 2) co-invest in an infrastructure for innovation: investment in higher education, improved university-government-industry linkages, greater R&D, encouragement of "co-opetition" or collective entrepreneurship; 3) promote innovation- and customer-oriented government: cut costs, improve quality of life, attract knowledge workers, provide services and interactions with citizens on-line; 4) foster the transformation to a digital economy: legal framework that encourages electronic commerce and use of the internet, new telecommunications technologies, public internet access; 5) foster civic collaboration: encourage formation of "social capital" in the community, economic policy councils, regional collaborative networks. Saskatchewan has seen some developments in most of these areas in the 1990s, ranging from increased discussion of the priority of education; to R&D partnerships in biotechnology; to advances in telecommunications and internet hook-ups; and provincial-level consultative councils as well as Regional Economic Development Authorities. All of these changes amount to beginnings.

However, the new economy cannot be met by piecemeal changes. To deal with what is likely to be a basic economic transformation, and to turn it and channel it into development within a defined locality, region, or province, will take not a grab-bag of small, independent measures, but a closely integrated set of forceful and far-reaching strategies that go beyond what is usually conceived of as economics. According to Manuel Castells, these strategies must encompass *cultural*, *economic*,

11. Ibid., 4, 38ff; the following quotations are from p. 38.

and *political* dimensions.[12] In the cultural dimension, policy must encourage a sense of place, regional and community identities, active collective memory, and it must do so in a positive and constructive way rather than through reactive tribalism. In the economic sphere, the main challenge is to understand where Saskatchewan fits in a free-flowing, information-based global economy. In politics, the corresponding tasks are to foster strong local governments and citizen participation to strengthen civil society. Each of these groups of policy measures is ineffective without being supported by the others. One might have the best economic policy conceivable, but without a sense of place and of common purpose, a regional society like Saskatchewan will disintegrate into competing and incoherent subunits incapable of action. Similarly, without strong local governments, without civil society, without citizens, there will no institutions capable of transforming regional identity into regional policy.

The point in the above list where informed members of the public would be hardest pressed to cite positive Saskatchewan examples would be the third item. If every institution in society will be transformed in some way, then this must include government, which has always been one of the biggest knowledge-based, service industries of all.

COMMUNITY ECONOMIC DEVELOPMENT

One of the concerns of government must be that the transformation to a new economy will benefit some parts of society more than others. Such problems have been true of every economic transformation in the past, and there is little reason to expect that current changes are inherently more egalitarian. Just as provincial policy must try to ensure that the province as a whole is not adversely affected by change, so, too, it must consider groups within the province who may be marginalized or adversely affected by change. The two questions are closely connected, for Saskatchewan as a whole cannot improve its quality of life if important groups in the provincial population do not do so. The province needs the talents and skills of all its people, not only of an elite. To make the province an attractive place for new-economy enterprises and workers means making it an attractive place, period.

"New Economy" thinking draws attention to growing businesses from within, and by so doing, it draws attention back to an area that has received little more than lip service in recent policy: the area of community economic development or CED. CED is one of those buzzwords that was misapplied so often that one frequently despairs of making the real meaning clear. Too often, CED has simply consisted of conventional economic development with the word "community" attached to make it sound better. Thus well-worn policies like granting incentives to attract plants, building infrastructure, supporting small businesses, were given a community veneer. But such policies were never the main points or the be-all-and-end-all of CED. Instead, CED refers to policies and approaches that develop people in their communities — enhance their skills, independence, ability to start and run successful ventures, and ability to work together toward common goals. CED is where the social and the economic gears mesh with each other to get work done.[13]

12. Castells, *The Informational City*.

13. On CED see David J.A. Douglas, *Community Economic Development in Canada*, 2 vols. (Toronto: McGraw-Hill Ryerson, 1994), and especially David J.A. Douglas's essay in that volume, "Contexts and Conditions of Community Economic Development in Canada: Government and Institutional Responses," I: 65–118.

There have been some advances toward creating a framework for CED in Saskatchewan. The regional development corporations of the 1980s gave way to the Regional Economic Development Authorities (REDAs) of the 1990s, whose purpose was, in effect, to rationalize the infrastructure for economic development, primarily in rural areas where many competing municipally based organizations existed. REDAs, as their name implies, are largely government-based, government-like agencies. Whether what they have done amounts to CED has depended very much on the nature of local leadership and priorities.

Frankly, governments have probably done so little genuine CED because it seemed too small-scale and uncertain to be worth much effort. Why develop people to work together as entrepreneurs, when we can (supposedly) just invite in someone who is already a successful entrepreneur? Why grow a myriad of diverse, small, community-based enterprises, when we can (apparently!) just pick one industry or one megaproject that will benefit thousands of people? But the failure of other forms of government economic intervention, and the reorientation of government away from planning results and towards facilitating process, should lead to a long, hard second look at CED as a significant economic strategy to be supported systematically by provincial policy. Concerns with unemployment, welfare rolls and welfare traps, and with communities that are bypassed by growth, are additional reasons to pursue CED strategies.

Community economic development differs in important ways from conventional economic development. Perhaps most importantly, it requires a shared community vision, it requires that people who have not been entrepreneurs learn to be entrepreneurial, and it requires that people who may be used to thinking individualistically learn to undertake entrepreneurship in a group setting. CED typically starts with a concerned neighbourhood, town, social-cultural group, or simply a group of citizens, who may not initially have a common understanding of their goals and problems, let alone with a common business plan. This means CED needs to start with community education, community outreach, with field workers, process facilitators, and adult educators. Such components have rarely been present in traditional economic-development programs. CED ventures only require start-up services and small-business services — the typical components of government economic development — at a later stage in their development. It is not an accident that, in Saskatchewan, a number of pioneering CED projects in the 1990s were initiated from within the social services department rather than the economic-development department; Quint Development Corporation in Saskatoon, and its associated housing and worker co-op enterprises and activities, was the first of these. CED brings the social and the economic together, and requires government agencies to work in new constellations and with new partners.

Community economic development mixes and produces all sorts of enterprises and services. It may well create new, private small businesses within the defined communities. Often it creates new social enterprises, nonprofits or co-operatives. It may even result in new public services or agencies. CED should not be seen as limited to a particular form of ownership. Its purpose is to produce economic development in whatever form is appropriate to the needs and resources of a community.

Because of the rural nature of Saskatchewan, CED has often been approached in terms of rural development; but with the urbanization of the population, and the growth of the Northern, Aboriginal population, city-neighbourhood and Northern development are equally relevant. In fact, while CED results are highly dependent on the nature of the community, the general process is relatively similar — it is possible to learn by analogy. Recently a Canadian CED newsletter published a list of "20 Clues to Rural Community Survival," based on research from the US Great Plains conducted by the Heartland Center for Leadership Development.[14] The "clues" in question are positive indications about the ability of a community to survive. They represent a list of factors important in CED, and are highly relevant to rural and northern Saskatchewan but also to marginalized urban populations: 1) evidence of community pride; 2) emphasis on quality in business and community life; 3) willingness to invest in the future; 4) participatory approach to community decision-making; 5) co-operative community spirit; 6) realistic appraisal of future opportunities; 7) awareness of competitive positioning; 8) knowledge of the physical environment; 9) active economic development program; 10) deliberate transition of power to a younger generation of leaders; 11) acceptance of women in leadership roles; 12) strong belief in and support for education; 13) problem-solving approach to providing health care; 14) strong multi-generational family orientation; 15) strong presence of traditional institutions that are integral to community life; 16) attention to sound and well-maintained infrastructure; 17) careful use of fiscal resources; 18) sophisticated use of information resources; 19) willingness to seek help from the outside; 20) conviction that, in the long run, you have to do it yourself.

The above list is another reminder that there is much to be learned from south of the border. The Great Plains states share much of our history, from agrarian populism to the strong development of rural co-operatives. They share similar current economic challenges. Some things are done better on our side of the border (health care springs to mind), but some things are done better to the south: such as government support for research and development, government support for agriculture and for rural co-operatives, and, in many cases, CED.

The list can also be turned on its head: instead of saying, these are signs for identifying promising communities, we can also say, these are the qualities to be developed in communities in order to enhance their chances of providing for their own survival. In effect, every program, policy, or intervention that contributes positively toward one of the twenty characteristics above, is at least partly an economic-development initiative. How do we help communities develop pride? What makes people willing to invest in their community's future? How can people learn about their immediate physical environment? What promotes leadership transition and development of new groups of leaders? What enhances the leadership roles of women? The answers to such questions are also economic development answers. The particular list of twenty items is of course not sacrosanct. What it hints at, however, is the importance of community identity, shared culture, connections among people, perceptions and attitudes, as determinants of development.

A number of writers have recently begun conceptualizing qualities like these as "social capital," which by analogy to financial capital is a multipurpose resource that can contribute to the success of almost any kind of venture.[15] At root, social

14. Vicki Luther, "20 Clues to Rural Community Survival," in *Making Waves* 10, no. 2 (1999): 5–7, based on Vicki Luther and Milan Wall, *Clues to Rural Community Survival* (Lincoln, NE: Heartland Center for Leadership Development, 1998), which contains useful case studies drawn from towns in mid-Western and Northern states.

15. The classic reading is Robert D. Putnam, "The Prosperous Community: Social Capital and Public Life," *The American Prospect* 13 (Spring 1993), http://epn.org/prospect/13/13putn.html as accessed on November 4, 1997. His book, *Making Democracy Work: Civic Traditions in Modern Italy* (Princeton: Princeton University Press, 1993) stresses the importance of social capital for democratic life.

capital consists of the ability of people to trust each other and work together effectively. Social capital relates to the capacity and resilience of communities, their ability to generate new ideas and put them into practice; it is a question of the quality of human resources. Of course social capital goes well beyond government's usual definition of economics; but an economic development strategy that does not consider social capital would fail to make full use of community resources and provide full benefits to communities. Saskatchewan's famously high rates of voluntarism and co-operation are indications that one of the province's strengths has been its social capital. But it is a separate question whether this stock of social capital is being replenished, whether it is being developed in communities where it is needed, and whether it is being tapped and put to productive use for economic development.

EDUCATION

Whether "new economy," "social capital," or "community economic development," all today's conceptions of economic change highlight the importance of education. Education is among other things perhaps the most important infrastructure program and economic development program for the twenty-first century. The infrastructure of the original First Nations economy included migration routes, buffalo jumps, and winter camps; for the fur economy, infrastructure was canoe routes and trading posts; the grain economy was built around surveyed land and railroads; the postwar resource economy was developed with highways into the north, with power and mines and forest-management areas. What will be the infrastructure of the new economy? Communications, to be sure, and information technology; but beyond that, the infrastructure of a knowledge economy consists of skills, education, and the institutions that foster these. There are some indications that the political system is picking up on the importance of education as a policy area: the 1999 provincial election featured more discussion of post-secondary education (in the form of Liberal and New Democratic promises for student aid) than in any election since the 1970s. But by absolute measures — high-school incompletion rates, percentage of population with post-secondary training — the problem is far more severe than political debate to date has reflected.

Today's economic challenges require us to think of education in new ways; sometimes, the best new thinking is by analogy. Leo Kristjanson, president of the University of Saskatchewan in the 1980s, was fond of comparing the role of education in today's society to the institution of homesteading in the pioneer, settler society. Settlers were given homestead land for only a nominal fee: in effect, government gave away vast tracts of land to those willing to settle it and invest their work in it. This was not exactly a handout, but rather a relatively egalitarian opportunity that could be realized only if those who received the land actually put their work into it. The result was an economic boom and the development of modern Saskatchewan. Kristjanson's point, of course, was that education is today's equivalent: an opportunity available to those willing to put their work into it; the basis for a new economic boom. In 1999, at the installation of one of Kristjanson's successors, Peter MacKinnon, Chief Perry Bellegarde presented a related metaphor by calling education the modern-day bison for Aboriginal people. Just as the bison provided the First Nations with raw materials for almost everything they needed, so education is the basic resource for today's economy.

Such comparisons of education to resources, to land or bison, is an appropriate metaphor for Saskatchewan. We are used to thinking about our economies having been based on resources. We need to think about them being based on people, and more particularly on people's education, abilities, and capacity to work together. Like the bison and the land, education is a tool or resource to be put into the hands of people, to make with what they will — not to be delivered over to corporations or micromanaged by governments. Education is development work, and it is an open-ended and populist form of development work that is not amenable to close control by planners and financial analysts.

But government, leaders in educational institutions, leaders in communities, and ordinary people do have to think about *what kind* of education, in general, is needed.

We are used to thinking of educational sectors as primary, secondary, and post-secondary. From the early years when completion of Grade 8 was a significant achievement, it became the norm, and then compulsory. Completion of Grade 12 is now the norm, and increasingly a complete post-secondary education is regarded as appropriate for the clear majority. It is important to state that the provincial economy has been well-served in the past by the successes of the public educational system at giving broad skills and knowledge to a large population. But Saskatchewan's achievements lag behind what is needed, particularly to keep pace with the rest of Canada. This task is becoming more important and more demanding, in that the new economy requires far more independence and creativity from citizens. This means education does have to change not only in quantity, but also in intensity and approach.

If there are key issues in education, from the point of view of economic development, they are these: quality; collaboration; technical education; apprenticeships; and informal or less-formal education.

Quality in education has many dimensions. It is important to recognize that some of these dimensions are resource-related (class sizes, preparation time, opportunities for instructors to upgrade and learn new techniques) while others are based on creativity and innovation. Very few aspects of educational quality are captured by industrial models of education that focus on standardization, objectified outcomes, and control by planners and administrators. As in the economy as a whole, such models measure the wrong things and stifle what actually makes for quality. A good example is provided by a recent issue of *Scientific American* that favourably highlighted science teaching in a Saskatoon high school compared to science teaching in other countries. What gave the Saskatoon school the edge was a "chaotic" learning environment in which students learned to seek answers and formulate theories for themselves rather than memorizing from a textbook; they came away excited by science and understanding it because they had *done* it, not just studied it.[16]

The last thing students will need in an information society is more information. What students will need from the educational system, at all levels, more than they ever needed it before, is the ability to handle information throughout their lives: they need concepts that organize information, analogies between different areas of knowledge, experience with different ideas, the ability to think and to communicate, the ability to keep learning. Knowing highly specialized techniques or information sets is not especially relevant because such techniques and information

16. On Bedford Road Collegiate Institute, see W. Wayt Gibbs and Douglas Fox, "The False Crisis in Science Education," *Scientific American* 281, no. 4 (October 1999): 91.

change so quickly. The history of technological change over the last two hundred years has been that, while new technologies have repeatedly transformed society, detailed study of each technology has not been a requirement for the vast majority of people. When, a century ago, the chemical and electrical industries created a new industrial revolution, there was indeed a need to train more chemists and electrical engineers; however, the larger change was in the number of office workers and managers needed by the newer and highly productive firms. To this extent it is a mistake to focus only on science and technology, or only on computers, as a way to prepare for the age of information technology. We should be educating large numbers of citizens to be white-collar and office workers, people who use and manage information, consultants and designers and researchers, deliverers of public and commercial services. These people need to be skilled enough, independent enough, and both scientifically and culturally literate enough to find their own places in the kinds of jobs that will be created in large numbers in the new economy: jobs that will use technology but not necessarily create it.

Interestingly, one of the characteristics of the new economy that may require the most rethinking from schools and educational institutions is its requirement for teamwork and collaboration. To train students to work as individuals is a reflection of the industrial-era economy; it conceptualizes education as a standardized individual good rather than as a social process. In the new economy, most people, most of the time, work in teams. Skill and experience in teamwork and collaboration is one of the most important "job skills" students can learn. There is another side to this: in a world of so much flexibility and teamwork, what do people believe in? What do they feel attached to? We should also view the development of senses of shared identities among students as one of the goals of twenty-first-century education. The more the world globalizes, the more we want Saskatchewan students to come to that world with a secure sense of a Saskatchewan identity.

At the post-secondary level, many of the goals of broad intellectual development and education in professions have been associated with the provincial universities, while technical institutes have sometimes been conceptualized as institutions where people are trained to the immediate requirements of specific jobs. Both kinds of institutions have performed their tasks well; however, in the grand scheme of things, it is apparent from interprovincial and international comparisons that the technical sector of postsecondary education is underdeveloped in Saskatchewan New-economy thinking would also suggest that the focus of technical education has been too narrow for what will be required in the future. Perhaps this is even one reason for the sustained enrolment pressure on universities, which promise access to more information-rich jobs. A possible implication is that the technical sector may need to become larger and more academic, even university-like in some respects; while more specific, short-term job-training programs should be located within industry instead of within public institutions.

Apprenticeship programs have long been one of the weak points of Saskatchewan and Canadian education. In other countries (and Germany comes to mind) apprentices are hired on a cost-shared basis between small enterprises and governments, with a reasonably secure promise of a real job at the end of the apprenticeship. The downfall of such programs is when apprentices do not actually get hired often enough into permanent jobs; then the program degenerates into wage subsidies for transient workers. The development of an effective apprenticeship system in which government and business both live up to their responsibilities would be the best way to address the job-specific training requirements of small and medium enterprises.

Finally, the roles of formal credentials and of ongoing, informal education need to be considered. Educational systems are coming under increasing pressure to provide credentials in nontraditional ways, based on assessments of unique combinations of student learning from different sources, or in partnership with other institutions. At the same time, there is continuing and perhaps growing demand for open-ended education, particularly for adults, that may or may not ever result in a credential. In effect, the relationship between education and credentials is being put into question in new ways. Informal, open-ended, and community-based education may be especially important in shaping social capital. How to support and if necessary credentialize such education could be a significant economic issue. The increasingly fluid boundaries are a reflection of changes in the educational sector that mirror changes in society, the economy, and government. One possible result is that all institutions may have to become involved, in different ways, in more informal or open-ended education. Perhaps we will see more schools and libraries, or other public institutions, or for that matter businesses, hosting events where technical or university personnel provide content for a general audience or a work force — or perhaps such learning will occur on the internet. While such education will come from many sources and head in many directions, Saskatchewan's network of regional colleges along with extension units in the larger institutions constitutes one set of nodes that might be expected to play a co-ordinating role.

In short, education is more important than ever before; and more flexible and creative educational structures and approaches, though they were perhaps always desirable, are now becoming imperative. The exact shape that twenty-first-century education will assume is difficult to foretell, but we can predict that education, along with other spheres of society, will indeed change. While education has broader purposes than simply serving the economy, the needs of the new economy and the information-based society will be part of the driving forces in educational change.

NEW GOVERNMENT

The traditional structure of modern government closely reflects the industrial model of organization, and has always done so: hierarchy, rigidity, strict functional specialization of sub-units, standardization and "mass production" of services. Not only Crown corporations, but line departments of government, are basically organized on the traditional corporate model. Efforts in recent decades to introduce private-sector management techniques into government seem to have changed this picture little, perhaps because techniques have been borrowed mostly from the more traditional end of the business spectrum. As in other spheres of society, the problem of such structures is their rigidity, their unresponsiveness to change, and their inability to inspire employee enthusiasm or public confidence. The symptom of the old structures, in government, is "program thinking": if a program exists, it is hard to think outside its boundaries to respond to new situations; if a problem arises for which no program exists, we do not know what to do, unless it is to create more programs. New issues in economic development, however, perhaps more typically involve a need for co-ordinating efforts by different departments, units, and regulatory agencies. Such a co-ordinated, multidisciplinary approach is difficult to organize within structures in which people work in separate boxes. As in other areas of society, there are also examples in government of the emergence of more innovative and responsive structures.

The new models imply organizing government, like other institutions, in a flexible way, with teams of specialists from different departments and units — perhaps even including knowledgeable people from outside government itself, in some cases — working around common themes that are close to the interests of citizens. One would expect to see a proliferation of departmental or interdepartmental committees, task forces, and project teams, each with a fair degree of autonomy to formulate and propose new policy and new common approaches, working on matters that are important issues in the lives of people and communities. In effect, such temporary units would be the nodes in a network model of government. They might deal with matters like childhood development (along the lines of the Action Plan for Children, one of the more successful policy-development initiatives of the 1990s, which involved a number of departments and programs), integration of work and family responsibilities in the lives of citizens (an issue raised by a task force in the 1995–99 government), introduction of New Generation Co-operatives into agricultural processing, electronic commerce, the education-employment interface, resource-based Northern economic development, or any area that spills over the boundaries of a single unit's mandate.

More flexible structures are problematic in government — more so than in the private sector — because of the importance of issues of accountability. Departments must be responsible to ministers, who must be responsible to the legislature, which must be accountable to the electors: the maintenance of this chain of responsibility is essential to preserving the appearance and reality of democratic control of government. Such considerations have to be recognized as important factors hindering the devolution of authority within government, factors which will tend to make civil servants seek prior approval for uncertain initiatives. Such risk-aversity is appropriate behaviour within a system of democratic accountability. However, there is considerable room for flexibility and innovation before democracy actually becomes undermined. In particular, forming autonomous and temporary units for the purpose of discussing, developing, and proposing policy does not necessarily change the systems for making decisions and implementing policy. In the future we are likely to see a dual system: a hierarchical structure for accountability, a network model for how creative work is done.

The changing social-economic environment touches on the question of the roles of elected and appointed officials in shaping policy and programs. Here there can be no mistake: it is increasingly the job of civil-service employees to learn to think outside the boxes of current government organization. To do this, they must have clear signals from above, supportive networks and training, and an environment of respect and trust. The job of elected officials is, first, to foster this environment; and second, to maintain trust and accountability to the public. There is no doubt that there is a tension in the politician's role, between spurring the civil service to be creative, and controlling its decisions. This tension has always existed, but is becoming if anything more severe. The politician, especially in the twenty-first century, has to be a specialist in communication and facilitation, a mediator of ideas between institutions and between cultures, an expert in social process. Simply to be a decision maker, a detail freak, a figurehead, or a popularizer does not fit the job description. What we need are politicians who are comfortable at the appropriate level of generality: who can seriously discuss big ideas, who can set general directions, who can hold out goals around which the public and government agencies can come together.

The real reason we will see new models of organizing work in government is that the old models successfully addressed the problems that they were suited to solving. The problems that remain or are emerging — today's problems, the problems of the new economy — are almost always ones that go beyond the established institutional roles and boundaries.

CONCLUSION

Recognition that Saskatchewan's economy has been transformed before, and is being transformed again. Acknowledgement that economic policies used in the past are ineffective today. A balanced approach supporting the strengths and addressing the weaknesses of private, public, and social forms of enterprise. Policies for the new economy. Community economic development, to draw in larger circles of people to share in and contribute to the economy. Priority for education and innovation in education. New concepts for how government works. This chapter has addressed these areas as overarching themes in economic development. There are many sectors and aspects that could be discussed and need to be discussed at length and have not been in this chapter: First Nations and Métis economic development; the future of agriculture; environmental sustainability; tourism; cultural industries, partnerships with labour unions and union-sponsored investment funds — there is a long list of economic issues and possibilities at the turn of the new century.

Economies exist to sustain people, and Saskatchewan's has done so historically by a succession of natural resource-based industries. As a province, we should both recognize and accept the importance of our natural environment and our location to who we are and what we do. Bison, furs, grain, hogs, pulp, minerals: to some extent we are our commodities. But while this is true, it also becomes a trap if we identify ourselves too closely with what we have produced in the past. We should go beyond our resource dependence when we can, and remember that extracting resources or producing a particular commodity is not, in itself, the final purpose of an economy. In fact, the resource-extraction mentality can be counterproductive when it leads to over-specialization, over-exploitation, narrow visions and environmental damage. Governments, educational institutions, businesses, and citizens alike are challenged to rethink their assumptions and their basic organizations and activities.

There is no guarantee of success. Saskatchewan could remain on the margin of the next economy, as it was on the margin of the last one.

To write today about economic development and about the role of government is risky. Our society is at a point when there are no clear answers, and when no one should pretend to expert knowledge. But society is not well-served when people in responsible positions — in organizations, businesses, universities, government — avoid the difficult questions. The last quarter-century has posed fundamental challenges to conventional ideas about the role of government and of political leadership in economic development. Easy assumptions about government planning and management of the economy, about megaprojects and job-creation programs, have been critically undermined by specific failures, by the fiscal crisis of the state, and by changing economic and social-cultural realities. Increasingly, Saskatchewan needs a new approach by government. It needs a new willingness by public officials to think outside their boxes. It needs a new kind of political leader who can set and communicate goals in a complex and fluid environment.

There are those who will disagree with the view presented here about the twenty-first-century economy and the role of government within it. Some will say that the information technology will be only for an elite. Presumably there were also people in the sixteenth century who argued that books would never catch on, that common people would never learn to read. Then as now, such critics were partly correct, especially in the short term; but missed the fundamentally transformative effect that certain kinds of technologies have on society as a whole. Others will say that governments have no business subsidizing postsecondary education because people, who may already be well-off, gain from it as individuals. To be consistent, people of such views would presumably have opposed giving valuable homestead land to settlers, and would instead have auctioned it, in the name of fairness, to whoever could pay. Such egalitarianism is admirable in its simplicity.

More generally, people may doubt that organizations and industries will actually change as much as predicted. The only answer to this is, first, that it is true that only time will tell, and also true that the change will not be total, and that new and old organizations will exist side by side; but finally, it is also true that similar doubts probably existed prior to each previous economic transformation. People should not categorically believe or disbelieve predictions of economic change. Instead, they should keep their heads up and their minds open — because economies really do go through transformations, and the ways in which these transformations are met make real differences to the lives of people.

TRANSITIONS IN RURAL SASKATCHEWAN

Bob Stirling

INTRODUCTION

The idea of "rural" conjures up the image of a quiet, traditional, unchanging way of life, an image which does not fit rural Saskatchewan. The theme of this chapter will be that the conjunction of factors which encouraged Saskatchewan's rural and farm people to develop a vigorous civil society during the decades after World War II have largely changed — to the detriment of their democratic project. Heavily influenced by the politics of "independent," small-scale family agriculture after World War II, rural Saskatchewan grasped important issues and championed important programs in health, education, co-operatives, transportation and others. But the politics of the future is not the politics of the past. In part, the relative importance of agriculture has itself declined. But more important has been the transformation of farming, increasing in scale but also growing more dependent upon non-farm interests, to a point where farm politics too is becoming dependent, for example mirroring the needs of agribusiness and being boxed in by patents and trade agreements. Yet trends are not inevitable. There are alternatives. The chapter ends by remembering some and pondering the political will to pursue them.

THE IMPORTANCE OF FARMING TO RURAL SASKATCHEWAN

It is true that other activities besides farming have, from time to time, sustained some rural communities in Saskatchewan. Furs, fishing and logging were historically important for northern communities. Several manufacturing establishments made a contribution in the south. But apart from agriculture, only mining and oil extraction have been important alternative reasons for southern rural communities to exist. Coal mining, largely confined to the southeast, began in the late 1800s. There have also been a few sodium sulphite and clay operations. Serious petroleum exploration began in the 1920s with some success — the town of Lloydminster was supplied with natural gas in 1934 and several urban refineries were built — but most of the fields were not developed until well after World War II. Similarly potash, found accidentally during oil exploration, was not developed commercially until the 1950s. In total, these non-agricultural primary products were important to only a handful of rural communities during the settlement phase, often playing a supportive role to farming.

While the same is true today, it is not for lack of non-farm economic activity. Saskatchewan's economy, like others' has become centred on trade and other services (see Figure 1). Over the past decade, total industrial production has accounted for one-fifth to one-quarter of the province's gross domestic product, while total

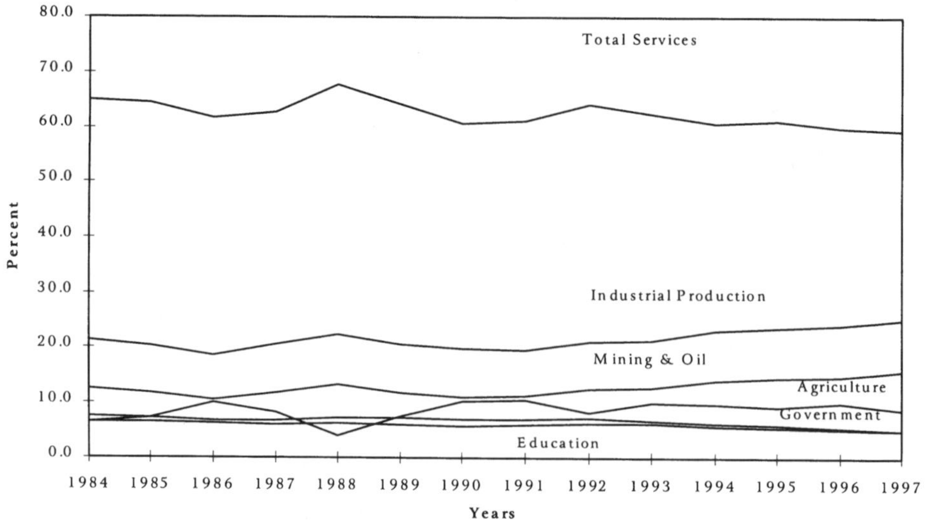

Figure 1: Saskatchewan Gross Domestic Product by Industry, 1984–1997.

services at times ran as high as two-thirds. The contribution of agriculture was characteristically variable, but also rather meagre at 10 percent or less. By comparison, mining and oil extraction accounted for 10–16 percent of provincial GDP and from 1984 to 1997 showed growth.

However these non-farm primary industries have not offered a solid basis for rural viability elsewhere and rural Saskatchewan is no doubt similar (Richards and Pratt, 1979: 159–62; Freudenburg and Gramling, 1998). For one thing, their level of technological specialization means that they support backward and forward linkages that are only modest at best. Typically the raw product is shipped unprocessed and few inputs are purchased locally. In some cases, like Alberta in the 1960s, their final demand linkages may have been strong since these primary industries — oil and gas in particular — contributed to strong employment growth. The rural Saskatchewan experience is different. Some of the employment growth has taken place in head offices and downstream facilities well removed from the local mine and well sites and often even outside of the province. Further, total employment in the non-farm primary industries is modest. Their employment in 1996 including fishing and trapping (230), forestry (2,585), mining and oil and gas wells (12,065), was only 3 percent of Saskatchewan's labour force compared to the 77,755 or 15.7 percent who worked in agriculture.

These industries can also contribute to final demand if their taxation and royalties can support strong state expenditures. This may have been true until the 1980s. Since then, royalties and resource revenues have been dropping. For example resource royalties and taxes dropped from $724 million (or 26.3 percent of the industries' sales) during the years of the Blakeney government (1979–1982) to $488 million (or 9.9 percent of sales) during the 1992–1997 period of the Romanow government. Almost one-third of total provincial revenues came from resource revenues during the Blakeney period compared to 10.2 percent during the Romanow period (Brown et al., 1999: Appendix 2).

Finally, the number of rural Saskatchewan communities where non-farm primary industries have an impact is small. Stabler and Olfert (1992: 62–65) found only 21 communities with mines nearby. In communities where mining employment was less than fifty, they found no difference in the viability of these communities compared to other communities between 1961 and 1990. Where mining employment was over fifty, the communities experienced population growth when the mines were first built and put into production, but their viability showed about the same pattern as other communities after that.

Compared to mining and oil extraction, local manufacturing has had a more beneficial effect on rural community viability although the pattern is stronger among larger, more viable centres with over 100 manufacturing employees (Stabler and Olfert, 1992: 65–76). Recently, this has been more true for the northern portion of the province's southern agricultural belt, where agriculture is more diversified and its consolidation has not advanced as far as in the south.

SUMMARY

Agriculture's contribution to the province's economy is comparatively modest but it makes a greater contribution to employment. This, plus the fact that the province's rural centres were largely built to service the farm sector suggests that farming continues to be the main ingredient in rural Saskatchewan's future. Mining and oil make a greater contribution to the province's economy but much less to employment. So the non-agricultural primary industries, plus manufacturing, may sustain a few communities but typically they play a supporting role to farming.

But what of the future of farming? Two decades ago, a respected agricultural economist reminded us of some negative consequences for rural communities as Saskatchewan's farms became fewer and larger: "larger and more mechanised farmers spend their money differently than smaller, low income farmers ... [and are willing] to travel many miles in order to possibly obtain a lower price" (Lee, 1980: 3). By then the negative consequences for rural communities of large-scale industrial farming had been identified in rural sociology (Goldschmidt, 1947, 1975; Lobao et al., 1993). In 1957, Saskatchewan's Royal Commission on Agriculture and Rural Life identified similar connections as it contemplated the future of rural life in light of the trend that it had identified for farms to get larger and fewer in number (chapter 8). One of the commissioners recognized that the implications of farm consolidation were not merely limited to farm economics when he observed that "[e]conomists and sociologists would agree, I am sure, that this trend (not yet a major concern in Saskatchewan) if carried to its logical conclusion, contains a very definite threat to our whole democratic setup" (Phelps, 1958). Is the trend in agriculture continuing to its "logical conclusion"? The next section takes up that question.

FARMERS' DEMOCRACY – THE PAST

The political life of prairie farming communities has been intimately tied to the interests of the agrarian petty bourgeoisie. Family farmers have different interests than industrial farmers, different relations with agribusiness, different internal dynamics, and different strategies of resistance. In many sectors of the economy, from mining and timbering to retail stores, the twentieth century has not been kind to the traditional petty bourgeoisie.[1] But family farmers resisted this trend for much

1. An example of their disappearance in Canadian mining is discussed in Clement, 1983, chapter 7. However, Clement's analysis of family farming in that volume is, in certain ways, an alternate view to the one presented in this chapter.

of the century. So will they go or won't they? I think the progressive era of their politics has been eclipsed, a case to be argued in this and the following sections.

The disappearance of family farming has two deep structural axes. One has to do with the challenge from outside, the growing penetration of agribusiness which has expanded old forms of market domination into areas such as farm knowledge and the nature of farm work. The other is internal to farming and is centred on the petty bourgeois need to own property. It heightens the competition between family farmers and as MacPherson (1962) has argued, limits their ability to resist the more powerful prerogatives of non-farm capital. Nevertheless, farm people have resisted, sometimes rather successfully, in spite of these structural constraints. How did they do it? A brief historical tour is in order.

The Era of the National Policy

The economy of the prairie region has been firmly rooted in staples production for several centuries. Indigenous peoples were drawn into the French and British colonial fur trade by the late 1600s. By the late 1800s, Canada's National Policy was recreating the region as an investment frontier and agricultural hinterland of central Canada (Fowke, 1957). The land was appropriated and surveyed, railways were built, and hundreds of thousands of potential farm families and those who would service their farm production were encouraged to settle the region. By the 1920s, rural society was firmly established on the basis of "family farming," wherein the family owns its farm capital but also does all, or most, of its farm work. Sometimes they are referred to as "independent commodity producers" or the "agricultural petty bourgeoisie" (Mann, 1990). Other forms, for example "bonanza" farms, more along industrial capitalist lines, were tried but could not cope as well as the family farms with low prices, high costs and the exigencies of nature (Friedmann, 1978; Morgan, 1960).

Family farming was also well suited to the needs of the fledgling Canadian economy. It produced virtually a monoculture of wheat in Saskatchewan, a staple that commercial capital would export while the thousands of individual farm families bought farm inputs and family needs, providing a home market for industrial capital. It was a "national" project that received vigorous support from the state. Indeed the staple, wheat, was one of the crucial elements leading to the emergence of Canada as an industrial nation (Macintosh, 1967; 1991: 78).

The first three decades of this century saw the population of the prairies grow by leaps and bounds; Saskatchewan's population grew tenfold. By 1931 its population was almost 922,000, about the size it would be for the rest of the century (see Table 1). Over two-thirds of the population was rural in 1931, while 61 percent resided on farms. The number of farms increased over 250 percent between 1906 and 1936, which saw the century's high point at over 142,300. The rural population built hundreds of rural centres of varying sizes, connected by a mushrooming system of railway branch lines (Artibise, 1981; Voisey, 1988).

Farm families on the prairies faced both drought and depression during the 1930s. The experience bankrupted farms and local businesses, broke families, disrupted farm production and put the national project on hold. Still, the number of Saskatchewan farms actually *increased* during the Great Depression as the labour reserve in the cities was driven back to the land to eke out an existence or receive state support.

Table 1: Rural and Urban Population and Number and Size of Farms, Saskatchewan, 1931–96

	1931	1941	1951	1956	1961	1966	1971	1976	1981	1986	1991	1996
Population												
Total	921,785	895,992	831,728	880,665	925,181	955,344	926,242	921,323	968,313	1,009,610	988,928	990,237
Urban	290,905	295,506	252,479	322,003	398,091	468,327	490,627	511,333	563,166	620,195	623,397	627,178
Rural	630,880	600,486	579,249	558,662	527,090	487,017	435,615	409,990	405,147	389,415	365,531	363,059
% Rural	68.4	67.0	69.6	63.4	57.0	51.0	47.0	44.5	41.8	38.6	37.0	36.7
Non-Farm	66,868	85,819	179,776	196,431	221,350	205,928	201,823	207,280	217,984	220,910	205,806	217,499
Farm	564,012	514,677	399,473	362,231	305,740	281,089	233,792	202,710	187,163	168,505	159,725	145,560
% Farm	61.2	57.4	48.0	41.1	33.0	29.4	25.2	22.0	19.3	16.7	16.2	14.7
Number of												
Farms	136,472	138,713	112,018	103,391	93,924	85,686	76,970	70,958	67,318	63,431	60,840	56,995
Average Farm Size												
Acres	408	432	550	607	686	763	845	923	974	1,036	1,091	1,152
Capital	9,325	6,459	17,787	22,384	30,504	57,332	71,008	161,969	465,976	460,838	421,364	536,121

Source: Statistics Canada, Annual Censuses; Saskatchewan Agriculture and Food, Agricultural Statistics 1997.

In other words, the settlement period resulted from a unique set of global forces. It created an objective class of family farmers and subjected them to the vagaries of world markets, hinterland status in a growing capitalist economy, and the uncertainty of nature magnified by the high degree of staples specialization and monoculture of Saskatchewan production. These were fertile conditions for developing political consciousness among the agrarian petty bourgeoisie. Indeed they founded co-operatives, actively involved themselves in political parties, strongly influenced the state and showed signs of fulfilling the Jeffersonian legacy of being the "backbone" of democracy. It was a period that nourished the growth of a social democratic form of agrarian populism (discussed elsewhere in this volume) which became one of rural Saskatchewan's important legacies (Conway, 1983; Laycock, 1990).

THE ERA OF THE KEYNESIAN COMPROMISE

World War II brought higher prices for farm commodities, vastly improved farm margins and the opportunity for farm families to accumulate capital. Gradually farm families and the family farm class became established and relatively secure. Here and elsewhere in the Canadian economy, and more broadly in the Western world, a post-World War II "Keynesian compromise" settled in over social and political relations and people's expectations concerning the role of the state in securing their future (Teeple, 1995 offers a detailed and systematic treatment of this argument.). In general, it turned the economy to mass production along Fordist lines, together with mass consumption through higher wages and incomes and growth in the welfare state for the lower classes. Confronted with unruly underclasses led by segments of workers and their unions but including farmers, fishermen and others, this was the price that capital was prepared to pay in order to stabilize capital accumulation and head off more serious change in capitalist class relations. Politically it involved a more fundamental advance of civil rights such as recognition of unions and collective bargaining, as well as collective marketing and marketing boards for farmers.

This was a fertile climate for the advancement of agrarian social democracy. It flourished in Saskatchewan not only by championing flagship social programs such as Medicare but also through improving the quality of rural life with rural electrification and other infrastructure projects, improved roads, the "larger school unit" campaign to put local education on a sounder financial and pedagogical footing, and greater, although not fundamental, attention to participatory democracy with activities such as the "Farm Radio Forum," the Royal Commission on Agriculture and Rural Life, and others. Its influence was also felt federally — albeit muted and twisted to suit more powerful national interests — in the form of marketing boards, international wheat agreements, various support and infrastructure programs, and policies to mitigate regional disparities. In other words, the hegemonic ideology of the Canadian Keynesian compromise after World War II had an agrarian component to it. On the one hand, and like the United States, there was the understanding — backed by state programs along Fordist lines — that food would be cheap for urban consumers, and that "progressive" farmers would do their best to increase productivity by adopting industrial technologies on the farm (Kenny et al., 1991). On the other hand, the state would attempt to make farm investment secure, upgrade the quality of rural life and make it possible for the sons and daughters of rural Canada to expect a brighter future, even if through opportunities for education and urban jobs.

Hegemonic ideologies not only exist at the level of the state and social formation, but they also penetrate the level of everyday life. The influence of agrarian social democracy was present at the local level with its emphasis on the informal rural culture of neighbourliness, community support and solidarity. The structural tendency toward individualism and competitiveness of the agrarian petty bourgeoisie was restrained somewhat by this ethos of co-operation and progressivism. The type of egalitarianism imagined in the vision of "building a New Jerusalem," a favourite metaphor of then CCF Premier Tommy Douglas, shows how the hegemony reached into institutions like the church, drawing on the social gospel (Smillie, 1991).

However, at the level of farm production, the seeds of a different ethic were being sown. Rising prices meant that for many farm families, capital accumulation once again became a likely possibility and a significant goal. As this orientation once again became embedded in social practices, the well-known trends for prairie farming began to reappear; growing farm size with fewer farms, reduced labour, increasing non-farm inputs, and a "progressive" drive toward industrial farming. In other words, agrarian resistance during the post-World War II period did have an effect. On the output side of farming, international wheat agreements, marketing boards and co-operatives served to blunt the influence of agribusiness. On the input side, however, it did nothing to limit the importance of property to farmers. So their competitive tendency to buy each other out, farming more land with fewer people, and the attendant ideology of progressivism, set the stage for heightened levels of agribusiness penetration to come. What appeared as calm and stability on the surface had a dialectical fury underneath.

FARMERS' "DEMOCRACY" – THE PRESENT

The 1970s brought a new stage of capitalism with profound effects on family farming the world over (McMichael, 1998). Still, it is not that the new era brought a different dynamics to prairie family farming or to capitalism. Saskatchewan farmers have always been integrated into capitalist markets. They have always produced for a world market, consumed on the domestic market, and faced agribusiness in both directions. But the opportunities for agribusiness to penetrate the farm sector increased in several ways. Responding to the typical forces that encourage concentration of wealth in other industries, agribusiness firms have consolidated and merged, growing larger and fewer while extending their global influence. Many of these multinationals are American firms or ones that have significant American interests. They demand and receive the benefits of a reinvigorated US imperialism. For Canada, this means taking continentalism to new heights, with much of Canadian capital aligning itself with American demands for "free" trade. One result for the farm sector is that programs that were secured under the post-World War II period such as marketing boards, public agricultural research and extension, and farm support programs, are seen as obstacles to capital accumulation by agribusiness or other sectors of capital. They have been quickly offered up in NAFTA and the WTO.

Partly for these reasons, and partly because of the internal dynamics of the agrarian petty bourgeoisie, farmers' ability to control their own economy, society and politics declined. At first a major weakness or "crack" in the class appeared to be a decline of the "middle" farmers (LaRimee and Buttel, 1991; Stirling and Conway, 1988). This was thought to be serious since these were the farm families that drew most of their income from farming and traditionally had been the hard-core participants in agrarian organizations (McCrorie, 1964). They carried the social democratic flags and were the wellspring of social democratic hegemony. Such class fracturing has long been seen as an indication of the demise of the agrarian class (for example, Lenin, 1971). It may help to explain changes in farmers' voting patterns or the ongoing hegemonic crisis in Prairie agriculture where farmers refuse to "speak with one voice." But it is only the outward show of deeper processes underlying prairie family farming.

I have mentioned above these deeper structural axes. One centres upon farmers' growing dependence on agribusiness for inputs, outputs and knowledge. The other focuses upon farmers' need to grow larger and therefore fewer in number. The fact that the first process produces low margins only adds a certain urgency to the second process. Indeed farm consolidation has occurred and will continue whether margins were low or high. In other words the particular set of global forces that have developed since the 1970s have increased farmers' dependence upon agribusiness and unleashed a new wave of competition between farmers. I will argue below that this has led to a form of dependent politics and the eclipse of agrarian social democracy. But first we should examine some examples of these changes at the farm level.

CHANGES IN FARMING — SOME ILLUSTRATIONS

I noted above how "family farms," not large-scale, industrial or "bonanza" farms, became the predominant form during the settlement period. Even as we begin the new century, only 2 percent of Saskatchewan's farms would not be classed as family farms (although some families have incorporated their farms or have written agreements, especially where more than one family operates the farm). Yet much of the industrial dynamics of non-farm industries can be found in farming as well. In spite of the dominance of family farms, the industrialization of farming is well underway. As in other industries, close margins and the need to accumulate capital encourage industrialization.

Prices for farm commodities are variable and low. World War II brought improved prices generally, but by 1987 the price of wheat reached an all-time low — even lower than its price during the Great Depression — in constant 1981 dollars (Fulton et al., 1989: 1). The pattern persisted over the next decade; wheat prices rebounded somewhat in the late 1980s, dropped even below the 1987 level in the early 1990s (accounting for inflation), recovered slightly at mid-decade, and headed downward again in the late 1990s! Similarly, hog and cattle prices were lower in 1998 than 10 years earlier and have not improved for several decades, except for their typical cycles. So are today's farm product prices exceptionally low or "crisis" prices? Hardly. Speaking about grains and oilseeds during the last two decades, University of Manitoba agricultural economist Daryl Kraft notes that there has been "a no-growth export market and at the same time ... new technology expanding yields by two percent a year" (*Western Producer*, August 26, 1999). This is a recipe for low prices. We recall times of good prices as if they were the standard but these are the exceptions; low farm prices appear to be the rule.

There are deeper reasons for the current low farm prices. Wealthy countries, particularly the United states, have used food commodities as a means to extend their imperial influence around the world. For more than a decade the US-EEC trade war has pushed grain prices down. Countries that were to have produced effective demand for Canadian food commodities, for example those that have recently come into the orbit of Western capital such as the old Soviet bloc countries, and others that have suffered setbacks in the new imperialism such as Japan and other Asian countries, have seen their economies seriously weakened (Brenner, 1998; McNally, 1999; Patnaik, 1999). Further, production and prices for many food commodities are heavily influenced by the retail chains, packing and processing firms which require a cheap, standard product (Winson, 1992; Heffernan, 1998). Recent forays by a few giant agribusiness firms to dominate the American broiler and hog sectors serve as examples.

Consider the case of hogs. About a dozen agribusiness firms began seriously raising hogs and contracting with large producers in the early 1990s. By mid-decade this strategy was marginalizing all but the largest producers. Four companies — Smithfield Foods, IBP, ConAgra and Cargill — controlled 60 percent of the US hog slaughter. Only 6 percent of all hogs were sold through public markets (Center for Rural Affairs, 1998: 3). The strategy was also vastly increasing the supply of hogs and driving prices ever lower. The hog industry was simply being restructured. For example in North Carolina, where the industrialization process is most advanced, hog numbers increased 433 percent between 1982 and 1996, while the number of farm producers dropped 74 percent. By 1998, Professor Grimes, a leading US livestock economist, warned of a "meltdown" if increasing hog production was not curtailed. But the industry, driven by its new dynamics and structure, could not "reverse" the trend, and the meltdown came. Since the hog market has become continental, Canadian producers were caught along with their US counterparts. Prices became so low that some producers destroyed pigs to cut their losses while others quit the business.

The state has played an active role in farm prices and restructuring farm production. For example, in the case of hogs, for most of this century American midwestern states like Nebraska and Iowa were the main producers. But the recent corporate dominance of the industry made its greatest strides in North Carolina, a state that offered low wages, few environmental controls, tax concessions and other forms of bonussing. Fearing lost investment opportunities, most of the other agricultural states and provinces joined in what became a frenzied attack on small independent hog producers. In Saskatchewan, the most visible example of this attack was the elimination of the hog marketing board in 1997 by an NDP government that claimed to be the heir of the very agrarian populist movements that struggled to put marketing boards in place originally. This action mirrored the elimination of hog marketing boards in Manitoba in 1995, and in Alberta in 1996, both by

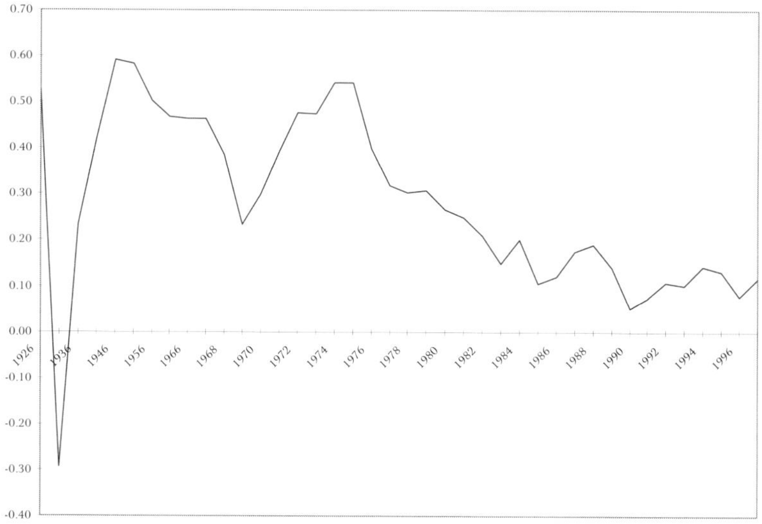

Figure 2: Net to Gross Income Ratio, Saskatchewan Farms, 1926–1997.

Conservative governments. Saskatchewan also established "Pork Central" in 1997, a government agency with a $1 million budget, devoted to encouraging large-scale hog barns and increasing provincial production threefold. Similar state and provincial agencies, indeed some with a similar name, appeared across the continent.[2]

It should not be surprising therefore that farm margins have become very thin. Figure 2 tracks the ratio of realized net farm income to gross farm income since the 1920s (note that before 1966, the data in Figure 2 are for five-year census intervals, after 1966 they are annual). From World War II until the mid-1970s, except for a brief period in the late 1960s and early 1970s, farm families, on average, claimed about half of their gross income as net income, the other half going for expenses. However, by the 1990s they claimed 10 percent or less, the other 90 percent going for expenses. Of course "expenses" include a wide range of items, some originating more distant from the farm than others. However, in 1997, for example, of total farm expenses (excluding depreciation), two categories of inputs — fertilizers and pesticides, and machinery repairs, fuels and lubricants — each accounted for just

2. The complex story of how each state and province moved to restructure their hog industries, while important, is beyond the scope of this chapter. The "intrigue" in Saskatchewan involved a hog marketing board, Saskatchewan Pork International (SPI) under siege from a handful of large producers with a mostly ideological mission to champion the "open" market. Unable to wrestle control of SPI from smaller producers, they successfully lobbied the NDP minister of Agriculture. When the minister told SPI that he intended to change the Act and remove its marketing powers, SPI contracted all of its hogs to two established packers in the province (it had a financial interest in both). However, this threatened the interests of other packers, particularly one owned by Saskatchewan Wheat Pool, a co-operative that had recently privatized and in the process renewed a close working relationship with the NDP government. The Pool's plan had been to vertically integrate the Saskatchewan hog industry with investment help from community groups, local economic development authorities, private investors and individual hog producers. Other investment groups proposed similar schemes. By undermining SPI's marketing powers, the minister altered the configuration of restructuring agents but did nothing to arrest or modify the restructuring process itself. Indeed, when the fortunes of large scale hog barns were threatened by coalitions of community and environmental groups and smaller producers who initially received a sympathetic ear from the environment department, the Department of Agriculture and Food went to bat for the large-scale investors. Versions of this story have been playing across North America especially during the last decade. (*Western Producer*, September 11, October 16, 23, 30, 1997; Center for Rural Affairs, 1998).

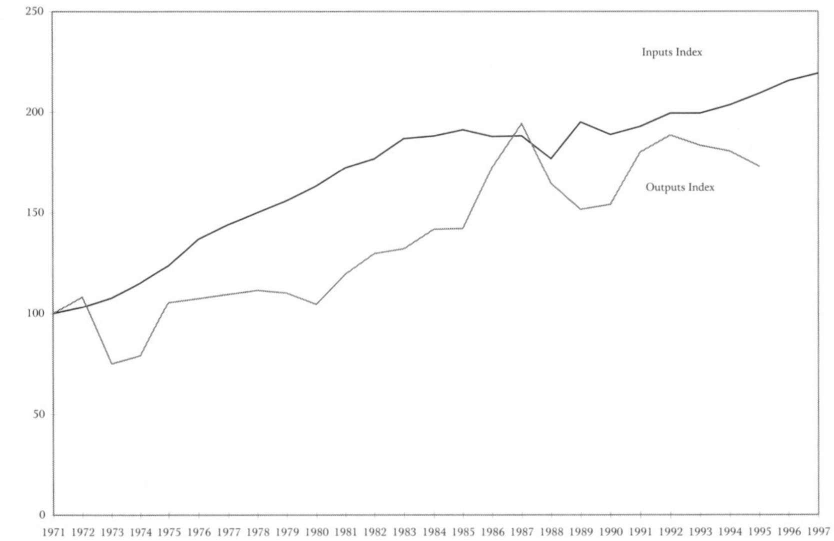

Figure 3: Index of Saskatchewan Farm Inputs and Outputs, 1971 = 100.

under one-quarter. These two types of purchased inputs alone made up almost half (47 percent) of farm operating expenses. By comparison, interest payments accounted for about 6.8 percent of operating expenses in 1997 (they had been well over 15 percent for most of the 1980s,) while property taxes accounted for 7.9 percent.

In fact there is a pattern of farmers' increasing dependence upon certain non-farm inputs (Figure 3). For example, the consumption of farm fuels has been essentially flat since 1971, but the consumption of fertilizers and pesticides has increased remarkably. Good data on pesticide sales is no longer readily available but, for example, the acres treated with wild oat herbicides increased between eight- and elevenfold from the early 1970s to the late 1980s. Fertilizer volumes, although generally quite variable, appear to have about doubled since the late 1980s. Overall, farm inputs, measured as total operating expenses plus depreciation in constant dollars, have more than doubled since 1971. Outputs have also increased although not to the same extent and the trend is characteristically unsteady in part due to the vagaries of weather, pests and other natural causes, perhaps made worse because of Saskatchewan's heavy emphasis on a modest range of crop production. The label "high input agriculture" certainly fits the Saskatchewan case.

Farmers are also becoming increasingly dependent upon marketing, processing and slaughtering firms. Signing marketing contracts to deliver commodities after harvest is now a common practice for some grains and speciality crops and arguably it reduces farmers' uncertainty and gives them more control over their daily activities. But where the contracts specify not only the quantity and quality of the product but also exactly how it will be produced, farmers' traditional control is diminished (Gertler, 1991). Such forms of vertical integration are currently more common for livestock and poultry products. For some commodities, like hogs in the US, where vertical integration is well advanced, so little is actually marketed through open markets that it is difficult to even determine a standard price. The agribusiness industry appears to see this as an inevitable wave of the future in which it extends greater influence over farming (*Western Producer*, September 16, 1999).

Another aspect of this increasing agribusiness penetration of farming lies in the growing control of farm knowledge, and therefore farm work. Proprietary knowledge is embedded in farm inputs and commodity contracts. In the case of machinery, the increased use of modular design where crucial parts are patented, definitely not "off-the-shelf," and virtually impossible to repair or modify on the farm, restricts farm knowledge and limits farmers' control over the nature of their work. Still, farmers' resistance here has been remarkable and probably aided by the extent to which the internal combustion engine has become deeply embedded in twentieth-century North American popular culture. By comparison, the make-up of farm chemicals has been heavily shrouded in secrecy and confusion. Although eager to use the pesticides and fertilizers, farmers have been generally reluctant to modify them or make their own (Stirling, 1998).

The process is being taken to new heights with the introduction of biotechnology and international trade agreements that protect intellectual property (Middendorf et al., 1998; McMichael, 1998; Shiva, 1997). This has allowed large firms to appropriate local farm knowledge or to replace it with other industrial, proprietary knowledge. Typically the practice takes the form of appropriating genetic material that has been in the public domain, and one of the bases underpinning decentralized forms of farming and, perhaps, rural democracy. At the national level, the newly acquired genetic stock is protected by "plant breeders' rights" and other patent laws. Consequently, firms can now require farmers to sign "use agreements" for the right to grow their patented varieties. The agreements usually forbid farmers from keeping seed from harvest to plant the next crop. Indeed the firms actively watch rural communities, and farmers who have not signed a current agreement that are "caught" with specimens of patented plants growing on their farms are sued or threatened into submission.

Certainly farmers resist this intrusion on their autonomy. At least one Saskatchewan farmer in this situation, found guilty of violating the patent on a genetically altered Canola, has countersued Monsanto, arguing that natural processes of cross-breeding, "spills" in transporting, wind drift and other normal farm practices can spread "proprietary" genes where they are not wanted (*Manitoba Co-operator*, August 19, 1999 and April 5, 2001). But more effective resistance to genetic property rights is hard for modern farmers to mount. Once again, it requires a limitation of the rights of property that does not fit well with farmers' petty bourgeois class location and the cultural and ideological trappings that go with it. Further, most of these genetic technologies appear well suited to other practices of large-scale, high-input farming, including family farming, where, during the growing period, labour is spread thinly over a large cultivated acreage, forcing the farm to rely heavily upon large machinery, fertilizers and industrial chemicals. In this circumstance, signing an agreement to use a company's patented crop that is resistant to its patented herbicide may be the only way a farm family knows to "keep its head above water" in the fight against weeds in a given year.

Farmers also engage in this high-input agriculture because there is no alternative. Of course there are alternatives such as organic and low-input agriculture, but with only some 1,000 certified organic farmers in Saskatchewan it is clear that most farmers don't yet take this alternative seriously. Perhaps it is too much to expect them to. Daily they have been bombarded by the claims for industrial agriculture in the farm press. Many carry substantial operating loans and/or loans for land, machinery or livestock; neither they nor their bankers tend to be keen to see the farm deviate from conventional practices. Equally important has been the role of the state.

Generous depreciation allowances have encouraged machinery purchases and from time to time tax abatements on farm fuels have encouraged their operation. Farm support programs and marketing structures have generally encouraged growth in farm size by benefiting families with large farms over small.

From at least the turn of the century, the state has played an even more intricate role in "fashioning" farmers, for example, through its "extension" activities in its departments of agriculture and universities, constructing a hegemonic social definition of the "good" farmer (Taylor, 1994. Taylor also shows how this had an impact upon agrarian politics in Manitoba during the early 1900s). Although the emphasis of state research and extension since World War II has been broadly on industrializing farming ("good" farmers should mechanize, use fertilizers and other chemicals, expand their farms, and maximize production), initially the state also played a role independent from agribusiness to the extent that many of its inventions — for example, new varieties and species — went into the public domain. However during the last two decades, as part of the general downsizing of the state, this role has been seriously cut back, opening the field as a new investment opportunity for agribusiness by also introducing plant breeders' rights and other measures discussed above. Today, the state largely champions an industrial definition of farming; indeed, in the short run at least, it would be hard for the state to operate otherwise since it has seriously hampered its own ability to consider and advocate alternatives.

Finally, of the many implications of the processes discussed in this section, one, the concentration of farm productive capital, needs to be added to the argument. Table 1 shows how the number of farms has declined since the Great Depression. Today there are only 50,000–55,000 farms in the province, and even some of these would be below a marginal size and hardly "farms" in a conventional sense. Similarly, the average size (acres) of farms has grown almost three fold since 1931.[3] But these familiar statistics do not adequately reveal the level of concentration of farm resources. Consider these examples: in 1976 the top 5 percent of Saskatchewan wheat farms controlled 16.7 percent of the total productive acres; by 1996 the top 5 percent controlled 19.8 percent of total acres while the bottom 50 percent of wheat farms controlled only 20.4 percent of total acres (these concentration figures are calculated from Statistics Canada, 1997, Cat. 93-358-XPB). The top 5 percent of farms raising cattle and calves in 1976 had 2.4 percent of the animals. By 1996 the top 5 percent (some 1,255 farms) had 25.6 percent, while the bottom 50 percent of farms had only 15.4 percent of the animals. Eighty-nine percent of all hens were on the top 150 chicken farms in 1996 compared to 57 percent held by the top 5 percent of farms in 1976. For hogs, the concentration is equally remarkable. In

3. Saskatchewan farmers have always emphasized crop production over livestock. In 1941, farms that drew most of their farm income from wheat, other grains and oilseeds accounted for two-thirds of all farms. These "grain" farms rose to about 80 percent by 1961 and the proportion has stayed in that range ever since. For example, in 1996, crop receipts accounted for 77 percent, and livestock receipts accounted for only 19 percent of total farm cash receipts in Saskatchewan. For Alberta farms the comparative figures were 46 percent for crops and 52 percent for livestock, while for Manitoba farms 58 percent of total receipts came from crops and 40 percent came from livestock. The point is not that Saskatchewan farms are more heavily specialized. Farming in Western economies is heavily specialized everywhere, including the prairies, in virtually every form of crop and livestock production. But Saskatchewan's emphasis on grains and oilseeds may increase the variability in farm income and certainly enhances the spatial domination of this form of monoculture. For example in 1981, wheat farms were the predominant type in all but one of Saskatchewan's 17 census divisions where farming is prevalent (Statistics Canada, 1984. Cat. no. 96-920, p. 97). The dominance of this type of farming has put a certain instability and "edge" to rural life and politics in the province.

1996, only 142 pig farms had 64 percent of the pigs, while the bottom 50 percent (1,424 farms) had only 3.3 percent of the pigs. The bottom half of the pig farm distribution harkens back to earlier eras when hogs were the "mortgage burners," the livestock that many farms had at least a few of because they were easily integrated into the total farm operation and they were vital to the farm's sustainability. Clearly the penetration of agribusiness into hog farming discussed earlier, and the processes of concentration in the farm sector itself have fundamentally restructured hog production. This has already happened in poultry and, without successful resistance, it will happen in the other farm commodities as well.

The point of presenting these data is not to lament the state of farming in Saskatchewan. This is simply the way farming is. Given the principles of managing industrial farms, there is nothing peculiar or untoward in these data, nothing that, in principle, would keep a competent farm business manager from building a financially viable farm operation. The point is simply that the number and nature of these modern farms is becoming vastly different from what were considered "family farms" in the past.

By imagining that these statistics represent the dominant restructuring trends for Saskatchewan farming, what can be said about its future? Bluntly, if the largest 5 percent of hog farms (142 farms) can produce two-thirds of the pigs, is there any strong commercial reason for the other 95 percent to exist? Or if the largest 5 percent of grain farms (2,850 farms) are showing us today a manageable level of farm scale and technology adoption, should we not expect that size and number of farms to become the norm in the future? Well, not entirely, for a host of reasons. For example, while farm markets are ruthless they are often chaotic, not following single tendencies. While agribusiness firms need to penetrate farming to expand their opportunities for investment and capital accumulation, their power and resources are not unlimited. Individually, farm families have always found ways to "go against the grain," nurturing their small farms with off-farm work or taking lower incomes. Collectively too, the agrarian petty bourgeoisie has dampened its inherent individualism and supported programs to the common good. Still, the forces of consolidation and corporate penetration in farming are strong and the determination to resist them among farm families is fractured, so while the number of farms may well decrease, more importantly we should expect farm production and wealth to concentrate heavily among the larger farms as the twenty-first century unfolds. That means that while the contribution of farming to rural employment will decline, an increasing portion will be paid workers. In other words, if farming continues to industrialize, its employment contribution will begin to look like that of mining or oil extraction. But what of its politics?

A POLITICS OF DEPENDENCY

This shift in the locus of control from the public domain, particularly farm families and the state, to agribusiness companies is an important mechanism for effecting the shift in the structure of farming that we are witnessing. The knowledge void is being filled, in part, by the very agribusiness firms that supply farm inputs and purchase farm commodities. It is also indicated by the growth of "professional crop scouts" who farmers hire for advice about fertilizer and pesticide applications, knowledge that once would have been obtained from others in the community, or the government or university extension agent. It is apparently a short step for farmers to turn over the management of their farms to these professionals. Faced with a wall of patented knowledge, increasingly farmers are fashioned as "business managers" who are either good or bad at calculating risk probabilities in their net income equations (*Manitoba Co-operator*, July 22, 1999).

This represents a de-skilling of the farm management role. It circumscribes the role of the family, reducing its influence to merely judgements on the adequacy of net farm income. It makes modifying the technology or even its application very difficult, if not illegal. So the social, political, environmental and economic considerations that used to be part of farm family decision making, are now embedded in the technology and typically must be taken on an "all or nothing" basis. In this circumstance, alternative sources of knowledge become crucial to farm families if they are to resist this form of agribusiness control. However, with a downsized state, they are left mostly to their own resources in developing and protecting this knowledge. Thus, organic and most alternate forms of farming are largely "do it yourself" propositions, where small cadres of dedicated farmers learn from each other.

As farm families increasingly depend on agribusiness for inputs, markets, and knowledge, their politics and approach to democracy changes toward a politics of dependency on agribusiness. They come to believe that their interests as independent commodity producers, and the interests of agribusiness, are the same, or at least that there is no alternative. But, as I argued above, neither is true. We are witnessing a diminution in the political will to resist.

First it is important to recognize that agrarian social democracy of the post-World War II era was not up to the challenge of redirecting farming or resisting the fundamental processes that set the direction for farming even in that era. Certainly it was a good vehicle for asking important questions and involving ordinary farmers and others in the analysis and debate. The work of the Saskatchewan Royal Commission on Agriculture and Rural Life mentioned above is a good example of how a vigorous civil society can be maintained. But when the answers came in, neither the social democratic government nor the broad mass of farmers could coalesce around effective strategies of resistance even though several, such as a land bank and producer co-operatives, were briefly tried. Since then, the locus of social democracy has become urban. Among urban social democrats, like urban society in Canada generally, rural and farm issues are alternatively ignored or exaggerated and often misunderstood. For these reasons it is, perhaps, not surprising that the Romanow government of the 1990s could find no strategy for farming and rural life that was consistent with its reform ideology of the past and effective at resisting the trends. It actively supported the industrialization of hog farming and appeared to draw its analysis from a segment of the co-op sector which is itself trying to become more openly capitalist. By keeping royalties on petroleum and minerals low, it reduced its own influence and made it financially impossible for the province to offer the level of support which industrial farming requires.

Still, it takes two to part company, and the paralysis of the Romanow government on rural and farm issues may not completely explain its inability to elect more than one MLA from a rural riding in the fall 1999 election. Faced with the kinds of farm trends discussed in the previous section, the earlier rural politics of progressivism and reform has been replaced with frustration and despair for many farm and rural residents. This is not, by any means, a phenomenon that is localized in rural Saskatchewan (for a discussion of the American plains case, see Dyer, 1998). On the political side, it engenders a great social amnesia, a collective forgetting by rural people especially about the strengths and successes of the resistances of their forebears, and a fundamental suspicion of the state. In the extreme, it shades off into xenophobic beliefs and fanciful theories about conspirators and the need for violence. On the social side, it challenges the collective tenets of the social gospel, substituting the individualism of various more fundamental interpretations of Christianity. In the extreme, it is reflected in suicide, family abuse and radical defences of patriarchy. Institutionally, the Reform Party (and its successor, the Canadian Alliance) has been successful in colonizing this rural politics of frustration and despair. Provincially, Reform's influence is seen in the Saskatchewan Party, which captured 25 of the 30 mostly rural ridings in the fall 1999 election, as well as in the eclectic coalitions that some farmers have created to oppose farm policies from the earlier eras of agrarian hegemony, such as the Canadian Wheat Board and regulated freight rates. Although Reform traces its lineage to agrarian progressives and some in today's rural right even see Tommy Douglas as their mentor, Brown convincingly argues that this is quite unwarranted even though they share some "xenophobic sentiments" that were present in earlier agrarian populist movements:

> None of their rhetoric or propaganda is directed against the railways, banks, mortgage companies and the commercial and industrial "big interests" who were the main targets of the agrarian populists of the past. Their wrath is directed instead at "big government," high taxes and welfare state institutions. (Brown, 1997: xxvii)

This tendency on the right also has no strategy for addressing the fundamental processes that underpin the decline of the family farm. Their recent farm demonstrations presented chilling demands to urban Saskatchewan. On the one hand the major demand is for farm support in the form of an immediate, one-time acreage payment. This is a very inequitable way to distribute support to farm families since large farmers with large acreages get the lion's share of the state support and are then potentially able to buy up more land, thus exacerbating the problem of rural and farm decline. As well, the amount demanded would create a state fiscal crisis. Further, the demand comes without conditions. While some call for long-term solutions, there is little mention of the need for regulations to sustain the number of farms or protect the environment. These would entail limitations on property which the agrarian petty bourgeoisie has always been reluctant to countenance.

The growing dependency in farm politics of the present shows us a likely scenario for farm politics of the future. At the moment, it is not qualitatively different from the past; family farming has always had to resist colonization by outside capital in order to maintain its independence. But, as I argued above, there have been changes in degree which are now beginning to yield a more fundamental, qualitative change.

DEMOCRACY FOR RURAL SASKATCHEWAN

Rural Saskatchewan still depends on farming for its economic and political viability. Family farming is in decline. Its numbers are dropping, the concentration of wealth is increasing, farming processes are becoming more industrialized as agribusiness increasingly controls them. Even local farm knowledge is being undermined. Arguably the spirit and will to farm is diminishing. With this goes the knowledge and determination on the part of farm people to reinvent civil society and energize a democratic project. Can there be no resistance?

The vagaries of political "will" are embedded, in part, in several contradictions of current farm politics. The agrarian populist right has not been able to find a way through its ideological fog to more fundamental strategies of rural sustainability.

But is that even part of its project? Rather, the right accepts the inevitability of family farm decline and has found a way to politically benefit from it in the current conjuncture of farm frustration and stress. For social democracy the crisis of "will" is perhaps more perplexing since its rhetoric makes the idea of the inevitability of family farm decline only uneasily accepted. But the Romanow government did accept it. Although the NDP government that succeeded Romanow has established a department of rural revitalization, the government seems deeply committed to an industrial model of agriculture. Further, the third way of modern social democracy appears to have no interest in the kind of policies that would reverse the growing inequalities or, in this case, put family farming on a sustainable path. In part it is illustrated by the Blair government in Britain, now reaping the consequences of its industrial agriculture policies in the virility of the outbreaks of Mad Cow and Foot-and-Mouth diseases.

Indeed a contradiction is even embedded in some farm groups' calls for a cash infusion from the state. On the one hand they believe the structure and dynamics of farming is inevitable. On the other hand, in the current crisis, they complain that no one — that is the state — is doing anything about it.

Nevertheless, there are signs of the revival of resistance. The traditional struggles to blunt the penetration of agribusiness continue to be important. On balance the history of marketing boards shows that they can modify market forces, giving farmers and the "public" more control. The spirited defence of the Canadian Wheat Board is one example.

The Achilles heal of the agrarian petty bourgeoisie has been its devotion to property. However, with our history of land banks and co-operative farms, we clearly already know ways of limiting the negative effects of capital concentration in farming. The task is to find a new form of farming where these can be put into practice. Not surprisingly, local groups of farm families are experimenting with ways to limit the negative effects of property using co-operatives and setting up land trusts. Without major movement in this area, "the market" and major agribusiness players will fundamentally transform farming.

As well, there must surely be environmental limits to high-input farming. Already many weeds are showing resistance to herbicides and bacteria, and resistance to drugs is common. The appearance of Chronic Wasting Disease in the province's domestic elk herd, and now also in the wild, is a bad omen not only for the industrial model of farming but for agriculture in general. This is one impetus for the growing trend among farmers to change to organic and low-input production. But it is the urban environmental and consumers' movements which are taking the lead on these issues. Farmers have joined this struggle and in the process, perhaps can convince urban Canada to also consider more broadly what the rural contours of a viable rural social environment should be. Further, farm and other women's organizations are playing a leadership role in this area. For the farm family and the rural community that we had in the past, with its own forms of domination, inequality and politics, is not only not viable in the future. Who would want it? The challenge is to build new social forms and for ordinary people to be able to take charge of that social project.

REFERENCES

Artibise, Alan (ed.). 1981. *Town and City*. Regina: Canadian Plains Research Center.

Brenner, Robert. 1998. "The Economics of Global Turbulence." *New Left Review* 229.

Brown, Lorne. 1997. "Introduction to the 1997 Reprint." In Paul F. Sharp, *The Agrarian Revolt in Western Canada: A Survey Showing American Parallels*. Regina: Canadian Plains Research Center.

Brown, Lorne, Joseph Roberts and John Warnock. 1999. *Saskatchewan Politics from Left to Right '44 to '99*. Regina: Hinterland Publications.

Center for Rural Affairs. 1998. *Spotlight on Pork III*. Walthill, NE: Center for Rural Affairs.

Clement, Wallace. 1983. *Class, Power and Property Essays on Canadian Society*. Toronto: Methuen.

Conway, John. 1983. *The West: The History of a Region in Confederation*. Halifax: James Lorimer.

Dyer, Joel. 1998. *Harvest of Rage: Why Oklahoma City is Only the Beginning*. Boulder, CO: Westview Press.

Fowke, Vernon. 1957. *The National Policy and the Wheat Economy*. Toronto: University of Toronto Press.

Friedmann, Harriet. 1978. "Simple Commodity Production and Wage Labour in the American Plains." *Journal of Peasant Studies* 6, no. 1: 71–100.

Fulton, Murray, Ken Rosaasen and Andrew Schmitz. 1989. *Canadian Agricultural Policy and Prairie Agriculture: A Study Prepared for the Economic Council of Canada*. Ottawa: Minister of Supply and Services.

Gertler, Michael. 1991. "The Institutionalization of Grower-Processor Relations in the Vegetable Industries of Ontario and New York." In William Friedland, Lawrence Busch, Frederick Buttel and Alan Rudy (eds.), *Towards a New Political Economy of Agriculture*. Boulder, CO: Westview Press.

Goldschmidt, Walter. 1947. *As You Sow*. New York: Harcourt and Brace.

Goldschmidt, Walter. 1975. "A Tale of Two Towns." In Catherine Lerza and Michael Jacobson (eds.), *Food for People, Not for Profit*. New York: Ballantyne, 70–73.

Heffernan, William D. 1998. "Agriculture and Monopoly Capital." *Monthly Review* 50, no.3: 46–59.

Kenny, Martin, Linda Lobao, James Curry and Richard Goe. 1991. "Agriculture in U.S. Fordism: The Integration of the Productive Consumer." In Friedland et al., *Towards a New Political Economy of Agriculture*.

LaRimee and Buttel. 1991. "The 'Disappearing Middle': A Sociological Perspective". In Friedland et al., *Towards a New Political Economy of Agriculture*.

Laycock, David. 1990. *Populism and Democratic Thought in the Canadian Prairies, 1910 to 1945*. Toronto: University of Toronto Press.

Lee, George. 1980. *Farm Size Now and in the Future*. Saskatoon: Division of Extension and Community Relations, University of Saskatchewan. Publication No. 444.

Lenin, V.I. 1971. "Preliminary Draft Thesis on the Agrarian Question." In *V.I. Lenin, Selected Works*. New York: International Publishers.

Lobao, Linda, Michael Schulman and Louis Swanson. 1993. "Still Going: Recent Debates on the Goldschmidt Hypothesis." Rural Sociology 58, no. 2: 277–88.

Mackintosh, W.A. 1967. *The Economic Background of Dominion-Provincial Relations*. Toronto: McClelland and Stewart Limited.

——. 1991. "Economic Factors in Canadian History." In Gordon Laxer (ed.), *Perspectives on Canadian Economic Development*. Toronto: Oxford University Press, 68–79.

MacPherson, C.B. 1962. *Democracy in Alberta: Social Credit and the Party System*. Toronto: University of Toronto Press.

Manitoba Co-operator

July 22, 1999. "Professional crop scouting set to explode?," by Gord Gilmour.

August 19, 1999. "Patent theft or environmental pollution? Monsanto and Saskatchewan farmer head for the courtroom."

September 30, 1999. "Few lines abandoned, Canadian rails say". By Alex Binkley.

April 5, 2001. "Monsanto wins patent case," by Murray Lyons.

Mann, Susan. 1990. *Agrarian Capitalism in Theory and Practice*. Chapel Hill: University of North Carolina Press.

McCrorie, James N. 1964. *In Union Is Strength*. Saskatoon: Centre for Community Studies.

McMichael, Philip. 1998. "Global Food Politics." *Monthly Review* 50, no. 3: 97–111.

McNally, David. 1999. "Turbulence in the World Economy." *Monthly Review* 51, no. 2: 38–52.

Middendorf, Gerald, Mike Skladany, Elizabeth Ransom, and Lawrence Busch. 1998. "New Agricultural Biotechnologies: The Struggle for Democratic Choice." *Monthly Review* 50, no. 3: 85–96.

Morgan, E.C. 1960. "The Bell Farm." *Saskatchewan History* 19, no. 2: 41–60.

Patnaik, Prabhat. 1999. "Capitalism in Asia at the End of the Millennium." *Monthly Review* 51, no. 3: 53–70.

Phelps, J.L. 1958. *Minority Report (Royal Commission on Agriculture and Rural Life)*. Regina: Queen's Printer.

Richards, John and Larry Pratt. 1979. *Prairie Capitalism: Power and Influence in the New West*. Toronto: McClelland and Stewart.

Royal Commission on Agriculture and Rural Life. 1957. *Service Centers. Report No. 12*. Regina: Queen's Printer.

Saskatchewan Agriculture and Food. 1998. *Agricultural Statistics 1997*. Regina: Statistics Branch, Saskatchewan Agriculture and Food.

Shiva, Vandana. 1997. *Biopiracy: The Plunder of Nature and Knowledge*. Toronto: Between the Lines.

Smillie, Ben. 1991. *Beyond the Social Gospel Church Protest on the Prairies*. Saskatoon: Fifth House Publishers.

Stabler, Jack and M.R. Olfert. 1992. *Restructuring Rural Saskatchewan: The Challenge of the 1990s*. Regina: Canadian Plains Research Center.

Stirling, Bob. 1998. "Farm Knowledge: Machines versus Biotechnology." In R. Hardy, J. Baker Segelken and N. Voionmaa (eds.), *Resource Management in Challenged Environments: NABC Report 9*. Ithaca N.Y.: National Agricultural Biotechnology Council, 147–55.

Taylor, Jeffery. 1994. *Fashioning Farmers: Ideology, Agricultural Knowledge and the Manitoba Farm Movement 1890–1925*. Regina: Canadian Plains Research Center.

Teeple, Gary. 1995. *Globalization and the Decline of Social Reform*. Toronto: Garamond Press.

Voisey, Paul. 1988. *Vulcan The Making of a Prairie Community*. Toronto: University of Toronto Press.

Western Producer

September 11, 1997. "Former hog official feels vindicated"; "Taiwan buys into Saskatchewan's hog future,"

October 16, 1997. "Japanese demand for pork fails to materialize."

October 23, 1997. "Pork rivalry spills into public"; "Kelvington barn's future in jeopardy."

October 30, 1997. "Ag minister faces heated fallout from decision on SPI"; "SPI death wrought in backroom dealings."

September 16, 1999. "Maple Leaf: trend guarantees supply, reduces volatility."

September 23, 1999. "Many farmers ready to throw in the towel," by Roberta Rampton.

Winson, Anthony. 1992. *The Intimate Commodity Food and the Development of the Ago-Industrial Complex in Canada*. Toronto: Garamond Press.

From Many Peoples, Strength: Demographics and Democracy in Saskatchewan's 1999 "Harvest Election"

Cora Voyageur and Joyce Green

INTRODUCTION

Saskatchewan's motto, *Multis E Gentibus Vires*, translates as "from many peoples, strength." The motto suggests something about the province's composition, but also something of its approach to difference and community. "From many peoples, strength" implies that Saskatchewan's population and culture are derived from many peoples, and that this diversity confers strength on the contemporary social and political project. It is a wonderful motto, constituting a public commitment to diversity and inclusion. Why, then, is the provincial legislature so homogeneous?

In this chapter, we examine Saskatchewan's demographic, economic and political profiles. We drew our demographic and economic information from Statistics Canada 1996 Census data. Our political profile focuses on the decade of the 1990s and more specifically on the 1999 Saskatchewan provincial election results that produced an NDP-Liberal coalition government. We drew the political data for the 1999 election from candidate lists provided by the party offices prior the election.

We examine the 1999 post-election legislature to assess the quality and nature of democratic representation in Saskatchewan's legislature. We found that politicians in Saskatchewan are typically white males and those elected to the legislature do not reflect the province's demographic makeup or its cultural diversity. It is important to understand why there is such a lack of presence of women, Aboriginal people, and other minorities; and why political power and democracy correlate with gender and race.

An analysis of race and gender, which has social, political and economic implications, suggests probabilities of life chances. In other words, in a society marred by racism, sexism, and inequitable distribution of wealth and power, we are not all equal. In this chapter, we look at the socio-economic population data and then suggest that it can be correlated with low rates of political participation in partisan politics. This correlation, in turn, negatively affects democracy: political representation is primarily a preserve of white men.

SASKATCHEWAN'S DEMOGRAPHIC PROFILE

Saskatchewan's geography extends to 651,900 square kilometers (Canex, 1988: 78) and 976,575 people inhabited the province in 1995 (Statistics Canada,

1999b).[1] This amounts to 3.2 percent of the Canadian population — coincidentally, a similar proportion to that of status Indians in the Canadian population. With 3.2 percent of the Canadian population, Saskatchewan is guaranteed representation in the Senate[2] and in the House of Commons,[3] and a share of equalization payments to meet the minimums of Canadian citizenship; status Indians get no such guarantees.

Despite being known for its agricultural base,[4] approximately half the population lives in urban areas. Indeed, over 42 percent of Saskatchewanians live in either Regina or Saskatoon (Statistics Canada:1999c).

Saskatchewan's people are, on average, slightly younger and slightly older than the Canadian norm. Twenty-three percent of Saskatchewanians are under the age of 15 years compared to 20 percent of the Canadian population (Statistics Canada, 1999c). However, 15 percent of people are over 65, compared with the Canadian average of 12 percent. This translates into a larger population requiring public services and a smaller tax base with which to support them. Women make up 51 percent of the population, and men 49 percent, consistent with the Canadian average. Aboriginal people are the largest minority population in the province, at least 11 percent of Saskatchewan's population (Statistics Canada, 1999a).[5] According to Statistics Canada, the size of Saskatchewan's families[6] has shrunk since 1971, when the average family had 3.7 members, to 3.0 in 1996. However, Aboriginal families tend to be larger, at an average of 4 persons. In addition, *Statistics Canada Daily January 13, 1998* notes that approximately one-third of Aboriginal children under the age of 15 resided in homes headed by a lone parent (primarily mothers), and we know that single mothers and their children are statistically likely to live in poverty. The report further states that the percentage of Aboriginal children living in lone-parent families increases to 46 percent in urban area households (Statistics Canada, 1998: 2).

Most folks are "home-grown," with about 81 percent of people born and raised in Saskatchewan. Another 13.6 percent of Saskatchewan residents were born outside its provincial borders but still within Canada. Only 5.4 percent of Saskatchewan's population was born outside of Canada with most of them from

---

1. The Saskatchewan Bureau of Statistics (SBS) cites the Saskatchewan population at 990,237 — a discrepancy of approximately 13,500 (SBS: http.www//gov.sk.ca/bureau.stats/pop/pop1.htm#Total). Saskatchewan Bureau of Statistics representatives were contacted about this discrepancy and could not offer an explanation since they too get their population numbers from Statistics Canada. For the purpose of this chapter we will use the original Statistics Canada figure of 976,575.
2. Saskatchewan currently has 6 seats in the Senate — 2 Liberals and 4 Progressive Conservatives (http://www.parl.gc.ca./common/senmember/ho...2789&OrgCId=103&Sect=hoccur&ProvCode=SK).
3. Saskatchewan has 14 seats in the House of Commons (http://www.parl.gc. ca/common/senmemb/ho...guage=E&Parl=37&ProvCOde=SK&Sect=hoccur).
4. Statistics Canada 1996 Census of Canada states that agriculture (as part of the goods-producing sector) employs 67,500 individuals while trade (as part of the service-producing sector which employs approximately 2.5 times more individuals than the Goods-producing sector) employs 76,600 individuals.
5. We say "at least" because a significant number of Aboriginal people do not participate in the census, and an indeterminate number do not choose to identify themselves as Aboriginal, leading to under-recording of the Aboriginal population. Even with this under-reporting, Saskatchewan's Aboriginal population is expected to be as much as 30 percent of the total population by the year 2010.
6. We use Statistics Canada's definition of family which is "a now-married couple (with or without never married sons or daughters of either or both spouses), a couple living common-law (with or without never married sons or daughters of either or both partners), or a lone parent of any marital status (with at least 1 never-married son or daughter living in the same dwelling).

Europe (27,945), the United Kingdom (9,530), and the United States (7,205). Most (37.4 percent) immigrated before 1961, and are now fully assimilated into the dominant society. The small "visible minority" population (2.6 percent) is overwhelmingly concentrated in Saskatoon and Regina.[7]

Aboriginal people constituted 11.4 percent or 111,230 of the population in 1995, and by definition are "home-grown." Aboriginal demographics differ from those of the dominant society. The average age of Aboriginals is a decade less at 25.5 years compared to 35.4 years for non-Aboriginals. Children under 15 years of age account for 35 percent of the Aboriginal population, compared with 20 percent for the total Saskatchewan population. The next youngest category, those between 15 and 24 years of age, is 20 percent of the Aboriginal population, compared with 13 percent for the total Saskatchewan population. Aboriginal youth are gaining academic credentials in unprecedented numbers, with a 94 percent increase of Indian post-secondary students between 1988 and 1997. Combined with the data showing higher birthrates for Aboriginal women than for non-Aboriginal women, these data suggest the Aboriginal constituency will be an important political and social force in the near future.

The Saskatchewan population is not as well educated as the Canadian population. Fewer people have high school graduation diplomas; 43.1 percent of Saskatchewanians didn't graduate from high school, compared with the national average of 36.8 percent. While 15.6 percent of Canadians hold university degrees, only 12.8 percent of Saskatchewanians have degrees (Statistics Canada, 1999d). Interestingly, both Aboriginal and settler women are slightly more likely to have finished high school than men and to have a university degree.

SASKATCHEWAN'S ECONOMIC PROFILE

Saskatchewan residents earn about 10 percent less personal income, at $22,541, than the Canadian average of $25,196. Income differences increase slightly when comparisons are drawn between Saskatchewan's *average household income* of $42,685 and the Canadian norm of $48,552. These data show a difference of approximately 12 percent.

However, averages can be deceiving. The distribution of wealth within Saskatchewan is uneven. Regina residents earn on average slightly more than the national average, but there are pockets of absolute poverty in the major urban centres and in some rural areas. Aboriginal people consistently earn less than non-Aboriginals: poverty is a high probability when correlated with race. First Nations communities in the prairie provinces typically have the poorest conditions when education, housing, employment and income are taken into consideration. Further, First Nations communities appear to be poorly integrated with the surrounding non-Aboriginal society and economy (Statistics Canada, 1999f). Constituencies with high Aboriginal populations have annual household incomes below the provincial average. For example, the Athabasca constituency, which is 67 percent Aboriginal, has an average annual household income of $30,957 (72.5 percent of the provincial average) and the Cumberland constituency, 68 percent Aboriginal,

7. Aboriginals are not considered by Statistics Canada to be a "visible minority" for demographic categories, so the category "visible minority" does not include Aboriginal people. For the purposes of this paper, the term "Aboriginal" is used when no distinction is made between peoples of First Nations and of Métis ancestry.

has an average annual household income of $38,697 (91 percent of the provincial average). The Canadian Council on Social Development found that Aboriginal people in fifteen Canadian cities were "more than twice as likely as non-Aboriginal people" and in Regina, were a scandalous four times more likely to live in poverty (O'Connor, 2000). Economic class has long been acknowledged as a factor determining personal political efficacy and electoral success. This means that poverty can serve as a barrier to both efficacy — the sense that one can affect politics — and to participation.

SASKATCHEWAN'S POLITICAL PROFILE IN THE 1990S

Saskatchewan has been considered the home of left-wing populism since the CCF, led by T.C. Douglas, first came to power in 1944.

According to political scientist Louise Carbert, NDP populism has made space for women in politics, through the agency of party elites, and for explicitly feminist analysis in government. The NDP government, in the 1991–1995 period, led rather than followed public opinion in pursuing woman-friendly policy, targeting issues such as labour standards, domestic violence, child care, and health care (Carbert 1997: 156–70). This policy concern has not, however, translated into a party commitment to increase women's political participation as candidates.

The NDP electoral platform also paid some, if only marginal, attention to Aboriginals. Again, the policy approach has been driven by party elites and by Aboriginal political elites, but not by the majority of Saskatchewan residents. Still, few Aboriginals have chosen to run as candidates and even fewer have been elected. In the 1991–1999 period, there were only two Aboriginal MLAs — Keith Goulet of the NDP and Buckley Belanger of the Liberals; in 1999, Belanger crossed the floor to join the NDP, and was re-elected in the 1999 provincial election.

The NDP re-election in 1995 resulted in a continuation of its policy agenda, although the dominance of neo-liberal ideology across Canada moved the NDP to the right and fostered a public commitment to the neo-liberal discourse of deficit and debt reduction and government restructuring. This is perhaps most evident in the last mandate, 1995 through to 1999, when government restructuring of health care, and policy responses since then, arguably affected women most often, and most negatively.[8]

The Saskatchewan Party was created in the 1995–1999 electoral term, from the remnants of the Progressive Conservatives and 5 Liberals.[9] After considerable infighting among the Liberals, including a caucus attack on leader Lynda Haverstock, renegade Liberals and PCs formed the Saskatchewan Party in 1997. This transformation explains the difference in parties and some members' political affiliations between the 1995 election and dissolution in 1999. Saskatchewan Party leader

8. Except for doctors (and even here the percentage of females is increasing), the majority of health-care professionals are female. This means that elimination of public-sector jobs in health care affects women. These jobs are among the best of women-dominated job sectors; hence their loss is a significant one. Reductions in funding and in institutional support (numbers of hospitals, and hospital beds, as well as numbers of nurses and so on) degrade the working conditions of those professionals who continue to work. Finally, hospitals' adoption of early-release strategies simply off-loads the care of sick people onto the family and community, where women take up most of it in their social roles as caregivers.

9. The Progressive Conservatives were unsuccessfully attempting to recover from political damage caused by a number of high-profile criminal prosecutions of former MLAs, cabinet ministers and party officials from the Devine administration.

Elwin Hermanson has stated a preference for undifferentiated equality among citizens and distaste for public policy initiatives directed at ameliorating the consequences of colonialism for Aboriginal peoples (Hermanson, 1999).

The 1999 NDP campaign materials suggested a policy platform with a mandate of inclusion that extended to women, Aboriginal people and visible minorities (New Democratic Party, 1999). The NDP legislative agenda has addressed some Aboriginal issues; for example, the NDP government has participated in the Treaty Land Entitlement process (Government of Saskatchewan, Aboriginal Affairs, 1999).

However, public opinion indicates many non-Aboriginal citizens are unaware of Aboriginal issues, and many are unsympathetic to them. The federal Canadian Alliance (formerly the Reform Party) has significant support in Saskatchewan, as is evident in the November 2000 federal election results where it won 10 of 14 Saskatchewan ridings. Yet, First Nations newspaper columnist Doug Cuthand writes "when it comes to aboriginal policy, the Alliance Party comes dead last... . It is a policy for rednecks and racists" (Cuthand, 2000). The Alliance's predecessor, the Reform Party, demonstrated antipathy towards progressive Aboriginal policy, such as equity hiring at the University of Saskatchewan decried by Saskatchewan Reform MP Jim Pankiw as "race-based" (*Leader-Post*, 2000) and the Nisga'a Treaty in British Columbia, rejected by the Reform Caucus as racist and unconstitutional (Mickleburgh, 1998, 1999; Rynard, 2000).

Despite its tradition of left-wing social-gospel populism, Saskatchewan demonstrably has a significant bloc of ideologically right-wing citizens. The Saskatchewan Party, ideologically neo-liberal and compatible with the federal Canadian Alliance, won a marginally higher percentage of the popular vote than the New Democrats in the 1999 election.

DEMOGRAPHIC REPRESENTATION IN SASKATCHEWAN'S LEGISLATURE IN THE 1990S

So how are Saskatchewan's political parties doing at running women and aboriginal candidates? Figure 1 shows a comparison of male, female and Aboriginal representation among MLAs when the NDP came into power in 1991, when they were re-elected in 1995, and when they dissolved the legislature to call the 1999 election.

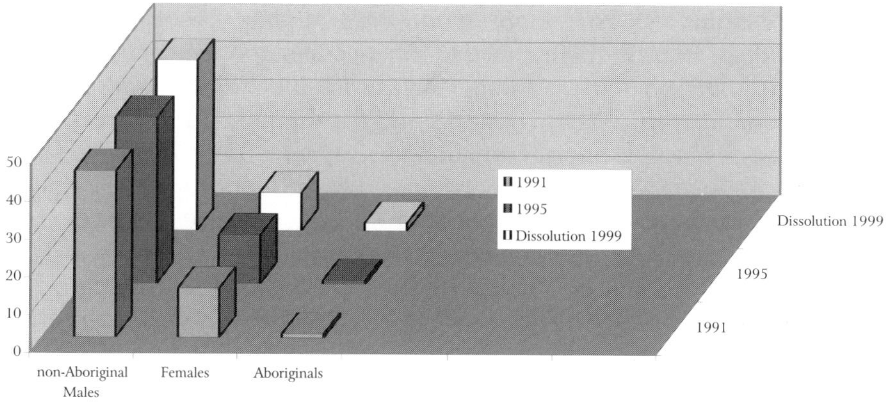

Figure 1: Comparison of Male, Female and Aboriginal Representation 1991, 1995 and at Dissolution in 1999.

In the 1991 election a total of 12 women were elected: 11 NDP and the Liberal leader, Lynda Haverstock. A second Liberal woman, Anita Bergman, won the 1994 by-election. At this point, women formed 20 percent of the NDP caucus, 17 percent of cabinet, and 20 percent of all MLAs in the legislature.

In the 1995 election, the NDP retained government status. A total of 13 women were elected to the Saskatchewan legislature: 10 NDP and 3 Liberal. This meant that women were 24 percent of the NDP caucus (which formed the government); 20 percent of cabinet ministers, and 20 percent of all MLAs in the House (Carbert 1997: 157–58).

Going into the election in 1999, the New Democratic Party held 41 of 58 seats or 71 percent of the seats in the legislature. The Saskatchewan legislature saw women as approximately 17 percent of MLAs while approximately 3 percent of MLAs (2 men) were Aboriginal.

THE HARVEST ELECTION

The writ was dropped on August 19, 1999, for the September 16 election. Elections in Saskatchewan are not normally called during harvest season, and the timing attracted much commentary and some hostility. Five parties — the NDP, the Saskatchewan Party, the Liberal Party, the New Green Alliance, and the Progressive Conservative Party — and two independent candidates, contested the election. Table 1 shows the distribution of seats between the political parties in the Saskatchewan legislature when the election was called on August 19, 1999.

Table 1: Saskatchewan Legislative Distribution at 1999 Dissolution by Party, Gender, Aboriginality, Total Seats and Percentage Representation of Total Legislative Seats

Party	Women		Aboriginal		Total Seats N=58	Provincial Total %
	Number	%	Number	%		
New Democratic Party	9	22	2	5	41	71
Saskatchewan Party	2	10	*	*	10	17
Liberal	*	*	*	*	5	9
Independent	1	*	*	*	1	1.5
Vacant	*	*	*	*	1	1.5

Source: Election Saskatchewan, 1999.
* denotes no representation.

A total of 206 people ran for election in 1999, for five political parties and as independent candidates. Forty-one of these candidates were women (one Aboriginal), and six were Aboriginal people (one woman and five men). Two Metis men ran for the NDP; one First Nations man ran for the Saskatchewan Party; and two men and one woman, all First Nations, ran for the Liberals. Fourteen women ran of a total of 58 New Democrat candidates, 3 women ran for the New Green Alliance's 16-candidate slate, 3 women ran of the total of 14 Progressive Conservatives, 7 women ran of 58 Liberals, and 14 women ran for the Saskatchewan Party slate of 58 candidates. No women ran as Independents. This totals 20 percent women candidates and just under 3 percent Aboriginal candidates. Twelve women and two Aboriginal men won their seats, for totals of 20.7 percent and 3.4 percent, respectively, of the 58 MLAs elected.

CONSTITUENCY PROFILES

Elections Saskatchewan categorizes constituencies as rural, urban, or rural/urban splits. Twenty-five of the 58 constituencies are urban, 24 are rural, and 9 are rural/urban splits. Approximately 44 percent of Saskatchewan's population lives in urban constituencies, while 40 percent lives in rural constituencies; the remaining 16 percent lives in the rural/urban splits. The population of constituencies varies considerably, despite the legal requirement that populations not vary by more than 5 percent between constituencies (25 percent in federal ridings), taking into account the need for representation of particular communities (Supreme Court of Canada, 1991). For example, the two northern ridings of Athabasca and Cumberland, which account for about one-third of the province's territory, are exempted by legislation from this population-to-representation formula, in recognition of the need to represent the dispersed northern population. Disparities in population are evident: consider the constituency of Regina-Qu'Appelle Valley, with the largest population at 20,180, while the geographically enormous constituency of Athabasca has the smallest number of voters, at 12,730. The difference between the two, 7,450, substantially exceeds the recommended degree of variance, but is permissible because of the principle of representing particular communities.

The data shows that Aboriginals make up 67 percent of the population in Athabasca (8,590/12,730) and 68 percent of the population in Cumberland (12,515/18,355).[10] Given what we know about the youth population in the Aboriginal community, a high percentage of these people could be under 18. Thus, the Aboriginal vote in the north is growing.

Average annual household incomes varied among constituency categories. The range within the categories is significant. For example, rural constituencies averaged $38,975 per household, but ranged from the low of $28,895 in Canora-Pelly to the high of $46,846 in Kindersley. Urban constituencies averaged $42,983, but ranged from $28,194 in Saskatoon Idylwyld to $62,146 in Regina Lakeview. The rural/urban split constituencies have the highest average at $52,560, but ranged from a low of $33,813 in Melville to a high of $74,917 in Regina Wascana Plains.

Clearly, political analysis of voting patterns must consider not only rural/urban designations, but the different economic location of voters in these constituencies. Moreover, good analysis will move beyond simple "household income" categories. In addition, women and Aboriginal people of both sexes are more likely to be poor than are white men. This means that income averages in constituencies do not take into account the dramatic differences in wealth distribution within constituencies, nor the different political issues this raises.

ELECTORAL CANDIDATES

The majority of candidates in 1999 — 165 of 206 (or 80 percent) — were men. Forty-one women (20 percent of candidates) ran (Elections Saskatchewan, 1999b). Table 2 describes the political candidates' gender, party affiliation and constituency locale.

Women were more likely to run in urban constituencies with 27 of the 41 female candidates, or 66 percent of women, running in urban areas. (Elections Saskatchewan, 1999b). Regina and Saskatoon, the largest cities with 42 percent of the provincial population, each had 10 women candidates. Eighteen of the 25 urban ridings were in Regina (9) and Saskatoon (9). Eight women (19 percent of female candidates) ran in rural constituencies. The remaining 7 women candidates

10. Based on Statistics Canada "mother tongue" Aboriginal total response questions.

Table 2: 1999 Saskatchewan Provincial Election Candidates by Political Party and Gender by Locale

Party	Locale			
	Urban	Rural	Urban/Rural	Total
New Democratic Party				
Male	18	21	5	44
Female	7	3	4	14
Total	25	24	9	58
New Green Alliance				
Male	8	4	1	13
Female	3	*	*	3
Total	11	4	1	16
Progressive Conservative				
Male	10	1	*	11
Female	3	*	*	3
Total	13	1	*	14
Liberal				
Male	21	22	8	51
Female	4	2	1	7
Total	25	24	9	58
Saskatchewan Party				
Male	15	21	8	44
Female	10	3	1	14
Total	25	24	9	58
Independent				
Male	1	1	*	2
Total	1	1	*	2
TOTAL	100	78	28	206

Source: Elections Saskatchewan: Twenty-Fourth General Election September 16, 1999 — List of Candidates Nominated, 1999.
* denotes no representation.

(15 percent) ran in the rural/urban split constituencies. Of the 6 Aboriginal candidates, all but one ran in rural ridings, with the one exception in a rural/urban split. All but one ran in the two northern constituencies where the majority of the population is Aboriginal.

Women's political participation cannot be attributed to progressive ideology of the populist left since both the Saskatchewan Party and the New Democrats ran the same number of women candidates (14 each). When the percentage of women candidates of parties' total candidates is calculated, all parties did better than the Liberals, who attracted only seven women in a field of 58 candidates. The New Green Alliance, environmentally focused and generally social democratic; and the Progressive Conservatives, generally neo-liberal and socially conservative, attracted 3 women each, with smaller candidate slates.

The NDP, the Saskatchewan Party, and the Liberal Party ran candidates in all 58 constituencies. The New Green Alliance, running in its first general election, fielded 16 candidates, while the Progressive Conservatives, running with no leader and no platform, fielded 14 candidates. Two persons also ran as independents. Individual constituencies had between 3 and 5 candidates.

ELECTION RESULTS

The NDP won re-election on September 16, 1999. However, and despite the premature and erroneous declarations of CBC TV and CTV that the NDP had won a majority government, the NDP won only 29 seats, half the 58 seats in the legislature.[11] Saskatchewan elections are decided on the plurality or "first-past-the-post" system, which can diverge from parties' share of the popular vote. Consider the results: the NDP won 29 of a possible 58 seats with 38.7 percent of the popular vote; the Saskatchewan Party won fewer seats (26) with a larger percentage of

Table 3: 1999 Election Results by Party, Gender and Aboriginality[12]

Party	Women		Aboriginal		Total Candidates
	Candidates	Elected	Candidates	Elected	
New Democratic Party	14	7	2	2	58
Saskatchewan Party	14	5	1	*	58
Liberal	7	*	3	*	58
New Green Alliance	3	*	*	*	16
Progressive Conservative	3	*	*	*	14
Independent	*	*	*	*	2
Total	41	12	6	2	206

Source: Elections Saskatchewan, 1999
* denotes no representation

the popular vote (39.6 percent); and the Liberal Party won only 3 seats (and was, by judicial decision, awarded a fourth in the Wood River constituency on January 26) despite earning 20.2 percent of the popular vote. The New Green Alliance, running in its first general election, won no seats, and had nearly 2 percent of the vote. Rather than govern with the chronic threat of a successful non-confidence motion, the NDP formed a coalition government with the Liberal Party on September 30, bringing two Liberals into cabinet and placing the third in the speaker's chair.

The Saskatchewan Party formed the official opposition, winning 26 seats. However, the results were not final, as the Wood River constituency produced a tie between Liberal Glen McPherson and Saskatchewan Party Yogi Huyghebaert. As of February 7, 2000, a judicial review determined that McPherson had won, but the Saskatchewan Party filed a petition under the Controverted Elections Act. The day prior to the court date, Mr. McPherson filed an "admission of undue election," which had the effect of rendering his election null and void. The seat was declared vacant. A by-election was called for June 26, 2000, and it was handily won by the Saskatchewan Party's Yogi Huyghebaert (Baker, 2001). The Saskatoon Southeast win by Pat Lorje for the NDP was also under judicial review, with Lorje declared the winner in December 1999.

Table 3 shows the election results by party, gender and Aboriginality. Clearly, there is only the most modest increase in the number of women winning elected office in Saskatchewan (from 17 percent at dissolution to 20.7 percent), and no increase at all in Aboriginal representation.

Aboriginal representation remains limited to the two northern constituencies, suggesting that Aboriginal candidates are only seldom recruited elsewhere and that the predominantly non-Aboriginal electorate does not view them positively.

Twelve white women were elected in all. Half the women who ran for the New Democrats (7) won, while 36 percent of Saskatchewan Party women candidates (5) were elected. This amounts to 21 percent of the 58 elected members of the legislature. This is consistent with observations from women's groups that politics in Saskatchewan remains male-dominated. During the election, Mavis Moore of the Canadian Federation of University Women said "there is still a fear here in

11. CBC TV's "Decision Desk" called the election for the NDP at 8:30 p.m.; CTV called it for the NDP 10 minutes earlier, well before the ballots were counted.

12. NDP, Saskatchewan Party and Liberal data obtained from party caucus offices in the legislature, January 26, 2000. New Green Alliance, Progressive Conservative and Independent candidate data obtained from the parties and from the Office of the Chief Electoral Officer during the election.

Saskatchewan of women in power," and Kripa Sekhar, vice-president of the National Action Committee on the Status of Women, stated that "women's issues are at the bottom of the agenda almost always" (Zakreski, 1999).

CONCLUSION

There are several socio-political consequences to the demographic data. Saskatchewan is more homogeneous than most other provinces. Most people are white, and share cultural, religious and historical beliefs. This contributes to community cohesion and shared cultural expectations and experiences. It also produces insularity, and discomfort with difference. White males hold the overwhelming majority of public elected positions. This shows a correlation between race, sex, success in electoral politics, and influence on political power. Women of all races and Aboriginal people of both sexes are under-represented in public life relative to their share of the general population. This raises questions about the nature and effectiveness of representative democracy. Are white males effectively representing women and Aboriginal people? Is proportional representation naturally a more democratic form of representation? Louise Carbert (1997) argues that during the 1991–1995 period the NDP government was "woman-friendly," and she attributes this to feminist influence on party elites. Can, and should, women and Aboriginal people rely on influence to shape public policy, or is greater representation in public life a part of healthy democratic practices?

We agree with Jane Arscott and Linda Trimble (1997: 4–5), that representation of women and other marginalized people requires the actual presence of these sectors of the population in partisan politics and especially in the legislature. An ideology of inclusion is a necessary condition for the effective representation of women, Aboriginals, and visible minorities in Saskatchewan. Further, we suggest the legislature must include a wider representation of citizens to be more effective at expressing inclusive democratic practices.

At present, the legislature is not very diverse. Pitifully few Aboriginals, no visible minorities, and a meager 21 percent women of all MLAs are included in the province's governance. Uniformity in the legislature is the antithesis of the provincial motto of "from many peoples, strength." It is a poor formula for representative democracy. All parties in Saskatchewan should seek to broaden their membership and candidate base, because diversity provides not only strength, but also potentially stronger democratic representation.

REFERENCES

Arscott, Jane and Linda Trimble. 1997. *In the Presence of Women: Representation in Canadian Governments*. Toronto: Harcourt Brace & Company, Canada, Ltd.

Baker, Jan. 2001. Conversation with Elections Saskatchewan Chief Electoral Officer, January 31, 2001.

Canadian Broadcasting Corporation. 1999. Decision Desk. September 16, 1999.

Canex Enterprises Inc. 1988. *Quick Canadian Facts*. Surrey: Webcom Ltd.

Carbert, Louise. 1997. "Governing on the Correct, the Compassionate, the Saskatchewan Side of the Border." In Arscott and Trimble, *In the Presence of Women*, 154–79.

Cuthand, Doug. 2000. "Nothing for aboriginals for Alliance Party." *Leader-Post*, November 14, 2000.

Elections Saskatchewan 1999. *Twenty-fourth General Election September 16, 1999 — List of Candidates Nominated, 1999*.

Hermanson, Elwin. 1999. Class lecture in Political Science 220-002, University of Regina, November 1999.

Government of Canada. 2001a. *Senators of Canada* (http://www.parl.gc.c./common/senmember/ho... 2789&OrgCId=103&Sect=hoccur&ProvCode=SK).

——. 2001b. *Members of Parliament. Commons* (http://www.parl.gc. ca/common/senmemb/ho... guage= E&Parl=37&ProvCOde=SK&Sect=hocur).

Government of Saskatchewan. 1999. *Treaty Land Entitlement*. Regina: Aboriginal Affairs.

Leader-Post. 2000. "Pankiw criticizes commission." March 10, 2000, A7.

Mickleburg, Ron. 1998. "Nisga'a' tribal leaders urge full turnout for historic treaty vote." *Globe and Mail*, November 7, 1998, A7.

——. 1999. "Nisga'a' treaty could cost $1.3 Billion, Reform says." *Globe and Mail*, February 11, 1999: A8.

New Democratic Party. 1999. Campaign Literature for Saskatchewan Election.

O'Connor, Kevin. 2000. "Native-white poverty gap huge." *Leader-Post*, April 18, 2000, A1.

Rynard, Paul. 2000. "Welcome In, But Check your Rights at the Door: The James Bay and Nisga'a' Agreements in Canada." *Canadian Journal of Political Science* 32: 211–43.

Saskatchewan Bureau of Statistics. 2000 [http://www.gov.sk.ca/bureau.stats/pop/popl htm#Total].

Statistics Canada. 1998. *The Daily January 17, 1998.*

——. 1999a. Statistics Canada 1996 Census Profile: Saskatchewan.

——. 1999b. Statistics Canada Census of Canada 1996, Saskatchewan [http ://ww2.statscan.ca/English /profil /Det...na& CSDNAME=Regina].

——. 1999c. [http://www.statscan.ca/english/Pgdb/People/Population/demo 01/htm].

——. 1999d. [http://www.statscan.ca:80/english/Pgdb/People/Education/educ41b.htm]; Statistics for Regina (Census Metropolitan Area).

——. 1999e. [http://www.statscan.ca.80/english/Pgdb/People /Families/famil61b.htm].

——. 1999f. Statistics Canada. *The Daily June 16, 1999.*

Zakreski, Dan. 1999. "Politics a man's game: women's groups." *Leader-Post*, September 2, 1999, C5.

First Nations and Saskatchewan Politics

James M. Pitsula

First Nations voters are an important element in Saskatchewan politics and are poised to become even more important. The facts speak for themselves. Saskatchewan has 58 provincial constituencies, 19 of which are located in Regina, Saskatoon, Moose Jaw and Prince Albert. Indian reserves are located in 22 of the remaining 39 seats. In 15 of these the number of Indians registered on the respective reserves and of voting age exceeds the margin of vote by which the constituency was won in 1995.[1] This estimate understates the potential impact of Aboriginal votes because it does not take into account registered Indians not resident on reserves, non-registered Indians, or Métis. In addition, demographic projections show that the Indian vote, already significant, will continue to grow in influence. Saskatchewan's registered Indian population is expected to increase from 7.8 percent of the province's total in 1990 to 13.45 percent by 2015.[2] As Perry Bellegarde, the chief of the Federation of Saskatchewan Indian Nations notes, as the Indian population grows, "so will its political clout and its ability to influence public policy in their favor."[3]

History has shaped the role of First Nations in the political culture of the province, and without an understanding of this history, both present and future are incomprehensible. From 1905, when the province of Saskatchewan came into existence, to World War II, Indians and non-Indians were two solitudes.[4] References to Indians in the official records of the province and the major newspapers were few and far between. Indians and non-Indians led separate lives and preserved separate identities. This was partly because the great majority of Indians lived in relative isolation on reserves and partly because the Constitution gave jurisdiction for "Indians and lands reserved for Indians" to the federal government. The treaties, which had been signed in the late 1800s and early 1900s, were with Ottawa, not Regina. Status Indians lived under the rules and regulations of the *Indian Act*, an Act of Parliament, and were subject to the supervisory authority of the federal Department of Indian Affairs. Saskatchewan Indians had little occasion to interact with the Saskatchewan government or its agencies.

1. David Smith, "Saskatchewan Perspectives," in *Saskatchewan and Aboriginal Peoples in the 21st Century: Social, Economic and Political Changes and Challenges* (Regina: Federation of Saskatchewan Indian Nations, 1997), 17.
2. Francois Nault et al., *Population Projections of Registered Indians, 1991–2015* (Ottawa: Statistics Canada, Population Projections Section, February 1993), 51, cited in Smith, "Saskatchewan Perspectives," 19.
3. Adam Killick, "Aboriginals Poised to Irrevocably Alter Political Landscape," *National Post*, February 7, 2000.
4. Smith, "Saskatchewan Perspectives," 7–9.

The barrier between the "two solitudes" began to break down as Indian population and off-reserve migration increased. On-reserve population grew 9 percent between 1941 and 1946, 15 percent between 1946 and 1951, 18 percent between 1951 and 1956, and 21 percent between 1956 and 1959. Movement away from the reserves increased from 1 percent of the total reserve population in 1942 to 3.7 percent in 1957.[5] Demographic change was accompanied by political innovation. The 1960s was the crucial decade in which a "quiet revolution" occurred in the relationship between First Nations and non-First Nations in Saskatchewan. The province is still sorting out the ramifications of this transformation. Historical conditions, it will be seen, go far towards explaining the two most salient features of Indian voting in Saskatchewan provincial elections: a relatively low voter turnout and a marked proclivity, since 1971, to support the NDP.

THE VANISHING INDIAN AND THE PERFORMING INDIAN

In the nineteenth and early twentieth centuries, there was a widespread assumption in Canada and the United States that Indian people were destined for extinction. Toronto painter Paul Kane set out in 1845 on a two-year journey through the West to capture on canvas images of the "vanishing Indian." A reviewer of his memoir, *Wanderings of an Artist among the Indians of North America* (1859) summed up the conventional wisdom of the day:

> One must make haste to visit the Red Men. Their tribes, not long since still masters of a whole world, are disappearing rapidly, driven back and destroyed by the inroads of the white race. Their future is inevitable... . The Indians are doomed; their fate will be that of so many primitive races now gone.[6]

Daniel Francis notes that the imminent disappearance of the Indian was "an article of faith among Canadians until well into the twentieth century."[7] The idea took two forms. One held that Indians were *literally* dying out, the other, that the Indian way of life was not sustainable in the presence of Euro-Canadian civilization. The former was based on the demographic reality of an Indian population declining as a result of disease, starvation, alcohol and poverty. The Native population in Canada fell from 108,500 in 1881 to 103,750 in 1915 at a time when the non-Native population was growing by leaps and bounds.[8] The 1921 Census found 110,814 registered Indians; ten years later, the number had increased to 122,911.[9] Curiously, even though the population decline had been arrested, the myth of the disappearing Indian stubbornly persisted.[10]

The other variant of the myth was that, even if Indians did not perish in the literal sense, they had been completely demoralized and had no future as distinct peoples and cultures. Anthropologist Diamond Jenness articulated this view in *The Indians of Canada*, published in 1932. He said that disease, alcohol, depletion of

5. Government of Canada, Joint Committee of the Senate and the House of Commons on Indian Affairs, *Minutes of Proceedings and Evidence*, No. 12, June 16–17, 1960, p. 1033.
6. J. Russell Harper (ed.), *Paul Kane's Frontier* (Toronto: University of Toronto Press, 1971), 41 as cited in Daniel Francis, *The Imaginary Indian: The Image of the Indian in Canadian Culture* (Vancouver: Arsenal Pulp Press, 1992), 23.
7. Francis, *The Imaginary Indian*, 53.
8. Ibid., 53.
9. Ibid., 54.
10. Ibid., 59.

game resources, and loss of traditional spiritual beliefs had robbed Indians of their life force: "Doubtless all the tribes will disappear."[11]

To the extent that Indians were not ignored or written off, they were seen as exotic remnants of a lost world. The phenomenon of the "performing Indian" was evident at travelling extravaganzas, such as Buffalo Bill's Wild West Show. Less dramatic perhaps, but more accessible for Saskatchewan residents, were Indian encampments at annual exhibitions and agricultural fairs. The *Leader-Post* described the scene at the Regina Exhibition in August 1945:

> Guests of the Regina fair board, about 90 of them — men, women, and papooses — have pitched their teepees in the camp ground west of the Grain Show building and for the entire week will take in the sights. The encampment is attracting hundreds of fair patrons, and on Monday children swarmed around the 13 teepees all day long, viewing with wonderment their red brothers.[12]

Fairs were entertainment and diversion, but also a place to display and promote economic development. They celebrated the progress made in the West since the arrival of Euro-Canadians. Daniel Francis speculates that the presence of Indians in traditional dress living in teepees on the edge of the Exhibition grounds served the purpose of reinforcing the contrast between modern, technological achievements and the primitive past.[13] Indians affirmed progress by exemplifying what it was not. Francis further suggests than the "performing" or "picturesque" Indians were "tame" Indians who did not pose a threat of any kind. They allowed non-Indians to satisfy curiosity about an Indian culture that was safely located in the past, without having to deal with the contemporary problems of Indian people.[14]

Another setting for the performing Indian was the historical pageant, one of the most impressive of which took place in the Qu'Appelle Valley near Lebret on August 16, 1925. Some 2,000 visitors, many of whom traveled by train from Regina, viewed the spectacle, and a cast of 3,500 Indians participated. According to Francis, "Indian customs were portrayed in the little Indian village built near the school. Indian ways of cooking, preparing food, tanning hides, canoe making and the domestic life of squaw and papoose, brave and chief were all depicted." The pageant presented three scenes: the coming of Champlain to Canada, La Vérendrye's arrival at Lake Huron, and the first appearance in the Qu'Appelle Valley of Father Hugonard, founder of the Indian residential school. Though wildly inaccurate as historical representations, the pageants communicated the idea that the arrival of Euro-Canadians was an unalloyed blessing for Indians.

When considering why Indians participated in such dramas, H.V. Nelles offers the explanation that participation enabled Indians "to present themselves as peoples with a history and a claim to the future also deserving of consideration."[15] At Lebret they had the opportunity to perform before the elite of the province, including Lieutenant-Governor Newlands, the Honourable J.M. Uhrich, Mr. Justice McKay, Judge Rimmer, M.A. MacPherson, MLA, Roman Catholic Archbishop

---

11. Diamond Jenness, *The Indians of Canada* (1932; Toronto: University of Toronto Press, 1977), 264 as cited in Francis, *The Imaginary Indian*, 56.
12. Regina *Leader-Post*, 1 August 1945.
13. Francis, *The Imaginary Indian*, 97.
14. Ibid., 102.
15. H.V. Nelles, *The Art of Nation-Building: Pageantry and Spectacle at Quebec's Tercentenary* (Toronto: University of Toronto Press, 1999), 178.

Mathieu, and Bishop Harding of the Anglican Church.[16] By acting in the pageant, albeit following somebody else's script, Indians proved that they had not vanished: "They were still there, in full view, on stage, claiming their share of the present too."[17]

INDIAN POLITICAL ORGANIZATION

The "vanishing Indian" and the "performing Indian" were constructs invented and fostered by non-Indians for their own purposes. They were concepts that had little to do with the reality of Indians' lives. Indians struggled to make their own voices heard and to organize politically, but faced a wall of opposition. Canadian government policies, especially before World War II, were based on repression of indigenous culture and coercive assimilation. The government imposed a full array of repressive measures covering all aspects of Indian life,[18] but, for the purposes of this study, the focus is political activity. An amendment to the *Indian Act* in 1880 empowered the superintendent general of the Department of Indian Affairs to impose the elective system of band government whether a band wanted it or not. This meant that traditional tribal leaders were deprived of their power since the government recognized as spokesmen for the band only those men elected according to the provisions of the *Indian Act*. The goal was to destroy the Indians' traditional political system. Indians responded by electing their traditional leaders, but the Act enabled the Department of Indian Affairs to depose such leaders for incompetence, immorality or intemperance.[19] The discretionary power enjoyed by the Department and the vagueness of the grounds for dismissal allowed Ottawa to force its policies on elected chiefs and councilors.[20] When band members re-elected the deposed leaders, the government passed an amendment to the *Indian Act* in 1884, barring persons deposed from office from standing for immediate re-election.[21]

J.R. Miller concludes that the government of Canada engaged in "a concerted attack on the aboriginal, autonomous and self-regulating qualities of Native Peoples, particularly in the West and North." He adds, however, that Indians did not passively accept victimization: "the efforts to reject political interference and legal superintendency were widespread, energetic and determined."[22] Initially, political action took the form of *ad hoc* petitions and protests.[23] It was not until World War I that an attempt was made to form a national Indian organization. Frederick Ogilvie Loft, a Mohawk war veteran, became president and secretary-treasurer in 1919 of the League of Indians of Canada. Chief Loft wrote letters to tribal leaders in Ontario, Quebec and the prairie provinces, calling for support for a united organization. The first meeting in Western Canada took place at Elphinstone, Manitoba

16. Regina *Leader*, August 17–18, 1925.

17. Nelles, *The Art of Nation-Building*, 181.

18. For an overview, see John L. Tobias, "Protection, Civilization, Assimilation: An Outline History of Canada's Indian Policy," in J.R. Miller (ed.), *Sweet Promises: A Reader on Indian-White Relations in Canada* (Toronto: University of Toronto Press, 1991).

19. Tobias, "Protection, Civilization, Assimilation," 134.

20. J.R. Miller, "The Historical Context of the Drive for Self-Government," in Richard Gosse, James Youngblood Henderson and Roger Carter (eds.), *Continuing Poundmaker and Riel's Quest: Presentations Made at a Conference on Aboriginal Peoples and Justice* (Saskatoon: Purich Publishing and the College of Law, University of Saskatchewan, 1994), 43.

21. Tobias, "Protection, Civilization, Assimilation," 134.

22. Miller, "The Historical Context of the Drive for Self-Government," 42–43.

23. Sarah Carter, *Lost Harvests: Prairie Indian Reserve Farmers and Government Policy* (Montreal: McGill-Queen's University Press, 1990), 115–16.

in June 1920, followed the next year by a meeting at Thunderchild Reserve in Saskatchewan. During the 1920s the League met annually in Saskatchewan under the leadership of Edward Ahenakew, an Anglican clergyman and graduate of Emmanuel College in Saskatoon. In 1929 the organization was revitalized and renamed the League of Indians in Western Canada. Its 1931 convention held at Saddle Lake, Alberta drew 1,344 delegates, including twenty-two chiefs and councilors from thirteen Saskatchewan reserves.[24]

In the 1920s and 1930s John Tootoosis, a grand-nephew of Chief Poundmaker, one of the towering figures of the 1885 resistance, emerged as one of Saskatchewan's most effective Indian leaders. His biographers, Jean Goodwill and Norma Sluman, recount an incident that prefigured his extraordinary impact on Indian and Saskatchewan politics:

> One evening when he was about twenty-five years old, John went to visit his aunt, Etoweskotawapew (Lodge With Two Doorways), his father's older sister who was married to Ewaysikan. During the course of the evening, his elderly aunt suddenly rose and began to go through her belongings. Then she came back and sat down holding a carefully wrapped bundle. As she began to unfold the many layers of cloth she spoke very seriously to John. "My nephew, I am going to give you something that belonged to your grandfather. It is your turn now to look after it." She leaned forward and put something into his hand. John looked down at a heavy silver medal in astonishment, sensing immediately that it was Poundmaker's long-missing treaty medal! His aunt explained softly that her father had secretly entrusted it into her care. In all the long years since then, even when everyone had been looking for it, she had kept it safe and hidden away until she was sure she had found the proper person to have it.[25]

Tootoosis worked as an organizer for the League, traveling by rail, wagon, horseback and even on foot to reserves all over the West. When Edward Ahenakew resigned in the 1930s, Tootoosis took over as president.[26] Then, in 1944, Andrew Paull, a Squamish Indian from British Columbia, took the initiative to revive a national Indian organization. He invited Indian leaders from across the country to a conference in Ottawa. Among those attending was John Tootoosis, who, after consulting with the League membership, gave his support to Paull's North American Indian Brotherhood (NAIB).[27]

The NAIB was not alone in representing Saskatchewan Indians. In the post-World War I period, three bands in the Qu'Appelle Valley — Pasqua, Piapot and Muscowpetung — formed an alliance to fight the seizure of Indian land under the *Soldier Settlement Act*. Changing its name in 1933 to the Protective Association for the Indians and Their Treaties, it fought for Indian treaty rights, lands and resources, improved education and economic welfare.[28] A third organization was the

---

24. Stan Cuthand, "The Native Peoples of the Prairie Provinces in the 1920s and 1930s," in J.R. Miller (ed.), *Sweet Promises: A Reader on Indian-White Relations in Canada* (Toronto: University of Toronto Press, 1991), 381–83

25. Jean Goodwill and Norma Sluman, *John Tootoosis* (1982; Winnipeg: Pemmican Publications, 1991), 137–38.

26. Delia Opekokew, *The First Nations: Indian Government and the Canadian Confederation* (Saskatoon: Federation of Saskatchewan Indians, 1980), 34–35.

27. Goodwill and Sluman, *John Tootoosis*, 179–82.

28. Ibid., 146; Opekokew, *The First Nations*, 31–34.

Association of Saskatchewan Indians. In June 1944, Dan Kennedy (Ochankugahe), an Assiniboine from Carry-the-Kettle reserve, wrote his friend Zachary Hamilton asking for an army tent "for us to hold another conference among ourselves during the Regina fair — for the purpose of forming an Indian organization."[29] The request epitomizes the transition from performing to politicized Indian. Kennedy knew that every year Indians from various reserves set up their teepees on the Exhibition grounds. What better opportunity could there be for launching a broadly based association?

Coincidentally, June 1944 marked a change of government in Saskatchewan. Voters terminated the reign of the Liberals and elected the province's first Co-operative Commonwealth Federation (CCF) administration. The new premier, Tommy Douglas, pursued a more activist Indian policy than any of his predecessors had done. He apparently took to heart the honorary chieftainship conferred on him in July 1945. When installed as Chief We-a-ga-sha (Red Eagle), he made a point of saying that he did not consider it an "empty honor" and asked his "fellow chiefs" to share their problems with him.[30]

True to his word, Douglas invited Indians from across the province to a conference in Regina beginning January 4, 1946. In his opening remarks, he was careful to say that he did not wish to impose solutions on Indian people ("for you know better what your problems are"), but rather "to cement you together so that you may speak with one voice in the councils of our nation."[31] The process of unification required delicate negotiations, but, by the end of February, the Saskatchewan branch of the North American Indian Brotherhood, the Protective Association for the Indians and Their Treaties, and the Association of Saskatchewan Indians came together to form the Union of Saskatchewan Indians. John Tootoosis was elected the first president.

The CCF government's intervention in Indian politics was a mixed blessing. On the one hand, the government helped Saskatchewan Indians coalesce into a united force. Joseph Dreaver, president of the Association of Saskatchewan Indians, acknowledged this by moving a vote of thanks on behalf of Indians "to their white friends who has [*sic*] assisted them in accomplishing a work which would have taken them a long, long while to complete, if they had not received help."[32] On the other hand, the connection with the CCF created problems because political enemies of the CCF became enemies of the Union. When the Union presented a brief on the *Indian Act* in 1947 to the Joint Committee of the Senate and House of Commons, Senator J.F. Johnston (Liberal-Saskatchewan) charged that the Union was largely a creation of the CCF and did not reflect authentic Indian opinion.[33] In addition, representatives of the Roman Catholic Church, deeply suspicious of CCF and its behind-the-scenes role, apparently sought to undermine the Union.[34]

29. Saskatchewan Archives Board (SAB), Saskatchewan History Society (SHS) 30, Dan Kennedy to Zachary Hamilton, June 17, 1944.

30. Regina *Leader-Post*, July 27, 1945.

31. SAB, R-834, Indians of North America, file 37, *The Union of Saskatchewan Indians*, March 1946.

32. Ibid.

33. Special Joint Committee of the Senate and the House of Commons on the *Indian Act, Minutes of Proceedings and Evidence*, No. 6, 21 March 1947, 247.

34. John Tootoosis, interview, IH-ST.02, July 14, 1976, University of Regina, SIFC Library/Canadian Plains Research Center, Indian History Film Project Records.

HOW INDIANS OBTAINED THE PROVINCIAL VOTE

Since a politician is not likely to take seriously a citizen without a vote, it might be assumed that Indians in Saskatchewan would eagerly accept the right to vote. Such was not the case. At the time that Premier Douglas encouraged the formation of the Union of Saskatchewan Indians, he also wanted to extend the provincial franchise to all Indians. Only Indian war veterans and their spouses were then allowed to vote in provincial and federal elections.[35] Certain "progressive" Indians, like Dan Kennedy and Joe Dreaver, supported Douglas, but others were strongly opposed. A group of chiefs and councilors meeting in Punnichy in July 1945 declared that having the vote "would cause the Indians to lose their Treaty rights, and that Indians, leaving the reserves, would be at a loss to compete with white men sufficiently to guarantee them a living."[36]

Part of the opposition arose from confusion over the term "enfranchisement." It means, of course, obtaining the right to vote, but it was also the word used in the *Indian Act* to denote the legal process by which an Indian lost Indian status and became a citizen with the same rights and responsibilities as other citizens. "Enfranchisement" encapsulated the assimilative purpose at the heart of Canadian government policy. Nonetheless, it is misleading to attribute opposition to the franchise solely to linguistic ambiguity. The fact of the matter was that for many Indians the provincial vote was conceptually linked to a larger question — would Saskatchewan Indians continue as a separate and distinct entity with collective rights or would they be increasingly integrated as equal individuals with the general population? Because of the controversy, Union of Saskatchewan Indians in 1947 officially opposed the vote, albeit in guarded language:

> This Organization does not favor the enfranchisement of Indians in Canada but does recognize the necessity of eventually assuming the responsibilities and duties of citizenship, as well as the rights thereof, but the franchise itself is a thing of which the Organization cannot approve as such.[37]

The hand of a skilled lawyer can be detected in the statement, which was drafted by Morris Shumiatcher, Premier Douglas's executive assistant who acted on behalf of the Union.[38]

The matter of the provincial franchise lay dormant until 1956 when the CCF government revived it. The cabinet appointed a Committee on Indian Affairs, which recommended, among other things, extending the vote and removing restrictions on the sale of liquor to Indians.[39] The government decided to hold a conference to sound Indian opinion. One hundred and three chiefs and councilors gathered at Valley Centre, Fort Qu'Appelle on October 30, 1958. Addressing the delegates, Premier Douglas emphasized two points. He promised that voting and liquor rights would not imperil treaty rights and neither would be granted without the consent of Indians.[40] John Tootoosis reminded the chiefs and councilors that they

35. Regina *Leader-Post*, February 25, 1947.

36. The Indian Missionary Record, July-August 1945.

37. Special Joint Committee of the Senate and the House of Commons on the *Indian Act, Minutes of Proceeding and Evidence*, No. 19, May 8, 1947, 1000.

38. Ibid., 947; Dr. Morris C. Shumiatcher, interview by author, July 19, 1992.

39. SAB, T.C. Douglas Papers, R-33.7 1291a, Committee on Indian Affairs, First Report, November 19, 1956.

40. Ibid., R-33.1 XLV 864d (49) 4/6, Provincial Conference of Indian Chiefs and Councilors, October 30–31, 1958.

had not consulted with the people on the reserves on these issues. His motion that the delegates defer making a decision for one year carried by a large majority.[41] A second major outcome of the conference was the formation of the Federation of Saskatchewan Indians (FSI), which came into being when the Union of Saskatchewan Indians,[42] led by Tootoosis, joined forces with the Queen Victoria Protective Association, led by William Joseph.

The next conference took place at Fort Qu'Appelle one year later on October 20–21, 1959. Once again, the Indian delegates resisted the provincial government's suggestion that they accept voting and liquor rights. The government manoeuvred to place a convoluted motion before the convention:

> Whereas in a political democracy the vote is a right and not a privilege, and whereas some Indians want the provincial vote and others do not want the vote, therefore be it resolved that the Federation of Saskatchewan Indians in conference assembled be not required to petition the Provincial Government on this question.[43]

Essentially, the government was trying to wriggle out of its promise not to extend the vote without a motion to that effect from the FSI assembly. The motion implied that silence from the assembly did not mean lack of consent. The complicated manoeuvering was to no avail; the resolution was almost unanimously rejected.

Douglas then made a key decision. On March 11, 1960 he announced in the Legislative Assembly that Indians would receive the provincial franchise. He noted that the Diefenbaker government had recently granted the federal vote, and British Columbia, Manitoba and Ontario had done the same in their respective jurisdictions without apparent adverse consequences. Douglas acknowledged breaking his promise not to proceed without Indian consent, and he gave three exculpatory reasons for his *volte-face*: voting would not threaten treaty rights, politicians would pay more attention to Indians if they were voters, and many younger Indians said they wanted the vote.[44] The announcement brought congratulations from Dan Kennedy, a resident of Carry-the-Kettle reserve, who wrote Douglas:

> Please convey my thanks to your colleagues for their good faith in the brotherhood of man. Without this instrument of defence [the vote] the Indian is a maverick in his own country — as you once aptly expressed it — "like a stray dog, unwanted and kicked about and that the politicians had no time for him."[45]

Chief William Joseph of the Big White Fish reserve, by contrast, collected money through the Meadow Lake and Loon Lake areas to pay for a protest trip to Ottawa and took to the air waves to exhort Indians not to participate in the upcoming provincial election.[46]

Thus, the provincial vote for Indians arrived with a broken promise in the midst of intense controversy. John Tootoosis, for one, saw a link between the manner of the

41. Ibid.

42. The Federation of Saskatchewan Indians became the Federation of Saskatchewan Indian Nations in 1982.

43. SAB, T.C. Douglas Papers, R-33.1 XLV 864e (49) 5/6, R. Woollam to T.C. Douglas and J.H. Sturdy, January 15, 1960.

44. Legislative Assembly of Saskatchewan, *Debates*, T.C. Douglas, March 11, 1960.

45. SAB, T.C. Douglas Papers, R-33.1, XLV 864e (49) 5/6, Dan Kennedy to T.C. Douglas, February 20, 1960.

46. Ibid., CXXXIII 961a (150) ½, R. Woollam to J.H. Sturdy, March 22, 1960.

vote's introduction and subsequent low voter turnout. He also perceived something sinister in the way voting rights and liquor rights were given at the same time:

> Getting back to the voting issue — the people didn't want the vote. It was Diefenbaker who shoved the federal vote down Indian throats — he never asked them whether they wanted it or not, he just gave them the federal vote. Later on Tommy Douglas did the same thing — he also went ahead and gave drinking privileges ... This is why Indians never voted much during elections, it wasn't their consent to have the vote — it was just given to them. One could also say that they were literally shoved into a pool of liquor. The reason why they gave the vote to Indians was only for the number of votes they could get from them and of course to use liquor along with it. For example, if I were on the side of Diefenbaker I would say to him if you give liquor to the Indians I'll get votes on your side — that's how they were going to use these things. That was the same with Tommy Douglas.[47]

THE QUIET REVOLUTION AND A NEW PARADIGM

Historians agree that in the 1960s the Quiet Revolution transformed the society, culture, economy and politics of the province of Quebec It is less widely known, but equally true, that in the same period a quiet revolution began in the relations between the Indian and non-Indian communities in Saskatchewan. In the words of Sally Weaver, who analyzed similar developments on the national scene, there was a paradigm shift from Indian policy based on individual rights and integration of Indians into the larger society to one based on Indian collective rights and self-government.[48] A fundamental realignment occurred in the terms of Indian/non-Indian coexistence.

In the early 1960s both of Saskatchewan's main political parties, the CCF and the Liberals, adhered to the old paradigm. Woodrow Lloyd, who succeeded Douglas as CCF leader and premier, declared in 1963: "There is a goal upon which most of us will readily agree. It is the steady integration of all minority groups into the mainstream of Canadian society." He went on to propose the removal of "the artificial division in public services between them [Indians] and all other Canadians," that is, elimination of the Department of Indian Affairs and delivery of services to Indians through the same channels as were used for other Canadians.[49] Ross Thatcher, who led the Liberals to victory in the April 1964 election, subscribed to the same integrationist policies. He agreed with Lloyd that the provincial government should provide services, including social welfare, health, education, natural resources and agriculture, to Indians.[50] Both the CCF and the Liberals held that Indians should not be separated out from the general population in the provision of government services.

In the course of the 1960s, one of the parties changed its policy, and the other did not. The Liberals, dominated by Thatcher's strong personality and firm convictions, made no concessions to the shifting terms of political discourse concerning

---

47. John Tootoosis, interview, IH-ST.02, July 14, 1976.

48. Sally M. Weaver, "A New Paradigm in Canadian Indian Policy for the 1990s," *Canadian Ethnic Studies* 22 (1990): 8–18.

49. SAB, F. Meakes Papers, R-74.1 II 3, E.I. Wood to all Chiefs, February 14, 1964, attached Dominion-Provincial Conference — Excerpt from Premier's Statement, November 1963.

50. SAB, J.R. Ross Barrie Papers, R-10 VII 48a, A Submission from the Government of Saskatchewan on the Administration of Indian Affairs, August 1964; Regina *Leader-Post*, October 29, 1964.

Indian/non-Indian relations. The CCF, by contrast, adapted its policy to new realities. It appointed in 1964 a Minorities Policy Committee and initiated a policy review. The name of the Committee itself indicates the mindset of the time. Indians were seen as one of a number of ethnic minorities, not as a group with distinct status and entitlement. The paradigm shift mentioned earlier involved the adoption of new language — from "ethnic minority" to "First Nations." The Committee produced a report that was approved by the CCF provincial convention in 1966. It affirmed the principle of "equality of opportunity," but added that "new opportunities must be seen, not as submerging the traditional Indian culture, but as a means to a more abundant life in which can be kept what is wanted from the past."[51] This may be contrasted with Premier Thatcher's 1969 statement:

> What is their [Indian] culture? Living in tents or dirty filthy shacks on a reserve? Culture is fine, but we've got to be realistic and bring them to where the jobs are, where the children are, where the children can go to school and where they can live in a decent house.[52]

The gulf between the two parties widened in the wake of the controversy over the Canadian government's 1969 statement on Indian policy, better known as the White Paper. The paper recommended abolishing all legal distinctions between Indians and other Canadians, dismantling the Indian Affairs Department, transferring delivery of Indian services from Ottawa to the provinces, and reviewing the treaties "to see how they can be equitably ended."[53] Thatcher praised the document, while Lloyd condemned it.[54] Lloyd played an important role in rethinking CCF Indian policy. He could see that the question was no longer, "What can the Government of Saskatchewan do for Indians?" The question was, "What kind of relationship should the Government of Saskatchewan have with the Indian community?" As soon as this question was asked, the door to Indian self-government was opened. The paradigm shift is evident in Lloyd's memorandum to the Saskatchewan NDP president in July 1969:

> "Program" [referring to the NDP Indian program] needs defining. Admittedly it should include "things" which a New Democratic Party government would undertake to do. Equally important, and indeed I think more important, is the necessity to define the kind of relationship we want to develop with members of the Indian community wherever such a community exists. This in turn involves some definition of the role for Indian people. It involves also a method of transferring certain essential authority to the Indians in their communities. Obviously if authority is to be meaningful there must at the same time be access to certain resources.[55]

Allan Blakeney, Lloyd's successor as party leader in 1970, continued in the same direction. He was quoted as saying, "Several years ago, a clear answer to discrimination was integration. That may now not be necessarily so."[56] In the run up to the

51. SAB, W.S. Lloyd Papers, R-61.8 XXI 106n 1/3, Cooperative Commonwealth Federation, Saskatchewan Section of the New Democratic Party, 1966 Provincial Convention, The Indian and Metis Minorities Policy Statement.

52. Regina *Leader-Post*, March 7, 1969.

53. Statement of the Government of Canada on Indian Policy, 1960.

54. Regina *Leader-Post*, August 5, 1969; SAB, A.E. Blakeney Papers, R-1143 X 1c, Statement of the Saskatchewan New Democratic Party on the Recent Federal Government Policy that the Provinces Would Assume Responsibility for Indian Programs and Services, July 30, 1969.

55. SAB, W.S. Lloyd Papers, R-61.8, XXI 119b 2/2, W.S. Lloyd to Bev Currie, July 16, 1969.

56. Regina *Leader-Post*, September 30, 1970.

June 1971 provincial election, an NDP strategy document pointed out that "the Indian culture is far from being destroyed, and any attempt to appeal for Indian votes on the basis of an invitation into the 'mainstream' will be politely received, but not accepted."[57] The party platform promised grants to enable Indians to make a "thorough study of treaty rights," as well as funds for "programs worked out in cooperation with Indian and Métis leaders and where feasible and desired by them, administered by their organizations."[58] Though not a recognition of Aboriginal self-government, it was a clear statement of moral and financial support for the central Indian and Métis organizations.

The Liberal Party under Ross Thatcher remained untouched by these policy developments. They were stuck in the old paradigm based on equality of citizenship and integration of Indians as individuals into the mainstream economy and society. NDP politicians joined the "quiet revolution" because they were more attuned to major changes occurring in the FSI. Under the leadership first of Walter Deiter[59] and then of David Ahenakew, the FSI emerged in the 1960s as a strong, effective organization offering positive alternatives to paternalistic government policies. The Federation evolved from a lobby group to a program delivery organization. Its budget increased from $70,000 in 1969 to $1.5 million in 1972, when it employed a staff of 119.[60] David Ahenakew himself used the term "quiet revolution" to describe the change that was taking place. In the mid-1960s he was employed as a job placement officer in the provincial government's Indian and Métis branch. His supervisor was John Ursan, who recalls this pivotal conversation with Ahenakew:

> After our meetings, he [Ahenakew] said, "My wife has invited you for dinner with our family." We had a lovely dinner. He said, "Do you like wild meat?" I said, "Yes, I like moose." "That's what we have, we have a piece of moose." And they cooked it up and we had a lovely dinner. I met the children — three beautiful kids. Then we sat with a glass of wine. We talked and at eight o'clock the kids came down from upstairs with their pyjamas and each said, "Good night, Mr. Ursan, it was nice meeting you," and, as the kids went back upstairs, David said to me, "That's what it's all about. If we can keep those kids from fighting your kids in the future and have a quiet revolution, then we've got it made, John." And I'll tell you those words just cut through me. They were beautiful. And that's how David approached this thing. The quiet revolution.[61]

The FSI (after 1982, the Federation of Saskatchewan Indian Nations (FSIN)) made the treaties the centre of concern and the foundation for the Indian/non-Indian relationship. The result of the process is evident in the *Statement of Treaty Issues: Treaties as a Bridge to the Future*, a document presented in 1998 by David M. Arnot, Treaty Commissioner for Saskatchewan, to FSIN Chief Perry Bellegarde and minister of Indian Affairs Jane Stewart. The paper states:

---

57. SAB, A.E. Blakeney Papers, R-800 III 25 16/38, Wylie Simmonds to Allan Blakeney et al., May 28, 1971.

58. Ibid., R-800 I 214 2/2, "New Deal for People," New Democratic Party of Saskatchewan, February 1971.

59. For the most complete discussion of Walter Deiter's career see Patricia Ann Deiter, "A Biography of Chief Walter P. Deiter" (Master's thesis, University of Regina, 1997).

60. Noel Dyck, "Representation and Leadership of a Provincial Indian Association," in Adrian Tanner (ed.), *The Politics of Indianness: Case Studies in Native Ethnopolitics in Canada* (St. John's, NF: St. John's Institute of Social and Economic Research, Memorial University of Newfoundland, 1983), 240.

61. John Ursan, interview with author, May 9, 1995.

> We are witnessing profound change in relations between the federal and provincial governments and First Nations in Saskatchewan. These changes are historic. A paradigm shift is occurring in our relations — from the paternalistic approach of the Indian Act, to a paradigm built upon the partnership of treaty relationships. ... Treaty First Nations wish to have responsible government, and to exercise jurisdiction rather than administer policies and programs not of their own making.[62]

FIRST NATIONS AND SASKATCHEWAN PROVINCIAL ELECTIONS

Most of the literature on Indian voting in provincial and federal elections focuses on the low participation rate and the presumed reasons for it. Roger Gibbons, in his study for the Royal Commission on Electoral Reform and Party Financing, found that in some northern polls in the 1984 and 1988 federal elections, Aboriginal voter turnout rates equaled or surpassed non-Aboriginal turnout rates. However, in the south, Aboriginal turnout was well below the Canadian norm of 75 percent. He argues that "low rates of electoral participation are symptomatic of distress within the political process and/or political community. When particular groups stand apart in this way, a low rate of participation suggests a significant degree of alienation and disaffection."[63] His conclusion is not surprising in light of the disadvantaged socio-economic standing of First Nations peoples in Canada. Although the United Nations ranks Canada third highest of all the countries in the world on the "Human Development Index," it ranks Aboriginal Canadians in the same category as Albania, Cuba, Paraguay and Iraq.[64] "Alienation and disaffection" from Canadian society and political processes are understandable responses.

David Bedford and Sidney Pobihushchy have a slightly different view in their study of voting in the Maritimes. They detect a decline in Indian voter participation in federal and provincial elections from the 1960s to the present, and they attribute the decline to "decolonization," the affirmation of Aboriginal nationalism and the recovery of Aboriginal traditions. "We are proposing that this change in consciousness — from Canadians who are Indians to members of the Maliseet or Micmac nations — is the most important reason for the decline in voter turnout."[65] Rather than seeing low turnout for provincial and federal elections as a sign of alienation, they see it as positive affirmation of belonging and identity.

Both Gibbons and Bedford/Pobihushchy assume that Indian voter turnout in provincial and federal provincial elections correlates directly with the degree of identification with province and country. Tim Schouls casts doubt on even this assumption. He points out that some Aboriginal leaders have advocated more

62. *Statement of Treaty Issues: Treaties as a Bridge to the Future*, transmitted to Chief Perry Bellegarde, Federation of Saskatchewan Indian Nations and the Honourable Jane Stewart, minister of Indian Affairs and Northern Development from the Honourable Judge David M. Arnot, Treaty Commissioner for Saskatchewan, October 23, 1998.

63. Roger Gibbons, "Electoral Reform and Canada's Aboriginal Population: An Assessment of Aboriginal Electoral Districts," in Robert A Milen (ed.), *Aboriginal Peoples and Electoral Reform in Canada, Research Studies for the Royal Commission on Electoral Reform and Party Financing* (Toronto: Dundurn Press, 1991), 158–60; 154.

64. United Nations Development Programme, *Human Development Report 1993* (Oxford: Oxford University Press, 1993), cited in Russel Lawrence Barsh, "Canada's Aboriginal Peoples: Social Integration or Disintegration?," *The Canadian Journal of Native Studies* 14, no. 1 (1994): 2.

65. David Bedford and Sidney Pobihushchy, "On-Reserve Status Indian Voter Participation in the Maritimes," *The Canadian Journal of Native Studies* 15, no. 2 (1995): 269.

Aboriginal representation in Parliament, not to forge links of common citizenship with non-Aboriginal Canadians, but rather to advance and facilitate Aboriginal self-government initiatives.[66] Ovide Mercredi states: "We do participate in the electoral process with the expectation and anticipation that we may be able to influence the better treatment of our people and the full enjoyment of our collective rights and freedoms."[67]

Russel Lawrence Barsh et al. studied the voting behaviour of three of the largest Alberta Aboriginal communities — Blood Tribe, Peigan Nation, and Four Nations — in 16 general elections and the 1992 constitutional referendum. They have found that Indian participation is poor and declining: "Among Bloods, for example, voter turnout in provincial elections was 44 percent of voter turnout for the riding as a whole before 1980, and this ratio fell to 20 percent for the period after 1980."[68] Participation in federal elections was somewhat higher than in provincial elections, though still low compared with non-Aboriginal voters.

To better understand the reasons for Alberta Aboriginals' voting or not voting, three university students conducted interviews with 99 eligible voters on the Peigan reserve. Nearly half of those interviewed (48.3 percent) felt they had "zero" impact on federal elections, 41.6 percent felt they had no impact on provincial elections, but only 11.5 percent felt the same way about Band elections.[69] Voting in Band elections was more than three times greater than in provincial or federal elections. Interestingly, no respondents argued that Aboriginal peoples should refrain from voting in provincial or federal elections because to do so would compromise their sovereignty. Instead, voters took a pragmatic view. They didn't vote because they didn't think voting was useful. The higher participation in federal as compared with provincial elections might reflect the perception that the Treaty relationship is with Ottawa.

The study of Indian voting in Saskatchewan elections is complicated by the fact that in many cases Indians and non-Indians vote in the same poll, making it impossible to separate the vote. This analysis, therefore, is confined to polls that are contained entirely within reserve boundaries. In 1960, the first Saskatchewan provincial election in which Indians had the right to vote, there was only one such poll, and in 1964, only two — not enough to yield meaningful evidence. In 1967, by contrast, there were 27 polls entirely within reserve boundaries (4,313 eligible voters), in 1971, 30 (5,881 eligible voters), and subsequently, at least 40 (from 7,558 to 14,061 eligible voters). This was the sample used to ascertain Indian voting participation and trends.

Figure 1 compares voting turnout among the general population in Saskatchewan elections from 1967 to 1995 with the turnout among Indian reserve voters. Not including 1995, when there was a sharp decline by the electorate as a whole, the overall rate of voter participation among the general population hovered at 80 percent. Among Indian voters, turnout averaged 49.8 percent. Thus, Indian voter

66. Tim Schouls, "Aboriginal Peoples and Electoral Reform in Canada: Differentiated Representation Versus Voter Equality," *Canadian Journal of Political Science* 29, no. 4 (December 1996): 739.

67. Ovide Mercredi, Testimony before the Royal Commission on Electoral Reform and Party Financing, April 19, 1990, quoted in Milen (ed.), *Aborginal Peoples and Electoral Reform in Canada*.

68. Russel Lawrence Barsh, Michelle Fraser, Faye Morning Bull, Toby Provost and Kirby Smith, "The Prairie Indian Vote in Canadian Politics 1965–1993: A Critical Case Study from Alberta," *Great Plains Research* 7 (Spring 1997): 10.

69. Ibid., 20.

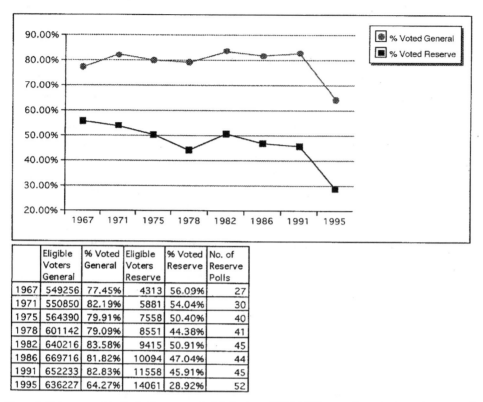

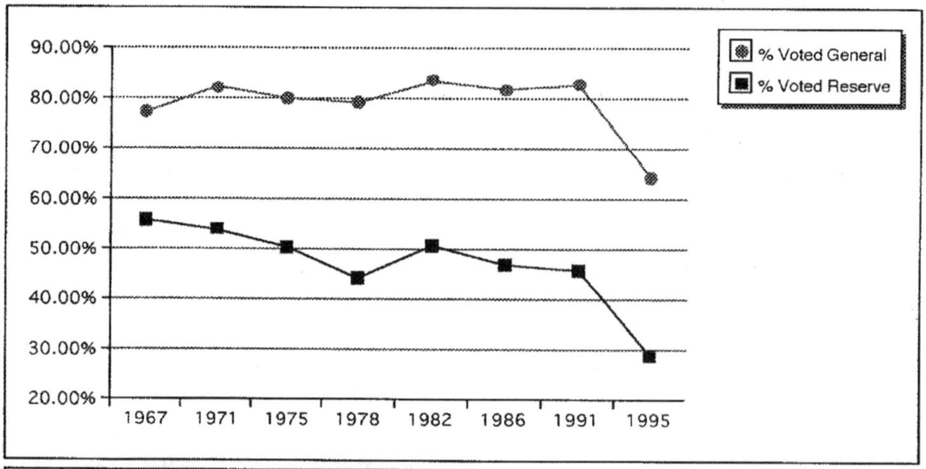

	Eligible Voters General	% Voted General	Eligible Voters Reserve	% Voted Reserve	No. of Reserve Polls
1967	549256	77.45%	4313	56.09%	27
1971	550850	82.19%	5881	54.04%	30
1975	564390	79.91%	7558	50.40%	40
1978	601142	79.09%	8551	44.38%	41
1982	640216	83.58%	9415	50.91%	45
1986	669716	81.82%	10094	47.04%	44
1991	652233	82.83%	11558	45.91%	45
1995	636227	64.27%	14061	28.92%	52

Figure 1. Voter turn-out in Saskatchewan provincial elections, 1967–1995: general population and reserve polls.

turnout over the period 1967 to 1991 was 62 percent of that of the general population. This is a significantly higher rate of Indian voter turnout than was found in the Alberta study.[70] Also, the Alberta study showed declining Indian voter turnout as compared with the general voting population. In Saskatchewan, no such relative decline is evident. Although Indian voter participation fell to 29 percent in 1995, general participation declined to 64 percent, which meant that Indian voter turnout was still 45 percent of the general turnout.

It might be objected that the reserve vote is a rural vote and that it would be more appropriate to compare it with the general rural vote in order to remove the extraneous variable of "urbanness." The Chief Electoral Officer for Saskatchewan defines the rural vote as including all constituencies except Regina, Saskatoon, Prince Albert, Swift Current, Yorkton and North Battleford. Figure 2, which compares the general rural vote with the Indian reserve vote, is virtually identical to Figure 1, which compares the total vote, rural and urban, with the Indian reserve vote. In other words, rural vote turnout is almost the same as general vote turnout, and it makes little difference whether we base the analysis on Figure 1 or Figure 2.

How are these numbers to be interpreted? In the first place, the relatively low Indian voter turnout can be partly attributed to historical factors. As mentioned above, the government of Canada from 1869 onward used the *Indian Act* to discourage and repress Indian political activity. When the controls started to be lifted after World War II, but especially in the 1960s, the extension of the vote to Indians

70. See footnote 61.

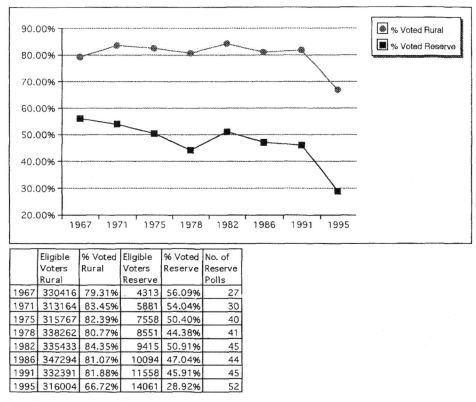

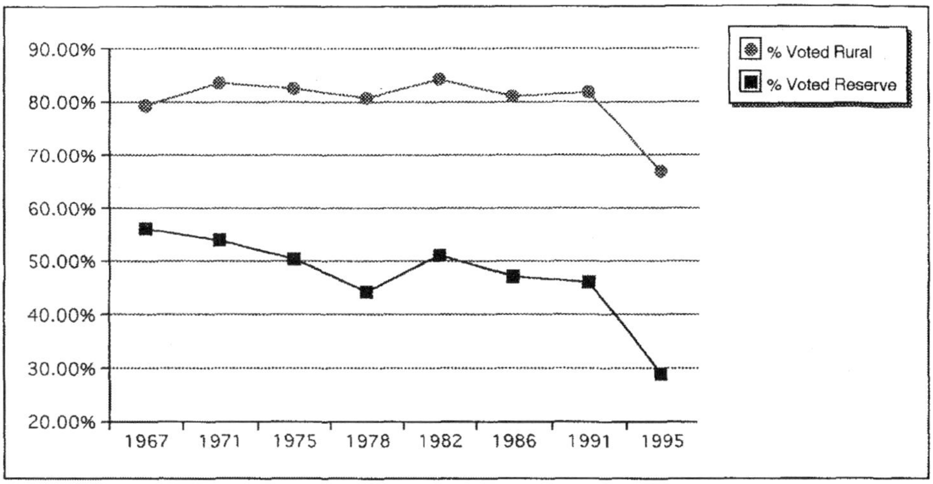

	Eligible Voters Rural	% Voted Rural	Eligible Voters Reserve	% Voted Reserve	No. of Reserve Polls
1967	330416	79.31%	4313	56.09%	27
1971	313164	83.45%	5881	54.04%	30
1975	315767	82.39%	7558	50.40%	40
1978	338262	80.77%	8551	44.38%	41
1982	335433	84.35%	9415	50.91%	45
1986	347294	81.07%	10094	47.04%	44
1991	332391	81.88%	11558	45.91%	45
1995	316004	66.72%	14061	28.92%	52

Figure 2. Voter turn-out in Saskatchewan provincial elections, 1967–1995: rural population and reserve polls.

was controversial. John Tootoosis and many other Indian leaders in Saskatchewan felt that the vote was foisted upon them. They were concerned about the link between voting and "enfranchisement," the term in the Indian Act for loss of Indian status. Premier Tommy Douglas called two provincial conferences of Indian chiefs and councilors and failed both times to have a resolution passed approving the provincial vote. In the end, he lost patience and gave the vote to Indians, breaking his promise not to do so without Indian consent.

The arguments made by Gibbons and others concerning the social and economic marginalization and alienation of Indian people are also relevant to Saskatchewan and help explain low voter turnout. However, we must explain the higher participation rate in Saskatchewan compared with Alberta and the fact that in Saskatchewan, unlike Alberta, Indian voter turnout is not significantly declining relative to the general population. Here the history of the Federation of Saskatchewan Indian Nations comes into play. The politicization and organization of First Nations, galvanized by leaders such as Walter Deiter and David Ahenakew in the 1960s and early 1970s and continued by their successors, has meant that Saskatchewan Indians have functioned more effectively as an organized political force than have their Alberta counterparts. It is likely that this translates into a greater mobilization of Indian voters in Saskatchewan provincial elections. It also means that strengthened First Nations institutions dedicated to self-government do not result in disengagement of Indian voters from the provincial political process. The contrary seems to be the case.

Figure 3 indicates the party preferences of reserve voters in provincial elections

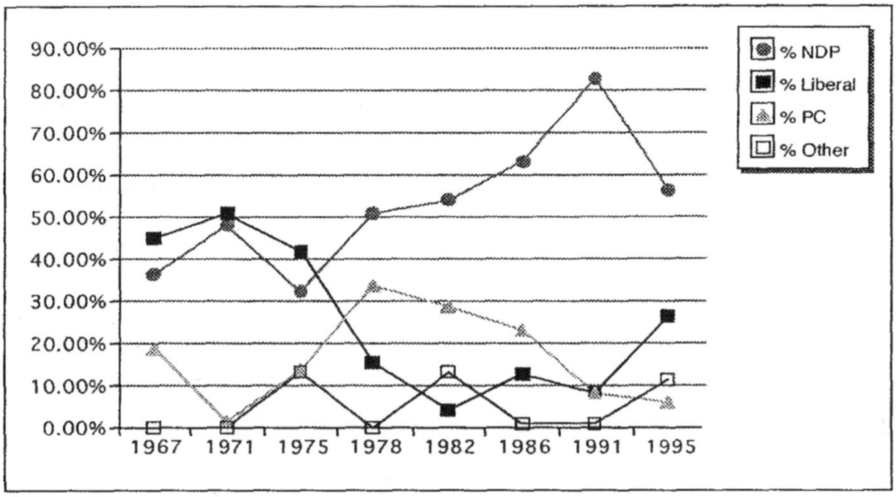

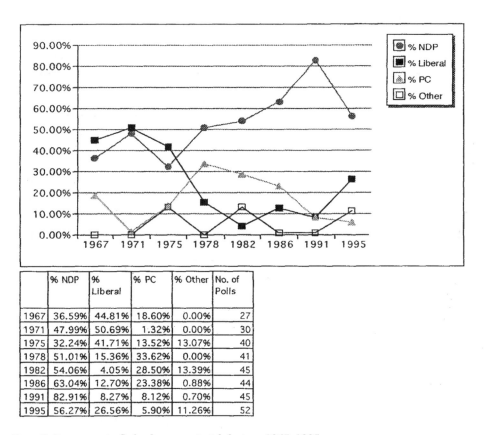

	% NDP	% Liberal	% PC	% Other	No. of Polls
1967	36.59%	44.81%	18.60%	0.00%	27
1971	47.99%	50.69%	1.32%	0.00%	30
1975	32.24%	41.71%	13.52%	13.07%	40
1978	51.01%	15.36%	33.62%	0.00%	41
1982	54.06%	4.05%	28.50%	13.39%	45
1986	63.04%	12.70%	23.38%	0.88%	44
1991	82.91%	8.27%	8.12%	0.70%	45
1995	56.27%	26.56%	5.90%	11.26%	52

Figure 3. Reserve vote in Saskatchewan provincial elections, 1967–1995.

from 1967 to 1995. Most of the time voters cast their ballots for one of the three mainstream parties. However, in 1975 candidates running as Independents garnered 13.07 percent of the reserve vote. In 1982, the Aboriginal People's Party of Saskatchewan captured 7.43 percent, while the Western Canada Concept Party and an Independent took 5.97 percent. In 1995, the United Aboriginal People's Party won 11.26 percent. With these exceptions the Indian vote has gone to the Liberals, the NDP and the Progressive Conservatives.

Figure 3 also shows that in 1967 the reserve vote favoured the Liberals (44.8 percent) over the NDP (36.6 percent) with the Progressive Conservatives trailing (18.6 percent). It is worth noting that when the Douglas government contemplated extending the franchise to Indians, it assumed that the Indian vote would be predominantly Liberal. A government committee chaired by John Sturdy in 1956 assumed that as many as 60 percent of Indians would vote Liberal and only 30 percent CCF.[71] The report based this projection on the belief that reserve Indians were under the influence of Indian agents, many of whom were political appointees of the federal Liberals. In addition, the majority of Indians were at least nominally Catholic, and Catholics in the province tended to support the Liberals. In fact, Angus Mirasty and William Charles, two Indian leaders from northern reserves, warned Douglas not to give Indians the vote for this very reason:

71. SAB, T.C. Douglas Papers, R-33.7 I 291A, Committee on Indian Affairs, First Report, November 19, 1956.

> I like to bring to your attention Mr. Douglas you must realize this and the members of your Cabinet that there are two thirds of the Indian people in Saskatchewan Roman Catholics and these Indians are pretty well dominated by their priests and you can be sure that those Indians, if they were to vote they would vote the way their Father the Priest, votes and you can be sure it won't be CCF either.[72]

In the 1971 election, when the Blakeney NDP defeated the Thatcher Liberals, the Liberals maintained their lead over the NDP in the reserve vote, but by a significantly reduced margin (50.7 percent compared to 48 percent). In 1975, the Liberals still led, but both Liberal and NDP votes were drained away to Independents who captured 13 percent of the total vote. From 1978 onward the Indian vote moved strongly to the NDP. Even when provincial voters as a whole turned to Grant Devine's Progressive Conservatives in 1982, 54.1 percent of the Indian vote stayed with the NDP and only 28.5 percent chose the Conservatives.

The trend in the reserve vote to the NDP really began in 1971 when significant gains were made on the Liberals. The 1975 election was something of an aberration because Independents cut into both NDP and Liberal votes, but especially the NDP. The pattern evident in 1971 resumed in 1978 and subsequently continued. A basic reason for the trend to the NDP is the "quiet revolution" of the 1960s and early 1970s. The NDP was first and most emphatic in recognizing and affirming the paradigm shift from small "l" liberal policies based on individual equality and integration to policies based on Indian treaty rights and self-government. The NDP, under Lloyd and Blakeney, was the first party to recognize and support the Federation of Saskatchewan Indian Nations, and that relationship appears to have continued in the Romanow era.

This chapter has emphasized the power of the past in shaping the role of First Nations in Saskatchewan politics, but what of the future? Without falling into the trap of crystal ball gazing, one can extrapolate certain general trends. The quiet revolution that began in the 1960s will control future political developments. The paradigm shift from liberal individualism and integration to partnership based on treaty relations appears irreversible. However, past experience suggests that strengthened First Nations self-government does not necessarily mean disengagement from provincial electoral politics. The two go hand in hand. It also appears likely that as the years go by and the quiet revolution turns into the status quo, the NDP will lose its predominance in the First Nations vote because its historical advantage will become less relevant. Finally and most obviously, the era of "two solitudes" is permanently over, and the First Nations role in Saskatchewan politics will become increasingly significant and influential.

72. Ibid., R-33.1 XLV 864c (49) 3/6, Angus Mirasty and William B. Charles to T.C. Douglas, April 9, 1956.

SASKATCHEWAN AND THE SOCIAL UNION

Gregory P. Marchildon and Brent Cotter

INTRODUCTION

The purpose of this chapter is to explain the government of Saskatchewan's unique and, at times, defining role in the social union discussions from the spring of 1995 until the signing of the Social Union Framework Agreement in February 1999. We begin with a review of Saskatchewan's historic role in building some of the key components of the "welfare state," the edifice upon which the modern social union has been constructed. With this background in mind, we explore the reasons for Saskatchewan's pro-active involvement in the first phase of the social union negotiations from 1995 to 1997, including the province's leadership in producing the National Child Benefit, the first pan-Canadian social program in thirty years. We then describe the next phases of the negotiations, from the autumn of 1997 until February 1999, which ultimately produced the Social Union Framework Agreement. We conclude with comments on the significance of what was achieved as well as the future potential — for both Saskatchewan and Canada — of the policies and processes agreed upon in these formative federal-provincial negotiations.

THE SASKATCHEWAN TRADITION AND THE CANADIAN SOCIAL UNION, 1944–1994

Saskatchewan has a long history of social policy experimentation going back to the first elected CCF government. In particular, the Douglas-Lloyd administrations, from 1944 to 1964, emphasized the positive role of the state in building greater security and accessibility out of the devastation of the Great Depression. To achieve this, the provincial government assembled a very motivated and able civil service, generally considered to have been the highest qualified in the country.[1] Highly professional but also ideologically motivated, the most senior officials in the government were dedicated to building a society where activist social policies would break down economic and social inequities.[2] This meshed well with the utopian desire of the provincial politicians to "forge a new, more equal society" and to "remake the nation in this new image."[3]

1. M. Brownstone, "The Douglas-Lloyd Governments: Innovation and Bureaucratic Adaptation," in Laurier LaPierre et al., *Essays on the Left* (Toronto: McClelland and Stewart, 1971), 64–80. Also see A.W. Johnson, "Biography of a Government: Policy Formulation in Saskatchewan, 1944–1961" (Ph.D. dissertation, Harvard University, 1963).

2. Robert I. McLaren, *The Saskatchewan Practice of Public Administration in Historical Perspective* (Lewiston, NY: Edwin Mellon, 1998), 112.

3. Christopher Dunn and David Laycock, "Innovation and Competition in the Agricultural Heartland" in Christopher Dunn and David Laycock (eds.), *The Provincial State* (Toronto: Copp, Clark Pitman, 1992), 225.

As befits such an ambitious agenda, the Douglas government, as well as the administrations that followed it, played a constructive and innovative role in the federal-provincial arena of formulating and implementing *national* social policy.[4] Ironically, Saskatchewan's traditionally pro-active intergovernmental stance can be traced to the failure of a series of policy proposals by the federal government at the Federal-Provincial Conference on Reconstruction in August 1945. The comprehensive federal plan included a federal-provincial shared-cost plan for the unemployable, a national pension plan for everyone over 70 years of age supplemented by the federal-provincial shared-cost program for the needy between the ages of 65 and 69, and a federal-provincial health insurance scheme in which the federal government would assume 60 percent of the costs of approved hospitalization and medical care plans. In putting forward the plan, the federal government argued that the constitutional "division of powers" should not prevent "any government, or governments in cooperation, from taking effective action."[5]

Agreeing with the sentiment expressed in the federal position, the Douglas government supported what amounted to a slightly amended version of the federal plan. But with Ontario and Quebec unwilling to accept the implicit centralizing tendency of the proposal, the federal plan was ultimately rejected. Disappointed, Douglas felt that the position staked out by Ontario and Quebec concerning provincial autonomy was too extreme. Unable to secure the federal-provincial agreement for a national health insurance plan, the Saskatchewan government proceeded on its own with a more modest hospitalization plan in 1947, a plan that nonetheless proved so popular that variations of it were adopted in British Columbia, Alberta and Newfoundland. It would take another 15 years before the province, again acting on its own, could introduce a more comprehensive medical care insurance system, comparable to what both Ottawa and Saskatchewan originally wanted in 1945.[6]

From Ottawa's perspective, the 1945 Conference outcome forced it to approach social policy in a much more incremental manner in the future, and to rely heavily on the spending power to induce provincial participation.[7] As a poor province with an ambitious social policy agenda, and with a pragmatism forced by the failure of the 1945 Conference, the Saskatchewan government became a willing partner in establishing future national shared-cost social programs on a piecemeal basis. These initiatives included: in 1948, health grants to encourage the construction and operation of health facilities; in 1951, a federal pension scheme for those over 70 supplemented by a federal-provincial pension scheme covering those from 65 to 69; in 1955, a federal-provincial social assistance scheme; a federal-provincial hospitalization program in 1957; and in 1968, a single-payer, universal medicare scheme.

In the case of the health care initiatives, the province went ahead on its own in terms of policy design and implementation as well as financing. The administration then pushed for national implementation through shared-cost financing after demonstrating the effectiveness and popularity of first hospitalization, then medicare, in one province.

During these negotiations, the Saskatchewan government consistently pushed

4. Johnson, "Biography of a Government," 556.
5. Quoted in Joan Price Boase, "Trends in Social Policy: Towards the Millenium," in Christopher Dunn (ed.), *Provinces: Canadian Provincial Politics* (Peterborough: Broadview Press, 1996), 451.
6. Malcolm Taylor, *Health Insurance and Canadian Public Policy* (Montreal: McGill-Queen's University Press, 1985).
7. Johnson, "Biography of a Government," 559–61.

two propositions. The first was support for the "equalization principle" — that the fiscal capacity of the provinces should be raised to the level where all could deliver "equal and sufficient" social and health services. As Tommy Douglas stated at the Dominion-Provincial Conference of 1960:

> The main argument for equalization (in fiscal capacity) lies in the concept that every Canadian citizen has an inalienable right to certain minimum standards of health, education and welfare, irrespective of where he may live in this broad Dominion... no nation is truly great which has depressed areas whose citizens must content themselves with a standard of services far below the national average. Such a policy could only foment resentment and recriminations; such a policy would eventually destroy the fabric of national unity.

The second principle pushed by the Saskatchewan government could be termed the "national interest principle" — the proposition that it was entirely legitimate and proper for the federal government to condition shared-cost grants to ensure that social and health services be adequate across Canada. At the same time, however, the principle was not an absolute. While conditional grants might be an effective way of starting a social program, the conditions they imposed would eventually suppress provincial innovation. In Douglas's view, "the time inevitably comes when the rigidities which encumber these grants outweigh their initial benefits."[8] Nonetheless, Douglas and his successors put their respective concerns about the constraining influence of the spending power aside in order to support its use in launching new national social programs.

In 1964, the Lloyd administration was defeated by Ross Thatcher. Despite the change of government, the Saskatchewan tradition continued for two reasons. First, some of the Douglas-Lloyd bureaucrats — nicknamed the Saskatchewan Mafia — moved to Ottawa and were instrumental in pushing an activist social policy agenda in the Pearson and Trudeau Liberal administrations. These civil servants kept in close touch with those they had left behind in Saskatchewan. Second, although Ross Thatcher had previously decried the collectivist ideology of the CCF/NDP, he decided against dismantling welfare and medicare programs once in office. His government was active in the negotiations leading to the Canada Assistance Plan in 1966. Medicare had become so popular after its implementation that Thatcher reversed his stand on "socialized medicine," and his administration participated in the negotiations that led to the introduction of medicare on a national basis in 1968.[9]

In the 1970s and 1980s, the province was preoccupied with a largely economic, as opposed to a social policy, agenda during both NDP and Progressive Conservative administrations. The Blakeney government concentrated on using revenues derived from natural resources as well as the vehicle of public ownership to diversify the provincial economy. While two social policy initiatives were implemented — the children's dental plan and the prescription drug plan — they remained solely provincial initiatives.[10] Social policy was also largely absent from

8. Statement by Premier Douglas at Dominion-Provincial Conference of 1960, quoted in Johnson, "Biography of a Government," 573.

9. Dale Eisler, *Rumours of Glory: Saskatchewan and the Thatcher Years* (Edmonton: Hurtig, 1987).

10. Paul Barker, "Decision Making in the Blakeney Years," *Prairie Forum* 19, no. 1 (Spring 1994): 65–79. Also see Steve Wolfson, "Use of Paraprofessionals: The Saskatchewan Dental Plan" and John Bury, "Reducing Drug Prices: The Saskatchewan Prescription Drug Plan" in Eleonor D. Glor (ed.), *Policy Innovation in the Saskatchewan Public Sector, 1971–82* (Toronto: Captus Press, 1997): 126–39, and 204–28. It is interesting to note that comprehensive dental and drug plans were put forward as

the federal-provincial relations agenda in the last three years of the Blakeney administration as the country became increasingly embroiled in the constitutional drama that pitted the separatist Parti Québécois government in Quebec against the Trudeau government in Ottawa.[11]

Following the election of Grant Devine's Conservatives in 1982, the provincial government became focused on its domestic economic agenda, investing in various megaprojects as well as supporting farm income during a sustained period of low agricultural commodity prices.[12] By this time, it had also become evident that the postwar economic boom had fizzled out. This meant that all governments — provincial and federal — were experiencing a growing gap between revenues and expenditures. The problem was made much worse in Saskatchewan by unprecedented government spending during the 1980s, and by the time the Romanow government was elected in October 1991, the province's debt was rapidly climbing to 40 percent of provincial gross domestic product.

While forced to repair the fiscal health of the province, the new administration also concentrated on social policy. In 1992, the Romanow government began the long process of moving from an illness model of medicare with its emphasis on critical care, hospitals and top-down decision making, to a wellness model with a greater emphasis on preventative care, in-home services and more responsive local governance. The following year, the administration introduced the Action Plan for Children to tackle the problems of inner-city poverty and education. The so-called Children's Action Plan also called for major changes to the provincial social assistance system, with a proposed Saskatchewan Child Benefit becoming the platform for a support system that would discriminate less between welfare recipients and the working poor. By putting the child benefit on the national agenda and converting it into a shared-cost program through an aggressive intergovernmental agenda, the Romanow government was able to speed up implementation. This was the domestic push behind the social union negotiations. The outside push came from a budgetary decision taken by the federal government alone.

SASKATCHEWAN AND THE FIRST PHASE OF THE SOCIAL UNION NEGOTIATIONS, 1995–1997

For provinces like Saskatchewan, the February 1995 federal budget was a watershed. Suddenly, without provincial consultation, Ottawa removed $8 billion in cash transfers to the provinces for health care, social assistance and post-secondary education. In one stroke, the postwar federal-provincial entente on shared-cost financing was shattered. Though all the provinces protested vociferously against the cuts, they were unable to convince the Chrétien government to reverse its decision.[13]

---

extensions of a proposed national medicare scheme in the Hall Commission on Health Services in 1964, but both were opposed at the time by Ontario and Quebec as unwarranted intrusions into provincial jurisdiction.

11. Allan Blakeney and Sandford Borins, *Political Management in Canada* (Toronto: University of Toronto Press, 1998), 162–68; Howard Leeson, "The Intergovernmental Affairs Function in Saskatchewan, 1960–1983," *Canadian Public Administration* 30, no. 3 (Fall 1987): 399–420; Roy J. Romanow, John D. Whyte and Howard A. Leeson, *Canada ... Notwithstanding: The Making of the Constitution, 1976–1982* (Toronto: Carswell-Methuen, 1984).

12. James M. Pitsula and Ken Rasmussen, *Privatizing a Province: The New Right in Saskatchewan* (Vancouver: New Star Books, 1991).

13. Gregory P. Marchildon, "'Constructive Entanglement': Intergovernmental Collaboration in Canadian Social Policy" in Donald Lenihan (ed.), *Collaborating Government: Is There a Canadian Way?* (Toronto: IPAC, 2000), 75.

A new block transfer fund — the Canada Health and Social Transfer, or CHST — was established.[14] Though as concerned as the other premiers about the sudden and unilateral withdrawal of cash from health care, education and the social safety net, Romanow also worried about the consequences of the new block transfer to the future of the federation. Publicly referring to the federal action as "un-Canadian," the Saskatchewan premier mused openly about the impact the cut would have on Ottawa's ability to enforce national standards in federal-provincial social programming.

Newfoundland Premier Clyde Wells shared Romanow's concern. Occupying the Chair of the Annual Premier's Conference (APC), he wanted the Conference that coming August to deal with the federal cuts but in as constructive a way as possible. Romanow agreed, and work began on an agenda that would have the provinces play a leadership role in shoring up the social union.

The choice of forum was interesting. For decades, premiers had been meeting on an annual basis. The APC offered a rare chance for premiers to get to know each other a little better as well as the opportunity to review a mixed bag of issues in private as well as a photo opportunity in public. It was, however, rarely used to do sustained work on any major interprovincial policy issue. Both Romanow and Wells wanted the 1995 APC to be different. With a new government in office in Toronto, and a newly elected PQ government in Quebec City that was still debating whether to attend the APC, Newfoundland and Saskatchewan with the support of a couple of other provinces carried the day on the idea of a single-theme Conference. By May, an APC working group of officials was established, and Saskatchewan officials were sent to Newfoundland in order to help prepare a draft text for the August Conference.

While the text was being prepared, some provinces continued to push for other items to be added to the agenda. Resisting most of these efforts, Wells did agree to add "internal trade" to the agenda as Quebec's price for attending the Conference. At the same time, Premier Jacques Parizeau made it clear that he would refuse to participate in the major "social union" agenda item. When the Conference opened in late August, the media focused on Parizeau's tortuous efforts to use the internal trade item to support his separatist agenda, and his refusal to participate in the main portion of the agenda.[15]

This contrasted sharply with the media's muted coverage of the premiers' initiative on the social union. In the closed meeting, the premiers reviewed the background papers on the challenges, issues and concerns common to all the provinces, the most substantive work ever prepared by officials for an APC. They then moved on to the common principles and underlying values that should be the foundation of future social policy reform as well as the processes that should be adopted in furthering the reforms. Finally, they created a Ministerial Council on Social Policy Reform and Renewal so that the necessary political tradeoffs in provincial positions across social policy domains could be made.

After the Quebec referendum in late October, the Ministerial Council began its work in earnest. The hope was that the government of Quebec would join the social

14. On the introduction of the CHST, see Thomas J. Courchene, *Redistributing Money and Power: A Guide to the Canada Health and Social Transfer* (Toronto: C.D. Howe Institute, 1995).

15. Romanow did everything he could — inside the meeting and outside — to prevent Parizeau from using the APC as a political platform to argue the advantages of Quebec seceding from the federation.

union negotiations after its proposal to negotiate separation from the rest of Canada was turned down, but Parizeau refused. In the past, Quebec's non-participation would have stopped the provinces dead. The close call of the referendum, however, meant that Quebec would continue to be reluctant to enter into the social union negotiations, while spelling out the costs of the other provinces waiting indefinitely for a "willing Quebec" to join the negotiations.

By December, the Ministerial Council had completed its "Report to Premiers." While rejecting federal unilateralism, the report also eschewed extreme decentralism. In deciding which order of government should be responsible and accountable for any given social program, constitutional jurisdiction was only one of eight questions that needed to be answered. The remaining seven questions were more instrumentalist or pragmatic in nature: How much personal contact is required to effectively provide the service or benefit? Is there a need to ensure flexibility in service design to meet local circumstances? Is there a national concern or national interest that needs to be addressed? Does one order of government already have an efficient delivery system in place? Is one order of government already involved in delivering services to a client group? Are related programs required to effectively manage the service? Can delivery by one government produce more effective outcomes?[16]

This list of questions perfectly reflected Saskatchewan's long-standing pragmatic approach to the federal-provincial dimensions of the Canadian social union. In particular, the province had always been bullish on the question of the extent to which the national interest was implicated in social policy. In fact, as the report was handed in to Romanow, the province was in the midst of making a major domestic social policy decision that was predicated on the national interest being invoked. At the core of the province's welfare redesign was a proposed Saskatchewan Child Benefit that would provide income to poorer families even while removing some of the barriers to work that existed in the current system. Concluding that it was neither feasible nor desirable for the province to implement the child benefit in isolation, the province introduced the concept of a federal-provincial — or *National* — Children's Benefit. This concept of the National Child Benefit, in which the federal government would be the principal service deliverer, was floated publicly in January 1996.

The difficulty with the Saskatchewan position was the federal government's initial unwillingness to join with the provinces in the social policy reform and renewal exercise. The federal cabinet and bureaucracy was split as to the merits of engagement, one group wanting a return to what it perceived as past federal hegemony of national social policy through the unilateral use of the spending power. The other group, responsive to the provinces' demand for respectful collaboration and recognizing the extent to which the provinces were both responsible and accountable for the vast majority of social program delivery in the country, advocated negotiations with the provinces.

Prime Minister Jean Chrétien allowed the debate to rage within his own government. Finally, on February 22, 1996, the Speech from the Throne identified the sustainability of social programs along with unity and economic uncertainty as the three major issues of concern to Canadians and, by implication, the Chrétien government. The prime minister then called for a First Ministers' Meeting (FMM) to deal with the social safety net, renewing Canada and job creation. Chrétien had

16. Ministerial Council on Social Policy Reform and Renewal, "Report to Premiers," December 1995.

finally tipped his hand in favour of engaging the provinces in their social policy reform and renewal exercise.

By the spring of 1996, the media had finally become intrigued with the concept of the National Child Benefit — the one concrete program that was emerging out of the social union discussions. Then, less than two weeks before the FMM, Romanow presented the National Child Benefit in a major speech in Ottawa in order to put additional pressure on the federal government.[17] Finally, on June 21, 1996, the prime minister accepted the majority of the provinces' report on Social Policy Reform and Renewal as well as the National Child Benefit proposal at the FMM and appointed Pierre Pettigrew as the federal minister responsible for the ongoing negotiations.

THE ORIGINS OF THE SOCIAL UNION FRAMEWORK NEGOTIATIONS, 1996–1997

Between June 1996 and February 1997, the National Child Benefit (NCB) was negotiated and then rolled out as the first major national social program in three decades. While most of the detailed work was done by ministers of Social Services and their officials, their work was cleared through the new Federal-Provincial-Territorial Ministerial Council. Under significant pressure to deliver the NCB before the federal budget was completed, the provincial ministers strove to broker an acceptable program with the federal government, and Pierre Pettigrew, in return, worked hard to ensure that room could be made in the 1997–98 budget for the first installment of the NCB.

At the same time, the provincial consensus on the other elements of the social union was beginning to fray. A division opened up (at least temporarily) between the larger and richer provinces and the smaller and poorer provinces. Heading into the August 1996 APC in Jasper, Alberta, Premier Harris of Ontario released a commissioned paper written by well-known economist Thomas Courchene. In the full ACCESS (A Convention on the Canadian Economic and Social Systems) version of his model, Courchene proposed that the provinces could, without Ottawa's participation, manage the Canadian social union.[18] Supporting the notion, Premier Klein of Alberta also argued that the new social union would not require enforcement of national standards in areas such as health care. With the background support of the premiers of the other smaller provinces, premiers Romanow and Tobin led the fight against a radically decentralized position, and slowly steered the provinces back to a consensus position.

Both sides in the provincial debate, however, agreed that the time had come for a clarification of the rules of engagement between the provinces and the federal government. Although they differed in their respective motivations, all provinces wanted a coordination protocol with Ottawa for the negotiation and management of social programs into the future. The 1995 federal budget cuts combined with process shortcomings originally identified in the *Report to Premiers* later that year spurred the premiers on.

17. Premier Roy Romanow, "Renewing Federalism: Why Social Reform is Necessary," speech for the Canadian Council on Social Development, Ottawa, May 24, 1996.

18. Thomas J. Courchene, "ACCESS: A Convention on the Canadian Economic and Social Systems," working paper prepared for the Ontario Ministry of Intergovernmental Affairs, August 1996 — republished with analysis in *Assessing ACCESS: Towards a New Social Union* (Kingston: Institute of Intergovernmental Relations, 1997).

The roadblocks preventing the negotiation of such a protocol were also large and obvious. The federal government had little incentive or desire to negotiate constraints on the use of its spending power. Moreover, given the near defeat in the Quebec referendum, Ottawa was looking for ways to become more — rather than less — involved in the daily lives of Canadian citizens. In other words, the federal government was attempting to claw back some of the central influence and authority it felt it had given up to the provinces in the recent past.

On the other side, Ontario and Alberta were becoming more hard line on the issue of shrinking and constraining the federal spending power. From this perspective, they looked forward to a day they could be joined by Quebec which was, traditionally, the most aggressive province on curtailing the spending power. From a very different perspective, Romanow was concerned about the very hard-line positions on the spending power. True to its history, Saskatchewan had a different view of the federal spending power. While wanting a protocol requiring a more collaborative use of the spending power, the province did not want to see the spending power so emasculated as to eliminate the potential for future federal-provincial funded social programming. As a consequence, Romanow supported the movement to get Ottawa to negotiate a coordination protocol with the provinces, but was prepared to fight hard for a spending power that would make possible "national" social programs with "national" standards.

At the Annual Premiers Conference in August 1997 in New Brunswick, two issues were paramount. The first was how to launch the negotiations for a coordination protocol or "framework agreement" on the social union. The second was how to provide some national leadership in light of the country's near defeat in the 1995 referendum. Both were to become linked in the Calgary Declaration the following month.

After agreeing that the time had come to negotiate a "broad framework agreement on the social union" to address the federal spending power and new processes to settle federal-provincial disputes as well as other issues, all premiers (except Lucien Bouchard, who had succeeded Parizeau as premier of Quebec) agreed to meet in Calgary the following month. The purpose of this further meeting was to work out a consensus position that would give federalist Quebecers some hope that the constitution might eventually be changed and brought in closer accordance with their view of Quebec's unique position within the federation, and included a commitment to pursue administrative changes with Ottawa that would improve the working of the federation for all Canadians.[19]

Although most premiers did not want to initiate another round of constitutional talks, they did want to send a message to Quebec that the potentially fundamental administrative reforms that they were initiating through the social union framework negotiations could eventually be followed by some constitutional change at an unspecified future date. This was the so-called "80/20" formulation used by Romanow to convince his colleagues and the general public: that 80 per cent of the change needed in Canada could be accomplished through administrative changes (such as were being proposed in the social union negotiations) but the final 20 percent of changes still needed to keep Quebec in the federation would have to be constitutional in nature.

---

19. 1997 Annual Premiers' Conference communiqué.

Romanow was strongly supported by Premier Frank McKenna at a Calgary meeting based upon the "80/20" formulation. However, a few of the other premiers felt that it was really up to Ottawa to deal with Quebec-specific changes. They were prepared to support the Calgary meeting only if they received some consideration in return from the federal government. In particular, they wanted a commitment in advance from the prime minister to hold an FMM and commit to negotiating a social union framework. Wanting to see the provinces make a positive statement concerning the future of Quebec in the federation, Chrétien agreed to hold an FMM before the end of the year. The Calgary meeting went ahead with the final communiqué recognizing the "uniqueness" of Quebec while calling for a coordination protocol on the management of social policy in the federation.

In October 1997, just days after the Calgary meeting, Frank McKenna announced his resignation as premier of New Brunswick. He called upon his closest provincial colleague, Roy Romanow, to take over his position as chair of the premiers and lead the preparation for the FMM.[20] He had not only agreed with Romanow's views concerning a positive "Plan A" agenda of inclusion for Quebec but he also promoted a similar agenda of inclusion for Ottawa as a partner in the social union, contrary to the more decentralist agendas of the larger provinces. McKenna also concluded that Romanow was in the best position to bridge the decentralist demands of provinces such as Ontario and Alberta on the one extreme, with the centralist elements within the federal government. There were more conciliatory voices in the provinces and in Ottawa but these would have to be forged into a meaningful consensus offering a compelling alternative to both decentralist and Ottawa-centred visions of the country's future.[21]

Initially, Romanow's main challenge lay in Ottawa. The federal government was worried about the short-term political — as well as long-term policy — consequences of negotiating a comprehensive agreement on managing Canada's social union without the participation of Quebec. Moreover, many in the federal cabinet felt that the provinces were far too radical in terms of constraining the central government's role in social policy. The concern was no doubt heightened by a document prepared by provincial officials on a proposed social union framework and then shared with federal officials that fall. In preparing for the FMM, federal officials tried to narrow the scope of the negotiations and lower expectations, preparing for a negotiation in which Ottawa would compromise as little as possible.

With insufficient time to narrow the gap between the premiers and the prime minister, however, Romanow found himself about to enter the FMM without agreement on basic content and objectives. Indeed, he was so concerned about the prime minister's commitment to the social union negotiations, that he felt obliged to write Chrétien that the chief outcome of the meeting "must be a commitment to negotiate a framework for the social union, including some agreement on scope, process and time frame."[22] At the actual FMM, which began on the evening of December 11 and continued through most of the next day, Romanow, on behalf of all the

20. The chairing of the premiers is a year-long interprovincial and federal-provincial coordinating role, rotating among the provinces, with transitions occuring just weeks before the APC generally held in August. Romanow would end up serving as chair of the premiers through the balance of Premier McKenna's term (1997–98) as well as his own term (1998–99).

21. These competing visions are set out in Marchildon, "Constructive Entanglement," 72–73.

22. Letter, Premier Roy Romanow to Prime Minister Jean Chrétien, November 26, 1997.

provinces, presented four priority subject areas for negotiation: a pan-Canadian mobility principle; rules surrounding the use of the federal spending power; mechanisms for federal-provincial dispute resolution; and roles and responsibilities in terms of intergovernmental collaboration on monitoring social policy outcomes and setting principles and standards.

Although Bouchard said Quebec was not prepared to participate in negotiations with the federal government on a social union framework, the prime minister had committed the federal government to negotiating with the remaining provinces and territories by the end of the FMM. Despite much argument over the wording of the final communiqué, the initial work plan presented by Romanow with only a few minor changes became the mandate for the framework negotiations.[23] All agreed to set a deadline on the negotiations of July 1998.

NEGOTIATING THE SOCIAL UNION FRAMEWORK AGREEMENT, 1998–1999

Intending to use the existing Ministerial Council on Social Policy Renewal as the vehicle for the federal-provincial negotiations, the provinces were keen to start. Ottawa was, however, not as prepared for the talks and consequently delayed the first meeting until the prime minister had carefully assigned both a minister and a team of negotiators. Instead of allowing Pierre Pettigrew to continue in his role as lead federal minister on the social union, Chrétien chose Anne McLellan, the minister of Justice, as Ottawa's ministerial lead. There was speculation that Pettigrew had developed a too collaborative relationship with the provinces, and that it would be unseemly for a federal minister from Quebec to lead negotiations in which the province of Quebec was not a participant. At the officials level, the federal task force on the social union was headed up by Alex Himelfarb, then an associate deputy minister in the Treasury Board Secretariat. For the purpose of these negotiations, federal provincial ministers recast themselves as the Ministers Responsible for the Social Union Framework Negotiations, with Saskatchewan (Bernhard Wiens) and Ottawa (McLellan) co-chairing. Quebec, an observer at the Ministerial Council on Social Policy Renewal, continued in its non-participatory role at the social union framework negotiations.

The delay involved in setting up the federal team allowed Ottawa to develop its own objectives. They involved three large themes that would be consistent throughout the negotiations: minimizing constraints on the federal spending power[24]; establishing meaningful provisions which would enhance the mobility of Canadian citizens across all provinces and territories; and maximizing accountability, government-to-government and government-to-citizen.[25]

23. The December 12, 1997, First Ministers' Meeting communiqué listed the objectives for negotiation as follows: "a set of principles for social policy, such as mobility and monitoring social policy outcomes; collaborative approaches to the use of the federal spending power; appropriate dispute settlement mechanisms between governments; clarifying ground rules for intergovernmental collaboration; and identifying processes for clarifying roles and responsibilities within various social policy sectors."

24. For a discussion of the federal spending power in Canada and other federations, see Ronald L. Watts, *The Spending Power in Federal Systems: A Comparative Study* (Kingston: Institute of Intergovernmental Relations, 1999).

25. For a commentary on the federal position, see Steven A. Kennett, "Securing the Social Union: A Commentary on the Decentralized Approach," Institute of Intergovernmental Relations, Queen's University research paper no. 34.

The federal spending power was not only the most contentious of the differences between both orders of government, it was also a flash point among the provinces.[26] Saskatchewan's challenge as chair of the provinces was to try and achieve (and keep) a provincial consensus even while pursuing its own position on such issues. Despite the province's best efforts, however, in the spring of 1998 the provinces insisted on preparing and releasing a common position paper with a tough position on the spending power as well as a strict discipline on provincial and federal "roles and responsibilities." Although uncomfortable with the position, Saskatchewan as chair was required to support the consensus. Ottawa rejected the provincial position outright. After deliberating for many weeks, McLellan presented an equally hard negotiating position at the Framework Ministers' meeting in late July 1998. Instead of an agreement by the FMM deadline, negotiators had reached an impasse.

Little progress had been made by the time the premiers met in Saskatoon for their annual meeting on August 10–11, 1998. With Romanow in the chair, the premiers bemoaned the apparent deadlock in the negotiations, but argued the necessity for a new, year-end deadline. But the surprise of the APC occurred when Lucien Bouchard announced that he was prepared to join his colleagues in the framework negotiations. While Quebec, he explained, had not previously agreed to join the negotiations in order not to acknowledge the legitimacy of the federal spending power in areas of exclusive provincial jurisdiction, it was now prepared to do so because of the provincial negotiating position on the spending power. This position, Bouchard concluded, was tantamount to a provincial veto of federal spending in areas of exclusive provincial jurisdiction. While the premier of Quebec went on to describe the spending power/opting-out provisions of the provincial position paper as essential, it was actually described as the "provincial consensus negotiating position" in the final conference communiqué.[27]

With the entry of Quebec into the negotiations, the provincial negotiating position became more rigid. Ottawa also became more wary, refusing to call a meeting of Framework Ministers (despite repeated calls from the provinces) throughout the fall of 1998. By early December, Ottawa complicated the framework negotiations by proposing a "Health Accord" that would establish federal-provincial ground rules specifically for the funding and delivery of public health care. This was to be, in Ottawa's eyes, a federal-provincial coordination protocol negotiated by the Health ministers, and might be a pre-condition to Ottawa signing any social union framework agreement.

Both sides seemed to be very far from any possible agreement when the second deadline of December 31, 1998, passed. Although the Framework Ministers had agreed to meet in Halifax on January 11–12, few expected any progress to be made. However, the unexpected intervened. Anne McLellan verbally set out a new federal position on the federal spending power that contemplated more constraints than previously put forward. As well, Ottawa's position on other aspects of the negotiations — mobility and dispute resolution in particular — were nudged closer to the provincial position. McLellan promised a written version of the federal position and ministers agreed to meet in Victoria at the end of the month to continue negotiations.

26. Gregory Marchildon, "A Step in the Right Direction," *Inroads* 9 (2000): 124–33.
27. Annual Premiers' Conference communiqué, August 11, 1998.

When the written version of the federal position was finally sent out, it was greeted with disappointment by the provinces. It did not, in their view, match the verbal commitments made by McLellan in Halifax. The meeting in Victoria was headed for confrontation. As a consequence, Saskatchewan officials held their own bilateral meetings with Ottawa's senior negotiators in an effort to bridge the growing gap. To this time, the provincial negotiating position had remained largely intact.[28] But Saskatchewan was losing patience with both the inflexibility and the hardness of the provincial position and signaled to the other provinces that it would consider tabling its own position if no movement was shown. When ministers arrived in Victoria, however, Saskatchewan found itself largely alone. The other provinces, led by Quebec, refused to modify the provincial position and, as a consequence, little progress was made with Ottawa during the meeting. With the most contentious issues remaining unresolved, the meeting adjourned without a firm commitment to a follow-up meeting. Everyone understood that the negotiations might soon end.

FIRST MINISTERS' NEGOTIATIONS AND THE SIGNING OF THE SOCIAL UNION FRAMEWORK AGREEMENT, 1999

In the meantime, premiers had been consulting one another on other issues. In particular, they were concerned about the upcoming federal budget and whether it would respond to their need for increases in block transfer spending for health care, given escalating costs and Ottawa's lack of effort in redressing the 1995 transfer cuts. At the same time, they were also adamantly opposed to signing any sort of "health accord" as a *quid pro quo* for more funding. On behalf of the premiers, Romanow discussed these matters with the prime minister and a compromise was reached. If the premiers made a written commitment to use any incremental funding through the block transfer for health care as well as "making information about the health system available to Canadians," the Prime Minister would agree to making health funding a priority in the next budget.[29] With the letter sent on January 22, the prime minister was able to say that the document amounted to a "Health Accord" and he was prepared to call an FMM to see if agreement on a social union framework could be achieved among First Ministers on February 4.

Chrétien was taking a calculated risk in calling the FMM given the distance between McLellan and her provincial Framework Ministers. He was well aware, however, of the deep divisions among the provinces, and the immediate desire of all premiers to get additional health funding (but through the CHST) in order to deal with the immediate problems they faced in their respective health sectors. Health care had by this time become the most important issue in the country. The Martin budget cuts of 1995 combined with provincial health care reforms had produced turmoil everywhere. The general public as well as health care practitioners and administrators were beginning to feel that the foundation of medicare itself might be shaky. In a way which the Framework Ministers and their officials had not fully digested, premiers were preoccupied with the funding and content of one social program — health care — rather than the federal-provincial management of social

28. By this point, provinces and territories had added a "dispute resolution" section to their paper. It contemplated a broad scope of issues that would be subject to dispute resolution and would make extensive use of third parties in the resolution of disputes.

29. Letter, Premiers and Territorial Leaders to Prime Minister Chrétien, January 22, 1999.

policy. Most notable was Premier Harris of Ontario, who wanted an immediate injection of new cash for health care plus a quick end to the social union negotiations in order to pave the way to an imminent provincial election.

On the day before the meeting, Chrétien forwarded to the premiers a proposed text for a social union framework agreement that was to form the basis of discussion at the FMM. Throughout the evening of February 3, Romanow held a series of meetings with the premiers to assess their willingness to support what was now becoming a package deal: 1) the Social Union Framework Agreement (SUFA) itself; 2) a substantial injection of new federal funding through the CHST for health care; and 3) the premiers' letter of January 22 substituting for a full-blown Health Accord. With the exception of Bouchard, all the premiers agreed to the deal, some suggesting minor revisions to the text language of the SUFA.

In addition to his other meetings on February 3, Romanow met with Bouchard privately for 90 minutes in a last-ditch effort to see if Quebec could sign an appropriately modified agreement. Nothing would convince the Quebec premier, however, and Romanow was left with a short list of changes to the SUFA sought by premiers from the rest of the country.

The meeting the next day was held privately at the prime minister's residence. The first two hours of discussion were devoted to health care changes and the inadequacy of funding. After the prime minister agreed to the first major investment in transfer funding since the Martin budget cuts of 1995, the discussion turned to the social union framework. Chrétien agreed to three changes to the text, including: a preamble to the Agreement, added at the request of the premiers; modest changes to the language referring to the relationship between the SUFA and Aboriginal people; and shortening, from four years to three years, the time within which the Agreement would be reviewed.

The final version of the agreement was signed early by all first ministers, with the exception of Bouchard, early in the afternoon. It was an exhausting — almost anticlimatic — end to years of negotiating a basic revision in the federal-provincial relationship in social policy.

CONCLUSION

It can fairly be said that Saskatchewan has significantly influenced Canada's social union, both in terms of the nature of our social programs and in terms of the model of federal-provincial engagement under which these programs have been created and managed. The quality of this fabric of social programs, from medicare to social safety nets to the more recent National Child Benefit are becoming recognized as part of Canada's identity. All of these programs have been developed within Saskatchewan's general philosophy of forging a better, more equal society for Canadians, and in many cases Saskatchewan led the way in the creation of the programs themselves.

More recently, tensions in the federal-provincial relationship — caused by Ottawa's unilateral reduction of its financial contributions to Canada's social programs — have emerged. To address these tensions, the provinces, led by Saskatchewan to an important extent, proposed new approaches to federal-provincial relations.

The SUFA is the most recent outcome of these efforts. It is the first of what is hoped to be an evolving commitment on the part of both orders of government in Canada to find healthier forms of intergovernmental engagement to ensure that the social needs of Canadians are met. The SUFA contains within it many of the values which have formed Saskatchewan's understanding of our federation. First, that Canadians want governments to design and deliver the best possible set of social programs. Second, that both orders of government have a legitimate role to play in the exercise of their various powers to achieve this goal. Third, that all Canadians should benefit from comparable levels of service in these programs and that Ottawa has an intermediating role to ensure that Canada's social programs are truly Canadian in scope. Fourth, that within a more general national framework, provinces are best placed to design and deliver programs suited to specific needs of their citizens. Fifth, that the work of governments must be collaborative rather than confrontational in the development and maintenance of national social programs. Sixth, that Canadians are entitled to know how well these programs are doing, and are entitled to contribute to their development. Finally, that these achievements will build and strengthen our country.

Whether recent developments, and the SUFA in particular, fulfill this vision is for others to determine. But that it reflects Saskatchewan's longstanding vision of what Canada should become cannot be questioned.

POLITICS AND THE MEDIA IN SASKATCHEWAN

Gerald B. Sperling and Kevin Wishlow

This is big time — three quarters of a billion dollars. It's not tiddly winks. We're dealing with marketing the message in the media and you know how important the media is.

Premier Grant Devine, November 5, 1990

The American Judge Murray Gurfein stated in his decision rejecting U.S. government efforts to ban the publication of the Pentagon Papers that a free society has a "cantankerous press, an obstinate press, an ubiquitous press..." and that such a press "must be suffered by those in authority in order to preserve the even greater values of freedom of expression and the right of the people to know."[1] In Saskatchewan, during the Devine years (1982–1991) and the Romanow years 1991–2001, the Saskatchewan media has been, in general, placid, supine and more invisible than "ubiquitous."

Every day we are inundated with what sometimes seems an infinite barrage of information — much of it packaged and filtered for our "easy" consumption. Yet this information, however palpable, is vital to the formulation of ideas we will use as citizens of a democratic society. The media, after all, is the primary means by which politicians and other interests in our society get their message to the public. Conversely, the media altruistically has the potential to convey public sentiments to our political leadership. It thus should come as no surprise that the increasing concentration of media ownership in Saskatchewan has been as contentious an issue here as it has been in other parts of the country and the world.

While this study attempts to use objective instruments to evaluate media coverage of politics in recent years, it is worth noting that practitioners in the media, both print and electronic, have considered themselves to be fair and unbiased in their reporting. During the Devine years, when a crusading media could have had a field day in its coverage of the shenanigans of the governing party, several of whose members ultimately were charged and convicted of a variety of criminal offenses, the Saskatchewan media had a rather calm and detached view of its work. For example, Frank Flegel, for many years news director of CKCK-TV, commented in 1991 that, over all, news coverage in the Devine years was fair. He said,

> In the last couple of years ... it would seem to me that the government would probably feel that the coverage has been more negative than positive and I think that if they have that perception, it is probably because

1. As quoted in Noam Chomsky, *Necessary Illusions: Thought Control in Democratic Societies* (Montreal: CBC Enterprises, 1989), 2.

> there have been more negative things happening insofar as the government has been concerned than there have been positive… . I think that after the '86 election when they changed the drug plan and the children's dental plans they took a lot of serious shots. I'm not sure that the government responded to those criticisms as effectively as they might have and I think that in those instances the coverage was probably more negative. But I don't think that you blame the messenger for that.
>
> I don't think that anything is objective. I have never believed that news is objective. News is subjective. It's a very subjective decision … what you cover and how you cover it. It's made by specific individuals with specific mindsets. But if you're going to run a good operation, then you have to make sure that the coverage is fair. And overall … I think the coverage was very fair.[2]

During the 1980s and 1990s, an important columnist in Saskatchewan was Armadale's Dale Eisler, whose columns appeared in the Regina *Leader-Post*, the Saskatoon *Star Phoenix*, and a raft of weeklies throughout the province. Asked at the end of the Devine era what he thought of media coverage in that period, Eisler commented:

> I think that on balance that media coverage has been pretty fair, evenly balanced … at the end of the day, the Government has been called to the account by the media as much as it should have been.[3]

Has coverage indeed been "fair and balanced," and if so, what does that mean?

This study will address three areas of the inquiry. First, it will ask whether news coverage in print and television in Saskatchewan supported the dominant ideological system. In other words, does news coverage in Saskatchewan favour the way things are, economically, politically, and socially? Second, the study will provide the results of a systematic analysis of the media's coverage of the 1999 Saskatchewan general election. A class analysis approach will provide the theoretical framework for the authors' interpretation of the results. Finally, using the results of a content analysis, the study will determine whether there is a correlation between the content of print and electronic media.

IPSCO, AND THE *LEADER-POST* – A CASE STUDY

This study rejects the notion that the media is a passive conduit through which the ideas of political leaders and other public interests objectively flow. Rather, the process of mediation — the selection of facts from the empirical world — cannot be distinguished from the subjective view of the author. Some studies, such as one prepared by the University of Calgary political science professor and right-wing columnist for the Hollinger chain, Barry Cooper, have readily noted a "discrepancy between the media world and world where we ordinarily live."[4] For Cooper, the media — in his case study, the CBC — constructed a "left-wing reality," which viewed the former USSR "as a regime more or less akin to Western liberal democracies."[5] Other writers, including Edward S. Herman and Noam Chomsky, have

2. Student interview with Frank Flegel, November 1990.
3. Interview with Dale Eisler, November 1990. Eisler now is a senior official with the federal government in the Department of Finance.
4. Barry Cooper, *Sins of Omission: Shaping the News at CBC TV News* (Toronto: University of Toronto Press, 1994), 225.
5. Ibid., 219.

come to quite the opposite conclusion. They argue that "the media serve the ends of a dominant elite."[6]

The two conclusions are seemingly contradictory, but the normative value that sustains them is the same: the idea that the news media must operate as a watchdog of the state, serving the interests of the greater public good. It is thus the role of the news media to ensure the government remains the servant of the people. In the words of the Supreme Court of Canada:

> Freedom of discussion is essential to enlighten public opinion in a democratic state. It cannot be curtailed without affecting the right of the people to be informed through sources independent of the government concerning matters of public interest. *There must be untrammeled publication of the news... . Democracy cannot be maintained without its foundation.*[7]

Integral to this understanding of the media is the belief that there must also be competition among those sources of information "independent of government" — no one source can hold a monopoly. Only through competition in the "marketplace of ideas," as John Stuart Mill perceived it, will the "truth" emerge.

Exactly what "truth" emerges is of course a matter of hot debate. Cooper's interpretation of the "truth" as delivered by the CBC assumes a journalistic culture set apart from the influences of a capitalist society — if anything, hostile to those influences. It is difficult to explain why journalists, most of whom were born and socialized in a society immersed in the tenets of Western liberalism, would with consistency construct views hostile to the culture in which they live. Cooper's argument starts to unravel with an examination of his methodological approach, which leans heavily on qualitative data compiled from the study of nearly 250 broadcasts, aired over the CBC during 1987 and 1988. Cooper was primarily concerned about how meaning was conveyed both orally and visually in CBC news and public affairs programs. His study used examples, such as the coverage of the opening of the fast-food chain McDonald's, to prove the CBC's pro-Soviet bent. What Cooper found problematic was the lack of criticism in the coverage of the company's partnership with the Soviet government.[8] At the heart of the issue was Cooper's abhorrence of stories that portrayed the Soviet Union in the midst of *glasnost* as a "progressive kind of place."[9]

The "truth," as Cooper saw it, challenged fundamental Western liberal precepts. But one can easily come to quite the opposite conclusion. Stories such as the opening of McDonald's in Moscow were conveyed uncritically by the CBC and other Western media precisely because they symbolized the decline of the Soviet Empire and the fall of communism itself. CBC journalists portrayed Soviet citizens "as being very much like us"[10] because they wanted them to be just "like us." As the Iron Curtain rusted out in the dying days of the Soviet Empire, Western elites relished the prospect of the triumph of capitalism in Eastern Europe. Large multinational corporations, including McDonald's, could now make money in what was once the bastion of communism.

---

6. Edward S. Herman and Noam Chomsky, *Manufacturing Consent: The Political Economy of the Mass Media* (New York: Pantheon Books, 1988), 1.
7. Cited in Robert Martin and Stuart Adam (eds.), *A Sourcebook of Canadian Law* (Ottawa: Carleton University Press, 1991), 26 (emphasis added).
8. Cooper, *Sins of Omission*, 53.
9. Ibid., 33.
10. Ibid.

Even though Cooper rejects the "mirror effect," he ultimately subscribes to the pluralist paradigm. In the context of such an approach the content of the stories journalists produce remains autonomous from the interests that employ them. Cooper's argument ignores the possibility that the state, which owns the CBC, and the advertisers that in part pay for news programming, would have any influence on news content. There are ample studies that suggest quite the opposite. One of the most famous is Edward Herman and Noam Chomsky's propaganda model. That model postulates the function of the media in a free and democratic society as primarily an agent of socialization, ensuring the public's acceptance of the dominant ideological system. Dominant interests of wealth and power determine what "real world" facts are newsworthy and how those facts are presented.

Herman and Chomsky identify five "filters": 1) concentrated ownership of mass-media firms and the ability of larger, more prestigious firms, to set the agenda for smaller news operations; 2) advertising revenue as necessary for the operation of media firms; 3) reliance on "official sources" such as state institutions for information; 4) pressure tactics such as advertising boycotts or public relations campaigns as a means of dealing with "undesirable" media content; and 5) the creation of an ideology that views communism as the primary threat against Western liberal democracies.[11] In the post-Soviet era the fifth filter might be interpreted to apply to any ideology that can be perceived as a threat to liberal democratic principles and ideals.

Variations of the "filters" approach have been employed in other studies. In a study of media ownership in Canada, James Winter, an associate professor of communication studies at the University of Windsor, applied his own version, the "trickle down theory." Winter contended that in "the news industry as in other industries, decisions are made by owners, either directly or indirectly."[12] Using a pragmatic approach, Winter reasoned that owners exercise influence by hiring "publishers who reflect their views, and who in turn hire and promote managers, who then hire and promote editors and journalists."[13] Journalists are not innately deviant individuals. Rather, they implicitly know what they can and cannot report if they are to either keep their jobs or get ahead.

Thus, news is essentially a management product shaped in the interests of the dominant groups that control its manufacture. Both Chomsky and Winter subscribe to a class analysis approach in their explanation of media content. Such a critique views the media, like the state itself, as an instrument of the capitalist class. The Western media championed the opening of a McDonald's in Soviet Moscow because it was in the interest of capitalists to do so.

The media, it can safely be predicted, behaves no differently in Saskatchewan. While this study is primarily concerned with an content analysis of the media in Saskatchewan as reflected in its treatment of the 1999 provincial election, it is salutary to examine the recent past, where the ideological tendencies of both the private press and the publicly owned media appear to have supported establishment views.

The Regina *Leader-Post* is now part of the Can-West Global media empire. In

11. Herman and Chomsky, *Manufacturing Consent,* 1–35.

12. James Winter, *Democracy's Oxygen: How Corporations Control the News* (Montreal: Black Rose Books, 1997), 86.

13. Ibid.

1990, it was still owned by the Siftons, the family that had dominated the print media in Saskatchewan for decades. In spite of the relatively small reach of the Sifton family outside of Saskatchewan, there are numerous examples of the *Leader-Post* in the 1990s treating businessmen with the kind of awe and respect that one would normally give to prophets and potentates. A dramatic example was the manner in which the paper dealt with IPSCO, Saskatchewan's only steel producing company.

The company's president, Roger Phillips, has been one of Saskatchewan's most outspoken opponents of government enterprise. He was a founding member of the Institute of Saskatchewan Enterprise, an ideological group advocating privatization in the province.

Phillips seems to be able to get prominent play in the *Leader-Post* paper whenever he wants it. On April 17, 1990, he appeared on the front page with information that turned out to be wrong. The way the *Leader-Post* handled this instance, and more importantly the way it responded to criticism of its handling of the issue, is revealing.[14]

The headline on page 1 of the paper on April 17, 1990 was: "IPSCO threatened by scrap import law." The story, by Gordon Brock, included a large colour photo of IPSCO scrap and an inset photo of Phillips himself. The essence of the story was that proposed regulations of the federal Department of the Environment would effectively destroy IPSCO because the company would have to take out $2.5 billion worth of bonds to protect itself against the possibility that the scrap metal that it imported contained hazardous waste. This amount was "just not available to a company whose net worth is less than $300 million," said Phillips. Furthermore, in the light of these regulations, Phillips said, "IPSCO would soon have to decide whether to shift all steel production in Regina to the United States." Interestingly, Phillips was the only source for this story. Nobody from Environment Canada, nor any other expert, was cited.

The next day, again on the front page, another story by Brock appeared: "IPSCO fears unfounded, Ottawa insists."[15] In this story a federal environment official was quoted as trying "to quell" IPSCO fears. Pointing out that the bond involved was only $5 million and not $2.5 billion, the official said, "importers who are confident that they are not bringing hazardous materials across the border can go about their business as usual." Nevertheless, Brock repeated all of Phillips' charges of the previous day, adding another one to the effect that the federal government was wrong in stating that the draft regulations in question were not part of the International Convention signed in Basel in 1989 in order to prevent the export of hazardous materials, a claim that was patently untrue.

Nevertheless, in the same issue of the *Leader-Post* on April 18, 1990 there was an editorial completely supporting Phillips' claims and suggesting that the new regulations may force the "abandonment of every manufacturing and resource industry."[16] Furthermore, also in this issue of the paper, there was yet another story reporting — without question — a provincial cabinet minister "blasting" the federal government

14. We wish to thank the late Dr. Ray Sentes of the University of Regina's political science department for providing us with his files on this matter, especially his correspondence with John Swan, editor of the *Leader-Post*. Among other things, Ray Sentes was a relentless critic of the "kept" press.
15. Gordon Brock, "Ipsco fears unfounded, Ottawa insists," *Leader-Post*, April 18, 1990.
16. "Environmental zeal needs practical side," *Leader-Post*, April 18, 1990.

for a "misguided attack on western Canadian steel producers."[17] Again, Phillips' charges were repeated.

On the following day, April 19, there was yet another story, "More recyclers oppose posting a bond," this time quoting opponents of the draft regulations as authoritative sources. Again there was a slighting reference to the federal official who "played down concerns that the new law would force IPSCO to cut steel production in Regina by half, or completely."[18]

Two days later, Bruce Johnstone, the *Leader-Post*'s financial editor, began a column on the issue as follows: "Earth Day Eve might not be the best time to throw darts at the zealots who make and enforce the laws to protect our environment."[19] He went on once again uncritically to repeat and support Phillips' version of events.

On April 24, the *Leader-Post* published a story citing union concerns about Phillips' threat to shut down the plant. Once again, his charges were repeated uncritically.[20]

Finally, on April 27, 1990, Bruce Johnstone wrote a story, "Phillips says it's unlikely government trying to close IPSCO," in which Phillips was quoted as saying that Environment Canada "appears to be backing away from the rigid position it took," and IPSCO will be keeping the maximum level of operations in Regina.[21] The article then went on to discuss IPSCO's "real problems" — high interest rates, declining sales, a high Canadian dollar, and so on.

On May 3, the late Ray Sentes, a professor of political science at the University of Regina, wrote a letter to the editor of the *Leader-Post*, John Swan, in which Sentes outlined his concerns about how the paper had handled the story. He asked that his communication be published in the paper either as a letter to the editor or as a reader's commentary, that is, an "op-ed" piece. He began his letter as follows: "From April 17 to April 27, 1990 Saskatchewan citizens were subject to one of the worst disinformation campaigns they had experienced in quite some time."[22] After surveying the *Leader-Post* articles in question, Sentes summarized his concerns:

> One, Phillips' claim, accepted by the *Leader-Post*, that the proposed regulations are unrelated to the Basel Convention is simply wrong. On the first page of the proposed regulation it states "Convention means the Basel Convention on the Control of Transboundary Movements of Hazardous wastes and their Disposal signed on 22 March 1989.
>
> Two, according to Environment Canada, IPSCO does not have to purchase a new bond unless it *knowingly* chooses to import scrap metals containing CFC's, or similar toxic substances. PCB's are already banned from Canada so unless IPSCO wants to deliberately import hazardous substances it has nothing to fear from the regulations.
>
> Three, according to Environment Canada if for whatever reason IPSCO chooses to purchase a bond as an extra precaution, a single bond for $5 million worth of coverage is required *not* the $2.5 billion worth alleged by Phillips and accepted by Brock and the *Leader-Post*.

---

17. Mark Wyatt, "New environmental law blasted," *Leader-Post*, April 18, 1990.
18. Gordon Brock, "More recyclers oppose posting a bond," *Leader-Post*, April 19, 1990.
19. Bruce Johnstone, "Some environmental laws counter-productive," *Leader-Post*, April 21, 1990.
20. Ann Kyle, "Ipsco union wants reassurances," *Leader-Post*, April 24, 1990.
21. Bruce Johnstone, "Phillips says it's unlikely government trying to close Ipsco," *Leader-Post*, April 27, 1990.
22. Ray Sentes, letter to John Swan, May 3, 1990.

> Since the above facts are accessible to anyone willing to look for them one is puzzled why IPSCO launched such a vitriolic campaign at this time.

Sentes speculated that perhaps IPSCO, having recently expanded operations in the United States, was planning to shift there anyway and was using alleged "oppressive" environmental regulations as an excuse. In his final paragraph, Sentes called upon IPSCO to come clean and he also demanded an explanation from the *Leader-Post*.

One would have thought that there would be no difficulty publishing the Sentes letter. There might have been a problem with length, but as for content, Sentes seemed to have made a point. Furthermore, Michael Sifton, the owner of the *Leader-Post* at the time, had been quite outspoken on his commitment to freedom of the press: "As my father taught me early in my newspaper career, we have a democracy because we had a free press. We don't have a free press because we have a democracy."[23]

On May 11, John Swan wrote back to Professor Sentes. His first substantive comment was, "This paper has certainly not engaged in a disinformation campaign, and, as editor, I frankly find that an odious accusation."[24] This response is curious since Sentes did not state that the *Leader-Post* had created this campaign. Indeed, Sentes had specifically wondered "why IPSCO had launched this vitriolic campaign at this time."

Swan went on to respond to Sentes' concern. He explained the fact that there was no reference to Environment Canada officials in the first front-page story by noting that the

> story arose out of a news conference held by IPSCO the previous day, Monday April 16. This happened to follow the Easter weekend and was on a day when most government offices, including those of Environment Canada, were closed.

The reporter, according to Swan, was thus unable to reach the appropriate official until April 17.

Brock makes no mention in his story that Environment Canada officials were not available. Did it occur to him or anyone at the *Leader-Post* that the timing of the news conference might not have been an accident? Furthermore, perhaps if Regina were not a one-newspaper town the reporter and his editor might have been moved to try and find anyone, including the minister of the Environment, at home — even on Easter Monday!

Swan then went on to admit that Phillips and the paper were wrong about the Basel Convention. More specifically he says, "In hindsight, it would appear there was a misunderstanding in interpreting dates... . There is no real excuse for that mistake or misinterpretation," which he admitted not only affected the news stories but also the editorial.

Swan concluded his letter as follows:

> I feel that many of the charges you make are unwarranted. In fact, as regards the IPSCO matter, I would suggest that it was a result of the follow-up by the *Leader-Post* (to the best of my knowledge, other news outlets did little similar follow-up) that a reasonably balanced picture emerged. If anything, these follow-up stories pointed to an initial overreaction by

23. *Royal Commission on Newspapers* (Hull, PQ: Ministry of Supply and Services, 1981), 28.
24. Swan-Sentes letter, May 11, 1990.

> IPSCO. I find it difficult to see how you can believe that the *Leader-Post* would have anything to gain from engaging in a "disinformation" campaign with IPSCO.
>
> Given the reasons outlined, we must decline publication of your letter, in its present form.

Swan's response raises several questions. For one thing, if an editorial was written on the basis of a mistake, why not write another one based on accurate facts? Furthermore, the words "overreaction by IPSCO" never appeared in the paper. Perhaps it would be better to ask what the paper would lose by treating the IPSCO story with the skepticism it deserved. What would it have lost by writing a strongly worded editorial attacking IPSCO's overreaction, if that were what it was?

The *Leader-Post*'s coverage of the IPSCO story in 1990 may not have been part of a conscious disinformation campaign, but the effect was the same as if it had been: Phillips "got in there first with the most," and the editorial writers and reporters followed with the same mistakes, creating credibility for what can only be called disinformation about Canada's environmental laws and regulations as they apply to IPSCO.

There are other examples that could be cited. The point, however, is that concentration of the media in private hands would appear to lead to critical acceptance of "news" generated by the business elite, a practice that supports the ideological status quo. Given this, the following hypothesis could be advanced: News coverage provided by Saskatchewan's major news operations supports the status quo in terms of the dominant ideological system. Given the print media's size, prestige, and resources relative to the television media, and mindful of Herman and Chomsky's five filters, a secondary hypothesis can also be advanced: there will be a direct correlation between newspaper content and that of television news.

To test these hypotheses we decided to use the 1999 Saskatchewan general election as a case study. We used thematic content analysis as a tool for examining coverage of the campaign. Six themes were identified that supported the dominant ideology or status quo, while six themes were identified as being associated with the counter-ideological position, challenging the status quo. Five additional categories were created representing themes in which there was either no context provided or an overtly ideological issue expressed. Table 1 outlines the themes used in the study and their codes. For each unit of analysis reviewed in the sample period, themes were systematically identified and noted, providing quantitative data on which to draw conclusions. The size of sample and quantity of data varied between newspaper and television coverage. For the *Leader-Post* and the *Star Phoenix*, the sample period spanned the first two weeks of the election campaign, August 20 to September 3, 1999. The sample period for television news coverage was shorter, concentrating on the 6:00 p.m. newscasts of the Regina operations of CBC, CTV, and Global for the three days of August 25–27. After encountering difficulties in obtaining detailed data for a longer period, we decided the sample was sufficiently large to determine a pattern.

For the purposes of the study, neo-liberalism is the dominant ideology or status quo. Neo-liberalism is defined as an economic, social, and political system that revives classic liberal notions demanding a diminished role of the state in society and the deregulation of the marketplace. (Paradoxically, neo-liberalism depends on the intervention of the state to subsidize the costs of production, including the education, training and reproduction of the labour force.) Relationships between

Table 1

CATEGORY	CODE	DESCRIPTION
Dominant Ideology 1	D1	Tax cuts, austerity budgeting, "trickle down" economics
Dominant Ideology 2	D2	Crime/public safety — emphasis on taking coercive measures to combat crime
Dominant Ideology 3	D3	Education — emphasis on skills and technical training
Dominant Ideology 4	D4	Health and social programs — emphasis on improving service by creating more efficient system
Dominant Ideology 5	D5	Pro-business platform — emphasis on providing economic incentives to capital interests to facilitate economic development. This includes subsidies and incentives to agricultural producers.
Dominant Ideology 6	D6	Opposition to state supported programs that infringe on civil liberties
Counter-ideology 1	C1	Progressive taxation policies — concept of requiring wealthier interests in society to pay a larger proportion of tax burden
Counter-ideology 2	C2	Poverty, rather than crime, viewed a major social problem
Counter-ideology 3	C3	Education — view education as more than skills training, but as something that builds a better society
Counter-ideology 4	C4	Health and social programs — recognition that current levels of funding are inadequate
Counter-ideology 5	C5	Labour issues — unemployment, low wages, pay equity, women's and minority group interests, workplace health and safety
Counter-ideology 6	C6	Recognition that even if state programs infringe on civil liberties, they can be reformed rather than "scrapped" or that such programs can be justified as essential to the greater public good
Analysis	A	General discussion of issues or issues that outwardly do not demonstrate significant ideological bent
Education-no context	E	Education discussed without context
Health-no context	H	Health discussed without context
Integrity	I	Integrity, honesty, corruption
Religion	R	Overt religious theme, such as school prayer, religious rights, and moral codes based on religious standards

individuals are presumed to be no more than contractual exchanges, transforming the notion of citizenship to that of consumer. With the reduced ability of the state to redistribute wealth, coercion becomes more acceptable as a method of social control.[25]

A counter-ideological position places a higher degree of emphasis on state intervention in society as a means of redistributing wealth. Such a position proposes that traditional or classical liberal rights guaranteeing individual equality are meaningless if there are not structural adjustments to the economy and society as a whole. The health and social welfare systems are inadequate not simply because they are "poorly run," but because they are underfunded. Thus inequities of wealth and power in society, not lax methods of social control, are the causes of social discord. In this approach, state-supported programs, including education and health, are primarily concerned with contributing to the greater public good, rather than catering solely to the interests of capital.[26]

To ensure consistency in the discussion of results, units of analysis for both newspaper and television coverage are referred to as news "stories." News "stories" are defined as self-contained descriptions of "real world" facts. The various formats utilized in television production were also noted. Table 2 provides a clarification of these differences.

25. See Gary Teeple, *Globalization and the Decline of Social Reform* (Toronto: Garamond Press, 1995),75–127; John Shields and B. Mitchell Evans, *Shrinking the State: Globalization and Public Administration "Reform"* (Halifax: Fernwood Publishing, 1998), 36–87, 116–24; Richard Shillington, "Tax System and Social Policy Reform" in Jane Pulkingham and Gordon Ternowetsky (eds.), *Remaking Canadian Social Policy: Social Security in the Late 1990s* (Halifax: Fernwood Publishing, 1996), 100–11.
26. Ibid.

Table 2

Term	Definition
Packaged report	Self-contained news story provided by reporter from location other than studio
Anchor read	Anchor reads news story "on camera" with no covering visuals
Voice-over	Anchor reads news story accompanied with visuals
Clip	A self-contained sound bite of a subject of news story accompanied with an anchor read or voice over
Studio interview	Anchor interviews subject or subjects of news story in studio

A thematic content analysis was chosen for a number of reasons. Such an analysis avoids some of the problems encountered when employing a simple "word count" approach. For example, counting the number of times "tax cut" appears in a particular sample could potentially distort the outcome. There might be a tendency to interpret the results out of context. A multitude of meanings can be applied to a specific word or phrase. As Kris Kripendorf writes, "breaking a highly organized message into separate sampling units invariably distorts the information contained in the resulting data."[27]

A thematic content analysis, however, is still potentially subject to the biases of the author. Still, an argument can be advanced that there is more likely to be a consensus regarding general themes. Such an analysis places a greater emphasis on how such concepts as "tax reduction," for example, are presented in the context of the story in which it appears. Observers, regardless of their ideological biases, are likely to agree on the general message being conveyed. The primary data collection does not concern itself with ideological issues, only with whether a particular theme emerges. If the theme, however, appears with a greater frequency than those themes associated with a counter-ideological position, a pattern then begins to emerge.

The greatest potential for subjective error in the study is in the determination of the dominant and counter-ideological positions and in the categorization of the respective themes. The results, however, should remain consistent with the definitions. Some themes were more difficult to identify than others. In stories that discussed "no-fault" insurance, we had to pay particular attention to the context provided in the story. If some "voices" in the ensuing discourse demanded that the program be "fixed" not "scrapped," then the theme was relegated to a counter-ideological category. Just because someone voiced displeasure with a particular program did not necessarily mean they were against it. In other instances, however, in which no context was provided, "no-fault" as an issue was placed in the dominant-ideological category, since the meaning conveyed to the observer was that "no-fault" as a government program was fundamentally bad. Other themes such as "tax cuts" were more easily identified. It was apparent from much of the discourse that all major political party leaders favored tax reductions. The only difference lay in their plan for implementing them.

NEWSPAPER ANALYSIS

The results obtained in the analysis overwhelmingly support the initial hypothesis. Both the content surveyed in the Regina *Leader-Post* and the Saskatoon *Star Phoenix* demonstrated a significant preference for dominant ideological themes over counter-ideological themes. In the *Leader-Post* 95.8 percent of all stories surveyed

27. Klaus Krippendorff, *Content Analysis: An Introduction to Its Methodology* (London: Sage Publications, 1980), 58.

Table 3

Table 3.1: Frequency of dominant-ideological themes

Media	D1		D2		D3		D4		D5		D6		Total		Total Stories in Sample
	#	%	#	%	#	%	#	%	#	%	#	%	#	%	
Leader-Post	30	41.7	5	6.9	2	2.8	6	8.3	25	34.7	1	1.4	69	95.8	72
Star Phoenix	28	34.2	6	7.3	3	3.7	7	8.5	28	34.2	1	1.2	73	89.0	82

Table 3.2: Frequency of counter-ideological themes

Media	C1		C2		C3		C4		C5		C6		Total		Total Stories in Sample
	#	%	#	%	#	%	#	%	#	%	#	%	#	%	
Leader-Post	0	0	2	2.8	2	2.8	9	12.5	8	11.1	1	1.39	22	30.6	72
Star Phoenix	0	0	2	2.4	2	2.44	11	13.4	10	12.2	1	1.2	26	31.7	82

Table 3.3: Frequency of other themes

Media	A		E		H		I		R		Total		Total Stories in Sample
	#	%	#	%	#	%	#	%	#	%	#	%	
Leader-Post	13	18.1	14	19.4	3	4.17	9	12.5	1	1.4	40	55.6	72
Star Phoenix	17	20.7	13	15.9	5	6.1	15	16.3	1	1.22	51	62.2	82

Table 3.4: Frequency with which dominant and counter-ideological themes appear in the same article

Media	Number of Articles	Total Number of Stories Sampled	Percentage
Leader-Post	10	72	13.9
Star Phoenix	9	82	11.0

Table 3.5: Frequency with which dominant-ideological themes appear on first page

Media	D1		D2		D3		D4		D5		D6		Total		Total Stories in Sample
	#	%	#	%	#	%	#	%	#	%	#	%	#	%	
Leader-Post	10	52.6	3	15.8	0	0	1	5.3	5	26.3	0	0	19	100	19
Star Phoenix	7	35.0	4	20	1	5	1	5	9	45.0	1	5.0	23	115	20

Table 3.6: Frequency of counter-ideological themes appearing on first page

Media	C1		C2		C3		C4		C5		C6		Total		Total Stories in Sample
	#	%	#	%	#	%	#	%	#	%	#	%	#	%	
Leader-Post	0	0	0	0	1	5.3	2	10.5	1	5.26	0	0	4	44.4	19
Star Phoenix	0	0	0	0	1	5.0	2	10.0	2	10.0	1	5.0	6	30.0	20

Table 3.7: Frequency with which other themes appear on first page

Media	A		E		H		I		R		Total		Total Stories in Sample
	#	%	#	%	#	%	#	%	#	%	#	%	
Leader-Post	5	26.3	5	26.3	3	15.8	6	31.6	19	100	19	100	19
Star Phoenix	4	20.0	4	20.0	2	10.0	6	30.0	0	0	16	80	20

contained dominant ideological themes, compared to 30.6 percent with counter-ideological themes. The results were relatively consistent with those of the *Star Phoenix*: 89 percent to 31.7 percent — a ratio of approximately 3 to 1. As Table 3.3 shows, other themes, those which were advanced either without context or had no overt ideological bent appeared in more than half of all stories, outweighing counter-ideological themes — but at a significantly lower margin than dominant themes. The frequency with which dominant and counter-ideological themes appeared in the same story was less than 14 percent in both the *Star Phoenix* and the *Leader-Post*. This means dominant ideological positions, such as austerity budgeting and tax cuts, were seldom questioned or scrutinized in the stories in which they appeared.

A smaller sample was taken that limited the analysis to front-page stories only. Tables 3.5 and 3.6 show an even higher frequency of dominant themes in both newspapers. By contrast, the frequency of counter-ideological themes remained relatively unchanged in the *Star Phoenix*. This was not the case in Regina's newspaper. The front-page sample saw counter-ideological themes jump close to 15 percent. Of greater significance was the increase in "other" themes. If Tables 3.3 and 3.7 are compared, "other" themes rose roughly 45 percent in the *Leader-Post* and close to 20 percent in the *Star Phoenix*.

The general statistical patterns revealed in the study, while valid, need to be put into context. To begin with, the high frequency of dominant ideological themes in the sample reflects, in part, the emphasis that "tax cuts" and the "farm crisis" received in the election campaign. Those two themes consistently were designated into categories D1 ("tax cuts") and D5 ("pro-business" incentives). The "farm crisis," for example, normally was linked to demands for government aid. In reality, such a demand constituted a plea for an economic incentive or subsidy to a business — a subsidy to capital. Calls for "tax cuts" were sometimes associated with demands for "farm aid." In an August 26 story of the *Leader-Post*, for example, reporter Bonnie Braden links the two themes: "so the Saskatchewan Party will help farmers by lowering the PST so agricultural inputs don't cost so much."[28] The major thrust of the story, however, included demands for a direct "payment" from the government, both provincial and federal, to farmers. As Braden notes in the opening paragraph, "It's now clear farmers won't be getting a wad of new cash from any of the three political parties immediately after the election."[29] The reporter then proceeded to elaborate on the agriculture platforms, clarifying the various leaders' calls for a federal aid package. In the case of this story, two themes were identified: "tax cuts" (D1) and "pro-business" incentives (D5).

The language of "tax cuts" is worthy of further discussion. Stories that contained demands for tax reduction consistently contained references to "job growth." The two concepts, in the logic of "trickle down" economics, were tied to the notion that only if business, and even consumers, were relieved of the shackles of taxation would liberated capital be readily poured into new investment that would create new jobs. *Star Phoenix* reporter Brigette Jobin's summation of Saskatchewan Party Leader Elwin Hermanson's position on taxation is a good example:

> If taxes aren't lowered, Hermanson says the province will continue to see poor job creation numbers, which will see people moving to neighboring

28. Bonny Braden, "Sask. Party offers to go to Ottawa," *Leader-Post*, August 26, 1999, p. A4.
29. Ibid.

> provinces. The fewer people Saskatchewan has, the smaller the tax base, which Hermanson said will hinder a government's ability to provide adequate services such as health care, infrastructure and education.[30]

Job creation or job growth in this context takes on a whole different meaning. Nowhere in the text is the concept of unemployment mentioned — the possibility that some Saskatchewan residents might have no job at all. The reader is left with the impression that "tax cuts" won't translate into spin-off employment for people who are without jobs. Rather, the message conveyed is quite the opposite: such cuts will keep in the province employed people who are being driven away because of high taxation.

In fact, in the entire sample there is not one person interviewed who had left the province for reasons of unemployment. A follow-up story on August 24 in the *Star Phoenix* chronicles the experience of Saskatchewan expatriate Colin May:

> Election promises of tax cuts don't mean much to Saskatchewan businessperson Colin May because he's already moved his family to the Alberta side of Lloydminster. May, who packed up his family and moved four years ago, said he has saved between $1,000 to $5,000 in taxes each year depending on the profits generated by his moving theatres located on both sides of the border.[31]

The story of Colin May hardly seems one of hopelessness or destitution. The authors note that May's brother, a partner in the family business, still lives in Saskatchewan. May left Saskatchewan not to secure a job, but to maximize his income. In both the former and latter *Star Phoenix* stories, no counter-ideological position was expressed. There was no qualification of the types of jobs or the expected rate of pay any new employment would generate in light of the proposed tax reductions. Did Saskatchewan's party leaders foresee more high-paying full-time positions, or simply more casual minimum wage jobs? In one story, appearing in both the *Star Phoenix* and the *Leader-Post*, some clarification is provided. The owner of a trailer and flatbed manufacturing plant complains high personal income taxes in Saskatchewan make it difficult to recruit highly skilled workers.[32] For the most part, however, the question was largely left unanswered within the context of stories in which the theme of "tax cuts" was present. What is more, as the statistics verify, there were relatively few dissenting voices.

Those dissenting voices that did appear were largely relegated to the inside pages. Two stories that appeared on page A6 of the *Star Phoenix* on August 31 are something of anomaly in this study in terms of their emphasis on counter-ideological themes and the headlines that drew the observer's eye to them: "Sask. Party has hidden agenda: critics"; "Parties alienating the poor, groups say." The first story opens with a summary of the Saskatchewan Party's platform, promising "more jobs, lower taxes, and safer streets." The summary is countered by an outline of the concerns of critics who fear a "hidden agenda" by the party:

> There's no mention, opponents point out, of programs for the poor and there's only a fleeting, threatening reference to labour. That has some

30. Brigette Jobin, "Hermanson touts tax relief message," *Star Phoenix*, August 23, 1999, p. A3.
31. Bonny Braden and Mark Wyatt, "Taxes driving Sask. Residents westward," *Star Phoenix*, August 24, 1999, p. A3.
32. Bonny Braden, "Sask Party courts rural businesses," *Star Phoenix*, August 28, 1999, p. A12; Bonny Braden, "Businessman keeps mind open," *Leader-Post*, August 28, 1999, p. A6.

> suggesting the party ... may have a hidden agenda to beat up on the poor and batter unions. Peter Gilmer of the Regina Anti-poverty Ministry said the party is already sending a frightening signal by promising to make most welfare recipients work for their cheques ... "by giving this huge tax break ... we're concerned that it will be on the backs of the poor."[33]

While the story goes to some length to elaborate on the concerns of Saskatchewan Party critics, it calls upon a "professional" expert to put their fears in perspective. David Smith, a professor of political science at the University of Saskatchewan, is quoted as saying there is no evidence that the Saskatchewan Party has a "hidden agenda ... to gut (social) spending."[34] Smith's presence in the story has the effect of discrediting — or at least neutralizing — the critics. By contrast, when Saskatchewan expatriate and businessperson Colin May lamented Saskatchewan's high tax burden, no professional expert was introduced in the same text as a counterbalance.

The second story on the same page of the *Star Phoenix* presents the counter-ideological position without a dissenting view. The story explains that social justice groups had written a letter to Saskatchewan's political parties demanding their response to the issue of poverty. Tony Haynes, social justice co-coordinator for the Catholic Diocese of Saskatoon, is attributed as commenting that the "election candidates are concentrating too much on tax reduction and not enough on social policy."[35] Both the counter-ideological themes of poverty (C2) and labour (C5) were identified in the story. Crime is not viewed in the story as a cause of social disharmony, but a product of the existing economic system:

> Haynes ... says many people are being alienated by faults in the economic system ... this group includes welfare recipients, the aged who see themselves as defenseless and a burden to society, youth who seem to be out of control, children living in poverty, the unemployed and underemployed, whose alternatives are food banks and petty crimes.[36]

The story also appeared in the *Leader-Post*, but on page A7 instead of page A6. Such cases certainly challenge the overall hypothesis of this study, but they must be kept in perspective given the small number of counter-ideological themes occurring in the sample. And as the study indicates, counter-ideological themes seldom appeared in stories without a counter-balancing dominant ideological theme.

In the latter two cases the voices of dissent came from specific interest groups. The one political party whose platform was characterized by counter-ideological positions, the New Green Alliance, was virtually absent from the coverage of both the *Leader-Post* and the *Star Phoenix*. On September 2, two weeks into the campaign, a story appearing on page A8 of the *Leader-Post* and page A6 of the *Star Phoenix* outlined the party's platform, emphasizing poverty, labour, and environmental issues. Granted, the New Green Alliance did not offer a full slate of candidates for election. Still, the fact remains: the issues advanced by either the New Green Alliance or other interests advancing counter-ideological positions did not receive front-page priority.

33. Martin O'Hanlon, "Sask Party has hidden agenda: critics," *Star Phoenix*, August 31, 1999, p. A6.

34. Ibid.

35. Brigette Jobin, "Parties alienating the poor, groups say," *Star Phoenix*, August 31, 1999, p. A6; Brigette Jobin, "Social issues not addressed," *Leader-Post*, August 31, 1999, p. A7.

36. Ibid.

37. Jason Warick,"Party announces platform," *Leader-Post*, September 2, 1999, p. A8; Jason Warick, "Green Alliance claims left-wing monopoly," *Star Phoenix*, September 2, 1999, p. A6.

These findings provide evidence that the newspaper media not only "mirrored" the agenda established by the party leaders, but framed the agenda as well. Poverty, or labour issues for that matter, never emerged to become an issue for the media in the election campaign. This does not mean dissenting voices were completely absent; it does mean they were given less emphasis, and relegated to the inside pages of both major dailies.

"Tax cuts," by contrast, repeatedly received front-page attention. This did not simply amount to journalists passively recording the content of the speeches of any one of the political leaders. Rather, the newspaper media played an active role in advancing issues. The lead story on the front page of the September 3 *Leader-Post* called upon "all three party leaders to guarantee to cut taxes as promised during the election campaign, or resign."[38] The demand, of course, did not come from the *Leader-Post* itself, but was attributed to Richard Truscott of the Canadian Taxpayers Federation. The story went so far as to quote Truscott as wondering about the sincerity of the party leaders promising to cut taxes if they did not sign the pledge with his organization: "We can infer that their commitment to tax relief, once the campaign is over, is softer than their colleagues."[39] All party leaders, with the exception of the New Democratic Party's Roy Romanow, were quoted as being willing to sign the pledge.

Truscott's comments were regularly recorded in both newspapers. But nowhere was there an explanation of what the Canadian Taxpayers Federation is, whom it represents, and of greater significance, to whom the organization is accountable. There seemed to be an assumption that the Canadian Taxpayers Federation is a watchdog agency committed to the interests of all taxpayers. But we are left only to speculate. Why, for example, did not the Regina Anti-Poverty Ministry receive the same priority in treatment? Are the impoverished not also taxpayers? Certainly they are. A simple calculation tells us that those individuals with lower incomes pay a higher proportion of their income on PST and GST than wealthier Canadians do.

There were other instances in which the newspapers framed the agenda of the election campaign. The results of a public opinion poll, sponsored in part by the *Leader-Post* and the *Star Phoenix* and published in both newspapers, warrant a more detailed examination. The breakdown of the results that appeared in the September 1 editions of both newspapers headlined voter confidence in the NDP to cut taxes: "On taxes, voters favour NDP"; "NDP favoured to cut taxes." The poll results identified tax relief as the most important issue among the electorate, and the NDP as the party believed to have the greatest credibility among voters in that regard. Respondents were polled on a variety of selected issues in addition to tax reduction: debt reduction, health care, education, agriculture, job creation, honesty/integrity, managing Crowns, crime/justice, and overall performance. Completely absent from the list of issues were those with counter-ideological themes, such as poverty or labour. Other issues such as health and education were offered without context.[40] Respondents could have easily said yes to health care as an issue of importance, believing that it meant more public funding should be devoted to the system when there is a possibility the designers of the survey intended something quite different.

38. Bruce Johnstone, "Two leaders OK tax pledge," *Leader-Post*, September 3, 1999, p. A1.

39. Ibid., quotation from Richard Truscott.

40. Randy Burton, "NDP favoured to cut taxes," *Star Phoenix*, September 1, 1999, pp. A1–A2; Randy Burton, "On taxes, voters favour NDP," *Leader-Post*, September 1, 1999, pp. A1–A2.

An issue that is advanced without context can be used to conceal an ideologically contentious policy or program.

This is precisely why the relatively high percentage in the sample of "other" themes — those in which no context was provided or an overt ideological bent existed — is significant. As indicated earlier in the discussion, the frequency of "other" themes was particularly more prevalent on the front pages of both newspapers. The *Leader-Post*'s and the *Star Phoenix*'s own opinion polls had revealed health care as the most important issue in the election campaign.[41] Yet, in 15.8 percent of all stories sampled on the front page of the *Leader-Post* and 10 percent of all stories sampled on the front page of the *Star Phoenix*, the health-care issue was mentioned without context.

One example is a story by Mark Wyatt, which appeared in both newspapers at the start of the campaign. He described the opposition parties as being concerned about "sub-standard health care."[42] Nowhere in the story is there an explanation of the type of health care system the opposition parties envisioned. Only in subsequent editions of both newspapers were both Liberal Party leader Melenchuk's and Saskatchewan Party Hermanson's positions on health care clarified.

Seven days later, in a third-page story in the *Star Phoenix*, Hermanson's position was put into context. The Saskatchewan Party leader believed more money could be found for health care by cutting back on administration.[43] No comparable story appeared that day in the *Leader-Post*. Liberal leader Jim Melenchuk's position on health care became clearer on September 2 — nearly two weeks after the beginning of the election campaign. In two stories, appearing on page A8 of the *Star Phoenix* and on page A5 of the *Leader-Post*, Melenchuk was said to favour eliminating health districts and cutting administrative staff in order to put more funding into health care.[44] When their positions were clarified, the opposition parties were considered in this study to express a dominant ideological theme: the idea that it was not under-funding that was causing service problems in health care, rather it was an inefficient bureaucracy. As has been the experience of other provinces, including Alberta, the concentration on efficiencies has sometimes translated into demands for the privatization of health-care delivery services.

Education was another election issue that was often discussed without context. As Table 3.3 shows, in over 19 percent of all stories in the *Leader-Post* and nearly 16 percent in of all stories in the *Star Phoenix*, education was mentioned without reference to a specific ideological approach. There was no analysis of whether education was primarily viewed as skills and technical training or whether education should have a broader purpose in society. Significant attention was paid in the newspaper coverage to the NDP's promise of one year of free tuition for first-year, post-secondary education. The discussion, however, seldom moved beyond the headline issue. Lacking was an analysis of the type of education system the party wanted to develop or the future of the system into which new students would be gaining free entrance. Instead, discussion frequently shifted to whether providing first-year students with a free education was indeed fair. One story that appeared in

41. Ibid.

42. Mark Wyatt, "The Battle Begins," *Leader-Post*, August 20, 1999, p. A1; Mark Wyatt, "Election September 16," *Star Phoenix*, August 20, 1999, p. A1.

43. Bonny Braden, "'Retro-Roy's' eight year's of failure," *Star Phoenix*, August 27, 1999, p. A3.

44. Mark Wyatt, "Health districts on Melenchuk's chopping block," *Star Phoenix*, September 2 , 1999, p. A8; Mark Wyatt, "Melenchuk promises health care purge," *Leader-Post*, September 2, 1999, p. A5.

both the *Leader-Post* and the *Star Phoenix* on September 3 had NDP Leader Roy Romanow defending the free-tuition promise amid angry complaints from high school students that any assistance for students should be based on merit alone. There was no further examination of education as an issue in the story, either in terms of the NDP or the platforms of the other parties.[45]

There were instances, however, when education was placed in context. Some clarification of the NDP's overall strategy for education was contained in an August 21 story of the *Star Phoenix*. Grade twelve students were characterized as applauding the program. The story provided some indication of why they should be positive about the program:

> Economic and Co-operative Development minister Janice MacKinnon said more education will be required in the "new economy." The credit will help students, but also create a more educated workforce.[46]

While MacKinnon's explanation of the NDP government's education strategy was still somewhat vague, the language she used was significant. The "new economy" is a popular "buzz word" associated with both "globalization" and neo-liberal regimes. Neo-liberals view education primarily as a method of skills and technical training to ensure business interests remain "competitive" in the global economy. Again, as with the treatment of health issues, the lack of context in the discussion of education can mask a particular ideological agenda. Issues are included uncritically by a media that seems to arbitrarily decide when and when not to place the rhetoric of politicians and other special interests under the microscope.

In other instances there was a tendency in the newspaper coverage to deflect the readers' attention away from ideologically charged issues entirely — framing issues in terms of integrity and honesty. Granted, voters in a democratic state have a right to demand that elected officials remain accountable to public interests. However, the preoccupation with themes of integrity and honesty seemed disproportionate, particularly when compared to non-contextual themes such as health and education or counter-ideological themes. In the first-page sample, stories with integrity as a theme accounted for 31.6 percent and 30 percent of all stories surveyed in the *Leader-Post* and the *Star Phoenix* respectively.[47] A recurring issue that in part contributed to the result was the allegation that the NDP had conducted illegal bingos in the 1980s for fundraising purposes. The allegations eventually went nowhere, because subsequent stories in both newspapers verified that it was indeed legal for political parties to reap the benefits of bingos during the period in question. While counter-ideological themes such as poverty and labour issues remained both infrequent and relegated to the inside pages, the alleged bingo scandal remained in the forefront.[48] Whether contrived or coincidental, the issue of integrity functions to divert the reader's attention away from more ideologically divisive issues. Integrity and honesty begin to dominate the election campaign, rather than pressing social issues.

45. Bonny Braden, "Students slam free tuition," *Star Phoenix*, September 3, 1999, pp. A1, A2; Bonny Braden, "Romanow faces the heat in Weyburn," *Leader-Post*, September 3, 1999, p. A7.

46. Jason Warick, "High school students cheer NDP tuition promise," *Star Phoenix*, August 21, 1999, p. A10.

47. See Tables 3.6 and 3.7 for a comparison to other themes.

48. Mark Wyatt, "NDP subject of police probe," *Star Phoenix*, August 26, 1999, p. A1; Mark Wyatt, "Premier questions timing of bingo complaint," *Star Phoenix*, August 26, 1999, p. A4; Mark Wyatt, "Disgruntled unionist behind bingo leaks," *Star Phoenix*, August 27, 1999, pp. A1–A2; Mark Wyatt, "RCMP eye NDP bingo complaint," *Leader-Post*, August 26, 1999, p. A1; Mark Wyatt. "Gunoff behind bingo allegations," *Leader-Post*, August 27, 1999, pp. A1–A2.

Integrity as a theme also functions to legitimize the media, in this case the newspaper media, as an objective mediator of "raw" information. The press is characterized as scrutinizing the "behaviour" of political officials in the public interest. One such example was reporter Mark Wyatt's treatment of NDP Premier Roy Romanow's tour of agricultural chemical producer AgrEvo's Saskatoon laboratories. Romanow's visit to the lab was preceded by an announcement that the chemical maker would receive a $450,000 grant from the Saskatchewan government to develop new wheat varieties.

Wyatt pointed out the seemingly contradictory position the NDP government took in giving AgrEvo the grant in light of earlier comments made by Romanow. At the national premiers' conference Romanow had called for a Federal Competition Bureau investigation into rising agriculture input costs. The irony, as Wyatt pointed out, was that Romanow's own government had now given money to a large corporation that manufactured agricultural chemicals. In the story, the premier defended the research grant, saying it would "create the right business climate" to facilitate economic growth.[49] Wyatt did raise the issue of whether the provincial government should be providing funding to large corporations allegedly contributing to the high cost of farm inputs. Still, the reporter's emphasis appeared to zero in on the integrity of Romanow's position. No real alternatives were examined. A question was never directly framed in the text of the story as to why the province did not provide funding to researchers employed by the University of Saskatchewan.

What becomes clear from the examination of the results of the study is that a concerted critical evaluation of the status quo was lacking in both the *Leader-Post* and the *Star Phoenix*. Dominant ideological themes were advanced, for the most part unchallenged. Yet the print media's seeming preoccupation with issues of integrity served to uphold the myth of objectivity. A broad assessment of the results demonstrated no overt partisan biases. The NDP's Roy Romanow was just as likely to advance a dominant ideological theme as the Saskatchewan Party's Elwin Hermanson or the Liberals' Jim Melenchuk. The print media characterized the leaders not by their commitment to tackle poverty, but by their commitment to reduce taxes.

TELEVISION ANALYSIS

Television news coverage, like that in the newspapers, did not present a critical view of the status quo. While there was some variance in the results among the three news operations — CBC, CTV, and Global — dominant ideological themes were consistently favoured over counter-ideological themes. As Table 4.1 indicates, Global had the greatest frequency of dominant themes with 90 percent, followed by the CBC with 80 percent, and CTV with 66.7 percent. CTV, as indicated in Table 4.2, had the lowest rate of counter-ideological themes, which were present in only 8.3 percent of stories sampled. This compares to the CBC in which counter-ideological themes were present in 46.7 percent of all stories and Global with 20 percent. By contrast, as can be seen in Table 4.3, nearly 60 percent of all stories reviewed on CTV contained "other" themes — those themes in which no context was provided or no overtly ideological position was taken. The result is roughly double those recorded by CBC and Global. Rarely did dominant and counter-

49. Mark Wyatt, "Premier tours AgrEvo headquarters," *Leader-Post*, August 24, 1999, p. A8.

Table 4

Table 4.1: Frequency of dominant-ideological themes (television news)

Media	D1		D2		D3		D4		D5		D6		TOTAL		Total Stories in Sample
	#	%	#	%	#	%	#	%	#	%	#	%	#	%	
CBC	5	33.3	3	20.0	0	0	1	6.7	2	13.3	1	6.7	12	80.0	15
CTV	2	16.7	1	8.3	0	0	0	0	3	25.0	2	16.7	8	66.7	12
Global	3	30.0	1	10.0	0	0	1	10.0	3	30.0	1	10.0	9	90.0	10

Table 4.2: Frequency of counter-ideological themes (television news)

Media	C1		C2		C3		C4		C5		C6		TOTAL		Total Stories in Sample
	#	%	#	%	#	%	#	%	#	%	#	%	#	%	
CBC	0	0	1	6.7	0	0	3	20.0	1	6.7	2	13.3	7	46.7	15
CTV	0	0	0	0	0	0	0	0	0	0	1	8.3	1	8.3	12
Global	0	0	0	0	0	0	1	10.0	0	0	1	10.0	2	20.0	10

Table 4.3: Frequency of other themes (television news)

Media	A		E		H		I		R		TOTAL		Total Stories in Sample
	#	%	#	%	#	%	#	%	#	%	#	%	
CBC	1	6.7	2	13.3	0	0	1	6.7	0	0	4	26.7	15
CTV	4	33.3	2	16.7	1	8.3	0	0	0	0	7	58.3	12
Global	0	0	1	10.0	1	10.0	1	10.0	0	0	3	30.0	10

Table 4. 4: Frequency with which dominant and counter -ideological themes appear in the same story (television news)

Media	Number of Stories	Total Number of Stories	Percentage
CBC	2	15	13.3
CTV	1	12	8.3
Global	1	10	10.0

ideological themes exist in the same story. As Table 4.4 shows, the frequency with which this occurred did not surpass 14 percent for any of the news operations in the sample.

A simple statistical breakdown does not completely convey the nature of the message that was delivered on television. The combination of audio and visual components and a somewhat less comprehensive analysis of "real" world facts, in contrast to the print medium, manufactured a message that was both focused and unmistakable. Both dominant and counter-ideological themes were delivered clearly and concisely. A good example was CTV's story that detailed NDP Premier Roy Romanow's campaign promise to hire more police officers in the province. The language used by the anchor to introduce the story was laden with both violent metaphors and trite expressions, leaving no mistake in the viewer's mind that the premier intended to use coercive tactics to deal with crime:

> The provincial election campaign has swept into Southern Saskatchewan... Premier Roy Romanow took on crime in a speech to a national gathering of police officers in Regina. As Manfred Joenck reports in tonight's "top story," Romanow has promised to give police officers the ammunition they need to make our cities safer.[50]

Reporter Manfred Joenck's packaged story continued in the same style:

50. CTV News, Regina, August 25, 1999, 6:00 p.m.

> Premier Romanow provided his view of crime and punishment at the Canadian Police Association convention being held in Regina ... [he] promised to double the money to fight gangs and also promised to get tough on young criminals that repeatedly break the law ... [he also promised to] put more police on the streets of Saskatchewan.[51]

Joenck's lead went directly into a clip from Romanow: "[the] simple fact of the matter is; the officer on the beat is the most effective way to fight crime and make our communities safer."[52] Romanow's message remained unchallenged for the remainder of the story — no counter-ideological position was expressed. Nor was there a follow-up story in the newscast that examined an alternative solution to crime.[53] The message was unmistakably clear: coercion is the most effective method of social control.

Global's coverage employed a similar style of presentation in the mediation of "real world" events. The news operation's treatment of a rally organized to protest the province's no-fault accident insurance program is one example. Reporter Tim Philisak's opening lines constructed a scenario that a gross injustice had taken place with the implementation of the no-fault program:

> They limped, hovelled, and wheeled their way into Victoria Park this afternoon. Close to one hundred people injured in automobile accidents over the last four years voiced their concern with no-fault insurance — a clause that does not allow those injured in accidents to sue drivers who caused the collision.[54]

The message delivered in the story, though not explicitly stated, was that no-fault insurance is fundamentally flawed because it curtails civil liberties. For this reason the story was deemed to contain a dominant ideological theme. By contrast, the CBC's interpretation of the same event understood the protestors' concerns in a different context. The CBC story characterized the victims as wanting "no-fault" fixed — a counter-ideological position.[55] In this instance the connotation was that there was nothing wrong in principle with the general concept of no-fault insurance, only that the existing program needed to be modified. Language, and ultimately the style of the presentation itself, was a vital element in the construction of the message.

The CBC's "top story" on August 27 applied a similarly "focused" technique to the examination of a counter-ideological theme: poverty. The packaged report prepared by Jonathan Shanks addressed the absence of poverty from the election campaign agenda. The anchor, Kristy Snell, introduced the story with a tone of urgency:

> a group of churches in Saskatchewan have sent a letter to the party leaders asking what they will do for the poor. Amid the flood of issues by Saskatchewan's political parties during the election campaign, the problem of poverty has been ignored.[56]

Within the text of the story itself, the reporter attempted to get each leader to clarify his party's position on the problem of poverty: the NDP's Romanow stated that more could be done to address the problem; the Saskatchewan Party's Hermanson declared, according to the reporter, that the "party won't be giving to the poor any

51. Ibid.
52. Ibid.
53. Ibid.
54. Global News, Regina, August 26, 1999, 6:00 p.m.
55. CBC News Hour, Regina, August 26, 1999, 6:00 p.m.
56. CBC News Hour, Regina, August 27, 1999, 6:00 p.m.

more," but would be offering "tax cuts" instead; and the Liberals' Melenchuk, in a sound bite, claimed that poverty wasn't a priority for his party. With the exception of Hermanson's offer of "tax cuts," the story maintained a counter-ideological position throughout. In his closing "standup" the reporter, Jonathan Shanks, made direct reference to the dominant neo-liberal regime:

> [there is] so little concern [for the poor] that none of the three major parties say a word about helping the poor in the platforms. Now, in what may be Saskatchewan's version of the "trickle down" economy, all three say their platform will eventually help the poor.[57]

The poverty story, however, remains an anomaly in terms of the television sample — even relative to CBC's overall coverage. On August 25, during a studio interview between the anchor and the reporters covering the election campaign, participants made no mention whatsoever of the "failure" of the political party leaders to advance poverty as an issue. Rather, the anchor in opening the discussion elaborated on how "tax breaks," more jobs, and free tuition for post-secondary education were the major campaign issues. There was little disagreement among the reporters, who also characterized the issue of tax relief as integrally linked to job creation.[58]

Their conclusion is substantiated by the results of the study — particularly in terms of "tax cuts." The impression the CBC panel of reporters might have left the viewer with is that it was politicians, and the electorate itself, who framed the election campaign agenda. But as the results of the study have already indicated, the television media played an active role in shaping the discourse of the campaign. As Table 4.1 demonstrates, in CBC news coverage the dominant ideological theme of tax reduction arose in 33.3 percent of the stories reviewed in the sample. That compared to 30 percent for Global, and 16.7 percent for CTV.

CTV's relatively lower rate of tax reduction stories was consistent with the overall pattern of its coverage. However, as we alluded to earlier, the frequency with which dominant ideological themes occurred in CTV's coverage was offset by the greater incidence of "other" themes. This distinction set CTV apart from the other two network newsrooms. Table 4.4 shows that 33.3 percent of stories fell into the "analysis" category — the general discussion of issues that outwardly do not demonstrate a significant ideological bent. On August 27 three "A" category stories appeared in the newscast line-up in succession. The first, a voice-over/clip, explained that Liberal leader Jim Melenchuk was in Regina on that day. In the clip Melenchuk did not discuss specific policy issues. Instead, he merely stated: "we have fresh ideas."[59] The second story, another voice-over/clip, highlighted Romanow's visit to a motion picture set. At a news conference, the premier congratulated Minds Eye Pictures of Regina on signing a multimillion dollar deal with Disney.[60] Both the CBC and Global newscasts indicated that Minds Eye Pictures had benefited from the NDP government's film employment tax credit. Moreover, the other two networks also included an appeal by Minds Eye Pictures for more tax concessions.[61] This information was completely absent from the CTV newscast.

57. Ibid.
58. CBC News Hour, Regina, August 25, 1999, 6:00 p.m.
59. Quoted in CTV News, Regina, August 27, 1999, 6:00 p.m.
60. Ibid.
61. CBC News Hour, Regina, August 27, 1999, 6:00 p.m.; Global News, Regina, August 27, 1999, 6:00 p.m.

And finally, in the last story, as an anchor read with a clip, viewers were told that Canadian National Railways was concerned that NDP campaign ads which showed Romanow on railway tracks would send the wrong message to people — that it's safe to walk on railway tracks. The anchor's reading was followed by a clip, which contained a sound bite from Romanow, who appeared to be caught off guard.

A number of theories might explain the high incidence of non-contextual themes in CTV's news coverage. The corporation had undergone a succession of staff cuts in recent years. A consolidation of shareholder interests over two years ago translated into more than 300 job losses. Successive rounds of layoffs since then had knocked more than 130 employees from the company's payroll. CTV's Saskatchewan operations were not spared, enduring cuts with each successive round.[62] It might be argued then that CTV simply lacked the resources to put a more comprehensive newscast together, regardless of its ideological content. Certainly, a class analysis paradigm, the one employed in this study, would explain corporate consolidation and "downsizing" as the natural outcome of the capitalist class maximizing its interests. But this is not the primary point of inquiry of the study. Rather, the question is not why the cuts occurred, but what function they have had on the mediation of the message.

Just as issues of integrity and honesty can function to legitimize the media's role as a defender of the public interest, so can ideologically neutral topics of discussion. Such stories as those providing information on Liberal leader Jim Melenchuk's whereabouts, for example, foster the perception of balance and objectivity. In the case of the voice-over/clip of Melenchuk, the story immediately followed a packaged report on the Saskatchewan Party leader's campaign tour. The story in turn preceded an ideologically neutral account of Romanow's campaign. With the absence of ideological content, the anchor's words became secondary to the visuals. In such instances it was not so important what the party leaders were saying, but what they were doing. The viewer was left to deduce that an impartial mediation of the events of the day had been undertaken: no party leader was favoured, they had all had their equal time on "the tube." Perhaps with the absence of any distinguishable ideological differences between the party leaders, the absence of meaningful dialogue becomes the logical next step in perpetuating the status quo. Why frame the agenda, when it can be muted entirely? This may be ultimate price of media concentration.

Nevertheless, as the results of the study have demonstrated, the agenda of Saskatchewan's television newsrooms was anything but muted. In most cases, when CTV provided a packaged report, the content more often than not supported the status quo. Even CBC's story that emphasized the absence of poverty from the election campaign appears to be an anomaly in the context of the overall results. Such anomalies, whether in the print media or in television, can be used to challenge the existence of a conspiracy established within the media organizations to "shut-out" counter-ideological issues.

As discussed earlier in this chapter, James Winter's "trickle down" approach is realized in the "chilling effect" on news content. Journalists, as paid employees of large media conglomerates, know what they can and cannot say in the mediation of

62. Anonymous, "More layoffs announced at CTV," Canoe Money News, August 26, 1999 [http://www.canoe.ca/MoneyNews/aug26_ctvjobs.html].

information in order to either "get ahead" or keep their jobs. This doesn't necessarily mean that all journalists — or news editors for that matter — are fully conscious of the "rules of the game." Those who do know the rules might have a heightened chance of reaping the meritorious awards of corporate culture. What is more, the "chilling effect" allows for momentary bouts of journalistic idealism that challenge the interests of the corporate owners.

But momentary bouts of journalistic idealism among television reporters are outweighed by an uncritical discourse that supports the status quo. As with the newspaper coverage, television newscasts less frequently advanced themes that conflicted with the dominant ideological regime. What viewers received was a fundamentally biased mediation of "real world" facts, supporting the interests of the dominant groups within society.

NEWSPAPERS VS. TELEVISION

The results of our content analysis suggest a direct relationship between newspaper and television news coverage during the provincial election campaign. While there is some variance between the results obtained in both samples, the evidence reviewed in this study supports our secondary hypothesis. As Table 5 shows, more than three-quarters, or nearly 8 out of 10 stories reviewed in both samples, contained dominant ideological themes. In contrast, counter-ideological themes existed in no more than three out of ten stories reviewed. The greatest disparity was in the presence of "other" themes — those themes in which no context was provided or an overt ideological position was taken. For the newspaper sample, these themes existed in nearly 60 percent of all stories. This compares to 38.3 percent for television. In terms of the relative ideological balance of stories, or the frequency that dominant and counter-ideological themes existed in the same story, the results for the newspaper and television samples were relatively the same: 12.5 percent vs. 10.5 percent.

The theoretical paradigm employed in this study explains the results from two perspectives. First, Saskatchewan's major urban daily newspapers, having greater prestige than the television newsrooms, framed the agenda for news coverage in the province. Second, the television and newspaper operations controlled by dominant interests, large corporate owners and, in the case of the CBC, the state, perpetuated the status quo. The latter scenario is difficult to prove, but the former explanation seems plausible given the underlying argument of the class analysis approach — particularly if we apply Winter's version of the "trickle down" theory.

A general assessment of both the television and newspaper coverage in the samples is that it was primarily reactive. The coverage depended heavily on news conferences, news releases, and staged photo opportunities. In terms of the newspapers, the coverage was so reactive that the *Leader-Post* and the *Star Phoenix* went so far as to generate opinion polls and then solicit public reaction to these polls! Even the CBC's headline story on poverty made no attempt to conceal the reactive newsgathering process. Anchor Kristy Snell introduced the story, telling viewers that "a group of churches in Saskatoon have sent a letter to party leaders asking what they will do for the poor." A letter from a group of churches was explicitly used as justification for a story on poverty, a procedure that is not sound journalistic inquiry.

Without an ongoing critical examination of the issues advanced by the party leaders in the election campaign, the message constructed by Saskatchewan's media becomes a hollow endorsement of the status quo. The form might vary between the

Table 5.
A comparison of the frequency themes occur in both newspapers and television

Theme	Newspaper (Average Percentage)	Television (Average Percentage)
Dominant ideology	92.4	79.0
Counter-ideology	31.5	25.0
"Other" themes	59.4	38.3
Frequency dominant and counter-ideological themes appear in the same story	12.5	10.5

newspapers and television, but the medium does not change the message. As evidenced by a comparison of the observations in both television and newspaper coverage, there is little or no competition of ideas in Saskatchewan, at least in the mainstream print and television media.

Elections are about people making choices in a democratic society. Yet the messengers that Saskatchewan voters relied upon in the 1999 provincial election to help them make a choice offered a narrow band of alternatives. The alternatives offered, whether in newspapers or television, amounted to little more than different shades of the same colour. As the three party leaders quibbled over the best way to cut taxes, the media failed to operate in the public interest and move the debate beyond superficial name-calling and rhetoric. The television and newspaper media operated together as a compact, with both media caught up in the dogma of the dominant ideology.

CONCLUSION

The primary objective of this study was to determine whether news coverage in Saskatchewan supported the dominant ideology or the status quo. We also sought to determine whether there was a relationship between newspaper and television news coverage. We provided one case study of such dominance from the early 1990s. Subsequently we conducted a thematic analysis of the news content of the 1999 elections coverage of the *Leader-Post*, the *Star Phoenix*, and the Regina operations of CBC, CTV, and Global television. Our hypotheses applied a class analysis approach, utilizing Herman and Chomsky's "propaganda" model and James Winter's "trickle down" theory.

It has been concluded that newspaper coverage, based upon the results of our analysis, supported the status quo or dominant ideological regime. Dominant ideological themes were advanced largely unchallenged — without substantial critical review. Issues such as integrity functioned to divert attention away from more ideologically contentious topics, while "legitimizing" the newspaper media as an "objective watchdog" of the state. At the same time, Saskatchewan's two major newspapers actively shaped the political agenda.

It has also been concluded that the Saskatchewan television media also favoured the dominant ideological regime in its news coverage. The "focused" style of the television media constructed a message that was concise and unmistakable. There was also a tendency, as demonstrated in CTV's news coverage, to apply greater significance to the visual elements of a story, over verbal content. We concluded that stories that contained no overt ideological issues served to create the perception of balance and objectivity. Like the newspaper media, the television newscasts reinforced the status quo.

Finally, we concluded that there was a direct relationship between the newspaper and television media. Despite differences in form and style, both media recorded remarkably similar results in the analysis. While we could not determine with certainty whether the newspaper media framed the agenda for television news coverage, we did conclude that both media were primarily reactive. This means journalists relied heavily on news conferences, news releases, and photo opportunities for the generation of news. We also concluded that both the newspapers and television newsrooms played an active role in shaping the agenda of the election campaign. As a result, Saskatchewan's newspaper and television media muted the competition of political ideas, functioning to perpetuate the status quo.

These conclusions are important for students of politics. If studies like this one continue to confirm such overt bias, we need to reexamine dominant ideas about how democratic elections are, or how democratic they can be. If, as Marshall McLuhan famously said, "the medium is the message," it is the message of the status quo.

APPENDIX A: ELECTORAL RESULTS, SASKATCHEWAN 1905–1999

General Election — December 13, 1905				
Political Party	Votes Cast	Percentage of Vote	Candidates Nominated	Candidates Elected
Liberal	17,812	52.25	25	16
Provincial Rights	16,184	47.47	24	9
Independent	94	.28	1	0
Totals	**34,090**	**100.00**	**50**	**25**

General Election — August 14, 1908				
Liberal	29,807	50.79	41	27
Provincial Rights	28,099	47.88	40	14
Independent-Liberal	394	.67	1	0
Independent	387	.66	2	0
Totals	**58,687**	**100.00**	**84**	**41**

General Election — July 11, 1912				
Liberal	50,004	56.96	53	45
Conservative	36,848	41.97	53	7
Independent	934	1.06	5	1
Totals	**87,786**	**99.99**	**111**	**53***

**There were 54 seats contested at the 1912 election, however Cumberland was declared void and only 53 people were elected. A by - election was held on September 8, 1913, to fill the vacancy which existed in Cumberland.*

General Election — June 26, 1917				
Liberal	106,552	56.68	58	51
Conservative	68,243	36.30	53	7
Non-Partisan	7,267	3.87	7	0
Independent	4,440	2.36	10	1
Labor	1,474	.78	2	0
Totals	**187,976**	**99.99**	**130**	**59**

General Election — June 9, 1921				
Liberal	93,983	51.39	60	46
Independent	46,556	25.73	35	7
Progressive	13,613	7.52	7	6
Conservative	7,133	3.94	4	2
Independent Conservative	6,295	3.48	3	1
Labor	6,034	3.33	3	0
Non-Partisan	3,735	2.06	3	0
Independent Labor	1,690	.93	1	0
Government	1,510	.83	1	0
Independent Non-Partisan	1,400	.77	1	0
Independent Pro-Government	Acclamation	—	1	1
Totals	**180,949**	**99.98**	**119**	**63**

General Election — June 2, 1925				
Liberal	127,751	51.51	62	50
Progressive	57,142	23.04	40	6
Conservative	45,515	18.35	18	3
Independent	8.703	3.51	6	2
Labor Liberal	4,704	1.90	1	1
Independent Liberal	2,653	1.07	1	1
Independent Conservative	1,545	.62	1	0
Totals	**248,013**	**100.00**	**129**	**63**

Political Party	Votes Cast	Percentage of Vote	Candidates Nominated	Candidates Elected
General Election — June 6, 1929				
Liberal	164,487	45.56	62	28
Conservative	131,550	36.44	40	24
Independent	32,729	9.07	17	6
Progressive	24,988	6.92	16	5
Liberal Labor	4,181	1.16	1	0
Economic Group	1,942	.54	3	0
Independent Liberal	1,160	.32	1	0
Totals	**361,037**	**100.01**	**140**	**63**
General Election — June 19, 1934				
Liberal	206,212	48.00	56	50
Conservative	114,923	26.75	52	0
Farmer-Labor	102,944	23.96	53	5
Independent	2,949	.69	3	0
Labor	1,420	.33	1	0
United Front	1,053	.25	3	0
Independent Liberal	133	.03	1	0
Totals	**429,634**	**100.01**	**169**	**55**
General Election — June 8, 1938				
Liberal	200,334	45.45	53	38
Co-operative Commonwealth Federation (CCF)	82,529	18.73	31	10
Social Credit	70,084	15.90	40	2
Conservative	52,315	11.87	24	0
Unity	9,848	2.23	3	2
Independent Labor	12,039	2.73	3	0
Labor Progressive	8,514	1.93	2	0
Independent	4,023	.91	2	0
Independent Conservative	828	.19	1	0
Independent Social Credit	228	05	1	0
Totals	**440,742**	**99.99**	**160**	**52**
General Election — June 15, 1944				
CCF	211,364	53.13	52	47
Liberal	140,901	35.42	52	5
Progressive Conservative	42,511	10.69	39	0
Labor Progressive	2,067	.52	3	0
Independent	705	.18	5	0
Social Credit	249	.06	1	0
Independent Liberal	5	.00	1	0
Totals	**397,802**	**100.00**	**153**	**52**
General Election — June 24, 1948				
CCF	236,900	47.56	52	31
Liberal	152,400	30.60	41	19
Social Credit	40,268	8.08	36	0
Progressive Conservative	37,986	7.63	9	0
Independent	11,088	2.23	5	1
Liberal-Progressive Conservative	9,574	1.92	3	0
Conservative Liberal	5,251	1.05	1	1
Independent Liberal	3,299	.66	1	0
Labor Progressive	1,301	.26	1	0
Totals	**498,067**	**99.99**	**149**	**52**

General Election — June 11, 1952				
Political Party	**Votes Cast**	**Percentage of Vote**	**Candidates Nominated**	**Candidates Elected**
CCF	291,705	54.06	53	42
Liberal	211,882	39.27	53	11
Social Credit	21,045	3.90	24	0
Progressive Conservative	10,648	1.97	8	0
Independent Progressive Conservative	1,542	.29	1	0
Independent	1,517	.28	3	0
Labor Progressive	1,151	.21	2	0
Independent Liberal	103	.02	1	0
Totals	**539,593**	**100.00**	**145**	**53**

General Election — June 20, 1956				
CCF	249,634	45.25	53	36
Liberal	167,427	30.35	52	14
Social Credit	118,491	21.48	53	3
Progressive Conservative	10,921	1.98	9	0
Independent	4,714	.85	2	0
Labor Progressive	536	.10	2	0
Totals	**551,723**	**100.01**	**171**	**53**

General Election — June 8, 1960				
CCF	276,846	40.76	55	37
Liberal	221,932	32.68	55	17
Progressive Conservative	94,737	13.95	55	0
Social Credit	83,895	12.35	55	0
Independent	1,417	.21	3	0
Communist	380	.06	2	0
Totals	**679,207**	**100.01**	**225**	**54***

**One seat declared void.*

General Election — April 22, 1964				
Liberal	269,402	40.40	58	32
CCF	268,742	40.30	59	25
Progressive Conservative	126,028	18.90	43	1
Social Credit	2,621	.39	2	0
Communist	68	.01	1	0
Totals	**666,861**	**100.00**	**163**	**58***

**One seat declared void.*

General Election — October 11, 1967				
Liberal	193,871	45.57	59	35
New Democratic Party	188,653	44.35	59	24
Progressive Conservative	41,583	9.77	41	0
Social Credit	1,296	.30	6	0
Totals	**425,403**	**99.99**	**165**	**59**

General Election — June 23, 1971				
New Democratic Party	248,978	54.99	60	45
Liberal	193,864	42.82	60	15
Progressive Conservative	9,659	2.13	16	0
Independent	189	.04	1	0
Communist	46	.01	1	0
Totals	**452,736**	**99.99**	**138**	**60**

Political Party	Votes Cast	Percentage of Vote	Candidates Nominated	Candidates Elected
General Election — June 11, 1975				
New Democratic Party	180,700	40.07	61	39
Liberal	142,853	31.67	61	15
Progressive Conservative	124,573	27.62	61	7
Independent	2,897	.64	5	0
Totals	**451,023**	**100.00**	**188**	**61**
General Election — October 118, 1978				
New Democratic Party	228,791	48.12	61	44
Progressive Conservative	181,045	38.08	61	17
Liberal	65,498	13.78	61	0
Independent	81	.02	2	0
Totals	**475,415**	**100.00**	**185**	**61**
General Election — April 26, 1982				
Progressive Conservative	289,311	54.07	64	55
New Democratic Party	201,390	37.64	64	9
Liberal	24,134	4.51	64	0
Western Canada Concept	17,487	3.26	40	0
Independent	1,607	.30	8	0
Aboriginal People's Party	1,156	.22	10	0
Totals	**535,085**	**100.00**	**250**	**64**
General Election — October 20, 1986				
Progressive Conservative	244,382	44.61	64	38
New Democratic Party	247,683	45.20	64	25
Liberal	54,739	9.99	64	1
Western Canada Concept	458	.08	9	0
Independent	358	.07	3	0
Alliance	237	.04	6	0
Communist	73	.01	1	0
Totals	**547,930**	**100.00**	**211**	**64**
General Election — October 21, 1991				
New Democratic Party	275,780	51.05	66	55
Progressive Conservative	137,994	25.54	66	10
Liberal	125,814	23.29	66	1
Independent	592	.11	8	0
Western Canada Concept	46	.01	1	0
Totals	**540,226**	**100.00**	**207**	**66**
General Election — June 21, 1995				
New Democratic Party	193,053	47.21	58	42
Liberal	141,873	34.70	58	11
Progressive Conservative	73,269	17.92	58	5
Independent	712	.17	4	0
Totals	**408,907**	**100.00**	**178**	**58**
General Election — September 16, 1999				
New Democratic Party	157,046	38.73	58	29
Saskatchewan Party	160,603	39.61	58	25
Liberal	81,694	20.15	58	4
New Green Alliance	4,101	1.01	16	0
Progressive Conservative	1,609	.40	14	0
Independent	422	.10	2	0
Totals	**405,475**	**100.00**	**206**	**58**

Appendix B: Premiers of Saskatchewan, 1905–2001

1905–1916	T. Walter Scott (Liberal)
1916–1922	William M. Martin (Liberal)
1922–1926	Charles A. Dunning (Liberal)
1926–1929	James G. ("Jimmy") Gardiner (Liberal)
1929–1934	J.T.M. Anderson (Conservative/Coalition)
1934–1935	James G. ("Jimmy") Gardiner (Liberal)
1935–1944	William J. Patterson (Liberal)
1944–1961	T.C. ("Tommy") Douglas (CCF)
1961–1964	Woodrow S. Lloyd (CCF)
1964–1971	W. Ross Thatcher (Liberal)
1971–1982	Allan E. Blakeney (New Democratic Party)
1982–1991	D. Grant Devine (Progressive Conservative)
1991–2001	Roy J. Romanow (New Democratic Party)
2001–	Lorne A. Calvert (New Democratic Party)

Appendix C: Lieutenant Governors of Saskatchewan, 1905–2001

1905–1910	Amédée E. Forget
1910–1915	George W. Brown
1915–1921	Richard S. Lake
1921–1930	Henry W. Newlands
1931–1936	Hugh E. Munroe
1936–1945	Archibald P. McNab
1945	Thomas Miller
1945–1948	Reginald J.M. Parker
1948–1951	John M. Uhrich
1951–1958	William J. Patterson
1958–1963	Frank L. Bastedo
1963–1970	Robert L. Hanbidge
1970–1976	Stephen Worobetz
1976–1978	George Porteous
1978–1983	C. Irwin McIntosh
1983–1988	Frederick W. Johnson
1988–1994	Sylvia O. Fedoruk
1994–1999	John E.N. ("Jack") Wiebe
1999–	Lynda Haverstock

Appendix D: Past Presidents and Chiefs Federation of Saskatchewan Indian Nations, 1958–Present

1958–1961	John Tootoosis
1961–1964	David Knight
1964–1966	Wilfred Bellegarde
1966–1968	Walter Dieter
1968–1978	David Ahenakew
1978–1979	Albert Bellegarde
1979–1986	Sol Anderson
1986–1994	Roland Crowe
1994–1998	Blaine Favel
1998–Present	Perry Bellegarde

— INDEX —

— Contributors —

Duane Adams was born in Brandon, Manitoba. He was raised in Alameda, Saskatchewan during the war years and moved to Regina with his mother Jane in 1941. Duane spent the majority of his life in Saskatchewan until his death on April 13, 2001 at the age of 60 from Lou Gehrig's disease. Duane took his original degrees in Commerce and Economics at the University of Saskatchewan. He went on to do a Master's and a PhD at the University of Berkley, California. As deputy minister of Saskatchewan Health from 1991–1997, Duane played a significant leadership role in transforming the province's health services. During this period Duane was instrumental in defining the vision for health reform in the province, and in particular for the adoption of the Wellness Model. For his contribution to provincial health reform, he was awarded the Lieutenant Governor's Medal for Outstanding Public Service in 1995.

Allan Blakeney has had a long and distinguished career in the public service of Saskatchewan. Born in Nova Scotia, he moved to Saskatchewan in 1950 to become secretary of Crown Corporations. He was elected as an MLA in 1960, and served in the cabinets of both T.C. Douglas and Woodrow Lloyd. He became leader of the NDP in Saskatchewan in 1970, and premier when the party won the election of 1971. He served as premier until 1982. Since then he has served in many capacities, both inside and outside Saskatchewan. Currently he is an adjunct professor in the Law School at the University of Saskatchewan, and an adjunct professor in the Department of Political Science at the University of Regina.

Brent Cotter is presently deputy minister of Intergovernmental and Aboriginal affairs, and deputy provincial secretary for the government of Saskatchewan. He graduated from the University of Saskatchewan with a Bachelor of Commerce and went on to do his law degrees at Dalhousie in Nova Scotia. From 1980 to 1993 he taught at the law school at Dalhousie, during which time he was also associate dean. Previous to his current position, he was deputy minister of Justice for Saskatchewan.

Dan de Vlieger is a professor of Political Science at the University of Regina. His academic interests include political parties and elections in Canadian and European contexts. He is a former dean of the Faculty of Arts at the University of Regina.

Brett Fairbairn is a professor of History at the University of Saskatchewan, and director of the Centre for the Study of Co-operatives. He teaches and does research on the history and development of co-operatives, community development, social movements, and democracy. His books include *Building a Dream: The Co-operative Retailing System in Western Canada, 1928–1988*; *Co-operatives and Community Development: Economics in Social Perspective* (as co-author); *Dignity and Growth: Citizen Participation in Social Change* (as co-editor); and most recently, *Canadian Co-operatives in the Year 2000: Memory, Mutual Aid, and the Millennium* (co-editor).

Joyce Green is an associate professor of Political Science at the University of Regina. Her areas of interest include Aboriginal decolonisation in Canada, Canadian constitutional and political transformations, citizenship theory, critical feminist, post-colonial, and neo-marxist theory.

Lynda Haverstock completed both a BEd and an MEd in the Education of

Exceptional Children, as well as a PhD in Clinical Psychology from the University of Saskatchewan. Haverstock spent years as an educator of children with special needs and as a practicing psychologist with an emphasis on working with farm families in crisis. She taught university classes in Special Education and Psychology, and has written articles in both fields. In April of 1989, Haverstock became the first woman elected leader of a political party in Saskatchewan. She remained leader of the Saskatchewan Liberal Party until November of 1995. Haverstock served as a member of the Legislative Assembly from 1991–1999. She was sworn into office as the province's nineteenth lieutenant governor on February 21, 2000.

MICHAEL JACKSON has been chief of Protocol for the government of Saskatchewan since 1980 and executive director of Protocol and Government House since 1998. He has BA and MA degrees from the University of Toronto and a doctorate in French literature from the University of Caen, France. He has coordinated a number of visits to Saskatchewan of the Queen and other members of the Royal Family, the governor general, and foreign heads of state. He was instrumental in establishing the Saskatchewan honours program in 1985 and has been secretary of the program since then. He also coordinated the introduction of the provincial Coat of Arms in 1986 and Great Seal in 1991. Dr. Jackson has published several articles on the Crown in Canada and is author of the educational booklet *The Canadian Monarchy in Saskatchewan*. In 1987 the Queen invested him as a Lieutenant of the Royal Victorian Order.

HOWARD A. LEESON was born in Lethbridge, Alberta. He received his MA and PhD from the University of Alberta. He moved to Saskatchewan (where his mother's family had homesteaded) in 1977 to work with the government of Saskatchewan. He later became deputy minister of Intergovernmental Affairs, and was involved in 1981 with Premier Blakeney and Deputy Premier Roy Romanow in the negotiations that culminated in the patriation of the Constitution. In 1982 he joined the faculty of the Department of Political Science at the University of Regina, where he still teaches. From 1992–1994 he returned to the public service to help negotiate the Charlottetown Agreement on the Constitution. He has published numerous books and articles on Canadian government and international relations.

GREGORY P. MARCHILDON, former deputy minister to the premier and cabinet secretary in Saskatchewan, is currently executive director of the Commission on the Future of Health Care in Canada.

COLLEEN MATTHEWS is Crown counsel for Saskatchewan Justice. She was employed in the Financial Institutions Section of the Department from 1995–1997 and prior to that was in private practice. She has worked in the deputy minister's office since 1997.

SARAH MCQUARRIE is an Honours student in the Department of Political Science at the University of Regina. Her academic interests include Saskatchewan politics and history as well as media/communications studies. She has been actively involved in the New Democratic Party of Saskatchewan and, more precisely, its youth wing, where she is currently serving a one-year term as youth vice-president. She is also employed as a science writer for the Communications Department of the University of Regina.

JAMES M. PITSULA is a professor of History at the University of Regina. He is author of three books, many chapters in books, and numerous scholarly articles.

Jocelyne Praud is an assistant professor in the Department of Political Science at the University of Regina. She has published articles on social democratic parties and women in politics in Ontario, Quebec, and France in Manon Tremblay and Caroline Andrew (eds.), *Women and Political Representation in Canada*, Jean-Pierre Beaud and Jean-Guy Prévost (eds.), *La social-démocratie en cette fin de siècle/Late Twentieth-Century Social Democracy*, *Politique et Sociétés*, *Peace Research*, and *Contemporary French Civilization* She has just edited a special issue on women's political representation in Fifth Republic France for the journal *Contemporary French Civilization*.

Ken Rasmussen is the assistant dean and an associate professor of public administration in the Faculty of Administration at the University of Regina. He has a PhD in Political Science from the University of Toronto specialising in public administration and public policy. He is the author of numerous articles on public management and public policy issues and is the co-author, with James M. Pitsula, of the book, *Privatizing a Province: The New Right in Saskatchewan*.

Merrilee Rasmussen has a BA and an MA in Political Science from the University of Regina, as well as an LLB and an LLM from the University of Saskatchewan. She worked for a number of years as legislative counsel and law clerk to the Saskatchewan legislature. She is in the private practice of law in Regina.

Michael Rushton is a professor of Economics at the University of Regina and a fellow of the Saskatchewan Institute of Public Policy. He received his PhD in Economics from the University of British Columbia. From 1998–2000 he was senior policy advisor in the Cabinet Planning Unit of the Saskatchewan government. He has also been a visiting scholar at Erasmus University, Rotterdam. His fields of interest include tax policy, intellectual property, and the economics of culture.

Gerald B. Sperling is a professor emeritus at the University of Regina where he taught Political Science and Journalism for thirty years. He was Head of the department of Political Science at the University of Regina from 1993–1999. He has co-authored or co-edited the following books: *Rain of Death: Acid Rain in Western Canada*; *Getting the Real Story: Propaganda and Censorship in South Africa*; *Whose Story? Reporting the Developing World After the Cold War*; and *Old Shandong*. He has worked as a freelance writer and broadcaster for several agencies including the *Financial Post*, *Canadian Business*, *Briarpatch*, CBC Radio and CBC TV, and CTV. Currently, as president of 4 Square Productions (Canada) Ltd., he is a producer of documentary films which have been, or will be, broadcast in Canada on CTV, CBC, Vision TV, History TV, Discovery Channel, SCN, and CLT.

Bob Stirling teaches Sociology at the University of Regina. He grew up on a farm in western Saskatchewan and holds an undergraduate degree in Agriculture (University of Saskatchewan), an MA (University of Alberta) and a PhD (Indiana University) in Sociology.

Cora Voyageur teaches in the Sociology Department at the University of Calgary. She received her PhD at the University of Alberta. Her academic research focuses primarily on the Aboriginal experience in Canada, including women's issues, justice, politics, employment, education, and economic development. She has conducted extensive community-initiated research with many First Nations and organizations within the Aboriginal community. She is a member of the Athabasca Chipewyan First Nation from Fort Chipewyan, Alberta.

John D. Whyte is deputy minister of Justice and deputy attorney general for the government of Saskatchewan. He served with the government of Saskatchewan as director of the Constitutional Law Branch of the Department of the Attorney General from 1979–1982. He was a professor of Law at Queen's University from 1969–1997 and dean of Law from 1987–1992.

Kevin Wishlow holds both a BA (Great Distinction) and an MA in Political Science from the University of Regina. In 2000 he was a privileged recipient of the Queen Elizabeth II Scholarship in Parliamentary Studies, in recognition of his academic achievements as an undergraduate student. His research interests concentrate in the area of Canadian politics, the media, human rights and international development. He is currently a sessional lecturer in political science at the University of Regina. Aside from his academic endeavours, Wishlow worked for fourteen years as a television journalist at a number of posts in both Saskatchewan and Manitoba, including CTV Saskatchewan.